Terrorism, 1980–1990

Terrorism, 1980–1990

A Bibliography

Amos Lakos

Westview Press
BOULDER • SAN FRANCISCO • OXFORD

This Westview softcover edition is printed on acid-free paper and bound in library-quality, coated covers that carry the highest rating of the National Association of State Textbook Administrators, in consultation with the Association of American Publishers and the Book Manufacturers' Institute.

Published in 1991 in the United States of America by Westview Press, Inc., 5500 Central Avenue, Boulder, Colorado 80301-2847, and in the United Kingdom by Westview Press, 36 Lonsdale Road, Summertown, Oxford OX2 7EW

Library of Congress Cataloging-in-Publication Data
Lakos, Amos, 1946–
Terrorism, 1980–1990 : a bibliography / by Amos Lakos.
p. cm.
Includes bibliographical references and index.
ISBN 0-8133-8035-9
1. Terrorism—Bibliography. I. Title.
Z7164.T3L343 1991
[HV6431]
016.3036′25—dc20 91-26865
CIP

Printed and bound in the United States of America

The paper used in this publication meets the requirements of the American National Standard for Permanence of Paper for Printed Library Materials Z39.48-1984.

10 9 8 7 6 5 4 3 2 1

CONTENTS

PREFACE

Terrorism as a modern phenomenon has been increasing during the last two decades. Media coverage of terrorism dramatizes each incident, and the theatrical quality of the incidents holds our attention. Although in reality very few people are actually subjected to political terrorism, the attention it elicits gives terrorists a disproportionate influence.

The literature of terrorism is comparatively new; most of the books and articles originate after 1965. The increase in terrorist activities during the last two decades has been accompanied by increased scholarly activity. In the 1970s we observed an explosion in output, with no real slackening in the 1980s. Terrorism is being studied by, among others, political scientists, psychologists, historians, lawyers and military and intelligence personnel. They are responsible for a flood of publications in the form of books, journal articles, reports, government documents, films, newspaper articles, fiction and so on.

This is my second large bibliography on the subject of terrorism. The earlier volume covered the English language literature from the mid-1960s to the mid-1980s. This bibliography covers English-language materials published during the decade of 1980-1990 and arranges them by major subject categories. I have attempted to add all 1980-1985 items which I may have overlooked in the earlier bibliography. Newspaper and newsmagazine articles are excluded from this listing. I have tried to keep duplicate entries to a minimum, although many entries could be classified under a number of categories. Interdisciplinary materials are linked by the subject index. Because of certain programming restrictions, I did not follow any prescribed style manual to the letter, but made efforts to be consistent with my entries, so that they are easily accessible to the reader.

The bibliography is organized into major chapters which are based on broad subject categories. Each chapter is divided by subsections and each subsection is further divided by form: books, journal articles and documents and reports, which include conference papers, government documents and dissertations. In each subsection entries are sorted alphabetically. The ***Reference Works*** section includes a listing of reference materials, mostly specific to terrorism, but also works of a more general nature which cover particular aspects of terrorism. This section includes chronologies of terrorist incidents, a list of bibliographies, indexes and abstracts, a list of relevant on-line databases and a list of periodicals which are devoted mainly to the subject of terrorism. The ***General Works*** section includes materials on definitions of terrorism, general historical analyses, general descriptions and studies of terrorism. ***Theories of Terrorism*** covers materials on the theoretical, religious and ideological foundations of terror and terrorist groups. ***Psychological and Social Aspects*** lists materials on terrorist motivation, psychological studies of violence, group dynamics and victimology. The chapter on ***Strategies and Tactics*** consists of nine sections, each one covering specific types of terror tactics such as assassinations, bombings, hostage incidents, maritime terror, aircraft hijackings, security of computer facilities. A large general section deals with general strategies and tactics. A special section covers urban guerrilla warfare. The last section lists materials dealing with state sponsorship of terrorist groups and state terror. This section covers both state terror, which is domestic in nature. and the use of terrorism by states as a tool in international relations. ***Counter Measures*** is a large chapter divided by eight sections, covering general anti-terrorist strategies and tactics, development of counter-terror policies and the effects of these measures on society at large. Four sections are organized by type of response: intelligence activities, bomb disposal operations, security measures against aircraft hijackings, airport security, maritime security and security measures to prevent and respond to hostage situations. The section on business security deals with the growing problem of businesses as targets of terrorism and with the many measures employed by them to counteract this trend. The section on simulation research lists some of the research into counter terrorism which uses simulation methodology. ***Domestic and International Law Aspects*** covers legal responses to terrorism, both in terms of domestic legislation and in the use of existing international law, such as extradition, in the pursuit of terrorists. Section two covers international organizations, international conventions and the difficulties of international legal cooperation. Section three covers legal aspects and conventions regarding civil aviation, airports and hijacking of aircraft. The ***Media and Terrorism*** chapter lists the growing literature which addresses the role of the media in covering terrorism and the effects of media coverage on the outcome of terrorist incidents and on society as a whole. ***Unconventional Terrorism Threats*** includes materials on the potential for nuclear blackmail by terrorists and on security measures to safeguard both military and civilian nuclear materials and facilities. This chapter also includes materials on biological and chemical weapons threats. Chapter X, ***Geographical Subdivision***, is the longest in the bibliography. It covers all aspects of terrorism, with emphasis on geographic locations and specific terrorist incidents. Arrangement is by continent, state and incident.

The last part of the bibliography consists of an author index and a subject index which greatly enhance the usefulness of the work.

Amos Lakos
Waterloo, Ontario

ACKNOWLEDGMENTS

This work would not have been possible without the generous cooperation and encouragement of my colleagues and superiors at the University of Waterloo Library. I would like to single out Murray Shepherd, Head Librarian, who supported the project wholeheartedly and was very helpful in my quest for research support and study leave. I also wish to acknowledge the help of Joanne Hadley from the Research Office, who guided me through my grant proposals.

Bibliographic research was supported by a grant from the University of Waterloo Social Sciences and Humanities General Research Grant Fund.

This bibliography was organized and indexed using the Foxpro database manager program. The programs used were written by Irwin Rodin. The final copy was produced with Wordperfect 5.1.

The contents and arrangement of this bibliography are my personal responsibility, as are any omissions, duplications, inaccuracies or mistakes. Any suggestions or corrections regarding this work will be most welcome.

A.L.

I

REFERENCE WORKS

This chapter lists reference materials dealing with the subject of terrorism. It provides a useful starting point for students and researchers investigating various aspects of terrorism. This bibliography covers English language materials only, but some of the sources listed include foreign language publications. Many of the sources listed here are regularly updated, and so reflect current developments.

Encyclopedias and dictionaries are useful starting points for research since they provide definitions as well as general and historic overviews to the subject. Biographical sources provide information on political figures, although the shadowy nature of terrorism precludes the easy availability of accurate biographical information on terrorists. Yearbooks are useful for updating and keeping abreast of terrorist activities and of the activities of the forces arraigned against them. Chronologies are good sources for getting an overview of terrorist activities and for verifying the many allegations that appear in the literature. Although I have listed as many bibliographies as possible, the student should note that many of the books, journal articles, government documents and dissertations listed in this bibliography also include useful bibliographies. Indexes and abstracts, whether of journals or newspaper articles or dissertations, are important tools for the study of terrorism. Although there is no exclusive subject index dedicated to the coverage of terrorism alone, there are many which cover some aspects of the subject. Many of the indexes are also available on databases which can be searched on-line through various vendors. Many of these databases are also available on CD-ROM. A list of these data bases and the systems through which they can be accessed is included. Many of these data bases are very current, a consideration of some importance in the study of terrorism.

As a professional librarian I am very much aware of the problem of access to materials. This chapter is an attempt to make students more aware of the many powerful reference sources available to them in their research work.

A. ENCYCLOPEDIAS AND GUIDES

1. ***Encyclopedia of World Crime: Criminal Justice, Criminology and Law Enforcement.*** Wilmette, IL.: Crime Books, 1990. 6 Vols.

2. Lentz, Harris M. ***Assassinations and Executions: A Encyclopedia of Political Violence, 1865-1986.*** Jefferson, NC.: McFarland & Co., 1988. 275p.

3. Nash, Jay R. ***Look for the Woman: A Narrative Encyclopedia of Female Poisoners, Kidnappers, Thieves, Extortionists, Terrorists, Swindlers, and Spies, from Elisabethan Times to the Present.*** New York: M. Evans, 1981. 408p.

4. Schmid, Alex P. ***Political Terrorism: A Research Guide to Concepts, Theories, Databases and Literature.*** Amsterdam: North-Holland, 1983. 585p.

5. _____, and Albert J. Jongman. ***Political Terrorism: A New Guide to Actors, Authors, Concepts, Data Bases, Theories and Literature.*** Rev. ed. New Brunswick, NJ.: Transaction Books, 1988. 700p.

6. Thackrah, John R. ***Encyclopedia of Terrorism and Political Violence.*** Routledge & Kegan Paul, 1987. 308p.

7. Wilson, Colin, and Donald Seaman. ***The Encyclopedia of Modern Murder, 1962-1982.*** New York: Putnam, 1985. 279p.

B. DICTIONARIES

8. Degenhardt, Henry W., ed. ***Revolutionary and Dissident Movements: An International Guide.*** London: Longman Group, 1988. 466p.

9. Gunson, C. A., et al. ***The Dictionary of Contemporary Politics of South America.*** London: Routledge, 1989. 314p.

10. McCrea, Barbara P., Jack C. Plano and George Klein. ***The Soviet Union and East European Political Dictionary.*** Santa Barbara, CA.: ABC-Clio, 1984. 367p.

11. Phillips, Claude. ***The African Political Dictionary.*** Santa Barbara, CA.: ABC-Clio, 1984. 245p.

12. Plano, Jack C., and Milton Greenberg. ***The American Political Science Dictionary. 7th ed.*** New York: Holt, Rinehart and Winston, 1985. 606p.

13. _____, and Roy Olton. ***The International Relations Dictionary.*** Santa Barbara, CA.: ABC-Clio, 1982. 488p.

14. Rolef, Susan H., ed. ***Political Dictionary of the State of Israel.*** New York: Collier Macmillan, 1988. 304p.

15. Rossi, Ernest, and Barbara P. McCrea. ***The European Political Science Dictionary.*** Santa Barbara, CA.: ABC-Clio, 1985. 432p.

16. _____, and Jack C. Plano. ***The Latin American Political Dictionary.*** Santa Barbara, CA.: ABC-Clio, 1980. 261p.

17. Shimoni, Y., ed. ***A Political Dictionary of the Arab World.*** Rev. ed. New York: Macmillan, 1988. 520p.

18. Ziring, Lawrence, and Eugene C.I. Kim, eds. ***The Asian Political Dictionary.*** Santa Barbara, CA.: ABC-Clio, 1986. 438p.

19. _____. ***The Middle East Political Dictionary.*** Santa Barbara, CA.: ABC-Clio, 1984. 452p.

C. BIOGRAPHICAL MATERIALS AND DIRECTORIES

20. ***Current Biography.*** New York: H.W. Wilson, 1965-.

21. Degenhardt, Henry W., comp. ***Political Dissent: An International Guide to Dissident, Extra-Parliamentary, Guerrilla and Illegal Political Movements.*** Detroit, MI.: Gale Research, 1983. 592p.

22. ***Dictionary of International Biography.*** London: International Biographical Center, 1964/65-.

23. Emerson, Ryan Q. ***Who's Who in Terrorism, 1984.*** Hollywood, FL.: International Research Center on Terrorism, 1984. 56p.

24. ***International Security Directory, 1987-88.*** Henley-on-Thames, Oxon.: R. Hazell, 1987. 108p. Annual.

25. Janke, Peter. ***Guerrilla and Terrorist Organizations: A World Directory and Bibliography.*** Brighton: Harvester Press, 1983. 531p.

26. Jongman, Albert J., and Alex P. Schmid. "World Directory of Terrorist and Other Organizations Associated with Guerrilla Warfare, Political Violence, and Protest." In: A. P. Schmid and A. J. Jongman. ***Political Terrorism.*** New Brunswick, NJ.: Transaction Books, 1988. pp. 485-496.

27. O Maolain, Ciaran, comp. ***The Radical Right: A World Directory.*** Santa Barbara: CA.: ABC-Clio, 1987. 500p.

28. Rosie, George. ***The Directory of International Terrorism.*** Edinburgh: Mainstream, 1986. 310p.

29. ***Terrorist Group Profiles.*** Washington, D.C.: U.S. Government Printing Office, 1988. 131p.

30. ***Who's Who in Germany.*** New York: Facts on File, 1980-.

31. ***Who's Who in Italy.*** New York: Facts on File, 1980.

32. ***Who's Who in the Arab World. 6th ed.*** Beirut: Publitec, 1981-82.

33. ***Who's Who.*** New York: St. Martin's Press, 1965-.

34. "World Directory on Dissent and Insurgency." ***TVI Journal,*** 2 (1981), 4-50.

D. YEARBOOKS

35. ***Annual Review of United Nations Affairs.*** Dobbs Ferry, NY.: Oceana, 1965-.

36. Crozier, Brian, ed. ***Annual of Power and Conflict.*** London: Institute for the Study of Conflict, 1973-.

37. Encyclopedia Britannica. ***Britannica Book of the Year.*** Chicago, 1965-.

38. ***The Europa Yearbook: A World Survey and Directory of Countries and International Organizations.*** London: Europa Publications, 1965-.

39. ***Facts on File.*** New York, 1965-.

40. Institute of World Affairs. ***The Yearbook of World Affairs.*** London: Stevens, 1965-.

41. International Association of Chiefs of Police. ***Police Yearbook.*** Gaithersburg, MD.:International Association of Chiefs of Police, 1967-.

42. International Institute for Peace and Conflict Research. ***SIPRI Yearbook of World Armaments and Disarmament.*** Stockholm: Almquist & Wiksell, 1968/69-.

43. ***International Yearbook and Statesman's Who's Who.*** London: Burke's Peerage, 1965-.

44. Israel. Police Headquarters. ***Israel Police Annual Report.*** Jerusalem, 1965-.

45. ***Keesing's Contemporary Archives.*** London: Longmans. Annual.

46. Legum, Colin, ed. ***Africa Contemporary Record.*** New York: Holmes & Meier, 1969-.

47. _____, ed. ***Middle East Contemporary Survey.*** New York: Holmes & Meier, 1978-.

48. Northern Ireland. Information Service. ***The Ulster Yearbook.*** Belfast: H.M.S.O., 1965-.

49. ***Political Handbook of the World.*** New York: McGraw-Hill, 1975-.

50. Saywell, John T., ed. ***Canadian Annual Review of Politics and Public Affairs.*** Toronto: University of Toronto Press, 1965-.

51. Scherer, John L. ***Terrorism: An Annual Survey. Vol. I and II.*** Minneapolis, MN.: J. L. Scherer, 1982-83.

52. _____. ***Terrorism.*** Minneapolis, MN.: J. L. Scherer, 1986-.

53. United Nations. Department of Social Affairs. ***United Nations Yearbook.*** New York, 1965-.

54. United States. Department of Justice. Federal Bureau of Investigation. ***Crime in the United States: Uniform Crime Reports.*** Washington, D.C.: U.S. Government Printing Office, 1965-.

55. _____. Department of State. Office of the Ambassador-at-Large for Counter-Terrorism. ***Patterns of Global Terrorism.*** Washington, D.C.: U.S. Government Printing Office, 1983-. Annual.

56. _____. National Criminal Justice Information and Statistics Service. ***Sourcebook of Criminal Justice Statistics.*** Washington, D.C.: U.S. Government Printing Office, 1973-.

E. CHRONOLOGIES

57. Bass, Gail V., and Bonnie J. Cordes. ***Actions Against Nonnuclear Energy Facilities: September 1981 - September 1982.*** RAND N-1980-SL. Santa Barbara, CA.: RAND Corporation, 1983. 29p.

58. "Chronology of Main International Terrorist Incidents in 1987." In: A. Merari and A. Kurz, et al. ***INTER: International Terrorism in 1987.*** Tel Aviv: Jaffee Center for Strategic Studies, 1988. pp. 85-112.

59. "Chronology of Main Terrorist Incidents in 1985." In: A. Merari, et al. ***INTER 85.*** Boulder, CO.: Westview Press, 1986. pp. 71-104.

60. "Chronology of Main Terrorist Incidents in 1988." In: A. Kurz, et al. ***INTER: International Terrorism in 1988.*** Tel Aviv: Jaffee Center for Strategic Studies, 1989. pp. 31-60.

61. "A Chronology of Significant Attacks on Israel and Israeli Reprisal Operations." ***TVI Journal,*** 5:4 (1985), 26-30.

62. "Chronology of Significant Terrorist Events in 1987." ***Terrorism,*** 9:4 (1987), 439-446.

63. "Chronology." In: S. R. Ontiveros, ed. ***Global Terrorism: A Historical Bibliography.*** Santa Barbara, CA.: ABC-Clio Press, 1986. pp. 145-168.

64. "A Chronology: Euroterrorist Actions 1984- April 1985." ***TVI Journal,*** 5:4 (1985), 18-21.

65. Dulaney, Richard C. ***Terrorism Chronology: 1981-1986: Incidents Involving U.S. Citizens or Property.*** Report No. 86-531F. Washington, D.C.: Congressional Research Service, Library of Congress, 1986. 9p.

66. Gardela, Karen, and Bruce Hoffman. ***The RAND Chronology of International Terrorism for 1986.*** RAND R-3890-RC. Santa Monica, CA.: RAND Corporation, 1990. 105p.

67. Hamizrachi, Yoram, and Beate Hamizrachi. "International Terrorist Events: 1987." In: Y. Alexander and A. H. Foxman, eds. ***The 1987 Annual on Terrorism.*** Dordrecht: Martinus Nijhoff, 1988. pp. 205-276.

68. _____. "International Terrorist Events, 1986." In: Y. Alexander, ed. ***The 1986 Annual on Terrorism.*** Dordrecht: Martinus Nijhoff, 1987. pp. 211-244.

69. "Incidents of Terrorism and Hijackings in the United States 1980-1983." ***TVI Journal,*** 5:1 (1984), 30-39.

70. Institute for the Study of Conflict. ***Political Violence and Civil Disobedience in Western Europe 1982.*** Conflict Studies, No. 145. London: Institute for the Study of Conflict, 1983. 31p.

71. Jenkins, Brian M., et al. ***A Chronology of Terrorist Attacks and the Other Criminal Actions Against Maritime Targets.*** RAND P-6906. Santa Monica, CA.: Rand Corporation, 1983. 26p.

72. Kurz, Anat. "Chronology of Main International Terrorist Incidents in 1986." In: A. Kurz, et al. ***INTER 86.*** Tel Aviv: Jaffee Center for Strategic Studies, 1987. pp. 79-114.

73. ***Latin America.*** London: Latin American Newsletter, 1965-.

74. Martin, Harry. ***A Chronology of Terrorist Incidents in France: January 1, 1985 - April 18, 1986.*** Washington, D.C.: Congressional Research Service, Library of Congress, 1986. 2p.

75. Mickolus, Edward F. ***Transnational Terrorism: A Chronology of Events, 1968-1979.*** Westport, CT.: Greenwood Press, 1980. 967p.

76. _____. Todd Sandler and Jean M. Murdock. ***International Terrorism in the 1980s: A Chronology of Events. v.1: 1980-1983.*** Ames: Iowa State University Press, 1989. 541p.

77. _____, et al. ***International Terrorism in the 1980s: A Chronology of Events. Vol, 2.: 1984-1987.*** Ames, IA.: Iowa State University Press, 1989. 794p.

78. "PLO Terrorism: 1976-1979." ***Middle East Review,*** 12:3 (1980), 49-52.

79. "The Path of Terrorism." ***Security Management,*** 25:9 (1981), 70-74.

80. "The Path of Terrorism." ***Security Management,*** 25:10 (1981), 63-79.

81. "The Path of Terrorism." ***Security Management,*** 25:12 (1981), 52-53.

82. "The Path of Terrorism." ***Security Management,*** 26:2 (1982), 53-58.

83. "The Path of Terrorism." ***Security Management,*** 26:5 (1982), 65-70.

84. "The Path of Terrorism." ***Security Management,*** 26:8 (1982), 75-79.

85. "The Path of Terrorism." ***Security Management,*** 26:9 (1982), 145-147.

86. "A Recap of 1980: The Path of Terrorism Around the World - Part I." ***Security Management,*** 25:7 (1981), 132-147.

87. "A Recap of 1980: The Path of Terrorism Around the World." ***Security Management,*** 25:8 (1981), 160-170.

88. Schechterman, Bernard. "Appendix: Worldwide Terrorism Since the World War II Period." In: M. Slann and B. Schechterman, eds. ***Multidimensional Terrorism.*** Boulder, CO.: Lynne Rienner, 1987. pp. 121-130.

89. Shahmon, Orit. "Chronology of Main International Terrorist Incidents in 1989." In: A. Kurz, et al. ***INTER: International Terrorism in 1989.*** Tel Aviv: Jaffee Center for Strategic Studies, 1990. pp. 87-105.

90. "TVI Update." ***TVI Journal,*** Vol. 1. 1980-. Update appears in each issue.

91. United States. Department of State. Bureau of Diplomacy. ***Significant Incidents of Political Violence Against Americans: 1988.*** Department of State Publication NO. 9718. Washington, D.C.: U.S. Government Printing Office, 1989. 43p.

92. _____._____. Office for Combatting Terrorism. ***Terrorist Skyjackings, January 1968 Through June 1982.*** Washington, D.C.: U.S. Department of State, 1982. 26p.

93. _____. Federal Aviation Administration. Office of Civil Aviation Security. ***Chronology of Hijackings of U.S. Registered Aircraft and Legal Status of Hijackers - - Updated: January 1, 1986.*** Washington, D.C.: Federal Aviation Administration, 1986. 56p.

94. _____._____._____. ***Explosions Aboard Aircraft - Updated: January 1, 1986.*** Washington, D.C.: Federal Aviation Adminitration, 1986. 23p.

95. _____._____._____. ***U.S. And Foreign Registered Aircraft Hijackings.*** Washington, D.C.: Federal Aviation Administration, 1986. 135p.

96. _____._____._____. ***Worldwide Significant Criminal Acts Involving Civil Aviation: January - December 1985.*** Washington, D.C.: Federal Aviation Administration, 1986. 30p.

97. _____. Library of Congress. Congressional Research Service. ***Iran Hostage Crisis: A Chronology of Daily Development Reports.*** Rockville, MD.: National Criminal Justice Reference Service, 1981. 425p.

98. Wootten, James P. ***Terrorist Incidents Involving U.S. Citizens or Property 1981-1989: A Chronology.*** Washington, D.C.: Library of Congress, Congressional Research Service, 1989. 15p.

99. "Worldwide Chronology of Terrorism - 1981." ***Terrorism,*** 6:2 (1982), whole issue.

F. BIBLIOGRAPHIES

1. Books

100. Bhan, Susheela, et al. ***Terrorism: An Annotated Bibliography.*** New Delhi: Concept Publishing, 1989. 338p.

101. Blackey, Robert. ***Revolutions and Revolutionists: A Comprehensive Guide to the Literature.*** War/Peace Bibliography Series # 17. Santa Barbara, CA.: ABC-Clio, 1982. 488p.

102. Deutsch, Richard. ***Northern Ireland, 1921-1974: A Selected Bibliography.*** New York: Garland, 1975. 142p.

103. Guth, D. J., and D. R. Wrone. ***The Assassination of John F. Kennedy: A Comprehensive Historical and Legal Bibliography, 1963-1979.*** Westport, CT.: Greenwood Press, 1980.

104. Lakos, Amos. ***The Nuclear Terrorism Threat: A Bibliography.*** Public Administration Series: Bibliography # P 1779. Monticello, Il.: Vance Bibliographies, 1985. 20p.

105. _____. ***Terrorism in the Middle East: A Bibliography.*** Public Administration Series: Bibliography, P-1842. Monticello, IL.: Vance Bibliographies, 1986. 39p.

106. _____. ***International Terrorism: A Bibliography.*** Boulder, CO.: Westview Press, 1986. 481p.

107. Mickolus, Edward F. ***The Literature of Terrorism: A Selectively Annotated Bibliography.*** Westport, CT.: Greenwood Press, 1980. 553p.

108. _____, and Peter A. Fleming. ***Terrorism, 1980-1987: A Selectively Annotated Bibliography.*** Westport, CT.: Greenwood Press, 1988. 328p.

109. Newton, Michael, and Judy A. Newton. ***Terrorism in the United States and Europe, 1800-1959: An Annotated Bibliography.*** New York: Garland, 1988. 522p.

110. Ontiveros, Suzanne R., ed. ***Global Terrorism: A Historical Bibliography.*** ABC-Clio Research Guides; 16. Santa Barbara, CA.: ABC-Clio Press, 1986. 168p.

111. Rao, Dittakavi N. ***Terrorism and Law: A Selected Bibliography of Articles, 1980-1985.*** Public Administration Series: Bibliography P-1958. Monticello, IL.: Vance Bibliographies, 1986. 9p.

112. Rupesinghe, Kumar. ***Ethnic Conflict and Human Rights in Sri Lanka: An Annotated Bibliography.*** Munich: Saur, 1989. 565p.

113. Signorielli, Nancy, and George Gerbner. ***Violence and Terror in the Mass Media: An Annotated Bibliography.*** Westport, CT.: Greenwood Press, 1988. 233p.

114. Smith, Myron J. Jr. ***The Secret Wars, Vol. 3. International Terrorism, 1968-1980.*** War/Peace Series 14. Santa Barbara, Ca.: ABC-Clio, 1980. 237p.

115. White, Anthony G. ***Recent Military Views of Counter Terrorism: A Selected Bibliography.*** Public Administration Series: Bibliography P-1960. Monticello, IL.: Vance Bibliographies, 1986. 6p.

116. _____. ***Recent Military Views of Terrorism: A Selected Bibliography.*** Public Administration Series: Bibliography P-1959. Monticello, IL.: Vance Bibliographies, 1986. 9p.

117. Wilcox, Laird. ***Bibliography on Terrorism, Assassination, Kidnapping, Bombing, Guerrilla Warfare and Countermeasures Against Them.*** Kansas City, MO.: Editorial Research Service, 1980.

118. _____. ***Master Bibliography on Political Psychology and Propaganda; Espionage and Intelligence Operations; and Terrorism and Assassination.*** Kansas, MO.: Editorial Research Service, 1985.

119. _____, comp. ***Guide to the American Right: Directory and Bibliography.*** Kansas City, MO.: Editorial Research Service, 1984.

120. _____, comp. ***Guide to the American Left: Directory and Bibliography.*** Kansas City, MO.: Editorial Research Service, 1984.

121. _____. ***Terrorism, Assasination, Espionage and Propaganda: A Master Bibliography.*** Olathe, KS.: Wilcox, 1989. 654p.

2. Journal Articles

122. Alexander, Yonah. "Selected Bibliography on the Legal Aspects of Terrorism." In: ***Israel Yearbook on Human Rights, Vol. 19. 1989.*** Dordrecht: Martinus Nijhoff, 1989. pp. 405-412.

123. Bazyler, Michael J., and Terry Porvin. "International Terrorism: A Selected Bibliography." ***Whittier Law Review,*** 8 (Summer 1986), 793-800.

124. Friedlander, Robert A. "Terrorism in the 70s - A Selective Bibliography." ***TVI Journal,*** 11:6 (July 1981), 2-9.

125. _____. "A Basic Library on Terrorism: Part I." ***TVI Journal,*** 2:6 (1981), 2-9.

126. Johnson-Champ, Debra S., Robert E. Lutz and Susan L. Streiker. "International Terrorism: A Legal Bibliography of Selected Issues and Sources." ***The International Lawyer,*** 20:3 (1986), 1084-1100.

127. Moreland, Richard L., and M. L. Berbaum. "Terrorism and the Mass Media - A Selected Bibliography." In: V. M. Bassiouni, ed. ***Terrorism, Law Enforcement and the Mass Media.*** Rockville, MD.: National Criminal Justice Reference Service, 1983. pp. 287-334.

128. _____. _____. "Terrorism and the Mass Media: A Researcher's Bibliography." In: A. H. Miller, ed. ***Terrorism: The Media and the Law.*** Dobbs Ferry, NY.: Transnational, 1982. pp. 191-216.

129. Norton, Augustus R. "Terror-Violence: A Critical Commentary and Selective Annotated Bibliography." In: ***Clandestine Tactics and Technology.*** Gaithersburg, MD.: International Association of Chiefs of Police, 1980. 16p.

130. Nudell, Mayer. "The Literature of Terrorism." ***Marine Corps Gazette,*** 69 (August 1985), 88-90.

131. Picard, Robert G., and Rhonda Sheets. "Terrorism and the News Media Research Bibliography, Part II." ***Political Communication and Persuasion,*** 4:2 (1987), 141-152.

132. _____. _____. "Terrorism and News Media: A Research Bibliography, Part I." ***Political Communication and Persuasion,*** 4:1 (1987), 65-70.

133. _____. _____. "Terrorism and the News Media: A Research Bibliography Part IV." ***Political Communication and Persuasion,*** 4:4 (1987), 325-326.

134. _____. _____. "Terrorism and the New Media Research Bibliography: Part III." ***Political Communication and Persuasion,*** 4:3 (1987), 217-221.

135. Saxena, Madhur. "International Terrorism: A Select Bibliography." In: R. P. Dhokalia and K. N. Rao, eds. ***Terrorism and International Law.*** New Delhi: Indian Society of International Law, 1988. pp. 137-151.

136. Schmid, Alex P., J. Brand and A. Van den Poel. "A Bibliography of Political Terrorism." In: A. P. Schmid and A. J. Jongman. ***Political Terrorism.*** New Brunswick, NJ.: Transaction Books, 1988. pp. 237-484.

3. Documents and Reports

137. Beanlands, Bruce, and Bruce Deacon. ***Counter-Terrorism Bibliography. No. 1988-14.*** Ottawa: Ministry of the Solicitor General of Canada, Police Research Demonstration Division, Police and Security Branch, 1989. 355p.

138. ***Civil Insurgency, 1964 - March 1982.*** Springfield, VA.: National Technical Information Service, 1982. 209p.

139. Crouch, T. W. ***Compilation of LIC (Low Intensity Conflict) References and Bibliography, Volume 2. CLIC Papers.*** SBI-AD-F000 131. Langley AFB, VA.: Army Air Force Center for Low Intensity Conflict, 1988. 48p.

140. _____. ***Compilation of References and Bibliography. Volume 1. An Annotated Bibliography on Low Intensity Conflict Taken from the Joint Low Intensity Conflict Project, Final Report. CLIC .*** Langley AFB, VA.: Army-Air Force Center for Low Intensity Conflict, 1987. 61p.

141. Failing, S. J. ***Terrorism, Guerrilla Warfare/Counterinsurgency/Low Intensity Conflict, and Revolutions: Report Bibliography.*** Colorado Springs, CO.: Air Force Academy, Library, 1986. 105p.

142. ***The Legal Aspects of International Terrorism.*** The Hague: The Hague Academy of International Law, Center for Studies and Research, 1988. 90p.

143. Leskovsek, Valentin. ***Terrorism: Bibliography-in-Brief, 1986-1987.*** Report 87-575L. Washington, D.C.: Library of Congress, Congressional Research Office, 1987. 10p.

144. ***Low Intensity Conflict: A Selected Bibliography.*** Carlisle Barracks, PA.: Army War College, 1986. 17p.

145. McKinley, Nancy P. ***Terrorism in International Relations: An Annotated Bibliography, 1975-1985.*** Report 86-567L. Washington, D.C.: Library of Congress, Congressional Research Service, 1986. 15p.

146. Metz, Sten. ***Literature of Low Intensity Conflict: A Selected Bibliography and Suggestions for Future Research (CLIC Papers).*** Langley AFB, CA.: Army-Air Force Center for Low Intensity Conflict, 1988. 32p.

147. Miller, Lester L. ***Terrorism: A Bibliography of Books and Periodical Articles.*** Fort Sill, OK.: Army Field Artillery School, 1981. 12p.

148. Shure, C., et al. ***Literature Review on Anti-Terrorism and Selected Bibliography on Terrorism.*** Springfield, VA.: Syllogistics, 1988. 40p.

149. Signorielli, Nancy. ***Violence and Terror in the Mass Media: Bibliography.*** Reports and Papers on Mass Communication. No. 102. Paris: UNESCO, 1988. pp. 29-45.

150. ***Terrorism: A Selected Bibliography.*** Fort McClellan, AL.: Army Military Police School, 1984. 238p.

151. ***Terrorism: A Selective Bibliography.*** Washington, D.C.: Department of Defence, Pentagon Library, 1984. 32p.

152. ***Terrorism: December 1974 - May 1990: A Bibliography from the NTIS Database.*** Springfield, VA.: National Technical Information Service (NTIS), 1990. 142p.

153. United States. Air Force Academy. Library. ***Terrorism, Guerrilla Warfare. Counterinsurgency, Low-Intensity Conflict and Revolutions: 1986-June 1988.*** Colorado Springs, CO.: U.S. Air Force Academy Library, 1988. 46p.

154. _____. Department of State. Library. ***Terrorism.*** Washington, D.C.: U.S. Government Printing Office, 1985. pp.11.

155. _____. Superintendent of Documents. ***Causes and Prevention of Violence.*** Washington, D.C.: U.S. Government Printing Office, 1980. 11p.

156. Vance, Mary. ***International Aspects of Terrorism: A Bibliography.*** Public Administration Series: Bibliography P-2742. Monticello, IL.: Vance Bibliographies, 1989. 17p.

G. INDEXES AND ABSTRACTS

157. ***ABC POL SCI.*** Santa Barbara, CA.: ABC Clio, 1964-.

158. ***Air University Library Index to Military Periodicals.*** Maxwell Air Force Base, AL.: Air University Library, 1965-.

159. ***Alternative Press Index.*** Baltimore, MD.: Alternative Press Center, 1969/70-.

160. ***America: History and Life.*** Santa Barbara, CA.: ABC-Clio, 1964/65-.

161. ***Business Periodicals Index.*** New York: H.W. Wilson, 1964/65-.

162. ***Canadian Periodical Index.*** Ottawa: Canadian Library Association, 1965-.

163. ***Catalog of Government Publications.*** London: Her Majesties Stationery Office, 1965-.

164. ***Communication Abstracts.*** Beverly Hills, CA.: Sage, 1978-.

165. ***Comprehensive Dissertation Index.*** Ann Arbor, MI.: University Microfilm International, 1861-.
166. ***Criminal Justice Abstracts.*** Buffalo, NY.: Willow Tree Press, 1969-.
167. ***Criminal Justice Periodicals Index.*** Ann Arbor, MI.: University Microfilms International, 1975-.
168. ***Criminology and Penology Abstracts.*** Amstelveen, Holland: Kugler, 1965-.
169. ***Current Military and Political Literature.*** Oxford: The Military Press, 1983-.
170. ***Dissertation Abstracts International.*** Ann Arbor, MI.: University Microfilms International, 1965-.
171. ***Historical Abstracts: Part B, Twentieth Century Abstracts (1914 to the Present).*** Santa Barbara, CA.: ABC-Clio, 1965-.
172. ***Index to Canadian Legal Periodical Literature.*** Montreal: Canadian Legal Periodical Literature, 1961-.
173. ***Index to Jewish Periodicals.*** Cleveland Heights, OH.: Index to Jewish Periodicals, 1964/65-.
174. ***Index to Legal Periodicals.*** New York: H.W. Wilson, 1965-.
175. ***Index to Social Sciences and Humanities Proceedings.*** Philadelphia, PA.: Institute for Scientific Information, 1979-.
176. ***Index to U.S. Government Periodicals.*** Chicago, IL.: Infordata International, 1974-.
177. ***Index to the Contemporary Scene.*** Detroit, MI.: Gale Research, 1973-.
178. ***International Bibliography of Political Science.*** London: Tavistock Publications, 1965-.
179. ***International Political Science Abstracts.*** Paris: International Political Science Association, 1965-.
180. ***Masters Abstracts.*** Ann Arbor, MI.: University Microfilms International, 1965-.
181. ***The Middle East: Abstracts and Indexes.*** Pittsburgh, PA.: Northumberland Press, 1978-.
182. ***Peace Research Abstracts Journal.*** Dundas, Ont.: Peace Research Institute, 1964/65-.
183. ***Police Science Abstracts.*** Amstelveen, Holland: Kugler, 1973-.
184. ***Political Science Abstracts. (Formerly the Universal Reference System).*** New York: IFI/Plenum, 1966-.
185. ***Psychological Abstracts.*** Arlington, VA.: American Psychological Association, 1965-.
186. ***Public Affairs Information Service. (PAIS).*** New York: Public Affairs Information Service, 1965-.
187. ***Quarterly Strategic Review.*** Boston, MA.: Center for International Security Studies of the American Security Council Foundation, Vol. 1-., 1977-.
188. RAND Corporation. ***Selected RAND Abstracts.*** Santa Monica, CA.: RAND Corporation, 1965-.
189. ***Reader's Guide to Periodical Literature.*** New York: H.W. Wilson, 1965-.
190. ***Sage Public Administration Abstracts.*** Beverly Hills, CA.: Sage, 1974/74-.
191. ***Social Sciences Index.*** New York: H.W. Wilson, 1974/75-.
192. ***Social Sciences and Humanities Index.*** New York: H.W. Wilson, 1965-1974. Continued by the Social Sciences Index.
193. ***Sociological Abstracts.*** San Diego, CA.: Sociological Abstracts, 1965-.
194. ***Television News Index and Abstracts: A Guide to the Videotape Collection of the Network Evening News Programs in the Vanderbilt Television News Archives.*** Nashville, TN.: Vanderbilt University News Archives, [1980-].

195. ***Terrorism: An International Resource File.*** Ann Arbor, MI.: University Microfilm International, 1986-.

196. United Nations. Dag Hammarskjold Library. ***United Nations Documents Index.*** New York, 1965-.

197. ***United States Political Science Abstracts.*** Pittsburgh, PA.: NASA Industrial Applications Center, University of Pittsburgh, 1975-.

198. United States. Library of Congress. Legislative Reference Service. ***Digest of Public General Bills and Selected Resolutions, with Index.*** Washington, D.C.: U.S. Government Printing Office, 1965-.

199. _____. Superintendent of Documents. ***Monthly Catalogue of U.S. Government Publications.*** Washington, D.C.: U.S. Government Printing Office, 1965-.

H. NEWSPAPER INDEXES

200. ***Canadian News Index.*** Toronto: Micromedia, 1977-.

201. ***Christian Science Monitor Index.*** Cornvallis, OR.: Helen M. Cropsey, 1965-.

202. ***New York Times Index.*** New York: New York Times, 1965-.

203. ***Newspaper Index. (To Chicago Tribune, Washington Post, Los Angeles Times and New Orleans Picayune).*** Worster, OH., 1972-.

204. ***Times, London.: Index to the Times.*** London: Times, 1965-.

I. DATABASES

205. ***Africa News.*** Available from NewsNet Inc.

206. ***America: History and Life.*** Available from DIALOG.

207. ***Asian Political News.*** Available from DATA-STAR, DIALOG.

208. ***Australian Public Affairs Information Service. (APAI).*** Available from OZLINE. Available on CD-ROM.

209. ***Aviation/Aerospace Online.*** Available from Aviation/Aerospace Online, DIALOG, Dow Jones News, MEAD DATA CENTRAL.

210. ***Biography Index.*** 1984-. Available from Wilsonline. Available on CD-ROM from H. W. Wilson.

211. ***Biography Master Index (BMI), Annual.*** Available from DIALOG.

212. ***Books in Print.*** 1900-. Available from BRS; DIALOG; UTLAS. Available on CD-ROM from Bowker.

213. ***British Official Publications (Non-HMSO).*** Available from DIALOG.

214. ***Business Periodicals Index.*** 1982-. Available from Wilsonline. Available on CD-ROM from H. W. Wilson.

215. ***CDMARC Bibliographic.*** Available on CD-ROM from the U.S. Library of Congress.

216. ***CIS Index.*** Available from DIALOG.

217. ***CODOC. (Cooperative Documents Project).*** 1901-. Available from CAN OLE.

218. ***Canadian Business and Current Affairs.*** 1982-. Available from CAN OLE; DIALOG. Available on CD-ROM from DIALOG.

219. ***Canadian News Index. (CNI).*** 1977-. Available from QL.

220. ***Canadian Periodical Index.*** Available from Info-Globe.

221. ***Canadian Press Newstex.*** 1981-. Available from QL.

222. ***The Catalogue of United Kingdom Official Publications.*** Available on CD-ROM from Chadwick-Healey.

223. ***Congressional Masterfile (1789-1969).*** Available on CD-ROM from C.I.S.

224. ***Congressional Masterfile 2 (1970-).*** Available on CD-ROM from C.I.S.

225. ***Congressional Records Abstracts.*** 1981-. Available from DIALOG; Public Affairs Information; SDC.

226. ***Country Report Services.*** Available from DATA STAR, MEAD DATA.

227. ***Criminal Justice Periodicals Index.*** 1975-. Available from DIALOG.

228. ***Cumulative Book Index.*** Available on WILSONLINE. Available on CD-ROM from H. W. Wilson.

229. ***Current Digest of the Soviet Press.*** Available from DIALOG, Knowledge Index, MEAD DATA.

230. ***Defence and Foreign Affairs.*** Current. Available from Mead Data Central.

231. ***Department of State Travel Advisory.*** Available from COMPUSERVE.

232. ***Dissertation Abstracts Online.*** 1861-. Available from BRS; DIALOG. Available on CD-ROM from UMI.

233. ***Facts on FILE: News Digest on CD-ROM.*** Available on CD-ROM from Facts on File.

234. ***Federal Index.*** 1976-1980. Available from DIALOG.

235. Fowler, W. W. ***Terrorism Data Bases: A Comparison of Missions, Methods and Systems.*** RAND N-1503-RC. Santa Monica, CA.: RAND Corporation, 1981. 42p.

236. ***G.P.O. Monthly Catalog.*** 1976-. Available from BRS; DIALOG. Available on CD ROM from OCLC, Silver Platter.

237. ***G.P.O. Publications Reference File.*** 1971-. Available from DIALOG.

238. ***General Periodicals Index.*** Available on CD-ROM from Information Access.

239. ***Globe and Mail Online.*** 1977-. Available from Infoglobe.

240. ***Government Documents Catalog Service.*** Available on CD-ROM from Auto-Graphics.

241. ***Government Publication and Periodicals.*** Available on CD-ROM from H. W. Wilson.

242. ***Government Publications Index.*** Available on CD-ROM from Information Access.

243. ***Historical Abstracts.*** 1973-. Available from DIALOG.

244. ***Index to Canadian Legal Literature.*** Available from INFO GLOBE.

245. ***Index to Legal Periodicals.*** Available from WILSONLINE. Available on CD-ROM from H. W. Wilson.

246. ***Index to U.S. Government Periodicals. (GOVT).*** 1980-. Available from BRS.

247. ***Jane's Defence and Aerospace News/Analysis.*** Available from DIALOG.

248. ***Law Enforcement and Criminal Justice Information Data Base.*** 1954-. Available from International Research & Evaluation.

249. ***Legal Resource Index.*** 1980-. Available from BRS; DIALOG.

250. ***MIDEAST File.*** 1979-. Available from DIALOG.

251. ***Magazine ASAP.*** 1983-. Available from DIALOG.

252. ***Magazine Index.*** 1959-. Available from BRS; DIALOG; Knowledge Index: Mead Data Central. Available on CD-ROM from Information Access.

253. ***Mental Health Abstracts.*** 1969-. Available from BRS; DIALOG.

254. ***The Middle East: Abstracts and Index.*** 1980-. Available from DIALOG.

255. ***NCJRS. (National Criminal Justice Reference Service).*** 1972-. Available from DIALOG.
256. ***NTIS. National Technical Information Service.*** Available on CD-ROm from DIALOG, OCLC.
257. ***National Newspaper Index.*** 1979-. Available from BRS.
258. ***New York Times - On Line.*** 1980-. Available from MEAD Data Central.
259. ***Newspaper Abstracts on Disk.*** Available on CD-ROM from UMI/DATA Courier.
260. ***OCLC Online Union Catalog.*** Available from OCLC.
261. ***OONL (CAN/MARC).*** 1973-. Available from CAN OLE.
262. ***PAIS International.*** 1976-. Available from BRS; DIALOG. Available on CD-ROM from PAIS, Silver Platter.
263. ***Periodical Abstracts on Disc.*** Available on CD-ROM from UMI/DATA Courier.
264. ***Psyc Info.*** 1967-. Available from BRS; DATA-STAR; DIALOG; SDC. Available on CD-ROM from Silver Platter.
265. ***Reader's Guide to Periodical Literature.*** Available on CD-ROM from H. W. Wilson.
266. ***SSIE Current Research.*** 1978-1982. Available from DIALOG.
267. Schmid, Alex P., Albert J. Jongman and R. Thysse. "Data and Data Bases on State and Non-State Terrorism." In: A. P. Schmid and A. J. Jongman. ***Political Terrorism.*** New Brunswick, NJ.: Transaction Books, 1988. pp. 137-175.
268. ***Social SciSearch.*** 1972-. Available from BRS; DIALOG; DIMDI. Available on CD-ROM.
269. ***Social Sciences Index.*** 1984-. Available from Wilson Line.
270. ***Sociological Abstracts.*** 1963-. Available from BRS; DATA-STAR; DIALOG. Available on CD-ROM from Silver Platter.
271. ***World Affairs Report.*** 1980-. Available from DIALOG.

J. PERIODICALS

272. ***Conflict.*** Available from Crane Russak.
273. ***The International Terrorism Newsletter.*** Available from C. M. Hellebush, ed. P.O. Box 22425, Louisville, KY.
274. ***Political Communication and Persuasion: An Interdisciplinary Journal.*** Available from Crane Russak.
275. ***TVI Journal (Terrorism, Violence, Insurgency Journal).*** Available from P.O. Box 1055, Beverly Hills, CA.
276. ***Terror Update.*** Edgeware, Middx.: Intel Publishing, 1986-.
277. ***Terrorism and Political Violence.*** Available from Frank Cass.
278. ***Terrorism: An International Journal.*** Available from Crane Russak.
279. ***Violence, Aggression, and Terrorism.*** Available from Decisions, Issues and Alternatives, Inc., CT.

II

GENERAL WORKS

The first part of this chapter deals with the unresolved issue of definition. The term terrorism has its roots in the French Revolution when terror was understood to mean state violence against domestic political opponents. Modern definitions are numerous and varied. Definitions vary according to one's political outlook, national allegiance and religious affiliation. Domestic terrorism is defined differently from international terrorism. Despite all these diversities of terrorism, most researchers agree that they all have violence or the threat of violence to advance some political end as the common element. This section includes materials that address directly the various aspects of definition. Materials dealing indirectly with the question of definition can be found in many of the other works included in this bibliography.

The main section of this chapter lists materials of general nature, including: general studies on all aspects of terrorism, covering causes, historical studies, studies on political violence, revolutions, organizational analyses, literature analyses and other types of materials which could not be easily classified into one of the more specific chapters.

A. DEFINITIONS OF TERRORISM

1. Journal Articles

280. Allemann, Fritz R. "Terrorism: Definitional Aspects." ***Terrorism***, 3:3-4 (1980), 185-190.

281. Collins, John M. "Definitional Aspects." In: Y. Alexander and C. K. Ebinger, eds. ***Political Terrorism and Energy***. New York: Praeger, 1982. pp. 1-14.

282. Farrell, William R. "Terrorism Is...?" ***Naval War College Review***, 33:3 (1980), 68-72.

283. Fattah, Ezzat A. "Terrorist Activities and Terrorist Targets: A Tentative Typology." In: Y. Alexander and J. M. Gleason, eds. ***Behavioral and Quantitative Perspectives on Terrorism***. New York: Pergamon Press, 1981. pp. 11-34.

284. Forte, David F. "Terror and Terrorism: There is a Difference." ***Ohio Northern University Law Review***, 13:1 (1986), 39-51.

285. Fraser, James, and Donald B. Vought. "Terrorism: The Search for Working Definitions." ***Military Review***, 67:7 (1986), 70-76.

286. Friedlander, Robert A. "Terrorism." In: ***Encyclopedia of Public International Law, Instalment 9: International Relations and Legal Cooperation in General Diplomacy and Consular Relations***. Amsterdam: North-Holland, 1986. pp. 371-376.

287. Georges-Abeyie, D. E., and Lawrence Haas. "Propaganda by Deed: Defining Terrorism." ***The Justice Reporter***, 2:3 (1982), 1-7.

288. Greaves, Douglas. "The Definition and Motivation of Terrorism." ***Australian Journal of Forensic Science***, 13 (June 1981), 160-166.

289. Hilmy, Nabil. "What is Terrorism? A Legal View." In: R. H. Ward and H. E. Smith, eds. ***International Terrorism: The Domestic Response***. Chicago, IL.: University of Illinois at Chicago, Office of International Criminal Justice, 1987. pp. 23-26.

290. Hitchens, Christopher. "Wanton Acts of Usage: Terrorism: A Cliche in Search of a Meaning." ***Harper's Magazine***, (September 1986), 66-70.

291. International Law Association. Committee on International Terrorism. "An Interim Report on 'War', 'Armed Conflict', and Terrorism." In: H. H. Han, ed. ***Terrorism, Political Violence and World Order***. Lanham, MD.: University Press of America, 1984. pp. 155-172.

292. Jenkins, Brian M. "The Study of Terrorism: Definitional Problems." In: Y. Alexander and J. M. Gleason, eds. ***Behavioral and Quantitative Perspectives on Terrorism***. New York: Pergamon Press, 1981. pp. 3-10.

293. Kupperman, Robert H. "Terrorism is International Warfare." In: B. Szumski, ed. ***Terrorism: Opposing Viewpoints***. St.Paul, MN.: Greenhaven Press, 1986. pp. 33-38.

294. Lador-Lederer, J. J. "Defining 'Terrorism' - A Comment." In: H. H. Han, ed. ***Terrorism, Political Violence and World Order***. Lanham, MD.: University Press of America, 1984. pp. 5-7.

295. Levitt, Geoffrey M. "Is "Terrorism" Worth Defining?." ***Ohio Northern University Law Review***, 13:1 (1986), 97-115.

296. Miller, Brian R. E. "Defining Political Terrorism." ***The Futurist***, 23:4 (1989), 16-17.

297. _____. "Defining Political Terrorism." ***Military Intelligence***, (March 1987), 22-23+.

298. Murphy, John F. "Defining International Terrorism: A Way Out of the Quagmire." In: ***Israel Yearbook on Human Rights, Vol. 19. 1989.*** Dordrecht: Martinus Nijhoff, 1989. pp. 13-38.

299. Netanyahu, Benjamin. "Defining Terrorism." In: B. Netanyahu, ed. ***Terrorism: How the West Can Win.*** New York: Farrar, Straus, Giroux, 1986. pp. 7-15.

300. Netanyahu, Benzion. "Terrorists and Freedom Fighters." In: B. Netanyahu, ed. ***Terrorism: How the West Can Win.*** New York: Farrar, Straus, Giroux, 1986. pp. 25-30.

301. Pasquino, Gianfranco. "Terrorism." In: J. Kuper, ed. ***Political Science and Political Theory.*** London: Routledge and Kegan, 1987. pp. 240-242.

302. Provizer, Norman W. "Defining Terrorism." In: M. Slann and B. Schechterman, eds. ***Multidimensional Terrorism.*** Boulder, CO.: Lynne Rienner, 1987. pp. 3-10.

303. _____. "Terrorism and the Terrors of Definition." ***Journal of Political Science,*** 14:1-2 (1986), 1-9.

304. Pyle, Christopher. "Defining Terrorism." ***Foreign Policy,*** 64 (Autumn 1986), 63-78.

305. Schmid, Alex P. "Concept." (First Chapter). In: A. P. Schmid. ***Political Terrorism: A Research Guide to Concepts, Theories, Data Bases and Literature.*** Amsterdam: SWIDOC, 1983. pp. 5-159.

306. Skubiszewski, Krzysztof. "Definition of Terrorism." In: ***Israel Yearbook on Human Rights, Vol. 19. 1989.*** Dordrecht: Martinus Nijhoff, 1989. pp. 39-54.

307. Standley, Tony. "Classifying Terrorism." In: H. Kochler, ed. ***Terrorism and National Liberation.*** Frankfurt: Verlag Peter Lang, 1988. pp. 67-78.

308. Taskiri, Muhammed Ali. "Terrorism: An Islamic Definition." ***Middle East Insight,*** 5 (November/December 1987), 32-36.

309. Teichman, J. "How to Define Terrorism." ***Philosophy,*** 64:250 (1989), 505-517.

310. Thackrah, John R. "Terrorism: A Definitional Problem." In: P. Wilkinson and A. M Stewart, eds. ***Contemporary Research on Terrorism.*** Aberdeen: Aberdeen University Press, 1987. pp. 24-44.

311. _____. "Terrorism: a Definitional Problem." ***RUSI & Brassey's Defense Yearbook,*** (1987), 181-204.

312. Thomas, Philip A., and Tony Standley. "Re-defining Terrorism." ***Australian Journal of Law and Society,*** 4 (1987) 61-84.

313. United States. Vice President's Task Force on Combatting Terrorism. "All Political Violence is Terrorism." In: B. Szumski, ed. ***Terrorism: Opposing Viewpoints.*** St.Paul, MN.: Greenhaven Press, 1986. pp. 16-21.

2. Documents and Reports

314. Hoffman, Robert A. ***Terrorism: A Universal Definition.*** Ph.D. Dissertation. Claremont, CA.: Claremont Graduate School, 1984. 216p.

315. Jenkins, Brian M. ***The Study of Terrorism: Definitional Problems.*** RAND P-6563. Santa Monica, CA.: RAND Corporation, 1980. 10p.

316. Tupman, W. A. ***Towards a Typology of Terrorism: Criticisms and Definitions in the Fields of Political Violence.*** Brookfield Paper No. 4. Exeter: University of Exeter, Centre for Police & Criminal Justice Studies, 1989. 9p.

B. GENERAL MATERIALS

1. Books

317. Adams, James. ***The Financing of Terror: Behind the PLO, IRA, Red Brigades and M19 Stand the Paymasters.*** New York: Simon & Schuster, 1986. 293p.

318. Adeniran, T., and Yonah Alexander. ***International Violence.*** New York: Praeger, 1983. 270p.

319. Alexander, Yonah, and Charles K. Ebinger. ***Political Terrorism and Energy: The Threat and Response.*** New York: Praeger, 1982. 258p.

320. _____, and Eli Tavin. ***Terrorists and Freedom Fighters.*** Fairfax, VA.: Hero Books, 1986. 180p.

321. _____, and Abraham H. Foxman, eds. ***The 1987 Annual on Terrorism.*** Dordrecht: Martinus Nijhoff, 1988. 257p.

322. _____, ed. ***The 1986 Annual on Terrorism.*** Dordrecht: Martinus Nijhoff, 1987. 358p.

323. _____, and Abraham H. Foxman, eds. ***The 1988-1989 Annual of Terrorism.*** Dordrecht: Martinus Nijhoff, 1990. 246p.

324. Anand, Vijay K. ***Terrorism and Security.*** New Delhi: Deep & Deep, 1984. 283p.

325. Anzovin, Steven, ed. ***Terrorism.*** The Reference Shelf Series. Vol. 58, No. 3. Glenwoods, CO.: Wilson, 1986. 192p.

326. Arnold, Terrell E., and Moorhead Kennedy. ***Think About Terrorism: The New Warfare.*** New York: Walker, 1987. 153p.

327. Bal, Doron, et al. ***Inter 84: A Review of International Terrorism in 1984.*** Tel Aviv: Tel Aviv University, Jaffee Center for Strategic Studies, 1985. 48p.

328. Bender, David L., and Bruno Leone, eds. ***Terrorism: Opposing Viewpoints.*** Opposing Viewpoints Series. St.Paul, MN.: Greenhaven Press, 1986. 240p.

329. Buckley, Alan D., and D. D. Olson, eds. ***International Terrorism: Current Research and Future Directions.*** Wayne, NJ.: Avery Publishing Group, 1980. 118p.

330. Calvert, Michael. ***Revolution.*** London: St.Martin's, 1984. 222p.

331. Carlton, David, and Carlo Schaerf, eds. ***Contemporary Terrorism: Studies in Sub-State Violence.*** London: Macmillan, 1981. 231p.

332. Chaliand, Gerard. ***Terrorism: From Popular Struggle to Media Spectacle.*** London: Sagi Books, 1987. 139p.

333. Chand, Attar. ***Terrorism, Political Violence and Security of Nations.*** Columbia, MO.: South Asia Books, 1988.

334. Chapman, Robert D. ***Crimson Web of Terror.*** Boulder, CO.: Paladin, 1980. 163p.

335. Cherniavsky, V., ed. ***The CIA on the Dock: Soviet Journalists on International Terrorism.*** Moscow: Progress Publishers, 1983. 176p.

336. Chomsky, Noam. ***Pirates & Emperors: International Terrorism in the Real World.*** Santa Monica, CA.: Claremont Press, 1986. 175p.

337. Clutterbuck, Richard L., ed. ***The Future of Political Violence: Destabilization, Disorder & Terrorism.*** London: St. Martin's Press, 1986. 232p.

338. Coker, Christopher. ***Terrorism.*** New York, CT.: Watts, 1986. 32p.

339. _____. ***Terrorism and Civil Strife.*** Conflicts in the 20th Century Series. New York: Watts, 1987. 64p.

340. Condit, D. M. ***Modern Revolutionary Warfare: An Analytical Overview.*** Kensington, MD.: American Institute for Research, 1983. 134p.

341. Connor, Michael. ***Terrorism: Its Goals, Its Targets, Its Methods - The Solutions.*** Boulder, CO.: Paladine Press, 1987. 272p.

342. Coyle, Dominick. ***Minorities in Revolt: Political Violence in Ireland, Italy and Cyprus.*** Cranbury, NJ.: Fairleigh Dickinson University Press, 1983. 253p.

343. Crenshaw, Martha. ***Terrorism, Legitimacy and Power: The Consequences of Political Violence.*** Middletown, CT.: Wesleyan University Press, 1983. 162p.

344. Dacor Bacon House Staff. ***Threat of International Terrorism.*** Dobbs Ferry, NY.: Oceana, 1988. 500p.

345. Dobson, Christopher, and Ronald Payne. ***War Without End: The Terrorists: An Intelligence Dossier.*** London: Harrap, 1986. 279p.

346. _____. _____. ***The Never Ending War.*** New York: Facts on File, 1987. 356p.

347. Ellingsen, Ellman, ed. ***International Terrorism as a Political Weapon.*** Oslo: The Norwegian Atlantic Committee, 1988. 71p.

348. Falk, Richard A. ***Revolutionaries and Functionaries: The Dual Face of Terrorism.*** New York: Dutton, 1988. 222p.

349. Foster, Levin W. ***A Menu for Terrorism.*** New York: Vantage, 1988.

350. Freedman, Lawrence Z., and Yonah Alexander, eds. ***Perspectives on Terrorism.*** Wilmington, DE.: Scholarly Resources, 1983. 254p.

351. _____, et al. ***Terrorism and International Order.*** Chatham House Special Paper. London: Routledge & Kegan Paul, 1986. 107p.

352. Freeman, Charles. ***Terrorism in Today's World.*** North Pomfret, VT.: David & Charles, 1980. 96p.

353. Frostmann, Herbert M. ***International Political Terrorism & the Approaching Emergence of the Authoritarian State.*** Albuquerque, NM.: American Classical College Press, 1981. 146p.

354. Goyal, Archana. ***Terrorism: Causes and Consequences.*** Bikaner, India: Institute of Environment, 1990. 129p.

355. Grosscup, Beau. ***The Explosion of Terrorism.*** Far Hills, NJ.: New Horizon, 1986. 340p.

356. Han, Henry H. ***Terrorism, Political Violence and World Order.*** Lanham, MD.: University Press of America, 1984. 767p.

357. Hanrahan, Gene Z. ***Terrorism 2000.*** Chapel Hill, N.C.: Documentary Publications, 1986. 300p.

358. Harris, Jonathan. ***The New Terrorism: Politics of Violence.*** New York: Messner, 1983. 160p.

359. Henrio, Ernst. ***Stop Terrorism.*** Moscow: Novosti Press Agency, 1982. 200p.

360. Herman, Edward. ***The Real Terror Network: Terrorism in Fact and Propaganda.*** Boston, MA.: South End Press, 1982. 252p.

361. _____, and Gerry O'Sullivan. ***The Terrorism Industry: The Experts and Institutions That Shape Our View of Terror.*** New York: Pantheon Books, 1989. 312p.

362. Hippchen, Leonard J., and Young S. Yim. ***Terrorism, International Crime and Arms Control.*** Springfield, IL.: C. C. Thomas, 1981. 293p.

363. Hopple, Gerald W. ***Transnational Terrorism: A Causal Modeling Approach.*** McLean, VA.: International Public Policy Research Corporation, 1980. 124p.

364. Hyde, M. O., and E. H. Forsyth. ***Terrorism - A Special Kind of Violence.*** New York: Dodd, Mead and Company, 1987. 117p.

365. ***International Terrorism & the CIA: Documents, Eyewitness Reports, Facts.*** London: Collets, 1983. 264p.

366. Klare, Michael T., and Peter Kornbluh. ***Low-Intensity Warfare: Counterinsurgency, Proinsurgency, and Antiterrorism in the Eighties.*** New York: Pantheon, 1988. 250p.

367. Koechler, Hans, ed. ***Terrorism and National Liberation: Proceedings of the International Conference on the Question of Terrorism.*** Frankfurt am Main: Peter Lang, 1988. 318p.

368. Kupperman, Robert H., and Jeff Kamen. ***Final Warning: Averting Disaster in the Age of Terrorism.*** New York: Doubleday, 1989. 242p.

369. Kurz, Anat, ed. ***Contemporary Trends in World Terrorism.*** New York: Praeger, 1987. 170p.

370. _____, et al. ***INTER 86: A Review of International Terrorism in 1986.*** Tel Aviv: Jaffee Center for Strategic Studies, 1987. 140p.

371. Laffin, John. ***War Annual 3: The World Conflict 1989; Contemporary Warfare Described and Analyzed.*** London: Brassey's Defence Publishers, 1989. 234p.

372. Laqueur, Walter Z. ***The Age of Terrorism.*** Boston, MA.: Little, Brown, 1987. 385p.

373. _____, and Yonah Alexander, eds. ***The Terrorism Reader.*** Rev. Ed. New York: New American Library, 1987. 416p.

374. Laur, Timothy M. ***The Handbook of International Terrorism & Political Violence.*** Boulder Creek, CA.: Aslan Press, 1987. 209p.

375. Lillich, Richard B., ed. ***Transnational Terrorism: Conventions and Commentary.*** Charlottesville, VA.: Michie Corp., 1982. 282p.

376. Livingstone, Neil C. ***The Weird World of Spooks, Counterterrorists, Adventurers, and not Quite Professionals.*** Lexington, MA.: Lexington Books, 1989. 437p.

377. Long, David E. ***The Anatomy of Terrorism.*** New York: Free Press, 1990. 244p.

378. Lopez, George A. ***Testing Theories of State Violence, State Terror & Repression.*** Boulder, CO.: Westview Press, 1990. 265p.

379. Mackey, Janet. ***Terrorism and Political Self-Determination: A Tragic Marriage We Could Help Decouple.*** Chicago, IL.: World Without War Council, 1980. 64p.

380. Merkl, Peter H. ***Political Violence and Terror: Motifs and Motivations.*** Berkeley, CA.: University of California Press, 1986. 380p.

381. Morgan, Robin. ***The Demon Lover: On the Sexuality of Terrorism.*** New York: Norton, 1989. 395p.

382. O'Ballance, Edgar. ***Terrorism in the 1980s.*** London: Arms and Armour Press, 1989. 127p.

383. O'Neill, Bard E., William R. Heaton and D. J. Alberts, eds. ***Insurgency in the Modern World.*** Boulder, CO.: Westview Press, 1980. 291p.

384. Oots, Kent L. ***A Political Organization Approach to Transnational Terrorism.*** Contributions to Political Science, No. 141. Westport, CT.: Greenwood Press, 1986.

385. Perdue, William D. ***Terrorism and the State: A Critique of Domination Through Fear.*** New York: Praeger, 1989. 229p.

386. Pisano, Vittorfranco S. ***Terrorist Dynamics: A Geographical Perspective.*** Arlington, VA: International Association of Chiefs of Police, 1988. 191p.

387. Purcell, Hugh. ***Revolutionary War: Guerrilla Warfare and Terrorism in Our Time.*** London: H. Hamilton, 1980. 96p.

388. Radu, Michael, ed. ***The New Insurgencies: Anticommunist Guerrillas in the Third World.*** Dobbs Ferry, NY.: Transaction Publishers, 1990. 306p.

389. Raynor, Thomas P. ***Terrorism.*** New York: Franklin Watts, 1982. 160p.

390. Reid, Edna F., ed. ***Terrorism.*** Resources on Contemporary Issues, Ser, No. 2. Ann Arbor, MI.: Pierian Press, 1986.

391. Rivers, Gayle. ***The Specialist: The Personal Story of an Elite Specialist in Covert Operations.*** London: Sidgwick & Jackson, 1985. 318p.

392. Rubenstein, Richard E. ***Alchemists of Revolution: Terrorism in the Modern World.*** New York: Basic Books, 1987. 266p.

393. Rubin, Barry, ed. ***The Politics of Terrorism: Terror as a State and Revolutionary Strategy.*** Washington, D.C.: Johns Hopkins University, Foreign Policy Institute. 1989. 236p.

394. Rudolph, Harold. ***Security, Terrorism and Torture: Detainee's Rights in South Africa and Israel: A Comparative Study.*** Capetown: Juta, 1984. 270p.

395. Santoro, Victor. ***Disruptive Terrorism.*** Boulder, CO.: Paladin Press, 1985. 135p.

396. Schamis, Gerardo J. ***War & Terrorism in International Affairs.*** New Brunswick, NJ.: Transaction Pubs, 1980. 100p.

397. Schechterman, Bernard, and Martin Slann, eds. ***Violence & Terrorism, 1990-1991.*** Guilford, CT.: Dushkin, 1989. 256p.

398. Schlagheck, Donna M. ***International Terrorism: An Introduction to Concepts and Actors.*** Lexington, MA.: Lexington Books, 1988. 163p.

399. Sederberg, Peter C. ***Terrorist Myths: Illusion, Rhetoric, and Reality.*** Englewood Cliffs, NJ.: Prentice-Hall, 1989. 168p.

400. Segaller, Stephen. ***Invisible Armies: Terrorism into the 1990s.*** San Diego, CA.: Harcourt, Brace, Jovanovich, 1987. 310p.

401. Selth, Andrew. ***Against Every Human Law: The Terrorist Threat to Diplomacy.*** Rushcutters Bay, N.S.W.: Australian National University Press, 1988. 219p.

402. Slann, Martin, and Bernard Schechterman, eds. ***Multidimensional Terrorism.*** Boulder, CO.: Lynne Rienner, 1987. 138p.

403. Slater, Robert O., and Michael Stohl, eds. ***Current Perspectives on International Terrorism.*** London: Macmillan Press, 1988. 270p.

404. Stohl, Michael, ed. ***The Politics of Terrorism.*** 2nd ed. New York: Marcel Dekker, 1983. 473p.

405. _____, ed. ***The Politics of Terrorism.*** 3rd ed. New York: Marcel Dekker, 1988. 622p.

406. Syrokomsky, V. ***International Terrorism and the C.I.A.*** Moscow: Progress Publishers, 1983. 264p.

407. Szumski, Bonnie, ed. ***Terrorism: Opposing Viewpoints.*** St.Paul, MN.: Greenhaven Press, 1986. 240p.

408. Taheri, Amir. ***Holy Terror: Inside the World of Islamic Terrorism.*** Bethesda, MD.: Adler & Adler, 1987. 332p.

409. Thompson, Loren B., ed. ***Low Intensity Conflict: The Pattern of Warfare in the Modern World.*** Lexington. MA.: Lexington Books, 1989. 207p.

410. Veenaskay Muakasa, Sahar. ***Terrorism and Political Destabilization.*** New York: Advance Research, 1986-. 2 Vols.

411. Wardlaw, Grant. ***Political Terrorism: Theory, Tactics and Counter-Measures.*** London: Cambridge University Press, 1982. 218p.

412. _____. ***Political Terrorism: Theory, Tactics & Counter Measures.*** New York: Cambridge University Press, 1989. 250p.

413. Warner, Martin, and Roger Crisp, eds. ***Terrorism, Protest and Power.*** Brookfield, VT.: Gower, 1990. 197p.

414. Weinberg, Leonard, and Paul Davis. ***Introduction to Political Terrorism.*** New York: McGraw-Hill, 1989. 234p.

415. White, Jonathan R. ***Terrorism: An Introduction: A Review of Domestic and International Terrorism for Police, Military and Security Forces.*** Pacific Grove, CA.: Brooks Cole, 1990.

416. Wilkinson, Paul. ***The New Fascists.*** London: Grant McIntyre, 1981. 179p.

417. _____. ***Terrorism and the Liberal State.*** 2nd rev ed. London: Macmillan, 1986.

418. _____, and Alasdair M. Stewart, eds. ***Contemporary Research on Terrorism.*** Aberdeen: Aberdeen University Press, 1987. 634p.

2. *Journal Articles*

419. Aaronson, Michael. "Terrorism or Freedom Fighting? A Minefield in International Relations." ***International Relations,*** 8:6 (November 1986), 611-634.

420. Abbott, Kenneth W. "Economic Sanctions and International Terrorism." ***Vanderbilt Journal of Transnational Law,*** 20:2 (March 1987), 289-328.

421. Abrams, Elliot. "Terrorist Wrongs Versus Human Rights." ***World Affairs,*** 146:1 (1983), 69-78.

422. Adam, Sunil. "Terrorism and International Relations." ***Strategic Analysis,*** (February 1987), 1325-1340.

423. Adams, James. "Banking on Terror." ***Penthouse,*** (November 1986), 40-42, 70-74.

424. _____. "The Financing of Terror." In: P. Wilkinson and A. M. Stewart, eds. ***Contemporary Research on Terrorism,*** Aberdeen: Aberdeen University Press, 1987. pp. 393-405.

425. Agyeman, Opoku. "Terrorism: The Northwestern View." ***Monthly Review,*** (May 1987), 43-53.

426. Ahmad, Eqbal. "Terrorists Struggle Against Oppressive Governments." In: B. Szumski, ed. ***Terrorism: Opposing Viewpoints.*** St.Paul, MN.: Greenhaven Press, 1986. pp. 58-61.

427. Albin, Cecilia. "The Politics of Terrorism: A Contemporary Survey." In: B. Rubin, ed. ***The Politics of Terrorism.*** Lanham, MD.: University Press of America, 1988. pp. 183-234.

428. Alexander, Yonah, Phil Baum and Raphael Danziger. "Terrorism: Future Threats and Responses." ***Terrorism,*** 7:4 (1985), 367-410.

429. _____, and Jaime Suchlicki. "Selected Papers from: International Terrorism: Threats and Responses." ***Terrorism,*** 10:1 (1987), 51-81.

430. _____. "Terrorism: Threats and Trends." ***Terrorism,*** 10:3 (1987), 213-216.

431. Amernic, Jerry. "Experiments in Terror." ***Quest,*** (November 1981), 62-65.

432. Amir, Menachem. "Political Terrorism and "Common Criminality": Some Preliminary Considerations." ***Violence, Aggression and Terrorism,*** 1:4 (1987), 371-402.

433. Anand, Vijay K. "Future Terrorism: Threats and Security." ***U.S.I. Journal,*** (April-June, 1985), 115-125.

434. Anderson, Bill. "Economics - Not Oppression - Motivates Terrorists." In: B. Szumski, ed.: ***Terrorism: Opposing Viewpoints.*** St. Paul, MN.: Greenhaven Press, 1986. pp. 62-68.

435. "Animal Rights Extremists Threaten Research." ***Law and Order,*** 6 (1990), 4-5.

436. Arnold, Ron. "Eco-Terrorism." ***Reason,*** 14 (February 1983), 31-36.
437. Arostegni, Martin C. "Special Report of Risks International." ***Terrorism,*** 7:4 (1985), 417-430.
438. Asencio, Diego, and Susan M. Livingston. "Terrorism: "The Original Cheap Shot"." ***World Affairs,*** 146:1 (1983), 42-53.
439. Asimov, Leonard, and Frederick D. Homer. "Democracies and the Role of Acquiescence in International Terrorism." In: M. Stohl and G. A. Lopez, eds. ***Terrible Beyond Endurance? The Foreign Policy of State Terrorism.*** Westport, CT.: Greenwood Press, 1988. pp. 35-58.
440. Ate, B. E. "Terrorism in the Context of Decolonization." In: H. Kochler, ed. ***Terrorism and National Liberation.*** Frankfurt: Verlag Peter Lang, 1988. pp. 79-86.
441. Atlantic Assembly. Working Group on Terrorism. "North Atlantic Assembly: Draft Interim Report." Y. Alexander, ed. ***The 1986 Annual on Terrorism.*** Dordrecht: Martinus Nijhoff, 1987. pp. 349-354.
442. "Atlas of Terrorism." ***Assets Protection,*** 6:2 (1981), 26-36.
443. Avery, William P. "Terrorism, Violence and the International Transfer of Conventional Armaments." In: Y. Alexander and J. M. Gleason, eds. ***Behavioral and Quantitative Perspectives on Terrorism.*** New York: Pergamon Press, 1981. pp. 329-342.
444. Azar, Edward. "Terrorism: A Global Perspective." ***Terrorism,*** 11:5 (1988), 348-349.
445. Barrett, David. "The Threat of Terrorism in a Broader Concept." In: B. Netanyahu, ed. ***International Terrorism: Challenge and Response.*** New Brunswick, NJ.: Transaction Books, 1981. pp. 122-127.
446. Barrett, Michael J. "Patterns in Terror." ***Defence and Diplomacy,*** 4:3 (March 1986), 40-43.
447. Bassiouni, M. Cherif. "Introduction: A Policy-Oriented Inquiry into the Different Forms and Manifestations of 'International Terrorism." In: M. C. Bassiouni, ed. ***Legal Responses to International Terrorism: U.S. Procedural Aspects.*** Dordrecht: Martinus Nijhoff, 1988. pp. xv-.
448. Beck, Barbara. "Terrorism Unlimited: Facts and Fallacies." ***Encounter,*** 69:4 (1988), 59-62.
449. Beeman, William D. "Terrorism: Community Based or State Supported?" ***American-Arab Affairs,*** (Spring 1986), 29-36.
450. Beer, D. "Terrorism." ***Social Education,*** 45:6 (1981), 480-482.
451. Begin, Menachem. "Freedom Fighters and Terrorists." In: B. Netanyahu, ed. ***International Terrorism: Challenge and Response.*** New Brunswick, NJ.: Transaction Books, 1981. pp. 39-46.
452. Bell, J. Bowyer. "An Overview." In: D. Carlton and C. Schaerf, eds. ***Contemporary Terror.*** London: Macmillan, 1981. pp. 21-36.
453. _____. "Old Trends and Future Reality." ***Washington Quarterly,*** 8:2 (1985), 25-36.
454. _____. "Terrorism and the Eruption of Wars." In: A. Merari, ed. ***On Terrorism and Combating Terrorism.*** Frederick, MD.: University Publications of America, 1985. pp. 41-52.
455. _____. "Explaining International Terrorism: The Elusive Quest." In: C. W. Kegley, ed. ***International Terrorism: Characteristics, Causes, Controls.*** New York: St. Martin's Press, 1990. pp. 178-184.
456. Belloff, Lord. "The Plague of Terrorism." ***RUSI: Journal of the Royal United Services Institute for Defence Studies,*** 127:1 (1982), 68-69.

457. Benson, Mike, M. Evans and Robert I. Simon. "Women as Political Terrorists." ***Research in Law, Deviance and Social Control,*** 4 (1982), 121-130.
458. Berman, Karl. "Bookstores Downplay Risk of Attacks." ***Business Insurance,*** 23:12 (1989), 16-17.
459. Berry, Nicholas O. "Theories on the Efficacy of Terrorism." In: P. Wilkinson and A. M. Stewart, eds. ***Contemporary Research on Terrorism.*** Aberdeen: Aberdeen University Press, 1987. pp. 293-306.
460. _____. "Theories on the Efficacy of Terrorism." ***Conflict Quarterly,*** 7 (Winter 1987), 7-20.
461. Beyl, R. A., et al. "International Terrorism: Proceedings of the International Terrorism Workshop held at the 88th Annual IACP Conference." ***Police Chief,*** 49:1 (1982), 112-130.
462. Bklash, S. "The Riddle of Terrorism." ***New York Review of Books,*** 34 (September 24, 1987), 12-16.
463. Blaufarb, Douglas S. "Terrorist Trends and Ties." ***Problems of Communism,*** 31:3 (1982), 73-77.
464. Bluhm, Louis H. "Trust, Terrorism and Technology." ***"Journal of Business Ethics,*** 6 (July 1987), 333-341.
465. _____. "International Terrorism: An Analysis of Some Fundamental Parameters and Issues." ***International Journal of Contemporary Sociology,*** 24:3-4 (July-October 1987), 141-153.
466. Blum, Robert. "Terrorism and the Uses of Rhetoric." ***Ohio University Law Review,*** 13:1 (1987), 31-38.
467. Bodansky, Yossef. "Issues in Terrorism Research." ***Terrorism,*** 12:1 (1989), 71-72.
468. Boyce, Daniel. "Narco-Terrorism." ***FBI Law Enforcement Bulletin,*** 56:10 (October 1987), 24-27.
469. Braungart, Richard G., and M. M. Braungart. "International Terrorism: Background and Response." ***Journal of Political and Military Sociology,*** 9:2 (1981), 263-288.
470. _____. _____. "Terrorism." In: A. P. Goldstein and L. Krasner, eds. ***Prevention and Control of Aggression.*** Elmsford, NY.: Pergamon Press, 1983. pp. 299-337.
471. Bremer, L. Paul. "Terrorism: Myths and Reality." In: E. Ellingsen, ed. ***International Terrorism as a Political Weapon.*** Oslo: The Norwegian Atlantic Committee, 1988. pp. 17-26.
472. Buckelew, Alvin H. "International Terrorism: Shadow on the Western World." ***Security Management,*** 30:4 (1986), 36-41.
473. Buckland, P. "Britain's Responsibility for Violence in Ireland and the Middle East: State Creation After the First World War." In: Y. Alexander and A. O'Day, eds. ***Ireland's Terrorist Dilemma.*** Dordrecht: Martinus Nijhoff, 1986. pp. 61-74.
474. Bull, Hedley. "The International Anarchy in the 1980s." ***Australian Outlook,*** 37:3 (December 1983), 132-137.
475. Byford, Lawrence. "Terrorism and Democracy." In: D. E. J. MacNamara and P. J. Stead, eds. ***New Dimensions in Transnational Crime.*** New York: John Jay Press, 1982. pp. 66-71.
476. Carlton, David. "The Future of Political Sub-State Violence." In: D. Carlton and C. Schaerf, eds. ***Contemporary Terror.*** London: Macmillan, 1981. pp. 90-111.
477. Cauley, Jon, and Todd Sandler. "Fighting World War III:A Suggested Strategy." ***Terrorism,*** 11:3 (1988), 181-196.

478. Cetron, Marvin. "The Growing Threat of Terrorism." ***The Futurist***, 23 (July/August 1989), 20-24.

479. _____, and Thomas O'Toole. "Encounters with the Future: A Forecast of Life into the 21st Century." ***TVI Journal***, 6:2 (1985), 5+.

480. Chalfont, Lord. "Terrorism and International Security." ***Terrorism***, 5:4 (1982), 309-324.

481. _____. "Terrorism and International Security." In: Y. Alexander and R. Latter, eds. ***Terrorism and the Media***. New York: Brassey's, 1990. pp. 12-22.

482. Charters, David. "Terrorism: A Survey of Recent Literature." ***Conflict Quarterly***, 7:4 (Fall 1987), 64-84.

483. "Charting Terrorism's Course." ***Security Management***, 31 (June 1987), 66-67.

484. Chomsky, Noam. "International Terrorism - Image and Reality." ***Crime and Social Justice***, 27:2 (1987), 172-200.

485. _____. "International Terrorism: Diplomacy by Other Means." ***Canadian Dimension***, 20:8 (February 1987), 37-40.

486. Christopher, Maura. "Terrorism's Brutal Impact - In Dollars and Cents." ***Scholastic Update***, (May 16, 1986),

487. Clark, R. "The Dimensions of Terrorism." In: H. Kochler, ed. ***Terrorism and National Liberation***. Frankfurt: Verlag Peter Lang, 1988. pp. 41-50.

488. Clark, Robert P. "Insurgents are not Crazy or Irrational - They are Different!." In: D. J. D. Sandole and I. Sandole-Staroste, eds. ***Conflict Management and Problem Solving***. London: Frances Pinter, 1987. pp. 197-198.

489. Clawson, Patrick. "Terrorism in Decline?." ***Orbis***, 32:2 (1988), 263-276.

490. Clutterbuck, Richard L. "Terrorism and Urban Violence." ***Proceedings of the Academy of Political Science***, 34:4 (1982), 165-175.

491. Cohen, Stephen P., and Harriet C. Arnone. "Conflict Resolution as the Alternative to Terrorism." ***Journal of Social Issues***, 44:2 (Summer 1988), 175-189.

492. Collins, J. G. "Terrorism and Animal Rights." ***Science***, 249:4967 (1990), 345.

493. Cooper, H. H. A. "Fiction May Become Fact." ***TVI Journal***, 4:1-3 (1983), 10-13.

494. Cordes, Bonnie J. "When Terrorists Do the Talking: Reflections on Terrorist Literature." ***Journal of Strategic Studies***, 10:4 (December 1987), 150-171.

495. _____. "When Terrorist Do the Talking - Reflections on Terrorist Literature." In: D. C. Rapoport, ed. ***Inside Terrorist Organizations***. New York: Columbia University Press, 1988. p. 150-171.

496. Corrado, Raymond R. "Female Terrorists: Competing Perspectives." In: C. T. Griffiths and M. Nance, eds. ***Female Offender***. Burnaby, B.C.: Simon Fraser University Criminology Research Centre, 1980. pp. 37-50.

497. "Covert Operations are Terrorism." In: B. Szumski, ed. ***Terrorism: Opposing Viewpoints***. St.Paul, MN.: Greenhaven Press, 1986. pp. 223-228.

498. Crelinsten, Ronald D. "Terrorism as Political Communication: The Relationship Between the Controller and the Controlled." In: P. Wilkinson and A. M. Stewart, eds. ***Contemporary Research on Terrorism***. Aberdeen: Aberdeen University Press, 1987. pp. 3-23.

499. _____. "Terrorism, Counterterrorism and National Security." In: P. Hanks and J. D. McCamus, eds. ***National Security: Surveillance and Accountability in a Democratic Society***. Cowansville, Que.: Les Editions Yvon Blais, 1990. pp. 207-226.

500. _____, and Denis Szabo. "International Political Terrorism: A Challenge for Comparative Research." ***Terrorism***, 3:3-4 (1980), 341-348.

501. _____. "Terrorism, Counter-Terrorism and Democracy: The Assessment of National Security Threats." ***Terrorism and Political Violence,*** 1:2 (April 1989), 242-269.
502. Crenshaw, Martha. "Conclusions." In M. Crenshaw, ed. ***Terrorism, Legitimacy and Power.*** Middletown, CT.: Wesleyan University Press, 1983. pp. 143-150.
503. _____. "Introduction: Reflections on the Effects of Terrorism." In M. Crenshaw, ed. ***Terrorism, Legitimacy and Power.*** Middletown, CT.: Wesleyan University Press, 1983. pp. 1-37.
504. _____. M. I. Midlarsky and Fumihiko Yoshida. "Why Violence Spreads: The Contagion of International Terrorism." ***International Studies Quarterly,*** 24:2 (1980), 262-298.
505. _____. _____. _____. "Rejoinder to Observations on 'Why Violence Spreads'." ***International Studies Quarterly,*** 24:2 (1980), 306-310.
506. _____. "An Organizational Approach to the Analysis of Political Terrorism." ***Orbis,*** 29:3 (1985), 465-488.
507. _____. "The Causes of Terrorism." ***Comparative Politics,*** 13:4 (July 1981), 379-399.
508. _____. "The Causes of Terrorism." In: C. W. Kegley, ed. ***International Terrorism: Characteristics, Causes, Controls.*** New York: St. Martin's Press, 1990. pp. 113-126.
509. "The Crime of World Terrorism." ***Scholastic Update,*** 118 (May 16, 1986), 2-129.
510. Dally, Peter. "Terrorism and East-West Tension: Peking Blames the U.S. and Israel." ***Asian Outlook,*** 21:7 (1986), 18-21.
511. Danforth, John C. "Terrorism Versus Democracy." in: B. Netanyahu, ed. ***International Terrorism: Challenge and Response.*** New Brunswick, NJ.: Transaction Books, 1981. pp. 115-121.
512. Delmas, Paul. "Terrorism and the Open Society." ***NATO Review,*** 30:5 (1982), 12-17.
513. _____. "Terrorism and the Open Society." In: H. H. Han, ed. ***Terrorism, Political Violence and World Order.*** Lanham, MD.: University Press of America, 1984. pp. 9-14.
514. Derrer, Douglas S. "Terrorism." ***U.S. Naval Institute Proceedings,*** 111 (May 1985), 190-203.
515. Deutsch, Antal. "On the Economics of Terrorism." ***Terrorism,*** 5:4 (1984), 363-366.
516. Devine, P. E., and R. J. Rafalko. "On Terror." ***Annals of the American Academy of Political and Social Science,*** 463 (1982), 39-53.
517. Dimitrijevic, Vojin. "Terrorism as International Provocation." ***Review of International Affairs,*** 36 (December 20, 1985), 5-7.
518. Dinstein, Yoram. "Terrorism and Human Rights." In: ***Festschrift in the Honor of Dr. George S. Wise.*** Tel Aviv: Tel Aviv University, 1982. pp. 72-81.
519. Doherty, Daniel A. "Carlos from 1970 to 1976: A Lesson in Transnational Terror." ***Joint Perspectives,*** 2 (Summer 1981), 70-79.
520. Donnelly, Frederick. "Linguistic Terrorism." ***Conflict Quarterly,*** 1:1 (1980), 31-35.
521. Dowling, Ralph E. "The Contributions of Speech Communication Scholarship to the Study of Terrorism: Review and Preview." ***Political Communication and Persuasion,*** 6:4 (1989), 289-310.
522. Dror, Yehezkel. "Terrorism as a Challenge to Democratic Capacity to Govern." In: M. Crenshaw, ed. ***Terrorism, Legitimacy and Power.*** Middletown, CT.: Wesleyan University Press, 1983. pp. 65-90.
523. _____. "High - Intensity Aggressive Ideologies as an International Threat." ***Jerusalem Journal of International Relations,*** 9:1 (March 1987), 153-172.

524. Duesbury, William C. "Softening the Final Option." ***TVI Report***, 6:3 (Winter 1986), 34-36.

525. Duncan, Keith, and Walter Isard. "A Thousand and One PH.D. Dissertation Topics: The Summary of the 1988 Third World Peace Science Congress," ***Conflict Management and Peace Science***, 10:2 (1989), 77-99.

526. Eby, L. "On Terrorism." ***International Journal on World Peace***, 4:2 (1987), 167-172.

527. Einstein, S. "An Interview with Dr. Robert Kupperman." ***Violence Aggression and Terrorism***, 1:4 (1987), 313-326.

528. _____. "An Interview with Mr. Brian Jenkins." ***Violence, Aggression and Terrorism***, 2:2 (1988), 99-118.

529. _____. "An Interview with Dr. Hans Horchem." ***Violence, Aggression and Terrorism***, 2:3 (1988), 199-220.

530. _____. "An Interview with Professor Jacques Leaute." ***Violence, Aggression and Terrorism***, 2:4 (1988), 295-306.

531. Eisenzweig, Uri. "Terrorism in Life and in Real Literature." ***Diacritics***, 18:3 (Fall 1988), 32-42.

532. Ellington, Lucien. "Teaching High School Students About Political Terrorism." ***Clearing House***, 56 (December 1982) 161-163.

533. Ellwood, Wayne. "Fear and Violence: The Roots of Terrorism." ***The New Internationalist***, 161 (1986), 4-6.

534. Epstein, David G. "Police, Terrorism and the Third World." ***Police Chief***, 52:4 (1986), 50-52.

535. Evans, Alona E. "Perspectives on International Terrorism." ***Willamette Law Review***, 17 (Winter 1980), 151-164.

536. Fagin, James A. "The Impact of Technology and Communications Upon International and Transnational Terrorism." ***International Journal of Comparative and Applied Criminal Justice***, 6:1-2 (1982), 85-98.

537. Falk, Richard A. "The Overall Terrorist Challenge in International Political Life." In: H. Kochler, ed. ***Terrorism and National Liberation.*** Frankfurt: Peter Lang, 1988. pp. 15-22.

538. _____. "Revolutionaries and Functionaries: The Dual Face of Terrorism." In: C. W. Kegley, ed. ***International Terrorism: Characteristics, Causes, Controls.*** New York: St. Martin's Press, 1990. pp. 39-44.

539. Fleming, Peter A., Michael Stohl and Alex P. Schmid. "The Theoretical Utility of Typologies of Terrorism: Lessons and Opportunities." In: M. Stohl, ed ***The Politics of Terrorism.*** New York: Marcel Dekker, 1988. pp. 153-196.

540. Ford, John W., and C. Casselman. "Balkanization of Western Hemisphere." In: H. H. Han, ed. ***Terrorism, Political Violence and World Order.*** Lanham, MD.: University Press of America, 1984. pp. 623-626.

541. Fraser, Hugh. "The Tyranny of Terrorism." In: B. Netanyahu, ed. ***International Terrorism: Challenge and Response.*** New Brunswick, NJ.: Transaction Books, 1981. pp. 23-32.

542. Freedman, Lawrence Z. "Terrorism and Strategy." In: ***Terrorism and International Order.*** London: Royal Institute of International Affairs, 1986. pp. 56-76.

543. Friedlander, Robert A. "Terrorism and National Liberation Movements: Can Rights Derive from Wrongs?" ***Case Western Reserve Journal of International Law***, 13 (Spring 1981), 281-289.

544. _____. "Terrorism and Self-Determination: The Fatal Nexus." ***Syracuse Journal of International Law and Commerce***, 7 (Winter 1979/80), 263-268.

545. Frost, Charles C. "Drug Trafficking, Organized Crime and Terrorism: The International Cash Connection." In: U. Ra'anan, et al. ***Hydra of Carnage.*** Lexington, MA.: Heath-Lexington Books, 1986. pp. 189-198.

546. Fulton, John S. "The Debate About Low-Intensity Conflict." ***Military Review***, 66:2 (1986), 62-67.

547. Galtung, Johan. "On the Causes of Terrorism and Their Removal." In: H. Kochler, ed. ***Terrorism and National Liberation***, Frankfurt: Verlag Peter Lang, 1988. pp. 51-66.

548. Galvin, Deborah M. "Women as Assassins - It's More Than a Shot in the Dark." ***TVI Journal***, 4:7-9 (1983), 6-11.

549. _____. "Women in the Role of Liberators." ***TVI Journal***, 3:12 (1983), 4-6.

550. Galyean, Thomas E. "Acts of Terrorism and Combat by Irregular Forces - An Insurance "War Risk"?." ***Comparative Juridical Review***, 21 (1984), 57-102.

551. Garner, Eric. "Correlates of State Terror: Militarism, Geopolitics and National Security Ideology." ***Chitty's Law Journal***, 32:1 (1984), 42-57.

552. Georges-Abeyie, D. E. "Political Crime and Terrorism: Toward an Understanding." In: G. R. Newman, ed. ***Crime and Deviance.*** Beverly Hills, CA.: Sage, 1980. pp. 313-332.

553. _____. "Toward the Development of a Terrorism Severity Index." ***Police Studies***, 6:4 (1983-84), 22-29.

554. _____. "Women as Terrorists." In: L. Z. Freedman and Y. Alexander, eds. ***Perspectives on Terrorism.*** Wilmington, DE.: Scholarly Resources, 1983. pp. 71-84.

555. _____. "Women as Terrorists." In: W. Laqueur, ed. ***The Terrorism Reader.*** New York: Meridian, 1987. pp. 260-266.

556. Gerringer, Arthur E. "Terrorism: 1986 Update." ***Law and Order***, 35:12 (December 1987), 67-72.

557. Gerson, Allan. "Terrorism and Turtle Bay." ***National Interest***, 11 (Spring 1988), 95-99.

558. Ghosh, Partha S. "International Terrorism: An Unending Malaise." ***Indian Journal of Social Science***, 2:4 (October-December 1989), 527-543.

559. Gibson, Fred E. "Terrorism: New Challenge for Government." In: B. Macdonald, ed. ***Terror.*** Toronto: Canadian Institute of Strategic Studies, 1987. pp. 4-10.

560. Goldie, L. F. E. "Profile of a Terrorist: Distinguishing Freedom Fighters from Terrorists." ***Syracuse Journal of International Law and Commerce***, 14:2 (Winter 1987), 125-139.

561. Govea, Rodger M. "Terrorism as a Political Science Offering." ***Teaching Political Science***, 8:1 (1980), 3-20.

562. Grachyov, A. "The Boomerang of Terrorism." ***New Times (Moscow)***, (October 26, 1987), 18-22.

563. _____. "Terrorism as a Method of Imperialist Foreign Policy." ***International Affairs***, (April 1982), 46-55.

564. _____. "Extremism and Terrorism in the Service of World Reaction." ***International Affairs***, (June 1981), 67-74.

565. Graham, David M. "Terrorism: What Political Status?" ***Round Table***, 284 (October 1981), 401-403.

566. Green, L. C. "Aspects of Terrorism." ***Terrorism***, 5:4 (1982), 373-400.

567. Greenberg, Joel. "Young Men Who Back Violence to Right Wrongs: How Do Terrorists Try to Justify Their Criminal Behavior?." ***Scholastic Update***, 118 (May 16, 1986), 4-6.

568. Griffith, E. "Terrorism. Part I and II." ***Security Gazette***, (December 1984), 10-11, 13-14; (January 1985), 14-15, 17.

569. Grimaldi, Michael A., et al. "Human Rights V. New Initiatives in the Control of Terrorism." ***American Society of International Law Proceedings***, (April 1985), 288-303.

570. Gross, Feliks. "Causation of Terror." In: W. Laqueur, ed. ***The Terrorism Reader.*** New York: Meridian, 1987. pp. 231-235.

571. Gurr, Ted R. "Some Characteristics of Political Terrorism in the 1960s." In: M. Stohl, ed. ***The Politics of Terrorism.*** 2nd ed. New York: Marcel Dekker, 1983. pp. 23-50.

572. _____. "Empirical Research on Political Terrorism: The State of the Art and How It Might Be Improved." In: R. O. Slater and M. Stohl, eds. ***Current Perspectives on International Terrorism.*** London: Macmillan, 1988. pp. 115-154.

573. _____. "Some Characteristics of Political Terrorism in the 1960s." In: M. Stohl, ed. ***The Politics of Terrorism.*** New York: Marcel Dekker, 1988. pp. 31-58.

574. _____. "Political Terrorism: Historical Antecedents and Contemporary Trends." In: T. R. Gurr, ed. ***Violence in America, Volume 2: Protest, Rebellion, Reform.*** Newbury Park, CA.: Sage Publications, 1989. pp. 201-230.

575. _____. "Terrorism in Democracies: Its Social and Political Bases." In: W. reich, ed. ***Origins of Terrorism.*** Cambridge: Cambridge University Press, 1990. pp. 86-102.

576. Gutteridge, William. "Summary of Discussions." In: D. Carlton and C. Schaerf, ed. ***Contemporary Terror.*** London: Macmillan, 1981. pp. 1-20.

577. Hacker, Frederick J. "Terror and Terrorism: Modern Growth Industry and Mass Entertainment." ***Terrorism***, 4 (1980), 143-160.

578. Halliday, Fred. "Terrorism in Historical Perspective." ***Arab Studies Quarterly***, 9:2 (1987), 139-148.

579. Hamilton, Donald R. "International Terrorism." ***Terrorism***, 11:4 (1988), 335-338.

580. Hamilton, Lawrence C., and James D. Hamilton. "Dynamics of Terrorism." ***International Studies Quarterly***, 26:4 (1982), 39-54.

581. Hatch, Orrin G. "Assessing the Cost of Terrorism." ***Connecticut Journal of International Law***, 2:2 (Spring 1987), 539-547.

582. Henze, Paul. "Organized Crime and Drug Linkages." In: U. Ra'anan, et al. ***Hydra of Carnage.*** Lexington, MA.: Heath-Lexington Books, 1986. pp. 171-188.

583. Hessman, James D. "Invisible Superpower - International Terrorism: The Major Threat of the 1990s." ***Sea Power***, 33:6 (June 1990), 43-44.

584. Hewitt, Christopher. "The Cost of Terrorism: A Cross-National Study of Six Countries." ***Terrorism***, 11:3 (1988), 169-180.

585. Heyman, Edward, and Edward F. Mickolus. "Observations on 'Why Violence Spreads'." ***International Studies Quarterly***, 24:2 (1980), 299-305.

586. Hildreth, Reed. "Terrorism Part III." ***Law and Order***, 36:8 (August 1988), 60-67.

587. _____. "Terrorism Part II." ***Law and Order***, 36:7 (July 1988), 61-67.

588. _____. "Terrorism Part I." ***Law and Order***, 36:6 (June 1988), 40-48.

589. Hocking, Jenny. "Terrorism and Counter Terrorism: Institutionalizing Political Order." ***Australia Quarterly***, (Spring 1986), 297-306.

590. Hopple, Gerald W. "Transnational Terrorism: Prospects for a Causal Modeling Approach." ***Terrorism,*** 6:1 (1982), 73-100.

591. Horowitz, Irving L. "The Routinization of Terrorism and its Unanticipated Consequences." In: M. Crenshaw, ed. ***Terrorism, Legitimacy and Power.*** Middletown, CT.: Wesleyan University Press, 1983. pp. 38-51.

592. Hruska, James M. "Terrorism: Is It War?." ***Military Police,*** (July 1988), 22-23.

593. Hunt, A. "A Civilized Sort of Terrorism." ***New Society,*** 76:1218 (1986), 10-11.

594. Hunter, Robert E., and Robert H. Kupperman. "Terrorism: Cancer of Civilization." ***American Legion,*** (June 1984), 16+.

595. "International Terrorism (Panel Discussion)." ***Police Chief,*** (March 1984), 94-98.

596. "International Terrorism in 1985: Main Features." In: A. Merari, et al. ***INTER 85.*** Boulder, CO.: Westview Press, 1986. pp. 4-12.

597. "Interview with Gerard Chaliand." ***TVI Report,*** 8:1 (1988), 1-7.

598. Ismail, Sadat. "Raid to Eradicate Terrorism." ***Pakistan Horizon,*** 39:2 (1986), 14-21.

599. Israel. Defence Forces Spokesman. "A Guide to Terrorist Leader's Codenames and Nicknames." In: Y. Alexander, ed. ***The 1986 Annual on Terrorism.*** Dordrecht: Martinus Nijhoff, 1987. pp. 297-300.

600. Jenkins, Brian M. "Areas of Consensus, Areas of Ignorance." In: B. Eichelman, D. Soskis and W. Reid, eds. ***Terrorism: Interdisciplinary Perspectives.*** Washington, D.C.: American Psychiatric Association, 1983. pp. 153-180.

601. _____, et al. "Forum: Terrorism and Political Violence." ***Orbis,*** 28:1 (1984), 5-52.

602. _____. "New Modes of Conflict." ***Orbis,*** 28:1 (1984), 5-15.

603. _____. "Statements About Terrorism." ***Annals of the American Academy of Political and Social Science,*** 463 (1982), 11-23.

604. _____. "Terrorism Prone Countries and Conditions." In: A. Merari, ed. ***On Terrorism and Combatting Terrorism.*** Frederick, MD.: University Publications of America, 1985. pp. 25-40.

605. _____. "Trends in International Terrorism." ***Journal of World Affairs,*** (Spring 1984), 40-48.

606. _____. "Terrorism Outlook for the 80's." ***Security Management,*** 25:1 (1981), 14-21.

607. _____. "Reflections on Recent Trends in Terrorism." ***Military Intelligence,*** (October-December 1984), 31-34.

608. _____. "Terrorism Cannot Be Eliminated." In: B. Szumski, ed. ***Terrorism: Opposing Viewpoints.*** St.Paul, MN.: Greenhaven Press, 1986. pp. 191-196.

609. _____. "The Future Course of International Terrorism." In: P. Wilkinson and A. M. Stewart, eds. ***Contemporary Research in Terrorism.*** Aberdeen: Aberdeen University Press, 1987. pp. 581-589.

610. _____. "The Future Course of International Terrorism." In: A. Kurz, ed. ***Contemporary Trends in World Terrorism.*** New York: Praeger, 1987. pp. 150-160.

611. _____. "Future Trends in International Terrorism." In: R. O. Slater and M. Stohl, eds. ***Current Trends on International Terrorism.*** London: Macmillan Press, 1988. pp. 246-266.

612. _____. "The Future Course of International Terrorism." ***Futurist,*** 21:4 (1987), 8-13.

613. _____. "International Terrorism: The Other World War." In: C. W. Kegley, ed. ***International Terrorism: Characteristics, Causes, Controls.*** New York: St. Martin's Press, 1990. pp. 27-38.

614. Johnson, Chalmers. "Perspectives on Terrorism." In: W. Laqueur, ed. ***The Terrorism Reader.*** New York: Meridian, 1987. pp. 267-288.

615. Johnson, Paul. "The Seven Deadly Sins of Terrorism." In: B. Netanyahu, ed. ***International Terrorism: Challenge and Response.*** New Brunswick, NJ.: Transaction Books, 1981. pp. 12-22.

616. _____. "The Seven Deadly Sins of Terrorism." In: H. H. Han, ed. ***Terrorism, Political Violence and World Order.*** Lanham, MD.: University Press of America, 1984. pp. 49-54.

617. _____. "The Cancer of Terrorism." In: B. Netanyahu, ed. ***Terrorism: How the West Can Win.*** New York: Farrar, Straus, Giroux, 1986. pp. 31-38.

618. _____. "The Seven Deadly Sins of Terrorism." In: C. W. Kegley, ed. ***International Terrorism: Characteristics, Causes, Controls.*** New York: St. Martin's Press, 1990. pp. 63-68.

619. Kackenmeister, John R. "Terrorism: That's War." ***Military Police,*** (April 1989), 30-32.

620. Kahn, Herman, William Brown and Leon Martel. "The Next 200 Years." ***TVI Report,*** 6:2 (1985), 5-11.

621. Kapetanovic, Goran. "International Terrorism: Legal and Political Aspects." ***Review of International Affairs,*** 36 (July 5-20, 1985), 8-11.

622. Karacan, Ismet. "Terrorism: Concepts and Constructs." In: ***International Terrorism and the Drug Connection.*** Ankara: Ankara University Press, 1984. pp. 202-223.

623. Karber, Phillip A., and R. William Mengel. "Political and Economic Forces Affecting Terrorism." In: P. J. Montana and G. S. Roukis, eds. ***Managing Terrorism.*** Westport, CT.: Quorum Books, 1983. pp. 23-40.

624. Kegley, Charles W. "The Characteristics, Causes, and Controls of International Terrorism: An Introduction." In: C. W. Kegley, ed. ***International Terrorism: Characteristics, Causes, Controls.*** New York: St. Martin's Press, 1990. pp. 1-10.

625. Kellen, Konrad. "Terrorists - What Are They Like? How Some Terrorists Describe Their World and Actions." In: B. M. Jenkins, ed. ***Terrorism and Beyond: An International Conference on Terrorism and Low-Level Conflict.*** Santa Monica, CA.: RAND Corporation, 1980. pp. 125-173.

626. Keller, John E. "Political Terrorism." ***Law and Order,*** 21:5 (1983), 25-33.

627. Kennedy, Richard T. "International Terrorism." ***Department of State Bulletin,*** (September 1981), 65-67.

628. Kessler, Richard J. "Terrorism and the Energy Industry." In: Y. Alexander and C. K. Ebinger, eds. ***Political Terrorism and Energy.*** New York: Praeger, 1982. pp. 85-106.

629. Kidder, Rushworth M. "Why Modern Terrorism? Three Causes Springing from the Seeds of the 1960s." In: C. W. Kegley, ed. ***International Terrorism: Characteristics, Causes, Controls.*** New York: St. Martin's Press, 1990. pp. 135-338.

630. Kirk, Richard M. "Political Terrorism and the Size of Government: A Positive Institutional Analysis of Violent Political Activity. ***Public Choice,*** 40:1 (1983), 41-52.

631. Kirkpatrick, Jeane J. "The Unauthorized Violence of Terrorism." ***Journal of Defence and Diplomacy,*** 2:11 (1984), 6-8.

632. Klamser, Robert. "Missionary Hostage - What Will Your Agency Do?." ***Evangelical Missions Quarterly,*** 24 (January 1988), 30-37.

633. Knauss, Peter, and D. A. Strickland. "Political Disintegration and Latent Terror." In: M. Stohl, ed. ***The Politics of Terrorism.*** 2nd. ed. New York: Marcel Dekker, 1983. pp. 77-118.

634. _____. _____. "Political Disintegration and Latent Terror." In: M. Stohl, ed. ***The Politics of Terrorism.*** New York: Marcel Dekker, 1988. pp. 85-126.

635. Koch, Noel. "Terrorism: The Undeclared War." ***Defence,*** (March 1985), 7-13.

636. Kooistra, Paul G. "What is Political Crime?" ***Criminal Justice Abstracts,*** 17:1 (1985), 100-105.

637. Kotzer, Sophia. "Statistical Tables." In: A. Kurz, et al. ***INTER 86.*** Tel Aviv: Jaffee Center for Strategic Studies, 1987. pp. 115-136.

638. _____. "Statistical Tables." In: A. Kurz, et al. ***INTER: International Terrorism in 1988.*** Tel Aviv: Jaffee Center for Strategic Studies, 1989. pp. 61-84.

639. _____. "Statistical Tables and Figures." In: A. Kurz, et al. ***INTER: International Terrorism in 1989.*** Tel Aviv: Jaffee Center for Strategic Studies, 1990. pp. 17-35.

640. Kupperman, Robert H. "On Terror and Civil Liberties." ***Harvard International Review,*** 7 (May-June 1985), 16-17.

641. _____. "Prospects for Terrorism in 1989." ***Terrorism,*** 12:2 (1989), 128-129.

642. Kurz, Anat. "International Terrorism in 1987: Main Features." In: A Merari and A. Kurz, et al. ***INTER: International Terrorism in 1987.*** Tel Aviv: Jaffee Center for Strategic Studies, 1988. pp. 5-16.

643. _____. "Introductory Essay." In: A. Kurz, ed. ***Contemporary Trends in World Terrorism.*** New York: Praeger, 1987. pp. 1-15.

644. _____, et al. "International Terrorism in 1988: Main Features." In: A. Kurz, et al. ***INTER: International Terrorism in 1988.*** Tel Aviv: Jaffee Center for Strategic Studies, 1989. pp. 5-16.

645. _____. "International Terrorism in 1989: Main Features." In: A. Kurz, et al. ***INTER: International Terrorism in 1989.*** Tel Aviv: Jaffee Center for Strategic Studies, 1990. pp. 6-16.

646. Langer, John H. "Recent Developments in Drug Trafficking: The Terrorist Connection." ***Police Chief,*** 52:4 (1986), 44-48.

647. Laqueur, Walter Z. "Terrorists and Spies." ***New Republic,*** 193:5 (July 29, 1985), 20-23.

648. _____. "The Futility of Terrorism." In: C. W. Kegley, ed. ***International Terrorism: Characteristics, Causes, Control.*** New York: St. Martin's Press, 1990. pp. 69-73.

649. _____. "Reflections on Terrorism." In: W. Laqueur, ed. ***The Terrorism Reader.*** New York: Meridian, 1987. pp. 378-391.

650. Latey, Maurice. "Terrorist Facts and Fancies." ***The World Today,*** 44 (February 1988), 35-37.

651. Leany, B. F. "Terrorism - A Summary." ***Australian Police Journal,*** 34:2 (1980), 100-109.

652. Leaute, Jacques. "Academics and Policy Makers." In: P. Wilkinson and A. M. Stewart, eds. ***Contemporary Research on Terrorism.*** Aberdeen: Aberdeen University Press, 1987. pp. 590-594.

653. Lighbody, Andy, and Joe Poyer. "Terror Worldwide." ***Combat Arms,*** 5 (November 1987), 76-85.

654. Livingstone, Neil C., and Terrell E. Arnold. "Democracy under Attack." In: N. C. Livingstone and T. E. Arnold, eds. ***Fighting Back: Winning the War Agaist Terrorism.*** Lexington, MA.: Lexington Books, 1985. pp. 1-10.

655. _____, ed. "Subnational Conflict: Special Issue." ***World Affairs,*** 146 (Winter 1983/84), 219-283.

656. _____, ed. "Terrorism (Symposium)." ***World Affairs***, 146 (Summer 1983), 3-116.

657. _____. "The Impact of Technological Innovation." In: U. Ra'anan, et al. ***Hydra of Carnage***. Le4xington, MA.: Heath-Lexington Books, 1986. pp. 137-154.

658. Livingstone, Susan M. "Terrorist Wrongs Versus Human Rights: An Interview with Assistant Secretary of State Elliott Abrams." ***World Affairs***, 146:1 (1983), 69-78.

659. Lodi, Sardar F. S. "Terrorism and Terrorists." ***Pakistan Army Journal***, 25:1 (1984), 59-63.

660. Long, David E. "Policy Implications of Handling Terrorist Incidents." In: J. R. Buckwalter, ed. ***International Terrorism: The Decade Ahead***. Chicago, IL.: University of Illinois at Chicago, Office of International Criminal Justice, 1989. pp. 1-11.

661. Lopez, George A., and Michael Stohl. "Editors' Conclusion: The Future of State Terrorism Research and Policy." ***Chitty's Law Journal***, 32:1 (1984), 57-63.

662. "Lost in the Terrorist Theater." ***Harpers***, (October 1984), 43-47+.

663. Ludwikowski, Rett R. "Aspects of Terrorism: Personal Reflections." ***Terrorism***, 10:3 (1987), 175-184.

664. Lynch, Michael J., and Graeme R. Newman. "The Meaning of Terrorism: Conflicting Views from the Left." ***Violence, Aggression and Terrorism***, 2:4 (1988), 307-328.

665. Mack, Andrew. "The Utility of Terrorism." ***The Australian and New Zealand Journal of Terrorism***, 14:4 (1981), 197-224.

666. Mahajan, S. K. "The Future of Urban Insurgency and Terrorism." ***U.S.I. Journal***, (October-December 1984), 80-87.

667. Marks, Edward. "The Implication of Political Terrorism for the Management of Foreign Policy and the Protection of Diplomacy." In: H. H. Han, ed. ***Terrorism, Political Violence and World Order***. Lanham, MD.: University Press of America, 1984. pp. 203-218.

668. Marshall, Jonathan. "The Business of Terrorism." ***Dial***, 3 (January 1982), 48-51.

669. Marshall, T. K. "A Pathologist's View of Terrorist Violence." ***Forensic Science International***, 36:1 (January 1988), 57-67.

670. Mastrangelo, Eugene. "International Terrorism: A Regional and Global Overview, 1987." In: Y. Alexander and A. H. Foxman, eds. ***The 1987 Annual on Terrorism***. Dordrecht: Martinus Nijhoff, 1988. pp. 5-26.

671. _____. "International Terrorism: A Regional and Global Overview, 1970-1986." In: Y. Alexander, ed. ***The 1986 Annual of Terrorism***. Dordrecht: Martinus Nijhoff, 1987. pp. 7-60.

672. _____. "International Terrorism: A Regional and Global Overview 1988-89 (June)." In: Y. Alexander and A. H. Foxman, eds. ***The 1988-1989 Annual of Terrorism***. Dordrecht: Martinus Nijhoff, 1990. pp. 3-38.

673. Mazrui, Ali, A. "The Third World and International Terrorism: Preliminary Reflections." ***Third World Quarterly***, 7:2 (April, 1985), 348-364.

674. McColm, R. B. "Terrorism and Human Rights Issues." ***Terrorism***, 10:1 (1987), 79-81.

675. Merari, Ariel. "International Terrorism in 1986: Main Features." In: A. Kurz, et al. ***INTER 86***. Tel Aviv: Jaffee Center for Strategic Studies, 1987. pp. 6-16.

676. Merkl, Peter H. "Approaches to the Study of Political Violence." In: P. H. Merkl, ed. ***Political Violence and Terror***. Berkeley, CA.: University of California Press, 1986. pp. 19-59.

677. Meyer, William H. "International Information Flows as a Determinant of Political Violence in Third World Nations: Fact or Fiction?." ***Social Science Quarterly***, 69:1 (1988), 24-39.

678. Mickolus, Edward F. "International Terrorism." In: M. Stohl, ed. ***The Politics of Terrorism.*** 2nd ed. New York: Marcel Dekker, 1983. pp. 221-254.

679. _____. "Tracking the Growth and Prevalence of International Terrorism." In: P. J. Montana and G. S. Roukis, eds. ***Managing Terrorism.*** Westport, CT.: Quorum Books, 1983. pp. 3-22.

680. _____. "Comment - Terrorists, Governments, and Numbers: Counting Things Versus Things That Count." ***Journal of Conflict Resolution***, 31:1 (March 1987), 54-62.

681. Miller, Abraham H. "A Time of Terror: How Democratic Societies Respond to Violence." ***Crime and Delinquency***, 26 (January 1980), 109-112.

682. Miller, Reuben. "The Literature of Terrorism." ***Terrorism***, 11:1 (1988), 63-88.

683. Mitchell, Christopher. "State Terrorism: Issues of Concept and Measurement." In: M. Stohl and G. A. Lopez, eds. ***Government Violence and Repression.*** Westport, CT.: Greenwood Press, 1986. pp. 1-26.

684. Monti, Daniel J. "The Relation Between Terrorism and Domestic Civil Disorders." ***Terrorism***, 4 (1980), 123-142.

685. Moore, R. M. "Terrorism: The Environment." ***International Lawyer***, 16 (Winter 1982), 135-138.

686. Motley, James B. "Perspective on Low-Intensity Conflict." ***Military Review***, 65:1 (January 1985), 2-11.

687. Mozaffari, Mehdi. "The New Era of Terrorism: Approaches and Typologies." ***Cooperation and Conflict***, 23:4 (December 1988), 179-198.

688. Mulgannon, Terry. "The Animal Liberation Front." ***TVI Journal***, 5:4 (1985), 39-43.

689. Mushkat, M. "Terrorism: The Soviet Attitude." ***International Problems***, 25:3-4 (Winter 1986), 14-31.

690. Nash, Collen A. "Profiles in Terror." ***Air Force Magazine***, 73:6 (June 1990), 58-61.

691. Nathan, J. A. "The New Feudalism." ***Foreign Policy***, 42 (Spring 1981), 156-166.

692. Nelson-Pallmeyer, Jack. "Low-Intensity Conflict: When Peace is War and War is Peace." ***Other Side***, 23 (November 1987), 24-29.

693. Netanyahu, Benzion. "Terrorist Causes are Lies." In: B. Szumski, ed. ***Terrorism: Opposing Viewpoints.*** St.Paul, MN.: Greenhaven Press, 1986. pp. 51-57.

694. "The New Left." ***TVI Journal***, 2:10 (1981), 3-8.

695. Newhouse, John. "Changing Targets." ***New Yorker***, 65 (July 10, 1989), 71-82.

696. _____. "International Terrorism in the Social Studies." ***Social Studies***, (1980), 14-17.

697. Nicholson, Michael. "Conceptual Problems of Studying State Terrorism." In: M. Stohl and G. A. Lopez, eds. ***Government Violence and Repression.*** Westport, CT.: Greenwood Press, 1986. pp. 27-44.

698. Norris, William F. "Terrorism: Random Violence with a Nightmare's Purpose." ***Air Defense Artillery***, (Fall 1985), 24-29.

699. Norton, Augustus R. "International Terrorism." ***Armed Forces and Society***, 7 (Summer 1981), 597-627.

700. _____. "Review Essay on Terrorism and the Liberal State." ***Armed Forces and Society***, 7:4 (Summer 1981), 598-625.

701. Norton, G. "Tourism and International Terrorism." ***The World Today***, 43:2 (February 1987), 30-32.

702. O'Brien, Conor Cruise. "Thinking About Terrorism: II." In: C. C. O'Brien. ***Passion and Cunning.*** London: Weidenfeld and Nicolson, 1988. pp. 234-237.

703. O'Neill, Bard E. "Insurgency: The Context of Terrorism." In: H. H. Han, ed. ***Terrorism, Political Violence and World Order.*** Lanham, MD.: University Press of America, 1984. pp. 173-202.

704. Oakley, Robert B. "Terrorism: Overview and Development." ***Department of State Bulletin,*** 85 (November 1985), 61-65.

705. _____. "Terrorism and Tourism." ***Department of State Bulletin,*** 86: 2115 (October 1986), 55-57.

706. _____. "International Terrorism." ***Foreign Affairs,*** 65:3 (1987), 611-629.

707. _____, and Parker W. Borg. "International Terrorism." ***Department of State Bulletin,*** 86:2113 (August 1986), 1-15.

708. Ochberg, Frank M. "List of Hypotheses and Assumptions on the Phenomenon of Terrorism." ***Terrorism,*** 3:3-4 (1980), 289-290.

709. "On Terrorism." ***Nation,*** 230 (February 9, 1980), 134-135.

710. Oppenheimer, Martin. "Terrorism is Sometimes Justified." In: B. Szumski, ed. ***Terrorism: Opposing Viewpoints.*** St.Paul, MN.: Greenhaven Press, 1986. pp. 86-89.

711. "Organizations Responsible for International Terrorist Incidents in 1985." In: A. Merari, et al. ***INTER 85.*** Boulder, CO.: Westview Press, 1985. pp. 125-130.

712. "Organizations Responsible for International Terrorist Incidents in 1986." In: A. Kurz, et al. ***INTER 86.*** Tel Aviv: Jaffee Center for Strategic Studies, 1987. pp. 137-140.

713. "Organizations Responsible for International Terrorist Incidents in 1988." In: A. Kurz, et al. ***INTER: International Terrorism in 1988.*** Tel Aviv: Jaffee Center for Strategic Studies, 1989. pp. 85-90.

714. Padia, Chandrakala. "Terrorism: An Analysis." ***Indian Journal of Political Science,*** 49:3 (July-September 1988), 351-358.

715. Pattackas, A. N. "Trends in Terrorism: The Experts Comment." ***Security Management,*** 29 (October 1985), 121-122.

716. "Patterns of International Terrorism." ***Security Management,*** 26:9 (1982), 148-151.

717. Perez, Frank H. "Impact of International Terrorism." ***Department of State Bulletin,*** (January 1982), 55-57.

718. Phillips, Robert. "The War and Ethics Program at the University of Connecticut." ***Terrorism,*** 12:1 (1989), 72-73.

719. "Politics and the World." ***Canada and the World,*** 50 (February 1985), 3-4.

720. Porter, Jack N. "Neo-Nazism, Neo-Fascism, and Terrorism: A Global Trend?." ***Judaism,*** 31 (Summer 1982), 311-321.

721. Post, Jerrold M., and Raphael Ezekiel. "Worlds in Collision, Worlds in Collusion: The Uneasy Relationship Between the Counterterrorism Policy Community and the Academic Community." ***Terrorism,*** 11:6 (1988), 503-510.

722. Probst, Peter S. "Terrorism: A Strategic Perspective." ***Terrorism,*** 11:4 (1988), 333-334.

723. Quainton, A. C. E. "Terrorism and Political Violence: A Permanent Challenge to Governments." In: M. Crenshaw, ed. ***Terrorism, Legitimacy and Power.*** Middletown, CT.: Wesleyan University Press, 1983. pp. 52-64.

724. Quandt, William B. "The Multi-Dimensional Challenge of Terrorism: Common Misperceptions and Policy Dilemmas." In: C. W. Kegley, ed. ***International Terrorism: Characteristics, Causes, Controls.*** New York: St. Martin's Press, 1990. pp. 74-80.

725. Quarles, Chester L. "The Threat of Terrorism to Missionaries: Meeting the Challenge." ***International Bulletin of Missionary Research***, 12 (October 1988), 161-162+.

726. _____. "Can Terrorism Be Understood?." ***Criminologist***, 12:3 (1988), 131-138.

727. _____. "Danger Appraisals in Developing Nations." ***Journal of Security Administration***, 11:1 (1989), 22-43.

728. "RAND Report: Review of Trends in International Terrorism." ***TVI Journal***, 5:3 (1985), 37-38.

729. Rackley, Frank. "Measures of the Impact and Appeal of Terrorism." In: D. C. Rapoport and Y. Alexander, eds. ***The Rationalization of Terrorism.*** Frederick, MD.: University Publications of America, 1982. pp. 91-100.

730. Rada, S. E. "Transnational Terrorism as Public Relations?" ***Public Relations Review***, 11 (Fall 1985), 26-33.

731. Raditsa, Leo. "The Source of World Terrorism." ***Midstream***, 27:10 (1981), 42-48.

732. Rapoport, David C. "Inside Terrorist Organizations: Introduction." ***Journal of Strategic Studies***, 10:4 (December 1987), 1-12.

733. _____. "The International World as Some Terrorists Have Seen It: A Look at a Century of Memoirs." ***Journal of Strategic Studies***, 10:4 (December 1987), 32-58.

734. _____. "The International World as Some Terrorists have Seen It - A Look at a Century of Memoirs." In: D. C. Rapoport, ed. ***Inside Terrorist Organizations.*** New York: Columbia University Press, 1988. pp. 32-58.

735. Reid, Edna F. "An Analysis of Terrorism Literature: A Bibliometric and Content Analysis Study." In: A. Van der Laan and A. A. Winters, eds. ***The Use of Information in a Changing World.*** Amsterdam: Elsevier Science Publishers, 1984. pp. 253-265.

736. Revel, Jean Francois. "A Good Season for Terrorism." ***Encounter***, (April 1987), 37-39.

737. Revell, Oliver B. "Terrorism: A Review of 1989 and Prospects for 1990." ***Terrorism***, 12:6 (1989), 379-382.

738. "A Review of Explicit and Implicit Propositions About Women as Terrorists." ***Resources for Feminist Research***, 13:4 (December-January 1986), 20-22.

739. Risks International. "Special Report: Significant Regional Developments, October - December 1984." ***Terrorism***, 8:2 (1985), 165-183.

740. _____. "Regional and Entity Analysis by Target, 1986." In: Y. Alexander, ed. ***The 1986 Annual on Terrorism.*** Dordrecht: Martinus Nijhoff, 1987. pp. 203-204.

741. _____. "Statistical Overview." In: Y. Alexander, ed. ***The 1986 Annual on Terrorism.*** Dordrecht: Martinus Nijhoff, 1987. pp. 205-210.

742. Roberts, Adam. "Terrorism and International Order." In: ***Terrorism and International Order.*** London: Royal Institute of International Affairs, 1986. pp. 7-25.

743. Rosenne, Meir. "Terrorism: Who Is Responsible? What Can Be Done?" ***World Affairs***, 148:3 (Winter 1986), 169-172.

744. _____. "Terrorism: Who Is Responsible; What Can Be Done?." In: Y. Alexander, ed. ***The 1986 Annual on Terrorism.*** Dordrecht: Martinus Nijhoff, 1987. pp. 309-314.

745. Rosetti, Joe. "Violence in the Year 2000." ***TVI Report***, 6:2 (1985), 5-12.

746. Rubenstein, Richard E. "The Noncauses of Terrorism." In: C. W. Kegley, ed. ***International Terrorism: Characteristics, Causes, Controls.*** New York: St. Martin's Press, 1990. pp. 127-134.

747. Rubin, Alfred P. "Proceedings of the ILA Committee on International Terrorism (August 1984)." ***Terrorism,*** 8:4 (1986), 379-412.

748. Rupprecht, Reinhard. "Description of a Research Project to Study the Causes of Terrorism." In: B. M. Jenkins, ed. ***Terrorism and Beyond: An International Conference on Terrorism and Low-Level Conflict.*** Santa Monica, CA.: RAND Corporation, 1980. pp. 115-118.

749. Russell, Charles A. "Profile of a Terrorist." ***Terrorism Report,*** 1:1 (1980), 1-2.

750. Rustin, Bayard. "Democracy and Terrorism." In: B. Netanyahu, ed. ***International Terrorism: Challenge and Response.*** New Brunswick, NJ.: Transaction Books, 1981. pp. 201-207.

751. Saddy, Fehmi. "International Terrorism, Human Rights, and World Order." ***Terrorism,*** 5:4 (1982), 325-352.

752. Sandler, Todd, et al. "Economic Methods and the Study of Terrorism." In: P. Wilkinson and A. M. Stewart, eds. ***Contemporary Research on Terrorism.*** Aberdeen: Aberdeen University Press, 1987. pp. 376-389.

753. Saper, Bernard. "On Learning Terrorism." ***Terrorism,*** 11:1 (1988), 13-28.

754. Sater, William F. "The Terrorist Threat to Travellers." ***TVI Report,*** 6:4 (1986), 19-21.

755. Savage, J. A. "Radical Environmentalists: Sabotage in the Name of Ecology." ***Business and Society Review,*** (Summer 1986), 35-37.

756. Saxena, J. N. "Terrorism and Human Rights." In: R. P. Dhokalia and K. N. Rao, eds. ***Terrorism and International Law.*** New Delhi: Indian Society of International Law, 1988. pp. 42-50.

757. Schelling, Thomas C. "The Phenomenon of Terrorism." ***Terrorism,*** 3:3-4 (1980), 303-304.

758. Schlagheck, Donna M. "The Superpowers, Foreign Policy, and Terrorism." In: C. W. Kegley, ed. ***International Terrorism: Characteristics, Causes, Controls.*** New York: St. Martin's Press, 1990. pp. 170-177.

759. Schmid, Alex P. "Goals and Objectives of International Terrorism." In: R. O. Slater and M. Stohl, eds. ***Current Perspectives on International Terrorism.*** London: Macmillan, 1988. pp. 47-87.

760. Selth, Andrew. "International Terrorism and the Challenge to Diplomacy." ***Terrorism,*** 10:2 (1987), 103-112.

761. _____. "Terrorist Studies and the Threat to Diplomacy." ***Australian and New Zealand Journal of Criminology,*** 19:2 (1986), 114-119.

762. _____. "International Terrorism: A New Kind of Warfare." ***RUSI, Journal of the Royal United Services Institute for Defense Studies,*** 132:1 (March 1987), 65-71.

763. Shank, Gregory, Paul Takagi and Bob Gould. "The State of Terrorism." ***Crime and Social Justice,*** 25 (1986), i-v.

764. Shastri, Ravi. "Insurgency and Drugs: The Deadly Alliance." ***Strategic Analysis,*** (April 1987), 39-52.

765. Sherman, Arnold. "'Terrorist' Versus 'Freedom Fighters': The Implications of Alternative Constructions of Reality." In: D. J. D. Sandole and J. Sandole-Staroste, eds. ***Conflict Management and Problem Solving.*** London: Francis Pinter, 1987. pp. 194-198.

766. Shestack, Jerome J. "Of Private and State Terror - Some Preliminary Observations." ***Rutgers Law Journal,*** 13 (Spring 1982), 453-463.

767. Shultz, George. "Terrorism: The Challenge to the Democracies." ***Vital Speeches***, 50:22 (September 1, 1984), 674-677.

768. _____. "Terrorism and the Modern World." ***Terrorism***, 7:4 (1985), 431-447.

769. _____. "The Challenge to Democracies." In: B. Netanyahu, ed. ***Terrorism: How the West Can Win.*** New York: Farrar, Straus, Giroux, 1986. pp. 16-24.

770. _____. "Terrorism and the Modern World." In: W. Laqueur, ed. ***The Terrorism Reader.*** New York: Meridian, 1987. pp. 345-349.

771. Shultz, Richard H., and Stephen Sloan. "International Terrorism: The Nature of the Threat." In: R. H. Shultz and S. Sloan, eds. ***Responding to the Terrorist Threat.*** New York: Pergamon Press, 1980. pp. 1-7.

772. _____. _____. "Terrorism: An Objective Act, A Subjective Reality." In: R. H. Shultz and S. Sloan, eds. ***Responding to the Terrorist Threat.*** New York: Pergamon Press, 1980. pp. 245-254.

773. _____. "Recent Regional Patterns." In: U. Ra'anan, et al. ***Hydra of Carnage.*** Lexington, MA.: Heath-Lexington Books, 1986. pp. 95-124.

774. _____. "Conceptualizing Political Terrorism: A Typology." In: A. D. Buckley and D. D. Olson, eds. ***International Terrorism: Current Research and Future Directions.*** Wayne, NJ.: Avery, 1980. pp. 9-18.

775. _____. "Conceptualizing Political Terrorism." In: C. W. Kegley, ed. ***International Terrorism: Characteristics, Causes, Controls.*** New York: St. Martin's Press, 1990. pp. 45-50.

776. Sick, Gary. "The Political Underpinnings of Terrorism." In: C. W. Kegley, ed. ***International Terrorism: Characteristics, Causes, Controls.*** New York: St. Martin's Press, 1990. pp. 51-54.

777. Silverstein, Martin E. "Hypotheses on Terrorism." ***Terrorism***, 3:3-4 (1980), 329-333.

778. Simon, Jeffrey. "Misunderstanding Terrorism." ***Foreign Policy***, (Summer 1987), 104-120.

779. _____. "The Future of Political Risk Analysis." ***TVI Journal***, 5:2 (Fall 1984), 23-25.

780. _____. "Global Perspective: The Year of the Terrorist." ***TVI Report***, 6:3 (Winter 1986), 1-3.

781. Simpson, John R. "International Terrorism: Crimes Against the World." ***Security Management***, 30:4 (1986), 44-46.

782. Slater, Robert O., and Michael Stohl. "Introduction: Towards a Better Understanding of International Terrorism." In: R. O. Slater and M. Stohl, eds. ***Current Perspectives on International Terrorism.*** London: Macmillan Press. 1988. pp. 1-11.

783. Smith, G. Davidson. "Political Violence in Animal Liberation." ***Contemporary Review***, 247:1434 (1985), 26-31.

784. Smylie, Robert F., ed. "Terrorism: Perceptions and Reflections." ***Christian Society***, 78 (May-June, 1988), 3-62.

785. Snall, I., and D. Lowe. "The Hate Movement Today - A Chronicle of Violence and Disarray." ***Terrorism***, 10:4 (1987), 345-364.

786. "Special Focus: International Terrorism." ***The Police Chief***, 56 (March 1989), 16-63.

787. "Statistical Tables: Terrorism: April - June 1982." ***Terrorism***, 6:3 (1983), 497-500.

788. "Statistics: Terrorism: January - September 1981." ***Terrorism***, 5:4 (1982), 371-372.

789. "Statistics: Terrorism: October 1981 - March 1982." ***Terrorism***, 6:1 (1982), 105.

790. Steinitz, Mark S. "Insurgents, Terrorists and the Drug Trade." ***Washington Quarterly***, 8:4 (1985), 141-153.

791. _____. "Insurgents, Terrorists and the Drug Trade." In: W. Laqueur, ed. ***The Terrorism Reader.*** New York: Meridian, 1987. pp. 327-336.

792. Sterling, Claire. "Threat from Left and Right." ***Society,*** 19:3 (1982), 82-83.

793. Stohl, Michael. "Conclusion: Issues and Controversies Concerning Contemporary Political Terrorism." In: M. Stohl, ed. ***The Politics of Terrorism.*** 2nd Ed. New York: Marcel Dekker, 1983. pp. 446-462.

794. _____, and George A. Lopez. "Introduction." In: M. Stohl and G. A. Lopez, eds. ***State as Terrorist.*** Westport, CT.: Greenwood Press, 1984. pp. 3-10.

795. _____. "The Three Worlds of Terrorism." ***TVI Journal,*** 3:6 (July 1982), 4-11.

796. _____. "National Interests and State Terrorism in International Affairs." In: M. Stohl, ed. ***The Politics of Terrorism.*** New York: Marcel Dekker, 1988. pp. 273-294.

797. _____. "Terrorists Vary Their Tactics in 1st, 2nd, and 3rd Worlds." ***TVI Journal,*** 3:6 (1982), 4-12.

798. _____. "Demystifying the Mystery of International Terrorism." In: C. W. Kegley, ed. ***International Terrorism: Characteristics, Causes, Controls.*** New York: St. Martin's Press, 1990. pp. 81-96.

799. Sundberg, Jacob W. F. "What Have We Learned at the Conference?" ***International Journal of Group Tensions,*** 12:1-4 (1982), 161-172.

800. Szabo, Denis, and Ronald D. Crelinsten. "International Political Terrorism: A Challenge for Comparative Research." ***Terrorism,*** 3 (1980), 341-348.

801. Szulkin, Robert, and Richard Weisberg. "Editor's Preface. Symposium - Terror in the Modern Age: The Vision of Literature, the Response of Law." ***Human Rights Quarterly,*** 5:2 (1983), 109-112.

802. "Tables." In: A. Merari, et al. ***INTER 85.*** Boulder, CO.: Westview Press, 1986. pp. 105-124.

803. Taulbee, James L. "Raiders of the Leased Art: A Note on Mercenary Coup Strike Forces." ***Conflict,*** 7:2 (1987), 197-210.

804. Taylor, Clyde D. "Links Between International Narcotics Trafficking and Terrorism." ***Department of State Bulletin,*** 85 (August 1985), 69-74.

805. Taylor, Maxwell, and Helen Ryan. "Fanaticism, Political Suicide and Terrorism." ***Terrorism,*** 11:2 (1988), 91-112.

806. "Terrorism and Drug Trafficking: A Lethal Partnership." ***Security Management,*** 28 (June 1984), 44-46.

807. "Terrorism is Here to Stay: An Interview with R. H. Kupperman." ***Military Intelligence,*** 1:4 (1985), 33, 66.

808. "Terrorism, Pure and Complex." ***Commonweal,*** (December 14, 1984), 675-676.

809. "Terrorism." ***World Press Review,*** 32 (September 1985), 35-40.

810. "Terrorism." ***American Legion Magazine,*** 120 (June 1986), 15-21+.

811. "Terrorism: A Growth Industry." In: ***Strategic Survey 1985-1986.*** London: Institute for International Studies, 1986. pp. 19-27.

812. "Terrorism: A National Issues Seminar: The Brookings Institution Advanced Study Program." ***World Affairs,*** 146:1 (1983), 79-113.

813. Thackrah, John R. "Contemporary Terrorism." ***Government and Opposition,*** 17:1 (Winter 1982), 127-128.

814. Thomas, Philip A., and Tony Standley. "Classifying Terrorism." In: H. Koechler, ed. ***Terrorism and National Liberation.*** Frankfurt am Main: Peter Lang, 1988. 67-78.

815. Thornton, Richard C. "Nuclear Superiority, Geopolitics and State Terrorism." ***Global Affairs,*** 1:4 (1986), 14p.

816. Trent, Darrell M. "The New Religion: Terrorism." ***Human Rights,*** 8:4 (1980), 10-13.

817. Turk, Austin T. "Political Crime." In: R. F. Meier, ed. ***Major Forms of Crime.*** Newbury Park, CA.: Sage Publications, 1984. pp. 119-135.

818. _____. "Notes on Criminology and Terrorism." In: W. S. Laufer and F. Adler, ed. ***Advances in Criminological Theory, Vol. 1.*** New Brunswick, NJ.: Transaction Books, 1989. pp. 17-29.

819. Tyagi, Yogesh K. "Political Terrorism: National and International Dimensions." In: R. P. Dhokalia and K. N. Rao, eds. ***Terrorism and International Law.*** New Delhi: Indian Society of International Law, 1988. pp. 8-30.

820. Vatikiotis, P. J. "The Spread of Islamic Terrorism." In: B. Netanyahu, ed. ***Terrorism: How the West Can Win.*** New York: Farrar, Straus, Giroux, 1986. pp. 77-84.

821. Wallace, Gerry. "Area Bombing, Terrorism and the Death of Innocents." ***Journal of Applied Philosophy,*** (March 1989), 3-15.

822. Ward, Dick. "Narco-Terrorism Grows as a World Threat." ***C. J. International,*** 6:1 (January 1990), 1,6+.

823. Wardlaw, Grant. "Perspectives on Terrorism: A Review Article." ***The Australian and New Zealand Journal of Criminology,*** 16:4 (1984), 264-276.

824. _____. "Terrorism: A Challenge to International Stability." ***Pacific Defence Reporter,*** 12: 6-7 (December 1985/January 1986), 65-67.

825. _____. "Linkages Between Illegal Drugs Traffic and Terrorism." ***Conflict Quarterly,*** 8:3 (Summer 1988), 5-26.

826. _____. "Terrorism: Apparent Lull Hides Serious Picture." ***Pacific Defense Reporter,*** 15 (December 1988 - January 1989), 106-108.

827. Warner, John. "The Relationship Between Terrorism and Drug Trafficking." ***Police Chief,*** 3:3 (1984), 94-97.

828. _____. "Terrorism and Drug Trafficking: A Lethal Partnership." ***Security Management,*** 28:5 (1984), 44-46.

829. Weil, Sherri L. "Terrorist Expert Yonah Alexander: Scholar in an Uncharted Field." ***Georgetown Magazine,*** (March April 1983), 10-12.

830. "Western States' Policies and International Terrorism in 1985." In: A. Merari, et al. ***INTER 85.*** Boulder, CO.: Westview Press, 1986. pp. 13-30.

831. Westrate, David L. "How are Drug Trafficking and Terrorism Related?" ***Narcotics Control Digest,*** 15:11 (1985), 1-4.

832. _____. "Drug Trafficking and Terrorism." ***Drug Enforcement,*** 12:1 (Summer 1985), 19-24.

833. Westrum, R. "Vulnerable Technologies - Accident, Crime and Terrorism." ***Interdisciplinary Science Reviews,*** 11:4 (1986), 386-391.

834. Whealey, R. H. "On Terrorism." ***International Journal on World Peace,*** 4:2 (1987), 26-29.

835. Whitaker, Reg. "Who are the Real Terrorists." ***Canadian Dimension,*** (July-August 1986), 40.

836. "Who Will Terrorists Target in 1984?." ***TVI Journal,*** 3:2 (1982), 3-8.

837. Wilkinson, Paul. "Pathways Out of Terrorism for Democratic Societies." In: E. Moonman, ed. ***The Violent Society.*** London: Frank Cass, 1987. pp. 138-154.

838. _____. "Terrorism: International Dimensions." In: W. Gutteridge, ed. ***The New Terrorism.*** London: Mansell, 1986. pp. 29-56.

839. Will, George. "Calculating the Public Interest." In: B. Netanyahu, ed. ***International Terrorism: Challenge and Response.*** New Brunswick, NJ.: Transaction Books, 1981. pp. 208-213.

840. Williams, Arnold. "The International Threat." ***Terrorism,*** 10:3 (1987), 225-226.

841. Wilson, Michele, and John Lynxwiler. "Abortion Clinic Violence as Terrorism." ***Terrorism,*** 11:4 (1988), 263-274.

842. Windsor, Philip. "Terrorism and International Order." ***The Atlantic Community Quarterly,*** 25 (Summer 1987), 201-209.

843. Wolf, John B. "Assessing the Performance of a Terrorist and an Anti-Terrorist Organization." In: D. E. J. MacNamara and P. J. Stead, eds. ***New Dimensions in Transnational Crime.*** New York: John Jay Press, 1982. pp. 72-102.

844. Wolfgang, Marvin E. "Surveying Violence Across Nations: A Review of the Literature, With Research and Policy Recommendations." ***International Review of Criminal Policy,*** 37 (1981), 62-95.

845. Woods, B. F. "Terrorism: The Continuing Crisis." ***Police Chief,*** 48 (May 1981), 48-49.

846. Woolf, S. J. "Prototypes and Terrorists." ***Society,*** 18:4 (1981), 28-29.

847. "World Terrorism Intelligence Report." ***Security Systems Digest,*** 12:26 (December 23, 1981), 10-12.

848. Wright, Robin. "Terrorist Act to Achieve Freedom." In: B.: Szumski, ed. ***Terrorism: Opposing Viewpoints.*** St.Paul, MN.: Greenhaven Press, 1986. pp. 47-50.

849. _____. "The Rage of the Children." ***TVI Report,*** 7:3 (1987), 35-39.

850. Yerushalmi, Mordechai. "A "Control Code" Model of Terrorism." In; R. H. Ward and H. E. Smith, eds. ***International Terrorism: The Domestic Response.*** Chicago, IL.: University of Illinois at Chicago, Office of International Criminal Justice, 1987. pp. 77-84.

851. Zawodny, J. K. "Infrastructures of Terrorist Organizations." ***Conflict Quarterly,*** 1:4 (1980), 24-31.

852. _____. "Infrastructure of Terrorist Organizations." In: L. Z. Freedman and Y. Alexander, eds. ***Perspectives on Terrorism.*** Wilmington, DE.: Scholarly Resources, 1983. pp. 45-60.

853. Zilka, Orit, and Sophia Kotzer. "Statistical Tables." In: A. Merari and A. Kurz, et al. ***INTER: International Terrorism in 1987.*** Tel Aviv: Jaffee Center for Strategic Studies, 1988. pp. 113-135.

854. Zimmermann, Ekkart. "Political Violence and Other Strategies of Opposition Movements: A Look at Some Recent Evidence." ***Journal of International Affairs,*** 40:2 (Winter/Spring 198&), 325-351.

855. Zirschky, J. "Environmental Terrorism." ***Journal of Water Pollution Control Federation,*** 60:7 (1988), 1206-1210.

856. Zusman, Lynne. "Terrorism: The Issues Confronting a Free Society." ***ABA Law and National Security Intelligence Report,*** 8:9 (1986), 1,8-9.

857. Zwi, Anthony, and Antonio Ugalde. "Toward an Epidemiology of Political Violence in the Third World." ***Social Science and Medicine,*** 28:7 (1989), 633-642.

3. Documents and Reports

858. ***The 1980's: Decade of Confrontation. Proceedings of the 8th National Security Affairs Conference, 1981.*** Washington, D.C.: National Defence University, 1981. 326p.

859. Barrett, B. A., et al. ***Mobilization and Defence Management Technical Reports Series. International Terrorism: The DOD Approach.*** Washington, D.C.: Industrial College of the Armed Forces, Research Department, 1983. 63p.

860. Borg, Parker W. ***International Terrorism: Breaking the Cycle of Violence.*** Occasional Paper No. 8. Washington, D.C.: Center for the Study of Foreign Affairs, 1987.

861. Bremer, L. Paul. ***Terrorism: Its Evolving Nature.*** Washington, D.C.: U.S. Department of State, Bureau of Public Affairs, 1989. 5p.

862. Burns, Thomas E. ***United States and Western European Terrorist Groups: Current Status and Future Perspectives.*** Carlisle Barracks, Pa.: Army War College, 1982. 69p.

863. Carr, S. R. ***Book Analysis: Terrorism - How the West Can Win.*** Maxwell AFB, AL.: Air Command and Staff College, 1988. 31p.

864. Charters, David, Graham Dominick and Maurice A. Tugwell. ***Trends in Low Intensity Conflict.*** ORAE Extramural Paper No. 16. Ottawa: Operational Research and Analysis Establishment, Department of National Defence, 1981. 315p.

865. Cheason, J. M. "Terrorist Risk Exposure: A Bayesian Approach." Paper Presented to the, ***National Meeting of the Academy of Criminal Justice***, held in 1980, at Oklahoma City.

866. Cline, Ray. "Endemic Nature of Political Terrorism in the 1980s." Paper Presented at the ***Conference on Political Terrorism and Energy: The Threat and Response***, held on May 1, 1980 at Georgetown University, Washington, D.C.

867. Cordes, Bonnie J., et al. ***A Conceptual Framework for Analyzing Terrorist Groups.*** RAND R-3151. Santa Monica, CA.: RAND Corporation, 1985. 114p.

868. _____. ***Trends in International Terrorism, 1982-1983.*** RAND R-3183-SL. Santa Monica, CA.: RAND Corporation, 1984. 54p.

869. _____. ***When Terrorists Do the Talking: Reflections on Terrorist Literature.*** RAND P-7365. Santa Monica, CA.: Rand Corporation, 1987. 38p.

870. Crelinsten, Ronald D. "Terrorism as Political Communication: The Relationship Between the Controller and the Controlled." Paper Presented at the ***Conference on Domestic Security: Issue for Democracy***, held on May 8, 1986, at York University, Toronto.

871. Crenshaw, Martha. "An Organizational Approach to the Analysis of Political Terrorism." Paper Presented at the ***13th World Congress of the International Political Science Association***, held on July 15-20, 1985, in Paris.

872. _____. "How Terrorism Ends." Paper Presented to the ***Annual Meeting of the American Political Science Association***, held in September 1987, in Chicago.

873. _____. "The Meaning of Terrorism for World Order." Paper Presented at the ***24th Annual Convention of the International Studies Association***, held on April 5-9, 1983 in Mexico City.

874. _____. "The State of Terrorism as an International Problem." Paper Presented at the ***Annual Meeting of the International Studies Association,*** held on March 18-22, 1980 in Los Angeles, CA.

875. _____. "Incentives for Terrorism." In: B. G. Curtis, ed. ***Outthinking the Terrorist - An International Challenge, Proceedings.*** Rockville, MD.: National Criminal Justice Reference Service, 1985. pp. 15-24.

876. Curtis, B. G., ed. ***Conflict and Confrontation in a Civilized Society.*** Proceedings of the 8th Annual Symposium on the Role of Behavior Science in Physical Security, held on June 7-8, 1983 in Springfield, VA. 87p.

877. _____, ed. ***Symmetry and Asymmetry of Global Adversary Behavior.*** Proceedings of the 9th Annual Symposium on the Role of Behavior Science in Physical Security, held on April 3-4, 1984 in Springfield, VA. 94p.

878. Danner, Malcolm A. ***Contemporary Terrorism.*** Carlisle Barracks, PA.: Army War College, 1982. 45p.

879. Dowling, Ralph E., and Richard Nitcavic. ***Visions of Terror: A Q-Methodological Analysis of American Perceptions of International Terrorism.*** San Francisco, CA.: Mass Communication and Public Address Divisions, SCA Convention, 1989.

880. Farrell, William R. "High Risk Violence and Terrorism: A Distinction with a Difference?." Paper Presented at the ***Spring Conference of the National Capital Area Political Science Association,*** held on February 27, 1982 in Washington, D.C.

881. Fowler, W. W. ***An Agenda for Quantitative Research on Terrorism.*** RAND P-6591. Santa Monica, CA.: RAND Corporation, 1980. 11p.

882. Frankel, Norman. "Political Terrorism: Causes and Prognosis: The Cases of Israel and Northern Ireland." Paper Presented at the ***Annual Convention of the International Studies Association,*** held on October 16-18, 1980 at the Loyola University of Chicago.

883. Friedlander, Robert A. ***Terrorism: Documents of International and Local Control.*** 5 Vols. Dobbs Ferry, NY.: Oceana, 1979-.

884. Galtung, Johan. "On the Causes of Terrorism and their Removal." Paper Presented to the ***International Progress Organization Conference on the Question of Terrorism,*** held on March 19-21, 1987 in Geneva.

885. Garrigan, Timothy B., and George A. Lopez. ***Terrorism: A Problem of Political Violence.*** Croton-on-Hudson, NY.: Learning Resources in International Studies, 1980. 40p.

886. Govea, Rodger M. "Distinction Without Purpose: The Study of Political Terrorism." Paper Presented at the ***24th Annual Convention of the International Studies Association,*** held on April 5-9, 1983 in Mexico City.

887. Grosscup, Beau. "Terrorism, Neoconservatism and the Crisis of Liberal Democracy." Paper Presented at the ***American Political Science Association Convention,*** held in August 1980, in Washington, D.C. 29p.

888. Gurr, Ted R. ***Empirical Research on Political Terrorism: The State of the Art and How it Might be Improved.*** Boulder, CO.: Center for Comparative Politics, University of Colorado, 1986. 55p.

889. Gwin, S. R. ***Terrorism - A Global Perspective.*** Carlisle Barracks, PA.: Army War College, 1987. 41p.

890. Heather, Randall. ***Terrorism, "Active Measures", and SDI.*** Toronto: The Mackenzie Institute for the Study of Terrorism, Revolution and Propaganda, 1987. 37p.

891. Helms, Andrea R. C. "Democracy Under Fire: Liberalism and the Terrorist Challenge." Paper Presented to the, ***30th Annual Meeting of the Society for the Study of Social Problems***, held on August 21-24, 1981.

892. Holloway, James, Joel Lisker and Victoria Toensing. ***International Terrorism.*** Charlottesville, VA.: The Center for Law and National Security, 1986. 30p.

893. Jenkins, Brian M., ed. ***Terrorism and Beyond: An International Conference on Terrorism and Low-level Conflict.*** RAND R-2714-DOE/DOJ/DOS/RC. Santa Monica, CA.: RAND Corporation, 1982. 287p.

894. _____. ***Some Reflections on Recent Trends in Terrorism.*** RAND P-6897. Santa Monica, CA.: RAND Corporation, 1983. 8p.

895. _____. ***Terrorism in the 1980s.*** RAND P-6564. Santa Monica, CA.: RAND Corporation, 1980. 13p.

896. _____. ***Testimony Before the Committee on the Judiciary.*** RAND P-6962. Santa Monica, CA.: RAND Corporation, 1984. 10p.

897. _____. ***Future Trends in International Terrorism.*** RAND P-7176. Santa Monica, CA.: Rand Corporation, 1985. 30p.

898. Keefe, Gail A. "The Existence of Violence in Nonviolent Protest Groups." In: ***Terrorism: Special Studies, 1985-1988, First Supplement.*** Bethesda, MD.: University Publications of America, 1989. Reel 3. Frames 0915-end. 89p.

899. Kellen, Konrad. ***On Terrorists and Terrorism.*** RAND N-1942-RC. Santa Monica, CA.: RAND Corporation, 1982. 54p.

900. Kellett, Anthony. ***International Terrorism: A Retrospective and Prospective Examination.*** ORAE Report, No. R78. Ottawa: Department of National Defence, 1981. 72p.

901. Khawaldeh, Mohammed. ***International Terrorism.*** Maxwell Air Force Base, AL.: U.S. Air War College, 1987. 24p.

902. Killeen, John E., and Robert A. Hoffman. ***Coping With Terrorism: A Concept Paper.*** Maxwell Air Force Base, AL.: U.S. Air War and Command College, 1987. 186p.

903. Kissane, Thomas P. ***The Theoretical Literature on Terrorism: A Sociological Interpretation.*** Ph.D. Dissertation. New York: Fordham University, 1989. 221p.

904. Kubiak, Anthony J. ***Phobos and Performance: The Stages of Terror.*** Ph.D. Dissertation. Milwaukee, WI.: The University of Wisconsin in Milwaukee, 1988. 274p.

905. Kunciw, J. L. ***Profile of a Terrorist.*** Maxwell AFB, AL.: Air Command and Staff College, 1988. 44p.

906. Kupperman, Robert H., et al. ***Low Intensity Conflict. Main Report and Appendices. 2 Vols.*** NTIS AD-A137 260/6 and AD-137 261/4. Washington, D.C.: Kupperman and Associates, 1983. 83p. & 193p.

907. Kurz, Anat, et al. ***INTER: International Terrorism in 1988.*** Tel Aviv: Jaffee Center for Strategic Studies, 1989. 90p.

908. _____, et al. ***INTER: International Terrorism in 1989.*** Tel Aviv: Jaffee Center for Strategis Studies, 1990. 110p.

909. Lopez, George A. "Terrorism and Alternative Worldviews." In: Paper Presented to the, ***Southwest International Studies Association Conference***, held in 1981, at San Antonio, TX.

910. _____. "Dealing with Terrorism in the 1980s: A World Order Approach." Paper Presented at the ***24th Annual Convention of the International Studies Association***, held on April 5-9, 1983 in Mexico City.

911. _____. "Terrorism, Worldviews and Problems of Policy." Paper Presented at the ***Annual Meeting of the International Studies Association,*** held in March 1982 in Cincinnati, Ohio.

912. MacDonald, Brian, ed. ***Terror.*** Toronto: Canadian Institute of Strategic Studies, 1986. 170p.

913. Markides, Kyriacos. "Terrorism: The Functional Equivalent of War." Paper Presented at the ***24th Annual Convention of the International Studies Association,*** held on April 5-9, 1983 in Mexico City.

914. McAndrew, William R. ***Determinants and Justifications for the Use of Terrorist Violence in Separatist Situations.*** Master's Thesis. Houston, TX.: Rice University, 1987.

915. McBrien, J. R. "Face of Terrorism: Policy Making and the Eye of the Beholder." In: ***Proceedings of the 9th Annual Symposium on the Role of Behavioral Science in Physical Security,*** held on April 3-4, 1984 at Springfield, VA. pp.21-26.

916. McGurn, William. ***Terrorist or Freedom Fighter? The Cost of Confusion.*** Institute for European Defence & Strategic Studies. No. 25. (April 1987). 59p.

917. Merari, Ariel, ed. ***On Terrorism and Combating Terrorism: Proceedings of an International Seminar, Tel Aviv, 1979.*** Frederick, MD.: University Publications of America, 1985. 188p.

918. _____, et al. ***Inter 85: A Review of International Terrorism in 1985.*** Tel Aviv: Jaffee Center for Strategic Studies; Boulder, CO.: Westview Press, 1986. 130p.

919. _____, and Anat Kurz, et al. ***INTER: International Terrorism in 1987.*** Tel Aviv: Jaffee Center for Strategic Studies, 1988. 140p.

920. Mickolus, Edward F. "Studying Terrorism in the 1980s: Looking Backward and Forward." Paper Presented at the ***Symposium on International Terrorism,*** held on December 2-3, 1985 at the Defence Intelligence College, Washington, D.C.

921. _____. "Studying Terrorist Incidents: Issues in Conceptualization and Data Acquisition." Paper Presented at the ***Annual Meeting of the International Studies Association,*** held on March 18-22, 1980, in Los Angeles, CA. 31p.

922. Moayedoddin, Mohsen. ***International Terrorism: Three Case Studies.*** Ph.D. Dissertation. Claremont, CA.: Claremont Graduate School, 1982. 139p.

923. Mohsen, Raed A. ***The Communicative, Persuasive, and Agitational Aspects of Revolutionary "Terrorism".*** Ph.D. Dissertation. Bowling Green, OH.: Bowling Green State University, 1987. 111p.

924. Myers, Michael. ***Terrorism: A Discussion Guide.*** New York: Coalition for Alternatives in Jewish Education, 1986-87. 20p.

925. Nanes, Allan S. "International Terrorism." In: ***Major Studies and Issue Briefs of the Congressional Research Service, 1984-1985 Supplement.*** Frederick, MD.: University Publications of America, 1985. Reel VIII. pp. 0407-0424.

926. _____. ***Changing Nature of International Terrorism.*** Report 85-625F. Washington, D.C.: Library of Congress, Congressional Research Service, 1985. 14p.

927. _____. ***International Terrorism.*** Issue Brief 81141. Washington, D.C.: Library of Congress, Congressional Research Service, 1985. 17p.

928. Oakley, Robert B. ***Terrorism: Overview and Developments.*** Washington, DC.: U.S. Department of State, Bureau of Public Affairs, 1985. 5p.

929. Oots, Kent L. ***Transnational Terrorism: A Political Organization Approach.*** Ph.D. Dissertation. DeKalb, IL.: Northern Illinois University, 1984. 213p.

930. Purkitt, Helen. "International Terrorism: A Systematic Study of Past, Present, and Future Trends in Transnational Violence." Paper Presented at the ***Annual Convention of the International Studies Association***, held on March 18-22, 1980 in Los Angeles, CA.

931. Reid, Edna F. ***An Analysis of Terrorism Literature: A Bibliometric and Content Analysis Study.*** D.L.S.. Los Angeles, CA.: University of Southern California, 1983.

932. Reinares, Fernando. "Political Terrorism as a Form of Collective Action." Paper Presented at the ***12th World Congress of Sociology***, held on July 3-9, 1990 in Madrid.

933. Romano, Anne T. ***Terrorism: An Analysis of the Literature.*** Ph.D. Dissertation. New York: Fordham University, 1984. 146p.

934. Sayre, Robert M. ***International Terrorism: A Long Twilight Struggle: August 15, 1984.*** Washington, D.C.: U.S. Department of State, Bureau of Public Affairs, 1984.

935. Simon, Jeffrey. ***Misperceiving the Terrorist Threat.*** RAND R-3423-RC. Santa Monica, CA.: RAND Corporation, 1987. 17p.

936. Snitch, Thomas H. "Political Separatism and Terrorism: A Global Overview." Paper Presented at the ***Annual Convention of the International Studies Association***, held on October 29-31, 1981 at the University of Florida.

937. Stohl, Michael. "The Superpower and International Terrorism." Paper Presented to the ***13th Annual World Congress of the International Political Science Association***, held on July 15-20, 1985, in Paris.

938. ***Terrorism and International Order.*** Chatham House Special Paper. London: Royal Institute of International Affairs, 1986. 112p.

939. ***Terrorism: Special Studies, 1975-1985.*** Frederick, MD.: University Publications of America, 1986. 5 microfilm reels with printed guide.

940. ***Terrorism: Special Studies, 1985-1988, First Supplement.*** Bethesda, MD.: University Publications of America, 1989. 5 microfilm reels.

941. Tromp, Hylke. "A Survey of the Contemporary Spread of Terrorism." Paper Presented at the ***24th Annual Convention of the International Studies Association***, held on April 5-9, 1983 in Mexico City.

942. United States. Central Intelligence Agency. ***International Terrorism in 1979.*** Washington, D.C.: U.S. Government Printing Office, 1980. 30p.

943. _____._____. ***Patterns of International Terrorism: 1980.*** Washington, D.C.: U.S. Government Printing Office, 1981. 31p.

944. _____. Congress. House. Committee on Foreign Affairs. Subcommittee on Arms Control, International Security and Science and on International Operations. ***International Terrorism, 1985: Hearing and Markup on H.R. 2822.*** 99th Cong, 2nd sess. Washington, D.C.: U.S. Government Printing Office, 1985.

945 ._____._____._____._____. Subcommittee on Arms Control, International Security and Science. ***Impact of International Terrorism on Travel: Joint Hearings.*** Serial (99-48). 99th Cong., 2nd sess. Washington, D.C.: U.S. Government Printing Office, 1988. 432p.

946. _____._____. Senate. Committee on Appropriations. Subcommittee on Foreign Operations. ***International Terrorism: Hearings.*** 98th Cong., 2nd sess. Washington, D.C.: U.S. Government Printing Office, 1985. 29p.

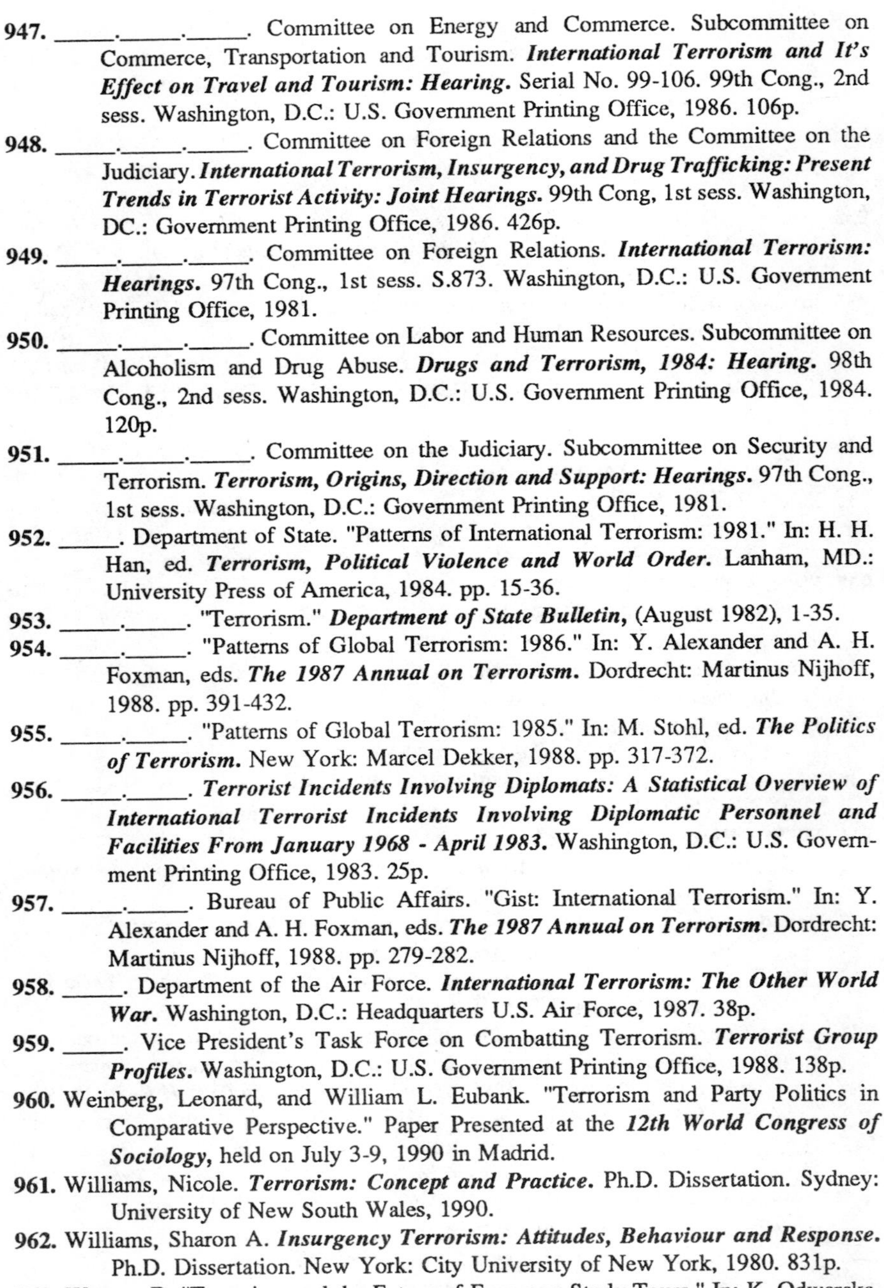

947. _____._____._____. Committee on Energy and Commerce. Subcommittee on Commerce, Transportation and Tourism. ***International Terrorism and It's Effect on Travel and Tourism: Hearing.*** Serial No. 99-106. 99th Cong., 2nd sess. Washington, D.C.: U.S. Government Printing Office, 1986. 106p.

948. _____._____._____. Committee on Foreign Relations and the Committee on the Judiciary. ***International Terrorism, Insurgency, and Drug Trafficking: Present Trends in Terrorist Activity: Joint Hearings.*** 99th Cong, 1st sess. Washington, DC.: Government Printing Office, 1986. 426p.

949. _____._____._____. Committee on Foreign Relations. ***International Terrorism: Hearings.*** 97th Cong., 1st sess. S.873. Washington, D.C.: U.S. Government Printing Office, 1981.

950. _____._____._____. Committee on Labor and Human Resources. Subcommittee on Alcoholism and Drug Abuse. ***Drugs and Terrorism, 1984: Hearing.*** 98th Cong., 2nd sess. Washington, D.C.: U.S. Government Printing Office, 1984. 120p.

951. _____._____._____. Committee on the Judiciary. Subcommittee on Security and Terrorism. ***Terrorism, Origins, Direction and Support: Hearings.*** 97th Cong., 1st sess. Washington, D.C.: Government Printing Office, 1981.

952. _____. Department of State. "Patterns of International Terrorism: 1981." In: H. H. Han, ed. ***Terrorism, Political Violence and World Order.*** Lanham, MD.: University Press of America, 1984. pp. 15-36.

953. _____._____. "Terrorism." ***Department of State Bulletin,*** (August 1982), 1-35.

954. _____._____. "Patterns of Global Terrorism: 1986." In: Y. Alexander and A. H. Foxman, eds. ***The 1987 Annual on Terrorism.*** Dordrecht: Martinus Nijhoff, 1988. pp. 391-432.

955. _____._____. "Patterns of Global Terrorism: 1985." In: M. Stohl, ed. ***The Politics of Terrorism.*** New York: Marcel Dekker, 1988. pp. 317-372.

956. _____._____. ***Terrorist Incidents Involving Diplomats: A Statistical Overview of International Terrorist Incidents Involving Diplomatic Personnel and Facilities From January 1968 - April 1983.*** Washington, D.C.: U.S. Government Printing Office, 1983. 25p.

957. _____._____. Bureau of Public Affairs. "Gist: International Terrorism." In: Y. Alexander and A. H. Foxman, eds. ***The 1987 Annual on Terrorism.*** Dordrecht: Martinus Nijhoff, 1988. pp. 279-282.

958. _____. Department of the Air Force. ***International Terrorism: The Other World War.*** Washington, D.C.: Headquarters U.S. Air Force, 1987. 38p.

959. _____. Vice President's Task Force on Combatting Terrorism. ***Terrorist Group Profiles.*** Washington, D.C.: U.S. Government Printing Office, 1988. 138p.

960. Weinberg, Leonard, and William L. Eubank. "Terrorism and Party Politics in Comparative Perspective." Paper Presented at the ***12th World Congress of Sociology,*** held on July 3-9, 1990 in Madrid.

961. Williams, Nicole. ***Terrorism: Concept and Practice.*** Ph.D. Dissertation. Sydney: University of New South Wales, 1990.

962. Williams, Sharon A. ***Insurgency Terrorism: Attitudes, Behaviour and Response.*** Ph.D. Dissertation. New York: City University of New York, 1980. 831p.

963. Wymar, B. "Terrorism and the Future of European Study Tours." In: K. Odwarska, ed. ***Proceedings of the Eleventh European Studies Conference.*** Omaha, NE.: Department of Political Science, University of Nebraska, 1986. pp. 315-317.

III

THEORIES OF TERRORISM

This chapter lists works dealing with the theoretical foundations of terrorism. The works examine the philosophies, doctrines and ideologies of modern terrorist movements. Examination of this literature shows no unifying doctrine. Instead, one finds fragmentation of theories which reflect the diverse nature of causes, beliefs, and goals of terrorist movements. Nevertheless, some common patterns can be observed. One such pattern is the process of accelerated modernization and its widespread social and political consequence. Rapid technological, economic, political and social change has profound influence on many traditional societies. These factors are having major social and psychological effects in many parts of the world. Totalitarian ideologies and religious radicalism give terrorist groups their major ideological impetus and moral self-justification. All these elements influence the theories and the ideologies which are used to defend acts of political violence which have come to be called terrorism.

1. Books

964. Bauhn, Per Roald. ***Ethical Aspects of Political Terrorism: The Sacrifice of the Innocent.*** Melbourne, FL.: Krieger, 1989. 179p.

965. Chomsky, Noam. ***The Culture of Terrorism.*** Boston, MA.: South End Press, 1988. 268p.

966. Feibleman, James K. ***From Hegel to Terrorism: And Other Essays on the Dynamic Nature of Philosophy.*** Atlantic Highlands, NJ.: Humanities Press, 1985.

967. Johnson, James T., and John Kelsay, eds. ***Cross, Crescent, and Sword: The Justification and Limitation of War in Western and Islamic Tradition.*** Westport, CT.: Greenwood Press, 1990. 236p.

968. Laffin, John. ***Holy War, Islam Fights.*** London: Grafton Books, 1990. 240p.

969. O'Sullivan, Noel. ***Terrorism, Ideology and Revolution.*** Brighton: Wheatsheaf Books, 1986. 232p.

970. Rapoport, David C., and Yonah Alexander, eds. ***The Morality of Terrorism: Religious and Secular Justifications.*** New York: Pergamon Press, 1982. 377p.

971. _____. _____, eds. ***The Rationalization of Terrorism.*** Frederick, MD.: University Publications of America, 1982. 233p.

2. Journal Articles

972. Adams, Tom. "Strategy and Philosophy of Terrorism." ***Military Intelligence,*** 7:2 (April-June 1981), 21-23.

973. _____. "Terrorism: The Philosophy, The Strategy." ***Engineer,*** 11:3 (Winter 1981-82), 14-17.

974. Amjad-Ali, Charles W., and Lester Edwin J. Ruiz. "Terrorism: A Logocentric Moral Issue or an Expression of the Plurality of Human Dwelling." ***Chitty's Law Journal,*** 32:1 (1984), 33-42.

975. Amon, Moshe. "The Phoenix Complex: Terrorism and the Death of Western Civilization." In: L. Z. Freedman and Y. Alexander, eds. ***Perspectives on Terrorism.*** Wilmington, DE.: Scholarly Resources, 1983. pp. 13-18.

976. _____. "Religion and Terrorism: A Romantic Model of Secular Gnosticism." In: D. C. Rapoport and Y. Alexander, eds. ***The Rationalization of Terrorism.*** Frederick, MD.: University Publications of America, 1982. pp. 80-90.

977. _____. "The Unravelling of the Myth of Progress." In: D. C. Rapoport and Y. Alexander, eds. ***The Morality of Terrorism.*** New York: Pergamon Press, 1982. pp. 62-76.

978. Barrett, William. "Morality and the Present Peril." ***Parameters,*** 11 (March 1981), 47-49.

979. Becker, Jillian. "Another Final Battle on the Stage of History." In: P. Wilkinson, ed. ***British Perspectives on Terrorism.*** London: Allen and Unwin, 1981. 89-106.

980. Begg, John D. "Holy Terror! The Third World's War Against Modernity." ***Defense Transportation Journal,*** 43 (April 1987), 10-13.

981. Bell, Donald H. "Comment: The Origins of Modern Terrorism." ***Terrorism,*** 9:3 (1987), 307-311.

982. Blakesley, Christopher L. "The Modern Blood Feud: Thoughts on the Philosophy of Terrorism." ***Catholic Lawyer,*** 33 (Summer 1990), 177-201.

983. Bookbinder, Paul. "Terrorism: Left and Right." ***Present Tense,*** 13:3 (1986), 54-56.

984. Bose, A. "Possibility of Peaceful Revolution and Role of Revolutionary Terrorism." ***Economic and Political Weekly,*** 24:9 (March 4, 1989), 479-480.

985. Bozeman, Adda B. "Closed Societies and the Resort to Violence." In: U. Ra'anan, et al. ***Hydra of Carnage.*** Lexington, MA.: Heath-Lexington Books, 1986. pp. 19-48.

986. Brainerd, Gideon R. "Terrorism: The Theory of Differential Effects." ***Conflict,*** 5:3 (1984), 233-245.

987. Burmudez, Francisco Morales. "On Terrorism: Some Philosophical Considerations." ***Global Affairs,*** 1:2 (1986), 11-18.

988. Burtchaell, James T. "Moral Response to Terrorism." In: N. C. Livingstone and T. E. Arnold, eds. ***Fighting Back: Winning the War Against Terrorism.*** Lexington, MA.: Lexington Books, 1985. pp. 191-212.

989. Calvert, Peter. "Terror in the Theory of Revolution." In: N. O'Sullivan, ed. ***Terrorism, Ideology, and Revolution.*** Boulder, CO.: Westview Press, 1986. pp. 27-48.

990. Cantelon, John. "Terrorism and the Moral Majority." In: H. H. Han, ed. ***Terrorism, Political Violence and World Order.*** Lanham, MD.: University Press of America, 1984. pp. 65-72.

991. _____. "Violence: An Educational and Religious Perspective." In: H. H. Han, ed. ***Terrorism, Political Violence and World Order.*** Lanham, MD.: University Press of America, 1984. pp.65-72.

992. Capitanchik, David. "Terrorism and Islam." In: N. O'Sullivan, ed. ***Terrorism, Ideology, and Revolution.*** Boulder, CO.: Westview Press, 1986. pp. 115-131.

993. Carmichael, D. J. C. "Of Beasts, Gods, and Civilized Men: The Justification of Terrorism and of Counterterrorist Measures." ***Terrorism,*** 6:1 (1982), 1-26.

994. Chaliand, Gerard. "Terrorism - A Means of Liberation?." ***Terrorism and Political Violence,*** 1:1 (January 1989), 21-27.

995. Coady, C. A. J. "The Morality of Terrorism." ***Philosophy,*** (January 1985), 47-69.

996. Cooper, H. H. A. "An Imam's Absence Makes the Heart Grow Darker." ***TVI Journal,*** 4:10-12 (1983), 7-10.

997. Crenshaw, Martha. "Theories of Terrorism: Instrumental and Organizational Approaches." ***Journal of Strategic Studies,*** 10:4 (December 1987), 13-31.

998. _____. "Theories of Terrorism - Instrumental and Organizational Approaches." In: D. C. Rapoport, ed. ***Inside Terrorist Organizations.*** New York: Columbia University Press, 1988. pp. 13-31.

999. Decter, Midge. "The Theory of Grievances." In: B. Netanyahu, ed. ***Terrorism: How the West Can Win.*** New York: Farrar, Straus, Giroux, 1986. pp. 190-192.

1000. Dimitrijevic, Vojin. "The Non-Aligned Movement and International Terrorism." ***Social Thought and Practice,*** 29:(3-5), (March-June 1989), 56-69.

1001. Dinse, John. "Ideological Orientation of Contemporary Left Terrorism." In: H. H. Han, ed. ***Terrorism, Political Violence and World Order.*** Lanham, MD.: University Press of America, 1984. pp. 79-86.

1002. _____. "The Role of Violence in Marx's Theory of Revolution." In: H. H. Han, ed. ***Terrorism, Political Violence and World Order.*** Lanham, MD.: University Press of America, 1984. pp. 59-64.

1003. Dugard, John. "International Terrorism and the Just War." In: D. C. Rapoport and Y. Alexander, eds. ***The Morality of Terrorism.*** New York: Pergamon Press, 1982. pp. 77-98.

1004. Eby, L. "Peace Versus Terrorism - Rejoinder." ***International Journal on World Peace***, 5:3 (1988), 10-14.

1005. Elias, Norbert. "Civilization and Violence." ***Telos***, 54 (Winter 1982-83), 134-154.

1006. Erickson, Richard J. "What is Terrorism and How Serious is the Threat?." ***Quarterly Journal of Ideology***, 11:3 (July 1987), 9-25.

1007. Ferracuti, Franco. "Theories of Terrorism." In: ***International Terrorism and the Drug Connection.*** Ankara: Ankara University Press, 1984. pp. 225-239.

1008. Ferrarotti, Franco. "Terrorism and the Catholic Ethic." ***Worldview***, 26:11 (November 1983), 18-19.

1009. Fleming, Marie. "Propaganda by the Deed: Terrorism and Anarchist Theory in Late Nineteenth-Century Europe." ***Terrorism***, 1:4 (1980), 1-24.

1010. Foley, Tom. "International Terrorism: Code Word and Reality." ***Political Affairs***, 64 (November 1984), 15-21.

1011. Furet, Francois. "Terrorism and Democracy." ***Telos***, 65 (Fall 1985), 75-86.

1012. George, David. "Distinguishing Classical Tyrannicide from Modern Terrorism." ***Review of Politics***, 50:3 (Summer 1988), 390-419.

1013. _____. "Terrorists or Freedom Fighters." In: M. Warner and R. Crisp, eds. ***Terrorism, Protest and Power.*** Brookfield, VT.: Society for Applied Philosophy, 1990. pp. 54-67.

1014. Gerstein, Roberts. "Do Terrorists Have Rights?" In: D. Rapoport and Y. Alexander, eds. ***The Morality of Terrorism.*** New York: Pergamon Press, 1982. pp. 290-307.

1015. Giuffrida, Louis O. "Dealing with the Consequences of Terrorism - We Are Not Yet Where We Must Be." ***Terrorism***, 10:1 (1987), 71-75.

1016. Gobetz, Edward. "Terrorism and Objective Moral Principles: Comment." ***International Journal of World Peace***, 4:4 (October - December, 1987), 40-50.

1017. Goertzel, Ted. "The Ethics of Terrorism and Revolution." ***Terrorism***, 11:1 (1988), 1-12

1018. Graham, Gordon. "Terrorists and Freedom Fighters." ***Philosophy of Social Action***, 11 (October-December 1985), 43-54.

1019. Grosscup, Beau. "The Neoconservative State and the Politics of Terrorism." ***New Political Science***, 8 (Spring 1982), 39-62.

1020. Gurr, Ted R. "Tyrants and Terrorists." ***Society***, 23:6 (1986), 81-84.

1021. _____, and Mark Irving Lichbach. "Forecasting Internal Conflict: A Competitive Evaluation of Empirical Theories." ***Comparative Political Studies***, 19:1 (1986), 3-38.

1022. _____. "The Political Origins of State Violence and Terror: A Theoretical Analysis." In: M. Stohl and G. A. Lopez, eds. ***Government Violence and Repression.*** Westport, CT.: Greenwood Press, 1990. pp. 45-72.

1023. Halliday, Fred. "The Cult of the Gun." ***Marxism Today***, (January 1987), 24-26.

1024. Hampson, Norman. "From Regeneration to Terror: The Ideology of the French Revolution." In: N. O'Sullivan, ed. ***Terrorism, Ideology, and Revolution.*** Boulder, CO.: Westview Press, 1986. pp. 49-66.

1025. Harff, Barbara. "Genocide as State Terror." In: M. Stohl and G. A. Lopez, eds. ***Government Violence and Repression.*** Westport, CT.: Greenwood Press, 1986. pp. 165-188.

1026. Hartle, Anthony E. "Military Ethic in an Age of Terror." ***Parameters***, 17:2 (Summer 1987), 68-75.

1027. Held, Virginia. "Violence, Terrorism, and Moral Inquiry." ***Monist,*** 67 (October 1984), 605-626.

1028. Hocking, Jenny. "Orthodox Theories of 'Terrorism': The Power of Politicised Terminology." ***Politics,*** 19:2 (1984), 103-110.

1029. Hoffman, Bruce. "The Contrasting Ethical Foundations of Terrorism in the 1980s." ***Terrorism and Political Violence,*** 1:3 (July 1989), 361-377.

1030. Hubbard, David G. "Terrorism is Criminal Activity." In: B. Szumski, ed. ***Terrorism: Opposing Viewpoints.*** St.Paul, MN.: Greenhaven Press, 1986. pp. 26-32.

1031. Hughes, Martin. "Terrorism and National Security." ***Philosophy,*** 57 (January 1982), 5-26.

1032. Ivianski, Zeev. "The Terrorist Revolution: Roots of Modern Terrorism." ***Journal of Strategic Studies,*** 10:4 (December 1987), 127-149.

1033. _____. "The Terrorist Revolution - Roots of Modern Terrorism." In: D. C. Rapoport, ed. ***Inside Terrorist Organizations.*** New York: Columbia University Press, 1988. pp. 129-149.

1034. _____. "Sources of Inspiration for Revolutionary Terrorism: The Bakunin-Nechayev Alliance." ***Conflict Quarterly,*** 8:3 (Summer 1988), 49-68.

1035. Jamali, M. F. "Peace Versus Terrorism." ***International Journal on World Peace,*** 5:3 (1988), 10-14.

1036. Juergensmeyer, Mark. "The Logic of Religious Violence." ***Journal of Strategic Studies,*** 10:4 (December 1987), 172-193.

1037. _____. "The Logic of Religious Violence." In: D. C. Rapoport, ed. ***Inside Terrorist Organizations.*** New York: Columbia University Press, 1988. pp. 172-193.

1038. Kampf, Herbert A. "Terrorism, the Left Wing, and the Intellectuals." ***Terrorism,*** 13:1 (1990), 23-52.

1039. Kaplan, Abraham. "The Ethics of Terror." In: B. Eichelman, D. Soskis and W. Reid, eds. ***Terrorism: Interdisciplinary Perspectives.*** Washington, D.C.: American Psychiatric Association, 1983. pp. 5-30.

1040. Kavolis, Vytantas. "Models of Rebellion." In: D. C. Rapoport and Y. Alexander, eds. ***The Morality of Terrorism.*** New York: Pergamon Press, 1982. pp. 43-61.

1041. Kedourie, Elie. "Political Terrorism in the Muslim World." In: B. Netanyahu, ed. ***Terrorism: How the West Can Win.*** New York: Farrar, Straus, Giroux, 1986. pp. 70-76.

1042. _____. "Political Terror in the Muslim World." ***Encounter,*** 68:2 (1987), 12-16.

1043. Kemp, Jack. "A False Symmetry." In: B. Netanyahu, ed. ***Terrorism: How the West Can Win.*** New York: Farrar, Straus, Giroux, 1986. pp.193-195.

1044. Kennedy, Moorhead. "The Root Causes of Terrorism: Terrorism and Retribution Will Be a Self-Perpetrating Phenomenon Unless We Seek to Understand Its Sources." ***Humanist,*** 46 (September/October 1986), 5-9+.

1045. Khatchadourian, Haig. "Terrorism and Morality." ***Journal of Applied Philosophy,*** 5 (October 1988), 131-145.

1046. Kirkpatrick, Jeane J. "The Totalitarian Confusion." In: B. Netanyahu, ed. ***Terrorism: How the West Can Win.*** New York: Farrar, Straus, Giroux, 1986. pp. 56-60.

1047. _____. "Terrorist Goals Do Not Justify Terrorism." In: B. Szumski, ed. ***Terrorism: Opposing Viewpoints.*** St.Paul, MN.: Greenhaven Press, 1986. pp. 119-122.

1048. Kolakowski, Leszek. "Terrorism and the Concept of Legitimacy." In: B. Netanyahu, ed. ***Terrorism: How the West Can Win.*** New York: Farrar, Straus, Giroux, 1986. pp. 48-51.

1049. Kramer, Martin. "The Moral Logic of Hizballah." In: W. Reich, ed. ***Origins of Terrorism.*** Cambridge: Cambridge University Press, 1990. pp. 131-160.

1050. Krauthammer, Charles. "Terrorism is Murder." In: B. Szumski, ed. ***Terrorism: Opposing Viewpoints.*** St. Paul, MN.: Greenhaven Press, 1986. pp. 39-42.

1051. Kutner, Luis. "The Revolt of Planet Earth." ***Common Law Lawyer,*** 11:5-6 (1986), 1-36.

1052. Laqueur, Walter Z. "Reflections on Terrorism." ***Foreign Affairs,*** 65:1 (Autumn 1986), 86-100.

1053. _____. "The Futility of Terrorism: Second Thoughts on Terrorism." In: W. Z. Laqueur, ed. ***The Political Psychology of Appeasement: Finlandization and Other Unpopular Essays.*** New Brunswick, NJ.: Transaction, 1980. pp. 101-125.

1054. _____. "Terrorism Reconsidered." ***NATO's 16 Nations,*** 32:7 (November 1987), 33-34.

1055. Leeman, Richard W. "Rhetoric and Value in Terrorism." In: M. Slann and B. Schechterman, eds. ***Multi-Dimensional Terrorism.*** Boulder, CO.: Lynne Rienner, 1987. pp. 45-56.

1056. _____. "Terrorism as Rhetoric: An Argument of Values." ***Journal of Political Science,*** 14:1-2 (1986), 33-42.

1057. Levy, Rudolph. "Terrorism and Communism: A History and Profile, Conclusion." ***Military Intelligence,*** (October-December 1980), 26-33.

1058. _____. "Terrorism and Communism: A History and Profile, Part 1." ***Military Intelligence,*** (September 1980), 17-25.

1059. Lewis, Bernard. "Islamic Terrorism?" In: B. Netanyahu, ed. ***Terrorism: How the West Can Win.*** New York: Farrar, Straus, Giroux, 1986. pp. 65-69.

1060. Lopez, George A. "National Security Ideology as an Impetus to State Violence and State Terror." In: M. Stohl and G. A. Lopez, eds. ***Government Violence and Repression.*** Westport, CT.: Greenwood Press, 1986. pp. 73-96.

1061. Louch, A. R. "Terrorism: The Immorality of Belief." In: D. C. Rapoport and Y. Alexander, eds. ***The Morality of Terrorism.*** New York: Pergamon Press, 1982. pp. 267-274.

1062. Machan, Tibor R. "Terrorism and Objective Moral Principles." ***International Journal of World Peace,*** 4:4 (October-December 1987), 31-39.

1063. Maranto, Robert. "The Rationality of Terrorism." In: M. Slann and B. Schechterman, eds. ***Multidimensional Terrorism.*** Boulder, CO.: Lynne Rienner, 1987. pp. 11-18.

1064. _____. "The Rational Terrorist: Toward a New Theory of Terrorism." ***Journal of Political Science,*** 14:1-2 (1986), 16-24.

1065. Martin, Richard C. "Striving in the Path of Allah: Toward an Understanding of Religious Violence in Text and Context." Paper Presented at the ***Terrorism: An International Conference,*** held on April 17-19, 1986 at Aberdeen University, Aberdeen. pp. 55-71.

1066. Maynes, Charles W. "All Political Violence is Not Terrorism." In: B. Szumski, ed. ***Terrorism: Opposing Viewpoints.*** St. Paul, MN.: Greenhaven Press, 1986. pp. 22-25.

1067. McConnell, Jeff. "The Counterterrorists at the Fletcher School." ***Boston Review,*** 11:4 (August 1986), 20-21.

1068. McFarlane, Robert C. "Terrorism and the Future of Free Society." ***Terrorism***, 8:4 (1986), 315-326.

1069. McGurn, William. "Terrorism is Never Justified." In: B. Szumski, ed. ***Terrorism: Opposing Viewpoints.*** St.Paul, MN.: Greenhaven Press, 1986. pp. 90-95.

1070. Metz, Steven. "The Ideology of Terrorist Foreign Policies in Libya and South Africa." ***Conflict***, 7:4 (1987), 379-402.

1071. Miguens, Jose E. "Magical Aspects of Political Terrorism." ***Diogenes***, 126 (January 1985), 17-32.

1072. Moravia, Alberto. "The Terrorist Esthetic." ***Harper's***, 274 (June 1987), 37-19+.

1073. Morrison, P. R. "Limits to Technocratic Consciousness - Information Technology and Terrorism as Example." ***Science, Technology & Human Values***, 11:4 (1986), 4-16.

1074. Murphy, John F. "Clandestine Warfare: Morality and Practical Problems Confounded." ***Washington and Lee Law Review***, 39 (Spring 1982), 377-379.

1075. Musacchio, John M., and Arnon Rozen. "Fundamentalist Fervor: Islamic Terrorism in the '80s." ***Security Management***, 32:11 (November 1988), 54-64+.

1076. Naidu, M. V. "Religionism, Rationalism and Violence: A Study in Religious Terrorism." ***Peace Research***, 21:2 (May 1989), 1-12+.

1077. Nathan, J. A. "International Terrorism and the Moral Structure of International Society." In: D. C. Rapoport and Y. Alexander, eds. ***The Rationalization of Terrorism.*** Frederick, MD.: University Publications of America, 1982. pp. 115-135.

1078. Newman, Graeme R., and Michael J. Lynch. "From Feuding to Terrorism - The Ideology of Vengeance." ***Contemporary Crises***, 11:3 (1987), 223-242.

1079. Nielsen, Kai. "Political Violence and Ideological Mystification." ***Journal of Social Philosophy***, 13 (May 1982), 25-33.

1080. "Nihilism and Terrorism." ***New Republic***, 195:13 (1986), 9-11.

1081. Noakes, Jeremy. "The Origins, Structure and Functions of Nazi Terror." In: N. O'Sullivan, ed. ***Terrorism, Ideology, and Revolution.*** Boulder, CO.: Westview Press, 1986. pp. 67-87.

1082. O'Brien, Conor Cruise. "Thinking About Terrorism." ***The Atlantic***, 257:6 (June 1986), 62-66.

1083. _____. "Thinking About Terrorism: I." In: C. C. O'Brien. ***Passion and Cunning.*** London: Weidenfeld and Nicolson, 1988. pp. 226-233.

1084. O'Sullivan, Noel. "Terrorism, Ideology and Democracy." In: N. O'Sullivan, ed. ***Terrorism, Ideology, and Revolution.*** Boulder, CO.: Westview Press, 1986. pp. 3-27.

1085. Oruka, H. Odera. "Legal Terrorism and Human Rights." ***Praxis International***, 1 (January 1982), 376-385.

1086. Parekh, Bhikhu. "Gandhi's Theory of Non-Violence: His Reply to the Terrorists." In: N. O'Sullivan, ed. ***Terrorism, Ideology, and Revolution.*** Boulder, CO.: Westview Press, 1986. pp. 178-204.

1087. Petrakis, Gregory. "Terrorism: Multinational Corporation and Nation State: The Anarchist's Rationale for Terrorism." ***Law and Order***, 28:7 (1980), 14, 16-18.

1088. _____. "Terrorism: Multinational Corporation and the Nation State: The Anarchist's Rationale For Terrorism, Part Two." ***Law and Order***, 28:6 (1980), 22-24.

1089. Phillips, Robert. " Terrorism: Historical Roots and Moral Justifications." In: M. Wagner and R. Crisp, eds. ***Terrorism, Protest and Power.*** Brookfield, VT.: Society for Applied Philosophy, 1990. pp. 68-80.

1090. _____. "The Roots of Terrorism." ***Christian Century***, 103:12 (April 9, 1986), 355-357.

1091. Pipes, Daniel. "The Scourge of Suicide Terrorism." ***The National Interest***, 4 (Summer 1986), 95-99.

1092. Possony, Stefan T. "Kaleidoscopic Views of Terrorism." ***Terrorism***, 4 (1980), 89-122.

1093. Pottenger, John R. "Liberation Theology: Its Methodological Foundations for Violence." In: D. C. Rapoport and Y. Alexander, eds. ***The Morality of Terrorism***. New York: Pergamon Press, 1982. pp. 99-126.

1094. Quinton, A. C. E. "Reflection on Terrorism and Violence." In: M. Warner and R. Crisp, eds. ***Terrorism, Protest and Power***. Brookfield, VT.: Society for Applied Philosophy, 1990. pp. 35-43.

1095. Rapoport, David C. "Fear and Trembling: Terrorism in Three Religious Traditions." ***American Political Science Review***, 78:3 (1984), 658-677.

1096. _____. "Rebel Terror: Introduction to Part 3." In: D. C. Rapoport and Y. Alexander, eds. ***The Morality of Terrorism***. New York: Pergamon Press, 1982. pp. 219-228.

1097. _____. "Religious Terror: Introduction to Part 1." In: D. C. Rapoport and Y. Alexander, eds. ***The Morality of Terrorism***. New York: Pergamon Press, 1982. pp. 3-12.

1098. _____. "Terror and the Messiah: An Ancient Experience and Some Modern Parallels." In: D. C. Rapoport and Y. Alexander, eds. ***The Morality of Terrorism***. New York: Pergamon Press, 1982. pp. 13-42.

1099. _____. "Why Does Religious Messianism Produce Terror?." In.: P. Wilkinson and A. M. Stewart, eds. ***Contemporary Research on Terrorism***. Aberdeen: Aberdeen University Press, 1987. pp. 72-88.

1100. _____. "Messianism and Terror." ***Century Magazine***, 19 (January/February 1986), 30-39.

1101. _____. "Messianic Sanctions for Terror." ***Comparative Politics***, 20:2 (January 1988), 195-214.

1102. _____. "Sacred Terror: A Contemporary Example from Islam." In: W. Reich, ed. ***Origins of Terrorism***. Cambridge: Cambridge University Press, 1990. pp. 103-130.

1103. _____. "Religion and Terror: Thugs, Assassins, and Zealots." In: C. W. Kegley, ed. ***International Terrorism: Characteristics, Causes, Controls***. New York: St. Martin's Press, 1990. pp. 146-157.

1104. Revel, Jean Francois. "Democracy Versus Terrorism." In: B. Netanyahu, ed. ***Terrorism: How the West Can Win***. New York: Farrar, Straus, Giroux, 1986. pp. 196-198.

1105. Roberts, Adam. "Ethics, Terrorism and Counter-Terrorism." ***Terrorism and Political Violence***, 1:1 (January 1989), 48-69.

1106. Romerstein, Herbert. "Political Linkages and Apparatus." In: U. Ra'anan, et al. ***Hydra of Carnage***. Lexington, MA.: Lexington Books, 1986. pp. 59-76.

1107. Rose, Gregory F. "Revolution, Culture and Collective Action." ***Journal of Political Science***, 14:1-2 (Spring 1986), 25-32.

1108. Sandler, Todd, John T. Tschirhart and Jon Cauley. "A Theoretical Analysis of Transnational Terrorism." ***American Political Science Review***, 77:1 (1983), 36-54.

1109. Schechterman, Bernard. "Irrational Terrorism." In: M. Slann and B. Schechterman, eds. ***Multidimensional Terrorism.*** Boulder, CO.: Lynne Rienner, 1987. pp. 19-32.

1110. Scheuer, Jeffrey. "Moral Dimensions of Terrorism." ***Fletcher Forum,*** 14:1 (Winter 1990), 145-160.

1111. Schmid, Alex P. "Theories." (Second Chapter). In: A. P. Schmid. ***Political Terrorism: A Research Guide to Concepts, Theories, Data Bases and Literature.*** Amsterdam: SWIDOC, 1983. pp. 160-244.

1112. _____. "Violence as Communication: The Case of Insurgent Terrorism." In: E. Jahn and Y. Sakamoto, eds. ***Elements of World Instability: Armaments, Communication, Food, International Division of Labour.*** Frankfurt am Main: Campus Verlag, 1981. pp. 147-170.

1113. Schrastetter, Rudolph. "Theses on Terrorism." ***Terrorism,*** 3:3-4 (1980), 305-309.

1114. Sick, Gary. "Terrorism: Its Political Uses and Abuses." ***SAIS Review,*** 7:1 (Winter-Spring 1987), 11-26.

1115. Simmons, Carolyn H., and J. R. Mitch. "Labelling Public Aggression: When is it Terrorism?" ***Journal of Social Psychology,*** 125:2 (April, 1985), 245-251.

1116. Smylie, Robert F. "Terrorism Probing the Dynamics." ***Christian Society,*** 78 (May-June 1988), 6-36.

1117. Sonnleitner, M. W. "Of Logic and Liberation - Fannon on Terrorism." ***Journal of Black Studies,*** 17:3 (March 1987), 287-304.

1118. Stackhouse, Max L. "Torture, Terrorism and Theology: The Need for a Universal Ethic." ***Christian Century,*** 103:29 (October 8, 1986), 861-863.

1119. Stohl, Michael. "The Superpowers and International Terrorism." In: M. Stohl and G. A. Lopez, eds. ***Government Violence and Repression.*** Westport, CT.: Greenwood Press, 1986. pp. 207-234.

1120. _____. "Demystifying Terrorism: The Myths and Realities of Contemporary Political Terrorism." In: M. Stohl, ed. ***The Politics of Terrorism.*** New York: Marcel Dekker, 1988. pp. 1-30.

1121. Strentz, Thomas. "Radical Right vs. Radical Left: Terrorist Theory and Threat." ***Police Chief,*** 57:8 (August 1990), 70-75.

1122. Taussig, Michael. "Culture of Terror - Space of Death, Roger Casement's Putuyamo Report and the Explanation of Torture." ***Comparative Studies in Society and History,*** 26:3 (1984), 467-497.

1123. "Terror's Roots Many and Tangled." ***TVI Journal,*** 3:8 (1982), 8-14.

1124. Tololyan, Khachig. "Martyrdom as Legitimacy: Terrorism, Religion and Symbolic Appropriation in the Armenian Diaspora." In: P. Wilkinson and A. M. Stewart, eds. ***Contemporary Research on Terrorism.*** Aberdeen: Aberdeen University Press, 1987. pp. 89-103.

1125. _____. "Cultural Narrative and the Motivation of the Terrorist." ***Journal of Strategic Studies,*** 10:4 (December 1987), 217-236.

1126. _____. "Cultural Narrative and the Motivation of the Terrorist." In: D. C. Rapoport, ed. ***Inside Terrorist Organizations.*** New York: Columbia University Press, 1988. pp. 217-236.

1127. Turner, Billy M. "Security and Social Inquiry - Terrorism as a Quasi-Religious Phenomenon." ***Journal of Security Administration,*** 8:1 (June 1985), 57-68.

1128. Vitiuk, V. V. "Toward an Analysis and Evaluation of the Evolution of Terrorism." ***The Soviet Review,*** 21:4 (1980-81), 85-106.

1129. Vought, Donald B. "Terror and Counterterror. Good? Bad? Ugly?." ***Quarterly Journal of Ideology***, 11:3 (July 1987), 27-43.

1130. Walzer, Martin. "What's Terrorism - And What Isn't." ***Dissent***, 33:3 (1986), 274-275.

1131. Wardlaw, Grant. "Terrorism, Counter-Terrorism, and the Democratic Society." In: M. Stohl and G. A. Lopez, eds. ***Government Violence and Repression.*** Westport, CT.: Greenwood Press, 1986. pp. 189-206.

1132. Wellmer, Albrecht. "Terrorism and Social Criticism." ***Telos***, 48 (Summer 1981), 65-79.

1133. West, Louis J. "Cults, Liberty and Mind Control." In: D. C. Rapoport and Y. Alexander, eds. ***The Rationalization of Terrorism.*** Frederick, MD.: University Publications of America, 1982. pp. 101-107.

1134. Wilkins, Burleigh T. "Terrorism and Consequentialism." ***Journal of Value Inquiry***, 21 (1987), 141-151.

1135. Wilkinson, Paul. "Some Observations on the Relationships Between Terrorism and Freedom." In: M. Warner and R. Crisp, eds. ***Terrorism, Protest and Power.*** Brookfield, VT.: Society for Applied Philosophy, 1990. pp. 44-53.

1136. _____. "The Sources of Terrorism: Terrorists' Ideologies and Beliefs." In: C. W. Kegley, ed. ***International Terrorism: Characteristics, Causes, Controls.*** New York: St. Martin's Press, 1990. pp. 139-145.

1137. _____. "Ethical Defenses of Terrorism - Defending the Indefensible." ***Terrorism and Political Violence***, 1:1 (January 1989), 7-20.

1138. _____. "Pathology and Theory." In: W. Laqueur, ed. ***The Terrorism Reader.*** New York: Meridian, 1987. pp. 236-245.

1139. Wilson, James. "Thinking About Terrorism." ***Commentary***, 72:1 (July 1981), 34-39.

1140. Wolpin, Miles. "State Terrorism and Repression in the Third World: Parameters and Prospects." In: M. Stohl and G. A. Lopez, eds. ***Government Violence and Repression.*** Westport, CT.: Greenwood Press, 1986. pp. 97-164.

1141. Wouk, Herman. "Sadness and Hope: Some Thoughts on Modern Warfare." ***Naval War College Review***, 33:5 (September- October 1980), 4-12.

1142. Zoppo, Ciro. "The Moral Factor in Interstate Politics and International Terrorism." In: D. C. Rapoport and Y. Alexander, eds. ***The Rationalization of Terrorism.*** Frederick. MD.: University Publications of America, 1982. pp. 136-153.

3. Documents and Reports

1143. Bauhn, Per Roald. ***Ethical Aspects of Political Terrorism: The Sacrificing of the Innocent (Rights and Violence).*** Ph.D. Dissertation. Lunds: Lunds Universitet, 1989. 184p.

1144. Beecroft, David R. ***The Conspiracy Theory of Terrorism: Analysis and Application.*** Master's Thesis. Sacramento, CA.: California State University, 1986. 88p.

1145. Brusitus, J. M. ***Terrorism: Crime or War.*** Carlisle Barracks, PA.: Army War College, 1987. 23p.

1146. Campbell, James. ***The Concept of Violence: An Examination of Its Ideological Uses.*** Ph.D. Dissertation. Belfast: Queen's University, 1986. 286p.

1147. "The Conspiracy Theory of Terrorism: Analysis and Application." In: ***Terrorism: Special Studies, 1985-1988, First Supplement.*** Bethesda, MD.: University Publications of America, 1989. Reel 3, Frames 0821-0914. 94p.

1148. Desloover, Michael Marc. ***Terrorism vs Democracy: A Study in the Effect Terrorism Has on the Political Systems it Attempts to Influence.*** Master's Thesis. Louisville, KY.: University of Louisville, 1986. 83p.

1149. Galtung, Johan. ***On Violence in General and Terrorism in Particular.*** Omslagsside Papers, No. 72. Oslo: University of Oslo, 1980. 27p.

1150. Hazelip, A. Charles. ***Twelve Tenets of Terrorism: An Assessment of Theory and Practice.*** Ph.D. Dissertation. Tallahassee, FL.: Florida State University, 1980. 344p.

1151. Hoffman, Bruce. ***The Contrasting Ethical Foundations of Terrorism in the 1980s.*** RAND P-7416. Santa Monica, CA.: Rand Corporation, 1988. 24p.

1152. Kader, Omar M. ***Contemporary Political Terror: Comparing the Use of Violence by National Liberation and Ideological Groups.*** Ph.D. Dissertation. Los Angeles, Ca.: University of Southern California, 1981.

1153. Moore, Terrence L. ***The Nature and Evaluation of Terrorism.*** Ph.D. Dissertation. Pittsburgh, PA.: University of Pittsburgh, 1987. 346p.

1154. Overbey, B. F. ***Terror and Reprisal: An Ethical Perspective.*** M.A. Thesis. Alexandria, VA.: Army Military Personnel Center, 1985. 64p.

1155. Rapoport, David C. "Why Does Messianism Produce Terror." Paper presented at the ***81st Annual Meeting of the American Political Science Association,*** held on August 28 - September 1, 1985 in New Orleans, LA. 22p.

1156. Said, Edward W. ***The Essential Terrorist.*** Washington, D.C.: General Union of Palestinian Students U.S.A., 1987. 13p.

1157. Shelly, M., and F. Moos. "Notes on a Theory of Terrorism." In: ***Proceedings of the 9th Symposium on the Psychology in the Department of Defence,*** held on April 18-20, 1984 at Colorado Springs, CO. pp. 30-34.

1158. Tupman, W. A. ***Beyond Terrorism: Toward a Theory of Scenarios of Political Violence.*** Brookfield Paper No. 1. Exeter: University of Exeter, Centre for Police & Criminal Justice Studies, 1987. 32p.

1159. Van Til, L. John. ***Moral Dimensions of Terrorism.*** Special Report, No. 32. Grove City, PA.: Public Policy Education Fund, 1985. 4p.

IV

PSYCHOLOGICAL AND SOCIAL ASPECTS OF TERRORISM

Materials listed in this chapter examine the psychological and sociological aspects of terrorism. The literature deals with psychological and social characteristics of individual terrorists, the characteristics of terrorist groups and their dynamics. Personal and group attributes of terrorists, as well as their social, educational and ideological milieu are analyzed. The literature looks at the question of mental instability of terrorists. Section B analyzes the growing concern of society with the victim of terrorist acts. Materials in this section cover studies on behavioral patterns of victims and the emotional, psychological and physical stress experienced by survivors of terrorist incidents. The sections also covers studies dealing with the recuperation of victims.

A. PSYCHOLOGICAL AND SOCIAL ASPECTS

1. Books

1160. Alexander, Yonah, and John M. Gleason, eds. ***Behavioral and Quantitative Perspectives on Terrorism.*** New York: Pergamon Press, 1981. 396p.
1161. Arnold, Terrell E. ***The Violence Formula: Why People Lend Sympathy and Support to Terrorism.*** Lexington, MA.: Lexington Books, 1988. 202p.
1162. Eichelman, Burr, David A. Soskis and William H. Reid. ***Terrorism: Interdisciplinary Perspectives.*** Washington, D.C.: American Psychiatric Association, 1983. 186p.
1163. Friedlander, Robert A. ***Terror - Violence: Aspects of Social Control.*** New York: Oceana, 1983. 299p.
1164. ***Psychological Operations in Guerrilla Warfare.*** New York: Vintage Books, 1985. 124p.
1165. Reich, Walter, ed. ***Origins of Terrorism: Psychologies, Ideologies, Theologies, States of Mind.*** Cambridge: Cambridge University Press, 1990. 289p.
1166. Taylor, Maxwell. ***The Terrorist.*** London: Brassey's Defense Publishers, 1988. 205p.
1167. Tobias, R. ***They Shoot to Kill - A Psycho-Survey of Criminal Sniping.*** Boulder, CO.: Paladin Press, 1981. 268p.
1168. Turk, Austin T. ***Political Criminality: The Defiance and Defence of Authority.*** Beverly Hills, CA.: Sage, 1982. 231p.

2. Journal Articles

1169. Alexander, Yonah. "Terrorism as a Sociopolitical Phenomenon." ***International Journal of Group Tensions,*** 12:1-4 (1982), 41-61.
1170. Altemeyer, Bob. "Marching in Step: A Psychological Explanation of State Terror." ***Sciences,*** 28:2 (March-April 1988), 30-38.
1171. Bandura, Albert. "Mechanisms of Moral Disengagement." In: W. Reich, ed. ***Origins of Terrorism.*** Cambridge: Cambridge University Press, 1990. pp. 161-191.
1172. "Behavioral Science: Its Potential in the War Against Terrorism." ***TVI Journal,*** 2:1 (1981), 6-10.
1173. Bell, J. Bowyer. "Psychology of Leaders of Terrorist Groups." ***International Journal of Group Tensions,*** 12:1-4 (1982), 84-104.
1174. Ben-Eli, Tzion, and Miriam Sela. "Terrorists in Nahariya: Description of Coping Under Stress." ***Israeli Journal of Psychology and Councelling in Education,*** 13 (September 1980), 94-101.
1175. Billig, Otto. "The Lawyer Terrorist and His Comrades." ***Political Psychology,*** 6:1 (1985), 29-46.
1176. _____. "The Lawyer Terrorist." In: ***Psychiatry: The State of the Art, Vol. 6.*** New York: Plenum, 1985. pp. 391-398.
1177. Bollinger, L. "Terrorist Conduct as a Result of a Psychological Process." In: ***Psychiatry: The State of the Art, Vol. 6.*** New York: Plenum, 1985. pp. 387-390.

1178. Cairns, Ed, and Ronnie Wilson. "Coping with Political Violence in Northern Ireland." ***Social Science and Medicine***, 28:6 (1989), 621-624.

1179. _____. _____. "Mental Health Aspects of Political Violence in Northern Ireland." ***International Journal of Mental Health***, 18:1 (1989), 38-56.

1180. Clarke, James W. "Emotional Deprivation and Political Deviance: Some Observations on Governor Wallace's Would-Be Assassin, Arthur B. Bremer." ***Political Psychology***, (Spring/Summer 1981/82), 84-115.

1181. Cordes, Bonnie J. "Euroterrorists Talk About Themselves: A Look at the Literature." In: P. Wilkinson and A. M. Stewart, eds. ***Contemporary Research on Terrorism***. Aberdeen: Aberdeen University Press, 1987. pp. 318-336.

1182. Corrado, Raymond R. "A Critique of the Mental Disorder Perspective of Political Terrorism." ***International Journal of Law and Psychiatry***, 4:3-4 (1981), 293-309.

1183. Crayton, John W. "Terrorism and the Psychology of the Self." In: L. Z. Freedman and Y. Alexander, eds. ***Perspectives on Terrorism***. Wilmington, DE.: Scholarly Resources, 1983. pp. 33-44.

1184. Crenshaw, Martha. "The Psychology of Political Terrorism." In: M. G. Hermann, ed. ***Political Psychology***. San Francisco, CA.: Jossey-Bass, 1986. pp. 379-413.

1185. _____. "The Subjective Reality of the Terrorist: Ideological and Psychological Factors in Terrorism." In: R. O. Slater and M. Stohl, eds. ***Current Perspectives on International Terrorism***. London: Macmillan, 1988. pp. 12-46.

1186. _____. "The Logic of Terrorism: Terrorist Behavior as a Product of Strategic Choice." In: W. Reich, ed. ***Origins of Terrorism***. Cambridge: Cambridge University Press, 1990. pp. 7-24.

1187. _____. "Questions to Be Answered, Research to Be Done, Knowledge to Be Applied." In: W. Reich, ed. ***Origins of Terrorism***. Cambridge: Cambridge University Press, 1990. pp. 247-260.

1188. Curran, Peter S., and W. Gregg. "Psychiatric Aspects of Terrorist Violence in Northern Ireland 1969 to 1989." ***Medico-Legal Journal***, 58:2 (Spring 1990), 83-96.

1189. _____. "Psychiatric Aspects of Terrorist Violence: Northern Ireland 1969-1987." ***British Journal of Psychiatry***, 153 (October 1988), 470-475.

1190. Daly, L. N. "Terrorism - What Can The Psychiatrist Do?" ***Journal of Forensic Sciences***, 26:1 (1981), 116-122.

1191. De Dunayevich, J. B., and Janine Puget. "State Terrorism and Psychoanalysis." ***International Journal of Mental Health***, 18:2 (1989), 98-112.

1192. De Mause, Lloyd. "The Real Target Wasn't Terrorism." ***Journal of Psychohistory***, 13:4 (1986), 413-426.

1193. Dolev, E. "Medical Aspects of Terrorist Activities." ***Military Medicine***, 153:5 (1988), 243-244.

1194. DuBoe, Wendy L. "Why Western Terrorists Join and Quit." In: B. Rubin, ed. ***The Politics of Counterterrorism***. Lanham, MD.: University Publications of America, 1990. pp. 189-220.

1195. Duffy, John C. "Common Psychological Themes in Societies Reaction to Terrorism and Disasters." In: J. C. Duffy, ed. ***Health and Medical Aspects of Disaster Preparedness***. New York: Plenum, 1990. 123-130.

1196. _____. "Common Psychological Themes in Societies' Reaction to Terrorism and Disasters." ***Military Medicine***, 153:8 (1988), 387-390.

1197. Dutter, Lee E. "Ethno - Political Activity and the Psychology of Terrorism." ***Terrorism***, 10:3 (1987), 145-163.

1198. Ebbert, Bruce W. "The Mental Health Response Team." ***The Police Chief***, 53:4 (1986), 36-37.

1199. Eichelman, Burr, and A. C. Hartwig. "Ethical and Consultation Issues in the Behavioral Sciences and Terrorism." ***Behavioral Sciences and the Law***, 1:2 (1983), 9-18.

1200. _____. "Ethics in Hostage Encounters." In: B. Eichelman, D. Soskis and W. Reid, eds. ***Terrorism: Interdisciplinary Perspectives.*** Washington, D.C.: American Psychiatric Association, 1983. pp. 49-64.

1201. Ferracuti, Franco. "A Sociopsychiatric Interpretation of Terrorism." ***Annals of the American Academy of Political and Social Science***, 463 (1982), 129-141.

1202. _____, and Francesco Bruno. "A Psychiatric Comparative - Analysis of Left and Right Wing Terrorism in Italy." In: ***Psychiatry: The State of the Art, Vol. 6.*** New York: Plenum, 1985. pp. 399-406.

1203. _____. _____. "Psychiatric Aspects of Terrorism in Italy." In: I. L. Barak-Glantz and C. R. Huff, eds. ***The Mad, the Bad and the Different: Essays in Honor of Simon Dinitz.*** Lexington, MA.: Lexington Books, 1981. pp. 199-213.

1204. Finn, Geraldine. "Taking Gender into Account in the 'Theatre of Terror': Violence, Media, and the Maintenance of Male Dominance." ***Canadian Journal of Women and the Law***, 3:2 (Summer-Fall 1989), 375-394.

1205. Freedman, Lawrence Z. "Terrorism: Problems of the Polistaraxic." In: L. Z. Freedman and Y. Alexander, eds. ***Perspectives on Terrorism.*** Wilmington, DE.: Scholarly Resources, 1983. pp. 3-12.

1206. _____. "Why Does Terrorism Terrorize?" In: D. C. Rapoport and Y. Alexander, eds. ***The Rationalization of Terrorism.*** Frederick, MD: University Publications of America, 1982. pp. 17-28.

1207. _____. "Why Does Terrorism Terrorize?" ***Terrorism***, 6:3 (1983), 389-402.

1208. Fried, Risto. "The Psychology of Terrorism." In: B. M. Jenkins, ed. ***Terrorism and Beyond: An International Conference on Terrorism and Low-Level Conflict.*** Santa Monica, CA.: RAND Corporation, 1980. pp. 119-124.

1209. _____. "Question on Terrorism." ***Terrorism***, 3:3-4 (1980), 219-238.

1210. Friedlander, Robert A. "The Psychology of Terrorism: Contemporary Views." In: P. J. Montana and G. S. Roukis, eds. ***Managing Terrorism.*** Westport, CT.: Quorum Books, 1983. pp. 41-54.

1211. Galvin, Deborah M. "The Female Terrorist: A Socio-Psychological Perspective." ***Behavioral Sciences and the Law***, 1:2 (1983), 19-32.

1212. Gibbs, Jack P. "Conceptualization of Terrorism." ***American Sociological Review***, 54:3 (June 1989), 329-340.

1213. Gibson, Kerry. "Children in Political Violence." ***Social Science and Medicine***, 28:7 (1989), 659-667.

1214. Gunn, John, and Gisli Gudjonsson. "Using the Psychological Stress Evaluator in Conditions of Extreme Stress." ***Psychological Medicine***, 18:1 (1988), 235-238.

1215. Hacker, Frederick J. "Contagion and Attraction of Terror and Terrorism." In: Y. Alexander and J. M. Gleason, eds. ***Behavioral and Quantitative Perspectives on Terrorism.*** New York: Pergamon Press, 1981. pp. 73-85.

1216. _____. "Dialectic Interrelations of Personal and Political Factors in Terrorism." In: L. Z. Freeman and Y. Alexander, eds. ***Perspectives on Terrorism.*** Wilmington, DE.: Scholarly Resources, 1983. pp. 19-32.

1217. Handler, Jeffrey S. "Socioeconomic Profile of an American Terrorist: 1960s and 1970s." ***Terrorism***, 13:3 (1990), 195-214.

1218. Harris, F. Gentry. "Hypothetical Facts or Ingredients of Terrorism." ***Terrorism***, 3:3-4 (1980), 239-244.

1219. Hartman, Geoffrey. "The Response to Terror: Introductory Notes. ***Human Rights Quarterly***, 5:2 (1983), 113-115.

1220. Hubbard, David G. "A Glimmer of Hope: A Psychiatric Perspective." In: C. M. Bassiouni, ed. ***International Terrorism and Political Crimes.*** Springfield, IL.: C. C. Thomas, 1982. pp. 27-32.

1221. _____. "The Psychodynamics of Terrorism." In: T. Adeniran and Y. Alexander, eds. ***International Violence.*** New York: Praeger, 1983. pp. 43-53.

1222. James, Patrick, and Ronald D. Crelinsten. "Terrorism's Real Danger." ***Humanist in Canada***, 20:3 (Fall 1987), 5-8+.

1223. Jenkins, Brian M. "The Terrorist Mindset and Terrorist Decisionmaking: Two Areas of Ignorance." ***Terrorism***, 3:3-4 (1980), 245-250.

1224. Jonas, Adolphe D. "Introduction." ***Terrorism***, 3:3-4 (1980), 257-264.

1225. Kampf, Herbert A. "On the Appeal of Extremism to the Youth of Affluent, Democratic Societies." ***Terrorism***, 4 (1980), 161-194.

1226. Kaplan, Abraham. "The Psychodynamics of Terrorism." In: Y. Alexander and J. M. Gleason, eds. ***Behavioral and Quantitative Perspectives on Terrorism.*** New York: Pergamon Press, 1981. pp. 35-50.

1227. Kissane, Thomas P. "A Reexamination of Hacker's Typology." ***International Journal of Comparative and Applied Criminal Justice***, 13:2 (Fall 1989), 39-44.

1228. Knutson, Jeanne N. "Social and Psychodynamic Pressures Toward a Negative Identity: The Case of an American Revolutionary Terrorist." In: Y. Alexander and J. M. Gleason, eds. ***Behavioral and Quantitative Perspectives on Terrorism.*** New York: Pergamon Press, 1981. pp. 105-152.

1229. _____. "The Terrorist's Dilemmas: Some Implicit Rules of the Game." ***Terrorism***, 4 (1980), 195-222.

1230. Kucuk, Eyub. "Political Terrorism as a Means of Psychological Warfare and Propaganda." ***Socialist Thought and Practice***, 21 (August 1981), 76-88.

1231. Lanceley, F. J. "Antisocial Personality as a Hostage Taker." ***Journal of Police Science and Administration***, 9:1 (1981), 28-34.

1232. Lotto, D. J. "On Terrorist Groups. (Correspondence)." ***International Journal of Group Psychotherapy***, 37:3 (July 1987), 459-461.

1233. Loughrey, G. C., et al. "Post-Traumatic Stress Disorder and Civil Violence in Northern Ireland." ***British Journal of Psychiatry***, 153 (October 1988), 554-560.

1234. Martin, Jay. "The Fictional Terrorist." ***Partisan Review***, 55:1 (1988), 69-81.

1235. McClenon, James. "Terrorism as Persuasion: Possibilities and Trends." ***Sociological Focus***, 21:1 (January 1988), 53-66.

1236. McKenzie, Ian K. "Hostage - Captors Relationships: Some Behavioral and Environmental Determinants." ***Police Studies***, 7:4 (1984), 219-223.

1237. _____. "Psychological Effects of Kidnapping and Hostage-Taking." ***Police Studies***, 10:2 (1987), 96-102.

1238. Merari, Ariel, and Nehemia Friedland. "Social Psychological Aspects of Political Terrorism." In: S. Oskamp, ed. ***International Conflict and National Public Policy Issues.*** Applied Social Psychology Annual; 6. Beverly Hills, CA.: Sage, 1985. pp. 185-206.

1239. _____. _____. "Social Psychological Aspects of Political Terrorism." ***Applied Social Psychology Annual***, 6 (1985), 185-205.

1240. _____. "Problems Related to the Symptomatic Treatment of Terrorism." ***Terrorism***, 3:3-4 (1980), 279-283.

1241. Merkl, Peter H. "In the Mind of the Terrorist: An Interview with Merkl, Peter." ***The Center Magazine***, 19:2 (1986), 18-24.

1242. _____. "Conclusion: Collective Purposes and Individual Motives." In: P. H. Merkl, ed. ***Political Violence and Terror.*** Berkeley, CA.: University of California Press, 1986. pp. 335-374.

1243. Moos, Rudolph H., and Jeanne A. Schaefer. "Coping with Violence and Disaster." ***Violence Aggression and Terrorism***, 1:3 (1987), 217-240.

1244. Ochberg, Frank M. "Sociopolitical Climate of Contemporary Terrorism." ***International Journal of Group Tensions***, 12:1-4 (1982), 62-83.

1245. Olin, W. Ronald, and David G. Born. "A Behavioral Approach to Hostage Situations." ***FBI Law Enforcement Bulletin***, 52:1 (1983), 18-24.

1246. Oots, Kent L. "Biopolitics and Terrorist Behavior." In: Y. Alexander and A. H. Foxman, eds. ***The 1987 Annual on Terrorism.*** Dordrecht: Martinus Nijhoff, 1988. pp. 41-60.

1247. _____. "An Individual-Level Model of Terrorist Contagion." In: Y. Alexander, ed. ***The 1986 Annual on Terrorism.*** Dordrecht: Martinus Nijhoff, 1987. pp. 109-126.

1248. _____. "Organizational Perspectives on the Formation and Disintegration of Terrorist Groups." ***Terrorism***, 12:3 (1989), 139-152.

1249. Ottenberg, P. "Terrorism: No Hostages Are Innocent." ***Psychiatric Annals***, 10:5 (1980), 11-22.

1250. Pankuv, Yu. "Anti-Social Psychology of Ultra-Leftist Terrorism." In: W. Laqueur, ed. ***The Terrorism Reader.*** New York: Meridian, 1987. pp. 358-362.

1251. Post, Jerrold M. "Notes on a Psychodynamic Theory of Terrorist Behavior." ***Terrorism***, 7:3 (1984), 241-256.

1252. _____. "Individual and Group-Dynamics of Terrorist Behavior." In: ***Psychiatry: The State of the Art, Vol. 6.*** New York: Plenum, 1985. pp. 381-386.

1253. _____. "Rewarding Fire with Fire - Effects of Retaliation on Terrorist Group Dynamics." ***Terrorism***, 10:1 (1987), 23-36.

1254. _____. "The Psycho-Logic of Terror: Terrorist Behavior as a Product of Psychological Forces." Paper Presented at the ***Interdisciplinary Research Conference on the Psychology of Terrorism***, held on March 16-18, 1987, at the Woodrow Wilson International Center for Scholars in Washington, D.C.

1255. _____. "Hostilite, Conformite, Fraternite: The Group Dynamics of Terrorist Behavior." ***International Journal of Group Psychotherapy***, 36:2 (April 1986), 211-224.

1256. _____. "Rewarding Fire with Fire? Effects of Retaliation on Terrorist Group Dynamics." In: A. Kurz, ed. ***Contemporary Trends in World Terrorism.*** New York: Praeger, 1987. pp. 103-115.

1257. _____. "Terrorist Psycho-logic: Terrorist Behavior as a Product of Psychological Forces." In: W. Reich, ed. ***Origins of Terrorism.*** Cambridge: Cambridge University Press, 1990. pp. 25-42.

1258. _____. "Current Understanding of Terrorist Motivation and Psychology: Implications for a Differentiated Antiterrorist Policy." ***Terrorism***, 13:1 (1990), 65-68.

1259. Puget, Janine. "Social Violence and Psychoanalysis in the Argentinian Context." ***British Journal of Psychotherapy***, 5:3 (Spring 1989), 363-369.

1260. Reich, Walter. "Understanding Terrorist Behavior: The Limits and Opportunities of Psychological Inquiry." In: W. Reich, ed. ***Origins of Terrorism.*** Cambridge: Cambridge University Press, 1990. pp. 261-280.

1261. Reid, William H. "Terrorism and the Social Sciences: The Psychiatrist's Role." ***Violence, Aggression and Terrorism***, 3:1-2 (1989), 101-118.

1262. Rice, Berkeley. "Between the Lines of Threatening Messages." ***Psychology Today***, 15 (September 1981), 52-59.

1263. Rigamer, Elmore F. "Psychological Management of Children in a National Crisis." ***Journal of the American Academy of Child Psychiatry***, 25:3 (May 1986), 364-369.

1264. Rofe, Yacov. "The Effects of War Environment on Dreams and Sleep Habits." In: C. Spielberger, ed. ***Stress and Anxiety.*** Vol. 8. Washington, D.C.: Hemisphere, 1982. pp. 67-79.

1265. Rogers, Rita. "On Emotional Responses to Nuclear Issues and Terrorism." ***Psychiatric Journal of the University of Ottawa***, 5:3 (1980), 147-152.

1266. Rootes, C. "Living With Terrorism." ***Social Attitudes***, 1:6-7 (1980), 46-49.

1267. Roucek, Joseph S. "Terrorism in its Sociological Aspects." ***Sociologia Internationalis***, 18 (1980), 1-2, 97-110.

1268. Rubin, Jeffrey Z., and Nehemia Friedland. "Theater of Terrorism." ***Psychology Today***, 20:3 (March 1986), 18-28.

1269. _____. _____. "Terrorists and Their Audience: Theater of Terror." ***Current***, 284 (July/August 1986), 36-39.

1270. Russell, Charles A., and Bowman H. Miller. "Profile of a Terrorist." In: L. Z. Freedman and Y. Alexander, eds. ***Perspectives on Terrorism.*** Wilmington, DE.: Scholarly Resources, 1983. pp. 45-60.

1271. Sagarin, Edward, and Robert J. Kelly. "Political Deviance and the Assumption of Responsibility." ***Deviant Behavior***, 7:3 (1986), 217-242.

1272. Salewski, Wolfgang D. "The Latest Theory Recognized by Sociological Science Research in Terrorism and Violence." ***Terrorism***, 3:3-4 (1980), 297-301.

1273. Shanmugam, T. E. "Terrorism and Terrorists." ***Journal of Social and Economic Studies, New Series***, 1:4 (October-December 1984), 357-364.

1274. Shaw, Eric D. "Political Terrorists: Dangers of Diagnosis and an Alternative to the Psychopathology Model." ***International Journal of Law and Psychiatry***, 8:3 (1986), 359-368.

1275. Sipe, Robert B. "Sandinista Psychology and Contra Terrorism: An Eyewitness Report on Nicaragua Libre." ***Issues in Radical Therapy***, 11:4 (1985), 16-19, 50-52.

1276. Soskis, David A. "Behavioral Scientists and Law Enforcement Personnel: Working Together on the Problem of Terrorism." ***Behavioral Sciences and the Law***, 1:2 (1983), 47-58.

1277. _____. "Law Enforcement and Psychiatry: Forging the Working Alliance." In: B. Eichelman, D. A. Soskis and W. Reid, eds ***Terrorism: Interdisciplinary Perspectives.*** Washington, D.C.: American Psychiatric Association, 1983. pp. 129-146.

1278. Strentz, Thomas. "The Terrorist Organizational Profile: A Psychological Role Model." In: Y. Alexander and J. M. Gleason, eds. ***Behavioral and Quantitative Perspectives on Terrorism.*** New York: Pergamon Press, 1981. pp. 86-104.

1279. _____. "A Terrorist Psychosocial Profile: Past and Present." ***FBI Law Enforcement Bulletin***, 57 (April 1988), 13-19.

1280. Sulwold, L. "Biographical Features of Terrorists." In: ***Psychiatry: The State of the Art, Vol. 6.*** New York: Plenum, 1985. pp. 407-409.

1281. Targ, Harry R. "Societal Structure and Revolutionary Terrorism: A Preliminary Investigation." In: M. Stohl, ed. ***The Politics of Terrorism.*** 2nd. ed. New York: Marcel Dekker, 1983. pp. 119-144.

1282. _____. "Societal Structure and Revolutionary Terrorism: A Preliminary Investigations." In: M. Stohl, ed. ***The Politics of Terrorism.*** New York: Marcel Dekker, 1988. pp. 127-152.

1283. Taylor, Maxwell. "Terrorist Behavior." ***Police Journal***, 58:3 (1985), 195-202.

1284. "Terrorism: Psyche or Psychos?" ***TVI Journal***, 3:9 (1982), 3-11.

1285. Turco, R. M. "Psychiatric Contributions to the Understanding of International Terrorism." ***International Journal of Offender Therapy and Comparative Criminology***, 31:2 (1987), 153-162.

1286. Turk, Austin T. "Social Dynamics of Terrorism." ***Annals of the American Academy of Political and Social Science***, 463 (1982), 119-128.

1287. Turner, James T. "A Systematic Conceptualization of Acts of Terror." ***Journal of Police and Criminal Psychology***, 1 (March 1985), 36-40.

1288. _____. "Hostage-Takers in Health Care Settings." ***Psychiatric Clinic North America***, 11:4 (1988), 649-664.

1289. Wardlaw, Grant. "Psychology and the Resolution of Terrorist Incidents." ***Australian Psychologist***, 18:2 (1983), 179-190.

1290. _____. "Behavioral Science vs. Terrorism." ***TVI Journal***, 2:1 (1981), 6-12.

1291. Wolman, Benjamin B. "Psychology of Followers of Terrorist Groups." ***International Journal of Group Tensions***, 12:1-4 (1982), 105-121.

1292. Wright, Fred, and Phyllis Wright. "Violent Groups." ***Group***, 6:2 (Summer 1982), 25-34.

1293. Zawodny, J. K. "Infrastructures of Terrorist Organizations." ***Violence Aggression and Terrorism***, 1:1 (1987), 27-40.

3. Documents and Reports

1294. Baeyer-Kaette, W. "A Left-Wing Terrorist Indoctrination Group." Paper Presented to the ***1983 Annual Meeting of the International Society of Political Psychology***, held in July 1983, in Oxford, England.

1295. Curtis, B. G., and Lawrence Visniesky, eds. ***Supplemental Proceedings of the 10th Annual Symposium on the Role of Behavioral Science in Physical Security - Outthinking the Terrorist: An International Challenge.*** Washington, D.C.: Defence National Agency, 1985. 44p.

1296. Ferracuti, Franco. "Psychiatric Aspects of Italian Left Wing and Right Wing Terrorism." Paper Presented to the ***7th World Congress of Psychiatry***, held in July 1983 in Vienna, Austria.

1297. Galvin, John R. ***Psychologic Aspects of Terrorism.*** Carlisle Barracks, PA.: Army War College, 1983. 15p.

1298. Groebel, J. "Quantitative Sociometry in Human-Aggression: Research Applied in a Study on German Terrorist Groups." Paper Presented to the ***Sixth Biennial Meeting of the International Society for Research on Aggression,*** held on July 12-15, 1984, in Turku, Finland.

1299. Groen, J. J. "The Interdisciplinary Behavioral-Study of War and Terrorism as a Way Towards Prevention and Substitution by Other, Less Violent and Destructive Forms of Resolutions of Group Conflicts." Paper Given ***To the Sixth Biennial Meeting of the International Society for Research on Aggression,*** held on July 12-15, 1984, in Turku, Finland.

1300. Jenkins, Brian M. "Some Observations on the Behavior of the Terrorist Adversary." In: ***Proceedings of the 8th Annual Symposium on the Role of the Behavioral Science in Physical Security,*** held on June 7-8, 1983 in Springfield, VA. pp. 5-14.

1301. Knutson, Leslie K. ***A Psychological Profile of 'Terrorists': A Comparison of Judicial and Psychological Signifiers.*** Ph.D. Dissertation. Berkeley, CA.: California School of Professional Psychology, 1990.

1302. Kostick, Gary T. ***The Study of the Physical and Psychological Impact of Terrorism on Americans and Their Families Residing in Europe.*** Sacramento, CA.: California State University at Sacramento, 1987. 112p.

1303. Labuscagne, Ockert D. J. ***A Criminological Perspective on Terrorism as a Crime Phenomenon.*** Master's Thesis. Johannesburg: University of South Africa, 1986.

1304. MacNair, Douglas G. "Social Psychology of Selective Violence in Society: Terrorism." In: ***Proceedings of the 8th Annual Symposium on the Role of Behavioral Science in Physical Security,*** held on June 7-8, 1983, in Springfield, VA. pp. 15-24.

1305. Martinez, P. ***Combatting Terrorism Through Study of the Genetic Psychology of Terrorist Leaders: The Early Development of the Terrorist Mind.*** Master's Thesis. Monterey, CA.: Naval Postgraduate School, 1989. 123p.

1306. McAllister, Ian, and Richard Rose. ***Can Violent Political Conflict Be Resolved by Social Change.*** Studies in Public Policy. No. 103. Glasgow: University of Strathclyde, Centre for the Study of Public Policy, 1982. 24p.

1307. Miller, Bowman H. ***The Language Component of Terrorism Strategy: A Text-based, Linguistic Case Study of Contemporary German Terrorism.*** Ph.D. Dissertation. Washington, D.C.: Georgetown University, 1983. 434p.

1308. Montville, Joseph F. ***Nationalism, Sectarianism and Political Violence: Aggressive and Defense Behaviours of Threatened and Separatist Minorities.*** Washington, D.C.: Interdisciplinary Research Committee, 1987. 30p.

1309. Nagley, Andrew G. ***Changing People's Reaction to Terrorism.*** Master's Thesis. Denton, TX.: North Texas State University, 1988. 62p.

1310. Oots, Kent L. "Organizational Perspectives on the Formation and Disintegration of Terrorist Groups." Paper Presented at the ***Annual Meeting of the International Studies Association - Southwest,*** held on March 29 - April 1, 1989 in Little Rock, AR.

1311. Pearlstein, Richard M. ***Lives of Disquieting Desperation: An Inquiry into the Mind of the Political Terrorist.*** Ph.D. Dissertation. Chapel Hill, NC.: University of North Carolina, 1986. 628p.

1312. Post, Jerrold M. "Psychological Insights on Political Terrorism." Paper Presented at the ***24th Annual Convention of the International Studies Association,*** held on April 5-9, 1983 in Mexico City.

1313. Rachman, S. J. ***Psychological Approaches to Organized Aggression.*** London: London University, Institute of Psychiatry, 1987. 45p.

1314. Rose, Richard. ***Can Violent Political Conflict Be Resolved by Social Change?.*** Studies in Public Policy, No. 103. Glasgow: Centre for the Study of Public Policy, University of Strathclyde, 1982.

1315. Rossow, A. F. ***Problems in Determining the Motivation of Terrorists.*** Maxwell AFB, AL.: Air War College, 1986. 28p.

1316. Schoen, Glenn C. ***The Correlation Between Ideological Intensity and Terrorist Activity as a Predictive Indicator of Terrorist Behaviour.*** Columbus, OH.: Ohio State University, 1987. 80p.

1317. Strinkowski, Nicholas C. ***The Organizational Behavior of Revolutionary Groups.*** Ph.D. Dissertation. Evanston, IL.: Northwestern University, 1985. 312p.

1318. Taylor, Maxwell. ***Psychological Approaches to Terrorism: A Selective Review.*** U.S. Army Research Institute, DAJA 45-84-11-0400. Cork, Ireland: Department of Applied Psychology, 1986. 40p.

1319. Whitley, Julian L. ***An Examination of Terrorism from a Psychological and Historical Perspective.*** Master's Thesis. Tacoma, WA.: Pacific Lutheran University, 1981. 83p.

B. VICTIMOLOGY

1. Books

1320. Ochberg, Frank M., and David A. Soskis. ***Victims of Terrorism.*** Boulder, CO.: Westview Press, 1982. 200p.

2. Journal Articles

1321. Adler, J., et al. "Terrorist Bombing Experience During 1975-79. Casualties Admitted to the Shaare Zedek Medical Center." ***Israeli Journal of Medical Science,*** 19:2 (1983), 189-193.

1322. Asencio, Nancy Rodriguez. "Managing the Crisis of Hostage Families." In: N. C. Livingstone and T. E. Arnold, eds. ***Beyond the Iran-Contra Crisis.*** Lexington, MA.: D.C. Heath & Lexington Books, 1988. pp. 155-172.

1323. Ayalon, Ofra. "Children as Hostages." ***Practitioner,*** 226:1372 (1982), 1773-1781.

1324. Beck, Betty. "Terrorist Victim Has Never Given Up." ***U.S. Navy Medicine,*** 72:10 (October 1981), 14-17.

1325. Blum, Robert, and Robert I. Simon. "After the Terrorist Incident: Psychotherapeutic Treatment of Former Hostages." ***American Journal of Psychotherapy,*** 41:2 (1987), 194-200.

1326. Clark, M. A., et al. "Investigation of Incidents of Terrorism Involving Commercial Aircraft." ***Aviation, Space, And Environmental Medicine,*** 60:7 II (1989), 55-59.

1327. "Compensating Victims of Terrorism: The Current Framework in the United States." ***Texas International Journal,*** (Spring/Summer 1987), 383-401.

1328. Corbett, William T. "Sidestep the Victim Syndrome." ***Security Management,*** 31 (June 1987), 56-59.

1329. Corrado, Raymond R., and Eric Tompkins. "A Comparative Model of the Psychological Effects on the Victims of State And Anti-State Terrorism." ***International Journal of Law and Psychiatry,*** 12:4 (Fall 1989), 281-293.

1330. Dreman, Solly B., and E. C. Cohen. "Children of Victims of Terrorist Activities: A Family Approach to Dealing with Tragedy." ***American Journal of Family Therapy,*** 10:2 (1982), 39-47.

1331. _____. _____. "Children of Victims of Terrorism Revisited - Integrating Individual and Family Treatment Approaches." ***American Journal of Orthopsychiatry,*** 60:2 (1990), 204-209.

1332. _____. "Children of Victims of Terrorism in Israel - Coping and Adjusting in the Face of Trauma." ***Israel Journal of Psychiatry and Related Sciences,*** 26:4 (1989), 212-222.

1333. Eitinger, Leo. "The Effects of Captivity." In: F. M. Ochberg and D. A. Soskis, eds. ***Victims of Terrorism.*** Boulder, CO.: Westview Press, 1982. pp. 73-94.

1334. Eth, S. "Long-Term Effects of Terrorism on Children." ***Western Journal of Medicine,*** 147:1 (1987), 73-74.

1335. Fearey, Robert A. "Relations With the Victim's Family." In: M. F. Herz, ed. ***Diplomats and Terrorists.*** Washington, D.C.: Institute for the Study of Diplomacy, 1982. pp. 60-62.

1336. Fields, Rona M. "Psychological Sequelae of Terrorization." In: Y. Alexander and J. M. Gleason, eds. ***Behavioral and Quantitative Perspectives on Terrorism.*** New York: Pergamon Press, 1984.

1337. _____. "Research on the Victims of Terrorism." In: F. M. Ochberg and D. A. Soskis, eds. ***Victims of Terrorism.*** Boulder, CO.: Westview Press, 1982. pp. 137-148.

1338. _____. "Victims of Terrorism: The Effects of Prolonged Stress." ***Evaluation and Change,*** (1980), 76-83.

1339. Flynn, Edith E. "Victims of Terrorism: Dimensions of the Victim Experience." In: P. Wilkinson and A. M. Stewart, eds. ***Contemporary Research on Terrorism.*** Aberdeen: Aberdeen University Press, 1987. pp. 337-356.

1340. Frederick, C. J. "Psychic Trauma in Victims of Crime and Terrorism." In: G. R. Vandenbos and B. K. Bryant, eds. ***Cataclysms, Crises and Catastrophes: Psychology in Action.*** Washington, D.C.: American Psychological Association, 1987. pp. 55-108.

1341. Gulley, Myra I. "Support Systems and Mental Health Involvement with Victims of the Beirut and Greek Bombing Incidents." ***Medical Bulletin,*** 43:2 (February 1986), 11-12.

1342. Harkis, Barbara A. " The Psychopathology of the Hostage Experience - A Review." ***Medicine, Science and the Law,*** 26:13 (1986), 48-52.

1343. Hassel, Conrad V. "Interactions of Law Enforcement and Behavioral Science Personnel." In: F. M. Ochberg and D. A. Soskis, eds. ***Victims of Terrorism.*** Boulder, CO.: Westview Press, 1982. pp. 165-172.

1344. Hatcher, Chris. "A Conceptual Framework in Victimology: The Adult and Child Hostage Experience." In: P. Wilkinson and A. M. Stewart, eds. ***Contemporary Research on Terrorism.*** Aberdeen: Aberdeen University Press, 1987. pp. 357-375.

1345. Hellman, P. "One Woman's Will to Live." ***Reader's Digest,*** (July 1985) 73-78.

1346. Hill, Peter, and Peter Friend. "The Angriest Hostage: Hijacked, He Couldn't Get Even, So He Got Mad." ***Life,*** (April 1986), 50-54, 59-61, 64.

1347. Hillman, Robert G. "The Psychopathology of Being Held Hostage." In: L. Z. Freedman and Y. Alexander, eds. ***Perspectives on Terrorism.*** Wilmington, DE.: Scholarly Resources, 1983. pp. 157-168.

1348. Jenkins, Brian M. "Reentry." In: B. M. Jenkins, ed. ***Terrorism and Personal Protection.*** Stoneham, MA.: Butterworth, 1985. pp. 426-434.

1349. Kleinman, Stuart B. "A Terrorist Hijacking: Victim's Experiences Initially and 9 Years Later." ***Journal of Traumatic Stress,*** 2:1 (January 1989), 49-58.

1350. Lahad, Shmuel, and Ada Abraham. "Preparing Teachers and Pupils for Coping with Stress Situations: A Multi-Model Program." ***Israeli Journal of Psychology and Counselling in Education,*** 16 (September 1986), 196-210.

1351. Lanza, Marilyn L. "Victims of International Terrorism." ***Issues in Mental Health Nursing,*** 8:2 (1986), 95-107.

1352. Lunde, Inge, and Ole Vedel Rasmussen. "The Treatment and Rehabilitation of Victims of Torture." ***International Journal of Mental Health,*** 18:2 (1989), 122-130.

1353. McEwen, Michael T. "Psychological Operations Against Terrorism: The Unused Weapon." ***Military Review,*** 66:1 (June 1986), 59-67.

1354. Miller, Abraham H. "Responding to the Victims of Terrorism: Psychological and Policy Implications." In: R. Shultz and S. Sloan, eds. ***Responding to the Terrorist Threat: Security and Crisis Management.*** New York: Pergamon Press, 1980. pp. 93-104.

1355. Mitchell, Jack. "Botched Relations with Relatives." In: M. F. Herz, ed. ***Diplomats and Terrorists.*** Washington, D.C.: Institute for the Study of Diplomacy, 1982. pp. 44-47.

1356. Niehous, William F. "Surviving Captivity II: The Hostages Point of View." In: B. M. Jenkins, ed. ***Terrorism and Personal Protection.*** Stoneham, MA.: Butterworth, 1985. pp. 423-425.

1357. Ochberg, Frank M. "A Case Study: Gerard Vaders." In: F. M. Ochberg and D. A. Soskis, eds. ***Victims of Terrorism.*** Boulder, CO.: Westview Press, 1982. pp. 9-36.

1358. _____. "Hostage Victims." In: B. Eichelman, D. A. Soskis and W. Reid, eds. ***Terrorism: Interdisciplinary Perspectives.*** Washington, D.C.: American Psychiatric Association, 1983. pp. 83-88.

1359. _____, and David A. Soskis. "Planning for the Future: Means and Ends." In: F. M. Ochberg and D. A. Soskis, eds. ***Victims of Terrorism.*** Boulder, CO.: Westview Press, 1982. pp. 173-190.

1360. _____. "Victims of Terrorism." ***Journal of Clinical Psychiatry,*** 41:3 (1980), 73-74.

1361. _____. "The Victims of Terrorism." In: R. H. Moos, ed. ***Coping With Life Crises.*** New York: Plenum, 1986. pp. 367-384.

1362. Olsson, Peter A. "The Terrorist and the Terrorized: Some Psychoanalytic Considerations." ***Journal of Psychohistory,*** 16:1 (Summer 1988), 47-60.

1363. Oots, Kent L., and Thomas C. Wiegele. "Terrorist and Victim: Psychiatric and Physiological Approaches from a Social Science Perspective." ***Terrorism,*** 8:1 (1985), 1-32.

1364. _____. _____. "Terrorist and Victim: Psychiatric and Physiological Approaches from a Social science Perspective." In: W. Laqueur, ed. ***The Terrorism Reader,*** New York: Meridian, 1987. pp. 246-259.

1365. Pergamenter, Ruth. "Crisis Intervention With Child-Care Personnel in an Israeli Border Kibbutz." In: C. Spielberger, ed. ***Stress and Anxiety, Vol. 8.*** Washington, D.C.: Hemisphere, 1982. pp. 355-360.

1366. Pyper, P. C., and W. J. H. Graham. "Analysis of Terrorist Injuries Treated at Craigavon Area Hospital, Northern Ireland, 1972-1980." ***Injury,*** 14:4 (1983), 332-338.

1367. Rejai, Mostafa. "The Professional Revolutionary: A Profile." ***Air University Review,*** (March-April 1980), 86-90.

1368. Rigamer, Elmore F. "Stresses of Families Abroad." ***Travel Medicine International,*** 3:3 (1985), 137-140.

1369. Rosenberg, B., et al. "Burns Due to Terroristic Attacks on Civilian Populations from 1975 to 1979." ***Burns,*** 9:1 (1982), 21-23.

1370. Roth, Walton T. "The Meaning of Stress." In: F. M. Ochberg and D. A. Soskis, eds. ***Victims of Terrorism.*** Boulder, CO.: Westview Press, 1982. pp. 37-58.

1371. Roy, D. "Gunshot and Bomb Blast Injuries: A Review of Experience in Belfast." ***Journal of Royal Society of Medicine,*** 75:7 (1982), 542-545.

1372. Rutherford, W. H. "Bomb Injuries in Urban Terrorism." In: A. G. MacMahon and M. Jooste, eds. ***Disaster Medicine.*** Capetown: A. Balkema, 1980. pp. 135-139.

1373. Schneider, Hans Joachim. "Victims of Terrorism." In: H. J. Schneider, ed. ***The Victims in International Perspective.*** Berlin: Walter DeGruyter, 1982.

1374. Scott, B. A., et al. "The Beirut Terrorist Bombing." ***Neurosurgery,*** 18:1 (1986), 107-110.

1375. "Seminar on the Protection of Victims of Violence in the 1980s." ***Terrorism,*** 9:2 (1987), 215-224.

1376. Siegel, Ronald K. "Hostage Hallucinations: Visual Imagery Induced by Isolation and Life Threatening Stress." ***Journal of Nervous and Mental Disease,*** 172:5 (May 1984), 264-272.

1377. Silverstein, Martin. "Surviving Terrorism." ***Washington Quarterly,*** 5:4 (1982), 175-180.

1378. Simon, Robert I., and R. A. Blum. "After the Terrorist Incident: Psychotherapeutic Treatment of Former Hostages." ***American Journal of Psychotherapy,*** 41 (April 1987), 194-200.

1379. Soskis, David A., and Frank M. Ochberg. "Concepts of Terrorist Victimization." In: F. M. Ochberg and D. A. Soskis, eds. ***Victims of Terrorism.*** Boulder, CO.: Westview Press, 1982. pp. 105-136.

1380. _____. "Helping Victims: Psychiatrist's Most Valuable Role in Terrorist Situations, Task Force Concludes." ***Psychiatric News,*** 17:19 (1982), 5,10,29.

1381. _____, and Ofra Ayalon. "A Six-Year Follow-Up of Hostage Victims." ***Terrorism,*** 7:4 (1985), 411-416.

1382. Strentz, Thomas. "The Stockholm Syndrome: Law Enforcement Policy and Hostage Behavior." In: F. M. Ochberg and D. A. Soskis, eds. ***Victims of Terrorism.*** Boulder, CO.: Westview Press, 1982. pp. 149-164.

1383. _____. "The Stockholm Syndrome - Law Enforcement Policy and Ego Defences of the Hostage." In: F. Wright, C. Bahn and R. W. Rieber, eds. ***Forensic Psychology and Psychiatry.*** New York: New York Academy of Sciences, 1980. pp. 137-150.

1384. Symonds, Martin. "Victim Responses to Terror: Understanding and Treatment." In: F. M. Ochberg and D. A. Soskis, eds. ***Victims of Terrorism.*** Boulder, CO.: Westview Press, 1982. pp. 95-104.

1385. _____. "Victim Responses to Terror." In: F. Wright, C. Bahn and R. W. Rieder, eds. ***Forensic Psychology and Psychiatry.*** New York: New York Academy of Sciences, 1980. pp. 129-136.

1386. _____. "Victimization and Rehabilitative Treatment." In: B. Eichelman, D. A. Soskis and W. Reid, eds. ***Terrorism: Interdisciplinary Perspectives.*** Washington, D.C.: American Psychiatric Association, 1983. pp. 69-82.

1387. Tinklenberg, J. "Coping with Terrorist Victimization." In: F. M. Ochberg and D. A. Soskis, eds. ***Victims of Terrorism.*** Boulder, CO.: Westview Press, 1982. pp. 59-72.

1388. Turner, James T. "Factors Influencing the Development of the Hostage Identification Syndrome." ***Political Psychology,*** 6:4 (December 1985), 705-711.

1389. Van der Ploeg, Henk M., and Wim C. Kleijn. "Being Held Hostage in the Netherlands: A Study of Long-Term Aftereffects." ***Journal of Traumatic Stress,*** 2:2 (April 1989), 153-169.

1390. Zafrir, A. "Community Therapeutic Intervention in Treatment of Civilian Victims After a Major Terrorist Attack." In: C. Spielberger, ed. ***Stress and Anxiety, Vol. 8.*** Washington, D.C.: Hemisphere, 1982. pp. 303-316.

1391. Zuckerman, B. C. "The Effect of Border Tension on the Adjustment of Kibbutzim and Moshavim on the Northern Border of Israel: A Path Analysis." In: C. Spielberger, ed. ***Stress and Anxiety. Vol. 8.*** Washington, D.C.: Hemisphere, 1982. pp. 81-91.

3. Documents and Reports

1392. Cowley, R. Adams, ed. ***Emergency Medical Services: Proceedings of the First Conference.*** held on June 13- 17, 1982, in Baltimore. Washington, D.C.: U.S. Government Printing Office, 1982.

1393. _____. Sol Edelstein and Martin E. Silverstein, eds. ***Mass Casualties, A Lessons Learned Approach: Accidents, Civil Disorders, Natural Disasters, Terrorism.*** Washington, D.C.: National Highway Safety Administration, 1982. 372p.

1394. Dane, Leila F. ***The Iran Hostage Wives: Long-Term Crisis Coping.*** Ph.D. Dissertation. Florida Institute of Technology, 1984. 241p.

1395. United States. Congress. House. Committee on Foreign Affairs. ***Victims of Terrorism Compensation Act.*** Washington, D.C.: U.S. Government Printing Office, 1985. 39p.

1396. _____._____._____._____. Subcommittee on International Operations. ***Victims of Terrorism Compensation Act: Markup.*** 99th Cong., 1st sess. Washington, D.C.: U.S. Government Printing Office, 1986. 106p.

1397. American Psychiatric Association. "Ethical Dimensions of Psychiatric Intervention in Terrorist and Hostage Situations: A Report." In: B. Eichelman, D. Soskis and W. Reid, eds. ***Terrorism: Interdisciplinary Perspectives.*** Washington, D.C.: American Psychiatric Association, 1983. pp. 181-186.

V

STRATEGIES AND TACTICS OF TERRORISM

Terrorists have used almost any imaginable type of operation to achieve their goals. The goal may be to capture public attention, to influence public policy, to bring about some imaginable ideological, national or religious change or just pure vengeance. Violence is employed in an attempt to force authorities to concede to the terrorist demands. This chapter lists terrorist tactics in general and by specific type of activities such as assassinations, bombings, hostage takings, aircraft hijackings, maritime terror, etc. Subsection G examines guerrilla warfare and subsection H examines state sponsorship of terrorist groups. It is becoming increasingly evident that terrorist acts, especially those of international character are supported directly or indirectly by some states. The logistical infrastructure needed for many of these operations is so complicated and expensive, that it is clear that terrorist groups could not carry out many of their acts without some kind of state support. Since the collapse of communist regimes in Eastern Europe, the complicity of these states with various terrorist organizations has been uncovered. Some of this information has been published in the press, but it does not yet show up in the scholarly literature. Additional information on terrorist tactics can be found in many of the references cited in the geographic subdivision sections.

A. GENERAL WORKS

1. Books

1398. Dobson, Christopher, and Ronald Payne. ***The Terrorists: Their Weapons, Leaders, and Tactics.*** Revised Edition. New York: Facts on File, 1982. 262p.

1399. Hanle, Donald J. ***Terrorism: The Newest Face of Warfare.*** Pergamon-Brassey's Terrorism Library, Vol, 1. Washington: Pergamon-Brassey's, 1989. 272p.

1400. Kegley, Charles W., ed. ***International Terrorism: Characteristics, Causes, Controls.*** New York: St. Martin's, 1990. 280p.

1401. Lodge, Juliet, ed. ***The Threat of Terrorism.*** Brighton: Wheatsheaf, 1988. 280p.

1402. McForan, Desmond. ***The World Held Hostage: The War Waged by International Terrorism.*** London: Oak-Tree Books, 1986. 262p.

1403. O'Neill, Bard E. ***Insurgency & Terrorism: Inside Modern Revolutionary Warfare.*** New York: Pergamon Press, 1990. 171p.

1404. Rapoport, David C., ed. ***Inside Terrorist Organizations.*** New York: Columbia University Press, 1988. 259p.

2. Journal Articles

1405. Adams, James. "The Financing of Terror." ***TVI Report,*** 7:3 (1987), 30-35.

1406. Ahern, Jerry. "Techniques of Weapon Concealment." ***TVI Journal,*** 1:4 (1980), 9-11.

1407. Alexander, Yonah. "Narco-Terrorism: Some Strategic Considerations. ***Crossroads,*** 20 (1986), 55-71.

1408. Biddle, W. "It Must Be Simple and Reliable." ***Discover,*** 7 (June 1986), 22-31.

1409. Chapman, Robert D. "New Terrorist Weapon - Protocol 2." ***Security Management,*** 25:7 (1981), 46-49.

1410. Clarke, Philip C. "Drugs and Terrorism: The Deadly Alliance." ***The American Legion,*** 121:2 (1986), 16-17, 54-55.

1411. Clifford, Mark. "Terror Tactics Threat." ***Far Eastern Economic Review,*** 139 (February 18, 1988), 32-33.

1412. Corsi, Jerome R. "Terrorism as a Desperate Game: Fear, Bargaining and Communication in the Terrorist Event." ***Journal of Conflict Resolution,*** 25 (March 1981), 47-85.

1413. Dellow, John. "Terrorism - The Military Bypassed?." ***RUSI,*** 132:1 (1987), 13-16.

1414. Donelan, Michael. "Terrorism: Who is A Legitimate Target?." ***Review of International Studies,*** 13 (July 1987), 229-33.

1415. Duncan, Evan. "Terrorist Attacks on U.S. Official Personnel Abroad." ***Assets Protection,*** 6:4 (1981), 36-40.

1416. Ehrenfeld, Rachel, and Michael Kahan. "The 'Doping' of America: The Ambivalence of the Narco-Terrorist Connection and a Search for Solutions." In: P. Wilkinson and A. M. Stewart, eds. ***Contemporary Research on Terrorism.*** Aberdeen: Aberdeen University Press, 1987. pp. 241-255.

1417. Findlay, Mark. "Organized Crime as Terrorism." ***Australian Quarterly,*** 58:3 (Spring 1986), 286-296.

1418. Fromkin, David. "The Strategy of Terrorism." In: C. W. Kegley, ed. ***International Terrorism: Characteristics, Causes, Controls.*** New York: St. Martins Press, 1990. pp. 55-62.

1419. Gillan, L. "Oil Field Terrorism: Nobody Wants the Bomb." ***World Oil,*** (October 1981), 140-142.

1420. Grabosky, P. N. "The Urban Context of Political Terrorism." In: M. Stohl, ed. ***The Politics of Terrorism.*** New York: Marcel Dekker, 1988. pp. 59-84.

1421. Hoeber, Francis P. "Terrorism, Sabotage and Telecommunications." ***International Security Review,*** 7 (Fall 1982), 289-304.

1422. Hurwitz, Elliott. "Terrorists and Chemical/Psychological Weapons." ***Naval War College Review,*** 35:3 (1983), 36-40.

1423. Im, Eric I., Jon Cauley and Todd Sandler. "Cycles and Substitutions in Terrorist Activities: A Spectral Approach." ***Kyklos,*** 40:2 (1987), 238-255.

1424. Janke, Peter. "Nationalist and Separatist Terrorism." In: A. Kurz, ed. ***Contemporary Trends in World Terrorism.*** New York: Praeger, 1987. pp. 16-23.

1425. Jenkins, Brian M. "The Future Course of International Terrorism." ***TVI Journal,*** 6:2 (1985), 3-7.

1426. _____. "New Modes of Conflict." ***Orbis,*** 28:1 (1984), 5-16.

1427. Joyal, Paul M. "A Case Study in Terrorism." ***Terrorism,*** 12:2 (1989), 120-122.

1428. Kennedy, Richard T. "International Terrorism." ***Defence Transportation Journal,*** (September 1981), 65-69.

1429. Ketcham, Christine C., and Harvey J. McGeorge. "Terrorist Violence: Its Mechanics and Countermeasures." In: N. C. Livingstone and T. E. Arnold, eds. ***Fighting Back: Winning the War Against Terrorism.*** Lexington, MA.: Lexington Books, 1985. pp. 25-34.

1430. Killeen, John E. "Terrorism: A Misunderstood Form of Low-Intensity Warfare." ***Quarterly Journal of Ideology,*** 11:3 (July 1987), 57-72.

1431. Lisker, Joel. "International Threats." ***Terrorism,*** 10:1 (1987), 54-58.

1432. Livingstone, Neil C. "Low-Level Violence and Future Targets." ***Conflict,*** 2:4 (1980), 351-382.

1433. _____. "Is Terrorism Effective?" ***International Security Review,*** (Fall 1981), 387-409.

1434. Mathur, Krishnan. "Terrorists' Objectives." ***Terrorism,*** 12:1 (1989), 69-70.

1435. McClure, Brooks. "Operational Aspects of Terrorism." ***Willamette Law Review,*** 17 (Winter 1980), 165-184.

1436. McDonald, Donald. "In the Minds of Terrorists: An Interview with Peter Merkl." ***The Center Magazine,*** (January/February 1986), 18-24.

1437. McGeorge, Harvey J. "Kinetics of Terrorism." ***World Affairs,*** 146:1 (1983), 23-41.

1438. _____. "Reversing the Trend on Terror." ***Defense and Foreign Affairs,*** (April 1988), 16-22.

1439. Monday, Mark. "Power Grid has been Vulnerable for Years." ***TVI Journal,*** 3:10 (1982), 5-7.

1440. Moore, Larry R. "Women On The Dark Side." ***Security Management,*** 30:6 (1986), 47-50.

1441. Motley, James B. "Terrorist Warfare: Assessment." ***Military Review,*** (June 1985), 45-57.

1442. _____. "International Terrorism: A New Mode of Warfare." ***International Security Review,*** 6 (Spring 1981), 93-123.

1443. Olsen, Janice. "An Examination of Terrorist Techniques." ***Crossroads,*** 17:1 (1987), 2.

1444. "Patterns of Global Terrorism: 1984." ***Terrorism,*** 9:4 (1987), 409-446.

1445. Perez, Frank H. "Terrorist Target: The Diplomat." ***Department of State Bulletin,*** 82 (August 1982), 22-28.

1446. _____. "Terrorist Target: The Diplomat." In: H. H. Han, ed. ***Terrorism, Political Violence and World Order.*** Lanham, MD.: University Press of America, 1984. pp. 37-48.

1447. Perlstein, Gary R. "The Changing Face of Terrorism: From Regicide to Homicide." ***International Journal of Offender Therapy and Comparative Criminology,*** 30:3 (1986), 187-193.

1448. Petrakis, Gregory. "Terrorism: The Terrorist as a Surrogate Soldier." ***Law and Order,*** 28:9 (1980), 31-32, 34, 36, 38.

1449. RAND Corporation. "Terrorism and Beyond." ***TVI Report,*** 6:2 (1985), 512-513.

1450. Rapoport, David C. "Inside Terrorist Organizations: Introduction." In: D. C. Rapoport, ed. ***Inside Terrorist Organizations.*** New York: Columbia University Press, 1988. pp. 1-12.

1451. Rawles, James W. "High-Technology Terrorism." ***Defense Electronics,*** 22:1 (January 1990), 74-78.

1452. Sandler, Todd, and Harvey E. Lapan. "The Calculus of Dissent: An Analysis of Terrorists' Choice of Targets." ***Synthese,*** 76 (August 1988), 245-261.

1453. Selth, Andrew. "Diplomats as Terrorist Targets: An Historical Overview." ***Australian Foreign Affairs Record,*** 56 (July 1985), 597-603.

1454. Shackley, Theodore G., Robert L. Oatman and Richard A. Finney. "Enviroterrorism." ***Chief Executive,*** (July - August 1990), 34-37.

1455. Simpson, Charles M. "Paranoia as a Weapon in Unconventional Warfare." ***Army,*** 34:4 (1984), 30-33.

1456. Smart, Ian. "International Terrorism." ***Behind the Headlines,*** 44:3 (February 1987), 1-19.

1457. Stephens, Hugh S., and Douglas G. MacNair. "Red Star in the Morning." ***Defense Transportation Journal,*** 42:2 (1986), 12-14.

1458. Stinson, J. L. "CTT Update: Terrorist Trends." ***Police Chief,*** 52 (April 1986), 41-42.

1459. "Terrorism: When Knowledge is a Weapon." ***TVI Journal,*** 4:10-12 (1983), 4-7.

1460. Tomkins, Thomas C. "The Terrorist Arsenal - Part I." ***TVI Report,*** 6:3 (Winter 1986), 27-33.

1461. _____. "The Terrorist Arsenal - Part 2." ***TVI Report,*** 6:4 (1986), 51-56.

1462. Truby, David. "The Complete Terrorist Arsenal." ***Gung-Ho,*** (January 1987), 36-65.

1463. Ward, Richard H. "The Terrorist Connection: A Persuasive Network." ***Police Studies,*** 8:4 (1985), 189-197.

1464. Wardlaw, Grant. "Terrorism: The Threat Remains, But..." ***Pacific Defense Reporter,*** (December 1987/January 1988), 57-60.

1465. Waugh, William L. "The Values in Violence: Organizational and Political Objectives of Terrorist Groups." ***Conflict Quarterly,*** 3:4 (1983), 5-19.

1466. Wilhelm, Kirk R. "Islamic Terrorism: Understanding the Threat." ***Security Management,*** 30:4 (1986), 32-35.

1467. Wilkinson, Paul. "The Real-World Problems of the Terrorist Organization and the Problem of Propaganda." In: A. Merari, ed. ***Terrorism and Combating Terrorism.*** Frederick, MD.: University Publications of America, 1985. pp. 69-86.

1468. _____. "Support Mechanisms in International Terrorism." In: R. O. Slater and M. Stohl, eds. ***Current Perspectives on International Terrorism.*** London: Macmillan, 1988. pp. 88-114.

1469. Wright, Jeffrey W. "Terrorism: A Mode of Warfare." ***Military Review,*** (October 1984), 35-45.

1470. Young, P. Lewis. "Covert Arms Dealing." ***TVI Report,*** 6:2 (1985), 23-28.

3. Documents and Reports

1471. American Bar Association. Committee on Law and National Security. ***Terrorism: The Issues Confronting a Free Society.*** New York: American Bar Association, 1986. 19p.

1472. Charters, David, and Maurice A. Tugwell. ***Trends in International Terrorism.*** Fredericton, New Brunswick: Centre for Conflict Studies, 1980. 124p.

1473. Crenshaw, Martha. "The Strategic Development of Terrorism." Paper Presented at the ***1985 Annual Meeting of the American Political Science Association,*** held on August 29 - September 1, 1985, in New Orleans.

1474. Fowler, W. W., and Helen Purkitt. "Temporal Trends in International Terrorism 1968 to 1979: An Analysis Using Poison and Contagion Models." Paper Presented at the ***Annual Convention of the International Studies Association,*** held on March 1980.

1475. Hanle, Donald J. ***Terrorism: An Analysis of Terrorism as a Form of Warfare.*** Master's Thesis. Monterey, CA.: Naval Postgraduate School, 1987. 247p.

1476. Holland, Carol Sue. "The Black, the Red and the Orange: System Terrorism Versus Regime Terror." Paper Presented to the ***30th Annual Meeting of the Society for the Study of Social Problems,*** held on August 21-24, 1981, in Toronto.

1477. Jenkins, Brian M. ***Embassies Under Siege: A Review of 48 Embassy Takeovers, 1971-1980.*** RAND-R-2651-RC. Santa Barbara, CA.: RAND Corporation, 1981. 38p.

1478. _____. ***New Modes of Conflict.*** RAND-R-3009-DNA. Santa Monica, CA.: RAND Corporation, 1983. 20p.

1479. _____. ***International Terrorism: The Other World War.*** Santa Monica, CA.: Rand Corporation, 1985. 29p.

1480. Osborne, J. S. ***Diplomatic Privilege and Immunity - Abuse and Exploitation by International Terrorists.*** M.A. Thesis. Monterey, CA.: Naval Postgraduate School, 1985. 71p.

1481. Quainton, A. C. E. "Terrorism and Low-Level Conflict." Paper Presented to the ***American Society for Industrial Security,*** held on September 25, 1980 in Miami.

1482. Revell, Oliver B. "Motives and Tactics of Terrorist Groups." In: ***Proceedings of the 9th Annual Symposium on the Role of Behavioral Science in Physical Security,*** held on April 3-4, 1984 in Springfield, VA.

1483. Sharif, Idris Sadiq. ***The Success of Political Terrorist Events: An Analysis of Terrorist Tactics and Victim Characteristics, 1968-1977.*** Ph.D. Dissertation. Washington, D.C.: Howard University, 1990. 211p.

1484. United States. Department of State. Bureau of Diplomatic Security. Threat Analysis Division. ***Lethal Terrorist Actions Against Americans, 1973-1986.*** Washington, D.C.: U.S. Government Printing Office, 1986. 80p.

1485. _____._____. Office for Combatting Terrorism. ***Terrorist Attacks Against Diplomats.*** Washington, D.C.: U.S. Government Printing Office, 1981. 8p.

1486. Wilkinson, Paul. ***Terrorist Targets and Tactics: New Risks to World Order.*** Conflict Studies 236. London: Research Institute for the Study of Conflict and Terrorism, 1989.

B. ASSASSINATIONS

1. Books

1487. Clarke, James W. ***American Assassins: The Darker Side of Politics.*** Princeton, NJ.: Princeton University Press, 1982. 321p.

1488. Ford, Franklin L. ***Political Murder: From Tyrannicide to Terrorism.*** Cambridge, MA.: Harvard University Press, 1985. 423p.

1489. Sterling, Claire. ***The Time of the Assassins.*** New York: Holt, Rinehart and Winston, 1985. 264p.

2. Journal Articles

1490. "Assassination and Anarchy." ***TVI Journal,*** 2:10 (1981), 8-11.

1491. "The Assassins, Whose Hand on the Trigger?" ***TVI Journal,*** 2:8 (1981), 6-12.

1492. Clarke, James W. "American Assassins: An Alternative Typology." ***British Journal of Political Science,*** 2 (January 1981), 81-104.

1493. "The Female Assassin." ***TVI Journal,*** 4:7-9 (1983), 6-11.

1494. Little, Philip W. "Abduction and Assassination Reconsidered." ***TVI Report,*** 8:3 (1989), 16-19.

1495. Rosenzweig, S. "On Assassination: A Democratic Outlook." ***Aggressive Behavior,*** 7 (1981), 265-274.

1496. Schmookler, A. "Assassinations: The Problem Is Not That The World Is Sick." ***Terrorism,*** 5:4 (1982), 367-369.

1497. Snitch, Thomas H. "Terrorism and Political Assassinations: A Trans-National Assessment, 1968-80." ***Annals of the American Academy of Political and Social Science,*** 463 (1982), 54-68.

3. Documents and Reports

1498. Eden, Charles. ***Assassination: A Military View.*** Carlisle Barracks, PA.: U.S. Army War College, 1987. 26p.

1499. Snitch, Thomas H. ***Assassination and Political Violence 1968-1978: An Event Data Approach.*** Washington, D.C.: American University, 1980.

C. BOMBINGS

1. Journal Articles

1500. Brismar, B., and L. Bergenvald. "The Terrorist Bomb Explosion in Bolognia, Italy, 1980: An Analysis of the Effects and Injuries Sustained." ***Journal of Trauma,*** 22:3 (1982), 216-220.

1501. Casswell, A., D. G. Hardy and D. F. Scott. "Bombs for Kicks." ***Practitioner,*** 226:1363 (1981), 111-119.

1502. Charan, Bhagwat. "The Philosophy of the Bomb." In: W. Laqueur, ed. ***The Terrorist Reader.*** New York: Meridian, 1987. pp. 137-139.

1503. Georges-Abeyie, D. E. "The Social Ecology of Bomb Threats: Dallas, Texas." ***Journal of Black Studies,*** 13:3 (March 1983), 305-320.

1504. "Keep It Simple and Reliable." ***Discover,*** 7:6 (June 1986), 22-31.

1505. "Letterbombs." ***TVI Journal,*** 1:3 (1980), 6-10.

1506. Nice, David C. "Abortion Clinic Bombings as Political Violence." ***American Journal of Political Science,*** 32:1 (1988), 178-195.

1507. Salamanca, Beth A. "Vehicle Bombs: Death on Wheels." In: N. C. Livingstone and T. E. Arnold, eds. ***Fighting Back: Winning the War Against Terrorism.*** Lexington, MA.: Lexington Books, 1985. pp. 35-48.

1508. Sharon, Yosef. "Survey of Selected Terrorist Devices." In: ***Anti Terrorism - IDENTA - 85.*** Boulder, CO.: Westview Press, 1985. pp. 138-141.

1509. Wardlaw, Grant. "The Year of the Bomb (and more to come)." ***Pacific Defence Reporter,*** (December 1983/January 1984), 31-34.

2. Documents and Reports

1510. Kindel, Stephen. ***Off-The-Shelf Technology.*** McLean, VA.: Science Applications International, 1987. pp. 97-102.

1511. Morris, Bruce L. "Structural Damage to Building Frames From Accidental or Terrorist Explosions." Paper Presented to the ***Explosives Safety Seminar,*** held on August 24-26, 1982, at Norfolk, VA. Vol 1. 27p.

1512. United States. Department of Justice. Federal Bureau of Investigation. ***Bomb Summary, 1984.*** Washington, D.C.: U.S. Government Printing Office, 1985. 21p.

D. HOSTAGE AND KIDNAPPING INCIDENTS

1. Books

1513. Antokol, Norman, and Mayer Nudell. ***No One is Neutral: Political Hostage Taking in the Modern World.*** Medina, OH.: Alpha, 1990. 252p.

1514. Cooper, H. H. A. ***The Hostage Takers.*** Boulder, CO.: Paladin Press, 1980. 100p.

1515. Miller, Abraham H. ***Terrorism and Hostage Negotiations.*** Boulder, CO.: Westview Press, 1980. 134p.

1516. Moorehead, Caroline. ***Hostages to Fortune: A Study of Kidnapping in the World Today.*** New York: Atheneum, 1980. 305p.

2. Journal Articles

1517. Arnold, Terrell E. "Hostage Taking: Restoring Perspective After the Iran-Contra Crisis." In: N. C. Livingstone and T. E. Terrell, eds. ***Beyond the Iran-Contra Crisis.*** Lexington, MA.: D.C. Heath & Lexington Books, 1988. pp. 39-52.

1518. Aston, Clive C. "Hostage - Taking: A Conceptual Overview." In: D. Carlton and C. Schaerf, ed. ***Contemporary Terror.*** London: Macmillan, 1981. pp. 75-89.

1519. Bahn, C. "Hostage Taking - the Takers, the Taken and the Context - Discussion." ***Annals of the New York Academy of Sciences,*** 347 (June 20, 1980), 151-156.

1520. _____. "Hostage Taking - The Takers, The Taken and the Context - Discussion." In: F. Wright, C. Bahn and R. W. Rieber, eds. ***Forensic Psychology and Psychiatry.*** New York: New York Academy of Sciences, 1980. pp. 151-156.

1521. Baumann, Carol E. "Diplomatic Kidnappings." In: B. M. Jenkins, ed. ***Terrorism and Personal Protection.*** Stoneham, MA.: Butterworth, 1985. pp. 23-45.

1522. Capotorto, Gerardo. "How Terrorists Look at Kidnappings." In: B. M. Jenkins, ed. ***Terrorism and Personal Protection.*** Stoneham, MA.: Butterworth, 1985. pp. 2-7.

1523. _____. "How Terrorists Look at Kidnappings." ***TVI Journal,*** 5:3 (1985), 8-10.

1524. Clutterbuck, Richard L. "The Year of the Hostages." In: ***Annual of Power and Conflict, 1980-81.*** London: Institute for the Study of Conflict, 1981. pp. 1-9.

1525. Duncan, Evan, William Z. Slany and David F. Trask. "Hostage Incidents: Examples in Modern History." ***Department of State Bulletin,*** (March 1981), 23-28.

1526. Knutson, Jeanne N. "Dynamics of the Hostage Taker: Some Major Variants." ***Annals of the New York Academy of Sciences,*** 347 (June 20, 1980), 117-128.

1527. Russell, Charles A. "Kidnapping as a Terrorist Tactic." In: B. M. Jenkins, ed. ***Terrorism and Personal Protection.*** London: Butterworth, 1985. pp. 8-22.

1528. Sandler, Todd, and J. L. Scott. "Terrorist Success in Hostage-Taking Incidents: An Empirical Study." ***Journal of Conflict Resolution,*** 31 (March 1987), 35-53; 54-62.

1529. "TVI Special Report on Kidnapping." ***TVI Report,*** 7:4 (1987), 1-29.

1530. Wilkinson, Paul. "Kidnap and Ransom." In: P. Wilkinson and A. M. Stewart, eds. ***Contemporary Research on Terrorism.*** Aberdeen: Aberdeen University Press, 1987. pp. 390-392.

3. Documents and Reports

1531. Arostegni, Martin C. ***Kidnapping as a Terrorist Tactic, 1975-1981.*** Bureau of Operations and Research, International Association of Chiefs of Police, 1982. 22p.

E. CIVIL AVIATION ASPECTS

1. Books

1532. Ashwood, Tom. ***Terror in the Sky.*** New York: Stein & Day, 1986. 240p.

2. Journal Articles

1533. "Bomb Destroyed Pan Am 747." ***Flight International,*** 135:4146 (January 1989), 2-3.

1534. Brown, David A. "Bomb Destroys Pan Am 747 in Blast Over Scotland." ***Aviation Week and Space Technology,*** 130:1 (1989), 28-29.

1535. Bruce, J. "Terrorists Graduate to Sabotage." ***Jane's Airport Review,*** (June 1990), 3-4.

1536. Carew-Jones, David. "The Hijacking of Ku 422: A Hostage's Account." ***TVI Report,*** 8:3 (1989), 43-51.

1537. Cooper, H. H. A. "Skyjacking: The Threat to Corporate Aviation." ***TVI Journal,*** 1:5 (1980), 2-6.

1538. _____. "Airlines are Forgotten Target." ***TVI Journal,*** 3:10 (1982), 2-3.

1539. Crenshaw, William A. "Civil Aviation: Target for Terrorism." ***The Annals of the American Academy of Political and Social Science,*** 498 (July 1988), 60-69.

1540. Dawson, Humphrey G. "Civil Aviation, Hijacking and International Terrorism: An Historical and Legal Review." ***International Business Lawyer,*** 15:2 (1987), 53-66.

1541. Feiler, Stuart I. "Terrorism: Is It Winning?." ***Hotels and Restaurants International,*** 20 (September 1986), 71-72.

1542. Gal-Or, Noemi. "The Pendulum of Arab International Civil Transportation Terrorism." In: Y. Alexander, ed. ***The 1986 Annual on Terrorism.*** Dordrecht: Martinus Nijhoff, 1987. pp. 177-190.

1543. Holden, Robert T. "The Contagiousness of Aircraft Hijacking." ***American Journal of Sociology,*** 91:4 (1986), 874-904.

1544. Jenkins, Brian M. "The Terrorist Threat to Commercial Aviation." ***TVI Report,*** 9:3 (1990), 1-6.

1545. Maxwell, Evan. "Bomb on the Loose! A Terrorist and a Bomb were Reported on a Passenger Plane." ***Reader's Digest,*** 129 (July 1986), 86-90.

1546. Merari, Ariel. "International Terrorism and Civil Aviation." In: A. Merari and A. Kurz, et al. ***INTER: International Terrorism in 1987.*** Tel Aviv: Jaffee Center for Strategic Studies, 1988. pp. 71-84.

1547. Moorehead, Caroline. "Terrorism in the Air." ***New Society,*** 72:1174 (1985), 471-472.

1548. Sochor, Eugene. "Terrorism in the Sky - the Rhetoric and Realities of Sanctions." ***Terrorism,*** 10:4 (1987), 311-328.

3. Documents and Reports

1549. Crenshaw, William A. ***Terrorism and the Threat to Civil Aviation.*** Ph.D. Dissertation. Miami, FL.: University of Miami, 1987. 207p.

1550. Jenkins, Brian M. ***The Terrorist Threat to Commercial Aviation.*** RAND P-7540. Santa Monica, CA.: Rand Corporation, 1989. 13p.

1551. United States. Congress. House. Committee on Energy and Commerce. Subcommittee on Commerce, Transportation and Tourism. ***International Terrorism and Its Effects on Travel and Tourism: Hearing.*** 99th Cong., 2nd sess. Washington, D.C.: U.S. Government Printing Office, 1986. 104p.

1552. _____._____._____. Committee on Foreign Affairs and Committee on Public Works and Transportation. ***Impact of International Terrorism on Travel: Joint Hearings.*** 99th Cong., 2nd sess. Washington, D.C.: U.S. Government Printing Office, 1986. 432p.

1553. _____. Department of State. ***Terrorist Skyjackings: A Statistical Overview of Terrorist Skyjackings From January 1968 Through June 1982.*** Washington, D.C.: U.S. Government Printing Office, 1982. 25p.

1554. _____. Department of Transportation. Federal Aviation Administration. Office of Aviation Medicine. ***Master List of All Hijacking Attempts, Worldwide, Air Carrier, and General Aviation.*** Washington, D.C.: U.S. Department of Transportation, Updated Periodically.

1555. _____._____._____. Office of Civil Aviation Security. ***U.S. Registered Aircraft Hijacking Statistics, 1961 - to Present.*** Washington, D.C.: U.S. Government Printing Office, 1986. 19p.

1556. _____._____._____._____. ***Criminal Acts Against Civil Aviation, 1988.*** Washington, D.C.: U.S. Government Printing Office, 1989. 39p.

F. MARITIME TERROR

1. Books

1557. Mueller, G. O. W., and Freda Adler. ***Outlaws of the Ocean - The Complete Book of Contemporary Crime on the High Seas.*** New York: Hearst Marine Books, 1985. 354p.

2. Journal Articles

1558. Allen, Thomas B. "The Enemies of All Mankind - Piracy and Terrorism Combine to Create New Dangers for Mariners." ***Sea Power,*** 28 (October 1985), 48-52.

1559. Breemer, J. S. "Offshore Energy Terrorism: Perspectives on a Problem." ***Terrorism,*** 6:3 (1983), 455-468.

1560. Ellen, Eric F. "Violence at Sea." ***TVI Report,*** 7:2 (1987), 20.

1561. Fleming, Diana, and Kellogg Fleming. "Siege at Larnaca: A Cruising Couple's Brush with Terrorism." ***Cruising World,*** 11 (December 1985), 94-97.

1562. "Greece Victim of Worst Ever Maritime Terrorist Attack." ***Commercial Crime International,*** 6:2 (July 1988), 1-2.

1563. Halberstam, Malvina. "Terrorist Acts Against and On Board Ships." In: ***Israel Yearbook on Human Rights, Vol. 19. 1989.*** Dordrecht: Martinus Nijhoff, 1989. pp. 331-342.

1564. Jenkins, Brian M. "Potential Threats to Offshore Platforms." ***TVI Report,*** 8:2 (1988), 1-10

1565. MacBain, Merle. "Will Terrorism Go To Sea?" ***Sea Power,*** (January 1980), 15-24.

1566. _____. "Will Terrorism Go to Sea." ***Security Management,*** (August 1980), 76-77+.

1567. MacNair, Douglas G. "Terrorism in the Marine Environment." In: B. M. Jenkins, ed. ***Terrorism and Beyond: An International Conference on Terrorism and Low-Level Conflict.*** Santa Monica, CA.: RAND Corporation, 1980. pp. 273-276.

1568. Matt, A. R. "Maritime Terrorism: An Unacceptable Risk." ***Ocean Industry,*** (February 1981), 65-69; (March 1981), 93-98; (April 1981), 59+.

1569. _____. "Maritime Terrorism: Unacceptable Risk." ***Officer,*** 57 (September 1981), 18-19.

1570. Menefee, Samuel P. "Maritime Terror in Europe and the Mediterranean." ***Marine Policy,*** 12:2 (April 1988), 143-152.

1571. _____. "Piracy, Terrorism, and the Insurgent Passenger: A Historical and Legal Perspective." In: N. Ronzitti, ed. ***Maritime Terrorism and International Law.*** Dordrecht: Martinus Nijhoff, 1990. pp. 43-68.

1572. Mueller, G. O. W., and Freda Adler. "Terrorism at Sea: Passengership Targets." ***Violence Aggression and Terrorism,*** 1:4 (1987), 327-342.

1573. Raizner, Jeff. "Achille Lauro was the 'Wrong Ship'." ***Journal of Defense and Diplomacy,*** 5 (August 1987), 19-20.

1574. Simpson, Howard R. "Soft Targets for Terrorists?." ***TVI Report,*** 8:3 (1989), 15-16.

1575. Stephens, Hugh W. "Not Merely the Achille Lauro: The Threat of Maritime Terrorism and Piracy." ***Terrorism,*** 9:3 (1987), 285-296.

1576. "Terrorists Seize Cruise Ship in Mediterranean." ***Department of State Bulletin,*** 85 (December 1985), 74-77.

1577. Truver, Scott C. "Maritime Terrorism, 1985." ***U.S. Naval Institute Proceedings,*** 112:5 (1986), 160-173.

3. Documents and Reports

1578. Cardinal, Eric, Josephine Holz and Dennis Kerr. ***The Achille Lauro: A Study in Terror.*** New York: National Broadcasting Company, 1987. 20p.

1579. Jenkins, Brian M. ***Potential Threat to Offshore Platforms.*** RAND P-7406. Santa Monica, CA.: Rand Corporation, 1988. 21p.

G. COMPUTER FACILITIES

1. Journal Articles

1580. Campbell, Douglas E. "Computer Contagion." ***Security Management,*** 32:10 (October 1988), 83-84.

1581. _____. "Computer Sites: Targets for Destruction." ***Security Management,*** 32:7 (July 1988), 56-60.

1582. Etheridge, James, and John Lamb. "DP: The Terror Target." ***Datamation,*** (February 1986), 44-46.

1583. Lamb, John, and James Etheridge. "DP: The Target of Terror: Attacks on Computer Centers are Becoming More Common in Countries all Over the World." ***Datamation,*** 32 (February 1, 1986), 44-46.

1584. Lloyd, Andrew. "DP: An Easy Target: While Terrorists Attacks Usually Endanger People, Europeans Fear Computers Are Being Threatened as Well." ***Datamation,*** 26 (June 1980), 99-100.

1585. Murphy, Ian A. "E.D.I.T.: Electronic Deceptions, Interception and Terrorism: The Radio Shack Reality!." ***Data Processing and Communications Security,*** 12:3 (Summer 1988), 13-16.

1586. Rozen, Arnon, and John M. Musacchio. "Computer Sites: Assessing the Threat." ***Security Management,*** 32:7 (July 1988), 40-47+.

1587. "Terrorism and Computers." ***The Futurist,*** 22 (January-February 1988), 45-46.

1588. Yearwood, Ellen A. "Data Bank Control." In: M. C. Bassiouni, ed. ***Legal Responses to International Terrorism: U.S. Procedural Aspects.*** Dordrecht: Martinus Nijhoff, 1988. pp. 249-276.

H. GUERRILLA WARFARE

1. Books

1589. Atkinson, Alexander. ***Social Order and the General Theory of Strategy.*** London: Routledge & Keegan, 1981. 305p.

1590. Chaliand, Gerard, ed. ***Guerrilla Strategies: Revolutionary Warfare and Counterinsurgency: An Historical Anthology from the Long March to Afghanistan.*** Berkeley, CA.: University of California Press, 1982. pp. 353.

1591. Clutterbuck, Richard L. ***Terrorism and Guerrilla Warfare: Forecasts and Remedies.*** New York: Routledge, 1990. 235p.

1592. Guevara, Che. ***Guerrilla Warfare.*** Lincoln, NE.: University of Nebraska Press, 1985. 430p.

1593. Marighella, Carlos. ***Manual of the Urban Guerrilla.*** Chapel Hill, NC.: Documentary Publications, 1985. 110p.

1594. ***War in Peace: Conventional and Guerrilla Warfare Since 1945.*** New York: Harmony Books, 1985. 336p.

2. Journal Articles

1595. Elliott, R. J. "Are Urban Guerrillas Invincible?" ***Commonweal,*** (June-July 1980), 5-9.

1596. Grabosky, P. N. "The Urban Context of Political Terrorism." In: M. Stohl, ed. ***The Politics of Terrorism.*** 2nd ed. New York: Marcel Dekker, 1983. pp. 51-76.

1597. Guillen, Abraham. "Urban Guerrilla Strategy." In: C. Chaliand, ed. ***Urban Guerrillas.*** Berkeley, CA.: University of California Press, 1982. pp. 317-323.

1598. Harkabi, Yehoshafat. "Guerrilla Warfare and Terrorism." In: A. Merari, ed. ***On Terrorism and Combatting Terrorism.*** Frederick, MD.: University Publications of America, 1985. pp. 19-24.

1599. Little, M. R. "The Evolution and Future of Revolutionary Guerrilla Warfare and Terrorism." ***R.U.S.I.: Journal of the Royal United Services Institute for Defence Studies,*** 129:2 (1984), 33-38.

1600. Maechling, Charles. "Insurgency and Counterinsurgency: The Role of Strategic Theory." ***Parameters,*** 14:3 (Autumn 1984), 32-41.

1601. McGeorge, Harvey J., and Christine C. Ketcham. "Sabotage: A Strategic Tool for Guerrilla Forces." ***World Affairs,*** 146:3 (1983/84), 249-256.

1602. O'Neill, Bard E. "Insurgency: A Framework for Analysis." In: B. E. O'Neill, ed. ***Insurgency in the Modern World.*** Boulder, CO.: Westview Press, 1980. pp. 1-44.

1603. Rentner, Kevin S. "Terrorism in Insurgent Strategies." ***Military Intelligence,*** (January-March 1985), 48-51.

1604. Rougeron, Camille. "The Historical Dimension of Guerrilla Warfare." In: G. Chaliand, ed. ***Guerrilla Strategies.*** Berkeley, CA.: University of California Press, 1982. pp. 35-51.

1605. Sarkesian, Sam C. "Low - Intensity Conflict: Concepts, Principles and Policy Guidelines." ***Air University Review,*** (January-February 1985), 4-23.

1606. Stahel, Albert A. "Dynamic Models of Guerrilla Warfare." In: V. Luterbacher and M. D. Ward, eds. ***Dynamic Models of International Conflict.*** Boulder, CO.: Lynne Rienner, 1985. pp. 354-372.

1607. Viljoen, C. L. "Revolutionary Warfare: The Scourge of the Civilized World." ***Paratus,*** 34:8 (August 1983), 22-23, 36.

1608. Williams, John W. "Carlos Marighela: The Founder of Urban Guerrilla Warfare." ***Terrorism,*** 12:1 (1989), 1-20.

3. Documents and Reports

1609. McLaurin, R. D., and R. Miller. ***Urban Counterinsurgency: Case Studies and Implications for U.S. Military Forces.*** HEL-TM-14-89. Springfield, VA.: Abbott Associates, 1989. 153p.

1610. _____. _____. ***Military Forces in Urban Antiterrorism.*** HEL-TM-12-89. Springfield, VA.: Abbott Associates, 1989. 165p.

1611. Thomas, Walter R. ***Guerrilla Warfare: Causes and Conflict.*** Washington, D.C.: National Defence University, Research Directorate, 1981. 91p.

1612. United States. Central Intelligence Agency. ***Psychological Operations in Guerrilla Warfare.*** New York: Vintage, 1985.

1613. Ya, Deau. ***Terrorism and Guerrilla Warfare: An Essay on People's War and Revolution.*** Ph.D. Dissertation. Aberdeen: University of Aberdeen, 1986.

I. STATE SPONSORSHIP

1. Books

1614. Cline, Ray, and Yonah Alexander. ***Terrorism: The Soviet Connection.*** Washington, D.C.: Center for Strategic and International Studies, Georgetown University, 1984. 165p.

1615. _____. _____. ***Terrorism as State Sponsored Covert Warfare.*** Fairfax, CA.: Hero Books, 1986. 128p.

1616. Levitt, Geoffrey M. ***Democracies Against Terror: The Western Response to State-Supported Terrorism.*** The Washington Papers 134. New York: Praeger, 1989. 142p.

1617. Murphy, John F. ***State Support of International Terrorism: Legal, Political and Economic Dimensions.*** Boulder, CO.: Westview Press, 1989. 128p.

1618. Pincher, Chapman. ***The Secret Offensive: Active Measures: A Saga of Deception, Disinformation, Subversion, Terrorism, Sabotage and Assassination.*** London: Sidgwick & Jackson, 1985. 314p.

1619. Stohl, Michael, and George A. Lopez. ***State as Terrorist: Dynamics of Governmental Violence and Repression.*** Westport, CT.: Greenwood Press, 1984. 202p.

1620. _____. _____, eds. ***Government Violence & Repression: An Agenda for Research.*** Contributions to Political Science Series, No. 148. Westport, CT.: Greenwood Press, 1986. 288p.

1621. _____. _____, eds. ***Terrible Beyond Endurance? The Foreign Policy of State Terrorism.*** Westport, CT.: Greenwood Press, 1988. 360p.

2. Journal Articles

1622. Alexander, Yonah. "Nation-States Support of Terrorism and Political Violence: Case of the U.S.S.R.." In: H. H. Han, ed. ***Terrorism, Political Violence and World Order.*** Lanham, MD.: University Press of America, 1984. pp. 219-228.

1623. _____. "Terrorism and the Soviet Union." In: A. Merari, ed. ***On Terrorism and Combating Terrorism.*** Frederick, MD.: University Publications of America, 1985. pp. 101-118.

1624. _____. "International Terrorism and the Soviet Connection." In: M. Hough, ed. ***Revolutionary Warfare and Counter Insurgency.*** Pretoria, South Africa: Institute for Strategic Studies, University of Pretoria, 1984.

1625. _____. "Some Perspectives on Terrorism and the Soviet Union." ***International Security Review,*** 7 (Spring 1982), 35-45.

1626. _____. "Terrorism in Soviet Strategy." In: R. S. Cline, J. A. Miller and R. E. Kanet, eds. ***Western Europe in Soviet Global Strategy.*** Boulder, CO.: Westview Press, 1987. pp. 81-90.

1627. Alexiev, Alex. "The Kremlin and the Pope." ***Ukrainian Quarterly,*** 39:4 (1983), 378-388.

1628. Almond, Harry H. "The Use of Organized Groups By States as Vehicles to Promote Their Foreign Policy." In: H. H. Han, ed. ***Terrorism, Political Violence and World Order.*** Lanham, MD.: University Press of America, 1984. pp. 229-266.

1629. Anderson, Lisa. "Qaddafi and the Kremlin." ***Problem of Communism,*** 34:5 (September-October 1985), 29-44.

1630. Arens, Moshe. "Terrorist States." In: B. Netanyahu, ed. ***Terrorism: How the West Can Win.*** New York: Farrar, Straus, Giroux, 1986. pp. 93-97.

1631. Asa, M. "Forms of State Support to Terrorism and the Possibility of Combating Terrorism by Retaliating Against Supporting States." In: A. Merari, ed. ***On Terrorism and Combating Terrorism.*** Frederick, MD.: University Publications of America, 1985. pp. 119-134.

1632. Boiter, Albert. "Terrorism and Linkage: Moscow's Reaction." ***Political Communication and Persuasion,*** 1:3 (1981), 301-306.

1633. Brady, Donald R., and John F. Murphy. "The Soviet Union and International Terrorism." ***The International Lawyer,*** 16:1 (1982), 139-148.

1634. Brenchley, Frank. "Diplomatic Immunities and State-Sponsored Terrorism." In: W. Gutteridge, ed. ***The New Terrorism.*** New York: Facts on File, 1986. pp. 85-110.

1635. Bukovsky, Vladimir. "The Curse of Complicity." In: B. Netanyahu, ed. ***International Terrorism: Challenge and Response.*** New Brunswick, NJ.: Transaction Books, 1981. pp. 350-358.

1636. Carnes, Colland F. "Soviet Intelligence Support to International Terrorism." ***American Intelligence Journal,*** (January 1986), 18-23.

1637. Carns, Cal. "Terrorism and Soviet Intelligence." ***American Intelligence Journal,*** (Spring 1981), 5-7.

1638. Casey, William J. "The International Linkages - What Do We Know?." In: U. Ra-anan, et al. ***Hydra of Carnage.*** Lexington, MA.: Lexington Books, 1986. pp. 5-16.

1639. Chalfont, Lord. "Overcoming the Climate of Appeasement." In: B. Netanyahu, ed. ***International Terrorism: Challenge and Response.*** New Brunswick, NJ.: Transaction Books, 1981. pp. 79-89.

1640. Chambliss, W. J. "State-Organized Crime: The American Society of Criminology, 1988 Presidential Address." ***Criminology,*** 27:2 (May 1989), 183-208.

1641. Chapman, Robert D. "State Terrorism." ***Conflict,*** 3:4 (1981), 283-298.

1642. Cline, Ray. "The Strategic Framework." In: B. Netanyahu, ed. ***International Terrorism: Challenge and Response.*** New Brunswick, NJ.: Transaction Books, 1981. pp. 90-100.

1643. _____. "Terrorism: Seabed for Soviet Influence." ***Midstream,*** 26 (May 1980), 5-8.

1644. _____. "Soviet Footprints in St.Peter's Square." ***Terrorism,*** 7:1 (1984), 53-56.

1645. Commager, Henry Steele. "Both Superpowers Encourage Terrorism." In: B. Szumski, ed. ***Terrorism: Opposing Viewpoints.*** St.Paul, MN.: Greenhaven Press, 1986. pp. 175-177.

1646. Crenshaw, Martha. "Is International Terrorism Primarily State-Sponsored?." In: C. W. Kegley, ed. ***International Terrorism: Characteristics, Causes, Controls.*** New York: St. Martin's Press, 1990. pp. 163-169.

1647. Crozier, Brian. "Soviet Support for International Terrorism." In: B. Netanyahu, ed. ***International Terrorism: Challenge and Response.*** New Brunswick, NJ.: Transaction Books, 1981. pp. 64-72.

1648. De Borchgrave, Arnaud. "Unspiking Soviet Terrorism." ***International Security Review,*** 7 (Spring 1982), 3-16.

1649. De Vernisy, Jacques. "The New International Terrorism: Militant Regimes Develop a Deadly Alternative to Traditional Diplomacy." ***World Press Review,*** (November 1980), 23-25.

1650. Dunn, Michael C. "Iran Shi'ite International." ***Defence and Foreign Affairs,*** (August 1985), 34-35, 39.

1651. Duval, Raymond D., and Michael Stohl. "Governance by Terror." In: M. Stohl, ed. ***The Politics of Terrorism.*** 2nd ed. New York: Marcel Dekker, 1983. pp. 179-220.

1652. _____. _____. "Governance by Terror." In: M. Stohl, ed. ***The Politics of Terrorism.*** New York: Marcel Dekker, 1988. pp. 231-272.

1653. Ehrenfeld, Rachel. "Narco-Terrorism: The Soviet Connection." ***Defense and Diplomacy,*** 8:9 (September 1990), 11-15.

1654. Emerson, S. A. "Exposing the Terror Trade: Details of Communist Regimes' Involvement in Terrorism Against the West." ***American Enterprise,*** 1 (1990), 64-68.

1655. Evans, Ernest. "Juggling A Two Edged Sword." ***TVI Journal,*** 2:7 (1981), 2-13.

1656. Francis, Samuel T. "The Soviet Union Sponsors Terrorism." In: B. Szumski, ed. ***Terrorism: Opposing Viewpoints.*** St.Paul, MN.: Greenhaven Press, 1986. pp. 145-151.

1657. Goldberg, Arthur J. "The Shoot-Out at the Libyan Self-Styled People's Bureau: A Case of State-Supported International Terrorism." ***South Dakota Law Review,*** 30 (Winter 1984), 1-7.

1658. Great Britain. British Information Services. "International Terrorism: British Government Breaks Diplomatic Relations with Syria." In: Y. Alexander, ed. ***The 1986 Annual on Terrorism.*** Dordrecht: Martinus Nijhoff, 1987. pp. 257-259.

1659. Gregor, A. James. "Some Thoughts on State and Rebel Terror." In: D. C. Rapoport and Y. Alexander, eds. ***The Rationalization of Terrorism.*** Frederick, MD.: University Publications of America, 1982. pp. 56-66.

1660. Halperin, Ernst. "Terrorism: Moscow's Motive." ***International Security Review,*** 7 (Spring 1982), 69-78.

1661. Haselkorn, Avigdor. "How Qaddafi's Indirect Strategy is Working." ***Current Issues,*** (July 1987), 111-117.

1662. Henze, Paul. "The Plot to Kill the Pope." ***Survey: A Journal of East and West Studies,*** 27:118-119 (1983), 2-21.

1663. _____. "International Terrorism: The Russian Background and the Soviet Linkage." In: ***NATO in the 1980's.*** Istanbul: Doyuran Matbaasi, 1983. pp. 119-143.

1664. Herman, Edward. "Soviet-Backed Terrorism is U.S. Propaganda." In: B. Szumski, ed. ***Terrorism: Opposing Viewpoints.*** St.Paul, MN.: Greenhaven Press, 1986. pp. 152-159.

1665. _____. "U.S. Sponsorship of International Terrorism: An Overview." ***Crime and Social Justice,*** 27 (1987), 1-32.

1666. Herzog, Haim. "Opening Remarks: State Support for International Terrorism." In: B. Netanyahu, ed. ***International Terrorism: Challenge and Response.*** New Brunswick, NJ.: Transaction Books, 1981. pp. 49-51.

1667. Jenkins, Brian M. "The American Response to State-Sponsored Terrorism." In: S. L. Spiegel, M. A. Heller and J. Goldberg, eds. ***The Soviet-American Competition in the Middle East.*** Lexington, MA.: Lexington Books, 1988. pp. 183-190.

1668. Johns, Milton C. "The Reagan Administration's Response to State-Sponsored Terrorism." ***Conflict***, 8:4 (1988), 241-259.

1669. Kegley, Charles W., T. Vance Sturgeon and Eugene R. Wittkopf. "Structural Terrorism: The Systemic Sources of State-Sponsored Terrorism." In: M. Stohl and G. A. Lopez, eds. ***Terrible Beyond Endurance? The Foreign Policy of State Terrorism.*** Westport, CT.: Greenwood Press, 1988. pp. 13-34.

1670. Krauthammer, Charles. "The New Terrorism." ***New Republic***, (August 13-20, 1984), 11-13.

1671. Ledeen, Michael A. "Soviet Sponsorship: The Will to Disbelieve." In: B. Netanyahu, ed. ***Terrorism: How the West Can Win.*** New York: Farrar, Straus, Giroux, 1986. pp. 87-92.

1672. Leidhold, Wolfgang. "Alien Sharks in the Lagoon? Libyan Activities in the South Pacific." ***TVI Report***, 8:2 (1988), 11-20.

1673. Levitt, Geoffrey M. "The Western Response to State-Supported Terrorism." ***Terrorism***, 11:1 (1988), 53-62.

1674. Lewellen, Ted C. "The U.S. and State Terrorism in the Third World." In: M. Stohl and G. A. Lopez, eds. ***Terrible Beyond Endurance? The Foreign Policy of State Terrorism.*** Westport, CT.: Greenwood Press, 1988. pp. 85-118.

1675. Lichenstein, Charles. "State-Sponsored Terrorism - Some Reflections." ***Global Affairs***, 1:2 (1986), 1-10.

1676. Livingstone, Neil C., and Terrell E. Arnold. "The Rise of State - Sponsored Terrorism." In: N. C. Livingstone and T. E. Arnold, eds. ***Fighting Back: Winning the War Against Terrorism.*** Lexington, MA.: Lexington Books, 1985. pp. 11-24.

1677. Lopez, George A. "A Scheme for the Analysis of Government as Terrorist." In: M. Stohl and G. A. Lopez, eds. ***State as Terrorist.*** Westport, CT.: Greenwood Press, 1984. pp. 59-82.

1678. _____, and Michael Stohl. "Studying the State as Terrorist - A Conclusion and Research Agenda." In: M. Stohl and G. A. Lopez, eds. ***State as Terrorist.*** Westport, CT.: Greenwood Press, 1984. pp. 183-202.

1679. _____. _____. "State Terrorism: From the Reign of Terror to Nineteen Eighty--Four." ***Chitty's Law Journal***, 32:1 (1984), 14-33.

1680. Mason, T. David, and Dale A. Krane. "The Political Economy of Death Squads: Toward a Theory of the Impact of State-Sanctioned Terror." ***International Studies Quarterly***, 33:2 (June 1989), 175-198.

1681. _____. "Nonelite Response to State-Sanctioned Terror." ***Western Political Quarterly***, 42:4 (1989), 467-492.

1682. McCamant, John F. "Governance Without Blood: Social Science's Antiseptic View of Rule; or, The Neglect of Political Repression." In: M. Stohl and G. A. Lopez, eds. ***The State as Terrorist.*** Westport, CT.: Greenwood Press, 1984. pp. 11-42.

1683. McForan, Desmond, et al. "Terrorism - A Weapon of Soviet Subversion." ***International Journal on World Peace***, 6:4 (1989), 45-66.

1684. Merari, Ariel. "State Sponsorship of Middle Eastern Terrorism." In: A. Kurz, et al. ***INTER 86.*** Tel Aviv: Jaffee Center for Strategic Studies, 1987. pp. 17-35.

1685. Mickolus, Edward F. "What Constitutes State Support to Terrorists?." ***Terrorism and Political Violence***, 1:3 (July 1989), 287-293.

1686. Moss, Robert. "The Terrorist State." In: B.Netanyahu, ed. ***International Terrorism: Challenge and Response.*** New Brunswick, NJ.: Transaction Books, 1981. pp. 128-134.

1687. Nanes, Allan S. "Terrorism: How Can It be Combatted." ***Congressional Research Service Review***, 3:1 (1982), 2-4,24.

1688. Owen, David. "State Terrorism, Internationalism and Collective Action." ***Review of International Studies***, 13:2 (Spring 1987), 81-90.

1689. Pilgrim, M. K. "Financing International Terrorism." ***International Security Review***, 7:1 (Spring 1982), 47-68.

1690. Pipes, Richard. "The Roots of the Involvement." In: B. Netanyahu, ed. ***International Terrorism: Challenge and Response.*** New Brunswick, NJ.: Transaction Books, 1981. pp. 58-63.

1691. Probst, Peter S. "State-Supported Terrorism: Present and Future Trends." ***Terrorism***, 12:2 (1989), 131-133.

1692. Ra'anan, Uri. "Vulnerabilities of the International Support Apparatus." In: U. Ra'anan, et al. ***Hydra of Carnage.*** Lexington, MA.: Lexington Books, 1986. pp. 221-230.

1693. Rapoport, David C. "State Terror: Introduction to Part II." In: D. C. Rapoport and Y. Alexander, eds. ***The Morality of Terrorism.*** New York: Pergamon Press, 1982. pp. 127-132.

1694. Reagan, Ronald. "The New Network of Terrorist States." ***Terrorism***, 9:2 (1987), 101-112.

1695. Sanchez, Nestor D. "The Cuban Threat." ***Security Management***, 27:1 (1983), 55-60.

1696. Shultz, Richard H. "Soviet Global Strategy and Support for International Terrorist Groups." In: ***1980's: Decade of Confrontation.*** Washington, D.C.: National Defence University Press, 1981. pp. 243-265.

1697. Slann, Martin. "The State as Terrorist." In: M. Slann and B. Schechterman, eds. ***Multidimensional Terrorism.*** Boulder, CO.: Lynne Rienner, 1987. pp. 39-44.

1698. "Soviet Sponsorship of Middle-East Terror." ***Arab - Asian Affairs***, No. 9. March 1981.

1699. "State Supported Terrorism." ***Harvard International Review***, 7:6 (1986), 21-23.

1700. Sterling, Claire. "The State of the Art." In: U. Ra'anan, et al. ***Hydra of Carnage.*** Lexington, MA.: Lexington Books, 1986. pp. 49-56.

1701. _____. "The Great Bulgarian Cover-Up." ***The New Republic***, 192:21 (1985), 16-21.

1702. Stohl, Michael. "International Dimension of State Terrorism." In: M. Stohl, ed. ***The State as Terrorist.*** Westport, CT.: Greenwood Press, 1984. pp. 43-58.

1703. _____. "National Interests and State Terrorism in International Affairs." ***Political Science***, 31:1 (1984), 37-52.

1704. _____. "States, Terrorism and State Terrorism: The Role of the Superpowers." In: R. O. Slater and M. Stohl, eds. ***Current Perspectives on International Terrorism.*** London: Macmillan, 1988. pp. 155-205.

1705. Tamkoc, Metin. "International Terrorism: The Russian Connection." In: ***International Terrorism and the Drug Connection.*** Ankara: Ankara University, 1984. pp. 49-69.

1706. Terry, James P. "An Appraisal of Lawful Military Response to State Sponsored Terrorism." ***Naval War College Review***, (August 1986), 69-77.

1707. United States. Department of State. "Syrian Support for International Terrorism, 1983-6." In: Y. Alexander, ed. ***The 1986 Annual on Terrorism.*** Dordrecht: Martinus Nijhoff, 1987. pp. 339-348.

1708. Wallack, Michael. "Terrorism and "Compellence": New Risks for U.S. Allies with State Sponsored Terror." ***International Perspectives***, (November-December 1987), 13-16.

1709. Wardlaw, Grant. "Terrorism: State Involvement Adds New Dimension." ***Pacific Defence Reporter***, 11 (December 1984/January 1985), 59-60.

1710. _____. "Terror as an Instrument of Foreign Policy." ***Journal of Strategic Studies***, 10:4 (December 1987), 237-259.

1711. _____. "Terror as an Instrument of Foreign Policy." In: D. C. Rapoport, ed. ***Inside Terrorist Organizations***. New York: Columbia University Press, 1988. pp. 237-end.

1712. Warne, Richard N. "Soviets as Arms Merchants." ***Military Intelligence***, 7:1 (January-March 1981), 41-46.

1713. White, C. A. "'Official' Terrorism: On Behalf of the State." ***Canada and the World***, 50 (February 1985), 4-5.

1714. Wilkinson, Paul. "Can a State be 'Terrorist'?" ***International Affairs***, 57:3 (1981), 467-472.

1715. _____. "State Sponsored International Terrorism: The Problems of Response." ***World Today***, 40:7 (1984), 292-298.

1716. _____. "State Sponsorship and the Fight Against Terrorism." In: ***The Fight Against Terrorism***. Toronto: The Mackenzie Institute for the Study of Terrorism, Revolution and Propaganda, 1989. pp. 5-17.

1717. _____. "Uncomfortable Truths About International Terrorism." ***Across the Board***, 19 (January 1982), 78-84.

1718. Wolf, John B. "State-Directed Terrorist Squads." In: J. B. Wolf, ed. ***Antiterrorist Initiatives***. New York, NY.: Plenum Press, 1989. pp. 21-40.

1719. Yariv, Aharon. "Arab State Support for Terrorism." In: B. Netanyahu, ed. ***International Terrorism: Challenge and Response***. New Brunswick, NJ.: Transaction Books, 1981. pp. 73-78.

1720. Yefremov, Vasily. "Terrorism in the USA's Global Strategy." ***Supplement to Soviet Military Review***, 5 (1986), 54-55.

3. Documents and Reports

1721. Alexander, Yonah. ***State Sponsored Terrorism: Low Intensity Warfare***. Occasional Paper No. 3. London: Centre for Contemporary Studies, 1986. 16p.

1722. Becker, Jillian. ***The Soviet Connection: State Sponsorship of Terrorism***. Occasional Paper, No. 13. London: Institute for European Defence and Strategic Studies, 1985. 55p.

1723. Begines, Thomas J. ***An Ethical Response to State-Sponsored Terrorism***. Bethesda, MD.: University Publications of America, 1987. Reel 4. 154p.

1724. _____. ***Ethical Response to State Sponsored Terrorism***. Ph.D. Dissertation. Alexandria, VA.: Army Military Personnel Center, 1987. 157p.

1725. Bittman, Ladislav. "The Role of the Soviet Bloc Intelligence In International Terrorism: The View from Inside." Paper Presented at the ***Conference of the International Security Studies Program of the Fletcher School of Law and Diplomacy***, held in April 1985 at the Fletcher School.

1726. Brenchley, Frank. ***Diplomatic Immunities and State-Sponsored Terrorism.*** Conflict Studies, No. 164. London: Institute for the Study of Conflict, 1984. 24p.

1727. Chapin, Ari. "International Terrorism - An Elaboration on the Russian-Arab Link." Paper Presented at the ***Annual Meeting of the Academy of Criminal Justice,*** held on March 20, 1986 in Orlando, FL. 30p.

1728. Cline, Ray. ***State-Sponsored International Terrorism.*** Washington, D.C.: National Forum Foundation, 1985. 15p.

1729. De Borchgrave, Arnaud. ***State-Sponsored Terrorism: Truth and Consequences.*** Washington, DC.: Defense Nuclear Agency, 1985. pp. 21-29.

1730. Ehrenfeld, Rachel. ***Narco-Terrorism: The Kremlin Connection.*** The Heritage Lectures, 89. Washington, D.C.: The Heritage Foundation, 1986. 6p.

1731. Elad, Shlomi, and Ariel Merari. ***The Soviet Bloc and World Terrorism.*** Paper No. 26. Tel Aviv: Jaffee Center for Strategic Studies, Tel Aviv University, 1984. 81p.

1732. Erickson, Richard J. ***Legitimate Use of Military Force Against State Sponsored International Terrorism.*** Maxwell Air Force Base, AL.: Air University Press, 1989. 267p.

1733. Friedlander, Robert A. ***A Riddle Inside a Mystery Wrapped in an Enigma: Terrorism and the Soviet Connection.*** Gaithersburg, MD.: International Association of Chiefs of Police, 1982.

1734. Gurr, Ted R. "The Role of the State in Political Violence." Paper Presented to the ***13th Annual World Congress of the International Political Science Association,*** held on July 15-20, 1985, in Paris.

1735. Hoffman, Bruce. ***Recent Trends and Future Prospects of Iranian Sponsored International Terrorism.*** RAND R-3783-USDP. Santa Monica, CA.: RAND Corporation, 1990. 43p.

1736. Makki, Ahmed B. ***State-Sponsored Terrorism.*** Carlisle Barracks, PA.: U.S. Army War College, 1987. 23p.

1737. Morgenstern, Frederick L. ***International Terrorism: Soviet Connectivity.*** Maxwell Air Force Base, AL.: Air War College, 1986. 26p.

1738. Raine, Linnea P., ed. ***The International Implication of the Papal Assassination Attempt: A Case of State Sponsored Terrorism: A Report of the CSIS Committee on Terrorism.*** Significant Issues Series, v. 6. no. 20. Washington, D.C.: Center for Strategic and International Studies, 1985. 23p.

1739. Romerstein, Herbert. ***Soviet Support for International Terrorism.*** Washington, D.C.: The Foundation for Democratic Education, 1981.

1740. Stewart, Bernard L., ed. "Conference Report: State Supported Terrorism: The Threat and Possible Countermeasures." ***Terrorism,*** 8:3 (1986), 253-313.

1741. Tanham, George K., and Steven T. Hosmer. ***Countering Covert Aggression.*** RAND N-2412. Santa Monica, CA.: Rand Corporation, 1986. 28p.

1742. United States. Congress. House. Committee on Foreign Affairs. Subcommittee on Arms Control, International Security and Science. ***War Powers, Libya, and State Sponsorship of Terrorism: Hearings.*** 99th Cong., 2nd sess. Washington, D.C.: U.S. Government Printing Office, 1986. 382p.

1743. _____._____. Senate. Committee on Armed Services. ***State Sponsored Terrorism: Hearing.*** 99th Cong., 2nd sess. Washington, D.C.: U.S. Government Printing Office, 1986. 24p.

1744. _____._____._____. Committee on the Judiciary. Subcommittee on Security and Terrorism. ***Historical Antecedents of Soviet Terrorism: Hearings.*** 97th Cong., 1st Sess. Washington, D.C.: U.S. Government Printing Office, 1981.

1745. _____._____._____._____. ***The Role of Cuba in International Terrorism and Subversion.*** 97th Cong., 2nd sess. Washington, D.C.: U.S. Government Printing Office, 1982.

1746. _____._____._____._____. ***Terrorism: The Role of Moscow and its Subcontractors: Hearings.*** 97th Cong., 1st sess. Washington, D.C.: U.S. Government Printing Office, 1982.

1747. _____._____._____._____. ***State Sponsored Terrorism: Report.*** 99th Cong., 1st sess. Washington, D.C.: U.S. Government Printing Office, 1985. 186p.

1748. Utley, R. C. ***Soviet Surrogates in the Middle East.*** PC A02/MF A01. Fort Leavenworth, KS.: Army Command and General Staff College, 1981. 19p.

VI

COUNTER MEASURES TO TERRORISM

The increase in the number of terrorist incidents resulted in increased efforts to combat and contain and possibly eliminate them. The increased concern about terrorism is reflected in the amount of literature published on counter measure strategies and tactics. There is concern in Western democracies about the effectiveness of various counter measure tactics and about the potential negative social and political effects of excessive response. This reflects the different opinions about ways to combat terrorism in general and the methods used in isolated terrorist incidents. This chapter starts with a large general section which covers the general aspects of deterrence and response. The following sections examine specific types of counter measures, such as intelligence, bomb detection, hostage incidents crisis management and prevention, responses to aircraft hijackings and maritime terror. A whole chapter deals with business and executive security. The last section lists some of the simulation research studies.

A. GENERAL WORKS

1. Books

1749. Allan, Richard. ***Terrorism: Pragmatic International Deterrence and Cooperation.*** Occasional Paper Series, 19. Boulder, CO.: Westview Press, 1990. 71p.

1750. Becket, Ian F. W. ***Armed Forces and Modern Counter-Insurgency.*** New York: St.Martin's Press, 1985. 232p.

1751. Bolz, Frank, and Kenneth J. Dudonis. ***The Counter-Terrorism Handbook: Tactics, Procedures and Techniques.*** New York: Elsevier Science Publishers, 1990. 233p.

1752. Buckwalter, J. R., ed. ***International Terrorism: The Decade Ahead.*** Chicago, IL.: University of Chicago, Office of International Criminal Justice, 1989. 137p.

1753. Charters, David, and Maurice A. Tugwell, eds. ***Armies in Low-Intensity Conflict: A Comparative Analysis.*** London: Brassey's, 1989. 272p.

1754. Clutterbuck, Richard L. ***Kidnap, Hijack, and Extortion: The Response.*** New York : St.Martin's, 1987. 228p.

1755. Dewar, Michael. ***Weapons and Equipment of Counter Terrorism.*** New York: Sterling, 1988. 240p.

1756. Dobson, Christopher, and Ronald Payne. ***Counterattack: The West's Battle Against the Terrorists.*** New York: Facts on File, 1982. 198p.

1757. Farrell, William R. ***The U.S. Government Response to Terrorism: In Search of an Effective Strategy.*** Boulder, CO.: Westview Press, 1982. 142p.

1758. Fooner, M. ***Interpol: Issues in World Crime and International Criminal Justice.*** New York: Plenum Press, 1989. 244p.

1759. Gal-Or, Noemi. ***International Cooperation to Suppress Terrorism.*** London: Croom Helm, 1985. 390p.

1760. Hewitt, Christopher. ***The Effectiveness of Anti - Terrorist Policies.*** Lanham, MD.: University Press of America, 1984. 122p.

1761. Jenkins, Brian M., ed. ***Terrorism and Personal Protection.*** Stoneham, MA.: Butterworth, 1985. 451p.

1762. King, J. Andrew. ***Terrorism: A Practical Guide for Police.*** San Diego, CA.: EPS Publications, 1988. 240p.

1763. Lang, Walter N., et al. ***The World's Elite Forces: The Men, Weapons and Operations in the War Against Terrorism.*** London: Salamander Books, 1987. 224p.

1764. Livingstone, Neil C., and Terrell E. Arnold. ***Fighting Back: Winning the War Against Terrorism.*** Lexington, MA.: Lexington Books, 1985. 268p.

1765. _____. ***The Cult of Counterterrorism: The "Weird World" of Spooks, Counterterrorists, Adventurers, and Not-Quite Professionals.*** Lexington, MA.: Lexington Books, 1990. 437p.

1766. _____. ***The War Against Terrorism.*** Lexington, MA.: Lexington Books, 1982. 291p.

1767. Lodge, Juliet, ed. ***Terrorism: A Challenge to the State.*** New York: St. Martins Press, 1981. 247p.

1768. Morris, Eric, and Allan Hoe. ***Terrorism: Threat and Response.*** Basingstoke: Macmillan Press, 1987. 210p.

1769. Netanyahu, Benjamin. ***Terrorism: How the West Can Win.*** New York: Farrar, Straus, Giroux, 1986. 254p.

1770. Poland, James M. ***Understanding Terrorism: Groups, Strategies, and Responses.*** Englewood Cliffs, NJ.: Prentice Hall, 1988. 265p.

1771. Rivers, Gayle. ***War Against Terrorists: How to Win It.*** New York: Stein & Day, 1986. 256p.

1772. Rosenthal, Uriel, M. T. Charles and P. Hart, eds. ***Coping with Crises: The Management of Disasters, Riots and Terrorism.*** Springfield, IL.: Charles C. Thomas, 1989. 485p.

1773. Rubin, Barry, ed. ***The Politics of Counterterrorism: The Ordeal of Democratic States.*** Lanham, MD.: University Publications of America, 1990. 220p.

1774. Ryan, Paul. ***The American Rescue Mission: Why It Failed.*** Annapolis, MD.: Naval Institute Press, 1985. 185p.

1775. Seger, Karl A. ***The Antiterrorism Handbook: A Practical Guide to Counteraction Planning and Operations for Individuals, Businesses and Government.*** San Francisco, CA.: Presidio Press, 1990. 230p.

1776. Shackley, Theodore G., et al. ***You're the Target: Coping with Terror and Crime.*** New York: New World, 11989. 168p.

1777. Shultz, Richard H., and Stephen Sloan, eds. ***Responding to the Terrorist Threat: Security and Crisis Management.*** New York: Pergamon Press, 1980. 261p.

1778. _____, et al. ***Guerrilla Warfare and Counterinsurgency: U.S.-Soviet Policy in the Third World.*** Lexington, MA.: Lexington Books, 1989. 431p.

1779. Siljander, R. P. ***Terrorist Attacks: A Protective Service Guide to Executives, Bodyguards and Policemen.*** Springfield, IL.: C. C. Thomas, 1980. 339p.

1780. Smith, G. Davidson. ***Combating Terrorism.*** New York: Routledge, 1990. 336p.

1781. Thompson, Leroy. ***The Rescuers: The World's Top Anti-Terrorist Units.*** Boulder, CO.: Paladin Press, 1986. 248p.

1782. Trager, Oliver, ed. ***Fighting Terrorism: Negotiation or Retaliation.*** New York: Facts on File, 1986. 233p.

1783. Tucker, H. H., ed. ***Combating the Terrorists: Democratic Responses to Political Violence.*** New York: Facts on File, 1988. 210p.

1784. Ward, Richard H., and Harold E. Smith. ***International Terrorism: Operations Issues.*** Chicago, IL.: Office of International Criminal Justice (OICJ), 1988. 190p.

1785. _____, and Ahmed G. Ezeldin, eds. ***International Responses to Terrorism: New Initiatives.*** 2nd ed. New York: Prentice-Hall, 1990. 171p.

1786. Waugh, William L. ***International Terrorism: How Nations Respond to Terrorism.*** Salisbury, NC.: Documentary Publications, 1982. 326p.

1787. _____. ***Terrorism and Emergency Management: Policy and Administration.*** New York: Marcel Dekker, 1990. 215p.

1788. Wolf, John B. ***Fear of Fear: A Survey of Terrorist Operations and Control in Open Societies.*** New York: Plenum Press, 1981. 235p.

1789. Yallop, H. J. ***Protection Against Terrorism.*** Chichester: Barry Rose, 1980. 92p.

2. Journal Articles

1790. Abrams, Elliot. "Drug Wars: The New Alliance Against Traffickers and Terrorists." ***Department of State Bulletin,*** 86 (April 1986), 89-92.

1791. Alexander, Joseph H. "Countering Tomorrow's Terrorism." ***U.S. Naval Institute Proceedings,*** 107 (July 1981), 44-50.

1792. Alon, Hanan. "Can Terrorism be Deterred? Some Thoughts and Doubts." In: A. Kurz, ed. ***Contemporary Trends in World Terrorism.*** New York: Praeger, 1987. pp. 125-131.

1793. _____. "Terrorism and Countermeasures: Analysis Versus a Participant's Observations." In: B. M. Jenkins, ed. ***Terrorism and Beyond: An International Conference on Terrorism and Low-Level Conflict.*** R-2714-DOE/DOJ/DOS/RC. Santa Monica, CA.: RAND Corporation, 1982. pp. 233-242.

1794. Amir, Menachem. "Combatting Terrorism." In: R. H. Ward and H. E. Smith, eds. ***International Terrorism: The Domestic Response.*** Chicago, IL.: University of Illinois at Chicago, Office of International Criminal Justice, 1987. pp. 41-58.

1795. Amos, John W., and R. H. S. Stolfi. "Controlling International Terrorism: Alternatives Palatable and Unpalatable." ***Annals of the American Academy of Political and Social Science,*** 463 (1982), 69-83.

1796. "Anti - Surveillance Security." ***TVI Journal,*** 1:9 (1980), 2-3.

1797. "Anti-Terrorism: New Priority in Foreign Policy." ***Editorial Research Reports,*** 1 (1981), 229-248.

1798. Aranha, J. D. "Countering Terrorism: The Vulnerability of the Road." ***Law Enforcement News,*** 9:16 (1983), 1, 6-7, 14.

1799. Arnold, Terrell E., and Neil C. Livingstone. "Fighting Back." In: N. C. Livingstone and T. E. Arnold, eds. ***Fighting Back: Winning the War Against Terrorism.*** Lexington, MA.: Lexington Books, 1985. pp. 229-248.

1800. _____. "Rewriting the Rules of Engagement." In: N. C. Livingstone and T. E. Arnold, eds. ***Fighting Back: Winning the War Agaist Terrorism.*** Lexington, MA.: Lexington Books, 1985. pp. 175-190.

1801. Aruri, Naseer H., and John J. Carroll. "The War on Terrorism." ***Christian Society,*** 78 (March-April 1987), 45-51.

1802. Aston, Clive C. "Restrictions Encountered in Responding to Terrorist Sieges: An Analysis." In: R. H. Shultz and S. Sloan, ed. ***Responding to the Terrorist Threat.*** New York: Pergamon Press, 1980. pp. 59-92.

1803. Atkinson, Scott E., et al. "Terrorism in a Bargaining Framework." ***Journal of Law and Economics,*** 30:1 (April 1987), 1-21.

1804. Ball, George. "Retaliatory Attacks Will Not Eliminate Terrorism." In: B. Szumski, ed. ***Terrorism: Opposing Viewpoints.*** St.Paul, MN.: Greenhaven Press, 1986. pp. 204-208.

1805. Barclay, Glen. "Selective Assassination: An Answer to the Terrorist's Trade." ***Pacific Defence Reporter,*** 13:8 (February 1987), 37,43.

1806. Bassiouni, M. Cherif. "International Control of Terrorism: Some Policy Proposals." ***International Review of Criminal Policy,*** 37 (1981), 44-54.

1807. _____. "Terrorism, Law Enforcement and the Mass Media: Perspectives, Problems, Proposals." ***Journal of Criminal Law and Criminology,*** 72:1 (1981), 1-51.

1808. Bavly, Dan. "Terrorism Can and Should Be Contained." ***Terrorism,*** 10:2 (1987), 127-132.

1809. Beeman, William D. "Stricter Penalties Will Not Eliminate Terrorism." In: B. Szumski, ed. ***Terrorism: Opposing Viewpoints.*** St.Paul, MN.: Greenhaven Press, 1986. pp. 215-217.

1810. Bell, J. Bowyer. "Unconventional War: The Army in the Year 2000." In: R. H. Kupperman and W. J. Taylor, eds. ***Strategic Requirements for the Army to the Year 2000.*** Lexington, MA.: Lexington Books, 1984. pp. 171-186.

1811. Beres, Louis Rene. "Terrorism, Insurgency and Geopolitics: The Errors of U.S. Foreign Policy." ***California Western International Law Journal,*** 17:1 (Winter 1987), 161-174.

1812. _____. "Current Debate: Should Terrorists be Assassinated?." ***Tikkun,*** 3 (July-August 1988), 76-77.

1813. Bienen, H., and R. Gilpen. "Economic Sanctions as a Response to Terrorism." ***Journal of Strategic Studies,*** 3:1 (1980), 89-98.

1814. Bierly, Jerome F. "Planning a Counterterrorist Exercise." ***Military Police,*** (June 1990), 24-26.

1815. Billiere de la, Peter. "International Cooperation, Intelligence and Technology." In: R. Clutterbuck, ed. ***The Future of Political Violence.*** London: Macmillan, 1986. pp. 185-193.

1816. Billing, John C. "Terrorism and the Secure Landscape." ***Landscape Architecture,*** 76:4 (July-August 1986), 58-63.

1817. Bishop, James. "Toward Safer Embassies." ***TVI Report,*** 7:3 (1987), 3-4.

1818. Blair, Robert A. "Fighting Terrorism: A Dissenting View." ***World Affairs,*** 146:1 (1983), 114-116.

1819. Blumenfeld, Eric. "'No' to Terrorism in Any Guise." In: B. Netanyahu, ed. ***International Terrorism: Challenge and Response.*** New Brunswick, NJ.: Transaction Books, 1981. pp. 318-324.

1820. Boge, Henrick. "Control of Terrorist Threat." ***Police Chief,*** 52:3 (1985), 133-136.

1821. Bornmann, Karl Gerhard. "Modern Weapons and Equipment Increase the Striking Power of Counter-Terrorist Groups." ***Military Technology,*** 6 (August 1982), 155-158+.

1822. Bossard, Andre. "Interpol and Law Enforcement: Response to Transnational Crime." ***Police Studies,*** 11:4 (Winter 1988), 177-182.

1823. _____. "The War Against Terrorism: The Interpol Response." In: R. H. Ward and H. E. Smith, eds. ***International Terrorism: The Domestic Threat.*** Chicago, IL.: University of Illinois at Chicago, Office of International Criminal Justice, 1987. pp. 1-10.

1824. Bowman, M. E. "The Military Role in Meeting the Threat of Domestic Terrorism." ***Naval Law Review,*** 39 (1990), 209-220.

1825. Boyes, Jon L. "C3I Technologies: A Deterrent to Terrorism." ***Terrorism,*** 10:3 (1987), 271-274.

1826. Boyle, Francis A. "Military Responses to Terrorism." ***American Society of International Law Proceedings,*** (1987), 287-297.

1827. Brady, Julio A. "The Threat of Terrorism to Democracy: A Criminal Justice Response." ***Terrorism,*** 8:3 (1986), 205-214.

1828. Braybrooke, Marcus. "Is There a Meaningful Response?." In: E. Moonman, ed. ***The Violent Society.*** London: Frank Cass, 1987. pp. 155-167.

1829. Bremer, L. Paul. "Counterterrorism Strategies and Programs." ***Terrosism,*** 10:4 (1987), 337-344.

1830. _____. "Combatting International Terrorism." ***TVI Report,*** 7:3 (1987), 1-3.

1831. Brosio, Maulio. "Fighting Terror Within the International Framework." In: B. Netanyahu, ed. ***International Terrorism: Challenge and Response.*** New Brunswick, NJ.: Transaction Books, 1981. pp. 313-317.

1832. Brown, John. "Planning for the Worst: Terrorism." ***Direction,*** (Spring-Summer 1986), 4-6.

1833. Burchael, James T. "Framing a Moral Response to Terrorism." In: C. W. Kegley, ed. ***International Terrorism: Characteristics, Causes, Controls.*** New York: St. Martin's Press, 1990. pp. 213-218.

1834. Burgess, William H. "Special Operations Forces and the Challenge of Transnational Terrorism." ***Military Intelligence,*** (April-June, 1986), 8-15, 48.

1835. _____. "Countering Global Terrorism." ***Military Review,*** 66:6 (June 1986), 72-80.

1836. Burns, Arnold. "Ten Commandments to Deal with Terrorism." ***ADL Bulletin,*** (1987), 1-11.

1837. Burwitz, Richard. "Equipment for Police Counterterrorist Efforts." ***The Police Chief,*** 56:3 (1989), 57-62.

1838. Bush, George. "The U.S. and the Fight Against International Terrorism." In: B. Netanyahu, ed. ***International Terrorism: Challenge and Response.*** New Brunswick, NJ.: Transaction Books, 1981. pp. 332-337.

1839. Campbell, Julian M., and Glenn E. Farrell. "Tips for Countering Terrorism." ***Military Intelligence,*** 11:2 (1985), 33-37.

1840. Capotorto, Gerardo. "Avoiding Capture and Surviving Captivity." In: B. M. Jenkins, ed. ***Terrorism and Personal Protection.*** Stoneham, MA.: Butterworth, 1985. pp. 395-406.

1841. "The Car and Driver: A Defensive Weapon." ***TVI Journal,*** 2:5 (1981), 5-13.

1842. Charters, David. "Organization, Selection and Training of National Response Teams - A Canadian Perspective." ***Conflict Quarterly,*** 1:3 (1980), 26-30.

1843. _____. "Security Forces in an Open Society." ***Coflict Quarterly,*** 1:2 (1980), 8-14.

1844. _____. "Terrorism and the 1984 Olympics." ***Conflict Quarterly,*** 3:4 (1983), 37-47.

1845. _____. "Terrorism and Political Crime: The Challenge of Policing in the Global Village." In: D. J. Loree, ed. ***Future Issues in Policing.*** Ottawa: Canadian Police College, 1989. pp. 79-106.

1846. Chmelir, William C. "Terrorism and Transportation in the 1990s." ***Defense Transportation Journal,*** 46:4 (August 1990), 22-24.

1847. Clifford, W. "Terrorism and Overkill." ***Terrorism,*** 5:3 (1981), 281-286.

1848. Coetzee, P. J. "Urban Terror and Counter-Measures." In: M. Hough, ed. ***Revolutionary Warfare and Counter Insurgency.*** Pretoria, South Africa: Institute for Strategic Studies, University of Pretoria, 1984.

1849. Colwell, William Lee. "Reacting to Terrorism: Don't Fuel the Fire." ***Security Management,*** 29:2 (1985), 22-25.

1850. "Commonwealth Co-operation in the Containment of Terrorism." ***Parliamentarian,*** 67:4 (1986), 148-151.

1851. "Confronting Terrorism (Symposium)." ***Police Chief,*** 54 (May 1987), 28-38.

1852. Cooper, H. H. A., and Richard W. Kobetz. "Advanced Counterterrorism Training." ***Assets Protection,*** (November/December 1980), 21-24.

1853. Cordesman, Anthony H. "After the Raid - The Emerging Lessons from the U.S. Attack on Libya." ***Armed Forces,*** 5:8 (1986), 355-360.

1854. Crawshaw, Simon. "Countering Terrorism: The British Model." In: R. H. Ward and H. E. Smith, eds. ***International Terrorism: The Domestic Response.*** Chicago, IL.: University of Illinois at Chicago, Office of International Criminal Justice, 1987. pp. 11-22.

1855. Crenshaw, Martha. "On Terrorism and Counterterrorism." In: E. A. Kolodziej and P. M. Morgan, eds. ***Security and Arms Control, Volume 2: A Guide to International Policymaking.*** Westport, CO.: Greenwood Press, 1989. pp. 269-296.

1856. Cruse, Charles. "Rise in International Terrorism: Can It Be Halted?." ***Hawk,*** (March 1987), 100-108.

1857. Daskal, Steven E. "The Insurgency Threat and Ways to Defeat It." ***Military Review,*** (January 1986), 28-41.

1858. Davidson, Ian. "U.S., E.C. Disagree on How to Deal with Terrorism: Reaction to U.S. Raid on Libya Underscores Differences Over the Use of Military Force." ***Europe: Magazine of the European Community,*** (May 1986), 16-17.

1859. Davis, Forrest L. "Countering Terrorism in the Trenches." ***Infantry,*** 77:6 (November-December 1987), 31-35.

1860. De Capua, Michael L. "Police Planning for Terrorism." ***Police Chief,*** 52:4 (1986), 31-33.

1861. De Janos, Sigmund J. A. "Riot Control Tactics." ***TVI Journal,*** 1:12 (1980), 2-7.

1862. Dederer, Ann F., and Timothy P. Coffey. "Developing a Counterterrorism Tracking System." ***Signal,*** 42:10 (June 1988), 131-136.

1863. Degeneste, H. I., and John P. Sullivan. "EMS, The Police Response to Terrorism." ***Police Chief,*** 54:5 (1987), 36, 38, 40.

1864. Derrer, Douglas S. "Countering Terrorism, Part II." ***U.S. Naval Institute Proceedings,*** (February 1986), 72-77.

1865. _____. "Countering Terrorism, Part I." ***U.S. Naval Institute Proceedings,*** (January 1986), 50-57.

1866. Digenova, Joseph. "Continuing the Fight Against Terrorism." ***Terrorism,*** 12:2 (1989), 118-120.

1867. Dittmer, Clark M. "Combating Terrorism Abroad: State Department Initiatives." ***The Police Chief,*** 56:3 (1989), 24-29.

1868. Dreher, E. T., and J. W. Manger. "Investigating Terrorism." In: J. J. Grau and B. Jacobson, ed. ***Criminal and Civil Investigation Handbook.*** New York: McGraw-Hill, 1981. pp. 3-17.

1869. Droge, Dolf. "Revive the Quarantine to Stop Terrorism." ***Armed Forces Journal International,*** (July 1986), 82-83.

1870. Dror, Yehezkel. "Facing Unconventional Terrorism." In: ***Anti Terrorism, IDENTA 85.*** Boulder, CO.: Westview Press, 1985. pp. 26-31.

1871. Dunkin, T. "Terrorists Beware: Werbell's Cobra School." ***Soldier of Fortune,*** 5:1 (1980), 46-50.

1872. Dziak, John J. "Military Doctrine and Structure." In: U. Ra'anan, et al. ***Hydra of Carnage.*** Lexington, MA.: Lexington Books, 1986. pp. 72-92.

1873. "Economic Sanctions to Combat International Terrorism." ***Department of State Bulletin,*** 86:2115 (October 1986), 27-31.

1874. "Eliminating Terrorist Surprise?" ***TVI Journal,*** 3:7 (1982), 11-13.

1875. Evans, Ernest. "The Reagan Administration's Policy Toward Revolutionary Movements." ***Conflict Quarterly,*** 3:1 (1982), 55-61.

1876. Ezeldin, Ahmed G. "International Aspects of Terrorism and the Need for Cooperation." In: R. H. Ward and H. E. Smith, eds. ***International Terrorism: The Domestic Response.*** Chicago, IL.: University of Illinois at Chicago, Office of International Criminal Justice, 1987. pp. 85-92.

1877. Falk, Richard A. "Rethinking Counter-Terrorism." In: M. Kaldor and P. Anderson, eds. ***Mad Dogs: The U.S. Raids on Libya.*** London: Pluto Press, 1986. pp. 124-141.

1878. _____. "Rethinking Counter-Terrorism." ***Scandinavian Journal of Development Alternatives,*** 6:2-3 (June-September 1987), 19-36.

1879. Farrell, William R. "Organized to Combat Terrorism." In: N. C. Livingstone and T. E. Arnold, eds. ***Fighting Back: Winning the War Against Terrorism.*** Lexington, MA.: Lexington Books, 1985. pp. 49-58.

1880. _____. "Responding to Terrorism: What, Why and When." ***Naval War College Review,*** (January-February 1986), 47-52.

1881. Feith, Douglas J. "International Responses." In: U. Ra'anan, et al. ***Hydra of Carnage.*** Lexington, MA.: Lexington Books, 1986. pp. 265-286.

1882. Felton, John. "Reagan, Hill Move to Bolster Embassy Security." ***Congressional Quarterly Weekly Report,*** 42 (September 29, 1984), 2401-2403.

1883. Finn, Kim E., and William E. Chmelir. "Meeting the Terrorist Challenge." ***Defense Transportation Journal,*** 45 (June 1989), 11-12+.

1884. Fitzpatrick, Thomas K. "Prudent Traveller - A Basic Primer." ***Assets Protection,*** 5:6 (1980), 25-29.

1885. Flores, David A. "Export Controls and the U.S. Effort to Combat International Terrorism." ***Law and Policy in International Business,*** 13:2 (1981), 521-590.

1886. "Forgetting Rights, The Wrong Road in Counterinsurgency." ***TVI Journal,*** 3:1 (1982), 6-8.

1887. Foster, Simeon E. "Terrorism: Facing an Ugly Reality." ***All Hands,*** 822 (September 1985), 2-6.

1888. Foster, Stewart. "Maintaining a Co-ordinated Approach to Counter-Terrorism." ***Australian Quarterly,*** 58:3 (Spring 1986), 321-325.

1889. Fowler, John M. "Counterterrorism Precautions." ***Military Police Journal,*** 11 (Spring 1984), 8-9.

1890. Fraser, James. "First-Response Training: Critical Incident Management.' ***Police Chief,*** 57:8 (August 1990), 68-69.

1891. Frey, Bruno S. "Fighting Political Terrorism by Refusing Recognition." ***Journal of Public Policy,*** 7:2 (April-June 1987), 179-188.

1892. Friedland, Nehemia. "National Responses to Political Terrorism." ***Social Science Newsletter,*** 21 (January/April 1983), 21-26.

1893. _____. "Fighting Political Terrorism by Refusing Recognition: A Critique of Frey's Proposal." ***Journal of Public Policy,*** 9:2 (April-June, 1989), 207-240.

1894. Friedlander, Robert A. "When Will the Madness End?." ***University of Toledo Law Review,*** 18:1 (Fall 1986), 125-131.

1895. Fuchs, Ron. "Terrorism: War of the World." ***Airman,*** 30:2 (1986), 28-31.

1896. Funkhouser, Preston L. "Terrorism as an Element of War: A Primer for the SOF (Special Operations Force) Soldier." ***Special Warfare,*** 1 (April 1988), 12-17.

1897. Fuselier, G. W. "What Every Negotiator Would Like His Chief to Know." ***FBI Law Enforcement Bulletin,*** 55:3 (1986), 12-15.

1898. Gallagher, R. H. "Crisis Management: The Need - The Response." In: ***Clandestine Tactics and Technology.*** Gaithersburg, MD.: International Association of Chiefs of Police, 1980.

1899. Garrett, H. Lawrence III. "Terrorism and the Use of Military Force." ***Defense,*** (May-June 1987), 26-32.

1900. Gates, David F. "The Role of Analysis in Combatting Modern Terrorism." ***FBI Law Enforcement Bulletin,*** 58:6 (1989), 1-5.

1901. Gazit, Shlomo. "Risk, Glory and the Rescue Operation." ***International Security,*** 6:1 (Summer 1981), 111-135.

1902. Geldenhuys, J. J. "Rural Insurgency and Countermeasures." In: M. Hough, ed. ***Revolutionary Warfare and Counter Insurgency.*** Pretoria, South Africa: Institute for Strategic Studies, University of Pretoria, 1984.

1903. Georges-Abeyie, D. E. "Terrorism and the Liberal State: A Reasonable Response." ***Police Studies,*** 4:3 (1981), 34-53.

1904. Gibbs, George. "Equipments for Internal Security and Anti-Terrorist Operations." ***Asian Defence Journal,*** 10 (October 1981), 87-91.

1905. Gilan, Linda. "Oil Fields Terrorism: Nobody Wants the Bomb." ***World Oil,*** 193 (October 1981), 140-142.

1906. Glendon, Robert P. "Ploting a Rational Response to Political Terrorism." ***Risk Management,*** (September 1981), 28-30+.

1907. Goldman, Joseph R. "Terrorism and the Role of Security Strategies." ***Journal of Political Science,*** 14:1-2 (Spring 1986), 10-15.

1908. _____. "Counterterrorism." In: M. Slann and B. Schechterman, eds. ***Multidimensional Terrorism.*** Boulder, CO.: Lynne Rienner, 1987. pp. 33-38.

1909. Green, L. C. "Terrorism and Its Responses." ***Terrorism,*** 8:1 (1985), 33-77.

1910. _____. "Niceties and Necessities: The Case for Diplomatic Immunity." ***International Perspectives,*** 3 (April 1980), 19-23.

1911. Greenberg, Irwin. "Terrorism: Making the Response Fit the Act." In: D. J. D. Sandole and I. Sandole-Staroste, eds. ***Conflict Management and Problem Solving.*** London: Frances Pinter, 1987. pp. 199-200.

1912. Grodsky, Morris. "Combatting Terrorism: The Forensic Science Role." ***Assets Protection,*** 7:4 (1983), 10-13.

1913. Grondona, Mariano. "Reconciling International Security and Human Rights." ***International Security,*** 3 (Summer 1978), 3-16.

1914. Grotenroth, Mary Jo. "INTERPOL's Role in International Law Enforcement." In: M. C. Bassiouni, ed. ***Legal Responses to International Terrorism: U.S. Procedural Aspects.*** Dordrecht: Martinus Nijhoff, 1988. pp. 375-380.

1915. Gutteridge, William. "Countering Terrorism: Evaluating the Options." In: C. W. Kegley, ed. ***International Terrorism: Characteristics, Causes, Controls.*** New York: St. Martin's Press, 1990. pp. 245-252.

1916. _____. "Countering Terrorism." ***Journal of Defense and Diplomacy,*** (April 1988), 263-276.

1917. Hall, David. "Systematic Security." ***Journal of Defense and Security,*** 4:3 (1986), 53-54, 56.

1918. Hart, David C. "Antiballistic Update: Security in Fashion." ***TVI Journal,*** 1:11 (1980), 11-13.

1919. Hart, Kevin R. "The SJA in the Emergency Operations Centre: Advising the Commander During a Counterterrorism Operation." ***The Army Lawyer,*** (July 1988), 15-26.

1920. Hassel, Conrad V. "Preparing Law Enforcement Personnel for Terrorist Incidents." In: B. Eichelman, D. Soskis and W. Reid, eds. ***Terrorism: Interdisciplinary Perspectives.*** Washington, D.C.: American Psychiatric Association, 1983. pp. 117-128.

1921. Hatch, Orrin G. "Fighting Back Against Terrorism: When, Where, How?." ***Ohio Northern University Law Review,*** 13:1 (1986), 5-17.

1922. Hayden, H. T. "Antiterrorism Planning." ***Marine Corps Gazette,*** 72 (July 1988), 18-19.

1923. Heisey, D. Ray. "Reagan and Mitterand Respond to International Crisis: Creating Versus Transcending Appearances." ***Western Journal of Speech Communication,*** 50:4 (1986), 325-335.

1924. Helms, Andrea R. C. "Procedural Democracy and the Terrorist Threat." ***Police Studies,*** 4 (Winter 1982), 23-32.

1925. Henderson, Robert. "Use of Force: Wether and When?: Washington's Debate on Terrorism." ***International Perspective,*** (September/October, 1986), 17-19.

1926. Hensman, Jonathan R. "Taking Terrorism, Low-Intensity Conflict and Special Operations in Context." ***Marine Corps Gazette,*** 71:2 (1987), 44-50.

1927. Henze, Paul. "Coping with Terrorism." ***Fletcher Forum,*** 9 (Summer 1985), 307-323.

1928. Herring, Lynn, and James Fraser. "Overview of Terrorism for the Police Administrator." ***Police Chief,*** 54:3 (1987), 71-72+.

1929. Heyman, Edward. "The Diffusion of Transnational Terrorism." In: R. H. Shultz and S. Sloan, eds. ***Responding to the Terrorist Threat.*** New York: Pergamon Press, 1980. pp. 190-244.

1930. Heyman, M. N., ed. "Psychologist in Operational Support." ***Police Chief,*** 49 (January 1982), 124-129.

1931. Hill, Christopher. "The Political Dilemmas for Western Governments." In: ***Terrorism and International Order.*** London: Royal Institute of International Affairs, 1986. pp. 77-100.

1932. Hippler, Jochen. "Low-Intensity Warfare: Key Strategy for the Third-World Theatre." ***Middle East Report,*** 17:1 (1987), 32-38.

1933. Hoffacker, Lewis. "A Washington Perspective." In: M. F. Herz, ed. ***Diplomats and Terrorists.*** Washington, D.C.: Institute for the Study of Diplomacy, 1982. pp. 58-60.

1934. Hoffman, Bruce. "Commando Warfare and Small Raiding Parties as Part of a Counterterrorist Military Policy." ***Conflict,*** 7:1 (1987), 15-44.

1935. Hoffman, Robert A. "Policy Responses to International Terrorism." ***Quarterly Journal of Ideology,*** 11:3 (July 1987), 73-86.

1936. Horchem, Hans J. "Pre-Empting Terror." In: B. Netanyahu, ed. ***International Terrorism: Challenge and Response.*** New Brunswick, NJ.: Transaction Books, 1981. pp. 307-312.

1937. _____. "Perspectives on Terrorism - Terrorism Stalks the Globe." ***Security Management,*** 32:11 (November 1988), 128-132.

1938. "Interpol's Resolutions to Terrorism." ***TVI Journal,*** 6:1 (Summer 1985), 6-7.

1939. "Interpol's Response to Terrorism." ***TVI Journal,*** 6:1 (Summer 1985), 3-5.

1940. Isby, David C. "Special Operations Forces Response." ***Military Intelligence,*** 11:1 (January-March 1985), 24-27.

1941. Ivianski, Zeev. "'The Blow at the Center': The Concept and Its History." In: A. Merari, ed. ***On Terrorism and Combatting Terrorism.*** Frederick, MD.: University Publications of America, 1985. pp. 53-62.

1942. _____. "Provocation at the Center: A Study in the History of Counter-Terror." ***Terrorism,*** 3:3-4 (1980), 53-88.

1943. Jackson, Jeffrey. "Premonitions and Forewarnings." In: M. F. Herz, ed. ***Diplomats and Terrorists.*** Washington, D.C.: Institute for the Study of Diplomacy, 1982. pp. 22-25.

1944. Jarrett, James R. "Personal Survival Courses: A Matter of Choice." In: B. M. Jenkins, ed. ***Terrorism and Personal Protection.*** Stoneham, MA.: Butterworth, 1985. pp. 369-387.

1945. Jenkins, Brian M. "Defense Against Terrorism." ***Political Science Quarterly,*** 101:5 (1986), 773-786.

1946. _____. "The Possibility of Soviet-American Cooperation Against Terrorism." ***TVI Report,*** 9:1 (1989), 1-8.

1947. Jenkins, R. G. "Transportation Security: An MTMC Perspective." ***Defense Transportation Journal,*** 42:2 (April 1986), 15-17.

1948. Johnson, Chalmers. "A List of Hypotheses and Assumptions." ***Terrorism,*** 3:3-4 (1980), 251-255.

1949. Kara, Miles L. "Counterinsurgency Revisited." ***Military Intelligence,*** (January--March 1985), 34-36.

1950. Karkashian, J. E. "Too Many Things Not Working." In: M. F. Herz, ed. ***Diplomats and Terrorists.*** Washington, D.C.: Institute for the Study of Diplomacy, 1982. pp. 6-9.

1951. Keegan, George J. "The Preferred Route." In: B. Netanyahu, ed. ***International Terrorism: Challenge and Response.*** New Brunswick, NJ.: Transaction Books, 1981. pp. 338-342.

1952. Kellen, Konrad. "What Price Infiltration Into a Terrorist Group?." ***TVI Report,*** 6:4 (1986), 29-30.

1953. Kelly, Ross S. "Not Quit War, Not Quite Peace." ***Defence and Foreign Affairs,*** (May 1985), 36-43.

1954. Kemp, Jack. "The Unseen Hand." In: B. Netanyahu, ed. ***International Terrorism: Challenge and Response.*** New Brunswick, NJ.: Transaction Books, 1981. pp. 187-195.

1955. Kennedy, Richard T. "Combatting Terrorism." ***State,*** 236 (July 1981), 2-4.

1956. Kerr, Donald. "Coping with Terrorism." ***Terrorism,*** 8:2 (1985), 113-126.

1957. Kindel, Stephen. "Catching Terrorists." ***Science Digest,*** (September 1986), 37-41, 76-82.

1958. _____. "Off-the-Shelf Technology." ***Terrorism,*** 10:3 (1987), 281-284.

1959. King, Joseph. "Mounting an Undercover Operation." In: R. H. Ward and H. E. Smith, eds. ***International Terrorism: The Domestic Response.*** Chicago, IL.: University of Illinois at Chicago, Office of International Criminal Justice, 1987. pp. 37-40.

1960. Kisor, R. M. "INS Countermeasures Against Terrorists and Their Use of Fraudulent Documents." ***Police Chief,*** 55 (September 1988), 24-26.

1961. Kobetz, Richard W., and H. H. A. Cooper. "The Hardest Question." In: B. M. Jenkins, ed. ***Terrorism and Personal Protection.*** Stoneham, MA.: Butterworth, 1985. pp. 388-394.

1962. Krulak, Victor H. "Strategic Implications of "The Little War"." ***Strategic Review,*** 13:2 (1985), 31-36.

1963. Kupperman, Robert H. "Proposed Remedies and Preventive Methods." ***International Journal of Group Tensions,*** 12:1-4 (1982), 142-160.

1964. _____. "Terror, The Strategic Tool: Response and Control." ***Annals of the American Academy of Political and Social Science,*** 463 (1982), 24-38.

1965. _____, et al. "Terrorism: The Challenge to the Military in the 1990s." In: R. H. Kupperman and W. J. Taylor, eds. ***Strategic Requirements for the Army to the Year 2000.*** Lexington, MA.: Lexington books, 1984. pp. 187-208.

1966. _____, et al. "Terrorism: What Should We Do?." ***This World,*** 12 (Fall 1985), 31-84.

1967. LaTreill, D. R. "Dead Serious About Staying Alive." ***National Centurion,*** 2:5 (1984), 23-29.

1968. Laqueur, Walter Z. "Reflections on the Eradication of Terrorism." In: C. W. Kegley, ed. ***International Terrorism: Characteristics, Causes, Controls.*** New York: St. Martin's Press, 1990. pp. 207-212.

1969. Lasser, William. "Fighting Terrorism in Democratic Societies." In: M. Slann and B. Schechterman, eds. ***Multidimensional Terrorism.*** Boulder, CO.: Lynne Rienner, 1987. pp. 121-130.

1970. Lavery, Robert. "Incident Management: Target Studies." ***Police Chief,*** 48 (December 1981), 22-24.

1971. Lavey, Don. "Interpol: Fostering International Cooperation." ***The Police Chief,*** 56:3 (March 1989), 46-49.

1972. Laxalt, Paul. "The Agenda for International Action." In: B. Netanyahu, ed. ***Terrorism: How the West Can Win.*** New York: Farrar, Straus, Giroux, 1986. pp. 186-189.

1973. Leaute, Jacques. "Terrorism: Action and Reaction." In: ***International Terrorism and the Drug Connection.*** Ankara: Ankara University Press, 1984. pp. 289-294.

1974. Ledeen, Michael A. "Covert Operations Can Fight Terrorism." In: B. Szumski, ed. ***Terrorism: Opposing Viewpoints.*** St.Paul, MN.: Greenhaven Press, 1986. pp. 218-222.

1975. Lee, D. R., and Todd Sandler. "On the Optimal Retaliation Against Terrorists: The Paid-Rider Option." ***Public Choice,*** 61:2 (May 1989), 141-152.

1976. _____. "Free Riding and Paid Riding in the Fight Against Terrorism." ***American Economic Review,*** 78:2 (1988), 22-26.

1977. Lerner, Natan. "Sanctions and Counter-Measures Short of the Use of Force Against Terrorism." In: ***Israel Yearbook on Human Rights, Vol. 19. 1989.*** Dordrecht: Martinus Nijhoff, 1989. pp. 259-270.

1978. Levinson, Eric. "Car - Whose Weapon Is It?" ***Assets Protection,*** 6:5 (September/October 1981), 15-19.

1979. Levinson, J. "Documents and Forgery in Terrorist Operations." In: ***Anti Terrorism - IDENTA - 85.*** Boulder, CO.: Westview Press, 1985. pp. 63-71.

1980. Levy, Rudolph. "Countering the Terrorist Threat." ***Military Intelligence,*** (October--December 1984), 6-7.

1981. Lewis, Marlo. "Effective Retribution: Libya and Syria." ***Midstream,*** 32:9 (1986), 3-7.

1982. Lingo, E. J., et al. "Target - Terrorism." ***Police Chief,*** (April 1982), 51-65.

1983. Lipman, Ira A. "Living with Terrorism - Global Reality for American Interests." ***Security Management,*** 30 (January 1986), 81-82.

1984. Liu, Wen, Feng Luo and Yongchen Zhao. "International Terrorism and Countermeasures." ***Beijing Review***, 33 (July 16, 1990), 13-17.

1985. Livingstone, Neil C. "States in Opposition: The War Against Terrorism." ***Conflict***, 3:2-3 (1981), 83-142.

1986. _____. "Proactive Responses to Terrorism: Reprisals, Preemption and Retribution." In: N. C. Livingstone and T. E. Arnold, eds. ***Fighting Back: Winning the War Against Terrorism.*** Lexington, MA.: Lexington Books, 1985. pp. 109-132.

1987. _____. "Fighting Terrorism and the 'Dirty Little Wars'." ***Air University Review***, (March-April 1984), 4-16.

1988. _____. "Proactive Responses to Terrorism: Reprisals, Preemption, and Retribution." In: C. W. Kegley, ed. ***International Terrorism: Characteristics, Causes, Controls.*** New York: St. Martin's Press, 1990. pp. 219-227.

1989. _____. "Death of a Sanctuary." ***Sea Power***, 33:11 (November 1990), 29-30.

1990. "Low-Tech Threat to High-Tech: Marine Corps Forms Anti-Terror Security Forces." ***Officer***, 63 (December 1987), 23-26.

1991. Lynch, Edward. "International Terrorism: The Search for a Policy." ***Terrorism***, 9:1 (1987), 1-85.

1992. MacNair, Douglas G. "Incident Management - The Defensive Strategy." ***Journal of Security Administration***, 6:1 (1983), 7-15.

1993. Maechling, Lisa, and Yonah Alexander. "Security Risks to Energy Production and Trade." In: Y. Alexander and C. K. Ebinger, eds. ***Political Terrorism and Energy.*** New York: Praeger, 1982. pp. 107-140.

1994. Maghan, Jess, and Robert J. Kelly. "Terrorism and Corrections: The Incarcerated Radical." In: J. R. Buckwalter, ed. ***International Terrorism: The Decade Ahead.*** Chicago, IL.: University of Illinois in Chicago, Office of International Criminal Justice, 1989. pp. 29-53.

1995. Malley, Joseph A. "Preparing and Protecting Personnel and Property Prior to a Terrorist Attack." In: P. J. Montana and G. S. Roukis, eds. ***Managing Terrorism.*** Westport, CT.: Quorum Books, 1983. pp. 73-90.

1996. Marks, Edward. "Terrorism and the Policy Response." ***TVI Report***, 6:4 (1986), 10-15.

1997. Marshall, T. K. "A Pathologist's Experience of Terrorist Violence." ***Medico-Legal Journal***, 56:1 (Winter 1988), 18-33.

1998. _____. "Forensic Aspects of Terrorism." ***Annals Academy of Medicine***, 13:1 (1984), 32-36.

1999. Martell, D. F. "FBI's Expanding Role in International Terrorism Investigations." ***FBI Law Enforcement Bulletin***, 56:10 (October 1989), 28-32.

2000. Marvil, David L. "The Role of the Federal Emergency Management Agency in Response to the Consequences of Terrorism." In: B. M. Jenkins, ed. ***Terrorism and Beyond: An International Conference on Terrorism and Low-Level Conflict.*** Santa Monica, CA.: RAND Corporation, 1980. pp. 266-272.

2001. Matteson, S. "Insurance, Against Terrorism: A New Defense." ***Security World***, 18:10 (1981), 20-24.

2002. McBrien, J. R. "How to Handle Terrorism." ***Terrorism***, 10:1 (1987), 67-70.

2003. McClure, Brooks. "How To Survive as a Senior Diplomat." In: M. F. Herz, ed. ***Diplomats and Terrorists.*** Washington, D.C.: Institute for the Study of Diplomacy, 1982. pp. 30-32.

2004. McCree, Arleigh. "Diversionary Devices." ***The Police Chief***, 53:4 (1986), 38-39.

2005. McGuire, Frank G. "Material I: Arming Against Terrorism." ***Journal of Defense and Diplomacy***, 4:3 (1986), 49-52.

2006. McKinnon, Raymond J. "Terrorism and DEA Foreign Operations." ***Drug Enforcement***, 12:1 (Summer 1985), 28.

2007. McNally, Richard. "After Vietnam: Living, Flying and Fighting Terrorism and 'Brush Fires'." ***Airman***, 31:9 (September 1987), 48-49.

2008. Meyer, Armin H. "The Three Facets of Terrorism." In: M. F. Herz, ed. ***Diplomats and Terrorists.*** Washington, D.C.: Institute for the Study of Diplomacy, 1982. pp. 55-58.

2009. Michelson, Richard S. "Terrorism: Does It Affect the Street Cop." ***Law and Order***, 31:2 (1983), 42-45.

2010. _____. "Understanding and Countering Terrorism." ***Campus Law Enforcement Journal***, 16:3 (May-June 1986), 40-42.

2011. Mickolus, Edward F. "Responding to Terrorism: Basic and Applied Research." In: S. Sloan and R. Shultz, eds. ***Responding to the Terrorist Threat: Prevention and Control.*** New York: Pergamon Press, 1980. pp. 174-189.

2012. Miller, Reuben. "Acts of International Terrorism - Governments Responses and Policies." ***Comparative Political Studies***, 19:3 (1986), 385-414.

2013. Milte, Kerry L., D. Shuvayev and Allen A. Bartholomew. "Political Violence and Its Assessment: Some Issues." ***Australian and New Zealand Journal of Criminology***, 13:2 (1980), 107-116.

2014. Mochary, M. V. "International Terrorism and the Investigation of Transnational Crime: Diplomatic Issues." In: J. R. Buckwalter, ed. ***International Terrorism: The Decade Ahead.*** Chicago, IL.: University of Illinois at Chicago, Office of International Criminal Justice, 1989. pp. 13-19.

2015. Mock, William B. T. "The INS Response to Terrorist Threats." In: M. C. Bassiouni, ed. ***Legal Responses to International Terrorism: U.S. Procedural Aspects.*** Dordrecht: Martinus Nijhoff, 1988. pp. 231-249.

2016. Moore, John N. "Global Order, Low Intensity Conflict and a Strategy of Deterrence." ***Naval War College Review***, (January-February 1986), 30-46.

2017. _____. "A Few Thoughts on Fighting Terrorism." ***Terrorism***, 10:1 (1987), 41-44.

2018. Moore, R. T. "Computerized Site Security Monitor and Response System." ***Journal of Security Administration***, 3:1 (1980), 29-41.

2019. Moran, Felix F. "In My Opinion - Security Foresight: A Rational Defense Against Terrorism." ***Air University Review***, 37:3 (1986), 94-103.

2020. Moss, Brenda. "Barricades Provide the Strength to Deter or Delay Intruders, Terrorists." ***Security***, 27:2 (February 1990), 40-43.

2021. Motley, James B. "Terrorist Warfare: Formidable Challenge." ***Fletcher Forum***, 9 (Summer 1985), 295-306.

2022. _____. "Coping with the Terrorist Threat." In: S. J. Cimbala, ed. ***Intelligence and Intelligence Policy in a Democratic Society.*** Ardsley on Hudson, NY.: Transnational Publications, 1987. pp. 165-176.

2023. _____. "The Case for a Multinational Strike Force." ***Journal of Defense and Diplomacy***, 4:3 (1986),

2024. _____. "Low Intensity Conflict: Global Challenge." ***Teaching Political Science***, 15:1 (Fall 1987), 15-23.

2025. Mullins, Wayman C. "Stopping Terrorism: The Problems Poised by the Organizational Infrastructure of Terrorist Organizations." ***Journal of Contemporary Criminal Justice***, 4:4 (1988), 214-228.

2026. Nadel, Seth R. "An Attitude Called Survival." ***TVI Journal***, 2:2 (1981), 2-4.

2027. Nagel, W. H. "A Social - Legal View on the Suppression of Terrorists." ***International Journal of the Sociology of Law***, 8:3 (1980), 213-226.

2028. Navasky, Victor. "Security and Terrorism." ***Nation***, 232 (February 14, 1981), 167-186.

2029. Nestlehutt, M. S. "Combatting Terrorism: Policies in the Making." ***TVI Report***, 6:4 (1986), 16-18.

2030. Netanyahu, Benjamin. "Terrorism: How the West Can Win." In: B. Netanyahu, ed. ***Terrorism: How the West Can Win.*** New York: Farrar, Straus, Giroux, 1986. pp. 199-226.

2031. _____. "Terrorism Can Be Eliminated." In: B. Szumski, ed. ***Terrorism: Opposing Viewpoints.*** St.Paul, MN.: Greenhaven Press, 1986. pp. 183-190.

2032. Newman, Robert P. "Making Marines Terror Resistant." ***Marine Corps Gazette***, 74:1 (January 1990), 20-21.

2033. Norton, John J. "Terrorism - The Police Response." ***The Police Chief***, 53:4 (1986), 8-27.

2034. Nudell, Mayer, and Norman Antokol. "Contingency Planning for Terrorism." ***Risk Management***, 33 (July 1986), 20-22+; 33 (August 1986), 30-32+.

2035. Nydele, Ann. "Practice: Designing for Terrorism and Other Aggressions." ***Architectural Record***, (January 1986), 37-43.

2036. _____. "Designing for Terrorism and Other Aggressions." ***TVI Report***, 7:1 (1987), 12-19.

2037. O'Brien, Conor Cruise. "Impediments and Prerequisites to Counter-Terrorism." In: C. W. Kegley, ed. ***International Terrorism: Characteristics, Causes, Controls.*** New York: St. Martin's Press, 1990. pp. 201-206.

2038. O'Brien, William V. "Counterterrorism: Lessons from Israel." ***Strategic Review***, 13:4 (1985), 32-44.

2039. _____. "Counterterror, Law and Morality." In: L. B. Thompson, ed. ***Low Intensity Conflict.*** Lexington, MA.: Lexington Books, 1989. pp. 187-208.

2040. _____. "Reprisals, Deterrence and Self Defence in Counterterror Operations." ***Virginia Journal of International Law***, 30:2 (Winter 1990), 421-478.

2041. _____. "Counter-Terror Deterrence/Defense and Just-War Doctrine." ***Theological Studies***, 48 (December 1987), 647-675.

2042. O'Keefe, Bernard. "Technology: An Introduction." ***Terrorism***, 10:3 (1987), 269-270.

2043. O'Leary, Brendan. "Terrorism: Review Article." ***British Journal of Criminology***, 28 (Winter 1988), 97-107.

2044. O'Neill, Bard E., and James B. Motley. "Global Terrorism: What Should the United States Do - Summary." In: ***1980's Decade of Confrontation.*** Washington, D.C.: National Defence University Press, 1981. pp. 237-242.

2045. Oakley, Robert B. "Combatting International Terrorism." ***Department of State Bulletin***, 85:2099 (June 1985), 73-77.

2046. _____. "Terrorism: The Fight." ***Army Quarterly***, 115 (April 1985), 167-180.

2047. _____. "Combatting International Terrorism." ***Drug Enforcement***, 12:1 (Summer 1985), 25-27+.

2048. _____. "Fighting International Terrorism." In: R.H. Ward and H. E. Smith, eds. ***International Terrorism: The Domestic Response.*** Chicago, IL.: University of Illinois at Chicago, Office of International Criminal Justice, 1987. pp. 127-133.

2049. Olin, W. Ronald. "Tactical Crisis Management: The Challenge of the 80's." ***FBI Law Enforcement Bulletin,*** 49:11 (November 1980), 20-25.

2050. _____. "Current Trends in the Terrorist War." ***The Police Chief,*** 53:4 (1986), 28-30.

2051. Oots, Kent L. "Bargaining with Terrorists: Organizational Considerations." ***Terrorism,*** 13:2 (1990), 145-158.

2052. Overton, James. "Interpol's Perspective on International Terrorism and Drug Trafficking." In: D. Rowe, ed. ***International Drug Trafficking.*** Chicago, IL.: University of Illinois at Chicago, Office of International Criminal Justice, 1988. pp. 5-14.

2053. "Overview of Terrorism for the Police Administrator. (Panel Discussion)." ***Police Chief,*** 54 (March 1987), 71-72+.

2054. Paderson, John G. "Defense Against Terrorism." ***Ordnance,*** 4:3 (Summer 1986), 22-24.

2055. Pagano, C. L. "An Active Patrol Force: The Strategic Essential." ***Police Chief,*** 56:3 (1989), 53-56.

2056. Palumbo, L. F. "In the Eyes of the Beholder." ***Security Management,*** 29 (October 1985), 115-116+.

2057. Partan, D. G., and F. A. Boyle. "Military Responses to Terrorism." In: ***Proceedings of the 81st Annual Meeting of the American Society of International Law.*** Washington, D.C.: American Society of International Law, 1990. pp. 287-296.

2058. Paschall, Rod. "Low-Intensity Conflict Doctrine: Who Needs It?" ***Parameters,*** 15:3 (Autumn 1985), 33-45.

2059. Patt, Douglas. "Counterterrorist Mandate." ***Military Intelligence,*** 8:3 (July-September 1982), 28-29+.

2060. Peres, Shimon. "The Threat and the Response." In: B. Netanyahu, ed. ***International Terrorism: Challenge and Response.*** New Brunswick, NJ.: Transaction Books, 1981. pp. 8-11.

2061. Perez, Frank H. "Combatting Terrorism in the 1980s." ***The Police Chief,*** (January 1982), 129-130.

2062. Perez, Martha B. "Clandestine Tactics and Technology." ***Police Chief,*** 48 (May 1981), 50-51.

2063. Petluck, R. "Forensic Ballistics in Counter-Insurgency Warfare." In: ***Anti Terrorism - IDENTA - 85.*** Boulder, CO.: Westview Press, 1988. pp. 72-80.

2064. Pockrass, Robert M. "Building a Civil Police Counter-Terrorist Team." ***Conflict,*** 8:4 (1988), 327-332.

2065. Pollak, R. "International Terrorism - A New Threat to Information Systems Security." In: ***Anti Terrorism - IDENTA - 85.*** Boulder, CO.: Westview Press, 1985. pp. 115-127.

2066. Pollick, Arthur L. "Terrorism: Communications Officer Tells How He Was Shot." ***State,*** 294 (November 1986), 6-8.

2067. Post, Jerrold M. "Group and Organizational Dynamics of Political Terrorism: Implications for Counterterrorist Policy." In: P. Wilkinson and A. M. Stewart, eds. ***Contemporary Research on Terrorism.*** Aberdeen: Aberdeen University Press, 1987. pp. 307-317.

2068. _____. "Countering Terrorist Strategies." ***Terrorism,*** 12:2 (1989), 129-131.

2069. "A Primer on Tailing." ***TVI Journal,*** 4:4-6 (1983), 6-13.

2070. Prodoroff, Allan. "Terrorists Want You." ***Airman,*** 26:9 (1983), 36-41.

2071. "Protecting the World from the Terrorist Threat." ***Police Chief,*** 52 (April 1986), 28-42+.

2072. Purkitt, Helen. "Dealing with Terrorism: Deterrence and the Search for an Alternative Model." In: M. Banks, ed. ***Conflict in World Society.*** Brighton: Wheatsheaf Books, 1984. pp. 161-173.

2073. Quainton, A. C. E. "Combatting Terrorism - A Strategy of Partnership." ***Police Chief,*** 47:5 (1980), 22-24.

2074. _____. "Moral and Ethical Considerations in Defining a Counter-Terrorist Policy." In: D. C. Rapoport and Y. Alexander, eds. ***The Rationalization of Terrorism.*** Frederick, MD.: University Publications of America, 1982. pp. 39-45.

2075. _____. "Terrorism: Policy, Action, and Reaction." In: L. Z. Freedman and Y. Alexander, eds. ***Perspectives on Terrorism.*** Wilmington, DE.: Scholarly Resources, 1983. pp. 169-176.

2076. Quarles, Chester L. "On Your Guard: Meeting the Threat of Terrorism." ***Evangelical Missions Quarterly,*** 23 (July 1987), 258-267.

2077. Quester, George H. "Eliminating the Terrorist Opportunity." In: R. D. Rapoport and Y. Alexander, eds. ***The Morality of Terrorism.*** New York: Pergamon Press, 1982. pp. 325-346.

2078. Rabin, Yitzhak. "An International Agency Against Terrorism." In: B. Netanyahu, ed. ***Terrorism: How the West Can Win.*** New York: Farrar, Straus, Giroux, 1986. pp. 182-185.

2079. Ramon, J. "Terrorism Takes Off." ***Security Management,*** 31 (June 1987), 62-64.

2080. Rao, T. S. Rama. "State Terror as a Response to Terrorism and Vice Versa." In: R. P. Dhokalia and K. N. Rao, eds. ***Terrorism and International Law.*** New Delhi: Indian Society of International Law, 1988. pp. 31-41.

2081. Rescorla, Richard. "In a Crisis: Managing the Unmanageable." ***TVI Journal,*** 2:2 (1981), 10-18.

2082. Revell, Oliver B. "No Hiding Place." ***Police,*** 21:8 (April-May 1989), 12,14,16.

2083. _____. "Counter Terrorism Planning and Operations." ***Police Chief,*** 57:8 (August 1990), 61-67.

2084. Richard, Marcel. "The Role of the Military in Countering Terrorism." In: B. Macdonald, ed. ***Terror.*** Toronto: Canadian Institute of International Studies, 1987. pp. 113-117.

2085. "Riot Control Tactics." ***TVI Journal,*** 1:12 (1980), 2-7.

2086. Roberts, Guy B. "Covert Responses: The Moral Dilemma." In: N. C. Livingstone and T. E. Arnold, eds. ***Fighting Back: Winning the War Against Terrorism.*** Lexington, MA.: Lexington Books, 1985. pp. 133-144.

2087. Robitaille, E. W. "Terrorism and the Role of the Police." ***Law and Order,*** 29:9 (1981), 57-59.

2088. "The Role of Technology in Combating Terrorism: A Symposium." ***Terrorism,*** 10:3 (1987), 211-287.

2089. Ronso, Lee. "TTAPS for Terrorists." ***Security Management,*** 30:12 (December 1986), 53-56.

2090. Roosevelt, Edith K. "Terrorism: High Tech Counterattack." ***Combat Arms,*** 5 (September 1987), 40-46.

2091. "Rooting Out A Root of Terror?" ***TVI Journal,*** 4:10-12 (1983), 7-11.

2092. Rosenstock, Robert. "Past Remedies: Successes and Failures." ***International Journal of Group Tensions,*** 12:1-4 (1982), 122-141.

2093. Rosenthal, Betsy R. "Countering International Terrorism: Building a Public Consensus." ***Whittier Law Review***, 8:3 (1986), 747-754.

2094. Rosetti, Joe. "Joining Forces in the Fight Against Terrorism." ***Security Management***, (December 1986), 41-43.

2095. Rothenberg, Elliot. "Terrorists Should Be Given Stricter Penalties." In: B. Szumski, ed. ***Terrorism: Opposing Viewpoints***. St.Paul, MN.: Greenhaven Press, 1986. pp. 209-214.

2096. Roukis, George S. "Negotiating with Terrorists." In: P. J. Montana and G. S. Roukis, eds. ***Managing Terrorism***. Westport, CT.: Quorum Books, 1983. pp. 109-122.

2097. Safir, Howard. "Courtroom Security: The International Scene." ***Security Management***, 33:6 (June 1989), 43-46.

2098. Sarkesian, Sam C. "Defensive Responses." In: U. Ra'anan, et al. ***Hydra of Carnage***. Lexington, MA.: Lexington Books, 1986. pp. 201-220.

2099. Sayre, Robert M. "The War of Words: Can Diplomacy Be Effective?" In: N. C. Livingstone and T. E. Arnold, eds. ***Fighting Back: Winning the War Against Terrorism***. Lexington, MA.: Lexington Books, 1985. pp. 85-94.

2100. _____. "Combating Terrorism." ***Asia-Pacific Defence Forum***, (Spring 1984), 29+.

2101. Scanlon, R. A. "Global Peace Keepers." ***Law Enforcement Technology***, 16:9 (October 1989), 34-36.

2102. Schembri, A. J. "'Blue Magic': Blueprint for Terror." ***Police Chief***, 40:12 (1981), 20-21.

2103. Schiller, David T. "From a National to an International Response." In: H. H. Tucker, ed. ***Combating the Terrorists***. New York: Facts on File, 1988. pp. 185-202.

2104. Schmid, Alex P. "Force or Conciliation? An Overview of Some Problems Associated with Current Anti-Terrorist Response Strategies." ***Violence, Aggression and Terrorism***, 2:2 (1988), 149-178.

2105. Scotti, Tony. "Transportation Security." In: B. M. Jenkins, ed. ***Terrorism and Personal Protection***. Stoneham, MA.: Butterworth, 1985. pp. 354-368.

2106. "Security in Fashion." ***TVI Journal***, 1:11 (1980), 11-13.

2107. Sederberg, Peter C. "Responses to Dissident Terrorism: From Myth to Maturity." In: C. W. Kegley, ed. ***International Terrorism: Characteristics, Causes, Controls***. New York: St. Martin's Press, 1990. pp. 262-280.

2108. Seger, Karl A. "Managing the Threat of Terrorism." ***Fire & Arson Investigation***, 37:1 (1986), 30-33.

2109. Shamgar, Meir. "Proposed Countermeasures for the Democratic World: Opening Remarks." In: B. Netanyahu, ed. ***International Terrorism: Challenge and Response***. New Brunswick, NJ.: Transaction Books, 1981. pp. 265-275.

2110. Shani, Joshua. "Airborne Raids: A Potent Weapon in Countering Transnational Terrorism." ***Military Intelligence***, (March-April 1984), 41-54.

2111. Shultz, George. "Low-Intensity Warfare: The Challenge of Ambiguity." ***"Department of State Bulletin***, 86 (March 1986), 15-18.

2112. Shultz, Richard H. "The State of the Operational Art: A Critical Review of Anti-Terrorist Programs." In: R. H. Shultz and S. Sloan, eds. ***Responding to the Terrorist Threat***. New York: Pergamon Press, 1980. pp. 18-58.

2113. _____. "Can Democratic Governments Use Military Force in the War Against Terrorism? The U.S. Confrontation with Libya." ***World Affairs***, 148:4 (1986), 205-215.

2114. _____. "On Low Intensity Conflict and National Security Policy: A Comparative Analysis." In: E. A. Kolodziej and P. M. Morgan, eds. ***Security and Arms Control, Volume 2: A Guide to International Policymaking.*** Westport. CO.: Greenwood Press, 1989. pp. 239-268.

2115. Silverstein, Martin. "Medical Technology in Combatting Terrorism." ***Terrorism,*** 10:3 (1987), 277-280.

2116. Simpson, Howard R. "Rivalry Among Counterterrorist Forces." ***TVI Journal,*** 5:3 (1985), 33-35.

2117. _____. "Organizing for Counter-Terrorism." ***Strategic Review,*** 10 (Winter 1982), 28-33.

2118. Sloan, Stephen. "In Search of a Counterterrorism Doctrine." ***Military Review,*** 66:1 (June 1986), 44-48.

2119. Smith, Brent, and James Fraser. "Countering Terrorism; The Development of an Instructional Model for Appropriate Military Involvement." ***Conflict Quarterly,*** 2:3 (1981), 30-39.

2120. Smith, G. Davidson. "Military Options in Response to State-Sponsored Terrorism." ***Terrorism and Political Violence,*** 1:3 (July 1989), 294-323.

2121. Spates, C. R., et al. "Intervention in Events of Terrorism." In: L. J. Hertzberg, G. F. Astrum, et al, eds. ***Violent Behavior: Assessment and Intervention. Vol. 1.*** Great Neck, MD.: PMA Publishing Corp., 1990. pp. 185-199.

2122. St. John, Peter. "Analysis and Response of a Decade of Terrorism." ***International Perspectives,*** (September-October 1981), 2-5.

2123. Standenmaier, William O., and Alan N. Sabrosky. "A Strategy of Counterrevolutionary War." ***Military Review,*** 65:2 (1985), 2-15.

2124. Stevens, James W., and David W. MacKenna. "Police Capabilities for Responding to Violent Criminal Activity and Terrorism." ***Police Studies,*** 11:3 (Fall 1988), 116-123.

2125. Stewart, Bernard L. "Terrorism: Are National Networks an Achilles' Heel?." ***Signal,*** 40:5 (1986), 31-39.

2126. _____. "The Role of Technology in Combatting Terrorism." ***Terrorism,*** 10:3 (1987), 211-212.

2127. Stewart, James. "The Complexity of Terrorism: A View from the Line." In: R. H. Ward and H. E. Smith, eds. ***International Terrorism: The Domestic Response.*** Chicago, IL.: University of Illinois at Chicago, Office of International Criminal Justice, 1987. pp. 59-64.

2128. Stohl, Michael, and James R. Brownell. "Research Design for a Study of Threat Communication and Audience Perception of Domestic Terrorism." ***Political Communication and Persuasion,*** 1:2 (1981), 209-215.

2129. _____. "Responding to the Terrorist Threat: Fashions and Fundamentals." In: M. Stohl, ed. ***The Politics of Terrorism.*** New York: Marcel Dekker, 1988. 579-599.

2130. Stratton, Ray E., and August G. Jannarone. "Toward a Strategic Targeting Doctrine for Special Operations Forces." ***Air University Review,*** 36:5 (July-August 1985), 24-29.

2131. Stuesser, Lee. "Active Defense: State Military Response to International Terrorism." ***California Western International Law Journal,*** 17:1 (Winter 1987), 1-42.

2132. Sulc, Lawrence B. "Counter-Terrorism - First Line, Last Line." ***Terrorism,*** 11:3 (1988), 241-246.

2133. Swanson, A. B. "Aid Programs to People to Offset Terrorism." In: H. Chesnutt, ed. ***Contributions of Technology to International Conflict Resolution.*** Oxford: Pergamon Press, 1987. pp. 23-26.

2134. "TVI Interview, Commander Ray Kendall, Secretary General of Interpol." ***TVI Journal,*** 6:1 (Summer 1985), 8-11.

2135. "TVI Interview, John Simpson, President of Interpol's General Assembly." ***TVI Journal,*** 6:1 (Summer 1985), 12-13.

2136. "Taking on Terrorism: An Interview with Professor Franco Ferracuti." ***Violence, Aggression and Terrorism,*** 3:4 (1989), 249-268.

2137. "Taking on Terrorism: An Interview with Professor Paul Wilkinson." ***Violence, Aggression and Terrorism,*** 3:3 (1989), 203-236.

2138. Tanay, E. "Pseudo-Political Terrorism." ***Journal of Forensic Sciences,*** 32:1 (1987), 192-200.

2139. Taylor, Robert W. "Managing Terrorist Incidents." ***The Bureaucrat,*** (Winter 1983-84), 53-58.

2140. "Terror in Tall Buildings." ***TVI Journal,*** 4:7-9 (1983), 2-3.

2141. "Terrorism (Symposium)." ***The Police Chief,*** 52 (April 1986), 28-54.

2142. "Terrorism in the 80's." ***Police Chief,*** (March 1985), 130-141.

2143. "Terrorist Threats Boosts Military Security Market." ***Corporate Security Digest,*** 4:10 (1990), 8-9.

2144. Thackrah, John R. "Army - Police Collaboration Against Terrorism." ***Police Journal,*** 56:1 (1983), 41-52.

2145. _____. "Reactions to Terrorism and Riots." In: J. R. Thackrah, ed. ***Contemporary Policing: An Examination of Society in the 1980's.*** London: Sphere, 1985. pp. 145-160.

2146. Thomas, James W. "Art of Anti-Terrorist Engineering." ***Naval Civil Engineering,*** 26:2 (Fall 1986), 18-19.

2147. Thompson, Michael. "Technology Against Terrorism." ***Security,*** 24:7 (July 1987), 36-40+.

2148. "To Be Abroad or Not to Be?" ***TVI Journal,*** 4:7-9 (1983), 3-6.

2149. Tovar, B. Hugh. "Active Responses." In: U. Ra'anan, et al. ***Hydra of Carnage.*** Lexington, MA.: Heath-Lexington, 1986. pp. 231-250.

2150. Trout, John E., and Curt P. Betts. "Security Engineering." ***Military Engineer,*** 80 (July 1988), 368-371.

2151. Truby, David. "Red Light for Blue Light." ***TVI Journal,*** 1:3 (1980), 2-5.

2152. Tugwell, Maurice A. "Tugwell's Terrorist." ***Canadian Lawyer,*** (November 1982), 16-18.

2153. Turner, Billy M. "Reacting to Terrorism: Demystifying the Terrorist Network." ***Security Management,*** 29:2 (1985), 26-29.

2154. _____. "Terrorist Attacks Upon Technological Systems." ***Journal of Security Administration,*** 7:2 (1984), 25-33.

2155. "U.S. Offers Rewards for Terrorists." ***Department of State Bulletin,*** 85 (December 1985), 77-80.

2156. United States. Department of State. Bureau of Public Affairs. "Economic Sanctions to Combat International Terrorism." ***Department of State Bulletin,*** 86:2115 (1986), 27-31.

2157. Van den Bergh, Harry. "Maintaining the Balance." In: B. Netanyahu, ed. ***International Terrorism: Challenge and Response.*** New Brunswick, NJ.: Transaction Books, 1981. pp. 283-288.

2158. Vlahos, Michael, and Michael Peck. "Counter-Terrorism: Another Look." ***Journal of Defense and Diplomacy***, 4:2 (February 1986), 7-9,61.

2159. Waghelstein, John D. "Post - Vietnam Counterinsurgency Doctrine." ***Military Review***, 65:5 (1985), 45-49.

2160. Wallace, J. "Firearms Examinations in a Terrorist Situation." In: ***Anti-Terrorism - IDENTA - 85.*** Boulder, CO.: Westview Press, 1985. pp. 52-62.

2161. "The War Against Terrorism." ***Harvard International Review***, 7 (May/June 1985), 4-23.

2162. Ward, Richard H. "The Investigation of Terrorist Activities." In: R. H. Ward and H. E. Smith, eds. ***International Terrorism: The Domestic Response.*** Chicago, IL.: University of Illinois at Chicago, Office of International Criminal Justice, 1987. pp. 119-126.

2163. Wardlaw, Grant. "Terrorism and Para-Military Forces." ***Pacific Defence Reporter***, 7:1 (1980), 46-51.

2164. _____. "The Armed Forces and Public Order Policing." ***Pacific Defence Reporter***, (October 1981), 44-48.

2165. _____. "Policy Dilemmas in Responding to International Terrorism." ***Australian Quarterly***, 58:3 (Spring 1986), 278-285.

2166. _____. "State Response to International Terrorism: Some Cautionary Comments." In: R. O. Slater and M. Michael, eds. ***Current Perspectives on International Terrorism.*** London: Macmillan Press, 1988. pp. 206-245.

2167. _____. "More Rational Approach Needed for Threat Assessment and Counter-Terrorist Policy." ***Pacific Defense Reporter***, (December 1986 - January 1987), 82-84.

2168. _____. "Terrorism: Security Needed but Don't Amplify the Threat." ***Pacific Defense Reporter***, 6:7 (December-January 1989-90), 87-89.

2169. Warner, Bruce W. "The Lessons of Munich: The Development of Western Anti-Terrorist Squads." ***TVI Journal***, 1:12 (1980), 9-20.

2170. Warner, John. "Countering Contemporary Terrorism." ***Police Chief***, 54:5 (1987), 28,31-32.

2171. Waugh, William L. "Integrating the Policy Models of Terrorism and Emergency Management." ***Policy Studies Review***, 6:2 (November 1986), 287-301.

2172. Webb, David. "Researching Terrorism: A Police Perspective." In: R. H. Ward and H. E. Smith, eds. ***International Terrorism: The Domestic Response.*** Chicago, IL.: University of Illinois at Chicago, Office of International Criminal Justice, 1987. pp. 99-106.

2173. Webster, William H. "Terrorism as a Crime. ***FBI Law Enforcement Bulletin***, 55:5 (1986), 11-13.

2174. Wegener, Ulrich K. "Defeating Terrorism." ***Military Engineer***, 79 (March-April 1987), 96-99.

2175. Western, T. F. "Countering Terrorism with the MAU." ***Marine Corps Gazette***, 70:3 (1986), 40-41.

2176. Whitcomb, G. E. "Blossoms, Bullets, Bombs, Bodies: A Mad Mixture." ***Police Journal***, 61:2 (April-June 1989), 131-135.

2177. Wilkinson, Paul. "Proposals for a Liberal - Democratic Government Response to Terrorism and Low - Intensity Violence at Domestic and International Levels." In: B. M. Jenkins, ed. ***Terrorism and Beyond: An International Conference on Terrorism and Low-Level Conflict.*** Santa Monica, CA.: RAND Corporation, 1980. pp. 203-232.

2178. _____. "Proposals to Government and International Responses to Terrorism." In: P. Wilkinson, ed. ***British Perspectives on Terrorism.*** London: Allen & Unwin, 1981. pp. 161-193.

2179. _____. "Proposals for Government and International Responses to Terror." ***Terrorism,*** 5:1-2 (1981), 161-193.

2180. _____. "Pathways Out of Terrorism for Democratic Societies." In: P. Wilkinson and A. M. Stewart, eds. ***Contemporary Research on Terrorism.*** Aberdeen: Aberdeen University Press, 1987. pp. 453-465.

2181. _____. "Terrorism Versus Liberal Democracy: The Problems of Response." In: W. Gutteridge, ed. ***The New Terrorism.*** London: Mansell, 1986. pp. 3-28.

2182. _____. "Trends in International Terrorism and the American Response." In: ***Terrorism and International Order.*** London: Royal Institute of International Affairs, 1986. pp. 37-55.

2183. Williams, Hubert. "Terrorism and Local Police." ***Terrorism,*** 8:4 (1986), 345-350.

2184. Wolf, John B. "Enforcement Terrorism." ***Police Studies,*** 3:4 (1981), 45-54.

2185. Woods, C. "Problems of International Terrorism." ***Australian Journal of Forensic Sciences,*** 12:2-3 (1979/80), 67-74.

2186. Yardley, Michael. "MACE a Multi-National Approach to Countering Terrorism." ***International Defence Review,*** (November 1986), 1621-1625.

2187. _____. "Combatting Terrorism." ***Armed Forces,*** 6 (April 1987), 161-165.

2188. Zartman, I. William. "Negotiating Effectively with Terrorists." In: B. Rubin, ed. ***The Politics of Counterterrorism.*** Lanham, MD.: University Publications of America, 1990. pp. 163-188.

3. Documents and Reports

2189. Alexander, Yonah, et al. ***Terrorism: What Should Be Our Response.*** Washington, D.C.: American Enterprise Institute, 1982. 25p.

2190. ***Anti Terrorism; Forensic Science; Psychology in Police Investigations: Proceedings of IDENTA-85, the International Congress on Techniques for Criminal Identification.*** Boulder, CO.: Westview Press, 1985. 424p.

2191. "Appendix III - INTERPOL's Resolution on Terrorism." In: M. C. Bassiouni, ed. ***Legal Responses to International Terrorism: U.S. Procedural Aspects."*** Dordrecht: Martinus Nijhoff, 1988. pp. 381-384.

2192. Ashby, Timothy. ***Winning the War Against Terrorism.*** Backgrounder, No. 4. Washington, D.C.: The Heritage Foundation, 1986. 9p.

2193. Bean, Harold G. ***Diplomats and Terrorists II: Overseas Security - Our People Are The Key.*** Washington, D.C.: Georgetown University, School of Foreign Service, 1987. 96p.

2194. Bedlington, Stanley S. ***Combatting International Terrorism: U.S. - European Cooperation and Political Will - Policy Paper.*** Washington D.C.: The Atlantic Council of the United States, 1986. 93p.

2195. Berrong, L. B., and P. T. Gerard. ***Combatting the Terrorist Threat.*** Carlisle Barracks, PA.: Army War College, 1985. 117p.

2196. Carlson, Joseph Ray, Jr. ***A Survey to Determine the Perceived Adequacy of Counter Terrorist Training of Security Guards at Anniston Army Depot.*** Ph.D. Dissertation. Hattiesburg, MS.: University of Southern Mississippi, 1986. 94p.

2197. Center for Law and Education of Americans for Effective Law Enforcement. ***Terrorism - Avoidance and Survival.*** Rockville, MD.: National Criminal Justice Reference Service, 1981. 33p.

2198. Charters, David, and Maurice A. Tugwell. ***Armies in Low-Intensity Conflict: A Comparative Study of Institutional Adaptation to New Forms of Warfare.*** ORAE Extra Mural Paper NO. 38. Ottawa: Operational Research and Analysis Establishment, 1985. 320p.

2199. Collins, John M. ***U.S. and Soviet Special Operations.*** Report 87-398S. Washington, D.C.: Library of Congress, Congressional research Service, 1986. 179p.

2200. Council of Europe. ***Combatting Terrorism: Collection of Texts.*** European Conference of Ministers Responsible for Combating Terrorism. Strasbourg: Council of Europe, 1986. 60p.

2201. Crenshaw, Martha. ***Terrorism and International Cooperation.*** Occasional Paper Series: 11. New York: Institute for East-West Studies, 1989. 89p.

2202. _____. "Incentives for Terrorism" Paper Presented at the ***Proceedings of the 10th Annual Symposium on the Role of Behavioral Science in Physical Security,*** held on April 23-24, 1985, in Washington, D.C. pp. 15-24.

2203. Curtis, B. G., ed. ***Outthinking the Terrorist: An International Challenge. Proceedings of the 10th Annual Symposium on the Role of Behavioral Science in Physical Security.*** Springfield, VA.: Defence Nuclear Agency, 1985. 110p.

2204. Daly, J. C., et al. ***Terrorism - What Should Be Our Response.*** Washington, D.C.: American Enterprise Institute for Public Policy Research, 1982. 27p.

2205. De Capua, Michael L. "Security System Engineering: Countering the Terrorist Engineering Services." Paper Presented at the ***1986 Carnahan Conference on Security Technology,*** held on May 14-16, 1986 at the University of Kentucky. pp. 39-41.

2206. De Vore, R. W., ed. ***Carnahan Conference on Security Technology: Electronic Crime Countermeasures: Proceedings.*** Lexington, KY.: University of Kentucky Press, 1988. 108p.

2207. Dixon, H. L. ***Low Intensity Conflict Overview, Definitions and Policy Concerns. CLIC Papers.*** SBI-AD-F000 145. Langley AFB, VA.: Army Air Force Center for Low Intensity Conflict, 1989. 48p.

2208. Evans, J. C., M. K. Pilgrim and C. J. Potter. ***Transition from Terrorist Event Management to Consequence Management, Executive Summary.*** Vienna, VA.: BDM Corporation, 1982. 62p.

2209. Ficuciello, A. ***Terrorism: Why: In Search of a Strategy to Defeat It.*** Carlisle Barracks, PA.: Army War College, 1985. 64p.

2210. Fuller, Cornell. ***Terrorism: Challenge and Response.*** Carlisle Barracks, PA.: U.S. Army War College, 1986. 29p.

2211. Gaines, G. P. ***Progress on a Multinational Policy Against Terrorism.*** Maxwell AFB, AL.: Air War College, 1989. 57p.

2212. Gal-Or, Noemi. ***International Cooperation in the Suppression of Terrorism.*** Ph.D. Dissertation. Geneva: University of Geneva, 1983. 439p.

2213. Gallis, Paul E., and James P. Wootten. ***Combatting State Sponsored Terrorism: Differing U.S. and West European Perspectives.*** Report 88-313F. Washington, D.C.: Library of Congress, Congressional Research Service, 1988. 55p.

2214. Goodpaster, Andrew J., et al. ***Combatting International Terrorism: U.S.- Allied Cooperation and Political Will.*** Washington, D.C.: The Atlantic Council of the United States, 1986. 72p.

2215. Gregory, Frank. ***Policing the Democratic State: How Much Force.*** Conflict Studies, No. 194. London: Centre for Security and Conflict Studies, 1986. 25p.

2216. Harper, James C. "Conducting Anti-Terrorism Operations and Contingency Planning for Risk Reduction of the Terrorist Threat." In: ***Terrorism: Special Studies, 1985-1988, First Supplement.*** Bethesda, MD.: University Publications of America, 1989. Reel 4. Frames 0001-0186. 186p.

2217. Herz, Martin F., ed. ***Diplomats and Terrorists: What Works, What Doesn't: A Symposium.*** Washington, D.C.: Institute for the Study of Diplomacy, Georgetown University, 1982. 69p.

2218. Hix, B. "Preparing Personnel to Live with a Protean Terrorist Threat." In: ***Proceeding of the 9th Annual Symposium on the Role of Behavioral Science in Physical Security,*** held on April 3-4,1984 in Springfield, VA. pp. 27-34.

2219. Hoffman, Bruce. ***The Prevention of Terrorism and Rehabilitation of Terrorists: Some Preliminary Thoughts.*** RAND P-7059. Santa Monica, CA.: RAND Corporation, 1985. 5p.

2220. _____. ***Commando Raids: 1946-1983.*** RAND N-2316-USDP. Santa Monica, CA.: Rand Corporation, 1985. 64p.

2221. Hosmer, Steven T., and George K. Tanham. ***Countering Covert Aggression.*** RAND N-2412. Santa Monica, CA.: Rand Corporation, 1986. 28p.

2222. Hough, M., ed. ***Revolutionary Warfare and Counter Insurgency.*** Pretoria, South Africa: Institute for Strategic Studies, University of Pretoria, 1984. 47p.

2223. Houle, E. H. ***Use of Military Force to Counter International Terrorism - A Policy Dilemma.*** Master's Thesis. Fort Leavenworth, KS.: Army Command and General Staff College, 1987. 188p.

2224. Jenkins, Brian M. "Asymmetries in Dealing with Terrorism." In: ***Proceedings of the 9th Annual Symposium on the Role of Behavioral Science in Physical Security,*** held on April 3-4, 1984, in Springfield, VA. pp. 39-47.

2225. _____. ***Combatting Terrorism: Some Policy Implications.*** RAND P-6666. Santa Monica, CA.: RAND Corporation, 1981. 11p.

2226. _____. ***Combatting Terrorism Becomes a War.*** RAND P-6988. Santa Monica, CA.: RAND Corporation, 1984. 7p.

2227. _____. ***Diplomats on the Front Line.*** RAND P-6748. Santa Monica, CA.: RAND Corporation, 1982. 11p.

2228. _____. ***Fighting Terrorism: An Enduring Task.*** RAND P-6585. Santa Monica, CA.: RAND Corporation, 1981. 8p.

2229. _____. ***International Terrorism: Choosing the Right Target.*** RAND P-6597. Santa Monica, CA.: RAND Corporation, 1981. 8p.

2230. _____. ***The Lessons of Beirut: Testimony Before the Long Commission.*** RAND N-2114-RC. Santa Monica, CA.: RAND Corporation, 1984. 13p.

2231. _____. ***Military Force May Not Be Ruled Out.*** RAND P-7103. Santa Monica, CA.: RAND Corporation, 1985. 4p.

2232. _____. ***A Strategy for Combating Terrorism.*** RAND P-6624. Santa Monica, CA.: RAND Corporation, 1981. 8p.

2233. _____. ***Talking to Terrorists.*** RAND P-6750. Santa Monica, CA.: RAND Corporation, 1982. 15p.

2234. _____. ***Terrorism: Between Prudence and Paranoia.*** RAND P-6946. Santa Monica, CA.: RAND Corporation, 1983. 5p.

2235. _____. ***Should Our Arsenal Against Terrorism Include Assassination.*** RAND P-7303. Santa Monica, CA.: Rand Corporation, 1987. 13p.

2236. _____. ***The Possibility of Soviet - American Cooperation Against Terrorism.*** RAND P-7541. Santa Monica, CA.: RAND Corporation, 1989. 20p.

2237. ***Joint Low-Intensity Conflict Project Final Report, Volume 1. Analytical Review of Low-Intensity Conflict.*** Langley AFB, VA.: Army-Air Force Center for Low Intensity Conflict, 1986. 248p.

2238. Jones, Arnold P. ***International Terrorism: Status of GAO's Review of the FBI's International Terrorism Program.*** Washington, D.C.: U.S. General Accounting Office, 1989. 9p.

2239. Kupperman, Robert H. ***The Challenge of Terrorism to the Military.*** Washington, D.C.: Army Science Board, 1982. 16p.

2240. _____. "Terrorism in the Decade Ahead - Adaptation, Technology and Response." In: ***The 1980's: Decade of Confrontation. Proceedings of the 8th Annual National Security Affairs Conference, 13-15 July, 1981.*** Washington, D.C.: National Defence University Press, 1981. pp. 265-284.

2241. _____. Edward Marks and Debra Van Opstal, eds. ***Combating Terrorism: A Matter of Leverage.*** Washington, D.C.: Center for Strategic and International Studies, 1986. 71p.

2242. Leeman, Richard W. ***The Rhetoric of Counter-Terrorism: A Strategy of Response.*** Ph.D. Dissertation. Adelphi, MD.: University of Maryland, 1990. 343p.

2243. Lum, Tom. ***Combatting Terrorism - A Response in Kind.*** Carlisle Barracks, PA.: U.S. Army War College, 1987. 21p.

2244. Mickolus, Edward F. ***Combatting International Terrorism: A Quantitative Analysis.*** Ph.D. Dissertation. New Haven, CT.: Yale University, 1981, 615p.

2245. Murphy, John F., et al. "International Cooperation in the Prevention and Suppression of Terrorism." In: R. W. Nelson and J. R. Hall, eds. ***Proceedings of the 80th Annual Meeting of the American Society of International Law,*** Washington, D.C.: American Society of International Law, 1988. pp. 386-407.

2246. Nelson, G. W. ***Terrorism: The Military Challenge.*** Carlisle Barracks, PA.: Army War College, 1987. 33p.

2247. O'Connor, M. F., and P. J. Sticha. ***Development of Decision Aids for Counter-Terrorist Applications.*** McLean, VA.: Decision and Designs, 1980. 100p.

2248. Oakley, Robert B. ***International Terrorism: Current Trends and the U.S. Response.*** Current Policy, No. 706. Washington, DC.: U.S. Department of State, Bureau of Public Affairs, 1985. 7p.

2249. ***Passports: Implications of Deleting the Birthplace in U.S. Passports.*** Washington, D.C.: General Accounting Office, National Security and International Affairs Division, 1987. 20p.

2250. Phillips, W. M. ***Evolution and Impact of Terrorism in the 20th Century and the U.S. Response.*** Maxwell AFB, AL.: Air War College, 1989. 83p.

2251. Rogers, Larry J. ***Executive Protection Against Acts of Terrorism Directed at the Private Residence.*** Lexington, KY.: Office of Engineering Services, University of Kentucky, 1986. pp. 107-111.

2252. Rogers, Marilyn R. ***Counterterrorism in the 1990's: A Framework for Dynamic Analysis.*** Master's Thesis. Las Vegas, NV.: University of Nevada, 1990. 125p.

2253. Rowe, Dennis. ***Considered Responses to Contemporary Terrorism in Democratic Societies.*** Chicago, IL.: University of Chicago, Office of International Criminal Justice, 1988. 56p.

2254. Rozen, Arnon, and John M. Musacchio. "Threat and Vulnerability Analyses of a Fuel Storage Facility Against Terrorists Attacks." In: R. W. De Vore, ed. ***Carnahan Conference on Security Technology: Electronic Crime Countermeasures.*** Lexington, KY.: University of Kentucky Press, 1988. pp. 83-87.

2255. _____. _____. "The Use of a Computerized Database of Terrorist Activities for Threat Assessment." In: R. W. DeVore, ed. ***Proceedings of the 1988 Carnahan Conference on Security Technology: Electronic Crime Countermeasures.*** Lexington, KY.: University of Kentucky Press, 1988. pp. 1-12.

2256. Scott, John L. ***The Deterrence of Terrorism: Terrorist Rationality and Government Signalling.*** Ph.D. Dissertation. Columbia, SC.: University of South Carolina, 1990. 125p.

2257. Sinisi, M. J. ***Network Security Issues.*** Master's Thesis. Wright-Patterson AFB, OH.: Air Force Institute of Technology, 1989. 149p.

2258. Sloan, Stephen. ***Beating International Terrorism: An Action Strategy for Preemption and Punishment.*** Maxwell AFB, AL.: Air University Library, 1986. 77p.

2259. Smith, G. Davidson. ***The Liberal Democratic Response to Terrorism: A Comparative Study of the Policies of Canada, the United States, and the United Kingdom.*** Ph.D. Dissertation. Aberdeen,: University of Aberdeen, 1986. 470p.

2260. Sobieck, Stephen M. ***Democratic Responses to Revolutionary Terrorism: A Comparative Study of Great Britain, Italy and West Germany.*** Ph.D. Dissertation. Claremont, CA.: Claremont Graduate School, 1990. 339p.

2261. Sterling, S. "Can American Craftsmanship and Technology Really Put a Dent in Terrorism." In: R. W. De Vore, ed. ***Proceedings of the 1988 Carnahan Conference on Security Technology: Electronic Crime Countermeasures.*** Lexington, KY.: University of Kentucky, 1988. pp. 53-58.

2262. Stinson, J. L., and Edward Heyman. "Analytic Approaches for Investigating Terrorist Crimes." In: ***Clandestine Tactics and Technology.*** Gaithersburg, MD.: International Association of Chiefs of Police, 1980. 43p.

2263. _____. "Unconventional Threat Assessment." In: ***Proceedings of the 6th Annual Symposium on the Role of Behavioral Science on Physical Security***, held on June 3-4, 1981, in Springfield, VA. pp. 171-188.

2264. Takeuchi, Jane, Fredric Solomon and W. Walter Menninger, eds. ***Behavioral Science and the Secret Service: Toward the Prevention of Assassination.*** Washington, D.C.: National Academy Press, 1981. 193p.

2265. Taylor, Maxwell. ***Discriminative Environmental Properties in Terrorist Environments: A Basis for Training.*** Alexandria, VA.: Army Research Institute for Behavioral and Social Sciences, 1990. 29p.

2266. ***Terrorism and the Military Professional.*** U.S. Naval Institute Professional Seminar Series. Annapolis, MA.: U.S Naval Institute, 1985. 45p.

2267. "Text of Summit Statement on International Terrorism." ***Security Systems Digest***, 17:10 (February 15, 1986), 9-10.

2268. Tomkins, Thomas C. ***Military Countermeasures to Terrorism in the 1980s.*** RAND N-2178-RC. Santa Monica, CA.: RAND Corporation, 1984. 38p.

2269. Tugwell, Maurice A., et al. ***Special Operations: Dominican Republic, Mayaguez, Mogadishu, Kolwezi, Kabul, Iranian Embassy London.*** Fort Bragg, NC.: Joint Special Forces Command, 1982. 276p.

2270. United Nations. General Assembly. Secretary General. "Measures to Prevent International Terrorism: Report." In: Y. Alexander and A. H. Foxman, eds. ***The 1987 Annual on Terrorism.*** Dordrecht: Martinus Nijhoff, 1988. pp. 325-344.

2271. United States. Advisory Commission on Public Diplomacy. ***Terrorism and Security: The Challenge for Public Diplomacy.*** Washington, D.C.: Advisory Commission on Public Diplomacy, 1985. 21p.

2272. _____. Congress. House. Committee on Foreign Affairs. ***Counter-Terrorism Policy and Embassy Security in Eastern Europe: Report.*** 100th Cong., 2nd sess. Washington, D.C.: U.S. Government Printing Office, 1988. 13p.

2273. _____._____._____._____. Subcommittee on International Operations. ***Security Procedures at U.S. Embassies: Hearings.*** Washington, D.C.: U.S. Government Printing Office, 1980. 243p.

2274. _____. Department of State. ***Report of the Secretary of State's Advisory Panel on Overseas Security.*** Washington, D.C.: U.S. Government Printing Office, 1985. 82p.

2275. _____._____. Bureau of Consular Affairs. ***A Safe Trip Abroad.*** Department of State Publication, 9493. Washington, D.C.: U.S. Government Printing Office, 1986. 4p.

2276. _____._____. Office of Public Communication. Editorial Division. ***Counterterrorism in the 1990s.*** Publ. No. 1243. Washington, D.C.: U.S. Government Printing Office, 1990. 4p.

2277. _____. Department of the Army. ***U.S. Army Counterterrorism Manual.*** Seattle, WA.: Lancer, 1984. 130p.

2278. _____. General Accounting Office. General Government Division. ***Counterterrorism: Role of INTERPOL and the U.S. National Central Bureau.*** Washington, D.C.: U.S. Government Printing Office, 1987. 44p.

2279. _____._____. National Security and International Affairs Division. ***Embassy Security: State Department Efforts to Improve Security Overseas.*** Washington, D.C.: U.S. General Accounting Office, 1986. 45p.

2280. Waters, D. C. ***Successful Anti-Terrorism Policies.*** Maxwell AFB, AL.: Air Command and Staff College, 1987. 40p.

2281. Waugh, William L. ***International Terrorism: Theories of Response and National Policies.*** Ph.D. Dissertation. University, Lafayette County: University of Mississippi, 1980. 350p.

2282. Wilkinson, Paul. "Terrorism - A Threat to Internal Security or a Weapon Against Tyranny: Problems of Municipal law Enforcement." Paper Presented to the ***8th Commonwealth Law Conference***, held on 1986 at Ocho Rios, Jamaica.

2283. Winkler, Carol. ***Argumentative Topoi in Presidential Responses to Hostage Situations: Truman to Reagan.*** Ph.D. Dissertation. Adelphi, MD.: University of Maryland, 1987. 296p.

2284. Woldman, Joel M. ***Security of U.S. Embassies and Other Overseas Civilian Installations.*** Report 85-11F. Washington, D.C.: Library of Congress, Congressional Research Service, 1985. 60p.

2285. Wootten, James P., and Raphael F. Perl. ***Anti-Terrorism Policy: A Pro-Con Discussion of Retaliation and Deterrence Options.*** Report 85-832F. Washington, D.C.: Library of Congress, Congressional research Service, 1985. 19p.

B. INTELLIGENCE ASPECTS

1. Books

2286. Cimbala, Stephen J., ed. ***Intelligence and Intelligence Policy in a Democratic Society.*** Dobbs Ferry, NY.: Transnational Publishers, 1987. 262p.
2287. Wolf, John B. ***Antiterrorist Initiatives.*** New York: Plenum Press, 1989. 218p.

2. Journal Articles

2288. Bayse, W. A. "Automated Systems' Reasoning Capabilities a Boon to Law Enforcement." ***Police Chief,*** 57:6 (June 1990), 48-52.
2289. Bottom, N. R., Jr. "Security Intelligence - A Definite Process is Necessary to Collect Intelligence." ***Journal of Security Administration,*** 5:1 (1982), 33-40.
2290. Campbell, Douglas E. "The Intelligent Threat." ***Security Management,*** 33:2 (February 1989), 19a-22a.
2291. Cline, Ray. "Technology and Intelligence." ***Terrorism,*** 10:3 (1987), 253-256.
2292. Coffman, John. "The Requirement: Intelligence, Protection, Counter-Measures." In: B. Macdonald, ed. ***Terror.*** Toronto: Canadian Institute of International Studies, 1987. pp. 118-126.
2293. Cooper, H. H. A. "American Foreign Legion Needed." ***TVI Journal,*** 3:4 (1982), 4-6.
2294. Crabtree, Richard D. "U.S. Policy for Countering Terrorism: The Intelligence Dimension." ***Conflict Quarterly,*** 6:1 (1986), 5-17.
2295. Crawshaw, Simon. "Anti-Terrorism Networks - Information and Intelligence for Fighting International Terrorism." ***Futurist,*** 23:2 (March-April 1989), 12-13.
2296. Davis, Robert B. "Changing Role for MI (Military Intelligence) in the 21st Century." ***Military Intelligence,*** 16:2 (April-June 1990), 32-35.
2297. Gallagher, Shaun. "Violence and Intelligence: Answers to the Irish Question." ***Political Communication and Persuasion,*** 2:2 (1983), 195-222.
2298. Gazit, Shlomo, and Michael Handel. "Insurgency, Terrorism and Intelligence." In: R. Gordon, ed. ***Intelligence Requirements for the 1980's: Counterintelligence.*** New Brunswick, NJ.: Transaction Books, 1980. pp. 125-147.
2299. Grutzius, Charles R. "An Approach to Low-Cost Information Dissemination." ***Terrorism,*** 10:3 (1987), 261-264.
2300. Hood, Horace E. "Terrorism and MAC Operations: The Intelligence Connection." ***Airlift Operations Review,*** 3 (October-December 1981), 16-20.
2301. "Intelligence in Terrorism Counteraction Course Prospectus." ***Military Intelligence,*** 11:2 (April-June 1985), 43-44.

2302. Jeffery, Keith. "Intelligence and Counter-Insurgency Operations: Some Reflections on the British Experience." ***Intelligence and National Security***, 2:1 (1987), 118-149.

2303. Krajick, K. "The Rise of Private Political Intelligence." ***Police Magazine***, 4 (September 1981), 22-23.

2304. Ledeen, Michael A. "Intelligence, Training and Support Components." In: U. Ra'anan, et al. ***Hydra of Carnage***. Lexington, MA.: Lexington Books, 1986. pp. 155-168.

2305. McEwen, Michael T. "Intelligence and PSYOP in Terrorism Counteraction." ***Military Intelligence***, (January-March 1984), 8-10.

2306. McGeorge, Harvey J. "A "Quest" for Using Information." ***Terrorism***, 10:3 (1987), 257-260.

2307. Motley, James B. "Coping with International Terrorism: The Role of U.S. Intelligence." ***Harvard International Review***, 7 (May/June 1985), 18-20.

2308. Ofri, Arie. "Intelligence and Counterterrorism." ***Orbis***, 28:1 (1984), 41-52.

2309. Oseth, John M. "Intelligence Controls and the National Interest." ***Parameters***, 11:4 (December 1981), 34.

2310. Oxford, Kenneth Sir. "Identifying the Terrorist." In: ***Legal Responses to the Terrorist Threat***. London: Institute for the Study of Conflict, 1988. pp. 7-12.

2311. Prince, James. "Is There a Role for Intelligence in Combatting Terrorism?." ***Conflict***, 9:3 (1989), 301-318.

2312. Ramsey, Thomas. "The Age of Information Technology." ***Terrorism***, 10:3 (1987), 265-268.

2313. Robertson, Ken G. "Intelligence, Terrorism and Civil Liberties." In: P. Wilkinson and A. M. Stewart, eds. ***Contemporary Research on Terrorism***. Aberdeen: Aberdeen University Press, 1987. pp. 549-569.

2314. _____. "Intelligence, Terrorism and Civil Liberties." ***Conflict Quarterly***, 7 (Spring 1987), 43-62.

2315. Rodriguez, Matt. "Intelligence Gathering: The Chicago Experience." In: R. H. Ward and H. E. Smith, eds. ***International Terrorism: The Domestic Response***. Chicago, IL.: University of Illinois at Chicago, Office of International Criminal Justice, 1987. pp. 27-36.

2316. Shepherd, A. "Anti-Hijack: a Change of Tactics." ***International Law Enforcement***, 3:6 (1986), 16-18, 20.

2317. Stewart, Bernard L. "Information and Communications: An Introduction." ***Terrorism***, 10:3 (1987), 251-252.

2318. Strohm, Gary D. "Electronic Intelligence vs. Terrorism." ***Military Intelligence***, (March 1987), 24-27.

2319. Sulc, Lawrence B. "Terrorism and the Importance of Intelligence." ***Terrorism***, 10:2 (1987), 133-138.

2320. Tuttle, A. C. "Secrecy, Covert Action, and Counterespionage: Intelligence Challenges for the 1990's." ***Harvard Journal of Law and Public Policy***, 12:2 (Spring 1989), 523-540.

2321. Vincent, Billie H. "Information Exchange: A Defense Against Terrorism." ***Security Management***, 27:8 (1983), 89-93.

2322. Waugh, William L. "Informing Policy and Administration: A Comparative Perspective on Terrorism." ***International Journal of Public Administration***, 12:3 (1989), 447-500.

2323. Yariv, Aharon. "The Role of Intelligence in Combatting Terrorism." In: A. Kurz, ed. ***Contemporary Trends in World Terrorism.*** New York: Praeger, 1987. pp. 116-124.

2324. _____. "Role of Intelligence in Combatting Terrorism." In: J. R. Buckwalter, ed. ***International Terrorism: The Decade Ahead.*** Chicago, IL.: University of Illinois at Chicago, Office of International Criminal Justice, 1989. pp. 63-71.

2325. Zindar, John M. "Tactical Intelligence Officer in Low Intensity Conflict." ***Military Intelligence,*** (January-March 1985), 46-47.

3. Documents and Reports

2326. Digenova, Joseph. "Terrorism, Intelligence and the Law." In: ***Proceedings of the 9th Annual Symposium on the Role of Behavioral Science in Physical Security,*** held on April 3-4, 1984, in Springfield, VA. pp. 53-59.

2327. Godson, Roy, ed. ***Intelligence Requirements for the 1980's. 5 Vols.*** Washington, D.C.: National Strategy Information Center, 1980-83.

2328. Jenkins, Brian M., Sorrel Wildhorn and M. M. Lavin. ***Intelligence Constraints of the 1970s and Domestic Terrorism: Executive Summary.*** RAND R-2939-DOJ. Santa Monica, CA.: RAND Corporation, 1982. 22p.

2329. Kornblum, A. N. ***Intelligence and the Law: Cases and Materials. Vol. 5. International Terrorism.*** Washington, D.C.: Defence Intelligence College, 1985.

2330. Lavin, M. M. ***Intelligence Constraints of the 1970's and Domestic Terrorism: Vol. II, A Survey of Legal, Legislative and Administrative Constraints.*** Santa Monica, CA.: RAND Corporation, 1982. 155p.

2331. Motley, James B. "The Threatened Role of Intelligence in Combatting Terrorism." In: ***The U.S. Strategy to Counter Domestic Political Terrorism.*** Washington, DC.: National Defense University Press, 1983. pp. 61-83.

2332. Wildhorn, Sorrel, Brian M. Jenkins and M. M. Lavin. ***Intelligence Constraints of the 1970s and Domestic Terrorism: Vol. 1. Effects of the Incidence, Investigation and Prosecution of Terrorist Activity.*** RAND N-1901-DOJ. Santa Monica, CA.: RAND Corporation, 1982. 179p.

2333. Wylie, A. C. ***Intelligence: Its Role in Counterterrorism.*** Arlington Hall Station, VA.: Army Intelligence and Threat Analysis Center, 1981. 23p.

C. COUNTER MEASURES - CIVIL AVIATION

1. Books

2334. Alexander, Yonah, and Eugene Sochor, eds. ***Aerial Piracy and Aviation Security.*** Dordrecht: Martinus Nijhoff, 1990. 224p.

2335. Emerson, Steven, and Brian Duffy. ***The Fall of Pan Am 103: Inside the Lockerbie Investigation.*** New York: G. P. Putnam's & Sons, 1990. 304p.

2336. Hubbard, David G. ***Winning Back the Sky: A Tactical Analysis of Terrorism.*** Old Saybrook, CT.: Saybrook Publ, 1987. 142p.

2. Journal Articles

2337. "Airports are the Target Again." ***Airports International,*** (1985), 14-18.

2338. Ashley, Steven. "Can Technology Stop Terror in the Air?." ***Popular Science,*** 227 (November 1985), 68-73.

2339. Barbash, G. I., et al. "Airport Preparedness for Mass Disaster: A Proposed Schematic Plan." ***Aviation, Space, and Environmental Medicine,*** 57:1 (1986), 77-81.

2340. Baumeister, Michel F. "Terrorism in Foreign Airports - Can Airlines be Held Responsible?." ***New Jersey Law Journal,*** 119 (June 11, 1987), 1.

2341. Beane, William F. "Cleared for Takeoff." ***Security,*** 23:10 (1986), 46-49.

2342. Ben-Ari, Mordechai. "Protecting the Airways." In: B. Netanyahu, ed. ***International Terrorism: Challenge and Response.*** New Brunswick, NJ.: Transaction Books, 1981. pp. 289-293.

2343. Berliner, Diane T., and L. Douglas Heck. "Thoughts on a Hijacking." In: M. F. Herz, ed. ***Diplomats and Terrorists.*** Washington, D.C.: Institute for the Study of Diplomacy, 1982. pp. 18-21.

2344. "Bitter Pills for the Public." ***TVI Journal,*** 1:5 (1980), 6-8.

2345. Blank, Joseph K. "Airport Security: Is It In The Bag?." ***Security Management,*** 30:1 (1986), 33-35.

2346. Bogan, J. A., David Truby and Mark Monday. "Passenger Screening - An Impractical Joke." ***TVI Journal,*** 1:5 (1980), 10-16.

2347. Brown, David A. "Investigators Expand Search for Debris from Bombed 747." ***Aviation Week and Space Technology,*** 130:2 (1989), 26-27.

2348. Brown, Peter J. "Viewpoint - Should Americans Sit Still for Hijackers?." ***Security Management,*** 30:4 (1986), 47-49.

2349. Cauley, Jon, and Eric I. Im. "Intervention Policy Analysis of Skyjacking and other Terrorist Incidents." ***American Economic Review,*** 78 (May 1988), 27-31.

2350. Chaseling, Trevor. "Aviation Security and Airlines." In: Y. Alexander and E. Sochor, eds. ***Aerial Piracy and Aviation Security.*** Dordrecht: Martinus Nijhoff, 1990. pp. 21-32.

2351. Clark, Gerald. "Air Terrorism: The Front Line is Everywhere." ***Reader's Digest (Canada),*** 130:781 (May 1987), 89-93.

2352. Colen, Mark S. "The Liability of a Security Company Handling Airport Security." ***TVI Report,*** 8:1 (1988), 12-14.

2353. "Combating Terrorism." ***Air Line Pilot,*** 55:4 (April 1986), 14-17.

2354. Conant, J. S. "Terrorism and Travel: Managing the Unmanageable." ***Journal of Travel Research,*** 26:4 (March 1988), 16-20.

2355. Corbett, William T. "Air Terrorism: Flight or Fright." ***Security Management,*** 33:9 (October 1989), 68-72.

2356. Crenshaw, Martha. "Civil Aviation: Target for Terrorism." ***Annals of the American Academy of Political and Social Science,*** 498 (July 1988), 60-69.

2357. Donoghue, J. A. "Terrorist Threat Spurs Security Technology Advances." ***Air Transport World,*** 23 (June 1986), 14-16.

2358. Duffy, Henry A. "How Can Terrorist Attacks Against Airline Passengers Be Prevented Most Effectively." ***Security System Digest,*** 17:9 (1986), 3-4.

2359. Emerson, Steven, and Richard Rothschild. "To Trap a Terrorist: American Agents Has Found Airplane Hijacker: But How Would They Nab Him?." ***Reader's Digest (Canada)***, 137:820 (August 1990), 49-53.

2360. Felton, John. "Hill Considers Ways to Boost Airport Security: Hijack Crisis Spurs Boycott Proposals." ***Congressional Quarterly Weekly Reports***, 43 (June 29, 1985), 1252-1253.

2361. Finger, Seymour M. "Security of International Civil Aviation: The Role of the ICAO." ***Terrorism***, 6:4 (1983), 519-528.

2362. "Freedom of the Airways." ***America***, (February 22, 1986), 130-131.

2363. Haggman, Bertil. "PAN AM 103 - The Swedish Connection." ***TVI Report***, 9:3 (1990), 23-25.

2364. Hill, Robin E. "Airport Violence and the Legal Principle." ***Terrorism and Political Violence***, 1:1 (January 1989), 78-106.

2365. Hopkins, Harry. "Sniffing Out Trouble." ***Flight International***, (June 28, 1986), 24-28.

2366. ICPO-Interpol. "Aircraft Hijacking: Trends Between 1980 and 1985." ***International Criminal Police Review***, 42:407 (1987), 23-27.

2367. "IFALPA Approves New Policies to Improve Airline Safety." ***Aviation Week and Space Technology***, 124:16 (April 1986), 32-33.

2368. Iglarsh, Harvey J. "Fear of Flying - Its Economic Costs." ***Terrorism***, 10:1 (1987), 45-50.

2369. Kelly, John H. "The Paris Hijacking: Operating Level Perspective." In: M. F. Herz, ed. ***Diplomats and Terrorists.*** Washington, D.C.: Institute for the Study of Diplomacy, 1982. pp. 16-18.

2370. Koch, Noel. "Terrorism and Aviation Security." ***Terrorism***, 13:1 (1990), 68-72.

2371. Koniak, Joel. "Access to Airport Security." ***Security Management***, 32:11 (November 1988), 145-175.

2372. Kotowski, A. "A Review of Modern X-Ray Screening Devices." ***ICAO Bulletin***, (October 1986), 22-23.

2373. Lally, Richard. "Passenger Safety and Aviation Security." ***Terrorism***, 10:3 (1987), 237-240.

2374. _____. "How Safe is Air Cargo from Terrorism?." ***Pacific Shipper***, (February 1986), 94-96.

2375. Lavery, Robert. "Flying can be Hazardous to Your Health." ***TVI Journal***, 3:8 (1982), 5-7.

2376. Leonard, Edward. "Hijacked: When His Wife and Son Died Aboard Egypt Air Flight 648, A Calgary Man Channelled his Rage into a Campaign to Protect Air Travellers from Terrorism." ***Saturday Night***, 101 (June 1986), 44-49.

2377. Levitt, Geoffrey M. "Collective Sanctions and Unilateral Action." In: Y. Alexander and E. Sochor, eds. ***Aerial Piracy and Aviation Security.*** Dordrecht: Martinus Nijhoff, 1990. pp. 95-124.

2378. Mackenzie-Orr, M. H. "Aviation Security in an Age of Terrorism." ***Australian Police Journal***, 43:2 (1989), 55-60.

2379. Magdelenat, Jean-Louis. "Liability for Damages Resulting from Air Terrorism." In: Y. Alexander and E. Sochor, eds. ***Aerial Piracy and Aviation Security.*** Dordrecht: Martinus Nijhoff, 1990. pp. 55-76.

2380. Mecham, Michael, and James Ott. "Increased Government Role Requested to Prevent Terrorism Against Aircraft." ***Aviation Week & Space Technology***, 130:1 (1989), 30-31.

2381. Mordoff, Keith M. "Security Levels Increased at Frankfurt, Heathrow." ***Aviation Week & Space Technology***, 130:2 (1989), 28-29.

2382. Murphy, Erin E. "A Rising War on Terrorists." ***IEEE Spectrum***, 26:11 (1989), 33-36.

2383. Ott, James. "FAA Security Panel Examines Means of Improving Defense Against Terrorists." ***Aviation Week & Space Technology***, 131:20 (1989), 75,77.

2384. _____. "ICAO Upgrades Security Unit as Part of Antiterrorist Effort." ***Aviation Week & Space Technology***, 130:18 (1989), 109,111.

2385. "Passenger Screening Gets High Marks." ***TVI Journal***, 1:5 (1980), 8-10.

2386. "Plain Truth About Plane Travel." ***TVI Journal***, 3:10 (1982), 2-5.

2387. Revell, Oliver B. "Aviation Security: A Global Issue." ***FBI Law Enforcement Bulletin***, 58 (July 1989), 8-11.

2388. Rush, Kenneth. "The Event Seen by the Ambassador." In: M. F. Herz, ed. ***Diplomats and Terrorists.*** Washington, D.C.: Institute for the Study of Diplomacy, 1982. pp. 12-15.

2389. Schneider, William J., and Richard P. Grassie. "Counting on Design." ***Security Management***, 33:9 (October 1989), 55-58.

2390. Scotti, Tony. "Don't Check Safety With the Luggage." ***TVI Journal***, 3:9 (1982), 2.

2391. "Security." ***Jane's Airport Review***, (October 1989), 13-18.

2392. Sharpe, Hal F. "The Investigation of Terrorist Incidents Involving Aircraft." ***Terrorism***, 13:2 (1990), 172-176.

2393. Sheppard, Paul, and Eugene Sochor. "Setting International Aviation Security Standards. In: Y. Alexander and E. Sochor, eds. ***Aerial Piracy and Aviation Security.*** Dordrecht: Martinus Nijhoff, 1990. pp. 3-20.

2394. Sochor, Eugene. "Conflicts in International Civil Aviation: Safeguarding the Air Routes." ***Conflict***, 8:4 (1988), 271-284.

2395. _____. "ICAO and Armed Attacks Against Civil Aviation." ***International Journal***, 44:1 (Winter 1988-1989), 134-170.

2396. Stewart, Bernard L. "Aviation Security: Cost and Technology." ***Terrorism***, 13:2 (1990), 168-171.

2397. "Surviving a Skyjacking." ***TVI Journal***, 2:1 (1981), 2-6.

2398. Taylor, Laurie. "Aerial Piracy - A Pilot Viewpoint." In: Y. Alexander and E. Sochor, eds. ***Aerial Piracy and Aviation Security.*** Dordrecht: Martinus Nijhoff, 1990. pp. 33-54.

2399. "Terror in the Skies: Who Should Pay the Price?." ***Syracuse Journal of International Law and Commerce***, 14 (Winter 1987), 209-235.

2400. "Terrorist Role Investigated in Trans World 727 Explosion." ***Aviation Week and Space Technology***, 124:14 (April 1986), 32-33.

2401. Thexton, Mike. "The Hijacking of PA 73: A Hostage's Account." ***TVI Report***, 8:3 (1989), 43-46.

2402. "The Ultimate Emergency." ***Business and Commercial Aviation***, 62:3 (March 1988), 58-64.

2403. Von Seyfried, Henry. "Surviving an Airplane Hijacking." ***Marine Corps Gazette***, 70:1 (1986), 38-39.

2404. Walker, Clive. "The World has Changed After Lockerbie." ***Jane's Airport Review***, (June 1990), 6-8.

2405. "The War Against Terrorism." ***Airline Executive***, 13:5 (May 1989), 44-45.

2406. Wilkinson, Paul. "Designing Effective National Aviation Security Systems: The Building Blocks for an Enhanced Global Response." ***Terrorism and Political Violence***, 1:3 (July 1989), 378-390.

3. Documents and Reports

2407. Brenchley, Frank. ***Living with Terrorism: The Problem of Air Piracy.*** Conflict Studies, No. 184. London: Institute for the Study of Conflict, 1986. 21p.

2408. Browne,, Marjorie Ann, and Ellen C. Collier. ***Foreign Airport Security: Diplomatic Framework and U.S. Policy.*** Issue Brief 85162. Washington, D.C.: Library of Congress, Congressional Research Service, 1987. 16p.

2409. Caskey, D. L., and M. T. Olascoaga. "The Systems Approach to Airport Security: The FAA/BWI Airport Demonstration Project." Paper Presented at the ***Carnahan Conference on Security Technology***, held on October 10, 1990 at the University of Kentucky, Lexington, KY. 21p.

2410. Gozani, T., et al. ***Explosive Detection System Bases on Thermal Neutron Analysis (TNA).*** Los Alamos, NM.: Los Alamos National Laboratories, 1989. 16p.

2411. Greneker, Eugene F., and Melvin C. McGee. "Planning for Physical Security to Counter the Airborne Threat." Paper Presented at the ***1986 Carnahan Conference on Security Technology***, held on May 14-16, 1986, at the University of Kentucky. pp. 5-7.

2412. Higgins, M. K. ***Airline Safety: A Comparative Analysis.*** Master's Thesis. Wright-Patterson AFB, OH.: Air Force Institute of Technology, 1987. 88p.

2413. Martin, J. P. ***Aviation Security: A System's Perspective.*** Albuquerque, NM.: Sandia National Laboratories, 1988. 35p.

2414. Olson, Harold W. "Security in Air Transportation." Paper Presented at the ***Meeting of the National Forum Foundation***, held on November 17, 1986 in Houston, TX. 6p.

2415. ***Response of International Organizations to Air Terrorism.*** Briefing Paper No. 24. Ottawa: United Nations Association in Canada, 1986. 5p.

2416. Roux, J. P. ***Security at Airports - Report.*** EP/PE Working Documents, A 2-208/85. Strassbourg: European Communities Committee on Transport, 1985-86. 18p.

2417. United States. Congress. House. Committee on Foreign Affairs. ***Antiterrorism Measures: The Adequacy of Foreign Airport Security: Staff Report.*** 99th Cong., 2nd sess. Washington, D.C.: U.S. Government Printing Office, 1986. 15p.

2418. _____._____._____._____. ***Foreign Airport Security.*** Washington, D.C.: U.S. Government Printing Office, 1989. 203p.

2419. _____._____._____._____. ***Report of the President's Commission on International Aviation Security and Terrorism: Hearing.*** 101st Cong., 2nd sess. Washington, D.C.: U.S. Government Printing Office, 1990. 109p.

2420. _____._____._____. Committee on Government Operations. ***Aviation Security: Are Our Airports Safe?.*** Washington, D.C.: U.S. Government Printing Office, 1985. 15p.

2421. _____._____._____._____. Subcommittee on Government Activities and Transportation. ***The Bombing of Pan Am Flight 103: A Critical Look at American Aviation Security: Hearings.*** 101st Cong., 1st sess. Washington, D.C.: U.S. Government Printing Office, 1990. 489p.

2422. _____._____._____. Committee on Public Works and Transportation. Subcommittee on Aviation. ***Oversight of Airport and Airline Security Programs: Hearings.*** 99th Cong., 1st sess. Washington, D.C.: U.S. Government Printing Office, 1985. 101p.

2423. _____._____._____._____._____. ***Aviation Security: Hearings.*** 101st Cong., 1st sess. Washington, D.C.: U.S. Government Printing Office, 1989. 419p.

2424. _____._____._____. Committee on Science, Space, and Technology. Subcommittee on Transportation, Aviation and Materials. ***Airport Security.*** Washington, D.C.: U.S. Government Printing Office, 1989. 80p.

2425. _____._____._____. Committee on the Judiciary. Subcommittee on Crime. ***Firearms Which Escape Detection at Airport Security Checkpoints: Hearings.*** 101st Cong., 1st sess. Washington: D.C.: U.S. Government Printing Office, 1989. 548p.

2426. _____._____. Senate. Committee on Appropriations. Subcommittee on Transportation and Related Agencies. ***Aviation Security: Hearing.*** 101st Cong., 1st sess. Washington, D.C.: U.S. Government Printing Office, 1989. 126p.

2427. _____._____._____. Committee on Commerce, Science and Transportation. Subcommittee on Aviation. ***Aviation Security: Hearing.*** 101st Cong., 1st sess. Washington, D.C.: U.S. Government Printing Office, 1989. 100p.

2428. _____. Federal Aviation Administration. Office of Civil Aviation Security. ***Semiannual Report to Congress on the Effectiveness of the Civil Aviation Security Program. January 1, 1987 - June 30, 1987.*** Washington, D.C.: U.S. Government Printing Office, 1987. 32p.

2429. _____. President's Commission on Aviation Security and Terrorism. ***Report to the President.*** Washington, D.C.: U.S. Government Printing Office, 1990. 182p.

2430. Wilkinson, Paul. ***The Lessons of Lockerbie.*** Conflict Studies, No. 226. London: Research Institute for the Study of Conflict and Terrorism, 1989. 30p.

D. COUNTER MEASURES - MARITIME TERROR

1. Books

2431. Cassese, Antonio. ***Terrorism, Politics and Law: The Achille Lauro Affair.*** Oxford: Polity Press, 1989. 162.

2. Journal Articles

2432. Barnett, R.W. "The U.S. Navy's Role in Countering Maritime Terrorism." ***Terrorism,*** 6:3 (1983), 469-480.

2433. Brenner, Philip J. "Bomb on Your Ship." ***Defense Transportation Journal,*** 46:4 (August 1990), 19-20.

2434. Chang, Dae H. "Aquatic Crime: New Directions Transnational Research." In: H. E. Smith, ed. ***Transnational Crime: Investigative Responses.*** Chicago, IL.: University of Illinois at Chicago, Office of International, Criminal Justice, 1989. pp. 79-88.

2435. "Fears Grow of More Terror Attacks on Ships." ***International Cargo Crime Prevention,*** 4:1 (May 1986), 1-2.

2436. Haines, S. W. "Criminal Violence at Sea - Observations on the Threat and Appropriate Responses." In: B. A. H. Parritt, ed. ***Violence at Sea.*** Paris: International Chamber of Commerce, 1986. pp. 93-107.

2437. Harlow, B. "Role of Military Force to Protect Ships and Ports Against Terrorists Attacks." In: B. A. H. Parritt, ed. ***Violence at Sea.*** Paris: International Chamber of Commerce, 1986. pp. 143-148.

2438. Hewer, C. "Precautions that Shipowners Could Take to Protect Their Vessels." In: B. A. H. Parritt, ed. ***Violence at Sea.*** Paris: International Chamber of Commerce, 1986. pp. 169-174.

2439. Jovanovic, Milorad. "Double Hijacking in the Meditterranean." ***Review of International Affairs,*** 36 (November 5, 1985), 23-25.

2440. Keane, P. T. "Maritime Terrorism: The U.S. Response." ***International Cargo Crime Prevention,*** 4:11 (March 1987), 5-6.

2441. Landi, Lando. "The Achille Lauro Trial and Its Aftermath." ***TVI Report,*** 7:1 (1987), 24-26.

2442. MacNair, Douglas G. "The Nature of the Beast - A Soliloque on Maritime Fraud, Piracy and Terrorism." ***Journal of Security Administration,*** 5:1 (1982), 41-47.

2443. _____, and Hugh W. Stephens. "Red Sky in the Morning: In the Wake of the Achille Lauro." ***Defense Transportation Journal,*** 42:2 (April 1986), 12-14.

2444. Maimone, Emanuel. "Maritime Vulnerability and Security." ***Terrorism,*** 10:3 (1987), 233-236.

2445. Mazzone, F. "Prevention of Terrorist Attack of a Ship While at Port or Sea." In: B. A. H. Parritt, ed. ***Violence at Sea.*** Paris: International Chamber of Commerce, 1986. pp. 149-167.

2446. Moore, Robert G. "The Price of Admiralty - II." ***TVI Report,*** 7:2 (1987), 16-20.

2447. _____. "Terror on the High Seas." ***Journal of Defense and Diplomacy,*** 5:8 (1987), 18-20, 62.

2448. _____. "The Price of Admiralty: The Regulatory Responses to Maritime Terrorism." ***TVI Report,*** 7:1 (1987), 27-29.

2449. "Shipping Around Terrorism ." ***Transportation and Distribution,*** 28:9 (September 1987), 28-30.

2450. Simon, Jeffrey. "The Implication of the Achille Lauro Hijacking for the Maritime Community." ***TVI Report,*** 7:1 (1987), 20-23.

2451. Stav, C. "Practical Measures to be Taken by Ports and Ship's Crews to Prevent an Attack and to Minimise the Risk when an Attack Occurs." In: B. A. H. Parritt, ed. ***Violence at Sea.*** Paris: International Chamber of Commerce, 1986. pp. 131-141.

2452. Stephens, Hugh W. "Maritime Terrorism and Piracy: Problems and Solutions in the Mid-1980s." In: Y. Alexander, ed. ***The 1986 Annual on Terrorism.*** Dordrecht: Martinus Nijhoff, 1987. pp. 165-176.

2453. _____. "Barriers to Port Security." ***Journal of Security Administration,*** 12:2 (December 1989), 29-41.

2454. Welham, M. G., and J. A. Welham. "Maritime Security." ***Defense Analysis***, 3:4 (December 1987), 371-373.

2455. "What You Need to Know About the PLO: In the Wake of the Achille Lauro Incident, Experts on Combatimg Terror Explain How to Protect Crews, Passengers and Ships." ***Maritime Engineering***, 198:11 (November 1986), 77-83.

2456. Wilkinson, Paul. "Navies in a Terrorist World." ***Jane's Naval Review***, (1986), 166-176.

2457. Williams, D. F. "Terrorism in the 90's: The Skull and Crossbone Still Flies." ***Police Chief***, 57:9 (September 1990), 47-50.

2458. Williams, Dave. "In the Wake of the Achille Lauro." ***Security Management***, 32:4 (April 1988), 57-59.

2459. Winkler, H. B. "Study of Need for Ocean Industry Protection." ***Journal of Security Administration***, 4:1 (1981), 11-25.

2460. "You Can Run, but You Can't Hide (Achille Lauro Affair)." ***Readers Digest***, 128:768 (April 1986), 111-115.

3. Documents and Reports

2461. Broughton, Hubert. ***Combatting Terrorism: A Guide for U.S. Naval Forces Afloat.*** Monterey, CA.: Naval Postgraduate School, 1985. 91p.

2462. Hubbard, E. F. ***Designing for Security: Protecting Our Shore Facilities from the Terrorist Threat.*** Master's Thesis. Gainesville, FL.: Florida University, 1988. 108p.

2463. ***International Symposium on Maritime Security and Terrorism.*** Arlington, VA.: ISIS Associates, 1981. 78p.

2464. Jenkins, Brian M. ***The Aftermath of the Achille Lauro.*** RAND P-7163. Santa Monica, CA.: Rand Corporation, 1985. 4p.

2465. Simon, Jeffrey. ***The Implications of the Achille Lauro Hijacking for the Marine Community.*** RAND P-7250. Santa Monica, CA.: Rand Corporation, 1986. 10p.

2466. United States. Coast Guard. ***Captain of the Port: (Maritime Counterterrorism) TRANSIT.*** Washington, D.C.: The Coast Guard, 1986. 23p.

2467. _____. Congress. House. Committee on Foreign Affairs. ***Overview of International Maritime Security: Hearing.*** 99th Cong., 1st sess. Washington, D.C.: U.S. Government Printing Office, 1986. 109p.

2468. _____._____._____._____. Subcommittee on International Operations. ***Aftermath of the Achille Lauro Incident: Hearing.*** 99th Cong., 1st sess. Washington, D.C.: U.S. Government Printing Office, 1986. 74p.

2469. _____. Department of Transportation. ***United Nations Maritime Agency Adopts Measures to Increase Security of Ports and Ships.*** Washington, D.C.: U.S. Government Printing Office, 1986. 2p.

2470. ***Violence at Sea: A Review of Terrorism, Acts of War and Piracy and Countermeasures.*** 2nd ed. International Chamber of Commerce No. 439. Paris: ICC, 1986. 267p.

E. COUNTER MEASURES - BOMBINGS

1. Books

2471. ***Handbook of Bomb Threats & Search Procedures.*** New York: Gordon Press, 1987.

2. Journal Articles

2472. Bozorgmanesh, Hadi. "Bomb and Weapon Detection." ***Terrorism,*** 10:3 (1987), 285-287.

2473. "Car Bombs - Defeating the Terrorist Weapon." ***TVI Journal,*** 3:1 (1982), 3-6.

2474. Coltharp, David R. "Designing Buildings Against Terrorists." ***Military Engineer,*** 79 (August 1987), 427-429.

2475. "Crime and International Terrorism: The New York Experience - Panel Discussion." ***Police Chief,*** (January 1982), 114-117.

2476. Eytan, Reuben. "Protecting Buildings Against Explosives." ***Terrorism,*** 10:3 (1987), 247-250.

2477. Frykberg, Eric R., and Joseph J. Tepas. "Terrorist Bombings: Lessons Learned from Belfast to Beirut." ***Annals of Surgery,*** 208:5 (1988), 569-576.

2478. Gray, Kenneth O. "Vehicle Access Control: Countermeasures Against Car-Bomb Attacks." ***Military Engineer,*** 79 (March-April 1987), 108-114.

2479. Hilburn, A. "Help Find This Mad Bomber." ***Reader's Digest,*** 135 (November 1989), 96-100.

2480. Howard, John W. "Designing the Embassy of the Future." ***Terrorism,*** 10:3 (1987), 241-242.

2481. Kennedy, Harold. "Unique School Teaches Latest Techniques to Thwart Terrorist--Style Bombing." ***Justice Assistance News,*** 2:3 (April 1981), 6-7.

2482. Kindillen, Robert E. "Putting the Brakes on Suicide Bombers." ***Security Management,*** 31:1 (January 1987), 97-103.

2483. Lavery, Robert. "They're not a Lemon in the Terrorist Arsenal." ***TVI Journal,*** 3:1 (1982), 3-6.

2484. Obe, John W., and David Williams. "UXB: Life on the Bomb-Line." ***Terror Update,*** 8 (May 1989), 4-5.

2485. Oehlsen, Nadia. "Prepare Your Campus for Bomb Threats." ***Campus Law Enforcement Journal,*** 17:2 (March-April 1987), 43-44.

2486. Passantino, Richard J. "Architectural Design and Physical Security." ***Terrorism,*** 10:3 (1987), 243-246.

2487. Rignault, D. P., and M. C. Deligny. "The 1986 Terrorist Bombing Experience in Paris." ***Annals of Surgery,*** 209:3 (1989), 368-373.

2488. Rogers, N. F. "Defuse Bomb Threats." ***Security Management,*** 27 (October 1983), 32-36.

2489. Rosenberg, Robert. "Tick...Tick...Tick: For the Guys in the Jerusalem Bomb Squad, Business is Booming." ***Playboy,*** 33:7 (July 1986), 86, 110, 131, 158-163.

2490. "Terrorism: Sturdy Barriers are Placed Around Department Buildings." ***State,*** (March 1984), 4-7.

2491. Wyatt, John. "Bomb Detection Needs New Approach." ***Terror Update***, 9 (July 1989) , 6-7.

2492. _____. "Defensive Search Operations - Beating the Bomber." ***International Defense Review***, 22 (October 1989), 27-31.

3. Documents and Reports

2493. Adams, K. G., and B. J. Roscoe. ***Vehicle Barriers: Emphasis on Natural Features.*** Albuquerque, NM.: Sandia National Laboratories, 1985. 112p.

2494. Deming, Romine. "High Speed Detection of Plastic Explosives." Paper Presented at the ***1986 Carnahan Conference on Security Technology***, held on May 14-16, 1986 at the University of Kentucky. pp. 79-81.

2495. ***Embassy of the Future: Recommendations for the Design of Future U.S. Embassy Buildings.*** Washington, D.C.: National Research Council, Building Research Board, 1986. 92p.

2496. Gozani, T., et al. "Explosive Detection System Bases on Thermal Neoutron Analysis (TNA)." Paper Presented at the ***Carnahan Conference on Security Technology***, held on October 3-5, 1989 in Zurich. 16p.

2497. ***Protection of Federal Office Buildings Against Terrorism.*** Washington, D.C.: National Research Council, Building Research Board, 1988. 61p.

2498. Swahlan, D. J. ***Anti-Terrorist Vehicle Crash Impact Energy Absorbing Barrier. (Patent Application).*** PAT-APPL-7-207 849. Albuquerque, NM.: Sandia National Laboratories, 1988. 21p.

2499. Thomas, C. H. ***Dissemination of Terrorist Threat Information: Who Should Be Warned.*** Carlisle Barracks, PA.: Army War College, 1990. 40p.

F. COUNTER MEASURES - HOSTAGE & KIDNAPPING INCIDENTS

1. Books

2500. ***American Hostages in Iran: The Conduct of a Crisis.*** Council on Foreign Relations. New Haven, CT.: Yale University Press, 1985. 443p.

2501. Bucheli, Fausto, and Robin Maxson. ***Hostage: The True Story of an American's 47 Days of Terrorist Captivity in Latin America.*** Grands Rapids, MI.: Zondervan, 1982. 293p.

2502. Cramer, Chris, and Sim Harris. ***Hostage.*** London: John Clare Books, 1982. 213p.

2503. Salinger, Pierre. ***America Held Hostage: The Secret Negotiations.*** Garden City, NY.: Doubleday, 1981. 349p.

2504. Sunday Times Insight Team. ***Siege.*** London: Hamlyn, 1980.

2505. Testrake, John, and David J. Wimbish. ***Triumph Over Terror on Flight 847.*** Old Tappan, NY.: Fleming H. Revell, 1987. 251p.

2. *Journal Articles*

2506. Abbott, Thomas E. "Time-Phase Model for Hostage Negotiation." ***The Police Chief***, 53:4 (1986), 34-35.

2507. Ackerman, "Mike" E. C. "Executive Kidnappings: The Role of the Recovery Consultant." ***International Lawyer***, 16:1 (1982), 155-160.

2508. _____. "The Hostage Recovery." In: B. M. Jenkins, ed. ***Terrorism and Personal Protection.*** Stoneham, MA.: Butterworth, 1985. pp. 293-301.

2509. Alexander, Arthur J. "An Economic Analysis of Security, Recovery, and Compensation in Terrorist Kidnappings." In: B. M. Jenkins, ed. ***Terrorism and Personal Protection.*** Stoneham, MA.: Butterworth, 1985. pp. 176-199.

2510. Andrew, R. J. "The Siege at Princess Gate: Attack on the Iranian Embassy." In: B. M. Jenkins, ed. ***Terrorism and Beyond: An International Conference on Terrorism and Low-Level Conflict.*** Santa Monica, CA.: RAND Corporation, 1980. pp. 243-246.

2511. Bolz, Francis A. "The Hostage Situation: Law Enforcement Options." In: B. Eichelman, D. Soskis and W. Reid, eds. ***Terrorism: Interdisciplinary Perspectives.*** Washington, D.C.: American Psychiatric Association, 1983. pp. 99-116.

2512. Born, David G., and W. Ronald Olin. "A Behavioral Approach to Hostage Situations." ***FBI Law Enforcement Bulletin***, 52:1 (1983), 18-24.

2513. Brown, William J. "Mediated Communication Flows During a Terrorist Event: The TWA Flight 847 Hijacking." Paper Presented at the ***Conference of the International Communication Association***, held In May 1987 in Montreal.

2514. Capotorto, Gerardo. "Further Thoughts on Negotiations." In: B. M. Jenkins, ed. ***Terrorism and Personal Protection.*** Stoneham, MA.: Butterworth, 1985. pp. 291-292.

2515. Charters, David. "Swift and Bold: An Appraisal of Hostage Rescue Operations." ***Conflict Quarterly***, 1:1 (1980), 26-33.

2516. Clutterbuck, Richard L. "Management of the Kidnap Risk." ***Terrorism***, 5:1-2 (1981), 125-138.

2517. _____. "Management of Kidnap Risk." In: P. Wilkinson, ed. ***British Perspectives on Terrorism.*** London: Allen & Unwin, 1981. pp. 125-138.

2518. _____. "Managing the Episode." In: B. M. Jenkins, ed. ***Terrorism and Personal Protection.*** Stoneham, MA.: Butterworth, 1985. pp. 232-249.

2519. _____. "Negotiations I: Negotiations with Kidnappers." In: B. M. Jenkins, ed. ***Terrorism and Personal Protection.*** Stoneham, MA.: Butterworth, 1985. pp. 250-261.

2520. Conley, J. M. "Terrorism Versus the United States: The Threat and Responses to Terrorist Kidnappings." ***Terrorism***, 12:6 (1989), 383-386.

2521. Cooper, H. H. A. "Hostageology." ***International Journal of Offender Therapy and Comparative Criminology***, 27 (1983), 94-96.

2522. Davidson, G. P. "Anxiety and Authority - Psychological Aspects for Police in Hostage Negotiation Situations." ***Journal of Police Science and Administration***, 9:1 (1981), 35-38.

2523. Dellow, John, and Alison Jamieson. "Kidnapping and Hostage Taking." In: ***Legal Responses to the Terrorist Threat.*** London: Institute for the Study of Conflict, 1988. pp. 51-66.

2524. "Developing an Effective Anti - Abduction Program." ***TVI Journal,*** 3:6 (1982), 2-4.

2525. Dolan, John T., and G. W. Fuselier. "A Guide for First Responders to Hostage Situations." ***FBI Law Enforcement Bulletin,*** 58:4 (1989), 9-13.

2526. Evans, Richard. "The West Held Hostage." ***Geographic Magazine,*** 61:8 (1989), 10-15.

2527. Friedland, Nehemia. "Hostage Negotiations: Dilemmas About Policy." In: L. Z. Freedman and Y. Alexander, eds. ***Perspectives on Terrorism.*** Wilmington, DE.: Scholarly Resources, 1983. pp. 201-212.

2528. _____. "Hostage Negotiations: Types, Processes, Outcomes." ***Negotiation Journal,*** 2:1 (1986), 57-72.

2529. Fuselier, G. W. "A Practical Overview of Hostage Negotiations, Part 1 and 2." ***FBI Law Enforcement Bulletin,*** 50:6 (1981), 2-6; 50-7 (1981), 10-15.

2530. _____, and Gary W. Noesner. "Confronting the Terrorist Hostage Taker." ***FBI Law Enforcement Bulletin,*** 59 (July 1990), 6-11.

2531. Glasgow, Matt. "If You Are Taken Hostage..." ***Soldiers,*** 35 (May 1980), 11-14.

2532. Hacker, Frederick J. "A Case Study of Hostage Negotiation." In: M. F. Herz, ed. ***Diplomats and Terrorists.*** Washington, D.C.: Institute for the Study of Diplomacy, 1982. pp. 1-5.

2533. Hassel, Conrad V. "Terrorism and Hostage Negotiation." In: D. J. D. Sandole and I. Sandole-Staroste, eds. ***Conflict Management and Problem Solving.*** London: Frances Pinter, 1987. pp. 184-193.

2534. Hermann, Margaret G., and Charles F. Hermann. "Hostage Taking, The Presidency and Stress." In: W. Reich, ed. ***Origins of Terrorism.*** Cambridge: Cambridge University Press, 1990. pp. 211-229.

2535. "Hostage Relief Operations." ***International Law Enforcement,*** 1:4 (1984), 5-7, 9, 11-12, 14-16, 18, 20.

2536. "Hostage Situation: Practice and Procedure." ***Security Management,*** 32:6 (June 1988), 128-129.

2537. "How to Survive the Terrorist Interrogation." ***TVI Journal,*** 2:8 (1981), 3-6.

2538. Hudson, Rex A. "Dealing with International Hostage-Taking: Alternatives to Reactive Counterterrorist Assaults." ***Terrorism,*** 12:5 (1989), 321-378.

2539. Jenkins, Brian M. "The Payment of Ransom." In: B. M. Jenkins, ed. ***Terrorism and Personal Protection.*** Stoneham. MA.: Butterworth, 1985. pp. 222-231.

2540. _____. "Some Simple Principles Based on Experience." In: M. F. Herz, ed. ***Diplomats and Terrorists.*** Washington, D.C.: Institute for the Study of Diplomacy, 1982. pp. 48-54.

2541. _____. "Talking to Terrorists." In: B. M. Jenkins, ed. ***Terrorism and Personal Protection.*** Stoneham, MA.: Butterworth, 1985. pp. 302-313.

2542. _____. "Children Held Hostage: When No Policy May Be the Best Policy." ***TVI Report,*** 8:4 (1989), 6-8.

2543. Laingen, Bruce. "Diplomats and Terrorism: A Former Hostage Looks at the Need for Physical Safety and Multilateral Accords." ***Foreign Service Journal,*** 58 (September 1981), 19-21.

2544. Lingo, E. J. "Proaction to the Terrorist Hostage - Taking Challenge: A Training Exercise." ***Police Chief,*** 49:4 (1982), 51-53.

2545. Malawer, Stuart S. "Rewarding Terrorism: The U.S. - Iranian Hostage Accords." ***International Security Review,*** (Winter 1981-1982), 477-496.

2546. Matwin, Stan, Stan Szpakowicz and Mike Connoly. "How to Talk to a Terrorist: An Expert System Approach." ***Canadian Police College Journal***, 12:2 (1988), 69-85.

2547. McGeorge, Harvey J. "Plan Carefully, Rehearse Throughly, Execute Violently: The Tactical Response to Hostage Situations." ***World Affairs***, 146:1 (1983), 59-68.

2548. Merari, Ariel. "Government Policy in Incidents Involving Hostages." In: A. Merari, ed. ***On Terrorism and Combating Terrorism.*** Frederick, MD.: University Publications of America, 1985. pp. 163-176.

2549. Michalowski, Wojtek. "How to Talk to a Terrorist: An Expert System Approach." ***Canadian Police College Journal***, 12:2 (1988), 69-85.

2550. Miller, Abraham H. "Terrorism and Hostage Taking: Lessons from the Iranian Crisis." ***Rutgers Law Journal***, 13 (Spring 1982), 513-529.

2551. Murphy, John F. "Report on Conference on International Terrorism: Protection of Diplomatic Premises and Personnel, Bellagio, Italy, March 8-12, 1982." ***Terrorism***, 6:3 (1983), 481-496.

2552. Newsom, David D. "The Diplomat's Task Versus Security." In: M. F. Herz, ed. ***Diplomats and Terrorists.*** Washington, D.C.: Institute for the Study of Diplomacy, 1982. pp. 9-11.

2553. Niehous, William F. "How to Survive as a Hostage." In: M. F. Herz, ed. ***Diplomats and Terrorists.*** Washington, D.C.: Institute for the Study of Diplomacy, 1982. pp. 33-36.

2554. _____. "Thoughts on What U.S. Reaction Should be After a Terrorist Strike - A Hostage Viewpoint." ***University of Toledo Law Review***, 18:1 (Fall 1986), 151-153.

2555. Nudell, Mayer, and Norman Antokol. "Negotiating for Life." ***Security Management***, 34:7 (1990), 56-64+.

2556. Ochberg, Frank M. "Negotiating with Terrorists." In: A. Merari, ed. ***On Terrorism and Combating Terrorism.*** Frederick, MD.: University Publications of America, 1985. pp. 177-188.

2557. Phillips, David A. "On Looking into the Barrel of a Gun." ***The Washingtonian***, (April 1980), 114-119.

2558. Pitts, Walter D. "Surviving as a Hostage." ***Marine Corps Gazette***, 70:1 (1986), 36-37.

2559. Pol, S. "Nations' Responses to Transnational Hostage Events: An Empirical Evaluation." ***International Interactions***, 14:1 (1988), 27-40.

2560. Porter, Richard E. "Military Hostages: What They Need to Know and Don't." ***Air University Review***, 33 (January/February 1982), 94-101.

2561. Potter, J. "Hostage Negotiation: It All Comes Down to Successful Stress Management." ***National Security***, (January 1989), 6-7.

2562. Quainton, A. C. E. "The Starr Case: A Bureaucracy Under Stress." In: M. F. Herz, ed. ***Diplomats and Terrorism.*** Washington, D.C.: Institute for the Study of Diplomacy, 1982. pp. 41-43.

2563. Quarles, Chester L. "Kidnapped: A "Successful Hostage" Will Emerge Alive." ***Evangelical Missionary Quarterly***, 23 (October 1987), 342-349.

2564. _____. "Kidnap Survival." ***Leaders***, 12:2 (1989), 136-138.

2565. Queen, Richard. "Review of the Terrorism Seminar by a Former Hostages." ***State***, 232 (March 1981), 15-16.

2566. Quigley, John. "Government Vigilantes at Large: The Danger to Human Rights From Kidnapping of Suspected Terrorists." ***Human Rights Quarterly,*** 10 (May 1988), 193-213.

2567. Reiser, Martin, and Martin Sloane. "The Use of Suggestibility Techniques in Hostage Negotiations." In: L. Z. Freedman and Y. Alexander, eds. ***Perspectives on Terrorism.*** Wilmington, DE.: Scholarly Resources, 1983. pp. 213-224.

2568. Richardson, Leon D., and K. Sinclair. "Negotiation III: The Richardson Negotiations." In: B. M. Jenkins, ed. ***Terrorism and Personal Protection.*** Stoneham, MA.: Butterworth, 1985. pp. 276-290.

2569. _____. "Surviving Captivity I: A Hundred Days." In: B. M. Jenkins, ed. ***Terrorism and Personal Protection.*** Stoneham, MA.: Butterworth, 1985. pp. 407-422.

2570. Rodman, Peter W. "The Hostage Crisis: How Not to Negotiate." ***Washington Quarterly,*** 4:3 (1981), 9-24.

2571. Sands, Jack M. "The Hostage Situation Decision Tree." ***TVI Journal,*** 1:8 (1980), 9-10.

2572. Schlossberg, Harvey. "Values and Organization in Hostage and Crisis Negotiation Teams." In: F. Wright, C. Bahn and R. W. Rieber, eds. ***Forensic Psychology and Psychiatry.*** New York: New York Academy of Sciences, 1980. pp. 113-116.

2573. Schoch, Bruce P. "Four Rules for a Successful Rescue." ***Army,*** 31 (February 1981), 22-25.

2574. Sen, S. "Handling Hostage Situations." ***Police Journal,*** 62:1 (1989), 49-55.

2575. Shaw, Eric D. "Political Hostages: Sanction and the Recovery Process." In: L. Z. Freedman and Y. Alexander, eds. ***Perspective on Terrorism.*** Wilmington, DE.: Scholarly Resources, 1983. pp. 143-156.

2576. Sick, Gary. "Taking Vows: The Domestication of Policy-Making in Hostage Incidents." In: W. Reich, ed. ***Origins of Terrorism.*** Cambridge: Cambridge University Press, 1990. pp. 230-246.

2577. Sloan, Stephen. "TWA Flight-847: Learning Hard Lessons." ***United States Naval Institute Proceedings,*** 112:2 (February 1986), 78-80.

2578. Soskis, David A., and Clinton R. Van Zandt. "Hostage Negotiation: Law Enforcement's Most Effective Nonlethal Weapon." ***Behavioral Sciences and the Law,*** 4:4 (Fall 1986), 423-435.

2579. Stanley, Richard. "Hostage Negotiations and the Stockholm Syndrome." ***Military Intelligence,*** (October-December 1984), 28-30.

2580. Starr, Richard C. "Callousness and Ineptitude in the State Department." In: M. F.Herz, ed. ***Diplomats and Terrorists.*** Washington, D.C.: Institute for the Study of Diplomacy, 1982. pp. 37-41.

2581. Strentz, Thomas. "Hostage Psychological Survival Guide." ***FBI Law Enforcement Bulletin,*** 56:11 (November 1987), 1-8.

2582. _____. "Negotiating with the Hostage-Taker Exhibiting Paranoid Schizophrenic Symptoms." ***Journal of Police Science and Administration,*** 14 (1986), 12-16.

2583. "TVI Interview: The Hostages and the Negotiator: Family Perspectives on the Bulgari Kidnapping." ***TVI Report,*** 8:3 (1989), 23-42.

2584. Wilkinson, Paul. "After Teheran." ***Conflict Quarterly,*** 1:4 (1981), 5-14.

2585. Wolfertz, Robert. "Surviving a Hostage Situation." ***Marine Corps Gazette,*** (June 1982), 18-20.

2586. Zeta, Dr. "Negotiations II: A Negotiator's Experience in a Latin American Kidnapping Case." In: B. M. Jenkins, ed. ***Terrorism and Personal Protection.*** Stoneham, MA.: Butterworth, 1985. pp. 262-276.

2587. Zoll, Donald A. "Coping with Hostage Taking: Lessons from the 19th Century." ***Military Review,*** 68:7 (1988), 67-78.

3. Documents and Reports

2588. Benjamin, Charles M. "The Iranian Hostage Negotiations: A Metagame Analysis." Paper Presented at the ***23rd Annual Convention of the International Studies Association,*** held on March 24-27, 1982 in Cincinnati, Ohio.

2589. Council of Europe. European Committee on Crime Problems. ***Extortions Under Terrorist Threats.*** Strasbourg: Council of Europe, 1986. 14p.

2590. Gore, R. L., and D. W. Reaney. ***Applicability of the Code of Conduct in a Terrorist Hostage Situation.*** Maxwell AFB, AL.: Air Command and Staff College, 1987. 41p.

2591. Gowin, W. C. ***Armed Intervention in Terrorist Hostage Situations: A Comparative Analysis.*** Master's Thesis. Wright-Patterson AFB, OH.: Air Force Institute of Technology, 1989. 88p.

2592. ***Hostage Negotiations: A Matter of Life and Death.*** International Security & Terrorism Series, No. 2. Upland, PA.: Diane Pubs, 1987. 42p.

2593. Pieczenik, Steve R. ***Hostage Negotiations with Terrorists.*** Ph.D. Dissertation. Cambridge, MA.: M.I.T., 1982.

2594. United States. Department of Justice. Drug Enforcement Administration. ***Terrorism, Avoidance and Survival.*** Washington, D.C.: U.S. Government Printing Office, 1981. 32p.

2595. _____. Department of State. Bureau of Diplomatic Security. ***Hostage Taking: Preparation, Avoidance, and Survival.*** Department of State Publication 9400. Washington, D.C.: U.S. Government Printing Office, 1989. 38p.

2596. Wolf, John B. "Hostage Extraction: A Comparative Analysis of the Options." In: ***Clandestine Tactics and Technology.*** Gaithersburg, MD.: International Association of Chiefs of Police, 1980. 22p.

G. BUSINESS SECURITY ASPECTS

1. Books

2597. Cole, Richard B. ***Executive Security: A Corporate Guide to Effective Response to Abduction and Terrorism.*** New York: Wiley - Interscience, 1980. 323p.

2598. Montana, Patrick J., and George S. Roukis, eds. ***Managing Terrorism: Strategies for the Corporate Executive.*** Westport, CT.: Quorum Books, 1983. 182p.

2599. Scotti, Tony. ***Executive Safety and International Terrorism: A Guide for Travellers.*** Englewood Cliffs, NJ.: Prentice-Hall, 1986. 220p.

2600. ***The Vulnerable 600: Top U.S. Corporations and Executives Most at Risk from Terrorist Attacks.*** Chapel Hill, NC.: Documentary Publications, 1986. 700p.

2. Journal Articles

2601. Ackerman, "Mike" E. C. "Protecting Businessmen Abroad." In: M. F. Herz, ed. ***Diplomats and Terrorists.*** Washington, D.C.: Institute for the Study of Diplomacy, 1982. pp. 26-29.

2602. Adkins, L., and William F. Niehous. "One Hostage's Experience." ***Dun's Review,*** 115:3 (1980), 60-66.

2603. Alexander, Arthur J. "Getting the Most from Scarce Resources." ***TVI Journal,*** 5:2 (1984), 26-32.

2604. Aranha, J. D. "VIP (Very Important Person) Protection - The Automobile." ***Professional Protection Magazine,*** 4:5 (January/February 1984), 36-41.

2605. Aristoff, Gregory P. "Insuring International Terrorist Risks." ***National Underwriter,*** 94 (July 9, 1990), 10-11+.

2606. Baron, Barbara. "Executive Protection: Security Firms Employ Special Skills, Services to Ensure Safety." ***Journal of Defense and Diplomacy,*** 5 (August 1987), 49-51.

2607. Blank, Joseph K., and Richard J. Gallagher. "Corporate Security Takes Off." ***Security Management,*** 26 (August 1982), 103-108.

2608. Brown, Peter J., and Terrell E. Arnold. "Counterterrorism as Enterprise: The Iran-Contra Investigations Spotlight the New Private Sector." In: N. C. Livingstone and T. E. Arnold, eds. ***Beyond the Iran-Contra Crisis.*** Lexington, MA.: D.C. Heath & Lexington Books, 1988. pp. 191-210.

2609. Buckelew, Alvin H. "The Threat of Technoterrorism." ***Security Management,*** 27 (November 1983), 38-42+.

2610. _____. "Security Without Constraints." ***Security Management,*** 31:6 (June 1987), 48-54.

2611. Business International Survey. "Corporate Risk Contingency Planning." ***International Lawyer,*** 13:1 (1982), 149-154.

2612. Business Risks International. "Regional and Entity Analysis by Target, 1987." In: Y. Alexander and A. H. Foxman, eds. ***The 1986 Annual on Terrorism.*** Dordrecht: Martinus Nijhoff, 1988. pp. 189-190.

2613. Campbell, H. E. "The Corporation as Hostage." ***Security Management,*** 28 (August 1984), 84-87.

2614. Carroll, John J. "Corporate Security: Top Management Mandate." ***Duns Review,*** 115 (January 1980),91-116.

2615. Cathey, P. "Ways to Combat Terrorism, Business Risk Overseas." ***Iron Age,*** (May 26, 1980), 26-29.

2616. "Choosing an Executive Car." ***TVI Journal,*** 3:4 (1982), 2-4.

2617. Colwell, William Lee. "Designing a Corporate Response to Terrorism." ***Police Chief,*** 52 (February 1985), 22-24.

2618. Cooper, H. H. A. "Getting Out: The Evacuation of Business Personnel." In: B. M. Jenkins, ed. ***Terrorism and Personal Protection.*** Stoneham, MA.: Butterworth, 1985. pp. 160-166.

2619. Copeland, Lennie. "Travelling: Safe or Sorry." ***Security Management,*** 31:9 (September 1987), 160-164.

2620. Corbett, William T. "Be on Your Toes." ***Security Management,*** (October 1986), 109-111.

2621. _____. "Fighting Back." ***Security Management,*** (August 1986), 42-44.

2622. Cowan, W. M. "Office Security: Thwarting the Terrorist Threat." ***Administrative Management***, 48 (June 1987), 14-16.

2623. D'Amore, Louis J., and Teresa E. Anuza. "International Terrorism: Implications and Challenge for Global Tourism" ***Business Quarterly***, 51:3 (November 1986), 20-29.

2624. "Danger on Our Doorsteps." ***Security Management***, 30:12 (December 1986), 49-52.

2625. Davis, E. D. "Combating Terrorism on the Corporate Level: The Emergence of Executive Protection Specialists in Private Security." ***Journal of Contemporary Criminal Justice***, 4:4 (1988), 241-251.

2626. De Janos, Sigmund J. A. "Corporate Security in the Electronic Age." ***TVI Journal***, 2:11 (1981), 3-8.

2627. "Equipping Executive Cars." ***TVI Journal***, 3:5 (1982), 2-4.

2628. Fairer-Smith, John. "Multinational Balancing Act: Risk and Profit in the Third World." ***TVI Journal***, 1:12 (1980), 7-9.

2629. Farnham, A. "Read This or We'll Cut off Your Ear." ***Fortune***, 122 (December 31, 1990), 88-90+.

2630. Fitzpatrick, Thomas K. "Buying an Armored Car: The Business-Like Approach Will Get better Mileage." ***TVI Journal***, 1:3 (1980), 13-17.

2631. Fruhauf, Henry. "Responding to Threats with the Wisdom of Solomon." ***Security Management***, 31:3 (March 1987), 47-50.

2632. Giuffrida, Louis O. "Physical Security: An Introduction." ***Terrorism***, 10:3 (1987), 231-232.

2633. Godfrey, David. "Terrorism and Banking." ***Terrorism***, 5:4 (1982), 353-362.

2634. Harrick, Phillip J. "Dangerous Waters." ***Security Management***, 33:11 (November 1989), 44-46+.

2635. Hartz, C. "Business Executives as International Terrorist Targets." In: J. R. Buckwalter, ed. ***International Terrorism: The Decade Ahead.*** Chicago, IL.: University of Illinois at Chicago, Office of International Criminal Justice, 1989. pp. 21-28.

2636. Harvey, M. G. "A New Corporate Weapon Against Terrorism." ***Business Horizons***, 28:1 (1985), 42-47.

2637. _____. "The Vanishing Multinational Marketing Executives: Protecting Them Against Terrorists." In: K. Bernhardt, et al. ***Changing Marketing Environments: New Theories and Applications.*** Chicago, IL.: American Marketing Association, 1981. pp. 51-53.

2638. _____. "Terrorists vs. the MNC." ***Public Relations Journal***, 39 (October 1983), 12-17.

2639. Hayes, James R. "International Terrorism and Violence: Corporate Response." ***Police Chief***, 49:1 (1982), 122-124.

2640. Healy, Richard J. "Protecting the Office." In: B. M. Jenkins, ed. ***Terrorism and Personal Protection.*** Stoneham, MA.: Butterworth, 1985. pp. 339-353.

2641. Heinly, D. R. "When Business Needs Protection Overseas." ***Security***, 24:6 (June 1987), 63-67.

2642. Iglarsh, Harvey J. "Studies in Business and Management." ***Terrorism***, 12:1 (1989), 64-65.

2643. _____. "Terrorism and Corporate Costs." ***Terrorism***, 10:3 (1987), 227-230.

2644. James, Patrick. "Terrorism and the Breakdown of International Order: The Corporate Dimension." ***Conflict Quarterly***, 8 (Summer 1988), 69-88.

2645. Jenkins, Brian M., Susanna W. Purnell and Eleanor S. Wainstein. "The Effects of Terrorism on Business." In: B. M. Jenkins, ed. ***Terrorism and Personal Protection.*** Stoneham, MA.: Butterworth, 1985. pp. 148-159.

2646. _____. "The Effects of Terrorism on Corporations." ***TVI Journal,*** 5:3 (1985), 4-6.

2647. _____. "The Payment of Ransom." ***TVI Report,*** 7:4 (1987), 22-26.

2648. Kelly, Robert J., and Jack Barnathan. "Perspectives on Terrorism - Out on a Limb: Executives Abroad." ***Security Management,*** 32:11 (November 1988), 117-127.

2649. Ketcham, Christine C., and Harvey J. II McGeorge. "Protection of Senior Executives." ***World Airlines,*** 146:3 (1983-84), 277-283.

2650. Kindel, Stephen. "Hazardous Duty." ***Savvy,*** (July 1986), 34-37.

2651. Kovsky, S. "Corporate Terrorism: A New Global Threat." ***Management Review,*** 79 (October 1990), 39-41+.

2652. Kupperman, Robert H. "Countering Terrorism: Time to Switch Tactics." ***Enterprise,*** (September 1982), 20-22.

2653. Leach, Norman S. "Executive Protection: An Ironclad Defense." ***Security Management,*** 34:2 (February 1990), 84-88.

2654. _____. "Terrorism in Your Own Backyard." ***Security Management,*** 33:5 (May 1989), 56-60.

2655. Lee, E. L. "Adopting an Executive Protection Program." ***Security Management,*** (February 1984), 26-29.

2656. Leibstone, Marvin. "Corporation Terror - Violence and the Business Community." In: ***Clandestine Tactics and Technology, Vol. 6.*** Gaithersburg, MD.: International Association of Chiefs of Police, 1980. 22p.

2657. Levinson, Eric. "For a High-Risk Office: Concrete Suggestions on "Target Hardening"." ***TVI Journal,*** 1:6 (1980), 2-8.

2658. _____. "The Car: Whose Weapon Is It?." ***TVI Journal,*** 2:5 (1981), 5-12.

2659. Lighbody, Andy. "How to Foil Terrorists: 101 Tips on How Not to Become a Victim." ***International Combat Arms,*** 4:6 (1986), 12, 15-16, 18, 20.

2660. Lipman, Ira A. "Viewpoint: Living with Terrorism - Global Reality for American Interests." ***Security Management,*** 30:1 (1986), 81-82.

2661. Littlejohn, Robert F. "When the Crisis is Terrorism." ***Security Management,*** (August 1986), 38-41.

2662. Livingstone, Neil C. "Fighting Terrorism: The Private Sector." ***Conflict,*** 3:2-3 (1981), 177-222.

2663. Mack, Toni. "Looking Out for Number One." ***Forbes,*** 134 (December 31, 1984), 126-127.

2664. Maddox, R. C. "Terrorism's Hidden Threat and the Promise for Multinational Corporations." ***Business Horizons,*** 33:6 (November - December 1990), 48-51.

2665. Malcher, A. "V.I.P. Close Protection and the Private Security Sector: An International Problem?." ***Police Journal,*** 62:3 (July-September 1989), 234-237.

2666. Marks, Jim. "Terrorism: An International Threat." ***Journal of Insurance,*** (September/October 1980), 13-18.

2667. McClure, Brooks. "Corporate Vulnerability - and How to Assess It." In: Y. Alexander and C. K. Ebinger, eds. ***Political Terrorism and Energy.*** New York: Praeger, 1982. pp. 209-228.

2668. _____. "Assessing Corporate Vulnerability." In: R. A. Kilmarx and Y. Alexander, eds. ***Business and the Middle East: Threats and Prospects.*** New York: Pergamon Press, 1982. pp. 200-216.

2669. McGeorge, Harvey J., and Charles F. Vance. "Executive Protection: Living Long in a Dangerous World." In: N. C. Livingstone and T. E. Arnold, eds. ***Fighting Back: Winning the War Against Terrorism.*** Lexington, MA.: Lexington Books, 1985. pp. 95-108.

2670. _____, and Christine C. Ketcham. "Protection of Senior Executives." ***World Affairs,*** 146:3 (1983/84), 277-283.

2671. Meserve, E. N. "Executive Protection." ***Journal of Security Administration,*** 5:1 (1982), 49-50.

2672. Messmer, Robert F. "Safe Houses for Business." ***Across the Board,*** 24 (January 1987), 45-52.

2673. Mitchell, Thomas H. "Corporate Security in an Age of Terrorism." ***Canadian Business Review,*** (Spring 1984), 31-36.

2674. Monday, Mark. "Dealing with Head-in-the-Sand Executives." ***TVI Journal,*** 3:12 (1983), 2-3.

2675. Montana, Patrick J., and S. M. Krinsky. "Organizations Serving the Executive Protection Field." In: J. P. Montana and S. M. Krinsky, eds. ***Managing Terrorism.*** Westport, CT.: Books, 1983. pp. 135-160.

2676. Morphew, Anthony J. "Corporate Extortion Insurance." ***TVI Report,*** 7:4 (1987), 27-29.

2677. Nadel, Seth R. "Ink is Also Red." ***TVI Journal,*** 2:2 (1981), 2-3.

2678. Newcomer, H. A., and J. W. Adkins. "Terrorism and the Business Executive." ***Personnel Journal,*** 59 (November 1980), 913-917.

2679. Nudell, Mayer. "Surviving a Terrorist Crisis." ***Risk Management,*** 32 (May 1985), 56-58+.

2680. O'Reilly, Brian. "Business Copes with Terrorism." ***Fortune,*** 113 (January 6, 1986), 47-48+.

2681. Passow, Sam. "Terrorism and Corporate Liability." ***TVI Journal,*** 5:2 (1984), 32-33.

2682. Pearson, Michael A., John K. Ryans and William L. Shanklin. "Counteracting Terrorism." ***Internal Auditor,*** 41 (April 1984), 24-27.

2683. Pizer, Harry. "Executive Protection: The View from the Private Security Sector." In: R. H. Shultz and S. Sloan, eds. ***Responding to the Terrorist Threat.*** New York: Pergamon Press, 1980. pp. 105-114.

2684. Pope, William. "Insuring Survival is the Only Policy." ***TVI Journal,*** 2:8 (1981), 5-7.

2685. Quarles, Chester L. "Kidnapped: Surviving the Ordeal." ***Security Management,*** 32:5 (May 1988), 40-44.

2686. Rescorla, Richard. "Adapting and Adopting: Tailoring the Company Security Plan to Meet the Terrorist Challenge." ***TVI Journal,*** 1:7 (1980), 7-12.

2687. _____. "Managing the Unmanageable." ***TVI Journal,*** 2:2 (1981), 10-17.

2688. Russell, Charles A. "Business Becoming Increasing Targets." In: P. J. Montana and G. S. Roukis, eds. ***Managing Terrorism.*** Westport, CT.: Quorum Books, 1983. pp.55-72.

2689. Russo, R. J. "Planning for Damage Control." ***Security Management,*** 33 (December 11, 1989), 97-99.

2690. Ryans, John K., and William L. Shanklin. "How Managers Cope With Terrorism." ***California Management Review,*** 23:1 (1980), 66-72.

2691. _____. _____. "Terrorism and the Multinational Company." ***Business,*** 30:2 (1980), 2-7.

2692. Schneider, Joseph S. "Business as a Terrorist Target: Experience and Response." ***Security Management***, 28:5 (1984), 86-92.

2693. Scotti, Tony. "Anti-Surveillance Security: The Key to Ambush Avoidance." ***TVI Journal***, 1:2 (1980), 2-3.

2694. _____. "Brief Notes in Morning Can Prevent Mourning." ***TVI Journal***, 3:6 (1982), 2-3.

2695. _____. "Careful Choice Needed for Executive Cars." ***TVI Journal***, 3:4 (1982), 2-3.

2696. _____. "Getting Right Car Isn't Automatic." ***TVI Journal***, 3:5 (1982), 2-3.

2697. _____. "More Ways to Tripping Up In a Car." ***TVI Journal***, 3:12 (1983), 7.

2698. _____. "That is How Terrorism Starts." ***TVI Journal***, 3:11 (1982), 3.

2699. _____. "A Calculated Assassination." ***Security Management***, 34 (November 1990), 26-31.

2700. "Security Directors on Terrorism: Putting the Problem into the Proper Perspective." ***Security Management***, 28 (August 1984), 79-83.

2701. Sessions, William S. "The Threat of Terrorism." ***Security Management***, 33:9 (September 1989), 10,12+.

2702. Shultz, George. "U.S. Government and Business: Our Common Defence Against Terrorism." ***Department of State Bulletin***, (March 1985), 10-12.

2703. _____. "Terrorism: A Threat to Business and Government." ***Security Management***, 29:4 (1985), 35-39.

2704. Stephens, David, and David MacKenna. "The Next Tool for Terrorists?." ***Security Management***, 32:12 (December 1988), 26-30+.

2705. United States. Department of State. Office for Combatting Terrorism. "Terrorist Attacks Against U.S. Businesses" ***Terrorism***, 8:2 (1985), 185-204.

2706. Wainstein, Eleanor S., and Susanna W. Purnell. "Effects of Terrorism on Business Operations." In: P. J. Montana and G. S. Roukis, eds. ***Managing Terrorism.*** Westport, CT.: Quorum Books, 1983. pp. 123-134.

2707. Wilkins, Keith. "A Minimanual on Surviving Business Trips." ***Internal Auditor***, 43 (October 1986), 22-28.

2708. Wurth, Don E. "The Proper Function and Use of the Private Sector Bodyguard." In: B. M. Jenkins, ed. ***Terrorism and Personal Protection.*** Stoneham, MA.: Butterworth, 1985. pp. 314-338.

3. Documents and Reports

2709. American Society for Industrial Security. ***Terrorism.*** ASIS Information Packet No. 2. Arlington, VA.: American Society for Industrial Security, 1986. 26p.

2710. Brinkerhoff, John R. ***Managing the Consequences of Terrorism.*** Fairfax, VA.: Data Memory Systems, Inc., November 3, 1986. 11p.

2711. Cook, William J. Jr. ***The Effect of Terrorism on Executives' Willingness to Travel Internationally.*** Ph.D. Dissertation. New York: City University of New York, 1990. 184p.

2712. ***How to Avoid, Prepare for & Survive Being Taken Hostage: A Guide for Executives & Travellers.*** International Security & Terrorism Series, No. 1. Upland, PA.: Diane Pubs, 1987. 54p.

2713. Jacobson, Kenneth H. ***The Corporation and International Terrorism.*** Menlo Park, CA.: Business Intelligence Program, SRI International, 1981. 20p.

2714. Murphy, G. M. "Terrorism: The Challenge to the Private Sector." Paper Presented to the ***Proceedings of the 9th Annual Symposium on the Role of Behavioral Sciences in Physical Security,*** held on April 3-4, 1984, in Springfield, VA. pp. 35-38.

2715. Purnell, Susanna W., and Eleanor S. Wainstein. ***The Problems of U.S. Businesses Operating Abroad in Terrorist Environments.*** RAND R-2842-DOC. Santa Monica, CA.: RAND Corporation, 1981. 103p.

2716. _____. ***How International Businesses Cope with Terrorism.*** RAND P-7294. Santa Monica, CA.: RAND Corporation, 1986. 16p.

2717. Stewart, Bernard L., ed. ***International Terrorism: The Threat to Industry.*** Arlington, VA.: SRI International, 1986. 116p.

2718. United States. Department of State. Bureau of Diplomatic Security. ***Countering Terrorism: Security Suggestions for U.S. Business Representatives Abroad.*** Washington, D.C.: U.S. Government Printing Office, 1986. 16p.

2719. _____._____. Office of the Ambassador-at-Large for Counter-Terrorism. ***Terrorist Attacks on U.S. Business Abroad.*** Washington, D.C.: U.S. Government Printing Office, 1986. 19p.

H. SIMULATION RESEARCH

1. Books

2720. Sloan, Stephen. ***Simulating Terrorism.*** Norman, OK.: University of Oklahoma Press, 1981. 158p.

2. Journal Articles

2721. Gilboa, Eitan. "The Use of Simulation in Combatting Terrorism." ***Terrorism,*** 5:3 (1981), 265-280.

2722. Gleason, John M. "Third World Terrorism: Perspectives for Quantitative Research." In: Y. Alexander and J. M. Gleason, eds. ***Behavioral and Quantitative Perspectives on Terrorism.*** New York: Pergamon Press, 1981. pp. 242-255.

2723. Hamilton, Lawrence C. "Dynamics of Insurgent Violence: Preliminary Findings." In: Y. Alexander and J. M. Gleason, eds. ***Behavioral and Quantitative Perspectives on Terrorism.*** New York: Pergamon Press, 1981. pp. 229-241.

2724. _____. "Political Kidnapping as a Deadly Game." ***Simulation and Games,*** 11:4 (1980), 387-402.

2725. Heyman, Edward, and Edward F. Mickolus. "Imitation by Terrorists: Quantitative Approaches to the Study of Diffusion Pattern in International Terrorism." In: Y. Alexander and J. M. Gleason, eds. ***Behavioral and Quantitative Perspectives on Terrorism.*** New York: Pergamon Press, 1981. pp. 175-228.

2726. Lavery, Robert. "Anti-Terrorism Games Can Save Money, Lives." ***TVI Journal,*** 2:12 (1981), 3-6.

2727. Martz, Harry F., and Mark E. Johnson. "Risk Analysis of Terrorist Attacks." ***Risk Analysis***, 7:1 (March 1987), 35-47.

2728. Mickolus, Edward F., and Edward Heyman. "ITERATE: Monitoring Transnational Terrorism." In: Y. Alexander and J. M. Gleason, eds. ***Behavioral and Quantitative Perspectives on Terrorism.*** New York: Pergamon Press, 1981. pp. 153-175.

2729. Miller, Reuben. "Game Theory and Hostage-Taking Incidents: A Case Study of the Munich Olympic Games." ***Conflict Quarterly***, 10:1 (Winter 1990), 12-33.

2730. Newman, F. H., and Lloyd W. Singer. "Simulation - A Key to Crisis Management Training." ***Security Management***, 26:9 (1982), 54, 56-58.

2731. Sloan, Stephen. "Simulating Terrorism: An Analysis of Findings Related to Tactical, Behavioral and Administrative Responses of Participating Police and Military Forces." In: R. H. Shultz and S. Sloan, eds. ***Responding to the Terrorist Threat.*** New York: Pergamon Press, 1980. pp. 115-133.

2732. Thompson, J. L. P. "Deprivation and Political Violence in Northern Ireland, 1922-1985: A Time-Series Analysis." ***Journal of Conflict Resolution***, 33:4 (December 1989), 676-699.

2733. Weimann, Gabriel, and Hans-Bernd Brosius. "The Predictability of International Terrorism: A Time-Series Analysis." ***Terrorism***, 11:6 (1988), 491-502.

3. Documents and Reports

2734. Daidone, H. F. "TAG. The Terrorist Game: A Systems Definition." In: J. S. Jackson and R. W. De Vore, eds. ***Carnahan Conference on Security Technology: Electronic Crime Countermeasures.*** Lexington, KY.: University of Kentucky Press, 1987. pp. 91-98.

2735. Mickolus, Edward F. ***International Terrorism: Attributes of Terrorist Events, 1968-1977 (ITERATE 2).*** Ann Arbor, MI.: Inter-University Consortium for Political and Social Research, 1982.

2736. Shore, C., et al. ***TRACKER: A Prototype Anti-Terrorism Research Data Base.*** Springfield, VA.: Syllogistics, 1987. 16p.

VII

DOMESTIC AND INTERNATIONAL LAW ASPECTS

The law is one of the main weapons used against terrorists. Most states apply their existing criminal codes when dealing with terrorists, but increasingly specific anti terror legislations have been adopted. As terrorism has become more international in scope, states have increased their collaboration in fighting it. These endeavors brought about interest in questions of international legal controls. We witness the development of international legal conventions to control terrorism. As there is a lack of consensus about the definition of terrorism, and states rarely have common interests and legal systems, the development of international laws is a slow process. As a result, existing legal agreements tend to be mainly bilateral in scope.

Section A covers the literature of domestic and international legislation, problems of jurisdiction and extradition. Section B covers materials dealing with various international organizations, such as the United Nations, the Organization of American States and the European Economic Community and their work in the area of legal agreements and conventions to counter terrorism. Section C deals with all legal aspects and legal conventions concerning civil aviation, airline security and aircraft hijackings.

A. DOMESTIC AND INTERNATIONAL LAW ASPECTS

1. Books

2737. Alexander, Yonah, and Allan S. Nanes, eds. ***Legislative Responses to Terrorism.*** International Studies on Terrorism, 1. Dordrecht: M. Nijhoff, 1986. 327p.

2738. Bassiouni, M. Cherif, ed. ***Legal Responses to International Terrorism: U.S. Procedural Aspects.*** International Studies in Terrorism, 4. Dordrecht: Martinus Nijhoff, 1988. 454p.

2739. Blischenko, Igor P. ***Terrorism and International Law.*** Moscow: Progress Publishers, 1984. 286p.

2740. Dewan, Vijay K. ***Law Relating to Terrorists.*** New York: State Mutual Book & Periodical Service, 1987. 400p.

2741. Dhokalia, R. P., and K. Narayana Rao, eds. ***Terrorism and International Law.*** New Delhi: Indian Society of International Law, 1988. 151p.

2742. Dubner, Barry H. ***The Law of International Sea Piracy.*** The Hague: Martinus Nijhoff, 1980. 176p.

2743. Gordon, E. ***Legal and Financial Aspects of Iranian Hostage Settlement. 2 Vols.*** Dobbs Ferry, NY.: Oceana, 1982.

2744. Murphy, John F. ***Punishing International Terrorists: The Legal Framework for Policy Initiatives.*** Totowa, NJ.: Rowman & Allanheld, 1985. 142p.

2745. Ronzitti, Natalino, ed. ***Maritime Terrorism and International Law.*** International Studies on Terrorism; 6. Dordrecht: Martinus Nijhoff, 1990. 185p.

2746. Satish, Chandra. ***International Terrorism and Its Control: Developing International Law and Operational Mechanisms.*** Allahabad, India: Vohra Publications, 1989. 122p.

2747. Scorer, Catherine, et al. ***The New Prevention of Terrorism Act: The Case for Repeal.*** New York: State Mutual Books, 1988.

2748. Suter, Keith. ***An International Law of Guerrilla Warfare: The Global Politics of Law Making.*** New York: St.Martin's Press, 1984. 192p.

2749. Van de Wijngaert, Christine. ***The Political Offence Exception to Extradition: The Delicate Problem of Balancing the Rights of the Individual and the International Public Order.*** Antwerp: Kluwer - Dewenter, 1980.

2750. Walker, Clive. ***The Prevention of Terrorism in British Law.*** Manchester: Manchester University Press, 1986. 272p.

2. Journal Articles

2751. Abramovsky, Abraham. "Extraterritorial Jurisdiction: The United States Unwarranted Attempt to Alter International Law in United States v. Yunis." ***The Yale Journal of International Law,*** 15 (Winter 1990), 121-161.

2752. _____. "The Political Offense Exception and the Extradition Process: The Enhancement of the Role of the U.S. Judiciary." ***Hastings International and Comparative Law Review,*** 13:1 (1989), 1-24.

2753. "The Achille Lauro Incident and the Permissible Use of Force." ***Loyola of Los Angeles International and Comparative Law Journal,*** 9 (1987), 481-497.

2754. Adams, Tom. "Law and the Lawless - Terrorism: The International Legal Perspective." ***TVI Journal,*** 1:9 (1980), 4-9.

2755. Adelman, Kenneth. "Extradition of Abu Eain: U.S. Justice at Work." ***World Affairs,*** 144 (Winter 1981/82), 290-295.

2756. Ader, Werner. "International Law and the Discretion of the State to Handle Hostage Incidents - Cui Bono?." ***German Yearbook of International Law,*** 31 (1988), 372-414.

2757. Aldridge, P., and C. Belsey. "Murder Under Duress - Terrorism and the Criminal--Law." ***International Journal for the Semiotics of Law-Revue,*** 2:6 (1989), 223-

2758. Alexander, Yonah, et al. "Legal Aspects of Terrorism." ***Terrorism,*** 12:L4 (1989), 297-316.

2759. Almond, Harry H. "The Legal Regulation of International Terrorism." ***Conflict,*** 3:2-3 (1981), 143-166.

2760. _____. "Limits and Possibilities of International Regulations of Terrorism." In: H. H. Han, ed. ***Terrorism, Political Violence and World Order.*** Lanham, MD.: University Press of America, 1984. pp. 493-510.

2761. _____. "Using the Law To Combat Terrorism." In: N. C. Livingstone and T. E. Arnold, eds. ***Fighting Back: Winning the War Against Terrorism.*** Lexington, MA.: Lexington Books, 1985. pp. 157-174.

2762. An-Na'im, Abdullahi Ahmed. "Islamic Ambivalence to Political Terrorism: Islamic Law and International Terrorism." ***German Yearbook of International Law,*** 31 (1988), 307-336.

2763. "An Analysis of the United States' Response to the Achille Lauro Hijacking." ***Boston College Third World Law Journal,*** 8 (Winter 1988), 137-149.

2764. Andrews, J. "The United Kingdom Prevention of Terrorism Act." ***European Law Review,*** 8 (1983), 205-208.

2765. "Appendix II - Extradition Treaty Between the Government of the United States of America and the Government of the Republic of Italy." In: M. C. Bassiouni, ed. ***Legal Responses to International Terrorism: U.S. Procedural Aspects.*** Dordrecht: Martinus Nijhoff, 1988. pp. 363-372.

2766. Arnold, Terrell E. "New Directions in Using the Law to Combat Terrorism." In: D. C. Livingstone and T. E. Arnold, eds. ***Beyond the Iran-Contra Crisis.*** Lexington, MA.: D.C. Heath & Lexington Books, 1988. pp. 211-224.

2767. "The Attempted Extradition of Mohammed Hamadei: Discretion and the U.S. - West German Extradition Treaty." ***Wisconsin International Law Journal,*** 8 (Fall 1989), 123-164.

2768. Awford, Ian. "Civil Liability Concerning Unlawful Interference with Civil Aviation." ***Air Law,*** 12:3 (June 1987), 120-142.

2769. Baker, Mark B. "The South American Legal Response to Terrorism." ***Boston University International Law Journal,*** 3 (Winter 1985), 67-97.

2770. _____. "Terrorism and the Inherent Right of Self-Defense." ***Houston Journal of International Law,*** 10:1 (Autumn 1987), 25-49.

2771. _____. "The Western European Legal Response to Terrorism." ***Brooklyn Journal of International Law,*** 13:1 (January 1987), 1-24.

2772. Bannoff, Barbara Ann, and Christopher Pyle. "'To Surrender Political Offenders': The Political Offense Exception to Extradition in United States Law." ***New York University Journal of International Law and Politics,*** 16:2 (Winter 1984), 169-210.

2773. Barnes, Rudolph C. "Special Operations and the Law." ***Military Review***, (June 1986), 49-58.

2774. Barr, Edward J. "Terrorism and International Law." ***Marine Corps Gazette***, 73 (October 1989), 32-33.

2775. Barr, Scott C. "The Dilemma of the Political Offence Exception: To Which Acts Should It Apply?." ***Hamline Journal of Public Law and Policy***, 10:1 (Spring 1989), 141-155.

2776. Bassiouni, M. Cherif. "The Political Offense Exception Revisited: Extradition Between the U.S. and the U.K. - A Choice Between Friendly Cooperation Among Allies and Sound Law and Policy." ***Denver Journal of International Law and Policy***, 15 (Winter-Spring 1987), 255-282.

2777. _____. "Effective National and International Action Against Organized Crime and Terrorist Criminal Activities." ***Emory International Law Review***, 4 (Spring 1990), 9-42.

2778. Baunach, Phyllis Jo. "The U.S. - U.K. Supplementary Extradition Treaty: Justice for Terrorists or Terror for Justice?." ***Connecticut Journal of International Law***, 2:2 (Spring 1987), 463-498.

2779. Bazyler, Michael J. "Capturing Terrorists in the 'Wild Blue Yonder': International Law and the Achile Lauro and Libyan Aircraft Incidents." ***Whittier Law Review***, 8:3 (1986), 685-709

2780. Beres, Louis Rene. "The Question of Terrorism Within the Framework of International Law." In: H. Kochler, ed. ***Terrorism and National Liberation.*** Frankfurt: Verlag Peter Lang, 1988. pp. 253-262.

2781. _____. "Terrorism and International Law." ***Florida International Law Journal***, 3:3 (Summer 1988) 291-306.

2782. Bernhardt, Peter J. "The Provisional Measures Procedure of the International Court of Justice Through U.S. Staff in Tehran: Fiat Institia, Pereat Curia?" ***Virginia Journal of International Law***, 20 (Spring 1980), 557-613.

2783. Berns, Walter. "Constitutional Power and the Defence of Free Government." In: B. Netanyahu, ed. ***Terrorism: How the West Can Win.*** New York: Farrar, Straus, Giroux, 1986. pp. 149-154.

2784. Berry, Steve M. "Combatting Terrorism: The Legislative Approach." ***TVI Report***, 9:3 (1990), 15-21.

2785. Bialos, J. P., and K. I. Juster. "The Libyan Sanctions: A Rational Response to State - Sponsored Terrorism?." ***Virginia Journal of International Law***, (Summer 1986), 799-855.

2786. Bishop, J. W. "Legal Measures to Control Terrorism in Democracies." In: B. Netanyahu, ed. ***International Terrorism: Challenge and Response.*** New Brunswick, NJ.: Transaction Books, 1981. pp. 294-306.

2787. Blakesley, Christopher L. "Terrorism, Law, and Our Constitutional Order." ***University of Colorado Law Review***, 60:3 (Summer 1989) 471-531.

2788. _____. "Jurisdiction as Legal Protection Against Terrorism." ***Connecticut Law Review***, 19:4 (Summer 1987), 894-943.

2789. _____. "Terrorism and the Constitution." ***Brigham Young University Studies***, 27 (Summer 1987), 197-216.

2790. _____. "Jurisdictional Issues and Conflicts of Jurisdiction." In: M. C. Bassiouni, ed. ***Legal Responses to International Terrorism: U.S. Procedural Aspects.*** Dordrecht: Martinus Nijhoff, 1988. pp. 131-180.

2791. _____. "The Evisceration of the Political Offense Exception to Extradition." ***Denver Journal of International Law and Policy,*** 15:1 (Summer 1986), 109-124.

2792. Bleich, J. David. "Reaction to Terrorism: A Jewish Law Caveat." ***Houston Journal of International Law,*** 11:2 (Spring 1989), 331-336.

2793. Blischenko, Igor P. "Acts of Terrorism Punishable Under International Law." In: H. Kochler, ed. ***Terrorism and National Liberation.*** Frankfurt: Verlag Peter Lang, 1988. pp. 281-.

2794. Blum, Yehuda Z. "The Legality of State Response to Acts of Terrorism." In: B. Netanyahu, ed. ***Terrorism: How the West Can Win.*** New York: Farrar, Straus, Giroux, 1986. pp. 133-138.

2795. _____. "The Gulf of Sidra Incident." ***American Journal of International Law,*** 80 (July 1986), 668-677.

2796. Boire, Martin C. "Terrorism Reconsidered as Punishment: Toward an Evaluation of the Acceptability of Terrorism as a Method of Societal Change or Maintenance." ***Stanford Journal of International Law,*** 20 (Spring 1984), 45-134.

2797. Bonner, David. "Combatting Terrorism in the 1990's: The Role of the Prevention of Terrorism (Temporary Provisions) Act 1989." ***Public Law,*** (Autumn 1989), 440-476.

2798. _____. "The Baker Review of the Northern Ireland (Emergency Provisions) Act 1978." ***Public Law,*** (Autumn 1984), 348-365.

2799. Bouffard, Dean K. "Extradition: Political Offense Exception: United States Court Creates a New Definition for Use Against International Terrorists." ***Suffolk Transnational Law Journal,*** 6:1 (1981-1982), 147-161.

2800. Boulton, J. W. "Maritime Order and the Development of the International Law of Piracy." ***International Relations,*** 7:5 (1983), 2335-2350.

2801. _____. "The Modern International Law of Piracy: Content and Contemporary Relevance." ***International Relations,*** 7:6 (1983), 2493-2511.

2802. Bowen, Elizabeth R. P. "Jurisdiction Over Terrorists Who Take Hostages: Efforts to Stop Terror-Violence Against United States Citizens." ***The American University Journal of International Law and Policy,*** 2:1 (1987), 153-202.

2803. Boyle, Francis A. "International Law in Time of Crisis: From the Entebbe Raid to the Hostages Convention." ***Northwestern University Law Review,*** 75 (December 1980), 769-856.

2804. _____. "Preserving the Rule of Law in the War Against International Terrorism." ***Whittier Law Review,*** 8 (Summer 1986), 735-745.

2805. Bremer, L. Paul. "Terrorism and the Rule of Law." ***Department of State Bulletin,*** 87 (August 1987), 83-86.

2806. Brownlee, Ian D. "Superior Orders - Time for a New Realism." ***Criminal Law Review,*** (June 1989), 396-411.

2807. Bury, Stephen. "The Political Offense Exception in United States Extradition Law: Eain vs. Wilkes." ***Brooklyn Journal of International Law,*** 8:2 (1982), 429-450.

2808. Calavita, Kitty. "'Law and Order' and the Anti-Terrorist Act of 1983." ***Crime and Social Justice,*** 20 (1983), 138-143.

2809. Caldwell, Jennifer. "International Terrorism (Emergency Powers) Act 1987." ***Auckland University Law Review,*** 6:1 (1988), 108-112.

2810. Carbonneau, T. E. "French Judicial Perspectives on the Extradition of Transnational Terrorists and Political Offence Exception." In: R. B. Lillich, ed. ***International Aspects of Criminal Law.*** Charlottesville, VA.: Michie Company, 1981. pp. 66-89.

2811. _____. "The Political Offence Exception as Applied in French Cases Dealing with the Extradition of Terrorists: The Quest for an Appropriate Doctrinal Analysis Revisited." In: ***Michigan Yearbook of International Legal Studies: Transnational Aspects of Criminal Procedures.*** 1983. pp. 209-243.

2812. _____. "Terrorist Acts - Crimes or Political Infractions? An Appraisal of recent French Extradition Cases." ***Hastings International and Comparative Law Review,*** 3:2 (Winter 1980), 265-298.

2813. "Case Concerning State Responsibility for Certain Acts of Terrorism - P.C. Jessup International Law Moot Court Competition 1988." ***ILSA Journal of International Law,*** 12 (Winter 1988), 171-281.

2814. Cassese, Antonio. "Terrorism and Human Rights." ***American University Law Review,*** 31 (Summer 1982), 945-958.

2815. _____. "The International Community's "Legal" Response to Terrorism." ***International and Comparative Law Quarterly,*** 38:3 (July 1989), 589-608.

2816. Chabner, Brandon S. "The Omnibus Diplomatic Security and Antiterrorism Act of 1986: Prescribing and Enforcing United States Law Against Terrorist Violence Overseas." ***UCLA Law Review,*** 37:5 (June 1990), 985-1024.

2817. Chatterjee, S. K. "Terrorism and Certain Legal Aspects of Human Rights." ***International Relations,*** 6:5 (1980), 749-768.

2818. Clark, James G. "Political Offenses in Extradition: Time for Judicial Abstention." ***Hastings International and Comparative Law Review,*** 5:1 (1981), 131-150.

2819. Clark, Roger S. "State Terrorism: Some Lessons from the Sinking of the Rainbow Warrior." ***Rutgers Law Journal,*** 20 (Winter 1989), 393-413.

2820. Cobb, Dawna M. "Prohibiting Indirect Assistance to International Terrorists: Closing the Gap in United States Law." ***Fordham International Law Journal,*** 6:3 (1983), 530-555.

2821. Coll, Alberto R. "The Legal and Moral Adequacy of Military Responses to Terrorism." ***American Society of International Law Proceedings,*** (1987), 297-307.

2822. Condorelli, Luigi. "The Imputability to States of Acts of International Terrorism." In: ***Israel Yearbook on Human Rights, Vol. 19. 1989.*** Dordrecht: Martinus Nijhoff, 1989. pp. 233-246.

2823. Connelly, Alpha. "Ireland and the Political Offence Exception to Extradition." ***Journal of Law and Society,*** 12:2 (1985), 153-182.

2824. Constantinople, George R. "Towards a New Definition of Piracy: The Achille Lauro Incident." ***Virginia Journal of International Law,*** 26:3 (1986), 723-753.

2825. Costello, Daniel C. "The Impact of the Constitution on the Anti-Terrorism Act of 1987." ***Maryland Journal of International Law and Trade,*** 13:2 (Spring 1989), 331-346.

2826. Cowen, Jon C. "The Omnibus Diplomatic Security and Antiterrorism Act of 1986: Faulty Drafting May Defeat Efforts to Bring Terrorists to Justice." ***Cornell International Law Journal,*** 21:1 (Winter 1988), 127-146.

2827. Cross, Susan L. "Export Controls - Foreign Policy Controls in Export Administration Act of 1979: The 1980 Amendment to the Antiterrorism Provisions." ***Texas International Law Journal,*** 16 (Summer 1981), 533-546.

2828. Cummings, Richard. "The PLO Case: Terrorism, Statutory Interpretation, and Conflicting Obligations under Domestic and Public International Law." ***Hastings International and Comparative Law Review***, 13:1 (Fall 1989), 25-70.

2829. Currin, Catherine N. "Extradition Reform and the Statutory Definition of Political Offenses." ***Virginia Journal of International Law***, 24:2 (1984), 419-458.

2830. D'Amato, Alfonse. "Terrorism: An International Responsibility." ***Ohio Northern University Law Review***, 13:1 (1986), 27-29.

2831. D'Amato, Anthony, and Alfred P. Rubin. "What Does Tel-Oren Tell Lawyers? Judge Bork's Concept of the Law of Nations is Seriously Mistaken." ***American Journal of International Law***, 79:1 (January 1985), 92-113.

2832. Davidson, Scott, and Rosario Priore. "The Problem of Frontiers." In: ***Legal Responses to the Terrorist Threat.*** London: Institute for the Study of Conflict, 1988. pp. 13-26.

2833. Dawkins, K. E. "Crimes (Internationally Protected Persons and Hostages) Act 1980." ***New Zealand Universities Law Review***, 9 (December 1981), 399-408.

2834. De Bernardi, Beth. "Congressional Intent and Conflicting Treaty Obligations: United States vs. Palestine Liberation Organization." ***Cornell International Law Journal***, 23 (Winter 1990), 83-105.

2835. De Schutter, Bart, and Christine Van de Wijngaert. "Coping with Non-International Armed Conflicts: The Borderline Between National and International Law." ***Georgia Journal of International and Comparative Law***, 13 (Winter 1983), 279-290.

2836. Derby, Daniel H. "A Democratic Response to Foreign Political Offenses: The Need for Legislation to Counter Anti-Terrorism Excesses." ***Touro Journal of Transnational Law***, 1:1 (Fall 1988), 1-55.

2837. _____. "Coming to Terms with Terrorism - Relativity of Wrongfulness and the Need for a New Framework." ***Touro Law Review***, 3:2 (Spring 1987), 151-201.

2838. Dhokalia, R. P. "Terrorism and International Law: Some Problems and Issues." In: R. P. Dhokalia and K. N. Rao, eds. ***Terrorism and International Law.*** New Delhi: Indian Society of International Law, 1988. pp. 6-7.

2839. Dickson, Brice. "The Prevention of Terrorism (Temporary Provisions) Act 1989." ***Northern Ireland Legal Quarterly***, 40:3 (Autumn 1989), 250-267.

2840. Dinstein, Yoram. "Coping Legally with Terrorism." ***Terrorism***, 10:1 (1987), 76-78.

2841. _____. "Terrorism as an International Crime." In: ***Israel Yearbook on Human Rights, Vol. 19. 1989.*** Dordrecht: Martinus Nijhoff, 1989. pp. 55-74.

2842. Donnelly, Patrick L. "Extraterritorial Jurisdiction Over Acts of Terrorism Committed Abroad: Omnibus Diplomatic Security and Antiterrorism Act of 1986." ***Cornell Law Review***, 72 (March 1987), 599-619.

2843. Dubner, Barry H. "Piracy in Contemporary National and International Law." ***California Western International Law Journal***, 21 (1990), 139-149.

2844. Dunlap, Charles J. "The Military Justice System and Command Accountability." ***Military Review***, 65 (February 1985), 45-53.

2845. Ellen, Eric F. "Contemporary Piracy." ***California Western International Law Journal***, 21 (1990), 123-128.

2846. Epps, Valerie. "Abolishing the Political Offense Exception." In: M. C. Bassiouni, ed. ***Legal Responses to International Terrorism: U.S. Procedural Aspects.*** Dordrecht: Martinus Nijhoff, 1988. pp. 203-218.

2847. Erny, Frederick M., and William G. Young. "The Political Offense Exception as Applicable to Terrorists: Judicial Interpretation and Legislative Reform." ***Duquesne Law Review***, 25:3 (1987), 481-518.

2848. Evans, Alona E. "Judicial Decisions." ***American Journal of International Law***, (April 1980), 433-450

2849. Everett, Robinson O. "Introduction: The Need For Careful Legal and Political Analysis of Terrorism." ***Ohio Northern University Law Review***, 13:1 (1986), 1-4.

2850. "Extradition Treaty Between India and Belgium." In: R. P. Dhokalia and K. N. Rao, eds. ***Terrorism and International Law.*** New Delhi: Indian Society of International Law, 1988. pp. 99-105.

2851. "Extradition Treaty Between India and Canada." In: R. P. Dhokalia and K. N. Rao, eds. ***Terrorism and International Law.*** New Delhi: Indian Society of International Law, 1988. pp. 92-98.

2852. Falvey, Anne. "Legislative Responses to International Terrorism: International and National Efforts to Deter and Punish Terrorists." ***Boston College International and Comparative Law Review***, 9:2 (1986), 323-359.

2853. Farhangi, Leslie S. "Insuring Against Abuse of Diplomatic Immunity." ***Stanford Law Review***, 38 (July 1986), 1517-1547.

2854. Fascell, D. B. "Combatting International Terrorism: The Role of Congress." ***Georgia Journal of International and Comparative Law***, (Winter 1986), 655-670.

2855. Feder, Linda Gerstel. "Distinguishing Terrorist Activities from Politically Motivated Acts Under the Political Offense Exception to Extradition." ***Temple International and Comparative Law Journal***, 1:1 (Fall 1985), 99-132.

2856. Feith, Douglas J. "Protocol I.: Moving Humanitarian Law Backwards." ***Akron Law Review***, 19 (Spring 1986), 531-535.

2857. _____. "Law in the Service of Terror - The Strange Case of the Additional Protocol." ***The National Interest***, 1 (Fall 1985), 36-47.

2858. _____. "The Law of War: The Terrorists are Rolled Back." ***The Atlantic Community Quarterly***, 25 (Summer 1987), 210-212.

2859. Fessler, E. Anthony. "Extraterritorial Apprehension as a Proactive Counterterrorism Measure." In: D. C. Livingstone and T. E. Terrell, eds. ***Beyond the Iran-Contra Crisis.*** Lexington, MA.: D.C. Heath & Lexington Books, 1988. pp. 225-324.

2860. Fields, Louis G. "Bringing Terrorists to Justice - The Shifting Sands of the Political Offense Exception." In: R. B. Lillich, ed. ***International Aspects of Criminal Law.*** Charlottesville, VA.: Michie Corporation, 1981. pp. 15-33.

2861. _____. "Terrorism: A Summary of Applicable U.S. and International Law." In: B. M. Jenkins, ed. ***Terrorism and Beyond: An International Conference on Terrorism and Low-Level Conflict.*** Santa Monica, CA.: RAND Corporation, 1980. pp. 247-265.

2862. _____. "Contemporary Terrorism and the Rule of Law." ***Military Law Review***, 113 (Summer 1986), 1-15.

2863. Findlay, D. Cameron. "Abducting Terrorists Overseas for Trial in the United States: Issues of International and Domestic Law." ***Texas International Law Journal***, 23:1 (Winter 1988), 1-53.

2864. Finnie, Wilson. "Rights of Persons Detained Under the Antiterrorist Legislation." ***Modern Law Review***, 45 (March 1982), 215-220.

2865. _____. "Old Wine in New Bottles? The Evolution of Anti-Terrorist Legislation." ***The Juridical Review***, (June 1990), 1-22.

2866. Fisher, Catherine C. "U.S. Legislation to Prosecute Terrorists: Antiterrorism or Legalized Kidnapping?." ***Vanderbilt Journal of Transnational Law***, 18 (Fall 1985), 915-959.

2867. Franck, Thomas M., and Deborah Niedermeyer. "Accommodating Terrorism: An Offence Against the Law of Nations." In: ***Israel Yearbook on Human Rights, Vol. 19. 1989***. Dordrecht: Martinus Nijhoff, 1989. pp. 75-130.

2868. _____, and Scott C. Senecal. "Porfiry's Proposition: Legitimacy and Terrorism." ***Vanderbilt Journal of Transnational Law***, 20:2 (March 1987), 195-234.

2869. Fraser, D. "If I had a Rocket Launcher - Critical Legal Studies as Moral Terrorism." ***Hastings Law Journal***, 41:4 (1990), 777-804.

2870. Friedlander, Robert A. "Terrorism and International Law: Recent Developments." ***Rutgers Law Journal***, 13 (Spring 1982), 493-511.

2871. _____. "Terrorism and the Law: Seeking Legal Remedies: Domestic and International." ***International Society of Barristers Quarterly***, 17:2 (1982), 298-306.

2872. _____. "The PLO and the Rule of Law: A Reply to Dr. Anis F. Kassim." ***Denver Journal of International Law***, 10:2 (Winter 1981), 221-235.

2873. _____. "Courting Legal Disaster." ***TVI Journal***, 3:1 (1982), 6-7.

2874. _____. "Framing Anti-Terrorism Legislation: Is It the People Vs. Terrorism or the State Vs. the People." ***TVI Journal***, 1:10 (1980), 2-4.

2875. _____. "When A Government Loses a Hostage at the Barricades." ***TVI Journal***, 3:11 (1982), 4-12.

2876. _____. "The U.S. Legislative Approach." In: M. C. Bassiouni, ed. ***Legal Responses to International Terrorism: U.S. Procedural Aspects***. Dordrecht: Martinus Nijhoff, 1988. pp. 3-24.

2877. _____. "The Orwellian Challenge: State Terrorism and International Law." ***Chitty's Law Journal***, 32:1 (1984), 4-13.

2878. _____. "Punishing Terrorists: a Modest Proposal." ***Ohio Northern University Law Review***, 13:1 (1986), 149-155.

2879. Fuller, S. N. "Extradition of Terrorists: An Executive Solution to the Limitations of the Political Offense Exception in the Context of Contemporary Judicial Interpretations of American Extradition Law." ***Suffolk Transnational Law Journal***, 11 (1988), 351-385.

2880. Gaja, Giorgio. "Measures Against Terrorist Acts Under International Law." In: N. Ronzitti, ed. ***Maritime Terrorism and International Law***. Dordrecht: Martinus Nijhoff, 1990. pp. 15-24.

2881. Gallagher, Richard J. "Kidnapping in the United States and the Development of the Federal Kidnapping Statute." In: B. M. Jenkins, ed. ***Terrorism and Personal Protection***. Stoneham, MA.: Butterworth, 1985. pp. 129-147.

2882. Gardes, Jeannemarie. "Exercising Extraterritorial Jurisdiction Over Terrorists." ***Criminal Justice Journal***, 10:2 (Spring 1988), 307-346.

2883. _____. "Terrorists on Trial: The Legal Dilemmas." ***Criminal Justice Journal***, 11:1 (Fall-Winter 1988), 235-265.

2884. Gasser, Hans-Peter. "Prohibition of Terrorist Acts in International Humanitarian Law." ***International Review of the Red Cross***, 253 (July-August, 1986), 200-212.

2885. Gearty, Conor. "The Rule of Law in an Emergency." ***Cambridge Law Journal***, 47:3 (November 1988), 332-334.

2886. George, B. J. "Federal Anti-Terrorist Legislation." In: M. C. Bassiouni, ed. ***Legal Responses to International Terrorism: U.S. Procedural Aspects.*** Dordrecht: Martinus Nijhoff, 1988. pp. 25-88.

2887. Gerber, Michael. "The Anti-Terrorism Act of 1987: Sabotaging the United Nations and Holding the Constitution Hostage." ***New York University Law Review,*** 65:2 (May 1990), 364-402.

2888. Gilbert, Geoffrey S. "Terrorism and the Political Offence Exception Reappraised." ***International and Comparative Law Quarterly,*** 34:4 (1985), 695-723.

2889. Ginossar, S. "Outlawing Terrorism." In: M. Kravitz, ed. ***International Summaries: A Collection of Selected Translations in Law Enforcement and Criminal Justice, Vol. 4.*** Rockville, MD.: National Criminal Justice Reference Service, 1980. pp. 229-232.

2890. Gold, Edgar. "International Shipping and the New Law of the Sea: New Directions for a Traditional Use?." ***Ocean Development and International Law,*** 20:5 (1989), 433-444.

2891. Goldie, L. F. E. "The "Political Offense" Exception and Extradition Between Democratic States." ***Ohio Northern University Law Review,*** 13:1 (1986), 53-95.

2892. _____. "Legal Proceedings Arising from the Achille Lauro Incident in the United States of America." In: N. Ronzitti, ed. ***Maritime Terrorism and International Law.*** Dordrecht: Martinus Nijhoff, 1990. pp. 107-128.

2893. _____. "Excursus on the Current State of the Admiralty Law on Wrongful Death in the United States of America." In: N. Ronzitti, ed. ***Maritime Terrorism and International Law.*** Dordrecht: Martinus Nijhoff, 1990. pp. 129-140.

2894. _____. "Terrorism, Piracy and the Nyon Agreements." In: Y. Dinstein, ed. ***International Law at a Time of Perplexity: Essays in Honour of Shabtai Rosenne.*** Dordrecht: Martinus Nijhoff, 1989. pp. 225-248.

2895. _____. "Low Intensity Conflict at Sea." ***Syracuse Journal of International Law and Commerce,*** 14 (1988), 597-637.

2896. Gooding, Gregory V. "Fighting Terrorism in the 1980's: The Interception of the Achille Lauro Hijackers." ***Yale Journal of International Law,*** 12:1 (Winter 1987), 158-179.

2897. Gouras, Eckhart K. "The Reform of West German Data Protection Law as a Necessary Correlate to Improving Domestic Security." ***Columbia Journal of Transnational Law,*** 24:3 (1986), 597-621.

2898. Grassie, Y. G. "Federally Sponsored International Kidnapping: An Acceptable Alternative to Extradition?." ***Washington University Law Quarterly,*** 64 (1986), 1205-1207.

2899. Green, L. C. "International Law and the Control of Terrorism." ***Dalhousie Law Journal,*** (April 1983), 236-256.

2900. _____. "Terrorism and the Courts." ***Manitoba Law Journal,*** 11:4 (1981), 333-358.

2901. _____. "Terrorism and the Law." ***Chitty's Law Journal,*** 30 (April 1982), 107-112.

2902. _____. "Is There an International Criminal Law?." ***Alberta Law Review,*** 21:2 (Spring 1983), 251-261.

2903. _____. "Terrorism and the Law of the Sea." In: Y. Dinstein, ed. ***International Law at a Time of Perplexity: Essays in Honour of Shabtai Rosenne.*** Dordrecht: Martinus Nijhoff, 1989. pp. 249-272.

2904. _____. "Terrorism and Armed Conflict: The Plea and the Verdict." In: ***Israel Yearbook on Human Rights, Vol 19. 1989.*** Dordrecht: Martinus Nijhoff, 1989. pp. 131-166.

2905. _____. "Terrorism, the Extradition of Terrorists and the 'Political Offence' Defence." ***German Yearbook of International Law,*** 31 (1988), 337-371.

2906. Greenberg, Ned. "Mendelsohn v. Meese: A First Amendment Challenge to the Anti-Terrorism Act of 1987." ***The American University Law Review,*** 39 (Winter 1990), 355-390.

2907. Greenwood, Christopher. "Terrorism and Humanitarian Law: The Debate over Additional Protocol I." In: ***Israel Yearbook on Human Rights, Vol. 19. 1989.*** Dordrecht: Martinus Nijhoff, 1989. pp. 187-208.

2908. _____. "International Law and the United States' Air Operation Against Libya." ***West Virginia Law Review,*** 89 (Summer 1987), 933-960.

2909. Groarke, J. P. "Revolutionaries Beware: The Erosion of the Political Offense Exception Under the 1986 United States - United Kingdom Supplementary Extradition Treaty." ***University of Pennsylvania Law Review,*** 136 (1988), 1515-1545.

2910. Grooms, Lloyd W., and Jane M. Samson. "The Political Offense Exception to Extradition: A 19th Century British Standard in 20th Century American Courts." ***Notre Dame Law Review,*** 59:4 (Summer 1984), 1005-1025.

2911. Grosman, Brian A. "Conspiracy: The Law's Pre-Emptive Strike." ***Conflict Quarterly,*** 2:2 (1981), 20-24.

2912. Gurovitsch, Kerry Ann. "Legal Obstacles to Combatting International State-Sponsored Terrorism." ***Houston Journal of International Law,*** 10:1 (Autumn 1987), 159-180.

2913. Halberstam, Malvina. "Terrorism." ***George Mason University Law Review,*** 9:1 (Winter 1986), 12-20.

2914. _____. "Symposium: The Use of Force Against Terrorist Bases." ***Houston Journal of International Law,*** 11:2 (1989), 307-336.

2915. Hall, J. W. "Possible Legal Solution to International Terrorism." ***Case and Comment,*** 85:2 (1980), 30-34, 36.

2916. Hannay, William M. "International Terrorism and the Political Offence Exception to Extradition." ***Columbia Journal of Transnational Law,*** 18 (1980), 381-412.

2917. _____. "Legislative Reform of the U.S. Extradition Statutes: Plugging the Terrorist's Loopholes." ***Denver Journal of International Law and Policy,*** 13 (Fall 1983), 53-84.

2918. _____. "The Legislative Approach to the Political Offense Exception." In: M. C. Bassiouni, ed. ***Legal Responses to International Terrorism: U.S. Procedural Aspects.*** Dordrecht: Martinus Nijhoff, 1988. pp. 115-128.

2919. Hansen, Mary Beth. "Extradition - The Role of the Political Offense Exception in Combating Terrorism." ***Suffolk Transnational Law Journal,*** 10:2 (Fall 1986), 441-471.

2920. Harke, Lance A. "The Anti-Terrorism Act of 1987 and American Freedoms: A Critical Review." ***University of Miami Law Review,*** 43:3 (1989), 667-719.

2921. Hassett, Joseph, John N. Moore and Joel Lisker. "Report on Legislative Responses to International Terrorism." ***Terrorism,*** 8:2 (1985), 147-163.

2922. Havers, Michael. "Legal Cooperation: A Matter of Necessity." ***International Lawyer,*** 21:1 (Winter 1987), 185-193.

2923. Heymann, P. B. "International Cooperation in Dealing with Terrorism: A Review of Law and Recent Practice." ***American University Journal of International Law and Policy,*** 6 (Fall 1990), 1-33.

2924. Horne, Andrew R. "Continued Confusion in Congressional Intent and the Hierarchy of Norms." ***Michigan Journal of International Law***, 10:3 (Summer 1989), 935-956.

2925. Imbalzano, Maria P. "In Re Mackin: Is the Application of the Political Offense Exception An Extradition Issue for the Judicial or the Executive Branch?." ***Fordham International Law Journal***, 5:1 (1981-82), 565-597.

2926. Intoccia, Gregory F. "International Legal and Policy Implications of an American Counter-Terrorist Strategy." ***Denver Journal of International Law and Policy***, 14 (Spring-Summer 1985), 121-146.

2927. _____. "American Bombing of Libya: An International Legal Analysis." ***Case Western Reserve Journal of International Law***, 19:2 (Spring 1987), 177-213.

2928. Iversen, Guy Casey. "Just Say No! United States Options to Extradition to the North of Ireland's Diplock Court System." ***Loyola of Los Angeles International and Comparative Law Journal***, 12:1 (December 1989), 249-280.

2929. Jackson, J. D. "The Northern Ireland (Emergency Provisions) Act 1987." ***Northern Ireland Legal Quarterly***, 39:3 (Autumn 1988), 235-257.

2930. Jackson, James K. "Legal Aspects of Terrorism." ***Parameters***, (Spring 1985), 39-51.

2931. _____. "Legal Aspects of Terrorism: An Overview." ***Army Lawyer***, (March 1985), 1-15.

2932. Janis, M. W. "Role of the International Court in the Hostage Crisis." ***Connecticut Law Review***, 13:2 (1981), 263-289.

2933. Jorgensen, Birthe. "Defending the Terrorists: Queen's Counsel Before the Courts of Northern Ireland." ***Journal of Law and Society***, 9 (Summer 1982), 115-126.

2934. Joseph, Zvi. "The Application of RICO to International Terrorism." ***Fordham Law Review***, 58:5 (April 1990), 1071-1084.

2935. Joyce, Anne. "Common Law Meets its Limits?." ***Harvard International Law Journal***, 29:2 (Spring 1988), 451-474.

2936. Joyner, Christopher. "Offshore Maritime Terrorism: International Implications and Legal Response." In: H. H. Han, ed. ***Terrorism, Political Violence and World Order.*** Lanham, MD.: University Press of America, 1984. pp. 443-466.

2937. _____. "Offshore Maritime Terrorism: International Implications and the Legal Response." ***Naval War College Review***, 36:4 (July-August 1983), 16-31.

2938. Juster, Kenneth I., and Irvin B. Nathan. "Law Enforcement Against International Terrorists: Use of the RICO Statute." ***University of Colorado Law Review***, 60:3 (1989), 553-570.

2939. Kalshoven, F. "'Guerrilla' and 'Terrorism' in Internal Armed Conflict." ***American University Law Review***, 33 (1983), 67-81.

2940. Kane, Terry Richard. "Prosecuting International Terrorists in United States Courts: Gaining the Jurisdictional Threshold." ***Yale Journal of International Law***, 12:2 (Summer 1987), 294-341.

2941. Kellett, Michael. "Extradition - The Concept of the Political Offense." ***The Liverpool Law Review***, 8:1 (1986), 1-22.

2942. Kennedy, David M., Torsten Stein and Alfred P. Rubin. "The Extradition of Mohammad Hamadei." ***Harvard International Law Journal***, 31 (Winter 1990), 5-35.

2943. Khan, Ali. "A Legal Theory of International Terrorism." ***Connecticut Law Review***, 19:4 (Summer 1987), 945-972.

2944. Kinneally, James J., III. "The Political Offense Exception: Is the United States - United Kingdom Supplementary Extradition Treaty the Beginning of the End?." ***The American University Journal of International Law and Policy,*** 2:1 (1987), 203-227.

2945. Kittrie, Nicholas N. "Patriots and Terrorists: Reconciling Human Rights with World Order." ***Case Western Reserve Journal of International Law,*** 13 (Spring 1981), 291-313.

2946. Koh, H. H. "Civil Remedies for Uncivil Wrongs: Combatting Terrorism Through Transnational Public Law Litigation." ***Texas International Law Journal,*** 22 (Spring/Summer 1987), 169-209.

2947. Konstantinov, Emil. "International Terrorism and International Law." ***German Yearbook of International Law,*** 31 (1988), 289-306.

2948. Kornblum, A. N., and L. M. Jachnycky. "America's Secret Court: Listening in on Espionage and Terrorism." ***Judges' Journal,*** (Summer 1985), 15-19+.

2949. _____. _____. "Politics, the Courts and Terrorism: Are the Laws Adequate?." ***Judge's Journal,*** (Winter 1987), 16-21.

2950. Kulman, Bradley G. "Eliminating the Political Offense Exception for Violent Crimes: The Proposed United States - United Kingdom Supplementary Extradition Treaty." ***Virginia Journal of International Law,*** 26:3 (1986), 755-783.

2951. Kutner, Luis. "Constructive Notice: A Proposal to End International Terrorism." ***Common Law Lawyer,*** 10:3 (May-June 1985), 1-16.

2952. Lagodny, Otto. "The Abolition and Replacement of the Political Offence Exception: Prohibited by International or Domestic Law." In: ***Israel Yearbook on Human Rights, Vol. 19. 1989.*** Dordrecht: Martinus Nijhoff, 1989. pp. 317-330.

2953. Larschan, Bradley. "Legal Aspects to the Control of Transnational Terrorism: An Overview." ***Ohio Northern University Law Review,*** 13:1 (1986), 117-148.

2954. _____. "Extradition, The Political Offense Exception and Terrorism: An Overview of the Three Principal Theories of Law." ***Boston University International Law Journal,*** 4:2 (1986), 231-284.

2955. Larson, David L. "Naval Weaponry and the Law of the Sea." ***Ocean Development and International Law,*** 18 (1987), 125-198.

2956. Leanza, Umberto, and Luigi Sico. "Compensation of Victims of Maritime Terrorism." In: N. Ronzitti, ed. ***Maritime Terrorism and International law.*** Dordrecht: Martinus Nijhoff, 1990. pp. 97-106.

2957. Legault, L. H. "Hostage Taking and Diplomatic Immunity." ***Manitoba Law Journal,*** 11:4 (1981), 359-365.

2958. Leich, Marian N. "Use of Force." ***American Journal of International Law,*** 80:3 (July 1986), 632-644.

2959. _____. "Four Bills Proposed by President Reagan to Counter Terrorism." ***American Journal of International Law,*** 78:4 (1984), 915-928.

2960. Leiser, Burton M. "Enemies of Mankind." In: B. Netanyahu, ed. ***Terrorism: How the West Can Win.*** New York: Farrar, Straus, Giroux, 1986. pp. 155-156.

2961. Levitt, Geoffrey M. "International Law and the U.S. Governments' Response to Terrorism." ***Whittier Law Review,*** 8:3 (1987), 755-762.

2962. _____. "The International Legal Response to Terrorism: A Reevaluation." ***University of Colorado Law Review,*** 60:3 (Summer 1989) 533-551.

2963. _____. "Combatting Terrorism Under International Law." ***University of Toledo Law Review,*** 18:1 (Fall 1986), 133-150.

2964. Lippman, Matthew. "The Political Offender Exception in International Extradition Law: Terrorism Versus Human Rights." ***International Journal of Comparative and Applied Criminal Justice***, 13:2 (Fall 1989), 45-59.

2965. Liput, Andrew L. "An Analysis of the Achille Lauro Affair: Towards an Effective and Legal Method of Bringing International Terrorists to Justice." ***Fordham International Law Journal***, 9:2 (1985-1986), 328-372.

2966. Livingstone, Stephen. "A Week is a Long Time in Detention: Brogan and Others v. United Kingdom: 1989." ***Northern Ireland Legal Quarterly***, 40 (Autumn 1989), 288-303.

2967. Lohr, M. F. "Legal Analysis of U.S. Military Responses to State-Sponsored International Terrorism." ***Naval Law Review***, 34 (1985), 1-48.

2968. Lomas, O. G. "The Executive and the Anti-Terrorist Legislation of 1939." ***Public Law***, (Spring 1980), 16-33.

2969. Lopez-Rey, Manuel. "Need for a New International - National Criminal Justice Order." ***Federal Probation***, (March 1984), 19-22.

2970. Lubet, Steven. "Extradition Reform: Executive Discretion and Judicial Participation in the Extradition of Political Terrorists." ***Cornell University Law Journal***, 15 (Summer 1982), 247-291.

2971. _____, and Morris Czackes. "The Role of the American Judiciary in the Extradition of Political Terrorists." ***Journal of Criminal Law and Criminology***, 71:3 (1980), 193-210.

2972. _____. "International Criminal Law and the "Ice-Nine" Error: A Disclosure on the Fallacy of Universal Solutions." ***Virginia Journal of International Law***, 28:4 (Summer 1988), 963-984.

2973. Ludwikowski, Rett R. "Political and Legal Instruments in Supporting and Combatting Terrorism: Current Developments." ***Terrorism***, 11:3 (1988), 197-212.

2974. Maechling, Charles. "Handcuffing Terrorism." ***Foreign Service Journal***, 64:1 (1987), 21-27.

2975. Magner, Eilis S. "Is a Terrorist Entitled to the Protection of the Law of Evidence?." ***The Sydney Law Review***, 11 (March 1988), 537-565.

2976. Matsuoka, Tama. "Extradition Law: Applicability of the Political Offense Exception. Eain V. Wilkes." ***Harvard International Law Journal***, 23:1 (1982), 124-131.

2977. McCarthy, John G. "The Passive Personality Principle and Its Use in Combatting International Terrorism." ***Fordham International Law Journal***, 13:3 (Spring 1990), 298-327.

2978. McCredie, Jeffrey A. "The Responsibility of States for Private Acts of International Terrorism." ***Temple International and Comparative Law Journal***, 1:1 (Fall 1985), 69-97.

2979. _____. "Contemporary Uses of Force Against Terrorism: The United States Response to Achille Lauro - Questions of Jurisdiction and Its Exercise." ***Georgia Journal of International and Comparative Law***, 16:3 (1986), 436-467.

2980. _____. "The April 14, 1986 Bombing of Libya: Act of Self-Defense or Reprisal?." ***Case Western Reserve Journal of International Law***, 19 (Spring 1987), 215-242.

2981. McCullough, Larry A. "International and Domestic Criminal Law Issues in the Achille Lauro Incident: A Functional Analysis." ***Naval Law Review***, 36 (Winter 1986), 53-108.

2982. McGinley, Gerald P. "The Achille Lauro Affair: Implications for International Law." ***Tennessee Law Review***, 52 (Summer 1985), 691-738.

2983. _____. "The Achille Lauro Case: A Case Study in Crisis Law, Policy and Management." In: M. C. Bassiouni, ed. ***Legal Responses to International Terrorism: U.S. Procedural Aspects.*** Dordrecht: Martinus Nijhoff, 1988. pp. 323-362.

2984. McGrath, Margaret. "Extradition: Another Irish Problem." ***Northern Ireland Legal Quarterly***, 34 (Winter 1983), 292-314.

2985. Menefee, Samuel P. "Yo Heave Ho: Updating America's Piracy Laws." ***California Western International Law Journal***, 21 (1990), 151-179.

2986. _____. "Terrorism at Sea - The Historical Development of an International Legal Response." In: B. A. H. Parritt, ed. ***Violence at Sea.*** Paris: International Chamber of Commerce, 1986. pp. 191-220.

2987. Meron, Theodore. "When Do Acts of Terrorism Violate Human Rights?." In: ***Israel Yearbook on Human Rights, Vol. 19. 1989.*** Dordrecht: Martinus Nijhoff, 1989. pp. 271-280.

2988. Meyer, Jurgen. "German Criminal Law Relating to International Terrorism." ***University of Colorado Law Review***, 60:3 (1989), 571-582.

2989. Miller, David W. "Extraterritorial Jurisdiction of Federal Criminal Law: The Assassination of Congressman Ryan." ***Lawyer of the Americas***, 14:1 (1982), 61-77.

2990. Moore, John N. "A Theoretical Overview of the Laws of War in a Post-Charter World, with Emphasis on the Challenge of Civil, 'Wars of National Liberation', Mixed Civil-International Wars and Terrorism." ***American University Law Review***, 31 (Summer 1982), 841-847.

2991. Moynihan, Daniel Patrick. "Terrorists, Totalitarianism and the Rule of Law." In: B. Netanyahu, ed. ***Terrorism: How the West Can Win.*** New York: Farrar, Straus, Giroux, 1986. pp. 41-43.

2992. Mullally, Kathe F. "Combatting International Terrorism: Limiting the Political Exception in Order to Prevent "One Man's Terrorism from Becoming Another Man's Heroism"". ***Villanova Law Review***, 31:5 (October 1986), 1495-1547.

2993. Munson, V. J. "Case Concerning United States Diplomatic and Consular Staff in Tehran." ***California Western International Law Journal***, (Summer 1981), 543-568.

2994. Murphy, John F. "Legal Controls and the Deterrence of Terrorism: Performance and Prospects." ***Rutger's Law Journal***, 13 (Spring 1982), 465-492.

2995. _____. "Recent International Legal Developments in Controlling Terrorism." ***Chinese Yearbook of International Law and Affairs***, 4 (1984), 97-127.

2996. _____. "The Future of Multilateralism and Efforts to Combat International Terrorism." ***Columbia Journal of Transnational Law***, 25:1 (fall 1986), 35-99.

2997. Murray, Matthew H. "The Torture Victim Protection Act: Legislation to Promote Enforcement of the Human Rights of Aliens in U.S. Courts." ***Columbia Journal of Transnational Law***, 25:3 (Summer 1987), 673-715.

2998. Neibergs, Paul. "The Limits of Extradition." ***Harvard International Review***, 9 (July/August 1987), 46-48.

2999. Nelson, William R. "Antiterrorist Legislation: A Comparative Analysis." ***Journal of Contemporary Criminal Justice***, 4:4 (1988), 203-213.

3000. _____. "Terrorist Challenge to the Rule of Law: The British Experience." ***Terrorism***, 13:3 (1990), 227-236.

3001. Noorani, A. G. "Terrorism and the Rule of Law." ***Economic and Political Weekly***, 23:48 (November 26, 1988), 2515-2516.

3002. Novotne, Alfred H. "Random Bombing of Public Places: Extradition and Punishment of Indiscriminate Violence Against Innocent Parties." ***Boston University International Law Journal***, 6:2 (Fall 1988), 219-251.

3003. Noyes, John E. "An Introduction to the International Law of Piracy." ***California Western International Law Journal***, 21 (1990), 105-121.

3004. O'Brien, Conor Cruise. "A Case for International Law - Coping with Terrorism." ***Center Magazine***, 20:2 (1987), 45-49.

3005. O'Brien, Francis W. "Irish Terrorists and Extradition: The Tuite Case." ***Texas International Law Journal***, 18 (1983), 249-272.

3006. O'Connor, Michael A. "International Extradition and the Political Offence Exception: The Granting of Political Offenders Status to Terrorists by United States Courts." ***New York Law School Journal of International and Comparative Law***, 4:3 (1983), 613-635.

3007. Oppermann, T. "The Part Played by International Law in Combatting International Terrorism." ***Law and State***, 25 (1982), 116-135.

3008. Paasche, F. W. "The Use of Force in Combatting Terrorism." ***Columbia Journal of Transnational Law***, 25:2 (1987), 377-402.

3009. Paris Court of Appeals. "The Francesco Piperno Case." ***Terrorism***, 4:1-4 (1980), 293-309.

3010. Parritt, B. A. H. "Maritime Terrorism and the Law." ***Lloyds Maritime and Commercial Law Quarterly***, 1 (February 1987), 18-21.

3011. Partan, D. G. "Terrorism: An International Law Offense." ***Connecticut Law Review***, 19:4 (Summer 1987), 751-797.

3012. Passas, Nikos. "Political Crime and Political Offender: Theory and Practice." ***Liverpool Law Review***, 8:1 (1986), 23-36.

3013. Pathak, R. S. "Global Terrorism: Legal Issues." In: R. P. Dhokalia and K. N. Rao, eds. ***Terrorism and International Law***. New Delhi: Indian Society of International Law, 1988. pp. 51-52.

3014. Patterson, K. J. "The Spectre of Censorship Under the International Terrorism (Emergency Powers) Act 1987." ***Victoria University of Wellington Law Review***, 18:3 (August 1988), 259-291.

3015. Paust, Jordan J. "Federal Jurisdiction over Extraterritorial Acts of Terrorism and Nonimmunity for Foreign Violators of International Law Under the FSIA and the Act of State Doctrine." ***Virginia Journal of International Law***, (Winter 1983), 191-251.

3016. _____. "Terrorism and 'Terrorism-Specific' Statutes." ***Terrorism***, 7:2 (1984), 233-239.

3017. _____. "Responding Lawfully to International Terrorism: The Use of Force Abroad." ***Whittier Law Review***, 8:3 (1986), 711-733.

3018. _____. ""Such a Narrow Approach" Indeed." ***Virginia Journal of International Law***, 29:2 (Winter 1989), 413-417.

3019. _____. "The Link Between Human Rights and Terrorism and Its Implications for the Law of State Responsibility." ***Hastings International and Comparative Law Review***, 11:1 (Fall 1987), 41-54.

3020. _____. "An Introduction To and Commentary on Terrorism and the Law." ***Connecticut Law Review***, 19:4 (Summer 1987), 697-749.

3021. _____. "Extradition and United States Prosecution of the Achille Lauro Hostage Takers: Navigating the Hazards." ***Vanderbilt Journal of Transnational Law***, 20:2 (March 1987), 235-257.

3022. Perry, Gregory C. "The Four Major Western Approaches to the Political Offense Exception to Extradition: From Inception to Modern Terrorism." ***Mercer Law Review***, 40:2 (1989), 709-735.

3023. Pilgrim, Caleb M. "Terrorism in National and International Law." ***Dickinson Journal of International Law***, 8:2 (Winter 1990), 147-202.

3024. Podhoretz, John. "The Pule of Law." ***The American Legion***, 120:6 (1986), 15, 49.

3025. Poland, James M. "Teaching "Terrorism" in Criminal Justice: Benefits and Problems." ***Journal of Police Science and Administration***, 14:3 (1986), 202-211.

3026. Pollock, Eileen R. "Terrorism as a Tort in Violation of the Law of Nations." ***Fordham International Law Journal***, 6 (Winter 1982), 236-260.

3027. "A Proposal to Deny Foreign Sovereign Immunity to Nations Sponsoring Terrorism." ***American University Journal of International Law and Policy***, 6 (Fall 1990), 77-109.

3028. Purdy, Chip. "Foreign Intelligence Surveillance Act: Unconstitutional Warrant Criteria Permit Wiretapping if a Possibility of International Terrorism is Found." ***San Diego Law Review***, 17 (July 1980), 936-977.

3029. Pyle, Christopher. "The Political Offense Exception." In: M. C. Bassiouni, ed. ***Legal Responses to International Terrorism: U.S. Procedural Aspects.*** Dordrecht: Martinus Nijhoff, 1988. pp. 181-202.

3030. Quigley, John. "Eliminating Terrorism: A Law and Justice Approach." ***Connecticut Journal of International Law***, 3:1 (Fall 1987), 47-70.

3031. Rafat, Amir. "The Iran Hostage Crisis and the International Court of Justice: Aspects of the Case Concerning United States Diplomatic and Consular Staff in Tehran." ***Denver Journal of International Law and Policy***, 10:3 (1981), 425-462.

3032. Raits, Vivian I. "Political Assassination and the Jurisdiction Question: Letelier V. Republic of Chile." ***Willamette Law Review***, 17:1 (1980), 291-301.

3033. Randall, Kenneth C. "Federal Questions and the Human Rights Paradigm." ***Minnesota Law Review***, 73:2 (December 1988), 349-424.

3034. _____. "Special U.S. Civil Jurisdiction." In: M. C. Bassiouni, ed. ***Legal Responses to International Terrorism: U.S. Procedural Aspects.*** Dordrecht: Martinus Nijhoff, 1988. pp. 89-114.

3035. Ravaschiere, Vincent P. "Terrorist Extradition and Political Offense Exception: An Administrative Solution." ***Virginia Journal of International Law***, 21 (Fall 1980), 163-183.

3036. Reagan, Ronald, and George Shultz. "United Kingdom - United States: Extradition Treaty Supplement Limiting Scope of Political Offenses to Exclude Acts of Terrorism." ***International Legal Materials***, 24:4 (July 1985), 1104-1109.

3037. Reisman, W. M. "An International Farce: The Sad Case of the PLO Mission." ***Yale Journal of International Law***, 14:2 (Summer 1989), 412-432.

3038. _____. "No Man's Land: International Legal Regulation of Coercive Responses to Protracted and Low Level Conflict." ***Houston Journal of International Law***, 11:2 (Spring 1989), 317-330

3039. _____. "The Tormented Conscience: Applying and Appraising Unauthorized Coercion." ***Emory Law Journal***, 32 (1983), 499-544.

3040. Richards, D. A. J. "Terror and the Law." ***Human Rights Quarterly,*** 5 (1983), 171-185.

3041. Roberts, Guy B. "Self-Help in Combatting State-Sponsored Terrorism: Self Defense and Peacetime Reprisals." ***Case Western Reserve Journal of International Law,*** 19:2 (Spring 1987), 243-293.

3042. Roberts, Kenneth. "The Legal Implications of Treating Terrorists as Soldiers." ***Conflict,*** 9:4 (1989), 375-388.

3043. Rodes, Robert E. "On Clandestine Warfare." ***Washington and Lee Law Review,*** 39 (Spring 1982), 333-372.

3044. Rogers, John M. "Prosecuting Terrorists: When Does Apprehension in Violation of International Law Preclude Trial?." ***University of Miami Law Review,*** 42:2 (November 1987), 447-465.

3045. Ronzitti, Natalino. "The Law of the Sea and the Use of Force Against Terrorists." In: N. Ronzitti, ed. ***Maritime Terrorism and International Law.*** Dordrecht: Martinus Nijhoff, 1990. pp. 1-14.

3046. _____. "The Prevention and Suppression of Terrorism Against Fixed Platforms on the Continental Shelf." In: N. Ronzitti, ed. ***Maritime Terrorism and International Law.*** Dordrecht: Martinus Nijhoff, 1990. pp. 91-96.

3047. Rostow, Eugene. "Overcoming Denial." In: B. Netanyahu, ed. ***Terrorism: How the West Can Win.*** New York: Farrar, Straus, Giroux, 1986. pp. 146-148.

3048. Roth, Paul. "Emergency Powers Legislation After the Repeal of the Public Safety Conservation Act." ***Otago Law Review,*** 6:4 (1988), 682-702.

3049. Roth, S. J. "Repatriation of Terrorist Prisoners." ***Patterns of Prejudice,*** 18:3 (July 1984), 47-50.

3050. Rowles, J. P., Guy B. Roberts and John F. Murphy. "Military Responses to Terrorism: Substantive and Procedural Constraints in International Law." In: ***Proceedings of the 81st Annual Meeting of the American Society of International Law.*** Washington, D.C.: American Society of International Law, 1990. pp. 307-319.

3051. Rubin, Alfred P. "Current Legal Approaches to International Terrorism." ***Terrorism,*** 7:2 (1984), 147-162.

3052. _____. "Current Legal Approaches to International Terrorism." In: H. H. Han, ed. ***Terrorism, Political Violence and World Order.*** Lanham, MD.: University Press of America, 1984. pp. 433-442.

3053. _____. "Terrorism and the Law of War." ***Denver Journal of International Law and Policy,*** 12 (Spring 1983), 219-235.

3054. _____, et al. "Should the Laws of War Apply to Terrorists." In: G. K. Walker, ed. ***Proceedings of the 79th Annual Meeting of the American Society of International Law.*** Washington, D.C.: American Society of International Law, 1987. pp. 109-125.

3055. _____. "Extradition and "Terrorist" Offenses." ***Terrorism,*** 10:2 (1987), 83-102.

3056. _____. "International Law Association Conference." ***Terrorism,*** 10:3 (1989), 189-210.

3057. _____. "The Law of Piracy." ***Denver Journal of International Law and Policy,*** 15 (Winter/Spring 1987), 173-233.

3058. _____. "Revising the Law of Piracy." ***California Western International Law Journal,*** 21 (1990), 129-137.

3059. Rubner, Michael. "Antiterrorism and the Writing of the 1973 War Powers Resolution." ***Political Science Quarterly,*** 102 (Summer 1987), 193-215.

3060. Ruff, Charles, M. H. Gallagher and W. L. Saunders. "Terrorism: Legal Aspects of Corporate Responsibility." In: B. M. Jenkins, ed. ***Terrorism and Personal Protection.*** Stoneham, MA.: Butterworth, 1985. pp. 200-221.

3061. Rumpf, Helmut. "International Legal Problems of Terrorism." ***Aussenpolitik,*** 36:4 (1985), 388-404.

3062. Ryan, Patrick J., and Robert J. Kelly. "Analysis of RICO and OCCA: Federal and State Legislative Instruments Against Crime." ***Violence, Aggression and Terrorism,*** 3:1-2 (1989), 49-100.

3063. Sacerdoti, Giorgio. "States' Agreements with Terrorists in Order to Save Hostages: Non-Binding, Void or Justified by Necessity?." In: N. Ronzitti, ed. ***Maritime Terrorism and International Law.*** Dordrecht: Martinus Nijhoff, 1990. pp. 25-42.

3064. _____. "Achille Lauro Judgement: International Terrorism Covered by Italian Law." ***Patterns of Prejudice,*** 21:3 (1987), 41-44.

3065. Sacopulos, Peter J. "Establishing Federal Jurisdiction Over International Terrorism." ***TVI Report,*** 9:1 (1989), 24-37.

3066. Samuels, Alec. "The Legal Response to Terrorism: The Prevention of Terrorism (Temporary Provisions) Act 1984." ***Public Law,*** (Autumn 1984), 365-370.

3067. _____. "Terrorism and English Law." ***Kingston Law Review,*** 10 (April 1980), 3-23.

3068. Sapiro, Miriam. "Extradition in an Era of Terrorism: The Need to Abolish the Political Offense Exception." ***New York University Law Review,*** 61:4 (1986), 654-702.

3069. Sassoli, Marco. "International Humanitarian Law and Terrorism." In: P. Wilkinson and A. M. Stewart, eds. ***Contemporary Research on Terrorism.*** Aberdeen: Aberdeen University Press, 1987. pp. 466-474.

3070. Saveri, Joseph R. "Extradition - Political Offense Exception - Violent Acts Commited in One State Which are Incidental to a Political Uprising in Another State are Extraditable Offenses." ***Virginia Journal of International Law,*** 26:4 (1986), 1001-1016.

3071. Sayre, Robert M. "Combatting Terrorism: American Policy and Organization." In: H. H. Han, ed. ***Terrorism, Political Violence and World Order.*** Lanham, MD.: University Press of America, 1984. pp. 481-492.

3072. Schachter, Oscar. "International Law in the Hostage Crisis: Implications for Future Cases." In: ***American Hostages in Iran.*** New Haven, CT.: Yale University Press, 1985. pp. 325-373.

3073. _____. "The Extraterritorial Use of Force Against Terrorist Bases." ***Houston Journal of International Law,*** 11:2 (Spring 1989), 309-316.

3074. _____. "The Lawful Use of Force by a State Against Terrorists in Another Country." In: ***Israel Yearbook on Human Rights, Vol. 19. 1989.*** Dordrecht: Martinus Nijhoff, 1989. pp. 209-232.

3075. Schaefer, Cindy V. "American Courts and Modern Terrorism: The Politics of Extradition." ***New York University Journal of International Law and Politics,*** 13 (Winter 1981), 617-643.

3076. Schiff, D. "A Note on Extradition and Terrorism." ***Atlantic Law Review,*** 21 (1983), 436-446.

3077. Schuetz, G. Gregory. "Apprehending Terrorists Overseas Under United States and International Law: A Case Study of the Fawaz Younis Arrest." ***Harvard International Law Journal,*** 29:2 (Spring 1988), 499-532.

3078. "A Sewing Lesson in Political Offense Determinations: Stitching-Up the International Terrorist's Loophole." ***Hastings International and Comparative Law Review***, 10 (Winter 1987), 499-524.

3079. Seymour, P. A. "The Legitimacy of Peacetime Reprisal as a Tool Against State-Sponsored Terrorism." ***Naval Law Review***, 39 (1990), 221-240.

3080. Shanks, Robert B. "Insuring Investment and Loans Against Currency Inconvertibility, Expropriation, and Political Violence." ***Hastings International and Comparative Law Review***, 9:3 (Spring 1986), 417-437.

3081. Sim, Joe, and Philip A. Thomas. "The Prevention of Terrorism Act: Normalising the Politics of Repression." ***Journal of Law and Society***, 10:1 (Summer 1983), 71-84.

3082. Simms, John S. "International Procedures for the Apprehension and Rendition of Fugitive Offenders." ***American Society for International Law Proceedings of the 74th Annual Meeting***, (1980), 274-289.

3083. Singer, Eric H. "Terrorism, Extradition, and FSIA Relief: The Letelier Case." ***Vanderbilt Journal of Transnational Law***, 19:1 (Winter 1986), 57-82.

3084. _____. "Terrorist Attacks on Nationals: The Lawful Use of Force Against Terrorist Bases on Foreign Soil." ***Terrorism and Political Violence***, 1:4 (October 1989), 435-465.

3085. Smith, Brent. "Antiterrorism Legislation in the United States: Problems and Implications." ***Terrorism***, 7:2 (1984), 213-232.

3086. _____. "State Anti-Terrorism Legislation in the United States: A Review of Statutory Utilization." ***Conflict Quarterly***, 8:1 (Winter 1988), 29-47.

3087. _____. "Anti-Terrorism Legislation in the United States." In; R. H. Ward and H. E. Smith, eds. ***International Terrorism: The Domestic Response.*** Chicago, IL.: University of Illinois at Chicago, Office of International Criminal Justice, 1987. pp. 107-118.

3088. Smith, Jeffrey H. "Terrorism and the Law: The Scope of the Problem." ***International Society of Barristers Quarterly***, 17:2 (1982), 267-273.

3089. Sofaer, Abraham D. "Fighting Terrorism Through Law." ***Department of State Bulletin***, 85 (October 1985), 38-42.

3090. _____. "The Political Offence Exception and Terrorism." ***Department of State Bulletin***, 85 (December 1985), 58-62.

3091. _____. "Terrorism and the Law." ***Foreign Affairs***, (Summer 1986), 901-922.

3092. _____. "The U.S. - U.K. Supplementary Extradition Treaty." ***Terrorism***, 8:4 (1986), 327-344.

3093. _____. "The Political Offence Exception and Terrorism." ***Denver Journal of International Law and Policy***, 15:1 (Summer 1986), 125-133.

3094. _____. "Terrorism and the Law -- 13th Sulzbacher Memorial Lecture." In: N. Wright, ed. ***Law and Current World Issues.*** Dobbs Ferry, NJ.: Oceana, 1987. pp. 131-174.

3095. _____. "The Sixth Annual Waldemar A. Solf Lecture in International Law: Terrorism, the Law, and the National Defense." ***Military Law Review***, 126 (Fall 1989), 89-124.

3096. _____. "Terrorism, the Law and the National Defense: Text of the Sixth Annual Waldemar A. Solf Lecture in International Law." ***Special Warfare***, 2:4 (Fall 1989), 12-28.

3097. _____. "Terrorism and the Law." In: W. Laqueur, ed. ***The Terrorism Reader.*** New York: Meridian, 1987. pp. 369-377.

3098. Solf, Waldemar. "International Terrorism in Armed Conflict." In: H. H. Han, ed. ***Terrorism, Political Violence and World Order.*** Lanham, MD.: University Press of America, 1984. pp. 467-480.

3099. _____. "A Response to Douglas J. Feith's Law in the Service of Terror - The Strange Case of the Additional Protocol." ***Akron Law Review,*** 20 (Fall 1986), 261-289.

3100. Starke, J. G. "International Terrorism and International Law." ***Australian Law Journal,*** 61:6 (June 1987), 311-313.

3101. "State Sponsored International Terrorism: A Symposium." ***Vanderbilt Journal of Transnational Law,*** 20 (March 1987), 195-363.

3102. "The Status of Treaties in United States Law - Reexamining the Last in Time Rule in Light of United States v. Palestine Liberation Organization." ***Villanova Law Review,*** 34 (November 1989), 1265-1294.

3103. Steckman, Laurence A. "Terrorism, Ideology and Rules of Law." ***Touro Journal of Transnational Law,*** 1:1 (Fall 1988), 213-256.

3104. Stein, Torsten. "Rendition of Terrorists: Extradition versus Deportation." In: ***Israel Yearbook on Human Rights. Vol. 19. 1989.*** Dordrecht: Martinus Nijhoff, 1989. pp. 281-296.

3105. Stephan, Paul B., III. "Constitutional Limits on the Struggle Against International Terrorism: Revisiting the Rights of Overseas Aliens." ***Connecticut Law Review,*** 19:4 (Summer 1987), 831-861.

3106. Sternberg, Kenneth S., and David L. Skelding. "State Department Determinations of Political Offense: Death Knell for the Political Offense Exception in Extradition Law." ***Case Western Reserve Journal of International Law,*** 15:1 (1983), 137-172.

3107. Stuby, G. "Humanitarian International Law and International Terrorism." In: H. Kochler, ed. ***Terrorism and International Liberation.*** Frankfurt: Verlag Peter Lang, 1988. pp. 237-252.

3108. Sucharitkul, Sompong. "International Terrorism and the Problem of Jurisdiction." ***Syracuse Journal of International Law and Commerce,*** 14:2 (Winter 1987), 141-181.

3109. _____. "Terrorism as an International Crime: Questions of Responsibility and Complicity." In: ***Israel Yearbook on Human Rights, Vol. 19. 1989.*** Dordrecht: Martinus Nijhoff, 1989. pp. 247-258.

3110. Sullivan, Dwight H. "Legal Restrictions on the Right to Use Force Against International Terrorism." ***ASILS International Law Journal,*** 10 (Winter 1986), 169-198.

3111. Sundberg, Jacob W. F. "Some Points of Interest and How to Go About Them." ***Terrorism,*** 3:3-4 (1980), 335-339.

3112. Sweeney, Jane C. "State-Sponsored Terrorism: Libya's Abuse of Diplomatic Privileges and Immunities." ***Dickinson Journal of International Law,*** 5:1 (Fall 1986), 133-165.

3113. Temple, Caleb L. "Terrorism and International Law: Two Barriers to Consensus." ***Conflict,*** 10:3 (1990), 215-226.

3114. "Terrorism and the Law: A Symposium." ***University of Colorado Law Review,*** 60 (1989), 447-600.

3115. "Terrorism and the Law: Protecting Americans Abroad: A Symposium." ***Connecticut Law Review,*** 19 (Summer 1987), 697-973.

3116. "Terrorism, Liberal Democracy and the Rule of Law." ***Bracton Law Journal,*** (1981), 34-42.

3117. "Terrorism." ***Behavioral Sciences and the Law,*** 1:2 (1983), 17-18, 31-32, 45, 57-58.

3118. "The Terrorist and Disruptive Activities (Prevention) Act, 1987." In: R. P. Dhokalia and K. N. Rao, eds. ***Terrorism and International Law.*** New Delhi: Indian Society of International Law, 1988. pp. 53-66.

3119. Terry, James P. "Iranian Hostage Crisis: International Law and United States Policy." ***Judge Advocate General (U.S. Navy) Journal,*** (Summer 1982), 31-79.

3120. _____. "Countering State-Sponsored Terrorism: A Law-Policy Analysis." ***Naval Law Review,*** 36 (Winter 1986), 159-186.

3121. _____. "State Terrorism: A Juridical Examination in Terms of Existing International Law." ***Journal of Palestinian Studies,*** 10:1 (1980), 94-117.

3122. Thompson, Duane K. "The Evolution of the Political Offence Exception in an Age of Modern Political Violence." ***Yale Journal of World Public Order,*** 9:2 (1983), 315-342.

3123. Thornberry, Patrick. "International Law and Its Discontents: The U.S. Raid on Libya." ***Liverpool Law Review,*** 8:1 (Winter 1986), 53-64.

3124. Toensing, Victoria. "The Legal Case for Using Force." In: N. C. Livingstone and T. E. Arnold, eds. ***Fighting Back: Winning the War Against Terrorism.*** Lexington, MA.: Lexington Books, 1985. pp. 145-156.

3125. _____. "Legal Approach." ***Terrorism,*** 11:4 (1988), 343-344.

3126. _____. "Legal Perspective on Terrorism." ***Terrorism,*** 12:1 (1989), 68-69.

3127. Tomasevski, K. "Some Thoughts on Constraints Upon the Approach of International Law to International Terrorism." ***Yugoslav Review of International Law,*** 27:1 (1980), 100-109.

3128. Touret, Denis G. "Terrorism and Freedom in International Law." ***Houston Journal of International Law,*** 2 (Spring 1980), 363-373.

3129. Trotter, Kimberly A. "Compensating Victims of Terrorism: The Current Framework in the United States." ***Texas International Law Journal,*** 22:2-3 (Spring-Summer 1987), 383-401.

3130. Tuggle, Bernie M., and Eain V. Wilkes. "Establishing the Parameters of the Political Offense Exception in Extradition Treaties." ***Denver Journal of International Law and Policy,*** 10:3 (1981), 596-602.

3131. Turk, Danilo. "International Law and Terrorism." ***Socialist Thought and Practice,*** 29:7-10 (July-September, 1989), 30-39.

3132. Turndorf, David. "The U.S. Raid on Libya: A Forceful Response to Terrorism." ***Brooklyn Journal of International Law,*** 12:1 (January 1988), 187-221.

3133. Tweedie, June, and Tony Ward. "The Gibraltar Shootings and the Politics of Inquests." ***Journal of Law and Society,*** 16:4 (Winter 1989), 464-476.

3134. "The United Kingdom's Obligation to Balance Human Rights and its Anti-Terrorism Legislation: The Case of Brogan and Others" ***Fordham International Law Journal,*** 13 (1989-1990), 328-360.

3135. "United States v. ? - International Responsibility for the Hijacking of TWA Flight 847." ***Arizona State Law Journal,*** 19:2 (1987), 325-370.

3136. "United States: 1984 Act to Combat International Terrorism." ***International Legal Materials,*** 24:4 (July 1985),1015-1018.

3137. "United States: Hanoch Tel-Oren v. Libyan Arab Republic et al.." ***International Legal Materials,*** 24:2 (March 1985), 370-434.

3138. Van de Wijngaert, Christine. "The Political Offence Exception to Extradition: How to Plug the "Terrorists' Loophole" Without Departing from Fundamental Human Rights." In: ***Israel Yearbook on Human Rights, Vol. 19. 1989.*** Dordrecht: Martinus Nijhoff, 1989. pp. 297-316.

3139. Venkataraman, R. "Terrorism: A Challenge to International Legal Order." In: R. P. Dhokalia and K. N. Rao, eds. ***Terrorism and International Law.*** New Delhi: Indian Society of International Law, 1988. pp. 1-5.

3140. Walker, Clive. "Legislation: Prevention of Terrorism (Temporary Provisions) Act 1984." ***The Modern Law Review,*** 47 (November 1984), 704-713.

3141. _____. "Reports of Committees: The Jellicoe Report on the Prevention of Terrorism (Temporary Provisions) Act 1976." ***The Modern Law Review,*** 46 (July 1983), 484-492.

3142. Walker, William M. "The International Law Applicable to Guerrilla Movements in Internal Armed Conflicts: A Case Study of Contra Attacks on Nicaraguan Farming Cooperatives." ***New York University Journal of International Law and Politics,*** 21:1 (Fall 1988), 147-194.

3143. Watson, Alan. "Law in a Reign of Terror." ***Law and History Review,*** 3:1 (Spring 1985), 163-168.

3144. Webster, William H. "Terrorism and the Law: The View of the Federal Bureau of Investigation." ***International Society of Barristers Quarterly,*** 17:2 (1982), 283-295.

3145. Weiner, Justus R. "Terrorism: Israel's Legal Responses." ***Syracuse Journal of International Law and Commerce,*** 14:2 (Winter 1987), 183-207.

3146. Wellbaum, Leslie Raissman. "International Human Rights Claims After Tel-Oren v. Libyan Arab Republic: Swan Song for the Legal Lohengrin?." ***Hastings International and Comparative Law Review,*** 9:1 (Fall 1985), 107-147.

3147. White, G. E. "The Marshall Court and International Law: The Piracy Cases." ***American Journal of International Law,*** 83 (October 1989), 727-735.

3148. Wilder, Shael H. "International Terrorism and Hostage Taking: An Overview." ***Manitoba Law Journal,*** 11:4 (1981), 367-386.

3149. Wilkinson, Paul. "The Laws of War and Terrorism." In: D. Rapoport and Y. Alexander, eds. ***The Morality of Terrorism.*** New York: Pergamon Press, 1982. pp. 308-324.

3150. _____. "Fighting the Hydra: International Terrorism and the Rule of Law." In.: N. O'Sullivan, ed. ***Terrorism, Ideology, and Revolution.*** Boulder, CO.: Westview Press, 1986. pp. 205-224.

3151. _____. "The Problem of International Terrorism with Particular Reference to the Maritime Environment." In: E. Ellingsen, ed. ***International Terrorism as a Political Weapon.*** Oslo: The Norwegian Atlantic Committee, 1988. pp. 55-71.

3152. _____. "Fighting the Hydra: Terrorism and the Rule of Law." In: C. W. Kegley, ed. ***International Terrorism: Characteristics, Causes, Controls.*** New York: St. Martin's Press, 1990. pp. 253-258.

3153. Williams, Sharon A. "International Law and Terrorism: Age-Old Problems, Different Targets." ***Canadian Yearbook of International Law,*** 26 (1988), 87-117.

3154. _____. "The Criminal Law Amendment Act 1985: Implications for International Criminal Law." ***Canadian Yearbook of International Law,*** 23 (1985), 226-245.

3155. Wise, Edward M. "Terrorism and the Problems of an International Criminal Law." ***Connecticut Law Review,*** 19:4 (Summer 1987), 799-830.

3156. Wright, Claudia. "The Prohibition Against Training and Support of Terrorist Organizations Act of 1984: Introduction." ***Journal of Palestine Studies,*** 13:3 (1984), 134-144.

3157. Young, J. R. "The Political Offence Exception in the Extradition Law of the United Kingdom: A Redundant Concept?." ***Legal Studies,*** 4 (1984), 211-223.

3158. Zagaris, Bruce, and David Simonetti. "Judicial Assistance Under U.S. Bilateral Treaties." In: M. C. Bassiouni, ed. ***Legal Responses to International Terrorism: U.S. Procedural Aspects.*** Dordrecht: Martinus Nijhoff, 1988. pp. 219-230.

3159. Zander, Michael. "Extradition of Terrorists from Ireland: A Major Judicial Setback." ***New Law Journal,*** 140 (April 6, 1990), 474-476.

3. Documents and Reports

3160. Barcella, E. Lawrence, Jr. ***Terrorism: The Law as an Effective Deterrent.*** Washington, DC.: Defense Nuclear Agency, 1985. pp. 89-92.

3161. Bassiouni, M. Cherif. "Human Rights vs New Initiatives in Control of Terrorism." In: G. K. Walker, ed. ***Proceedings of the 79th Annual Meeting of the American Society of International Law.*** Washington, D.C.: American Society for International Law, 1987. pp. 288-302.

3162. Baum, Phil, and Marc D. Stern. ***The Anti-Terrorism Act of 1987: A Response to its Critics.*** New York: American Jewish Congress, 1987. 13p.

3163. Chacon, Luis. "International Perspectives and the Legislative Role in Combating Terrorism." Paper Presented at the ***Fourth Symposium on International Terrorism,*** held in 1989 at the University of Chicago, Chicago, IL.

3164. Coates, Ken, ed. ***International Terrorism & International Law.*** Nottingham: Bernard Russell Peace Foundation, 1987. 122p.

3165. Cox, G. M. ***Legal Aspects of Terrorism.*** LL.M. Birmingham: University of Birmingham, 1980.

3166. Eig, Larry M. ***Comparison of Certain Provisions of the Proposed U.S. - United Kingdom Supplemental Extradition Treaty with the European Convention on the Suppression of Terrorism.*** Report 85-979A. Washington, D.C.: Library of Congress, Congressional Research Office, 1985. 7p.

3167. Great Britain. Parliament. House of Commons. ***Prevention of Terrorism (Temporary Provisions) Bill.*** London: H.M.S.O., 1988. 64p.

3168. _____._____. House of Lords. ***Prevention of Terrorism (Temporary Provisions) Bill.*** London: H.M.S.O., 1989. 65p.

3169. Green, L. C. ***The Tehran Embassy Incident and International Law.*** Toronto: Canadian Institute of International Affairs, 1980.

3170. Humphries, John. ***International Terrorism as a Lawful Form of Warfare: An Idea Whose Time Should Not Arrive.*** Maxwell Air Force Base, AL.: ACSC/EDCC, 1986. 54p.

3171. Jagelski, Jeanne. ***Statutes Authorizing Sanctions Against Countries Supporting International Terrorism.*** Report 86-1001A. Washington, D.C.: Library of Congress, Congressional Research Service, 1986. 9p.

3172. _____. ***Statutes Authorizing Sanctions Against Countries Supporting International Terrorism.*** Report 87-327A. Washington, D.C.: Library of Congress, Congressional Research Service, 1987. 10p.

3173. Jenkins, Brian M. ***Testimony Before the Senate Governmental Affairs Committee Regarding Senate Bill Against Terrorism.*** RAND P-6586. Santa Monica, CA.: Rand Corporation, 1981. 16p.

3174. Kuhn, Thomas M. ***Terrorism in International Law.*** L.L.D. Dissertation. Pretoria: University of South Africa, 1980.

3175. ***Legal Responses to the Terrorist Threat: An International Seminar, Washington, D.C., November 16-17, 1987.*** Conflict Special. London: Institute for the Study of Conflict, 1988. 97p.

3176. Moore, John N. ***International Law and the Fight Against Terrorism.*** Policy Forum, 3:5. Washington, D.C.: National Forum Foundation, 1986. 4p.

3177. NCCL Staff. ***Information Sheets on the Prevention of Terrorism Act, 1988.*** New York: State Mutual Books, 1988.

3178. Piper, Don C. "Documents Concerning the Achille Lauro Affair and Cooperation in Combatting International Terrorism." ***International Legal Materials,*** 24:6 (November 1985), 1509-1565.

3179. ***Prevention of Terrorism (Temporary Provisions) Act 1984: Elisabeth II. Chapter 8.*** London: H.M.S.O., 1984. 21p.

3180. ***Prevention of Terrorism (Temporary Provisions) Act 1989: Elisabeth II. Chapter 4.*** London: H.M.S.O., 1989. 72p.

3181. Rolnick, Michael P. ***Combatting Terrorism: Does the Law Fail.*** Master's Thesis. London: London School of Economics and Political Science, 1989. 28p.

3182. Sofaer, Abraham D. ***The Political Offence Exception and Terrorism.*** Washington, D.C.: U.S. Department of State, Bureau of Public Affairs, 1985. 5p.

3183. Terry, James P. ***Countering State-Sponsored Terrorism: A Law-Policy Analysis.*** Newport, RI.: Naval War College, 1986. 72p.

3184. Thomas, Kenneth R. ***Anti-Terrorism Act of 1987: Constitutional and Statutory Issues Which May Be Raised in Relations to its Interpretation and Enforcement.*** Report 88-382A. Washington, D.C.: Library of Congress, Congressional Research Service, 1988. 54p.

3185. Toensing, Victoria. "Discussion of the Factors Affecting Legislation on Terrorism: 535 and Counting." In: ***Proceedings of the 9th Annual Symposium on the Role of Behavior Science in Physical Security,*** held on April 3-4, 1984, in Springfield, VA. pp. 53-59.

3186. United States. Congress. House. ***Hostage Relief Act of 1980.*** HR 7085. Public Law 96-449. 96th Cong., 1st sess. Washington, D.C.: U.S. Government Printing Office, 1980. 8p.

3187. _____._____._____. Committee on Foreign Affairs. ***PLO Commitments Compliance Act: Report.*** 101 Cong., 2nd sess. Washington, D.C.: U.S. Government Printing Office, 1990. 32p.

3188. _____._____._____._____. ***Anti-Terrorism and Arms Export Amendments Act of 1989: Report.*** Washington, D.C.: U.S. Government Printing Office, 1989. 39p.

3189. _____._____._____._____. ***The Omnibus Diplomatic Security and Anti-Terrorism Act of 1986: Report.*** Washington, D.C.: U.S. Government Printing Office, 1986. 106p.

3190. _____._____._____._____. Subcommittee on International Security and Scientific Affairs and on International Operations. ***Legislation to Combat International Terrorism: Hearings and Markup, November 9, 1983 - September 26, 1984.*** 94th Cong., 1st sess. Washington, D.C.: U.S. Government Printing Office, 1984. 461p.

3191. _____._____._____. Committee on the Judiciary. ***Biological Weapons Anti-Terrorism Act of 1989: Report.*** 101st Cong., 2nd sess. Washington, D.C.: U.S. Government Printing Office, 1990. 15p.

3192. _____._____._____._____. Subcommittee on Civil and Constitutional Rights. ***Prohibition Against the Training or Support of Terrorist Organization Act of 1984: Hearings, August 2, 1984.*** 98th Cong., 2nd sess. Washington, D.C.: U.S. Government Printing Office, 1984. 75p.

3193. _____._____._____._____. Subcommittee on Crime. ***Extraterritorial Jurisdiction over Terrorist Acts Abroad: Hearings.*** 101st Cong., 1st sess. Washington, D.C.: U.S. Government Printing Office, 1990. 170p.

3194. _____._____._____._____._____. ***Antiterrorism Acts of 1986: Hearing.*** 99th Cong., 2nd sess. Washington, D.C.: U.S. Government Printing Office, 1987. 190p.

3195. _____._____._____._____._____. ***Terrorism Legislation: Hearing.*** 99th Cong., 2nd sess. Washington, D.C.: U.S. Government Printing Office, 1985. 42p.

3196. _____._____._____. Office of Legislative Information and Status. ***Congressional Bills Introduced Concerning Terrorism.*** Washington, D.C.: Congressional Research Service, 1988. 955p.

3197. _____._____. Senate. Committee on Foreign Relations. ***An Act to Combat International Terrorism: Report Together with Additional Views to Accompany S. 333.*** 96th Cong., 1st sess. Washington, D.C.: U.S. Government Printing Office, 1980.

3198. _____._____._____._____. ***Diplomatic Security Act - Hearings.*** Washington, D.C.: U.S. Government Printing Office, 1986. 158p.

3199. _____._____._____._____. ***Terrorism Legislation: Hearing.*** 99th Cong., 2nd sess. Washington, D.C.: U.S. Government Printing Office, 1986. 72p.

3200. _____._____._____._____. ***Diplomatic Security and Anti-Terrorism Act of 1986: Report.*** Washington, D.C.: U.S. Government Printing Office, 1986. 34p.

3201. _____._____._____._____. ***Central American Counterterrorism and Law Enforcement Professionalization Act of 1985: Report.*** Washington, D.C.: U.S. Government Printing Office, 1985. 30p.

3202. _____._____._____. Committee on Governmental Affairs. ***Omnibus Antiterrorism Act of 1979: Hearings on S. 333.*** 96th Cong., 1st sess. Washington, D.C.: U.S. Government Printing Office, 1980. 452p.

3203. _____._____._____._____. ***An Act to Combat International Terrorism: Report.*** 96th Cong., 2nd sess. Washington, D.C.: U.S. Government Printing Office, 1980. 64p.

3204. _____._____._____. Committee on the Judiciary. ***Rewards for Information Concerning Terrorist Acts.*** Washington, D.C.: U.S. Government Printing Office, 1984. 13p.

3205. _____._____._____._____. Subcommittee on Security and Terrorism. ***The Antiterrorism and Foreign Mercenary Act: Hearings on S. 2255.*** 97th Cong., 2nd sess. Washington, D.C.: U.S. Government Printing Office, 1983.

3206. _____._____._____._____._____. ***Legislative Initiatives to Curb Domestic and International Terrorism: Hearings.*** 98th Cong., 2nd sess. Washington, D.C.: U.S. Government Printing Office, 1984. 184p.

3207. _____._____._____._____._____. ***Legal Mechanisms to Combat Terrorism: Hearing.*** 99th Cong., 2nd sess. Washington, D.C.: U.S. Government Printing Office, 1986. 332p.

3208. _____._____._____._____._____. ***The United States Marshals Service Act of 1985: Hearing.*** 99th Cong., 2nd sess. Washington, D.C.: U.S. Government Printing Office, 1987. 141p.

3209. _____._____._____._____._____. ***Bills to Authorize Prosecution of Terrorists and Others Who Attack U.S. Government Employees and Citizens Abroad: Hearing.*** 99th Cong., 1st sess. Washington, D.C.: U.S. Government Printing Office, 1986. 103p.

3210. _____._____._____._____. Subcommittee on the Constitution. ***Supplementary Extradition Treaty Between the United States and the United Kingdom of Great Britain and Northern Ireland: Hearing.*** 99th Cong., 1st sess. Washington, D.C.: U.S. Government Printing Office, 1985. 198p.

3211. _____. General Accounting Office. National Security and International Affairs Division. ***Terrorism.*** Washington, D.C.: U.S. Government Printing Office, 1987. 25p.

3212. _____._____._____. ***Terrorism: Laws Cited Imposing Sanctions on Nations Supporting Terrorism.*** Washington, D.C.: U.S. Government Printing Office, 1987. 27p.

B. INTERNATIONAL ORGANIZATIONS AND CONVENTIONS

1. Books

3213. Dubin, Martin. ***International Terrorism: Two League of Nations Conventions, 1934-37.*** Milwood, NY.: Krauss International, 1990.

3214. Lambert, Joseph J. ***Terrorism and Hostages in International Law: A Commentary on the Hostages Convention 1979.*** Cambridge: Grotius, 1990. 454p.

3215. Murphy, John F. ***The United Nations and the Control of International Violence: A Legal and Political Analysis.*** Totowa, NJ.: Allanheld, Osmun, 1982.

2. Journal Articles

3216. "1988 Rome Convention for the Suppression of Unlawful Acts Against the Safety of Maritime Navigation." In: N. Ronzitti, ed. ***Maritime Terrorism and International Law.*** Dordrecht: Martinus Nijhoff, 1990. pp. 141-152.

3217. "1988 Rome Protocol for the Suppression of Unlawful Acts Against the Safety of Fixed Platforms Located on the Continental Shelf." In: N. Ronzitti, ed. ***Maritime Terrorism and International Law.*** Dordrecht: Martinus Nijhoff, 1990. pp. 153-158.

3218. "Appendix IV - European Convention on the Suppression of Terrorism." In: M. C. Bassiouni, ed. ***Legal Responses to International Terrorism: U.S. Procedural Aspects.*** Dordrecht: Martinus Nijhoff, 1988. pp. 419-422.

3219. "Appendix V - Council of Europe Recommendation No. R(82) Concerning International Co-operation in the Prosecution and Punishment of Acts of Terrorism (1982)." In: M. C. Bassiouni, ed. ***Legal Responses to International Terrorism: U.S. Procedural Aspects.*** Dordrecht: Martinus Nijhoff, 1988. pp. 423-436.

3220. "Appendix VI: 1972 United States Draft Convention for the Prevention and Punishment of Certain Acts of International Terrorism." In: M. C. Bassiouni, ed. ***Legal Responses to International Terrorism: U.S. Procedural Aspects.*** Dordrecht: Martinus Nijhoff, 1988. pp. 445-450.

3221. Aston, Clive C. "The United Nations Convention Against the Taking of Hostages: Realities or Rhetoric?" ***Terrorism,*** 5:1-2 (1981), 139-160.

3222. _____. "The United Nations Convention Against the Taking of Hostages: Realities or Rhetoric?" In: P. Wilkinson, ed. ***British Perspectives on Terrorism.*** London: Allen & Unwin, 1981. pp. 139-160.

3223. Carron, Michelle B. "Victim Compensation for Hostages of Terrorism Involving Aircraft: From Warsaw and Beyond." ***Suffolk Transnational Law Journal,*** 12:2 (Winter 1989), 395-409.

3224. Committee on International Terrorism. "International Terrorism: Fourth Interim Report of the Committee." ***Terrorism,*** 7:2 (1984), 123-146.

3225. "Council of Europe: Recommendation Concerning International Cooperation in the Prosecution and Punishment of Acts of Terrorism." ***International Legal Materials,*** 21:1 (1982), 199-201.

3226. Dinstein, Yoram. "Comments on the Fourth Interim Report of the ILA Committee on International Terrorism (1982)." ***Terrorism,*** 7:2 (1984), 163-168.

3227. _____. "International Cooperation in the Prevention and Suppression of Terrorism." ***Proceedings of the American Society of International Law,*** 80 (1986), 395-400.

3228. Fawcett, J. E. S. "Reform of the European Convention on Human Rights." ***Public Law,*** (1983), 468-476.

3229. Finger, Seymour M. "The United Nations and International Terrorism." In: C. W. Kegley, ed. ***International Terrorism: Characteristics, Causes, Controls.*** New York: St. Martin's Press, 1990. pp. 259-261.

3230. Finnie, Wilson. "The Prevention of Terrorism Act and the European Convention on Human Rights." ***Modern Law Review,*** 52:5 (September 1989), 703-710.

3231. Fitzgerald, Gerald F. "Aviation Terrorism and the International Civil Aviation Organization." ***Canadian Yearbook of International Law,*** 25 (1987), 219-241.

3232. Francioni, Francesco. "Maritime Terrorism and International Law: The Rome Convention of 1988." ***German Yearbook of International Law,*** 31 (1988), 263-288.

3233. Freestone, David. "The 1988 International Convention for the Suppression of Unlawful Acts Against the Safety of Maritime Navigation." ***International Journal of Estuarine and Coastal Law,*** 3:4 (November 1988), 305-327.

3234. Fried, Philip E. "International Agreements - Convention and Protocol from the International Conference on the Suppression of Unlawful Acts Against the Safety of Maritime Navigation." ***Harvard International Law Journal,*** 30:1 (Winter 1989), 226-236.

3235. Friedlander, Robert A. "Comment: Unmuzzling the Dogs of War." ***Terrorism,*** 7:2 (1984), 169-174.

3236. _____. "The Implausible Dream: International Law, State Violence, and State Terrorism." In: M. Stohl and G. A. Lopez, eds. ***Government Violence and Repression.*** Westport, CT.: Greenwood Press, 1986. pp. 235-268.

3237. Halberstam, Malvina. "Terrorism on the High Seas: The Achille Lauro, Piracy and the IMO Convention on Maritime Safety." ***American Journal of International Law,*** 82:2 (April 1988), 269-310.

3238. "International Law Association Paris Conference (1984)." ***Terrorism,*** 7:2 (1984), 199-212.

3239. Jenkins, Brian M. "International Terrorism: A New Challenge for the United Nations." In: J. G. Ruggie, ed. ***United Nations and the Maintenance of International Peace and Security.*** Dordrecht: Martinus Nijhoff, 1987. pp. 407-end.

3240. Jetter, Sherry L. "International Terrorism: Beyond the Scope of International Law: Tel Oren v. Libyan Arab Republic." ***Brooklyn Journal of International Law,*** 12:2 (1986), 505-552.

3241. Joyner, Christopher. "The UN Response to Terrorism: 1988 in Review." ***Terrorism,*** 12:2 (1989), 123-128.

3242. _____. "Suppression of Terrorism on the High Seas: The 1988 IMO Convention on the Safety of Maritime Navigation." In: ***Israel Yearbook on Human Rights, Vol. 19. 1989.*** Dordrecht: Martinus Nijhoff, 1989. pp. 343-370.

3243. _____. "The 1988 IMO Convention on the Safety of Maritime Navigation: Towards a Legal Remedy for Terrorism at Sea." ***German Yearbook of International Law,*** 31 (1988), 230-262.

3244. Kirgis, Frederic L. "Some Comments on Professor Rodes' Draft Convention." ***Washington and Lee Law Review,*** 39 (Spring 1982), 373-376.

3245. Kirsch, Philippe. "The 1988 ICAO and IMO Conferences: An International Consensus Against Terrorism." ***Dalhousie Law Journal,*** 12:1 (April 1989), 5-33.

3246. Lagodny, Otto. "The European Convention on the Suppression of Terrorism: A Substantial Step to Combat Terrorism?." ***University of Colorado Law Review,*** 60:3 (Summer 1989) 583-600.

3247. Lillich, Richard B. "Model American Convention on the Prevention and Punishment of Serious Forms of Violence." ***American Journal of International Law,*** 77 (July 1983), 662-668.

3248. Lockwood, Bert B., Jr. "The Model American Convention on the Prevention and Punishment of Certain Serious Forms of Violence Jeopardizing Fundamental Rights and Freedoms." ***Rutgers Law Journal,*** 13:3 (Spring 1982), 579-605.

3249. Lubet, Steven. "Taking the Terror Out of Political Terrorism: The Supplementary Treaty of Extradition Between the United States and the United Kingdom." ***Connecticut Law Review,*** 19:4 (Summer 1987), 863-893.

3250. McDonald, J. W. "The United Nations Convention Against the Taking of Hostages: the Inside Story." ***Terrorism,*** 6:4 (1983), 545-560.

3251. McRae, P., and J. Reiskind. "International Convention Against the Taking of Hostages." ***Canadian Yearbook of International Law,*** 19 (1981), 406-407.

3252. McWhinney, Edward. "International Terrorism: United Nations Projects for Legal Controls." ***Terrorism,*** 7:2 (1984), 175-184.

3253. Milde, M. "Draft Convention on the Marking of Explosives." ***Annals of Air and Space Law,*** 15 (1990), 155-182.

3254. Monday, Mark. "Bait or Debate? New Treaty may Make Police into Targets." ***TVI Journal,*** 1:3 (1980), 10-12.

3255. Moore, John N. "The Need for an International Convention." In: M. C. Bassiouni, ed. ***Legal Responses to International Terrorism: U.S. Procedural Aspects.*** Dordrecht: Martinus Nijhoff, 1988. pp. 437-444.

3256. Murphy, John F. "Comments on the Fourth Interim Report of the ILA Committee on International Terrorism (1982)." ***Terrorism,*** 7:2 (1984), 193-198.

3257. _____. "The United Nations and International Terrorism." In: H. H. Han, ed. ***Terrorism, Political Violence and World Order.*** Lanham, MD.: University Press of America, 1984. pp. 603-610.

3258. Pfeifenberger, Werner. "Chinese and Soviet Attitudes Towards Sub-State Violence in the U.N. Context." In: D. Carlton and C. Schaerf, eds. ***Contemporary Terror.*** London: Macmillan, 1981. pp. 66-74.

3259. Plant, Glen. "The Convention for the Suppression of Unlawful Acts Against the Safety of Maritime Navigation." ***The International and Comparative Law Quarterly,*** 39 (January 1990), 27-56.

3260. Pyle, Christopher. "International Cooperation in the Prevention and Suppression of Terrorism." ***Proceedings of the American Society of International Law,*** 80 (1986), 390-395.

3261. Rajput, R. S. "International Conventions on Aerial Hijacking: Ann Approach to Combat Terrorism." ***Indian Journal of Political Science,*** 51:1 (January-March 1990), 98-125.

3262. Ripp, Rudolph K. "The United Nations Commission on Human Rights." ***Terrorism,*** 6:4 (1983), 577-587.

3263. Rosenne, Shabtai. "The International Convention Against the Taking of Hostages, 1979." ***Israel Yearbook on Human Rights,*** 10 (1980), 109-156.

3264. Rosenstock, Robert. "International Convention Against the Taking of Hostages: Another International Community Step Against Terrorism." ***Denver Journal of International Law and Policy,*** 9 (Summer 1980), 169-195.

3265. Rubin, Alfred P. "International Cooperation in the Prevention and Suppression of Terrorism." ***Proceedings of the American Society of International Law,*** 80 (1986), 400-403.

3266. _____. "Report of the International Law Association's 63rd Conference (Warsaw): Legal Problems of Extradition in Relation to Terrorist Offenses (Working Session), 26 August 1988." ***Terrorism,*** 11:6 (1988), 511-530.

3267. Shamgar, Meir. "An International Convention Against Terrorism." In: B. Netanyahu, ed. ***Terrorism: How the West Can Win.*** New York: Farrar, Straus, Giroux, 1986. pp. 157-162.

3268. Shamwell, H. F. "Implementing the Convention on the Prevention and Punishment of Crimes Against Internationally Protected Persons, Including Diplomatic Agents." ***Terrorism,*** 6:4 (1983), 529-543.

3269. Silets, H. L. "Something Special in the Air and on the Ground: The Potential for Unlimited Liability of International Air Carriers for Terrorist Attacks Under the Warsaw Convention and its Revisions." ***Journal of Air Law and Commerce,*** 53:2 (Winter 1987), 321-374.

3270. Stewart, David. "The United Nations, Terrorism and Revolutionary Violence: A View from South Africa." In: H. H. Han, ed. ***Terrorism, Political Violence and World Order.*** Lanham, MD.: University Press of America, 1984. pp. 611-618.

3271. Sundberg, Jacob W. F. "Comments on the Fourth Interim Report of Committee on International Terrorism." ***Terrorism,*** 7:2 (1984), 185-192.

3272. Treves, Tullio. "The Rome Convention for the Suppression of Unlawful Acts Against the Safety of Maritime Navigation." In: N. Ronzitti, ed. ***Maritime Terrorism and International Law.*** Dordrecht: Martinus Nijhoff, 1990. pp. 69-90.

3273. Verwey, W. D. "International Hostages Convention and National Liberation Movements." ***American Journal of International Law***, 75 (January 1981), 533-546.

3274. Warbrick, Colin. "The European Convention on Human Rights and the Prevention of Terrorism." ***International and Comparative Law Quarterly***, 32 (January 1983), 82-119.

3275. _____. "The Prevention of Terrorism (Temporary Provision) Act 1976 and the European Convention on Human Rights: The McVeigh Case." ***International and Comparative Law Quarterly***, 32:3 (July 1983), 757-784.

3276. Wilensky, Roberta L. "Flying the Unfriendly Skies: The Liability of Airlines Under the Warsaw Convention for Injuries Due to Terrorism." ***Northwestern Journal of International Law And Business***, 8:1 (Spring 1987), 249-272.

3277. Yoder, A. "The Effectiveness of U.N. Action Against International Terrorism: Conclusion and Comments." ***Terrorism***, 6:4 (1983), 587-592.

3278. _____. "United Nations Resolution Against International Terrorism." ***Terrorism***, 6:4 (1983), 503-517.

3. Documents and Reports

3279. Constance, George W. ***Obstacles that Block U.N. Efforts to Control International Terrorism.*** Ph.D. Dissertation. New School for Social Research, 1981. 282p.

3280. Council of Europe. European Committee on Crime Problems. ***International Co-operation in the Prosecution and Punishment of Acts of Terrorism: Recomendation No. R (82) 1.*** Strasbourg: Council of Europe, 1983. 20p.

3281. European Economic Community. "Agreement Concerning the Application of the European Convention on the Suppression of Terrorism and the Member States." ***International Legal Materials***, 19:2 (1980), 325-327.

3282. Great Britain.Command Papers. ***International Convention Against Taking of Hostages.*** CMND 9100. London: H.M.S.O., 1983. 21p.

3283. International Civil Aviation Organization. ***International Standards and Recommended Practices: Security, Safeguarding International Civil Aviation Against Acts of Unlawful Interference.*** Montreal: International Civil Aviation Organization, 1986. 18p.

3284. James, R. D. ***Using the Protocols Additional to the Geneva Conventions of 12 August 1949 to Combat Acts of Terrorism.*** Master's Thesis. Wright-Patterson AFB.: Air Force Institute of Technology, 1989. 101p.

3285. Morgan, Edward M. ***International Convention Against the Taking of Hostages: Explanatory Documentation Prepared for Commonwealth Jurisdiction.*** London: Commonwealth Secretariat, 1989. 41p.

3286. Reiskind, J. "International Conventions on Terrorism and Canadian Criminal Law." In: ***Canadian Council on International Law: Proceedings of the Tenth Annual Conference.*** Ottawa: Canadian Council on International Law, 1981. pp. 68-78.

3287. Rubin, Alfred P. "Terrorism, Grave Breaches and the 1977 Geneva Protocols." In: J. R. Hall, ed. ***Proceedings of the 74th Annual Meeting of the American Society of International Law.*** Washington, D.C.: American Society of International Law, 1981. pp. 192-195.

3288. United Nations. General Assembly. ***Measures to Prevent International Terrorism Which Endanger or Takes Innocent Human Lives...etc.*** Report A/36/425. New York: United Nation, September 21, 1981. 108p.

3289. _____._____. ***Consideration of Effective Measures to Enhance the Protection, Security and Safety of Diplomatic and Consular Missions and Representatives.*** New York: United Nations, 1988. 34p.

3290. United States. Congress. House. Committee on Foreign Affairs. ***International Terrorism: A Compilation of Major Laws, Treaties, Agreements and Executive Documents: Report.*** 100th Cong., 1st sess. Washington, D.C.: U.S. Government Printing Office, 1987. 970p.

3291. _____._____. Senate. Committee on Foreign Relations. ***Maritime Counter-Terrorism Convention, with Related Protocol: Report.*** Washington, D.C.: U.S. Government Printing Office, 1989. 17p.

3292. Wilkinson, Paul. "Terrorism - A Threat to World Order - Need for a Code of International Criminal Law." Paper Presented to the ***8th Commonwealth Law Conference***, held on 1986 at Ocho Rios, Jamaica.

C. CIVIL AVIATION - LEGAL ASPECTS

1. Books

3293. Joyner, Nancy D. ***Aerial Hijacking as an International Crime.*** Dobbs Ferry, NY.: Oceana, 344p.

3294. McWhinney, Edward. ***Aerial Piracy and International Terrorism: The Illegal Diversion of Aircraft and International Law.*** 2nd ed. International Studies on Terrorism, 3. Dordrecht: Martinus Nijhoff, 1987. 264p.

2. Journal Articles

3295. Abeyratne, R. I. R. "Aerial Piracy and Extended Jurisdiction in Japan." ***International and Comparative Law Quarterly***, 33:3 (July 1984), 596-613.

3296. Bussutil, James J. "The Bonn Declaration on International Terrorism: A Non-Binding International Agreement on Aircraft Hijacking." ***International and Comparative Law Quarterly***, 31:3 (1982), 474-487.

3297. Chamberlain, Kevin. "Collective Suspension of Air Services with States Which Harbor Hijackers." ***International and Comparative Law Quarterly***, (July 1983), 616-632.

3298. Cope, Virginia. "Pan Am Crash Raises Complex Legal Issues." ***Trial***, 25:3 (March 1989), 88-90.

3299. Dempsey, Paul S. "Aerial Piracy and Terrorism: Unilateral and Multilateral Responses to Aircraft Hijacking." ***Connecticut Journal of International Law***, 2:2 (1987), 427-462.

3300. Duncan, J. C. "Battling Aerial Terrorism and Compensating the Victims." ***Naval Law Review***, 39 (1990), 241-268.

3301. Fingerman, Mark E. "Skyjacking and the Bonn Declaration of 1978: Sanctions Applicable to Recalcitrant Nations." ***California Western International Law Journal***, 10 (Winter 1980), 123-152.

3302. Ghislaine, Richard. "Air Transport Safety: Prevention and Sanctions." ***Annals of Air and Space Law***, 10 (1985), 209-216.

3303. Glassman, David L. "Keeping "The Wild" Out of "The Wild Blue Yonder": Preventing Terrorist Attacks Against International Flights in Civil Aviation." ***Dickinson Journal of International Law***, 4:2 (Spring 1986), 251-274.

3304. Gustafson, Glen. "Terrorist Attacks on Airport Terminals and Government Tort Liability: Is Moncur Distinguishable Under California Government Code Section 815.6?." ***Northrop University Law Journal of Aerospace, Energy and the Environment***, 7 (1986), 103-115.

3305. Haeck, Louis. "International Law and Air Piracy." In: B. Macdonald, ed. ***Terror.*** Toronto: Canadian Institute of International Studies, 1987. pp. 77-97.

3306. Leich, Marian N. "Contemporary Practice of the United States Relating to International Law." ***American Journal of International Law***, 77:4 (1983), 875-877.

3307. Lenett, M. G. "Implied Consent in Airport Searches - A Response to Terrorism, United-States vs. Pulidobaquerizo." ***American Criminal Law***, 25:3 (1988), 549-575.

3308. Levitt, Geoffrey M. "International Counterterrorism Cooperation: The Summit Seven and Air Terrorism." ***Vanderbilt Journal of Transnational Law***, 20:2 (March 1987), 259-287.

3309. McWhinney, Edward. "International and National Law, and Community Problem--Solving on Aerial Piracy." In: Y. Alexander and E. Sochor, eds. ***Aerial Piracy and Aviation Security.*** Dordrecht: Martinus Nijhoff, 1990. pp. 77-94.

3310. Morrison, Alastair. "Air Piracy." In: ***Legal Responses to the Terrorist Threat.*** London: Institute for the Study of Conflict, 1988. pp. 43-50.

3311. Richard, Ghislaine. "Airtransport Safety: Prevention and Sanctions." ***Annals of Air and Space Law***, 10 (1985), 209-216.

3312. Strantz, N. J. "Aviation Security and Pan Am Flight 103: What Have We Learned?." ***Journal of Air Law and Communication***, 56 (Winter 1990), 413-489.

3313. Wadegonkar, Damodar. "Hijacking and Conventional Law." ***Indian Journal of International Law***, 22:3-4 (1982), 360-374.

3. Documents and Reports

3314. Kaszczuk, Robert. ***Legal Limitations on the Use of Airpower Against Terrorist Activity.*** Maxwell Air Force Base, AL.: ACSC/EDCC, 1986. 33p.

3315. United States. Congress. House. Committee on Foreign Affairs. ***Aviation Security Improvement Act of 1990: Hearings.*** 101st Cong., 2nd sess. Washington, D.C.: U.S. Government Printing Office, 1990. 321p.

3316. _____._____. Senate. Committee on Foreign Relations. ***Airport Security Protocol: Report.*** Washington, D.C.: U.S. Government Printing Office, 1989. 17p.

3317. _____._____._____. Committee on the Judiciary. ***Aircraft Sabotage Act: Report.*** 98th Cong., 2nd sess. Washington, D.C.: U.S. Government Printing Office, 1984. 15p.

3318. _____. Federal Aviation Administration. Office of Civil Aviation Security. ***Legal Status of Hijackers.*** Washington, D.C.: Federal Aviation Administration, 1986. 15p.

VIII

MEDIA AND TERRORISM

Terrorist incidents have become almost everyday events. We watch terrorist incidents unfold on our television sets and read about them in newspapers. Terrorism is real life drama. Terrorists desire publicity and they plan their acts to achieve maximum media exposure. Many terrorist operations become symbolic acts, played out to the public and to governments in a macabre real life dramatic show.

Media coverage is payoff for terrorists and a real problem for crisis management. The media is constantly reexamining its terrorist incidents coverage policies. Media coverage may prolong certain situations and it may have significant political repercussions - as in the case of the Iranian Hostage Crisis. Other concerns relate to the subjectivity of media coverage, self censorship of media personnel, and intimidation of media personnel by terrorists - as was the case of most media personnel in Beirut. The dilemma of a democratic society which needs free access to information but needs to protect itself from possible negative effects of media coverage is demonstrated by the issues raised by the relationship between media and terrorism.

1. Books

3319. Adams, William C. ***Television Coverage of the Middle East.*** Norwood, NJ.: Ablex, 1983. 137p.

3320. Alexander, Yonah, and Robert G. Picard, eds. ***In the Camera's Eye: News Coverage of Terrorist Events.*** New York: Pergamon-Brassey's, 1990. 155p.

3321. _____, and Richard Latter, eds. ***Terrorism and the Media: Dilemmas for Government, Journalists, and the Public.*** New York: Pergamon-Brassey's, 1990. 145p.

3322. Bolling, Landrum R. ***Reporters Under Fire: U.S. Media Coverage of Conflicts in Lebanon and Central America.*** Boulder, CO,: Westview Press, 1985. 155p.

3323. Cathcart, Rex. ***The Most Contrary Region: The BBC in Northern Ireland.*** Belfast: Blackstaff Press, 1984. 306p.

3324. Chafets, Zeev. ***Double Vision: How the Press Distorts America's View of the Middle East.*** New York: Morrow, 1985. 349p.

3325. Clutterbuck, Richard L. ***The Media and Political Violence.*** London: Macmillan, 1981. 191p.

3326. Cox, Robert. ***The Sound of One Hand Clapping: A Preliminary Study of the Argentine Press in a Time of Terror.*** Washington, D.C.: Woodrow Wilson International Center for Scholars, 1980.

3327. Curtis, Liz. ***Ireland, The Propaganda War: The Media and the "The Battle for the Hearts and Minds".*** London: Pluto Press, 1984.

3328. Eliot, Philip, et al. ***Televising Terrorism: Political Violence in Popular Culture.*** New York: Scribner Books, 1984. 160p.

3329. Goldstein, Tom. ***The News at Any Cost: How Journalists Compromise Their Ethics to Shape the News.*** New York: Simon and Schuster, 1985. 301p.

3330. Hetherington, Alastair. ***News, Newspapers and Television.*** London: Macmillan, 1985. 329p.

3331. Hooper, Alan. ***The Military and the Media.*** Aldershot, Eng.: Gower, 1982.

3332. Karetzky, Stephen, and Peter Goldman. ***The Media's War Against Israel.*** New York: Steimatzky, 1985.

3333. Larson, James F. ***Television's Window on the World: International Affairs Coverage on the U.S. Networks.*** Norwood, NJ.: Ablex, 1984. 195p.

3334. Miller, Abraham H., ed. ***Terrorism: The Media and the Law.*** Dobbs Ferry, NY.: Transnational Publishers, 1982. 221p.

3335. Nimmorg, Dan D., and James E. Combs. ***Nightly Horrors: Crisis Coverage by Television Network News.*** Knoxville, TN.: University of Tennessee Press, 1985. 216p.

3336. O'Neill, Michael J. ***Terrorist Spectaculars: Should TV Coverage Be Curbed.*** New York: Priority Press/Twentieth Century Fund, 1986. 109p.

3337. Schlesinger, Philip, G. Murdock and Philip Elliott. ***Televising "Terrorism": Political Violence in Popular Culture.*** London: Comedia Publishers, 1983. 181p.

3338. Schmid, Alex P., and Janny F. A. De Graaf. ***Insurgent Terrorism and the Western News Media: An Exploratory Analysis with a Dutch Case Study.*** Leiden: Center for the Study of Social Conflicts, 1980. 490p.

3339. _____. _____. ***Violence as Communication: Insurgent Terrorism and the Western News Media.*** Beverly Hills, CA.: Sage, 1982. 283p.

2. Journal Articles

3340. Adams, William C. "The Beirut Hostages: ABC and CBS Seize an Opportunity: ABC News Got the Scoop on Hostage Interviews, but CBS Got the Better Story; A Comparison of the Two Networks Coverage of TWA Hijacking." ***Public Opinion***, 8 (August/September 1985), 45-48.

3341. Alexander, Yonah. "The Media and Terrorism." In: D. Carlton and C. Schaerf, eds. ***Contemporary Terrorism.*** London: Macmillan, 1981. pp. 50-65.

3342. _____. "Terrorism and the Mass-Media." In: ***Communications in a Changing World, Vol. 1.*** Brazilian Journalist Seminar. Washington, D.C.: Media Institute, 1982. pp. 84-94.

3343. _____. "Terrorism, The Media and the Police." In: H. H. Han, ed. ***Terrorism, Political Violence and World Order.*** Lanham, MD.: University Press of America, 1984. pp. 135-150.

3344. Altheide, David L. "Format and Symbols in TV Coverage of Terrorism in the United States and Great Britain." ***International Studies Quarterly***, 31:2 (June 1987), 161-176.

3345. _____. "Formats of Crises." ***National Forum***, 67:4 (Fall 1987), 12-14.

3346. _____. "Iran vs. U.S. TV News: The Hostage Story Out of Context." In: W. C. Adams, ed. ***Television Coverage of the Middle East.*** Norwood, NJ.: Ablex, 1981. pp. 128-158.

3347. Atwater, Tony. "Terrorism on the Evening News: An Analysis of Coverage of the TWA Hostage Crisis in "NBC Nightly News"." ***Political Communication and Persuasion***, 4:1 (1987), 17-24.

3348. _____, and Norma F. Green. "News Sources in Network Coverage of International Terrorism." ***Journalism Quarterly***, 65:4 (Winter 1988), 967-971.

3349. _____. "News Format in Network Evening News Coverage of the TWA Hijacking." ***Journal of Broadcasting and Electronic Media***, 33:3 (1989), 293-304.

3350. _____. "Network Evening News Coverage of the TWA Hostage Crisis." In: Y. Alexander and R. Latter, eds. ***Terrorism and the Media.*** New York: Brassey's, 1990. pp. 85-92.

3351. Ayanian, John Z., David L. Paletz and Peter A. Fozzard. "The I.R.A., the Red Brigades, and the F.A.L.N. in the New York Times." ***Journal of Communication***, 32:2 (Spring 1982), 162-170.

3352. Ayanian, Mark A., and John Z. Ayanian. "Armenian Political Violence on American Network News: An Analysis of Content." ***Armenian Review***, 40:1 (1987), 13-29.

3353. Baker, Brent. "The PAO and Terrorism." ***Military Media Review***, (July 1986), 10-11.

3354. Bar-Ilan, David. "Israel , The Hostages, and the Networks." ***Commentary***, 80:3 (1985), 33-37.

3355. Barendt, Eric. "Broadcasting Censorship. (Great Britain)." ***Law Quarterly Review***, 106 (July 1990), 354-361.

3356. Barton, Richard L., and Richard B. Gregg. "Middle East Conflict as a TV News Scenario: A Formal Analysis." ***Journal of Communication***, 32 (Spring 1982), 172-186.

3357. Bassiouni, M. Cherif. "Media Coverage of Terrorism: The Law and the Public." ***Journal of Communication***, 32:2 (1982), 128-143.

3358. _____. "Problems of Media Coverage of Nonstate - Sponsored Terror - Violence Incidents." In: L. Z. Freedman and Y. Alexander, eds. ***Perspectives on Terrorism.*** Wilmington, DE.: Scholarly Resources, 1983. pp. 177-200.

3359. _____. "Terrorism and the Media." ***Journal of Criminal Law and Criminology,*** 72 (Spring 1981), 1-55.

3360. Bazalgette, C., and R. Paterson. "Real Entertainment: The Iranian Embassy Siege." ***Screen Education,*** (1980), 55-67.

3361. Bennett, James R. "Page One Sensationalism and the Libyan "Hit Team."." ***Newspaper Research Journal,*** 4 (Spring 1983), 34-38.

3362. Bolling, Landrum R. "Insult to Injury: The Dan Mitrione Tragedy." In: M. F. Herz, ed. ***Diplomats and Terrorists.*** Washington, D.C.: Institute for the Study of Diplomacy, 1982. pp. 66-69.

3363. Bremer, L. Paul. "Terrorism and the Media." ***Department of State Bulletin,*** 87:2126 (September 1987), 72-75.

3364. _____. "Terrorism, the Media and the Government." ***Parameters,*** 18:1 (March 1988), 52-59.

3365. Brennan, Paul, et al. "The Northern Ireland Conflict in the French Press: Le Figaro, the Left-Wing Press, Le Monde, and the Religious Press." In: J. Darby, N. Dodge and A. C. Hepburn, eds. ***Political Violence: Ireland in a Comparative Perspective.*** Ottawa: University of Ottawa Press, 1990. pp. 83-102.

3366. Bromley, Michael. "War of Words: The Belfast Telegraph and Loyalist Populism." In: Y. Alexander and A. O'Day, eds. ***Ireland's Terrorist Trauma.*** New York: Harvester Wheatsheaf, 1989. pp. 213-233.

3367. Buddenbaum, Judith M. "Of Christian Freedom Fighters and Marxist Terrorists: The Image of SWAPO and the Namibian Independence Movement in the Religious and Secular Press." In: Y. Alexander and R. G. Picard, eds. ***In the Camera's Eye: News Coverage of Terrorist Events.*** New York: Braassey's, 1990. pp. 131-150.

3368. "CBS News Production Standards: Coverage of Terrorism." In: A. H. Miller, ed. ***Terrorism: Media and the Law.*** Dobbs Ferry, NY.: Transnational Publishers, 1982. pp. 157-158.

3369. "Calls for a Code on Terrorist Coverage." ***Broadcasting,*** 109 (July 22, 1985), 36-37.

3370. Catton, William R. "Militants and the Media." ***Indiana Law Journal,*** 53 (1978), 705-713.

3371. Chafets, Zeev. "Beirut and the Great Media Cover-Up." ***Commentary,*** 78:3 (1984), 20-29.

3372. Chalfont, Lord, et al. "Political Violence and the Role of the Media: Some Perspectives. ***Political Communication and Persuation,*** 1:1 (1980), 79-99.

3373. _____. "The Price of Sympathy." In: B. Netanyahu, ed. ***Terrorism: How the West Can Win.*** New York: Farrar, Straus, Giroux, 1986. pp. 126-130.

3374. _____. "Comment: Terrorism, Television and Philosophic Doubts." ***Terrorism,*** 0:3 (1987), 297-306.

3375. Chambers,, Thomas F. "A Willing Hostage: The News Media is Happy to Give Saturation Coverage to Terrorist Extremism." ***Canada and the World,*** 55:6 (February 1990), 21-23.

3376. "The Chicago Sun-Times and Daily News Standards for Coverage of Terrorism." In: A. H. Miller, ed. ***Terrorism: The Media and the Law.*** Dobbs Ferry, NY.: Transnational Publications, 1982. pp. 159-160.

3377. Chomsky, Noam. "Talking About Terrorism?." ***The National Reporter***, 28:1 (1986), 21-26.

3378. Clarke, James W. "Focusing Aggression: Some Observations of the Relationship Between Media Influences and Political Assassinations." In: H. H. Han, ed. ***Terrorism, Political Violence and World Order.*** Lanham, MD.: University Press of America, 1984. pp. 87-102.

3379. Clawson, Patrick. "Why We Need More but Better Coverage of Terrorism." ***Orbis***, 30 (Winter 1987), 701-710.

3380. _____. "Why We Need More but Better Coverage of Terrorism." In: C. W. Kegley, ed. ***International Terrorism: Characteristics, Causes, Controls.*** New York: St. Martin's Press, 1990. pp. 241-244.

3381. "Closer Look at Network Coverage of TWA Flight 847." ***Broadcasting***, 109 (August 5, 1985), 58-60.

3382. Clutterbuck, Richard L. "The Public and the Media in Situations of Terrorism and Disorder." ***Clandestine Facts and Technology***, 12:6 (1986), ;l;

3383. Cohen, Yoel. "The PLO: 'Guardian Angels of the Media'." ***Midstream***, (February 1983), 7-10.

3384. Collins, R. "Terrorism and the Mass Media." ***Inter Media***, 10:1 (1982), 48-50.

3385. Colvin, Teresa R. "Terrorism and the Media: Problems and Perspectives for Democratic Societies." ***Armed Forces Journal International***, (June 1985), 128-131.

3386. "Conference Report: Terrorism and the Media." ***Political Communication and Persuasion***, 3:2 (1985), 185-190.

3387. "Constitutional and Legal Issues Relating to News Media Coverage of Terrorism." In: M. C. Bassiouni, ed. ***Terrorism, Law Enforcement and the Mass Media.*** Rockville, MD.: National Criminal Justice Reference Service, 1983. pp. 150-186.

3388. Cooper, Thomas W. "Terrorism and Perspectivist Philosophy: Understanding Adversarial New Coverage." In: Y. Alexander and R. G. Picard, eds. ***In the Camera's Eye: News Coverage of Terrorist Events.*** New York: Brassey's, 1990. pp. 10-29.

3389. "The Courier Journal and Louisville (KY) Times Guidelines." In: A. H. Miller, ed. ***Terrorism: The Media and the Law.*** Dobbs Ferry, NY.: Transnational Publications, 1982. pp. 158-159.

3390. Cox, Robert. "Comments: The Media as a Weapon." ***Political Communication and Persuasion***, 1:3 (1981), 297-300.

3391. _____. "The Media as a Weapon." In: M. F. Herz, ed. ***Diplomats and Terrorists.*** Washington, D.C.: Institute for the Study of Diplomacy, 1982. pp. 63-65.

3392. Crelinsten, Ronald D. "Images of Terrorism in the Media: 1966-1985." ***Terrorism***, 12:3 (1989), 167-198.

3393. _____. "Terrorism and the Media: Problems, Solutions, and Counterproblems." ***Political Communication and Persuasion***, 6;4 (1989), 311-339.

3394. Cromer, Gerald. "The Roots of Lawlessness: The Coverage of the Jewish Underground in the Israeli Press." ***Terrorism***, 11:1 (1988), 43-52.

3395. Damm, C. A. "Media and Terrorism." ***Journal of Security Administration***, 5:1 (1982), 7-18.

3396. Davis, Richard. "The Manufacture of Propagandist History by Northern Ireland Loyalists and Republicans." In; Y. Alexander and A. O'Day, eds. ***Ireland's Terrorist Dilemma.*** Dordrecht: Martinus Nijhoff, 1986. pp. 145-178.

3397. De Borchgrave, Arnaud. "Censorship by Omission." In: B. Netanyahu, ed. ***Terrorism: How the West Can Win.*** New York: Farrar, Straus, Giroux, 1986. pp. 117-119.

3398. Decter, Midge. "A Need for Clarity." In: B. Netanyahu, ed. ***International Terrorism: Challenge and Response.*** New Brunswick, NJ.: Transaction Books, 1981. pp. 242-244.

3399. Delli Carpini, Michael, and B. A. Williams. "Terrorism and the Media: Patterns of Occurrence and Presentation, 1969-1980." In: H. H. Han, ed. ***Terrorism, Political Violence and World Order.*** Lanham, MD.: University Press of America, 1984. pp. 103-134.

3400. _____, and Bruce Williams. "Television and Terrorism: Patterns of Presentation and Occurrence." ***Western Political Quarterly,*** 40:1 (1987), 45-64.

3401. Der Derian, James. "The Importance of Shredding in Earnest: Reading the National Security Culture and Terrorism." In: I. Angus and S. Jhally, eds. ***Cultural Politics in Contemporary America.*** New York: Routledge, 1989. pp. 230-239.

3402. Diamond, Edwin. "The Coverage Itself: Why It Turned into 'Terrorvision'." ***TV Guide,*** 33 (September 21, 1985), 6-11.

3403. Dowling, Ralph E. "Terrorism and the Media: A Rhetorical Genre." ***Journal of Communication,*** 36:1 (1986), 12-24.

3404. _____. "Victimage and Mortification: Terrorism and Its Coverage in the Media." ***Terrorism,*** 12:1 (1989), 47-60.

3405. _____. "Terrorist Motivation: Media Coverage or Human Social Action?." ***Conflict Quarterly,*** 9:3 (Summer 1989), 41-53.

3406. _____. "The Terrorist and the Media: Partners in Crime or Rituals and harmless Observers?." In: Y. Alexander and A. H. Foxman, eds. ***The 1988-1989 Annual of Terrorism.*** Dordrecht: Martinus Nijhoff, 1989. pp. 227-244.

3407. Elkins, Michael. "Caging the Beasts." In: B. Netanyahu, ed. ***International Terrorism: Challenge and Response.*** New Brunswick, NJ.: Transaction Books, 1981. pp. 230-234.

3408. Elliott, Deni. "Family Ties: A Case Study of Coverage of Families and Friends During the Hijacking of TWA Flight 847." ***Political Communication and Persuasion,*** 5:1 (1988), 67-76.

3409. Elliott, Philip, G. Murdock and Philip Schlesinger. "Terrorism and the State: A Case Study of the Discourses of Television." ***Media, Culture & Society,*** 5:2 (1983), 155-177.

3410. Elmquist, Soren. "The Scope and Limits of Cooperation Between the Media and the Authorities." In: Y. Alexander and R. Latter, eds. ***Terrorism and the Media.*** New York: Brassey's, 1990. pp. 74-80.

3411. Ermlich, Ferdinand A. "Terrorism and the Media: Strategy, Coverage and Responses." ***Political Communication and Persuasion,*** 4:2 (1987), 135-140.

3412. Farnen, Russell F. "Terrorism and the Mass Media: A Systemic Analysis of a Symbiotic Process." ***Terrorism,*** 13:2 (1990), 99-144.

3413. Feith, Douglas J. "Israel, the Post, and the Shaft." ***Middle East Review,*** 12:4-13:1 (1980), 62-67.

3414. Finn, John E. "Media Coverage of Political Terrorism and the First Amendment: Reconciling the Public's Right to Know with Public Order." In: Y. Alexander and R. Latter, eds. ***Terrorism and the Media.*** New York: Brassey's, 1990. pp. 47-56.

3415. Friedland, Nehemia. "Desensitizing the Public to Terrorist Attacks: Methods and Dilemmas." In: A. Merari, ed. ***On Terrorism and Combating Terrorism.*** Frederick, MD.: University Publications of America, 1985. pp. 95-100.

3416. Friedlander, Robert A. "Iran: The Hostage Seizure, the Media and International Law." In: A. H. Miller, ed. ***Terrorism: The Media and the Law.*** Dobbs Ferry, NY.: Transnational Publishers, 1982. pp. 51-68.

3417. _____. "Public Information: A Deadly Weapon in Terrorist Hands." ***TVI Journal,*** 4:10-12 (Winter 1983), 4-6.

3418. Fuller, Linda K. "Terrorism as Treated by the Christian Science Monitor, 1977-1987." ***Political Communication and Persuation,*** 5:2 (1988), 121-137.

3419. "Furor over NBC's Abbas Interview." ***Broadcasting,*** 110 (May 12, 1986), 73-74.

3420. Gallimore, Timothy. "Media Compliance with Voluntary Press Guidelines for Covering Terrorism." In: Y. Alexander and R. G. Picard, eds. ***In the Camera's Eye: News Coverage of Terrorist Events.*** New York: Brassey's, 1990. pp. 103-120.

3421. Gerbner, George. "Symbolic Functions of Violence and Terror." In: Y. Alexander and R. Latter, eds. ***Terrorism and the Media.*** New York: Brassey's, 1990. pp. 93-99.

3422. _____. "Symbolic Functions of Violence and Terror." In: Y. Alexander and R. G. Picard, eds. ***In the Camera's Eye: News Coverage of Terrorist Events.*** New York: Brassey's, 1990. pp. 3-9.

3423. Ghareeb, Edmund. "The Middle East in the U.S. Media." ***The Middle East Annual,*** (1983), 185-210.

3424. Gilboa, Eitan. "Trends in American Attitudes Toward the PLO and the Palestinians." ***Political Communication and Persuation,*** 3:1 (1985), 45-68.

3425. _____. "Effects of Televised Presidential Addresses on Public Opinion: President Reagan and Terrorism in the Middle East." ***Presidential Studies Quarterly,*** 20:1 (Winter 1990), 43-54.

3426. Graham, Katharine. "The Media Must Report Terrorism." In: B. Szumski, ed. ***Terrorism: Opposing Viewpoints.*** St.Paul, MN.: Greenhaven Press, 1986. pp. 75-81.

3427. Greer, Herb. "Terrorism and the Media." ***Encounter,*** (August 1982), 67-74.

3428. Groebel, J. "Terrorism, Public-Opinion and the Media." ***Aggressive Behavior,*** 16:2 (1990), 124.

3429. Grossman, Lawrence K. "Television and Terrorism, A Common Sense Approach." ***TVI Report,*** 6:4 (1986), 1-5.

3430. "Guidelines of United Press International." In: A. H. Miller, ed. ***Terrorism: The Media and The Law.*** Dobbs Ferry, NY.: Transnational Publishers, 1982. pp.160.

3431. Hadar, Leon T. "Behind the New York Times Middle East Coverage." ***Middle East Review,*** 12:4-13:1 (1980), 56-62.

3432. Hale, Bob. "T.V. Hostage Coverage Cooled Hot Heads." ***Christian Century,*** 102 (August 28 - September 4, 1985), 773.

3433. Heid, Robin. "Should Government Control Media Reporting of Terrorism?." ***TVI Report,*** 6:4 (1986), 6-9.

3434. Hermon, John. "The Police, the Media and the Reporting of Terrorism." In: Y. Alexander and R. Latter, eds. ***Terrorism and the Media.*** New York: Brassey's, 1990. pp. 37-42.

3435. Herstgaard, Mark. "TV, Terrorism, and the White House." ***American Film,*** (December 1985), 38-39.

3436. Heumann, Joe. "U.S. Network Television: Melodrama and the Iranian Crisis." ***Middle East Review,*** 12:4-13:1 (1980), 51-56.

3437. Hickey, Neil. "The Battle for Northern Ireland: How TV Tips the Balance." ***TV Guide,*** 29 (September 26, 1981), 8-27.

3438. Hill, J. "Representing Violence: The British Cinema and Ireland." In: Y. Alexander and A. O'Day, eds. ***Ireland's Terrorist Dilemma.*** Dordrecht: Martinus Nijhoff, 1986. pp. 123-144.

3439. Hoge, James W. "Media and Terrorism." In: M. C.Bassiouni, ed. ***Terrorism, Law Enforcement and the Mass Media.*** Rockville, MD.: National Criminal Justice Reference Service, 1983. pp. 108-135.

3440. _____. "The Media and Terrorism." In: A. H. Miller, ed. ***Terrorism, The Media and the Law.*** Dobbs Ferry, NY.: Transnational Publishers, 1982. pp. 89-105.

3441. "Hostage Coverage Hindsight: Competition, Technology Shape the Story." ***Broadcasting,*** 109 (July 8, 1985), 33-34.

3442. "Is the Media Really Covering Terrorism." ***TVI Journal,*** 4:10-12 (1983), 2-4.

3443. Jaehnig, Walter B. "Police and Press in Great Britain - The Problem of Terrorism." In: M. C. Bassiouni, ed. ***Terrorism, Law Enforcement and the Mass Media.*** Rockville, MD.: National Criminal Justice Reference Service, 1983. pp. 250-272.

3444. Jamieson, Alison. "The Role of the Media." In: ***Legal Responses to the Terrorist Threat." In:*** London: Institute for the Study of Conflict, 1988. pp. 83-92.

3445. Jowell, Jeffrey. "Broadcasting and Terrorism, Human Rights and Proportionality." ***Public Law,*** (Summer 1990), 149-156.

3446. Joyce, Edward M. "Reporting Hostage Crises: Who's in Change of Television?." ***SAIS Review,*** 6 (Winter/Spring 1986), 169-176.

3447. Kalb, Marvin, et al. "The Networks and Foreign News Coverage." ***Washington Quarterly,*** 5:2 (1982), 39-52.

3448. Kehler, C. P., G. Harvey and R. Hall. "Perspectives on Media Control in Terrorist Related Incidents." ***Canadian Police College Journal,*** 6:4 (1982), 226-243.

3449. Kelly, Michael J., and Thomas H. Mitchell. "Transnational Terrorism and the Western Elite Press." ***Political Communication and Persuation,*** 1:3 (1981), 269-296.

3450. _____. _____. "Terrorism and the Western Press." ***Terrorism Report,*** 1:3 (1980), 1-2.

3451. Kirkaldy, John. "Northern Ireland and Fleet Street: Misreporting a Continuing Tragedy." In: Y. Alexander and A. O'Day, eds. ***Terrorism in Ireland.*** London: Croom Helm, 1983. pp. 171-200.

3452. _____. "English Cartoonists; Ulster Realities." In: Y. Alexander and A. O'Day, eds. ***Ireland's Terrorist Dilemma.*** Dordrecht: Martinus Nijhoff, 1986. pp. 109-122.

3453. Knight, G., and T. Dean. "Myth and the Structure of News." ***Journal of Communication,*** 32 (Spring 1982), 144-161.

3454. Krauthammer, Charles. "Partners in Crime." In: B. Netanyahu, ed. ***Terrorism: How the West Can Win.*** New York: Farrar, Straus, Giroux, 1986. pp. 111-113.

3455. Kupperman, Robert H., and Jeff Kamen. "When Terrorists Strike: The Lessons TV Must Learn." ***TV Guide,*** 37 (September 23-29, 1989), 18-22.

3456. Kurz, Philip. "Terrorism and TV." ***Television Broadcast,*** (July 1986), 44-48.

3457. Larson, James F. "Television and U.S. Foreign Policy: The Case of the Iran Hostage Crisis." ***Journal of Communication,*** 36:4 (1986), 108-130.

3458. Ledeen, Michael A. "The Bulgarian Connection and the Media." ***Commentary,*** 75:6 (June 1983), 45-50.

3459. Lee, A. McClung. "Mass Media Mythmaking in the United Kingdom's Interethnic Struggle." ***Ethnicity,*** 8 (1981), 18-30.

3460. Levy, Rudolph. "Terrorism and the Mass Media." ***Military Intelligence,*** 11:4 (1985), 34-39.

3461. Livingstone, W. D. "Terrorism and the Media Revolution." In: N. C. Livingstone and T. E. Arnold, eds. ***Fighting Back: Winning the War Against Terrorism.*** Lexington, MA.: Lexington Books, 1985. pp.213-228.

3462. _____. "New Media Strategies for Addressing Terrorism." In: N. C. Livingstone and T. E. Arnold, eds. ***Beyond the Iran-Contra Crisis.*** Lexington, MA.: D.C. Heath & Lexington Books, 1988. pp. 119-140.

3463. Lowenthal, Gerhard. "The Case of West Germany." In: B. Netanyahu, ed. ***International Terrorism: Challenge and Response.*** New Brunswick, NJ.: Transaction Books, 1981. pp. 223-229.

3464. Lower, E. W. "Violence in Northern Ireland: Is Media Coverage Tinged by Partisanship and Sensationalism?" ***Television and Radio Age,*** 30 (September 20, 1982), 44-48+.

3465. Lule, Jack. "The Myth of My Widow: A Dramatic Analysis of News Portrayal of a Terrorist Victim." ***Political Communication and Persuasion,*** 5:2 (1988), 101-120.

3466. _____. "Sacrifice and the Body on the Tarmac: Symbolic Significance of U.S. News About a Terrorist Victim." In: Y. Alexander and R. G. Picard, eds. ***In the Camera's Eye: News Coverage of Terrorist Events.*** New York: Brassey's, 1990. pp. 30-48.

3467. Martin, L. John. "The Media's Role in International Terrorism." ***Terrorism,*** 8:2 (1985), 127-146.

3468. _____. "The Media's Role in Terrorism." In: C. W. Kegley, ed. ***International Terrorism: Characteristics, Causes, Controls.*** New York: St. Martin's Press, 1990. pp. 158-162.

3469. _____, and Joseph Draznin. "Broadcast Gatekeepers and Terrorism." In: Y. Alexander and R. G. Picard, eds. ***In the Camera's Eye: News Coverage of Terrorist Events.*** New York: Brassey's, 1990. pp. 121-130.

3470. Maurer, Marvin. "The TWA Hijack - Television Embraces Terrorists." ***Midstream,*** 31:9 (1985), 10-12.

3471. Mazur, Allan. "Bomb Threats and the Mass Media: Evidence for a Theory of Suggestion." ***American Sociological Review,*** 47:3 (1982), 407-410.

3472. "Media Accused of Creating Terrorists." ***Editor and Publisher,*** (May 14, 1983), 116-132.

3473. "The Media: Hindrance of Help to Hostages?" ***Broadcasting,*** 109 (July 1, 1985), 27-28.

3474. Miller, Abraham H. "Terrorism, the Media and Law Enforcement: An Introduction." In: A. H. Miller, ed. ***Terrorism: The Media and the Law.*** Dobbs Ferry, NY.: Transnational Publishers, 1982. pp. 1-12.

3475. _____. "Terrorism, the Media , and the Law: A Discussion." In: A. H. Miller, ed. ***Terrorism: The Media and the Law.*** Dobbs Ferry, NY.: Transnational Publishers, 1982. pp. 13-50.

3476. Mitchell, Thomas H., and Michael J. Kelly. "Transnational Terrorism and the Western Elite Press." ***Political Communication and Persuation,*** 1 (1981), 269-296.

3477. Moffitt, Karin Anderson. "Regulating the Media's Coverage of Terrorist Activities." ***Computer-Law Journal,*** 8:3 (Summer 1988), 227-256.

3478. Montgomery, Louise F. "Media Victims: Reactions to Coverage of Incidents of International Terrorism Involving Americans." In: Y. Alexander and R. G. Picard, eds. ***In the Camera's Eye: News Coverage of Terrorist Events.*** New York: Brassey's, 1990. pp. 58-64.

3479. Morrison, Alastair. "Today's Terrorism: Fighting with Ideas." ***Journal of Defense and Diplomacy,*** 5:3 (March 1987), 7-9.

3480. Murphy, Jack. "Terrorism and the Media." In: R. H. Ward and H. E. Smith, eds. ***International Terrorism: The Domestic Response.*** Chicago, IL.: University of Illinois at Chicago, Office of International Criminal Justice, 1987. pp. 73-76.

3481. Murphy, Patrick V. "Police, The News Media and Coverage of Terrorism." In: M. C. Bassiouni, ed. ***Terrorism, Law Enforcement and the Mass Media.*** Rockville, MD.: National Criminal Justice Reference Service, 1983. pp. 136-158.

3482. _____. "The Police, The News Media and the Coverage of Terrorism." In: A. H. Miller, ed. ***Terrorism: The Media and the Law.*** Dobbs Ferry, NY.: Transnational Publishers, 1982. pp. 76-88.

3483. Nacos, Brigitte, David P. Fan and John T. Young. "Terrorism and the Print Media: The 1985 TWA Hostage Crisis." ***Terrorism,*** 12:2 (1989), 107-119.

3484. National News Council. "Paper on Terrorism." In: A. H. Miller, ed. ***Terrorism: The Media and the Law.*** Dobbs Ferry, NY.: Transnational Publishers, 1982. pp. 133-147.

3485. Nossek, Hillel. "The Impact of Mass Media on Terrorism, Supporters, and the Public at Large." In.: A. Merari, ed. ***On Terrorism and Combating Terrorism.*** Frederick, MD.: University Publications of America, 1985. pp. 87-94.

3486. O'Rourke, James S. "Terrorism and the Mass Media." ***Military Media Review,*** (July 1987), 73-76.

3487. _____. "Terrorism and the Mass Media." ***Military Media Review,*** (October 1987), 20-25.

3488. O'Sullivan, John. "Media Publicity Causes Terrorism." In: B. Szumski, ed. ***Terrorism: Opposing Viewpoints.*** St.Paul, MN.: Greenhaven press, 1986. pp. 75-81.

3489. _____. "Deny Them Publicity." In: B. Netanyahu, ed. ***Terrorism: How the West Can Win.*** New York: Farrar, Straus, Giroux, 1986. pp. 120-125.

3490. Obrien, P. "The Media and the Western Conception of Terrorism." In: H. Kochler, ed ***Terrorism and National Liberation.*** Frankfurt: Verlag Peter Lang, 1988. pp. 187-198.

3491. Paletz, David L., John Z. Ayanian and Peter A. Fozzard. "Terrorism on TV News: The IRA, the FALN and the RED Brigades." In: W. C. Adams, ed. ***Televisin Coverage of International Affairs.*** Norwood, NJ.: Aben, 1981. pp. 143-165.

3492. Palmerston, Patricia R. "The Rhetoric of Terrorism and Media Response to the Crisis in Iran." ***Western Journal of Speech Communication***, 52:2 (1988), 105-121.

3493. Parenti, Michael. "Soviet Terrorists, Bulgarian Pope Killers, and Other Big Lies." In: M. Parenti. ***Inventing Reality***, New York: St. Martin's Press, 1986. pp. 148-172.

3494. Pearlstein, Richard M. "Tuned-in Narcissus: The Gleam in the Camera's Eye." In: Y. Alexander and R. G. Picard, eds. ***In the Camera's Eye: News Coverage of Terrorist Events.*** New York: Brassey's, 1990. pp. 49-57.

3495. Perdue, William D. "The Selling of International Terrorism - The Reagan Administration, Israel and The American Media." In: H. Kochler, ed ***Terrorism and National Liberation.*** Frankfurt: Verlag Peter Lang, 1988. pp. 217-236.

3496. Picard, Richard. "News Coverage as the Contagion of Terrorism: Dangerous Charges Backed by Dubious Science." In: Y. Alexander and R. Latter, eds. ***Terrorism and the Media.*** New York: Brassey's, 1990. pp. 100-110.

3497. Picard, Robert G. "News Coverage as the Contagion of Terrorism: Dangerous Charges Backed by Dubious Science." ***Political Communication and Persuasion***, 3:4 (1986), 385-400.

3498. _____, and P. D. Adams. "Characterizations of Acts and Perpetrators of Political Violence in Three Elite U.S. Daily Newpapers." ***Political Communication and Persuasion***, 4:1 (1987), 1-10.

3499. _____. "Inciting Terrorism: Are the Media Guilty as Charged?." ***Security Management***, 32:1 (January 1988), 123-126, 128-129, 131.

3500. _____. "Conundrum of News Coverage of Terrorism." ***University of Toledo Law Review***, 18:1 (Fall 1986), 141-150.

3501. _____. "News Coverage as the Contagion of Terrorism: Dangerous Charges Backed by Dubious Science." ***TVI Report***, 7:3 (1987), 39-45.

3502. _____. "Press Relations of Terrorist Organizations." ***Public Relations Review***, 15:4 (1989), 12-23.

3503. _____. "Terrorism and Media Values: News Selection and the Distortion of Reality." In: Y. Alexander and A. H. Foxman, eds. ***The 1988-1989 Annual of Terrorism.*** Dordrecht: Martinus Nijhoff, 1990. pp. 219-226.

3504. _____. "Press Relations of Terrorist Organizations." ***TVI Report***, 9:4 (1990), 1-6.

3505. _____. "Journalists as Targets and Victims of Terrorism." In: Y. Alexander and R. G. Picard, eds. ***In the Camera's Eye: News Coverage of Terrorist Events.*** New York: Brassey's, 1990. pp. 65-74.

3506. Podhoretz, Norman. "The Subtle Collusion." In: B. Netanyahu, ed. ***International Terrorism: Challenge and Response.*** New Brunswick, NJ.: Transaction Books, 1981. pp. 235-241.

3507. Pohlmann, Marcus D., and Thomas P. Foley. "Terrorism in the 70s: Media's Connection." ***National Forum***, (Summer 1981), 33-35.

3508. Poland, James M., and Thomas R. Phelps. "Terrorism Increase Unlikely in U.S.." ***TVI Journal***, 2:2 (1981), 4-9.

3509. Prittie, Terence. "The British Media and the Arab-Israeli Dispute." ***Middle East Review***, 12:4-13:1 (1980), 67-71.

3510. Protheroe, Alan H. "Terrorism, Journalism and Democracy." In: Y. Alexander and R. Latter, eds. ***Terrorism and the Media.*** New York: Brassey's, 1990. pp. 64-70.

3511. Quester, George H. "Cruise-Ship Terrorism and the Media." ***Political Communication and Persuation,*** 3:4 (1986), 355-370.

3512. Rabe, Robert L. "The Journalist and the Hostage: How Their Rights Can Be Balanced." In: A. H. Miller, ed. ***Terrorism: the Media and the Law.*** Dobbs Ferry, NY.: Transnational Publishers, 1982. pp. 69-75.

3513. Rosen, Barry. "The Media Dilemma and Terrorism." In: Y. Alexander and R. Latter, eds. ***Terrorism and the Media.*** New York: Brassey's, 1990. pp. 57-60.

3514. Rosenberg, M. J. "Hijacking the Tube." ***Near East Report,*** 29:36 (1985).

3515. Salwen, Michael B., and Jung-Sook Lee. "News of Terrorism: A Comparison of the U.S. and South Korean Press." ***Terrorism,*** 11:4 (1988), 323-328.

3516. Scanlon, Joseph. "Coping with the Media: Police - Media Problems and Tactics in Hostage Takings and Terrorist Incidents." ***Canadian Police College Journal,*** 5:3 (1981), 129-148.

3517. _____. "Domestic Terrorism and the Media: Live Coverage of Crime." ***Canadian Police College Journal,*** 8:2 (1982), 154-178.

3518. _____. "Hijacking the Media." In: B. Macdonald, ed. ***Terror.*** Toronto: Canadian Institute of International Studies, 1987. pp. 98-107.

3519. Schlesinger, Philip. "Princes Gate, 1980: The Media Politics of Siege Management." ***Screen Education,*** 37 (1980), 29-54.

3520. _____. ""Terrorism," the Media, and the Liberal-Democratic State: A Critique of the Orthodoxy." ***Social Research,*** 48:1 (1981), 74-99.

3521. Schmid, Alex P. "Terrorism and the Media: The Ethics of Publicity." ***Terrorism and Political Violence,*** 1:4 (October 1989), 539-565.

3522. Schorr, Daniel. "The Encouragement of Violence." In: B. Netanyahu, ed. ***Terrorism: How the West Can Win.*** New York: Farrar, Straus, Giroux, 1986. pp. 114-116.

3523. Scotti, Tony. "The Media Doesn't Really Cover Terror-Violence." ***TVI Journal,*** 4:10-12 (1983), 2-3.

3524. Shipler, David K. "Future Domestic and International Terrorism: Media Perspective." ***Terrorism,*** 11:6 (1988), 543-545.

3525. Slack, Kenneth. ""Terrorvision" Censorship?." ***Christian Century,*** 102 (August 14-21, 1985), 724-725.

3526. Sobowale, Idowu A. "The Impact of the Mass Media on International Violence." In: T. Adeniran and Y. Alexander, eds. ***International Violence.*** New York: Praeger, 1983. pp. 221-230.

3527. Sommer, Michael, and Heidi Sommer. "The Project on Media Coverage of Terrorism: A Summary of National Surveys and Other Investigations, 1977-1979." In: A. H. Miller, ed. ***Terrorism: The Media and the Law.*** Dobbs Ferry, NY.: Transnational Publishers, 1982. pp. 161-190.

3528. _____. _____. "Project on Media Coverage of Terrorism - A Summary of National Surveys and other Investigations, 1977-1979." In: M. C. Bassiouni, ed. ***Terrorism, Law Enforcement and the Mass Media.*** Rockville, MD.: National Criminal Justice Reference System, 1983. pp. 220-249.

3529. Soustelle, Jacques. "Liberty or Licence?" In: B. Netanyahu, ed. ***International Terrorism: Challenge and Response.*** New Brunswick, NJ.: Transaction Books, 1981. pp. 250-252.

3530. Stein, M. L. "Covering Terrorism." ***Editor and Publisher,*** 119 (April 26, 1986), 18-19.

3531. _____. "Covering Terrorism Abroad: Peruvian Journalist Asks 'Foreign Press' to Scale down Reporting of Terrorist Acts." ***Editor and Publisher***, 119 (October 4, 1986), 28-29.

3532. Stock, Raymond. "Prestige at War: The New York Times and Le Monde in Lebanon, August1 - September 26, 1982." ***Middle East Journal***, 39:3 (1985), 317-340.

3533. Taylor, P. L. "The Installation Commander Versus on Aggressive News Media in an On-Post Terrorist Incident: Avoiding the Constitutional Collision." ***Army Lawyer***, (August 1986), 19-29.

3534. Terrell, Robert, and Kristina Ross. "The Voluntary Guidelines' Threat to U.S. Press Freedom." In: Y. Alexander and R. G. Picard, eds. ***In the Camera's Eye: News Coverage of Terrorist Events***. New York: Brassey's, 1990. pp. 75-102.

3535. "Terror in the News: Dramatic Functions of Press Coverage (Symposium)." ***Journal of Communication***, 32 (Spring 1982), 128-185.

3536. "Terrorism and the Media - An Issue of Responsible Journalism." In: M. C. Bassiouni, ed. ***Terrorism, Law Enforcement and the Mass Media***. Rockville, MD.: National Criminal Justice Reference Service, 1983. pp. 211-219.

3537. "Terrorism and the Media." In: B. Netanyahu, ed. ***Terrorism: How the West Can Win***. New York: Farrar, Straus, Giroux, 1986. pp. 229-240.

3538. "Terrorism and the Media: A Discussion." ***Harper's***, (October 1984), 47-58.

3539. Theberge, Leonard, and Yonah Alexander. "Terrorism and the Media in the 1980s." ***Political Communication and Persuation***, 2:3 (1984), 283-332.

3540. Thompson, Brian. "Broadcasting and Terrorism." ***Public Law***, (Winter 1989), 527-541.

3541. Timmerman, Kenneth R. "How the PLO Terrorized Journalists in Beirut." ***Commentary***, 75:1 (1983), 48-50.

3542. Tugwell, Maurice A. "Terrorism and Propaganda: Problem and Response." In: P. Wilkinson and A. M. Stewart, eds. ***Contemporary Research on Terrorism***. Aberdeen: Aberdeen University Press, 1987. pp. 409-418.

3543. _____. "Terrorism and Propaganda: Problems and Response." ***Conflict Quarterly***, 6 (Spring 1986), 5-15.

3544. Utley, Garrick. "When the Camera Trains Its Lens on the Terrorist." ***SPJ/SDX Journalism Ethics Report***, (1985-1986), 3-4.

3545. Van der Vat, Dan. "Terrorism and the Media." ***Index on Censorship***, 11 (April 1982), 25-27.

3546. Vanocur, Sander. "The Role of the Media." In: U. Ra'anan, et al. ***Hydra of Carnage***. Lexington, MA.: Heath-Lexington Books, 1986. pp. 259-264.

3547. Vitale, Joseph. "Reports: Production - TV and Terrorism." ***Channels of Communications***, 6:4 (1986), 12-13.

3548. Wall, James M. "Culture Clashes Need Cautious Interpretation." ***Christian Century***, 103:13 (April 16, 1986), 379-380.

3549. _____. "Terrorism Tempts T.V. to Waive Noble Right." ***Christian Century***, 102 (July 3-10, 1985), 635-636.

3550. Ward, Ken. "Ulster Terrorism: The U.S. Network News Coverage of Northern Ireland, 1968-1979." In: Y. Alexander and A. O'Day, eds. ***Terrorism in Ireland***. London: Croom Helm, 1983. pp. 201-212.

3551. Wattenberg, Ben. "A Politics of Freedom is the Answer." In: B. Netanyahu, ed. ***International Terrorism: Challenge and Response***. New Brunswick, NJ.: Transaction Books, 1981. pp. 245-249.

3552. Weimann, Gabriel. "Terrorists or Freedom Fighters? Labelling Terrorism in the Israeli Press." ***Political Communication and Persuation***, 2:4 (1985), 433-446.

3553. _____. "Theater of Terror: Effects of Press Coverage." ***Journal of Communication***, 33 (Winter 1983), 38-45.

3554. _____. "Conceptualizing the Effects of Mass-Mediated Terrorism." ***Political Communication and Persuasion***, 4:3 (1987), 213-216.

3555. _____. "Media Events: The Case of International Terrorism." ***Journal of Broadcasting and Electronic Media***, 31:1 (1987), 21-39.

3556. Weisbecker, Jane C. "Protecting Nuclear Materials in the Terrorist Age: The International Challenge." ***Brooklyn Journal of International Law***, 12:2 (1986), 305-338.

3557. Wilber, H. B. "The Role of the Media During a Terrorist Incident." ***FBI Law Enforcement Bulletin***, 54;4 (1985), 20-23.

3558. Wilkinson, Paul. "Terrorism, the Mass Media and Democracy." ***Contemporary Review***, 239:1386 (1981), 35-44.

3559. _____. "Terrorism and Propaganda." In: Y. Alexander and R. Latter, eds. ***Terrorism and the Media.*** New York: Brassey's, 1990. pp. 26-34.

3560. Wurth-Hough, S. "Network News Coverage of Terrorism: The Early Years." ***Terrorism***, 6:3 (1983), 403-421.

3561. Yeager, Carl H. "Vulnerabilities of the U.S. Network Systems to Sabotage or Terrorist Attack." ***TVI Report***, 9:3 (1990), 26-33.

3. Documents and Reports

3562. Barnathan, Jack. ***Aspects of Terrorism, the Police and the Media, a Study of Communication Patterns.*** New York: City University of New York, 1987.

3563. Bassiouni, M. Cherif. ***Terrorism, Law Enforcement and the Mass Media.*** Rockville, MD.: National Criminal Justice Reference Service, 1983. 361p.

3564. Clements, E. ***News Magazine and Network Television News Coverage of the Munich Olympic Crisis, 1972.*** Master's Thesis. Columbia, MO.: Missouri University, 1989. 132p.

3565. Cornelius, Debra A. ***The Packaging of Protest: Press Distortion and Image Dynamics in Radical and Mainstream Irish-American Sociopolitical Groups.*** Ph.D. Dissertation. Washington, D.C.: The George Washington University, 1990. 310p.

3566. Friedlander, Robert A. ***Terrorism and the Media: A Contemporary Assessment.*** Gaithersburg, MD.: International Association of Chiefs of Police, 1981. 22p.

3567. Gerbner, George. ***Violence and Terror in the Mass Media.*** Reports and Papers on Mass Communication. No. 102. Paris: UNESCO, 1988. pp. 7-26.

3568. Ghandour, Nabiha H. ***Coverage of the Arab World and Israel in American News Magazines Between 1975 and 1981: A Comparative Analysis.*** Ed.D. Dissertation. New York: Columbia University Teachers College, 1984. 257p.

3569. Hodgkins, S. E. ***Reporting of Terrorism by the Media.*** Master's Thesis. Wright--Patterson AFB, OH.: Air Force Institute of Technology, 1987. 89p.

3570. Jenkins, Brian M. ***The Psychological Implications of Media-Covered Terrorism.*** RAND-P6627. Santa Monica, CA.: RAND Corporation, 1981. 9p.

3571. Kelly, Michael J. ***The Media and Terrorism: An Examination of News Coverage of Armenian Terrorism in Canada.*** Ph.D. Dissertation. Ottawa: Carleton University, 1987.

3572. Kessler, James. ***The Media and Terrorism.*** Carlisle Barracks, PA.: U.S. Army War College, 1987. 27p.

3573. Latter, Richard. ***Terrorism and the Media: Ethical and Practical Dilemmas for Government, Journalists and Public.*** Wilton Park Papers, 1. London: H.M.S.O., 1990. 29p.

3574. Leon, Philip W. ***The Military, the Media, and International Terrorism.*** Carlisle Barracks, PA.: U.S. Army War College, 1986. 67p.

3575. Livingston, Steven. ***Terrorism, The News Media, and the State: Rethinking the Terrorism Spectacle.*** Ph.D. Dissertation. Seattle, WA.: University of Washington, 1990. 412p.

3576. Marino, Franco. ***Terrorism and the Media: An Investigation of Constructed Meaning.*** Master's Thesis. Burnaby, B.C.: Simon Fraser University, 1984.

3577. Media Institute. ***Terrorism and the Media in the 1980's.*** Washington, D.C.: Media Institute, 1984. 81p.

3578. Midgley, Sarah, and Virginia Rice, eds. ***Terrorism and the Media in the 1980's: The Proceedings of a Conference held on April 14, 1983.*** Washington, D.C.: Transnational Communications Center, 1984. 67p.

3579. Milburn, Michael, Brian Cistuli and Marjorie Garr. "Survey and Experimental Studies of the Effects of Television News on Individuals' Attribution About Terrorism." Paper Presented at the ***Annual Scientific Meeting of the International Society of Political Psychology,*** held on July 1-5, 1988 in New York.

3580. Ozyegin, Nejat. ***Construction of the "Facts" of Political Violence: A Content Analysis of Press Coverage.*** Master's Thesis. Philadelphia, PA.: University of Pennsylvania, Annenberg School of Communication, 1986.

3581. Palmerston, Patricia R. ***Terrorism and the Media: A Rhetorical Critical Analysis of the "Crisis in Iran".*** Ph.D. Dissertation. Minneapolis, MN.: University of Minnesota, 1984. 318p.

3582. Petentler, Charles W. ***The Impact of American Media's Coverage on Acts of Terrorism.*** Master's Thesis. Central Missouri State University, 1987. 99p.

3583. Picard, Robert G. "The Journalist's Role in Coverage of Terrorist Events." Paper presented at the ***Annual Conference of the Speech Communication Association,*** held in 1989 in San Francisco, CA. 17p.

3584. Steuter, Eric C. ***Ideology and the News: The Treatment of Terrorism in TIME Magazine.*** Master's Thesis. Halifax, N.S.: Dalhousie University, 1987.

3585. Tan, Che-Wei Zoe. ***Mass Media and Insurgent Terrorism: The Case of Belfast, 1916-1986.*** Ph.D. Dissertation. Ann Arbor, MI.: University of Michigan, 1987. 224p.

3586. United States. Congress. House. Committee on Foreign Affairs. Subcommittee on Europe and the Middle East. ***The Media, Diplomacy, and Terrorism in the Middle East: Hearing.*** 99th Cong., 1st sess. Washington, D.C.: U.S. Government Printing Office, 1986. 152p.

3587. _____. Department of State. "Guidelines for United States Government Spokespersons During Terrorist Incident." In: A. H. H. Miller, ed. ***Terrorism: The Media and the Law.*** Dobbs Ferry, NY.: Transnational Publishers, 1982. pp. 148-152.

3588. Wright, Joanne. ***Terrorist Propaganda: The Red Army Faction and the Provisional IRA, 1968-1986.*** Ph.D. Dissertation. Canberra: Australian National University, 1988.

IX

UNCONVENTIONAL TERRORISM THREAT

This chapter covers the literature dealing with the threat of unconventional weapons in the hands of terrorists. This literature is speculative in nature. It deals with the potential use of unconventional weapons. Among the topics we find nuclear blackmail, the vulnerability of nuclear facilities, weapons and materials. A large part of the literature covers various security methods designed to protects nuclear installations from potentially hostile elements. There appears to be consensus that while there is potential for nuclear terrorism, the utility of such terrorism is deemed to be relatively poor and therefore there is little probability of nuclear blackmail by independent terrorist groups. This may account for the decline of published materials on this subject in the 1980s. This chapter also lists materials on biological and chemical weapons as potential future terrorist weapons.

1. Books

3589. Beres, Louis Rene. ***Apocalypse: Nuclear Catastrophe in World Politics.*** Chicago, IL.: University of Chicago Press, 1980.

3590. _____. ***Terrorism and Global Security: The Nuclear Threat.*** 2nd rev. ed. Boulder, CO.: Westview Press, 1987. 156p.

3591. Cadwell, J. J. ***Nuclear Facility Threat Analysis and Tactical Response Procedures.*** Springfield, IL.: C. C. Thomas, 1983. 110p.

3592. Clark, Richard C. ***Technological Terrorism.*** Old Greenwich, CT.: Devin - Adair, 1980. 220p.

3593. Douglas, Joseph D. Jr., and Neil C. Livingstone. ***America the Vulnerable: The Threat of Chemical and Biological Warfare.*** Lexington, MA.: Lexington Books, 1987. 204p.

3594. Leventhal, Paul L., and Yonah Alexander, eds. ***Preventing Nuclear Terrorism: The Report and Papers of the International Task Force on Prevention of Nuclear Terrorism.*** Lexington, MA.: Lexington Books, 1987. 472p.

3595. _____. _____, eds. ***Nuclear Terrorism: Defining the Threat.*** Elmsford, NY.: Pergamon-Brassey's, 1986. 212p.

2. Journal Articles

3596. Albright, David. "Civilian Inventories of Plutonium and Highly Enriched Uranium." In: P. Leventhal and Y. Alexander, eds. ***Preventing Nuclear Terrorism.*** Lexington, MA.: Lexington Books, 1987. pp. 265-291.

3597. Alexander, Yonah. "Super Terrorism." In: Y. Alexander and J. M. Gleason, eds. ***Terrorism: Behavioral Perspectives.*** New York: Pergamon Press, 1980. pp. 343-362.

3598. _____. "Terrorism and High-Technology Weapons." In: Y. Alexander and L. Z. Freedman, eds. ***Perspectives on Terrorism.*** Wilmington, DE.: Scholarly Resources, 1983. pp. 225-240.

3599. _____. "Terrorism and the Nuclear Energy Industry: A Prelude to the Future?." ***Terrorism Report,*** 11 (1980), 3-5.

3600. American Bar Association. Committee on Law and National Security. "Terrorism Versus Society: The Technological War." ***Law and National Security Intelligence Report,*** 9:2 (1987), 1,4-5.

3601. Argyle, H. J. "Nuclear Security in a Sagebrush Environment." ***FBI Law Enforcement Bulletin,*** 51:9 (1982), 1-6.

3602. Badolato, Edward V. "Terrorism and Energy." In: Y. Alexander and A. H. Foxman, eds. ***The 1988-1989 Annual of Terrorism.*** Dordrecht: Martinus Nijhoff, 1990. pp. 145-170.

3603. Barth, Fritz J. "Stemming Nuclear Terrorism." ***United States Naval Institute Proceedings,*** 115:12 (December 1989), 54-59.

3604. Barton, John H. "The Civil Liberties Implications of a Nuclear Emergency." ***New York University Review of Law and Social Change,*** 10 (Winter 1981), 299-318.

3605. Bass, Gail V., et al. "Technical Note: Motivations and Possible Actions of Potential Criminal Adversaries of U.S. Nuclear Programs." ***Nuclear Safety***, 22:1 (January-February 1981), 21-25.

3606. Beckman, Robert L. "International Terrorism: The Nuclear Dimension - Conference Report." ***Terrorism***, 8:4 (1986), 351-378.

3607. _____. "Rapporteur's Summary." In: P. Leventhal and Y. Alexander, eds. ***Nuclear Terrorism: Defining the Threat.*** Elmsford, NY.: Pergamon-Brassey's, 1986. pp. 5-24.

3608. Bell, J. Bowyer. "A Future Free of Surprise." ***Society***, 17:5 (1980), 17-18.

3609. Berard, Stanley P. "Nuclear Terrorism: More Myth than Reality." ***Air University Review***, 36 (July/August 1985), 30-36.

3610. Beres, Louis Rene. "Subways to Armageddon." ***Society***, 20:6 (1983), 7-10.

3611. _____. "Preventing Nuclear Terrorism: Responses to Terrorist Grievances." In: P. Leventhal and Y. Alexander, eds. ***Preventing Nuclear Terrorism.*** Lexington, MA.: Lexington Books, 1987. pp. 146-159.

3612. _____. "Confronting Nuclear Terrorism." In: S. J. Cimbala, ed. ***Intelligence and Intelligence Policy in Democratic Society.*** Ardsley on Hudson: Transnational Publishers, 1987. pp. 177-196.

3613. _____. "Responding to the Threat of Nuclear Terrorism." In: C. W. Kegley, ed. ***International Terrorism: Characteristics, Causes, Controls.*** New York: St. Martin's Press, 1990. pp. 228-240.

3614. _____. "Confronting Nuclear Terrorism." ***Hastings International and Comparative Law Review***, 14 (Fall 1990), 129-154.

3615. Bradley, William A., et al. "Keeping Reactors Safe from Sabotage." ***Los Alamos Science***, (Summer-Fall 1981), 120-131.

3616. Buck, K. A. "Superterrorism - Biological, Chemical and Nuclear." ***Terrorism***, 12:6 (1989), 433-434.

3617. Bunn, George. "International Arrangements Against Nuclear Terrorism." In: P. Leventhal and Y. Alexander, eds. ***Preventing Nuclear Terrorism.*** Lexington, MA.: Lexington Books, 1987. pp. 339-359.

3618. Carlson, J. A. "It Can Happen in Centerville, U.S.A.: Nuclear Extortion." ***FBI Law Enforcement Bulletin***, 54 (September 1985), 1-4.

3619. Cobbe, James. "Supply Security of Coal and Uranium." In: Y. Alexander and C. K. Ebinger, eds. ***Political Terrorism and Energy.*** New York: Praeger, 1982. pp. 65-84.

3620. Crane, Alan Taft. "Physical Vulnerability of Electric Systems to Natural Disaster and Sabotage." ***Terrorism***, 13:3 (1990), 189-190.

3621. Cranston, Alan. "The Nuclear Terrorist State." In: B. Netanyahu, ed. ***Terrorism: How the West Can Win.*** New York: Farrar, Straus, Giroux, 1986. pp. 177-181.

3622. David, B. "The Capability and Motivation of Terrorist Organizations to Use Mass - Destruction Weapons." In: A. Merari, ed. ***On Terrorism and Combating Terrorism.*** Frederick, MD.: University Publications of America, 1985. pp. 145-156.

3623. Davies, Thomas D. "What Nuclear Means and Targets Might Terrorists Find Attractive?." In: P. Leventhal and Y. Alexander, eds. ***Nuclear Terrorism: Defining the Threat.*** Elmsford, NY.: Pergamon-Brassey's, 1986. pp. 54-91.

3624. De Vito, Donald A., and Lacy Suiter. "Emergency Management and the Nuclear Terrorism Threat." In: P. Leventhal and Y. Alexander, eds. ***Preventing Nuclear Terrorism.*** Lexington, MA.: Lexington Books, 1987. pp. 416-432.

3625. _____. "Mass Destruction." ***Terrorism,*** 10:3 (1987), 275-276.

3626. Denton, Jeremiah. "International Terrorism - The Nuclear Dimension." ***Terrorism,*** 9:2 (1987), 113-124.

3627. Depsres, John. "Intelligence and the Prevention of Nuclear Terrorism." In: P. Leventhal and Y. Alexander, eds. ***Preventing Nuclear Terrorism.*** Lexington, MA.: Lexington Books, 1987. pp. 321-330.

3628. Dixon, Herbert. "Physical Security of Nuclear Facilities." In: P. Leventhal and Y. Alexander, eds. ***Preventing Nuclear Terrorism.*** Lexington, MA.: Lexington Books, 1987. pp. 191-206.

3629. Easton, John J. "Electric Systems Vulnerabilities." ***Terrorism,*** 13:3 (1990), 183-188.

3630. Ebinger, Charles K. "Terrorism and the Nuclear Energy Industry: A Prelude to the Future?." ***Terrorism Report,*** 1:1 (198), 3-5.

3631. Ezeldin, Ahmed G. "Terrorism in the 1990's: New Strategies and the Nuclear Threat." ***International Journal of Comparative and Applied Criminal Justice,*** 13:2 (Fall 1989), 7-16.

3632. Falk, Richard A. "Inquiry and Morality." ***Society,*** 17:5 (1980), 18-21.

3633. Feld, Bernard T. "Nuclear Violence at the Non-Governmental Level." In: D. Carlton and C. Schaerf, eds. ***Contemporary Terror.*** London: Macmillan, 1981. pp. 37-49.

3634. Flood, Michael. "Nuclear Sabotage." In: A. R. Norton and M. H. Greenberg, eds. ***Studies in Nuclear Terrorism.*** Boston, MA.: G. K. Hall, 1979. pp. 123-138.

3635. Friedlander, Robert A. "Ultimate Nightmare: What if Terrorists Go Nuclear?" ***Denver Journal of International Law and Policy,*** 12 (Fall 1982), 1-11.

3636. _____. "Terrorism and Nuclear Decisions." ***Society,*** 23:2 (1986), 59-62.

3637. _____. "Public Information - A Deadly Weapon in Terrorist Hands." ***TVI Journal,*** 4:10-12 (1983), 4-6.

3638. Gallup, George. "Forecast 2000." ***TVI Journal,*** 6:2 (1985), 58-59.

3639. Gates, M. E. "The Nuclear Emergency Search Team." In: P. Leventhal and Y. Alexander, eds. ***Preventing Nuclear Terrorism.*** Lexington, MA.: Lexington Books, 1987. pp. 397-402.

3640. Gephart, Richard A., and Jeremiah Denton. "The New Nightmare: Nuclear Terrorism." In: P. Leventhal and Y. Alexander, eds. ***Nuclear Terrorism: Defining the Threat.*** Elmsford, NY.: Pergamon-Brassey's, 1986. pp. 144-158p.

3641. Giuffrida, Louis O. "How Can Government and Industry Effectively Respond?." In: P. Leventhal and Y. Alexander, eds. ***Nuclear Terrorism: Defining the Threat.*** Elmsford, NY.: Pergamon-Brassey's, 1986. pp. 92-123.

3642. Goldberg, Steven. "Civil Liberties and Nuclear Terrorism." In: P. Leventhal and Y. Alexander, eds. ***Preventing Nuclear Terrorism.*** Lexington, MA.: Lexington Books, 1987. pp. 403-415.

3643. Gordon, John C. "Biological Terrorism: A Direct Threat to Our Livestock Industry." ***Military Medicine,*** 151:7 (July 1986), 357-363.

3644. Greenberg, Eldon V. C., and Milton M. Hoenig. "The Front End of the Nuclear Fuel Cycle: Options to Reduce the Risks of Terrorism and Proliferation." In: P. Leventhal and Y. Alexander, eds. ***Preventing Nuclear Terrorism.*** Lexington, MA.: Lexington Books, 1987. pp. 298-318.

3645. Heim, M. "Reason as Response to Nuclear Terror." ***Philosophy Today,*** 28:4 (1984), 300-307.

3646. Higgins, C. E. "Energize! Nuclear Security." ***Security Management***, 32:5 (May 1988), 71-74.

3647. Hirsch, Daniel. "The Truck Bomb and Insider Threats to Nuclear Facilities." In: P. Leventhal and Y. Alexander, eds. ***Preventing Nuclear Terrorism.*** Lexington, MA.: Lexington Books, 1987. pp. 207-222.

3648. Hoenig, Milton M., and Paul L. Leventhal. "The Hidden Danger: Risks of Nuclear Terrorism." ***Terrorism***, 10:1 (1987), 1-21.

3649. Hooper, Richard R. "The Covert Use of Chemical and Biological Warfare Against United States Strategic Forces." ***Military Medicine***, 148:12 (December 1983), 901-912.

3650. Jacchia, Enrico. "European Nuclear Safeguards and Terrorism: A Personal Perspective." In: P. Leventhal and Y. Alexander, eds. ***Preventing Nuclear Terrorism.*** Lexington, MA.: Lexington Books, 1987. pp. 259-262.

3651. Jenkins, Brian M. "International Cooperation in Locating and Recovering Stolen Nuclear Materials." ***Terrorism***, 6:4 (1983), 561-577.

3652. _____. "Nuclear Terrorism and Its Consequences." ***Society***, 17:5 (1980), 5-15.

3653. _____. "Will Terrorists Go Nuclear." ***Orbis***, 29:3 (1985), 507-516.

3654. _____. "Is Nuclear Terrorism Plausible?." In: P. Leventahl and Y. Alexander, eds. ***Nuclear Terrorism: Defining the Threat.*** Elmsford, NY.: Pergamon-Brassey's, 1986. pp. 25-53.

3655. _____. "The Threat of Product Contamination." ***TVI Report***, 8:3 (1989), 1-3.

3656. _____. "Will Terrorists Go Nuclear?." In: W. Laqueur, ed. ***The Terrorism Reader.*** New York: Meridian, 1987. pp. 350-357.

3657. Joyner, Christopher. "The Rabta Chemical Factory Fire: Rethinking the Lawfulness of Anticipatory Self-Defence." ***Terrorism***, 13:2 (1990), 79-88.

3658. _____. "Chemoterrorism: Rethinking the Reality of the Threat." In: Y. Alexander and A. H. Foxman, eds. ***The 1988-1989 Annual of Terrorism.*** Dordrecht: Martinus Nijhoff, 1990. pp. 135-144.

3659. Julian, Thomas A. "Nuclear Weapons Security and Control." In: P. Leventhal and Y. Alexander, eds. ***Preventing Nuclear Terrorism.*** Lexington, MA.: Lexington Books, 1987. pp. 169-190.

3660. Keepin, G. Robert. "Nuclear Safeguards - A Global Issue." ***Los Alamos Science***, 1:1 (Summer 1980), 68-87.

3661. Kellen, Konrad. "The Potential for Nuclear Terrorism: A Discussion." In: P. Leventhal and Y. Alexander, eds. ***Preventing Nuclear Terrorism.*** Lexington, MA.: Lexington Books, 1987. pp. 104-133.

3662. _____, et al. "Technical Note: Motivations and Possible Actions of Potential Criminal Adversaries of U.S. Nuclear Programs." ***Nuclear Safety***, 22:1 (January-February 1981), 21-25.

3663. Kende, Istvan. "Terrorism, War, Nuclear Holocaust." ***International Social Science Journal***, 38:4 (1986), 529-538.

3664. Kerr, Donald. "Don Kerr on Nuclear Safeguards." ***Los Alamos Science***, 1:1 (Summer 1980), 138-139.

3665. Kindillen, Robert E. "Nuclear Plants Confront Modern Terrorism." ***Security Management***, 29 (October 1985), 119-120.

3666. Kirkwood, Craig W., and Stephen M. Pollock. "Multiple Attribute Scenarios, Bounded Probabilities, and Threats of Nuclear Theft." ***Futures***, 14 (December 1982), 545-553.

3667. Kohl, J., and A. Sud. "Fighting Toxic Terrorism." ***Alternatives***, 16:3 (1989), 12-14.

3668. Kupperman, Robert H. "Countering High Technology Terrorism." ***Scandinavian Journal of Development Alternatives,*** 3 (September 1984), 73-94.

3669. _____. "Government Response to Mass-Destruction Threats by Terrorists." In: A. Merari, ed. ***On Terrorism and Combating Terrorism.*** Frederick, MD.: University Publications of America, 1985. pp. 157-162.

3670. Laffey, J. K. "Nuclear Terrorism." ***Journal of Security Administration,*** 5:1 (1982), 57-74.

3671. Leventhal, Paul L., and Milton M. Hoenig. "The Hidden Danger - Risks of Nuclear Terrorism." ***Terrorism,*** 10:1 (1987), 1-22.

3672. _____, and Brahma Chellaney. "Nuclear Terrorism: Threat, Perception, and Response in South Asia." ***Terrorism,*** 11:6 (1988), 447-470.

3673. _____, and Milton M. Hoenig. "Nuclear Terrorism - Reactor Sabotage and Weapons Proliferation Risks." ***Contemporary Policy Issues,*** 8:3 (1990), 106-121.

3674. Livingstone, Neil C. "Megadeath: Radioactive Terrorism." In: Y. Alexander and C. K. Ebinger, eds. ***Political Terrorism and Energy.*** New York: Praeger, 1982. pp. 141-180.

3675. _____. "Vulnerability of Chemical Plants to Terrorism: An Examination." ***Chemical and Engineering News,*** 63:42 (September 21, 1985), 7-13.

3676. Louria, Donald B. "Monstrous Microbes: The Danger of Genetic Engineering." ***The Futurist,*** 15:5 (October 1981), 17-21.

3677. Luchaire, F. "Subnational Proliferation, Technology Transfers and Terrorism." In: A. M. Garfinkle, ed. ***Global Perspectives on Arms Control.*** New York: Praeger, 1984. pp. 113-132.

3678. Macbride, Sean. "Nuclear Terrorism." In: H. Koechler, ed. ***Terrorism and National Liberation.*** Frankfurt am Main: Peter Lang, 1988. pp. 35-40.

3679. Mackenzie, Alastair. "Nuclear Threat is Real: Terrorism." ***Pacific Defense Reporter,*** 15 (March 1989), 50-52.

3680. Mark, J. Carson, et al. "Can Terrorists Build Nuclear Weapons?." In: P. Leventhal and Y. Alexander, eds. ***Preventing Nuclear Terrorism.*** Lexington, MA.: Lexington Books, 1987. pp. 55-65.

3681. Marshall, Patrick G. "Obstacles to Bio-Chemical Disarmament." ***Editorial Research Reports,*** 24 (June 29, 1990), 366-378.

3682. Mastrangelo, Eugene. "Terrorist Activities by Region." In: P. Leventhal and Y. Alexander, eds. ***Preventing Nuclear Terrorism.*** Lexington, MA.: Lexington Books, 1987. pp. 134-145.

3683. Mazur, Allan. "Bomb Threats Against American Nuclear Energy Facilities." ***Journal of Political and Military Sociology,*** 11:1 (1983), 109-121.

3684. Meany, Daniel J. "Biochemicals - A New Threat." ***Terror Update,*** 9 (July 1989), 1-2.

3685. Mitic, Miodrag. "Convention on Physical Protection of Nuclear Materials." ***Review of International Affairs,*** 31 (March 5, 1980), 24-26.

3686. Moglewer, Sidney. "International Safeguards and Nuclear Terrorism." In: P. Leventhal and Y. Alexander, eds. ***Preventing Nuclear Terrorism.*** Lexington, MA.: Lexington Books, 1987. pp. 248-258.

3687. Mullen, Robert K. "Subnational Threats to Civil Nuclear Facilities and Safeguards Institutions." In: R. H. Shultz and S. Sloan, eds. ***Responding to the Terrorist Threat.*** New York: Pergamon Press, 1980. pp. 134-173.

3688. _____. "Nuclear Violence." In: P. Leventhal and Y. Alexander, eds. ***Preventing Nuclear Terrorism.*** Lexington, MA.: Lexington Books, 1987. pp. 231-247.

3689. _____. "Low-Intensity Terrorism Against Technological Infrastructures." In: N. C. Livingstone and T. E. Arnold, eds. ***Beyond the Iran-Contra Crisis.*** Lexington, MA.: D.C. Heath and Lexington Books, 1988. pp. 141-154.

3690. Murphy, John F. "Cooperative International Arrangements: Prevention of Nuclear Terrorism and the Extradition and Prosecution of Terrorists." In: P. Leventhal and Y. Alexander, eds. ***Preventing Nuclear Terrorism.*** Lexington, MA.: Lexington Books, 1987. pp. 360-380.

3691. Ne'eman, Yuval. "Mobilizing Intelligence Against Nuclear Terrorism: A Personal Perspective." In: P. Leventhal and Y. Alexander, eds. ***Preventing Nuclear Terrorism.*** Lexington, MA.: Lexington Books, 1987. pp. 331-336.

3692. Neuman, G. G. "Terrorism and the Nuclear Bomb: An Ominous Threat of a New Social Order." In: G. G. Neuman, ed. ***Origins of Human Aggression.*** New York: Human Sciences Press, 1987. pp. 164-173.

3693. Nunn, Sam, and John Warner. "Soviet Cooperation in Countering Nuclear Terrorism: The Role of Risk Reduction Centers." In: P. Leventhal and Y. Alexander, eds. ***Preventing Nuclear Terrorism.*** Lexington, MA.: Lexington Books, 1987. pp. 381-394.

3694. O'Keefe, Bernard. "How Can Nuclear Violence Be Prevented?." In: P. Leventhal and Y. Alexander, eds. ***Nuclear Terrorism: Defining the Threat.*** Elmsford, NY.: Pergamon-Brassey's, 1986. pp. 124-143.

3695. Petrakis, Gregory. "Terrorism - New Weapons Technology and Gun Barrel Philosophy for Terrorists." ***Law and Order,*** 28:8 (1980), 20-22, 24-26, 28.

3696. Pilat, Joseph F. "Antinuclear Terrorism in the Advanced Industrial West." In: Y. Alexander and C. K. Ebinger, eds. ***Political Terrorism and Energy.*** New York: Praeger, 1982. pp. 191-208.

3697. Pollack, Gerald L. "Severe Accidents and Terrorist Threats at Nuclear Reactors." In: P. Leventhal and Y. Alexander, eds. ***Preventing Nuclear Terrorism.*** Lexington, MA.: Lexington Books, 1987. pp. 66-77.

3698. Post, Jerrold M. "Prospects for Nuclear Terrorism: Psychological Motivations and Constraints." In: P. Leventhal and Y. Alexander, eds. ***Preventing Nuclear Terrorism.*** Lexington, MA.: Lexington Books, 1987. pp. 91-103.

3699. _____. "Prospects for Nuclear Terrorism: Psychological Motivations and Constraints." ***Conflict Quarterly,*** 7:3 (Summer 1987), 47-58.

3700. _____. "Superterrorism: Biological, Chemical, and Nuclear." ***Terrorism,*** 13:2 (1990), 165-168.

3701. "Protecting Nuclear Materials in the Terrorist Age: The International Challenge." ***Brooklyn Journal of International Law,*** 12 (March 1986), 305-338.

3702. Ramberg, Bennett. "Nuclear Plants - Military Hostages?." ***Bulletin of the Atomic Scientists,*** (March 1986), 17-21.

3703. _____. Daniel Hirsch and Stephanie Murphy. "Protecting Reactors From Terrorists." ***Bulletin of the Atomic Scientists,*** (March 1986), 22-25.

3704. "Report of the International Task Force on Prevention of Nuclear Terrorism, 25 June 1986." In: Y. Alexander, ed. ***The 1986 Annual on Terrorism.*** Dordrecht: Martinus Nijhoff, 1987. pp. 327-338.

3705. Ronfeldt, David F., and William F. Sater. "The Mindsets Of High-Technology Terrorists: Future Implications from an Historical Analog." In: Y. Alexander and C. K. Ebinger, eds. ***Political Terrorism and Response.*** New York: Praeger, 1982. pp. 15-38.

3706. Roosevelt, Edith K. "Germ War - Terrorism and the "New" Biology." ***Combat Arms,*** 4 (July 1986), 38-42.

3707. Rossnagel, Alexander. "Physical Protection of Special Nuclear Materials in the Federal Republic of Germany." In: P. Leventhal and Y. Alexander, eds. ***Preventing Nuclear Terrorism.*** Lexington, MA.: Lexington Books, 1987. pp. 223-230.

3708. Roy, Robin. "Physical Vulnerability of Electric Systems to Sabotage." ***Terrorism,*** 13:3 (1990), 191-194.

3709. Russett, Bruce M. "Who are Terrorists?" ***Society,*** 17:5 (1980), 16-17.

3710. Salmore, Barbara G., and Douglas W. Simon. "Nuclear Terrorism in Perspective." ***Society,*** 17:5 (1980), 21-24.

3711. Schelling, Thomas C. "Can Nuclear Terrorism Be Neutralized?" In: B. Netanyahu, ed. ***International Terrorism: Challenge and Response.*** New Brunswick, NJ.: Transaction Books, 1981. pp. 155-159.

3712. _____. "Thinking about Nuclear Terrorism." ***International Security,*** 6:4 (Spring 1982), 61-77.

3713. Shattuck, John. "Response." (Symposium: The Civil Liberties Implications of Nuclear Power Development) ***New York University Review of Law and Social Change,*** 10 (Winter 1981), 319-324.

3714. Sieghart, Paul. "Guarding Nuclear Materials and Civil Liberties." ***Bulletin of the Atomic Scientists,*** 36:5 (May 1980), 32.

3715. Slochower, Harry. "The Bomb and Terrorism: Their Linkage." ***American Imago,*** 39 (Fall 1982), 269-272.

3716. Spector, Leonard S. "Clandestine Nuclear Trade and the Threat of Nuclear Terrorism." In: P. Leventhal and Y. Alexander, eds. ***Preventing Nuclear Terrorism.*** Lexington, MA.: Lexington Books, 1987. pp. 78-88.

3717. _____. "Nuclear Proliferation: Who Next?." ***Bulletin of the Atomic Scientists,*** 43:4 (May 1987), 17-20.

3718. Sterling, Claire. "Responses to Terrorist Grievances: Another Perspective." In: P. Leventhal and Y. Alexander, eds. ***Preventing Nuclear Terrorism.*** Lexington, MA.: Lexington Books, 1987. pp. 160-164.

3719. Sullivan, John P., and Peter T. Caram. "Planning the Police Response to Chemical, Biological, or Nuclear Terrorism and Hazardous Material Incidents." ***TVI Report,*** 7:1 (1986), 31-36.

3720. Teller, Edward. "The Spectre of Nuclear Terrorism." In: B. Netanyahu, ed. ***International Terrorism: Challenge and Response.*** New Brunswick, NJ.: Transaction Books, 1981. pp. 141-145.

3721. Thompson, W. Scott. "Whose Order?" ***Society,*** 17:5 (1980), 24-25.

3722. Watkins, Charles A. "Terrorist Use of Biological Warfare Agents: A Threat to US Security." In: Y. Alexander, ed. ***The 1986 Annual on Terrorism.*** Dordrecht: Martinus Nijhoff, 1986. pp. 191-200.

3723. Webster, William H. "Chemical Weapon's Give the Poor Man's Answer to Nuclear Armaments." ***ROA National Security Report,*** 7:6 (1989), 6-10.

3724. Wolfe, Bertram, and Burton F. Judson. "The Back End of the Nuclear Fuel Cycle: An Update." In: P. Leventhal and Y. Alexander, eds. ***Preventing Nuclear Terrorism.*** Lexington, MA.: Lexington Books, 1987. pp. 292-297.

3725. Zilinskas, R. A. "Terrorism and Biological Weapons - Inevitable Alliance." ***Perspectives in Biology and Medicine,*** 34:1 (1990), 44-72.

3. Documents and Reports

3726. American National Standards Institute. ***Industrial Security for Nuclear Power Plants.*** ANSI Standard N18.17, Subcommittee ANS-3. Washington, D.C.: American Nuclear Society, n.d.

3727. Asseltine, James K. "What are Suitable Responses by Government and Industry to Terrorist Nuclear Threats or Violence." Paper Presented at the ***Conference on International Terrorism: The Nuclear Dimension,*** held on June 24, 1985. 7p.

3728. Bass, Gail V., et al. ***The Appeal of Nuclear Crimes to the Spectrum of Potential Adversaries.*** RAND R-2803-SL. Santa Monica, CA.: RAND Corporation, 1982. 56p.

3729. _____, et al. ***Motivation and Possible Actions of Potential Criminal Adversaries of U.S. Nuclear Programs.*** RAND R-2554-SL. Santa Monica, CA.: RAND Corporation, 1980. 84p.

3730. _____, et al. ***Motivation and Possible Actions of Potential Criminal Adversaries of U.S. Nuclear Programs: Executive Summary.*** RAND R-2554/1-SL. Santa Monica, CA.: RAND Corporation, 1980. 19p.

3731. _____, and Brian M. Jenkins. ***A Review of Recent Trends in International Terrorism and Nuclear Incidents Abroad.*** RAND N-1979-SL. Santa Monica, CA.: RAND Corporation, 1983. 73p.

3732. Beres, Louis Rene. ***Is it Plausible that Terrorists will Engage in Nuclear Violence?.*** Conference on International Terrorism: The Nuclear Dimension, 1985. 19p.

3733. Chellaney, Brahma, and Paul L. Leventhal. ***Nuclear Terrorism: Threat, Perception and Response in South Asia.*** Washington, D.C.: Nuclear Control Institute, 1989. 47p.

3734. Daubert, V. L. J., and Sue Moran. ***Origins, Goals, and Tactics of the U.S. Anti-Nuclear Protest Movement.*** RAND-N-2192-SL. Santa Monica, CA.: RAND Corporation, 1985. 117p.

3735. De Leon, Peter, et al. ***The Threat of Nuclear Terrorism: A Reexamination.*** RAND N-2706. Santa Monica, CA.: Rand Corporation, 1988. 16p.

3736. Donich, Terry. ***Nuclear Terrorism Effects Study.*** Livermore, CA.: Lawrence Livermore National Laboratory, 1983. 22p.

3737. _____. "Nuclear Terrorism Effects Study (1983)." In: ***Nuclear Weapons, Arms Control, and the Threat of Thermonuclear War: Special Studies: Second Supplement, 1983-1984.*** Frederick, MD.: University Publications of America, 1985. Reel IX: 0918-0936.

3738. Greene, Linwood G. ***Terrorism and the Communication Utilities: A National Security Concern.*** Carlisle Barracks, PA.: U.S. Army War College, 1989. 23p.

3739. Heineke, J. M. ***Insider Threat to Secure Facilities - Data Analysis.*** NUREG/CR--1234;UCRL-52744. Livermore, CA.: Lawrence Livermore Laboratory, 1980.

3740. Hoenig, Milton M., and Paul L. Leventhal. ***Nuclear Installations and Potential Risks: The Hidden Danger: Risks of Nuclear Terrorism.*** Washington, D.C.: The Nuclear Control Institute, 1987. 26p.

3741. Hoffman, Bruce. ***The Potential Threat to Commercial Nuclear Facilities.*** RAND P-7450. Santa Monica, CA.: Rand Corporation, 1988. 12p.

3742. _____. ***Terrorism in the United States and the Potential Threat to Nuclear Facilities.*** RAND R-3351-DOE. Santa Monica, CA.: Rand Corporation, 1986. 56p.

3743. _____, et al. ***A Reassessment of Political Adversaries of U.S. Nuclear Programs.*** RAND R-3363-DOE. Santa Monica, CA.: Rand Corporation, 1986. 29p.

3744. _____, et al. ***Inside Crime: The Threat to Nuclear Facilities and Programs.*** RAND R-3782-DOE. Santa Monica, CA.: RAND Corporation, 1990. 53p.

3745. International Task Force on Prevention of Nuclear Terrorism. ***Report.*** Washington, D.C.: Nuclear Control Institute, 1986. 33p.

3746. _____. "Report on Nuclear Terrorism." ***Bulletin of the Atomic Scientists,*** (1986), 38-44.

3747. Jenkins, Brian M. ***The Likelihood of Nuclear Terrorism.*** RAND P-7119. Santa Monica, CA.: RAND Corporation, 1985. 12p.

3748. _____. ***The Potential Criminal Adversaries of Nuclear Programs: A Portrait.*** RAND P-6513. Santa Monica, CA.: RAND Corporation, 1980. 8p.

3749. Judd, Bruce R., and A. Al-Ayat Rokaya. ***Inside Protection - A Report Card.*** Livermore, CA.: Livermore National Laboratory, 1986.

3750. Le Chene, Evelyn. ***Chemical and Biological Warfare: Threat of the Future.*** Mackenzie Paper, No. 11. Toronto: Mackenzie Institute for the Study of Terrorism, Revolution and Propaganda, 1989. 31p.

3751. Livingstone, Neil C., and Joseph D. Jr. Douglas. ***CBW: The Poor Man's Atomic Bomb.*** Cambridge, MA.: Institute for Foreign Policy Analysis, 1984. 36p.

3752. Mullen, S. ***Generic Adversary Characteristics and the Potential Threat to Licensed Nuclear Activities from Insiders.*** Washington, D.C.: Nuclear Regulatory Commission, 1981. 10p.

3753. Reinstedt, R. N., and J. L. Westbury. ***Major Crimes as Analogs to Potential Threats to Nuclear Facilities and Programs.*** RAND N-1498-SL. Santa Monica, CA.: RAND Corporation, 1980. 93p.

3754. Ronfeldt, David F., and William F. Sater. ***The Mindsets of High Technology Terrorists: Future Implications from an Historical Analog.*** RAND N-1610-SL. Santa Monica, CA.: RAND Corporation, 1981. 33p.

3755. Simon, Jeffrey. ***Terrorists and the Potential Use of Biological Weapons: A Discussion of Possibilities.*** R-3771-AFMIC. Santa Monica, CA.: RAND Corporation, 1989. 33p.

3756. Thornton, W. H. ***Modern Terrorism. The Potential for Increased Lethality. CLIC Papers.*** Langley AFB, VA.: Army-Air Force Center for Low Intensity Conflict, 1987. 19p.

3757. United States. Congress. House. Committee on Foreign Affairs. ***International Physical Security Standards for Nuclear Materials Outside the United States: Reports.*** 100th Cong., 1st sess. Washington, D.C.: U.S. Government Printing Office, 1988. 246p.

3758. _____._____._____. Committee on Interior and Insular Affairs. Subcommittee on General Oversight and Investigations. ***Threat of Sabotage and Terrorism to Commercial Nuclear Powerplants: Oversight Hearing.*** 100th Cong., 2nd sess. Washington, D.C.: U.S. Government Printing Office, 1988. 262p.

3759. _____._____. Senate. Committee on Governmental Affairs. ***Vulnerability of the Nation's Electric System to Multi-Site Terrorist Attack: Hearing.*** 101st Cong., 2nd sess. Washington, D.C.: U.S. Government Printing Office, 1990. 151p.

3760. _____._____._____. Committee on the Judiciary. ***Nuclear Powerplant Security and Anti-Terrorism Act of 1985: Report.*** Washington, D.C.: U.S. Government Printing Office, 1985. 15p.

3761. _____._____._____._____. ***The Biological Weapons Anti-Terrorism Act of 1989: Hearings.*** 101st Cong., 1st sess. Washington, D.C.: U.S. Government Printing Office, 1989. 135p.

3762. _____._____._____._____. Subcommittee on Technology and the Law. ***High-Technology Terrorism: Hearings.*** 101st Cong., 2nd sess. Washington, D.C.: U.S. Government Printing Office, 1989. 145p.

3763. _____. Defence Nuclear Agency. ***New Modes of Conflict.*** RAND R-3009-DNA. Santa Monica, CA.: RAND Corporation, 1983. 20p.

3764. _____. Nuclear Regulatory Commission.Office of Nuclear Material Safety and Safeguards. ***Security Training Symposium: Meeting the Challenge: Firearms and Explosives Recognition and Detection.*** Washington, D.C.: Nuclear Regulatory Commission, 1989. 298p.

X

GEOGRAPHIC SUBDIVISION

Terrorism is a worldwide phenomenon. Although some areas of the globe seem to be plagued by terrorism more than other areas, most states have experienced some sort of political violence. The references in this chapter, which is the longest in the bibliography, are organized by geographic area. The first section examines the aspect of networks of terror - the aspect of international cooperation between terror groups. The rest of the chapter is organized by continent and state. References identify various terrorist groups, specific terrorist incidents, domestic political aspects of states, counter measures in specific countries, rescue missions and other aspects dealing with terrorism.

As this bibliography cites only English language sources, the student should be aware of the large number of materials available in other languages. Some areas of conflict are very well covered - Northern Ireland and the Israeli-Palestinian conflict are well represented in the literature. The size of the English language literature may be a reflection of our own interest in a particular country, and may not reflect the amount of actual terrorist activity in that particular area. We can make a number of general observations: most terrorist acts in third world countries are of domestic nature; international terrorism seems to be directed mainly against western democracies; terrorism was almost unknown in the Soviet Union and other eastern block states - a situation which raises certain questions about the relationship between democracies and terrorism.

Additional materials related to this chapter can be found in all other parts of the bibliography.

A. TERROR NETWORKS

1. Books

3765. Hunter, Jack. ***The Terror Alliance.*** New York: Dorchester Publishing, 1984. 318p.
3766. Ra'anan, Uri, et al. ***Hydra of Carnage: International Linkages of Terrorism - The Witnesses Speak.*** Lexington, MA.: Heath - Lexington Books, 1986. 638p.
3767. Sterling, Claire. ***The Terror Network: The Secret War of International Terrorism.*** New York: Holt, Rinehart, 1981. 357p.

2. Journal Articles

3768. Alexander, Yonah. "International Network of Terrorism." In: Y. Alexander and C. K. Ebinger, eds. ***Political Terrorism and Energy.*** New York: Praeger, 1982. pp. 39-64.
3769. _____. "Terrorist Network." ***Defense and Diplomacy,*** 7 (September 1989), 36-41+.
3770. Alpher, Joseph. "The Khomeini International." ***Washington Quarterly,*** 3:4 (1980), 54-74.
3771. Coppola, Vincent. "The Fire This Time." ***Penthouse,*** (May 1986), 98-105.
3772. Gad, Z. "International Cooperation Among Terrorist Groups." In: A. Merari, ed. ***On Terrorism and Combating Terrorism.*** Frederick, MD.: University Publications of America, 1985. pp. 135-144.
3773. "International Terrorism: Interview with Dr. Ariel Merari." ***Defence Update International,*** 64 (1985), 44-46.
3774. "Italy's International Terrorist Links." ***TVI Journal,*** 3:7 (1982), 4-11.
3775. Kupperman, Robert H., and Darrell M. Trent. "The Terrorist International: The Past is Prologue and America is Vulnerable." ***Across the Board,*** 17 (February 1980), 50-68.
3776. Le Moyne, James. "The Guerrilla Network." ***New York Times Magazine,*** (April 16, 1986), 14-20, 69-71, 73-75, 79.
3777. Livingstone, Neil C. "Terrorism: The International Connection." ***Army,*** 30 (December 1980), 14-17, 20-21.
3778. Petrakis, Gregory. "Terrorism as a Transnational Phenomenon." ***Law and Order,*** 28:5 (1980), 26-30, 32-34, 36.
3779. Priore, Rosario. "International & Co-ordinated Terrorism." In: ***Legal Responses to the Terrorist Threat.*** London: Institute for the Study of Conflict, 1988. pp. 27-42.
3780. Shank, Gregory, and Thomas Polly. "The International Terrorist Network: A Right-Wing Conception of Academic Criminology." ***Crime and Social Justice,*** 17 (Summer 1982), 73-82.
3781. Sterling, Claire. "Unravelling the Riddle." In: B. Netanyahu, ed. ***Terrorism: How the West Can Win.*** New York: Farrar, Straus, Giroux, 1986. pp. 103-105.
3782. Stewart, Bernard L. "Terrorism: Are National Networks an "Achilles' Heel"?." In: A. Kurz, ed. ***Contemporary Trends in World Terrorism.*** New York: Praeger, 1987. pp. 140-149.
3783. Stohl, Michael. "International Network of Terrorism." ***Journal of Peace Research,*** 20:1 (1983), 87-94.

3784. Sundberg, Jacob W. F. "The Terrorist Conglomerate." In: Y. Alexander, ed. ***The 1986 Annual on Terrorism.*** Dordrecht: Martinus Nijhoff, 1987. pp. 127-142.

3785. Wilkinson, Paul. "Terrorism - Global Links." In: ***RUSI and Brassey's Defence Yearbook, 1984.*** London: Brassey's Defence Publishers, 1984. pp. 209-234.

3. Documents and Reports

3786. Great Britain. Foreign and Commonwealth Office. ***Libya and Irish ˈı rrorism.*** London: H.M.S.O., 1984.

3787. Katz, Shalom S. ***International Terrorism: The International Network and its Supporters.*** Master's Thesis. Ottawa: Carleton University, 1981.

B. UNITED STATES AND CANADA

a. UNITED STATES

1. Books

3788. Bayes, Jane H. ***Minority Politics and Ideologies in the United States.*** Novato, CA.: Chandler & Sharp, 1982.

3789. Beckwith, Charlie A. ***Delta Force.*** San Diego, CA.: Harcourt, Brace, Jovanovich, 1983. 310p.

3790. Bolz, Francis A., and E. Hershey. ***Hostage Cop - The Story of the New York City Police Hostage Negotiating Team and the Man Who Leads It.*** New York: Rawson, Wade, 1980. 334p.

3791. Buckelew, Alvin H. ***Terrorism and the American Response.*** San Rafael, CA.: MIRA Academic Press, 1984. 161p.

3792. Castellucci, John. ***The Big Dance: The Untold Story of Kathy Boudin and the Terrorist Family That Committed the Brink's Robbery Murders.*** New York: Dodd, Mead & Co., 1986. 336p.

3793. Celmer, Marc A. ***Terrorism, U.S. Strategy, and Reagan Policies.*** Contributions in Political Science, 173. New York:Greenwood Press, 1987. 132p.

3794. Dinges, John, and Saul Landau. ***Assassination on Embassy Row.*** New York: Pantheon Books, 1980. 411p.

3795. Evans, Ernest. ***Wars Without Splendor: The U.S. Military and Low-Level Conflict.*** Westport, CT.: Greenwood Press, 1987. 160p.

3796. Frankfort, Ellen. ***Kathy Boudin and the Dance of Death.*** New York: Stein and Day, 1984. 267p.

3797. Freed, Donald, and F. Landis. ***Death in Washington: The Murder of Orlando Letelier.*** London: Zed Press, 1980.

3798. Gunter, Michael M. ***Pursuing the Just Cause of Their People: A Study of Contemporary American Terrorism.*** Contribution in Political Science Series, No. 152. Westport, CT.: Greenwood Press, 1986. 192p.

3799. Leinwand, Gerald. ***America Kept Hostage: How Shall We Fight Terrorism.*** New York: Facts on File, 1990. 128p.

3800. Linedecker, Clifford L. ***The Swastika and the Eagle: Neo-Nazism in America Today.*** New York: A & W Pubs., 1983.

3801. Livingstone, Neil C., and Terrell E. Arnold, eds. ***Beyond the Iran-Contra Crisis: The Shape of U.S. Anti-Terrorism Policy in the Post Reagan Era.*** Lexington, MA.: Lexington Books, 1988. 339p.

3802. Mehdi, M. T. ***Terrorism: Why America is the Target.*** New York: New World Press, 1988. 128p.

3803. Melanson, Philip H. ***The Politics of Protection: Secret Service in the Terrorist Age.*** New York: Praeger, 1984. 215p.

3804. Mullins, Wayman C. ***Terrorist Organizations in the United States: An Analysis of Issues, Organizations and Responses.*** Springfield, IL.: Charles C. Thomas, 1988. 228p.

3805. Ward, Richard H., and Harold E. Smith, eds. ***International Terrorism: The Domestic Response.*** Chicago, IL.: University of Illinois at Chicago, Office of International Criminal Justice, 1987. 133p.

2. Journal Articles

3806. Alpert, Jane. "I Bombed the Federal Building." ***Rolling Stone,*** 348 (July 23, 1981), 20-23, 62-63.

3807. American Society for Industrial Security. "Uncle Sam's Antiterrorism Plan." ***Security Management,*** 24:2 (1980), 39-40, 42-45, 47-50.

3808. Anti Defamation League of B'nai B'rith.Civil Rights Division. "Neo-Nazi Skinheads: A 1990 Status Report." ***Terrorism,*** 13:3 (1990), 243-275.

3809. Aranha, J. D. "Terrorism at the Olympics." ***Midstream: A Monthly Jewish Review,*** 30:6 (1984), 10-11.

3810. _____. "Is the U.S. Soft on Terrorism?" ***Security Management,*** 29 (January 1985), 72-73.

3811. Arguelles, Lourdes. "The U.S. National Security State: The CIA and Cuban Emigre Terrorism." ***Race & Class,*** 23:4 (Spring 1982), 287-304.

3812. Arnold, Philip W. "Future Domestic and International Terrorism: The USIA Perspective." ***Terrorism,*** 11:6 (1988), 541-542.

3813. Aruri, Naseer H., and John J. Carroll. "U.S. Policy and Terrorism." ***American - Arab Affairs,*** 14 (Fall 1985), 59-70.

3814. Audsley, David. "Posse Comitatus: An Extremist Tax Protest Group." ***TVI Journal,*** 6:1 (Summer 1985), 13-16.

3815. Badolato, Edward V. "Terrorism and the U.S. Energy Infrastructure." ***Terrorism,*** 13:2 (1990), 159-164.

3816. Barkun, Michael. "Millenarian Aspects of 'White Supremacist' Movements." ***Terrorism and Political Violence,*** 1:4 (October 1989), 409-434.

3817. Blackely, Stephen B. "Capitol Security Strengthened After Terrorist Bomb Explodes." ***Congressional Quarterly Weekly Report,*** 41 (November 12, 1983), 2355-2358.

3818. Borg, Parker W. "The Evolution of U.S. Anti-Terrorism Policy." In: N. C. Livingstone and T. E. Arnold, eds. ***Beyond the Iran-Contra Crisis.*** Lexington, MA.: D.C. Heath and Lexington Books, 1988.

3819. Boyd, Richard W., and Martha Crenshaw. "The 99th Congress and the Response to International Terrorism." In: Y. Alexander and A. H. Foxman, eds. ***The 1987 Annual on Terrorism.*** Dordrecht: Martinus Nijhoff, 1988. pp. 451-480.

3820. Bremer, L. Paul. "Countering Terrorism: U.S. Policy in the 1980s and 1990s." ***Terrorism,*** 11:6 (1988), 531-537.

3821. _____. "Counterterrorism: Strategy and Tactics." In: Y. Alexander and A. H. Foxman, eds. ***The 1987 Annual on Terrorism.*** Dordrecht: Martinus Nijhoff, 1988. pp. 357-364.

3822. _____. "Continuing the Fight Against Terrorism." ***Terrorism,*** 12:2 (1989), 81-88.

3823. _____. "Practical Measures for Dealing with Terrorism." ***Department of State Bulletin,*** 88:2120 (March 1987), 1-4.

3824. _____. "U.S. Anti Terrorism Assistance Program." ***Department of State Bulletin,*** 88:2135 (June 1988), 61-63.

3825. Bridgeman, Edward R. "Violence as an Old Problem." ***TVI Journal,*** 2:10 (1981), 3-7.

3826. Buckelew, Alvin H. "Fighting Terrorism: Does the United States Need a New Response Structure?" ***Security Management,*** 29 (June 1985), 36-41+.

3827. _____. "The Reality of Terrorism in the U.S." ***Security Management,*** (February 1984), 42-51.

3828. Busby, Morris D. "U.S. Counterterrorism Policy in the 1980s and the Priorities for the 1990s." ***Terrorism,*** 13:1 (1990), 7-17.

3829. Bush, George. "Prelude to Retaliation: Building a Governmental Consensus on Terrorism." ***SAIS Review,*** 7:1 (Winter-Spring, 1987), 1-9.

3830. Cabot, Lon. "Terrorism: Closer Than You Think." ***All Hands,*** 1 (January 1983), 7-13.

3831. Camper, Frank. "The Sikh Terror Plot, Part One and Part Two." ***Penthouse,*** (April 1986), 40-42, 62-66, 161; (May 1986), 42-44, 68, 76, 120-123.

3832. Casey, William J. "The American Intelligence Community." ***Presidential Studies Quarterly,*** 12:2 (Spring 1982), 150-153.

3833. Chandler, Jerome G. "Terrorism: A Case of False Security." ***American Legion,*** 113 (July 1982), 18-22.

3834. Clawson, Patrick. "U.S. Options for Combating Terrorism." In: B. Rubin, ed. ***The Politics of Counterterrorism.*** Lanham, MD.: University Publications of America, 1990. pp. 3-31.

3835. _____. "Coping with Terrorism in the United-States." ***Orbis,*** 33:3 (1989), 341-356.

3836. Collier, Peter, and David Horowitz. "Doing It: The Inside Story of the Rise and Fall of the Weather Underground." ***Rolling Stone,*** 379 (September 10, 1982), 19, 21-24, 26, 29-30, 35-36, 95-96, 98, 100.

3837. Corbett, William T. "A Time to Redefine Policy?." ***Security Management,*** 34:6 (1990), 38-44.

3838. Cordes, Bonnie J. "Armenian Terrorism in America." In: ***International Terrorism and the Drug Connection.*** Ankara: Ankara University Press, 1984. pp. 155-166.

3839. _____. "Armenian Terrorism in America." ***TVI Journal,*** 5:1 (1984), 22-27.

3840. "Countering the Terrorist Threat in the U.S.." ***Security Management,*** 31:6 (June 1987), 40-41.

3841. Courter, James A. "Protecting Our Citizens: When to Use Force Against Terrorists." ***Policy Review,*** 36 (Spring 1986), 10-17.

3842. Criley, Richard L. "The Cult of the Informer Revisited: "Antiterrorism" Policy in the United States." ***Crime and Social Justice,*** 21-22 (1984), 183-190.

3843. Crowell, Lorenzo M. "U.S. Domestic Terrorism: An Historical Perspective." ***Quarterly Journal of Ideology***, 11:3 (July 1987), 45-56.

3844. Davis, L. J. "Ballad of an American Terrorist." ***Harper's***, (July 1986), 53-62.

3845. De Valderano, Ronald. "Terror: The War Against the West." ***Imprimis***, 17 (November 1988), 1-7.

3846. Decter, Midge. "Terrorists: Made in USA." ***Across the Board***, 19 (March 1982), 5-12+.

3847. _____. "Notes from the American Underground." ***Commentary***, 73:1 (1982), 27-33.

3848. Denton, Jeremiah. "New Senate Subcommittee is a Step Toward Terrorism Control in U.S." ***Conservative Digest***, (July 1981), 20-23.

3849. _____. "The Role of the Senate Sub-Committee on Security and Terrorism in the Development of U.S. Policy Against Terrorism." ***Ohio Northern University Law Review***, 13:1 (1986), 19-25.

3850. Di Laura, Arnold E. "Preventing Terrorism: An Analysis of National Strategy." ***SAIS Review***, 7:1 (Winter-Spring 1987), 27-38.

3851. Dieter, Alice. "When is a Peacemaker a Terrorist?." ***Witness***, 68:7 (July 1985), 6-8.

3852. Dieterich, Heinz. "Global U.S. State Terrorism: An Interview with Noam Chomsky." ***Crime and Social Justice***, 24 (1987), 96-109.

3853. Dixon, Alan J. "The Terror Next Time." ***Playboy***, 33:10 (October 1986), 96-98, 122, 156-157.

3854. Dizard, Wilson. "Terrorist Shots Heard Around the World." ***State***, (February 1985), 18-21.

3855. "Domestic Terrorism: Prevention in Court and Transit Systems." ***TVI Report***, 8:4 (1989), 16-18.

3856. Duncan, Evan. "Terrorist Attacks on U.S. Official Personnel Abroad." ***Department of State Bulletin***, 81 (April 1980), 34-37.

3857. _____. "Terrorist Attacks on U.S. Official Personnel Abroad, 1982-1984." ***Department of State Bulletin***, 85 (April 1985), 65-66.

3858. Elliff, John T. "The Attorney General's Guidelines for FBI Investigations." ***Cornell Law Review***, 69:4 (April 1984), 785-815.

3859. Englade, Kenneth F. "Terrorism: In the Name of God and Country." ***Liberty***, 76 (January-February 1981), 2-6.

3860. Evans, Ernest. "Toward a More Effective U.S. Policy on Terrorism." In: Y. Alexander and C. K. Ebinger, eds. ***Political Terrorism and Energy***. New York: Praeger, 1982. pp. 229-256.

3861. _____. "Higher Order Terrorism is Coming to the U.S.." ***TVI Report***, 2:1 (1981), 13-18.

3862. "Export Controls and the U.S. Effort to Combat International Terrorism." ***Law and Policy in International Business***, 13 (1981), 521-590.

3863. "FBI Analysis of Terrorist Incidents and Terrorist-Related Activities in the United States, 1985." In: Y. Alexander, ed. ***The 1986 Annual on Terrorism***. Dordrecht: Martinus Nijhoff, 1987. pp. 323-326.

3864. Farrell, William R. "Military Involvement in Domestic Terror Incidents." ***Naval War College Review***, 34 (July-August 1981), 53-66.

3865. _____. "Assessing Counter-Terrorism Policy." In: M. C. Bassiouni, ed. ***Legal Responses to International Terrorism: U.S. Procedural Aspects***. Dordrecht: Martinus Nijhoff, 1988. pp. 289-300.

3866. Faucher, Leo J. "FBI Statistics on U.S. Terrorism." ***Security Management***, 27:8 (1983), 95-98.

3867. "Felled by Terrorists: A Shipmate Comes Home." ***All Hands,*** (June 1985), 16-17.

3868. Fields, Louis G. "The Evolution of U.S. Counter-Terrorism Policy." In: M. C. Bassiouni, ed. ***Legal Responses to International Terrorism: U.S. Procedural Aspects.*** Dordrecht: Martinus Nijhoff, 1988. pp. 279-288.

3869. Finegan, Jay. "Targets for Terrorism?" ***Air Force Times,*** 45 (July 8, 1985), 53-54.

3870. Foster, Thomas W. "America's Insecure Borders in an Age of International Terrorism." ***Armed Forces Journal International,*** (February 1986), 80-82.

3871. Foxman, Abraham H., and Justin J. Finger. "Terrorism in the United States: 1987." In: Y. Alexander and A. H. Foxman, eds. ***The 1987 Annual on Terrorism.*** Dordrecht: Martinus Nijhoff, 1988. pp. 27-38.

3872. _____. _____. "Terrorism in the United States: An Overview, 1986." In: Y. Alexander, ed. ***The 1986 Annual on Terrorism.*** Dordrecht: Martinus Nijhoff, 1987. pp. 61-74.

3873. Francis, Samuel T. "The Jackal Reborn: The Brinks Robbery and Terrorism in the United States." ***International Security Review,*** 7:1 (1982), 99-124.

3874. _____. "Terrorism in the United States: Background and Prospects." In: H. H. Tucker, ed. ***Combating the Terrorists.*** New York: Facts on File, 1988. pp. 1-44.

3875. Franks, Lucinda. "The Seeds of Terror." ***New York Times Magazine,*** 131 (November 22, 1981), 34-76.

3876. Friedlander, Robert A. "So Proudly They Failed: The Reagan Administration and the Gradual Disintegration of U.S. Counter-Terror Policy." ***German Yearbook of International Law,*** 31 (1988), 415-447.

3877. Friedman, R. E. "In Search of a Counterterrorism Strategy." ***Terrorism,*** 12:6 (1989), 417-418.

3878. Gellman, Barton. "Though Terrorism May Be Hard to Define, This Administration Takes it Seriously." ***National Journal,*** 37 (September 12, 1981), 1631-1635.

3879. Gigliotti, Donna. "Security Teams are Visiting Posts, Teaching Self-Protection." ***State,*** 282 (October 1985), 13-16.

3880. Ginger, James, and Hubert Williams. "The Threat of International Terrorism in the United States: The Police Response." ***Terrorism,*** 10:3 (1987), 219-223.

3881. Gitlin, Todd. "White Heat Underground." ***Nation,*** 233 (December 19, 1981), 657, 669-674.

3882. Giuffrida, Louis O. "How Can Terrorism Be Stopped: The Domestic Front." ***Security Systems Digest,*** 15:16 (1984), 5-9.

3883. Gleason, John M. "A Poison Model of Incidents of International Terrorism in the United States." ***Terrorism,*** 4 (1980), 259-266.

3884. Gonzales, Lawrence. "The Targeting of America: A Special Report on Terrorism." ***Playboy,*** (May 1983), 88-92, 171-180.

3885. Gordon, Don. "Terrorism - Are We Losing the War?." ***Journal of Defence and Diplomacy,*** 4:3 (1986), 38-44.

3886. Gruen, George E. "The Anti-Terrorism Act of 1987 - An Update on the Controversy Surrounding Efforts to Close Down PLO Offices in the U.S.." ***Terrorism,*** 11:3 (1988), 235-240.

3887. Guillmartin, J. F. "Terrorism: Political Challenge and Military Response." In: W. P. Snyder and J. Brown, eds. ***Defense Policy in the Reagan Administration.*** Washington, D.C.: National Defence University, 1988. pp. 115-142.

3888. Gurr, Ted R. "Political Terrorism in the United States: Historical Antecedents and Contemporary Trends." In: M. Stohl, ed. ***The Politics of Terrorism.*** New York: Marcel Dekker, 1988. pp. 549-578.

3889. Hageman, Mary J. C. "Terrorism in the U.S.: The New K.K.K.." ***Violence, Aggression and Terrorism***, 1:4 (1987), 343-370.

3890. Harris, John W. "Domestic Terrorism in the 1980's." ***FBI Law Enforcement Bulletin***, 56:10 (October 1987), 5-13.

3891. Helgeland, John. "The Religion of Terrorism and the Mind of Gordon Kahl." ***TVI Report***, 8:1 (1988), 23-26.

3892. Herskowitz, Allen P. "Terrorism in the United States: We Can Defend Against It." ***Military Engineer***, 79 (March-April 1987), 88-91.

3893. Hertig, C. A. "The Threat of Terrorism in the United States." ***Police Chief***, 52 (June 1985), 48-49.

3894. Hinckley, R. H. "American Opinion Toward Terrorism - The Reagan Years." ***Terrorism***, 12:6 (1989), 387-400.

3895. Hoffman, Bruce. "The Cuban Anti-Castro Terrorist Movement." ***TVI Journal***, 5:1 (1984), 15-21.

3896. _____. "Terrorism in the United States During 1985." In: P. Wilkinson and A. M. Stewart, eds. ***Contemporary Research on Terrorism***. Aberdeen: Aberdeen University Press, 1987. pp. 230-240.

3897. _____. "Left-Wing Terrorism in the United States." ***Conflict Quarterly***, 6:4 (1986), 5-14.

3898. _____. "Terrorism in the United States: Recent Trends and Future Prospects." ***TVI Report***, 8:3 (1989), 4-10.

3899. _____. "Right Wing Terrorism in the United States." ***Violence Aggression and Terrorism***, 1:1 (1987), 1-26.

3900. _____. "Terrorism in the United States During 1985." ***TVI Report***, 6:3 (Winter 1986), 4-8.

3901. _____. "The Jewish Defence League." ***TVI Journal***, 5:1 (1984), 10-14.

3902. Hollis, Martin, and Steve Smith. "Roles and Reasons in Foreign Policy Decision Making." ***British Journal of Political Science***, 16 (July 1986), 269-286.

3903. Homer, Frederick D. "Government Terror in the United States: An Explanation of Containment Policy." In: M. Stohl and G. A. Lopez, eds. ***The State as Terrorist***. Westport, CT.: Greenwood Press, 1984. pp. 167-182.

3904. _____. "Terror in the United States: Three Perspectives." In: M. Stohl, ed. ***The Politics of Terrorism, 2nd ed.*** New York: Marcel Dekker, 1983. pp. 179-220.

3905. _____. "Terror in the United States: Three Perspectives." In: M. Stohl, ed. ***The Politics of Terrorism***. New York: Marcell Dekker, 1988. pp. 197-230.

3906. Houseworth, Joe. "U.S. Army Counterterrorism Course." ***Law and Order***, 31:1 (1983), 79-80.

3907. Hurt, Henry. "Search for a Terrorist Gang." ***Reader's Digest***, 127 (December 1985), 166-174.

3908. "Interview with Ed Best, Director of Security at the Los Angeles Olympics." ***TVI Journal***, 5:2 (1984), 1-6.

3909. Jacobs, M. J., and T. A. Watts-Fitzgerald. "Protection of Offshore Assets of the United States from Terrorist Activity." ***Natural Resources Lawyer***, 16 (1984), 569-595.

3910. Jenkins, Brian M. "American Terrorism: More Bombast or Bomb Blasts?" ***TVI Journal***, 1:4 (1980), 2-8.

3911. _____. "Terrorism in the United States." ***TVI Journal***, 5:1 (1984), 1-3.

3912. _____. "The Terrorist Threat to the Olympics." ***TVI Journal***, 5:1 (1984), 51+.

3913. _____. "The U.S. Response to Terrorism: A Policy Dilemma." ***TVI Journal***, 5:4 (1985), 31-35.

3914. _____. "A U.S. Strategy for Combatting Terrorism." ***Conflict***,

3915. _____. "The U.S Response to Terrorism: A Policy Dilemma." ***Armed Forces Journal International***, 122 (April 1985), 39+.

3916. Johnston, D. "Olympic Security." ***National Centurion***, 2:1 (1984), 25-30, 32+.

3917. Johnston, Robert J. "Security Arrangements for the Statue of Liberty Celebration." ***The Police Chief***, 56:3 (March 1989), 31-35+.

3918. Jones, P. M. "The U.S. Stand Against International Terrorism." ***Scholastic Update***, 118 (May 16, 1986), 19-20.

3919. Joyal, Paul M. "A View from Congress." ***Terrorism***, 11:4 (1988), 339-342.

3920. Joyner, Christopher. "In Search for an Anti-Terrorism Policy: Lessons from the Reagan Era." ***Terrorism***, 11:1 (1988), 29-42.

3921. Kaiser, Charles. "A Plague of Libyans." ***Rolling Stone***, 336 (February 5, 1981), 24-26.

3922. Kavey, Fred. "Animal Liberation: The New Trend in Terrorism." ***Guns & Ammo***, 29 (June 1985), 28-32.

3923. Kelly, Ross S. "Special Operations Reform in the Reagan Administration." In: N. C. Livingstone and T. E. Arnold, eds. ***Beyond the Iran-Contra Crisis***. Lexington, MA.: D.C. Heath & Lexington Books, 1988. pp. 85-118.

3924. Kemp, Geoffrey. "U.S. Support of Terrorists is Necessary." In: B. Szumski, ed. ***Terrorism: Opposing Viewpoints***. St.Paul, MN.: Greenhaven Press, 1986. pp. 133-136.

3925. Killam, E. W. "Terrorism: An Introduction for Rural Law Enforcement Officers." ***Law and Order***, 28:4 (1980), 38-44.

3926. King, Charles G., and Shelly King. "Fire as a Terrorist Weapon: An Analysis of the MOVE Confrontation asa Terrorist Attack." ***Fire Engineering***, (October 1986), 26-35.

3927. Kirka, Danica. "Terrorists in Vermont?." ***TVI Report***, 9:1 (1989), 12-14.

3928. Knutson, Jeanne N. "Toward a United States Policy on Terrorism." ***Political Psychology***, 5:2 (1984), 287-294.

3929. Kupperman, Robert H. "Terrorism and Public Policy: Domestic Impacts, International Threats." In: L. A. Curtis, ed. ***American Violence and Public Policy***. New Haven, CT.: Yale University Press, 1985. pp. 183-202.

3930. _____. "Vulnerable America." In: P. Wilkinson and A. M. Stewart, eds. ***Contemporary Research on Terrorism***. Aberdeen: Aberdeen University Press, 1987. pp. 570-580.

3931. _____. "Terrorism: What Should We Do?." ***This World***, 12 (1985), 31-84.

3932. Laingen, Bruce. "Future U.S. Policy and Action." ***Terrorism***, 11:6 (1988), 550-552.

3933. Lamb, Robert E. "How Much Security is Enough?." In: Y. Alexander and A. H. Foxman, eds. ***The 1987 Annual on Terrorism***. Dordrecht: Martinus Nijhoff, 1988. pp. 365-370.

3934. "Law Makers and Law Enforcers Discuss Domestic Terrorism." ***International Security Review***, 7 (Spring 1982), 79-98.

3935. Ledeen, Michael A. "Fighting Back." ***Commentary***, 80:2 (1985), 28-31.

3936. Lee, Martin A., and Kevin Coogan. "Killers on the Right." ***Mother Jones***, 13:4 (1987), 45-54.

3937. Lerner, Steve. "Terror Against Arabs in America: No More Looking the Other Way." ***New Republic***, 195 (July 28, 1986), 20-23.

3938. Liddy, Gordon L. "Rules of the Game." ***OMNI,*** 11:4 (January 1989), 42-44, 46+.

3939. Linn, Tom. "Puerto Rico's Terrorist Threat: A Strategic Problem." ***Defence and Foreign Affairs,*** 9 (October 1981), 24-27.

3940. Livingstone, Neil C. "Taming Terrorism: In Search of a New U.S. Policy." ***International Security Review,*** 7 (Spring 1982), 17-34.

3941. _____. "A New U.S. Antiterrorism Strategy for the 1990s." In: L. B. Thompson, ed. ***Low Intensity Conflict.*** Lexington, MA.: Lexington Books, 1989. pp. 77-108.

3942. Lopez-Rivera, Oscar. "Who is the Terrorist? The Making of a Puerto Rican Freedom Fighter." ***Social Justice,*** 16:4 (Winter 1989), 162-174.

3943. Lowe, David, and Irwin Suall. "Special Report: The Hate Movement Today: A Chronicle of Violence and Disarray." ***Terrorism,*** 10:4 (1987), 345-364.

3944. Luce, Phil. "Terrorist Actions Increasing." ***Conservative Digest,*** (February 1983), 39-41.

3945. Lupsha, Peter A. "The Problems of Domestic Intelligence and Terrorism." In: R. H. Ward and H. E. Smith, eds. ***International Terrorism: The Domestic Response.*** Chicago, IL.: University of Illinois at Chicago, Office of International Criminal Justice, 1987. pp. 65-72.

3946. Madison, Carol A. "Coping with Violence Abroad." ***Foreign Service Journal,*** (July/August 1985), 22-25.

3947. Maechling, Charles. "Containing Terrorism." ***Foreign Service Journal,*** (July/August 1984), 33-37.

3948. Maksudov, L. "The True Organizers of "International Terrorism"." ***International Affairs,*** 11 (November 1981), 30-36.

3949. Manor, F. S. "The New World Disorder: If Terrorism is War by Other Means, We Aren't Even Holding Our Positions." ***American Spectator,*** (June 1980), 19-21.

3950. Mariconde, R. J. "Terrorism in the United States." ***Journal of Security Administration,*** 5:1 (1982), 19-32.

3951. Martines, Lawrence J. "Thunder in the American Southwest." ***TVI Report,*** 7:4 (1987), 37.

3952. _____. "Trouble on the Reservation." ***TVI Report,*** 7:2 (1987), 39.

3953. Matheson, Michael. "The Role of the Reagan Administration." ***George Mason University Law Review,*** 9:1 (Winter 1986), 21-27.

3954. McEwen, Michael T., and Stephen Sloan. "Terrorism Preparedness on the State and Local Level: An Oklahoma Perspective". In: ***Clandestine Tactics and Technology.*** Gaithersburg, MD.: International Association of Chiefs of Police, 1980. 15p.

3955. _____. "Is Your Base Ready to Counteract Terrorism?" ***Air University Review,*** 35:6 (1984), 80-87.

3956. McGuire, P. C. "Posse Comitatus." ***National Sheriff,*** 35:5 (October-November 1983), 10-16, 18-20.

3957. Meese, Edwin, III. "U.S. Policy on Combating Terrorism." ***Security Management,*** 30:6 (1986), 51-52+.

3958. _____. "The Five Tiers of Domestic Action." In: B. Netanyahu, ed. ***Terrorism: How the West Can Win.*** New York: Farrar, Straus, Giroux, 1986. pp. 165-167.

3959. Melnichak, Joseph M. "Domestic Terrorism in America." ***TVI Journal,*** 6:1 (Summer 1985), 17-19.

3960. _____. "The "White Supremacy" Trial." ***TVI Report,*** 9:1 (1989), 14-18.

3961. _____. "Tactics of the Extreme Right in the Farm Crisis." ***TVI Report***, 6:3 (Winter 1986), 22-26.

3962. _____. "Hatred Continues...White Supremacists Update." ***TVI Report***, 8:1 (1988), 15-17.

3963. Methvin, Eugene H. "Terror Network, U.S.A." ***Reader's Digest***, (December 1984), 109-119.

3964. Miller, Abraham H., and J. S. Robbins. "The CIA, Congress, Covert Operations and the War on Terrorism." In: S. J. Cimbala, ed. ***Intelligence and Intelligence Policy in a Democratic Society***. Ardsley on Hudson, NY.: Transnational Publications, 1987. pp. 145-164.

3965. Miller, William J. "U.S. Embassies: Target for Terrorists." ***Security Management***, 30:6 (1986), 81-84.

3966. Milman, Joel, and Mark Dowie. "A Brazen Act of Terrorism: The Killing of Henry Liu." ***Mother Jones***, 10 (May 1985), 735-764.

3967. Monday, Mark, ed. "1984 Olympics Not All Fun and Games." ***TVI Journal***, 3:2 (1982), 8-12.

3968. Monroe, C. P. "Addressing Terrorism in the United States." ***Annals of the American Academy of Political and Social Science***, 463 (September 1982), 141-148.

3969. Motley, James B. "If Terrorism Hits Home, Will the Army Be Ready?" ***Army***, 34:4 (1984), 18-26.

3970. _____. "Target America: The Undeclared War." In: N. C. Livingstone and T. E. Arnold, eds. ***Fighting Back: Winning the War Against Terrorism***. Lexington, MA.: Lexington Books, 1985. pp 59-84.

3971. _____. "Terrorism." ***National Defense***, 69:40 (1985), 39-47.

3972. _____. "Terrorism: The US Targeted." ***Defense and Foreign Affairs***, (July 1988), 34-38.

3973. Mulgannon, Terry. "The Los Angeles Eight: Terrorists or Activists?." ***TVI Report***, 8:4 (1989), 1-6.

3974. Mullins, Wayman C. "Terrorism in the 90's: Predictions for the United States." ***Police Chief***, 57:9 (September 1990), 44-46.

3975. Murray, J. S. "Negotiating United States Policy to Counter Terrorism." ***Negotiation Journal***, 6:1 (1990), 15-22.

3976. Nadel, Seth R. "America's Counter Terrorism Teams: Teeming with Trouble." ***TVI Journal***, 1:10 (1980), 5-6.

3977. Nanes, Allan S. "Congressional Developments." ***Terrorism***, 6:1 (1982), 101-104.

3978. _____. "Congressional Developments." ***Terrorism***, 7:1 (1984), 71-72.

3979. _____. "Responding to the Terrorist Challenge." ***Congressional Research Service Review***, (June 1985), 17-19+.

3980. _____. "Congressional Developments: Terrorism." ***Terrorism***, 9:2 (1987), 207-214.

3981. Nathanson, B. "Operation Rescue - Domestic Terrorism or Legitimate Civil-Rights Protest." ***Hastings Center Report***, 19:6 (1989) 28-32.

3982. Nelson, Alan C. "Preventing the Entry of International Terrorists." ***The Police Chief***, 56:3 (March 1989), 50-52.

3983. "New York Provides Security for U.N. Anniversary Session." ***The Police Chief***, 53:4 (1986), 54-55.

3984. Nitcavic, Richard, and Ralph E. Dowling. "American Perceptions of Terrorism: A Q-Methodological Analysis of Types." ***Political Communication and Persuasion***, 7:3 (1990), 147-166.

3985. Noah, Timothy. "School for Scoundrels: Training Terrorists in Alabama." ***New Republic***, (August 26, 1985), 11-14.

3986. Olson, W. J. "Low-Intensity Conflict: The Challenge to the National Interest." ***Terrorism***, 12:2 (1989), 75-80.

3987. Oseth, John M. "Combatting Terrorism: The Dilemmas of a Decent Nation." ***Parameters***, (Spring 1985), 65-76.

3988. Ostrovitz, Nina Landfield, ed. "Terrorism: A National Issues Seminar." ***World Affairs***, 146:1 (1983), 79-113.

3989. "An Ounce of Prevention: Federal Government Initiative to Protect its Facilities." ***TVI Report***, 8:4 (1989), 12-16.

3990. Pearl, Marc. "Terrorism - Historical Perspectives on U.S. Congressional Action." ***Terrorism***, 10:2 (1987), 139-140.

3991. Pfaltzgraff, Robert L. "Implications for American Policy." In: U. Ra'anan, et al. ***Hydra of Carnage***. Lexington, MA.: Lexington Books, 1986. pp. 289-300.

3992. Phelps, Thomas R., and James M. Poland. "U.S. Terrorism - No Increase is Likely." ***TVI Journal***, 2:2 (1981), 4-10.

3993. Pinsky, Mark I. "The 'Quiet' Death of Alex Odeh: Terrorism Comes to Orange County." ***Present Tense,***, 13 (Winter 1986), 6-12.

3994. _____, and David Reyes. "Anti-Communist Faction Stalks Fearful Vietnamese." ***TVI Report***, 8:1 (1988), 33-36.

3995. Pizzo, Mark B. "The Terrorist Threat: Is the Navy Ready?" ***U.S. Naval Institute Proceedings***, 111 (November 1985), 121-125.

3996. Pomerantz, Steven L. "FBI and Terrorism." ***FBI Law Enforcement Bulletin***, 56:10 (October 1987), 14-17.

3997. "Powers of the State Governments and Governors to Meet a Terrorist Problem." ***TVI Journal***, 2:7 (1981), 46+.

3998. "The Presidential Candidates on Terrorism." ***TVI Report***, Special Edition. 8 (1988). 7p.

3999. Quainton, A. C. E. "U.S. Antiterrorism Program." ***Department of State Bulletin***, 80 (July 1980), 75-77.

4000. Quist, Burton C. "Implications of Terror." ***Marine Corps Gazette***, 70:1 (1986), 33-35.

4001. Rathburn, William. "LAPD's Role in Olympic Security." ***TVI Journal***, 5:3 (1985), 30-33.

4002. Reagan, Ronald. "'We Did Not Trade Weapons or Anything Else for Hostages'." In: Y. Alexander, ed. ***The 1987 Annual on Terrorism***. Dordrecht: Martinus Nijhoff, 1987. pp. 315-320.

4003. Rees, John. "Terrorism, U.S.A.." ***Conservative Digest***, 10:2 (1984), 11-13.

4004. Rees, Louise. "Foreign-Controlled Terrorists in the United States." In: Y. Alexander and A. H. Foxman, eds. ***The 1987 Annual on Terrorism***. Dordrecht: Martinus Nijhoff, 1988. pp. 85-156.

4005. "Report of the Congressional Committees Investigating the Iran-Contra Affair: Executive Summary." In: Y. Alexander and A. H. Foxman, eds. ***The 1987 Annual on Terrorism***. Dordrecht: Martinus Nijhoff, 1988. pp. 283-312.

4006. "Report on the Brinks Incident: New York State Policy Study Group on Terrorism." ***Terrorism***, 9:2 (1987), 169-206.

4007. Revell, Oliver B. "Terrorism in North America." In: V. S. Pisano, ed. ***Terrorist Dynamics: A Geographical Perspective***. Arlington, VA.: International Association of Chiefs of Police, 1988. pp. 127-183.

4008. _____. "International Terrorism in the United States." ***The Police Chief,*** 56:3 (1989), 16,19-20.

4009. _____. "Terrorism Today." ***FBI Law Enforcement Bulletin,*** 56:10 (October 1987), 1-4.

4010. Richman, Peter. "For Want of a Nail...The War Was Lost: Separation of Powers and the United States Counter-Terrorism Policy During the Reagan Years." ***Hastings Constitutional Law Quarterly,*** 17:3 (Spring 1990), 609-658.

4011. Ricks, Bob A. "Future Domestic and International Terrorism: The FBI Perspective." ***Terrorism,*** 11:6 (1988), 538-540.

4012. Ronso, Lee. "Hungry for Apple Pie." ***Security Management,*** 30 (August 1986), 34-36.

4013. _____. "Terrorist Attacks in CONUS." ***Marine Corps Gazette,*** 70:1 (1986), 35-36.

4014. Ross, Jeffrey Ian, and Ted R. Gurr. "Why Terrorism Subsides: A Comparative Study of Canada and the United States." ***Comparative Politics,*** 21:4 (July 1989), 405-426.

4015. Sallows, Karen. "The Terrorist Threat to Major Events." ***The Police Chief,*** 56:3 (March 1989), 38-45.

4016. Salmony, Steven E., and Richard Smoke. "The Appeal and Behavior of the Ku Klux Klan on Object Relations Perspective." ***Terrorism,*** 11:4 (1988), 247-263.

4017. Salzano, Carlo J. "Security of U.S. Ports Challenged by Thieves, Smugglers and Terrorists." ***Traffic World,*** 13:219 (1989), 11-18.

4018. Sample, Travis L. "The Existential Basis for Effecting a Coherent American Response to Terrorism." In: Y. Alexander and H. A. Foxman, eds. ***The 1987 Annual of Terrorism.*** Dordrecht: Martinus Nijhoff, 1988. pp. 157-186.

4019. Sarkesian, Sam C. "American Policy on Revolution and Counterrevolution: A Review of the Themes in the Literature." ***Conflict,*** 5:2 (1984), 137-184.

4020. Sater, William F. "Violence and the Puerto Rican Separatist Movement." ***TVI Journal,*** 5:1 (1984), 4-9.

4021. Scott, Peter Dale. "Northwards Without North: Bush, Counterterrorism, and the Continuation of Secret Power." ***Social Justice,*** 16:2 (Summer 1989), 1-30.

4022. Seddon, Alfred E. "The Domestic Threat: An FBI View." ***Terrorism,*** 10:3 (1987), 217-218.

4023. Sessions, William S. "The FBI's Mission in Countering Terrorism." ***Terrorism,*** 13:1 (1990), 1-6.

4024. Shank, Gregory. "Counterterrorism and Foreign Policy." ***Crime and Social Justice,*** 27 (1987), 33-65.

4025. _____. "Contragate and Counterterrorism: An Overview." ***Crime and Social Justice,*** 27 (1987), i-xx.

4026. Shultz, George, et al. "U.S. Airliner Hijacked: Passengers Held Hostage." ***Department of State Bulletin,*** (August 1985), 77-82.

4027. _____. "The U.S. Must Retaliate Against Terrorist States." In: B. Szumski, ed. ***Terrorism: Opposing Viewpoints.*** St.Paul, MN.: Greenhaven Press, 1986. pp. 197-203.

4028. _____. "The Struggle Against Terrorism." In: Y. Alexander and A. H. Foxman, eds. ***The 1987 Annual on Terrorism.*** Dordrecht: Martinus Nijhoff, 1988. pp. 347-356.

4029. _____. "The Struggle Against Terrorism." ***New York State Bar Journal,*** 62 (April 1990), 8-13+.

4030. Simpson, Howard R. "War of the Present." ***Foreign Service Journal,*** (October 1985), 27-30.

4031. Sloan, Stephen. "In Search of a Counterterrorism Doctrine." ***Military Review,*** 66:1 (1986), 44-48.

4032. Sofaer, Abraham D. "The War Powers Resolution and Antiterrorist Operations." ***Department of State Bulletin,*** 86 (August 1986), 68-71.

4033. Sprinzak, Ehud. "The Psychopolitical Formation of Extreme Left Terrorism in a Democracy: The Case of the Weathermen." In: W. Reich, ed. ***Origins of Terrorism.*** Cambridge: Cambridge University Press, 1990. pp. 65-85.

4034. Standenmaier, William O. "Options for U.S. National Strategy in the 1980s and Beyond." ***Naval War College Review,*** 34:3 (May-June 1981), 3-14.

4035. Stewart, Bernard L. "Domestic Vulnerabilities." ***Terrorism,*** 10:1 (1987), 51-53.

4036. Stinson, J. L. "Domestic Terrorism in the United States." ***Police Chief,*** 54:8 (1987), 62-65, 67, 69.

4037. Stocking, Kathleen. "Ann Arbor's Famous Radicals, Then and Now: A Personal Remembrance." ***Monthly Detroit,*** 5 (February 1982), 73-82.

4038. Stork, Joe. "Mad Dogs and Presidents." ***MERIP Middle East Report,*** 16 (May/June 1986), 6-10.

4039. Sweet, William. "Anti-Terrorism: New Priority in Foreign Policy." ***Editorial Research Reports,*** (March 27, 1981), 231-248.

4040. "TVI Interview: Ambassador Robert M. Sayre on Antiterrorist Policy." ***TVI Journal,*** 5:3 (1985), 1-3.

4041. Tanham, George K. "Getting the Priorities Right." ***Pacific Defense Reporter,*** (March 1987), 49,54.

4042. Taulbee, James L. "Retaliation, Deterrence, Terrorism and the Reagan Administration." ***Defence Analysis,*** 1:4 (1985), 281-283.

4043. "Terror is a War..." ***Marines,*** (March 1985), 12-13.

4044. "Terrorism and Attacks on Americans." ***National Defense,*** 74:453 (December 1989), 48-50.

4045. Terrorist Research and Analytical Center. "FBI Analysis of Terrorist Incidents in the United States: 1986." In: Y. Alexander and A. H. Foxman, eds. ***The 1987 Annual on Terrorism.*** Dordrecht: Martinus Nijhoff, 1988. pp. 191-202.

4046. "Terrorists Attacks on Foreign Service Posts Overseas." ***State,*** (May 1983), 6-9

4047. Toensing, Victoria. "Future U.S. Policy and Action: The Justice Department's Approach to Terrorism." ***Terrorism,*** 11:6 (1988), 553-557.

4048. Trent, Darrell M. "Reagan Administration Policy on International Terrorism." In: W. J. Taylor, S.A. Maaranen and J. W. Gong, eds. ***Strategic Responses to Conflict in the 1980s.*** Lexington, MA.: Lexington Books, 1984. pp. 93-98.

4049. Turner, Billy M. "America's Bull's Eye for Terrorists?" ***Security Management,*** 31 (June 1987), 42-46.

4050. "U.S. Support of Terrorists is Immoral (The Progressive)." In: B. Szumski, ed. ***Terrorism: Opposing Viewpoints.*** St.Paul, MN.: Greenhaven Press, 1986. pp. 128-132.

4051. "Uncle Sam's Antiterrorism Plan." ***Security Management,*** 24:2 (1980), 39-50.

4052. United States. Department of Justice. Federal Bureau of Investigation. "Terrorism at Home and Abroad: The U.S. Government View." In: M.Stohl, ed. ***The Politics of Terrorism.*** New York: Marcel Dekker, 1988. pp. 295-316.

4053. _____._____._____. Terrorist Research and Analytical Center. Counterterrorism Section. "Terrorism in the United States 1988." In: Y. Alexander and A. H. Foxman, eds. ***The 1988-1989 Annual of Terrorism.*** Dordrecht: Martinus Nijhoff, 1990. pp. 39-82.

4054. Vonier, Thomas. "Not a Fortress: The New Diplomatic Facilities Meant to Thwart Terrorism Need Not Be Unattractive nor Interfere with the Mission of the Foreign Service." ***Foreign Service Journal,*** 63 (June 1986), 22-26.

4055. Vought, Donald B. "Forging a Coherent, Tough Minded National Policy Toward Terrorism." ***TVI Report,*** 8:1 (1988), 39-46.

4056. Wallop, Malcolm. "The Role of Congress." In: U. Ra'anan, et al. ***Hydra of Carnage.*** Lexington, MA.: Heath-Lexington Books, 1986. pp. 251-258.

4057. Watkins, James D. "Countering Terrorism: A New Challenge to Our National Conscience." ***Sea Power,*** (November 1984), 35-37.

4058. Webster, William H. "Fighting Terrorism in the United States." In: B. Netanyahu, ed. ***Terrorism: How the West Can Win.*** New York: Farrar, Straus, Giroux, 1986. pp. 168-170.

4059. _____. "International Terrorism: The FBI's Response." ***International Business Lawyer,*** 15:2 (February 1987), 54-58.

4060. _____. "The FBI and the War Against Terrorism and Espionage." ***Law and National Security Intelligence Report,*** 7:12 (1985), 1-7.

4061. "Wegener and Beckwith Look at Olympics '84." ***TVI Journal,*** 3:2 (1982), 8-13.

4062. Weinberg, Yagil. "The Iran-Contra Crisis and Its Impact on U.S.-Israeli Counterterrorism Cooperation." In: D. C. Livingstone and T. E. Arnold, eds. ***Beyond the Iran-Contra Crisis.*** Lexington, MA.: D.C. Heath & Lexington Books, 1988. pp. 173-190.

4063. Weiss, Ellen R. "Islamic Terrorist Threat in U.S." ***TVI Journal,*** 5:1 (1984), 28-29.

4064. Wells, Ronald A. "Reagan and Terrorism." ***The Reformed Journal,*** 36:6 (June 1986), 2-3.

4065. White, Jonathan R. "The Road to Armageddon: Religion and Domestic Terrorism." ***Quarterly Journal of Ideology,*** 13:2 (1989), 11-21.

4066. Whitehead, John C. "Terrorism: The Challenge and the Response." ***Department of State Bulletin,*** 87:2119 (February 1987), 70-72.

4067. _____. "Contemporary Policy." ***Department of State Bulletin,*** (June 1986), 79-80.

4068. Whitehouse, Charles S. "Future U.S. Policy and Action: Defense Department Perspective." ***Terrorism,*** 11:6 (1988), 546-549.

4069. Wieviorka, Michel. "Defining and Implementing Foreign Policy: The U.S. Experience in Anti-Terrorism." In: Y. Alexander and A. H. Foxman, eds. ***The 1988-1989 Annual of Terrorism.*** Dordrecht: Martinus Nijhoff, 1989. pp. 171-202.

4070. Willenz, Eric. "U.S. Policy on Terrorism: In Search of an Answer." ***Terrorism,*** 9:3 (1987), 225-240.

4071. Williams, Hubert. "The Threat of International Terrorism in the United States: The Police Response." ***Terrorism,*** 10:3 (1987), 219-224.

4072. Winkler, Carol. "Presidents Held Hostage: The Rhetoric of Jimmy Carter and Ronald Reagan." ***Terrorism,*** 12:1 (1989), 21-30.

4073. Wohl, James P. "A Terrorists' Guide to the 1984 Olympics." ***Playboy,*** (May 1983), 90, 182-186.

4074. Woldman, Joel M. "Security of U.S. Embassies and Other Overseas Civilian Installations." ***Congressional Research Service Review,*** (April 1985), 2-3.

4075. Wood, Robert A. "Religion and the Radical Right: The Tie That Binds." ***TVI Report***, 8:1 (1988), 18-22.

4076. _____. "Gordon Kahl: The Legacy of an Extremist Hero." ***TVI Report***, 8:1 (1988), 27-32.

4077. _____. "Satanic Violence in North America." ***TVI Report***, 9:3 (1990), 7-14.

4078. Wootten, James P. "Terrorism: U.S. Policy Options." In: Y. Alexander and A. H. Foxman, eds. ***The 1987 Annual on Terrorism.*** Dordrecht: Martinus Nijhoff, 1988. pp. 433-450.

4079. _____. "Terrorism: U.S. Policy Options." In: Y. Alexander and A. H. Foxman, eds. ***The 1988-1989 Annual of Terrorism.*** Dordrecht: Martinus Nijhoff, 1990. pp. 203-218.

4080. Wurth, Don E. "Protecting the Olympic Torch." ***TVI Journal***, 5:3 (1985), 26-29.

4081. Zinni, A. C. "The Key to Defeating Terrorism." ***Marine Corps Gazette***, 69 (April 1985), 64-65.

4082. Zwerman, Gilda. "Domestic Counterterrorism: U.S. Government Responses to Political Violence on the Left in the Reagan Era." ***Social Justice***, 16:2 (Summer 1989), 31-63.

3. Documents and Reports

4083. American Arab Anti Discrimination Committee. ***The Effect of Anti-Terrorism on Arab-Americans.*** Washington, DC.: American-Arab Anti-Discrimination Committee, 1984. 5p.

4084. American Jewish Congress. ***Terrorism: Historical Perspective on U.S. Congressional Action.*** Washington, D.C.: American Jewish Congress, 1986. 7p.

4085. Anti Defamation League of B'nai B'rith.Civil Rights Division. ***"Propaganda of the Deed": The Far Right's Desperate Revolution.*** ADL Special Report. New York: Anti-Defamation League of B'nai B'rith. 11p.

4086. ***Aryan Nations Far Right Underground Movement.*** Atlanta, GA.: Center for Democratic Renewal, 1986. 64p.

4087. Bass, Gail V., et al. ***Options for U.S. Policy on Terrorism.*** RAND R-2764-RL. Santa Monica, CA.: RAND Corporation, 1981. 13p.

4088. Borg, Parker W. ***Policy Criteria for Responding to Terrorists.*** Washington, D.C.: Brookings Institution, 1986. 16p.

4089. Buckelew, Alvin H. ***Terrorism and the American Response: An Analysis of the Mechanisms Used by the Government of the United States in Dealing With National and International Terrorism.*** Ph.D. Dissertation. San Francisco, CA.: Golden Gate University, 1982. 264p.

4090. Celmer, Marc A. ***United States Response to International Terrorism: A Comprehensive Examination.*** Master's Thesis. Washington, D.C.: The American University, 1985. 312p.

4091. ***Combatting Terrorism: The Official Report of President Reagan's Cabinet Level Task Force Chaired by Vice President George Bush.*** International Security and Terrorism Series: No. 3. Upland, PA.: Diane Publishing Co., 1987. 42p.

4092. Crawford, Richard R. ***America's Response to International Terrorism.*** Carlisle Barracks, PA.: U.S. Army War College, 1986. 57p.

4093. Dearth, Douglas. ***Terrorism: Challenge and Response - The Search for National Strategy.*** Carlisle Barracks, PA.: U.S. Army War College, 1986. 124p.

4094. Eddie, Carroll T. ***Safeguards Against Terrorists: A Handbook for U.S. Military Personnel and Families.*** Maxwell Air Force Base, AL.: Air War College, 1986. 36p.

4095. Farrell, William R. ***The United States Government Response to Terrorism, 1972 - 1980: An Organizational Perspective.*** Ph.D. Dissertation. Ann Arbor, MI.: University of Michigan, 1981. 213p.

4096. Francis, Samuel T. ***The Terrorist Underground in the United States.*** Washington, D.C.: The Nathan Hale Institute, 1984.

4097. Garrett, H. Lawrence III. ***The Legality of Military Responses to Terrorism.*** Defence Issues 2:3. Washington, D.C.: American Forces Information Services, 1986. 4p.

4098. Ginger, James. ***Strategic Management of America's Counter-Terrorist Response: The Role of Boundary Spanning, Networking, and Collateral Organizations in Emergency Management.*** Ph.D. Dissertation. Blacksburg, VA.: Virginia Polytechnic Institute and State University, 1984. 476p.

4099. Hickey, Dennis Van V. ***Taiwan Agents in America: Silencing the Opposition or Combatting Terrorism.*** Austin, TX.: Department of Government, University of Texas at Austin, 1986. 25p.

4100. Hoffman, Bruce. ***Fixing the Blame: International Terrorism and Attacks on Americans.*** RAND P-7221. Santa Monica, CA.: Rand Corporation, 1986. 4p.

4101. _____. ***Recent Trends and Future Prospects of Terrorism in the United States.*** RAND R-3618. Santa Monica, CA.: Rand Corporation, 1988. 71p.

4102. _____. ***Terrorism in the United States During 1985.*** RAND P-7184. Santa Monica, CA.: Rand Corporation, 1986. 11p.

4103. Jenkins, Brian M. ***Let's Not Punish Ourselves for Beirut.*** Santa Monica, CA.: RAND Corporation, 1983. 5p.

4104. _____. ***Terrorism in the United States.*** RAND P-6474. Santa Monica, CA.: RAND Corporation, 1980. 17p.

4105. _____. ***Terrorism Between Prudence and Paranoia.*** RAND P-6949. Santa Monica, CA.: Rand Corporation, 1983. 5p.

4106. Johnson, Robert G. ***An Assessment of Perceptions of United States Army Provost Marshals Pertaining to Counterterrorism Policy and Programs on Army Installations.*** D.P.A. Dissertation. Athens, GA.: University of Georgia, 1981. 234p.

4107. Korntved, H. L. ***Terrorism: American Concerns.*** Maxwell AFB, AL.: Air Command and Staff College, 1987. 42p.

4108. Kumamoto, Robert D. ***International Terrorism and American Foreign Relations, 1945-1976.*** Ph.D. Dissertation. Los Angeles,CA.: University of California at Los Angeles, 1984. 410p.

4109. Laingen, Bruce. ***U.S. Options to Combat International Terrorism.*** Policy Forum, 3:4. Washington, D.C.: National Forum Foundation, 1986. 4p.

4110. Lawrence, John T. ***Intervention Forces: An American Necessity.*** Carlisle Barracks, PA.: U.S. Army War College, 1986. 21p.

4111. Livingstone, Neil C. ***People and Property: The Impact of Terrorism on U.S. Global Policy.*** Washington, DC.: The Brookings Institution, 1982. 29p.

4112. Miller, Clark L. ***"Let Us Die to Make Men Free," Political Terrorism in Post-Reconstruction Mississippi, 1877-1896. (Volumes I and II).*** Ph.D. Dissertation. Minneapolis, MN.: University of Minnesota, 1983. 703p.

4113. Miller, Reuben. ***Governments' Policies and Responses to Acts of International Terrorism.*** Ph.D. Dissertation. Denver, CO.:University of Denver, 1987. 481p.

4114. Mitchell, Thomas H. ***Politically-Motivated Terrorism in North America: The Threat and the Response.*** Ph.D. Dissertation. Ottawa: Carleton University, 1986.

4115. Morland, B. T. ***Covert Action as an Instrument of National Policy.*** Maxwell Air Force Base, AL.: U.S. Air War College, 1986. 35p.

4116. Moss, Donald E. "Domestic Terrorism: Threat Analysis and Countermeasures." Paper Presented at the ***9th Annual Symposium on the Role of Behavioral Science in Physical Security.*** held on April 3-4, 1984 at the Defense Nuclear Agency, Washington, D.C. pp. 7-19.

4117. Motley, James B. ***U.S. Strategy to Counter Domestic Political Terrorism.*** National Security Affairs Monograph Series 83-2. Washington, D.C.: National Defense University Press, 1983.

4118. _____. ***U.S. Counterterrorist Policy: An Analysis of its Strategy and Organization.*** Ph.D. Dissertation. Washington, D.C.: The Catholic University of America, 1983. 197p.

4119. Musolino, Mario J., and Valerie A. Willison. ***Report of the Policy Study Group on Terrorism.*** New York: Criminal Justice Institute, 1985. 140p.

4120. Nanes, Allan S. ***Anti-Terrorist Activities: Issues Raised by the Reagan Administration's Proposals.*** Washington, DC: Congressional Research Service, 1984. 26p.

4121. New York State. Criminal Justice Institute. ***Report of the New York State Policy Study Group on Terrorism.*** Albany, NY.: Criminal Justice Institute, 1985. 110p.

4122. Perez, Frank H. ***Current Trends in Terrorism and the U.S. Response.*** Washington, D.C.: U.S. Department of State, February 3, 1983. 6p.

4123. Phillips, Jimmy V. ***The Future of International Terrorism in California.*** Master's Thesis. Fullerton, CA.: California State University at Fullerton, 1988. 91p.

4124. Raines, Sam. ***Terrorism as a Perceived Threat to US Armed Forces Serving OCONUS and the Army's Program of Addressing That Threat.*** Carlisle Barracks, PA.: U.S. Army War College, 1986. 64p.

4125. Risks International. ***Terrorism in the United States.*** Alexandria, VA.: Risks International, 1982.

4126. Ross, Jeffrey Ian, and Ted R. Gurr. "Why Terrorism Subsides: A Comparative Study of Trends and Groups in Terrorism in Canada and the United States." Paper Presented at the ***Annual Meeting of the American Political Science Association,*** held in September 1987 in Chicago, IL.

4127. Ross, Richard J. ***A Study of Criminal Justice Policy as it Relates to Terrorism Within the United States.*** Ph.D. Dissertation. Los Angeles, CA.: University of Southern California, 1990.

4128. Sample, Travis L. ***The Existential Basis for Effecting a Coherent American Response to Terrorism.*** D.P.A. Los Angeles, CA.: University of Southern California, 1987.

4129. Sater, William F. ***Puerto Rican Terrorists: A Possible Threat to U.S. Energy Installations.*** RAND N-1764-SL. Santa Monica, CA.: RAND Corporation, 1981. 30p.

4130. Simon, Jeffrey. ***U.S. Countermeasures Against International Terrorism.*** RAND R-3840-C31. Santa Monica, CA.: RAND Corporation, 1990. 44p.

4131. Sloan, Stephen. ***Countering Terrorism in the Late 1980s and the 1990s, Future Threats and Opportunities for the United States.*** Maxwell Air Force Base, AL.: Air University, Airpower Research Institute, 1987. 31p.

4132. Steinberg, Jeffrey, et al. ***The Terrorist Threat to the 1984 Los Angeles Olympics: an EIR Multi-Client Special Report.*** New York: Executive Intelligence Review, 1984. 145p.

4133. Tarpley, John J. ***Terrorism: The Challenge and the Response.*** Carlisle Barracks, PA.: U.S. Army War College, 1986. 24p.

4134. Taylor, John B. ***An Historical Review of Olympic Terrorism: The Terrorist Threat to the 1984 Olympic Games and Proposed Security Countermeasures.*** Master's Thesis. Long Beach, CA.: California State University, 1982. 188p.

4135. United States. Congress. House. Committee on Armed Services. Investigations Subcommittee. ***Oversight Hearing on Physical Security at U.S. Military Bases.*** Washington, D.C.: U.S. Government Printing Office, 1983. 60p.

4136. _____._____._____._____._____. ***Physical Security at U.S. Military Bases.*** Washington, D.C.: U.S. Government Printing Office, 1981. 73p.

4137. _____._____._____._____. Readiness Subcommittee. ***U.S. Low Intensity Conflicts, 1899-1990.*** 101st Cong., 2nd sess. Washington, D.C.: U.S. Government Printing Office, 1990. 284p.

4138. _____._____._____. Committee on Foreign Affairs. ***Diplomatic Security.*** Washington, D.C.: U.S. Government Printing Office, 1985. 100p.

4139. _____._____._____._____. Subcommittee on Arms Control, International Security and Science. ***Antiterrorism Policy and Arms Export Controls: Hearing.*** 100th Cong., 2nd sess. Washington,D.C.: U.S.Government Printing Office, 1988. 129p.

4140. _____._____._____._____. Subcommittee on International Operations. ***The Diplomatic Security Program: Hearings and Markup, November 13, 1985 - March 6, 1986 on H.R. 4151.*** 99th Cong., 1st sess. Washington, D.C.: U.S. Government Printing Office, 1986. 340p.

4141. _____._____._____. Committee on the Judiciary. Subcommittee on Civil and Constitutional Rights. ***Federal Capabilities in Crisis Management and Terrorism: Oversight Hearings.*** 96th Cong., 1st sess. Washington, D.C.: U.S. Government Printing Office, 1980. 64p.

4142. _____._____._____._____._____. ***Terrorism: Oversight Hearing.*** 99th Cong., 1st sess. Washington, D.C.: U.S. Government Printing Office, 1987. 327p.

4143. _____._____._____._____._____. ***Domestic Security Measures Relating to Terrorism.*** Washington, D.C.: U.S. Government Printing Office, 1984. 138p.

4144. _____._____._____._____._____. ***CISPES and FBI Counterterrorism Investigations: Hearings.*** Washington, D.C.: U.S. Government Printing Office, 1989. 444p.

4145. _____._____._____. Permanent Select Committee on Intelligence. ***The FBI Investigation of CISPES: Hearings.*** Washington, D.C.: U.S. Government Printing Office, 1989. 36p.

4146. _____._____. Senate. Committee on Appropriations. Subcommittee on the Department of the Treasury, U.S.Postal Service, and General Government Appropriations. ***Drugs and Domestic Terrorism Threat to Arizona and the Southwest Border: Hearings.*** 99th Cong., 2nd sess. Washington, D.C.: U.S. Government Printing Office, 1986. 174p.

4147. _____._____._____. Committee on Armed Services. Subcommittee on Sea Power and Force Projection. ***To Combat Terrorism and Other Forms of Unconventional Warfare: Hearing.*** 99th Cong., 2nd sess. Washington, D.C.: U.S. Government Printing Office, 1987. 45p.

4148. _____._____._____. Committee on Governmental Affairs. ***Threat of Terrorism and Government Responses to Terrorism: Hearings.*** 101st Cong., 1st sess. Washington, D.C.: U.S. Government Printing Office, 1990. 113p.

4149. _____._____._____._____. ***Vulnerability of Telecommunications and Energy Resources to Terrorism: Hearings.*** 101st Cong., 1st sess. Washington, D.C.: U.S. Government Printing Office, 1989. 396p.

4150. _____._____._____. Committee on the Judiciary. Subcommittee on Security and Terrorism. ***FBI Oversight Hearings.*** 97th Cong., 2nd sess. Washington, D.C.: U.S. Government Printing Office, 1982.

4151. _____._____._____._____._____. ***Firearms Felonies by Foreign Diplomats: Hearings on S.2771.*** 98th Cong., 2nd sess. Washington, D.C.: U.S. Government Printing Office, 1985.

4152. _____._____._____._____._____. ***Domestic Security (LEVI) Guidelines: Hearings.*** 97th Cong., 2nd sess. Washington, D.C.: U.S. Government Printing Office, 1983. 587p.

4153. _____._____._____. Select Committee on Intelligence. ***The FBI and CISPES.*** Washington, D.C.: U.S. Government Printing Office, 1989. 138p.

4154. _____. Department of Justice. Federal Bureau of Investigation. ***Terrorism in the United States.*** Washington, D.C.: U.S. Government Printing Office, 1987-. Annual.

4155. _____._____._____. Terrorist Research and Analytical Center. ***FBI Analysis of Terrorist Incidents in the United States.*** Washington, D.C.: U.S. Government Printing Office, 1984-. Annual.

4156. _____. Department of State. Bureau of Diplomatic Security. ***Significant Incidents of Political Violence Against Americans, 1989.*** Washington, D.C.: U.S. Government Printing Office, 1990. 35p.

4157. _____._____. Bureau of Public Affairs. ***Combating Terrorism.*** Washington, D.C.: U.S. Government Printing Office, 1982. 30p.

4158. _____. Department of the Army. ***Personnel Security Precautions Against Acts of Terrorism.*** Washington, D.C.: U.S. Department of the Army, Headquarters, 1978 and 1983.

4159. _____. General Accounting Office. ***Domestic Terrorism: Prevention Efforts in Selected Federal Courts and Mass Transit Systems: Report.*** Washington, D.C.: U.S. Government Printing Office, 1988. 116p.

4160. _____. Vice President's Task Force on Combatting Terrorism. ***Public Report of the Vice President's Task Force on Terrorism.*** Washington, D.C.: U.S. Government Printing Office, 1986. 34p.

4161. Wilson, T. G. ***International Terrorism and the United States: Policy Considerations for the 1990's.*** Carlisle Barracks, PA.: Army War College, 1990. 114p.

4162. Wootten, James P. ***Terrorism: U.S. Policy Options.*** Washington, D.C.: Library of Congress. Congressional Research Service, 1989. 14p.

b. CANADA

1. Books

4163. De Vault, Carole, and William Johnson. ***The Informer: Confessions of an Ex-Terrorist.*** Toronto: Fleet Books, 1982. 282p.
4164. Fournier, Louis. ***FLQ: The Anatomy of an Underground Movement.*** Toronto: N.C. Press, 1984. 372p.
4165. Jacobs, Jane. ***The Question of Separatism: Quebec and the Struggle Over Sovereignty..*** New York: Random House, 1980.
4166. Jiwa, Salim. ***The Death of Air India Flight 182.*** London: Allen & Co., 1986.
4167. Loomis, Dan G. ***Not Much Glory: Quelling the FLQ.*** Ottawa: Deneau, 1985. 167p.
4168. Torrance, Judy. ***Public Violence in Canada, 1967-1982.*** Kingston, Ont.: McGill--Queens University Press, 1986.

2. Journal Articles

4169. Abrams, Terry. "Protecting the Spirit of the Winter Olympics." ***Security Management,*** 32:4 (April 1988), 38-49.
4170. "Action Directe Communique, Anti-Apartheid Bombings, September 4, 1985." ***Open Road, Vancouver,*** (Spring 1986)
4171. Aunger, Edmund A. "Political Violence in Canada: The Case of New Brunswick." In: J. Darby, N. Dodge and A. C. Hepburn, eds. ***Political Violence: Ireland in a Comparative Perspective.*** Ottawa: University of Ottawa Press, 1990. pp. 130-138.
4172. Bain, George A. "The Seizure of the Turkish Embassy in Ottawa." ***TVI Report,*** 6:2 (Fall 1985), 20-22.
4173. Beatty, Perrin. "Counter-Terrorism: The Role of the RCMP." ***Royal Canadian Mounted Police Gazette,*** 48:3 (1986), 1-3.
4174. Borovoy, Alan A. "Terrorism, Security and the Surveillance Powers of the Canadian Security Intelligence Service." In: P. Hanks and J. D. McManus, eds. ***National Security: Surveillance and Accountability in a Democratic Society.*** Cowansville, Que.: Les Editions Yvon Blais, 1990. pp. 243-246.
4175. Canada. Senate. Special Committee on Terrorism and the Public Safety. "Terrorism." In: Y. Alexander and A. H. Foxman, eds. ***The 1987 Annual on Terrorism.*** Dordrecht: Martinus Nijhoff, 1988. pp. 481-500.
4176. Charters, David. "The October Crisis: Implications for Canada's Internal Security." In: B. Macdonald, ed. ***Terror.*** Toronto: Canadian Institute of International Studies, 1987. pp. 55-72.
4177. Chisholm, Robert. "Current Trends and Canadian Interests." In: ***The Fight Against Terrorism.*** Toronto: The Mackenzie Institute for the Study of Terrorism, Revolution and Propaganda, 1989. pp. 19-30.

4178. Collins, Anne. "Trial by CSIS: All that the Canadian Secret Service has on Nicholas Moumdjian is Innuendo. But Innuendo May be All the Secret Service Needs to Kick Him Out of the Country." ***Saturday Night***, 104:8 (August 1989), 21-29+.

4179. Corrado, Raymond R. "Political Crime in Canada." In: R. Linden, ed. ***Criminology: A Canadian Perspective***. Toronto: Holt, Rinehart and Winston of Canada, 1987. pp. 295-319.

4180. "Counter-Measures (Against Terrorist Activity in Canada)." ***International Perspectives***, (September-October 1985), 11-13.

4181. Crelinsten, Ronald D. "Power and Meaning: Terrorism as a Struggle Over Access to the Communication Structure." In: P. Wilkinson and A. M. Stewart, eds. ***Contemporary Research on Terrorism***. Aberdeen: Aberdeen University Press, 1987. pp. 419-

4182. _____. "The Internal Dynamics of the FLQ During the October Crisis of 1970." ***Journal of Strategic Studies***, 10:4 (December 1987), 59-89.

4183. _____. "The Internal Dynamics of the FLQ During the October Crisis of 1970." In: D. C. Rapoport, ed. ***Inside Terrorist Organizations***. New York: Columbia University Press, 1988. pp. 59-89.

4184. _____. "Terrorism and Hostage Taking." In: J. M. MacLatchie, ed. ***Insights into Violence in Contemporary Canadian Society***. Ottawa: John Howard Society of Canada, 1987. pp. 250-254.

4185. "Embassy Attack." ***International Perspectives***, 40:2 (May-June 1985), 8-9.

4186. Gallagher, Tim. "Sikh Militants Fire on Their Own: A Conspiracy by Pro-Khalistan Terrorists is Linked to the Shooting of a Combative Editor." ***Western Report***, 3:34 (September 12, 1988), 30-33.

4187. _____, and Terry Johnson. "The Air India Breakthrough (Arrest of Reyat in England)." ***Western Report***, 3:5 (February 22, 1988), 42-43.

4188. Hadwen, John G. "The Phenomenon of Terrorism - A Canadian Perspective." In: B. Macdonald, ed. ***Terror***. Toronto: Canadian Institute of Strategic Studies, 1987. pp. 31-33.

4189. Inkster, N. D. "Counterterrorism: The Role of the RCMP." In: P. Hanks and J. D. McManus, eds. ***National Security: Surveillance and Accountability in a Democratic Society***. Cowansville, Que.: Les Editions Yvon Blais, 1990. pp. 253-260.

4190. Kaplan, Robert. "Canada's International Role in Combating Terrorism." In: B. Macdonald, ed. ***Terror***. Toronto: Canadian Institute of International Studies, 1987. pp. 145-149.

4191. Kelleher, James. "Fighting Terrorism and International Crime." In: Y. Alexander and A. H. Foxman, eds. ***The 1987 Annual on Terrorism***. Dordrecht: Martinus Nijhoff, 1988. pp. 371-376.

4192. _____. "The Counterterrorism Program of the Government of Canada: Recent Developments." In: P. Hanks and J. D. McManus, eds. ***National Security: Surveillance and Accountability in a Democratic Society***. Cowansville, Que.: Les Editions Yvon Blaise, 1990. pp. 247-252.

4193. Kelly, Michael J., and Thomas H. Mitchell. "The Story of Internal Conflict in Canada: Problems and Prospects." ***Conflict Quarterly***, 2:1 (1981), 10-17.

4194. _____. "The Seizure of the Turkish Embassy in Ottawa: Managing Terrorism and the Media." In: U. Rosenthal, M. T. Charles and P. Hart, eds. ***Coping with Crisis***. Sprigfield, IL.: Charles C. Thomas, 1989. pp. 117-138.

4195. McKinley, Michael, and R. Dolphin. "Bombers for Peace: The Alleged Cold Lake Plotters (Direct Action) are Stopped." ***Alberta Report,*** (February 7, 1983), 18-19.

4196. McMurtry, John. "States of Terror." ***Canadian Forum,*** 67:776-777 (February--March 1988), 6-8.

4197. "Mission Under Control." ***Liaison,*** 12:8 (1986), 4-11.

4198. Mitchell, Thomas H. "Terrorism and Hostage-Taking." In: J. M. MacLatchie, ed. ***Insights into Violence in Contemporary Canadian Society.*** Ottawa: John Howard Society of Canada, 1987. pp. 262-266.

4199. Perusse, Daniel. "Terror in Quebec City." ***Reader's Digest (Canada),*** 134:804 (August 1989), 108-114, 116+.

4200. "Revolutionary Cells and Rote Zora, Discussion Paper on the Peace Movement." ***Open Road (Vancouver),*** (Spring 1986)

4201. "Revolutionary Terrorism in Canada? It's Coming, Say the Experts." ***Liaison,*** 7:4 (1981), 2-7.

4202. Ross, Jeffrey Ian. "Attributes of Domestic Political Terrorism in Canada, 1960-1985." ***Terrorism,*** 11:3 (1988), 213-234.

4203. _____. "An Event Data Base on Political Terrorism in Canada: Some Conceptual and Methodological Problems." ***Conflict Quarterly,*** 8:2 (Spring 1988), 47-64.

4204. Rutan, Gerard F. "The Canadian Security Intelligence Service: Squaring the Demands of National Security with Canadian Democracy." ***Conflict Quarterly,*** 5:4 (Fall 1985), 17-30.

4205. Saunders, G. "RCMP (Royal Canadian Mounted Police) Special Emergency Response Team." ***Royal Canadian Mounted Police Gazette,*** 49:3 (1987), 1-7.

4206. Sewell, J. "Searching for Suspects (Direct Action)." ***Canadian Forum,*** (April 1983), 36-37.

4207. Shoniker, Peter A. "Canada: New Crossroads for International Terror." In: B. Macdonald, ed. ***Terror.*** Toronto: Canadian Institute of International Studies, 1987. pp. 43-54.

4208. Small, Alexis. "Living Dangerously." ***Canadian Lawyer,*** 13:8 (1989), 18-20.

4209. Smith, G. Davidson. "A Positive Approach to Terrorism: The Case for an Elite Counter-Force in Canada." ***RUSI Journal,*** 129 (September 1984), 17-22.

4210. _____. "The Military in Aid of the Civil Power: Limits in a Democratic Society." ***Canadian Defence Quarterly,*** 13 (Spring 1984), 27-33.

4211. Starnes, John. "Terrorism and the Canadian Security Intelligence Service." In: B. Macdonald, ed. ***Terror.*** Toronto: Canadian Institute of International Studies, 1987. pp. 137-144.

4212. Stevens, D. C. "International Terrorism: The Canadian Perspective." ***Defense Quarterly,*** 16:1 (Summer 1986), 39-41.

4213. Wallack, Michael. "Terrorism and Hostage Taking." In: J. M. MacLatchie, ed. ***Insights into Violence in Contemporary Canadian Society.*** Ottawa: John Howard Society of Canada, 1987. pp. 255-261.

4214. Whyte, Kenneth, et al. "Flight 182: An Omen for Alberta?" ***Alberta Report,*** 12 (July 8, 1985), 30-31.

3. Documents and Reports

4215. Beno, Ernest B. ***Canadian Public Policy for Countering Terrorism.*** Master's Thesis. Kingston, ON.: Queen's University, 1990. 88p.

4216. Canada. Security Intelligence Review Committee. ***Annual Report 1987-88.*** Ottawa: Security Intelligence Review Committee, 1988. 81p.

4217. Crelinsten, Ronald D. ***Limits to Criminal Justice in the Control of Insurgent Political Violence: A Case Study of the October Crisis of 1970.*** Ph.D. Dissertation. Montreal: University of Montreal, 1985. 591p.

4218. Fromm, Paul. ***Political Terrorism and the Peace Movement in Canada.*** C-Far Canadian Issues Series, 10. Toronto: Citizens for Foreign Aid Reform, 1985. 20p.

4219. Kavchak, Andrew. ***Canadian National Security and the CSIS Act.*** Mackenzie Paper No. 12. Toronto: Mackenzie Institute for the Study of Terrorism, Revolution and Propaganda, 1989. 40p.

4220. Kellett, Anthony. ***Contemporary International Terrorism and Its Impact on Canada.*** ORAE Report No. R100. Ottawa: Department of National Defence, 1988.

4221. Kelly, William M. ***Terrorism: The Report of the Senate Special Committee on Terrorism and the Public Safety.*** Ottawa: Senate, Special Committee on Terrorism and Public Safety, 1987. 151p.

4222. Macdonald, Donald. ***The Role of Parliaments Against Terrorism.*** Ottawa: Library of Parliament, Research Branch, 1987. 18p.

4223. Ross, Jeffrey Ian. "Domestic Political Terrorism in Canada: 1960-1985: A Statistical and Critical Analysis." Paper Presented at the ***Annual Meeting of the Canadian Political Science Association,*** held on June 6, 1987 in Hamilton, Ontario. 35p.

4224. Shoniker, Peter A. ***The Efficacy of Negotiation and Assault as a Response to the Terrorist Act of Hostage Taking in Urban Canada: An Evaluation of the Metropolitan Toronto Police Dept. Experience.*** M.A. Thesis. University of Ottawa, 1981.

4225. St. John, Peter. "Terrorist Threat to Canada." Paper Presented at the ***Canadian Association of Security and Intelligence Studies Meeting of the Learned Societies,*** held on June 11, 1988 in Windsor, Ontario.

C. EUROPE

a. GENERAL WORKS

1. Books

4226. Alexander, Yonah, and K. A. Myers, eds. ***Terrorism in Europe.*** London: Croom Helm, 1982. 216p.
4227. Aston, Clive C. ***A Contemporary Crisis: Political Hostage Taking and the Experience of Western Europe.*** Westport, CT.: Greenwood Press, 1982. 217p.
4228. Clutterbuck, Richard L. ***Terrorism, Drugs and Crime in Europe After 1992.*** London: Frank Cass, 1990. 231p.
4229. Gutteridge, William, ed. ***Contemporary Terrorism.*** New York: Facts on File, 1986. 226p.
4230. Harris, Geoffrey. ***The Dark Side of Europe: The Extreme Right Today.*** Edinburgh: Edinburgh University Press, 1990. 213p.
4231. Hill, Ray. ***The Other Face of Terror: Inside Europe's Neo-Nazi Network.*** London: Graffon, 1988. 315p.
4232. Mommsen, Wolfgang J., and G. Hirschfeld. ***Social Protest, Violence and Terror in Nineteenth and Twentieth Century Europe.*** London: Macmillan, 1982. 411p.
4233. Von Beyme, Klaus, ed. ***Right-Wing Extremism in Western Europe.*** London: Frank Cass, 1988. 110p.

2. Journal Articles

4234. Adams, Nathan M. "Profiteers of Terror: The European Connection." ***Reader's Digest,*** 129 (August 1986), 49-55.
4235. Adolph, Robert B. "Terrorism: The Causal Factors - The Italian Red Brigades and the West German Baader Meinhof Gang." ***Military Intelligence,*** 8:3 (1982), 49-57.
4236. Alexander, Yonah. "The European - Middle East Terrorist Connection." ***International Journal of Comparative and Applied Criminal Justice,*** 13:2 (Fall 1989), 1-5.
4237. Anderson, G. "Europeans Move to Thwart Terrorism." ***International Journal on World Peace,*** 4:3 (1987), 87-88.
4238. Aston, Clive C. "Political Hostage Taking in Western Europe: A Statistical Analysis. In: L. Z Freedman and Y. Alexander, eds. ***Perspectives on Terrorism.*** Wilmington, DE.: Scholarly Resources, 1983. pp. 99-130.
4239. _____. "Political Hostage-Taking in Western Europe." In: W. Gutteridge, ed. ***Contemporary Terrorism.*** New York: Facts on File, 1986. pp. 57-83.
4240. Bale, Jeffrey M. "Right Wing Terrorists and the Extraparliamentary Left in Post-World War II Europe: Collusion or Manipulation?." ***Berkeley Journal of Sociology,*** 32 (1987), 193-236.
4241. Besancon, Alain. "The First European Terrorists." In: B. Netanyahu, ed. ***Terrorism: How the West Can Win.*** New York: Farrar, Strauss, Giroux, 1986. pp. 44-47.
4242. Biggs-Davison, John. "Terrorism and the Superpowers." ***RUSI & Brassey's Defense Yearbook,*** (1987), 205-216.

4243. Blinken, A. J. "A Coalition of Violence in Europe - The New Terrorism." ***New Republic***, 192:3 (1985), 12-13.
4244. Clutterbuck, Richard L. "Terrorism and the Security Forces in Europe." ***Army Quarterly***, 111 (January 1981), 12-29.
4245. _____. "RUSI Forum: Terrorism, Political Violence and European Security." ***Armed Force***, (February 1986), 59-60.
4246. Coogan, Kevin, and Martin A. Lee. "Killers on the Right." ***Mother Jones***, 12:4 (1987), 40-46+.
4247. Corrado, Raymond R. "Ethnic and Ideological Terrorism in Western Europe." In: M.Stohl, ed. ***The Politics of Terrorism.*** 2nd ed. New York: Marcel Dekker, 1983. pp. 255-326.
4248. _____, and Rebecca Evans. "Ethnic and Ideological Terrorism in Western Europe." In: M. Stohl, ed. ***The Politics of Terrorism.*** New York: Marcel Dekker, 1988. pp. 373-444.
4249. Crozier, Brian. "International Terrorism: How NATO Became Impotent." ***The American Legion***, 120:6 (1986), 18-19, 54.
4250. Feltes, Thomas. "European Terrorism: Decline or Rebirth at the Beginning of the 1990's?." ***International Journal of Comparative and Applied Criminal Justice***, 13:2 (Fall 1989), 17-25.
4251. Freestone, David. "Legal Responses to Terrorism: Towards European Cooperation?" In: J. Lodge, ed. ***Terrorism - A Challenge to the State.*** Oxford: Martin Robertson, 1981. pp. 195-224.
4252. Frey, Linda, and Marsha Frey. "Terrorism in Early Modern Europe: The Camisard Revolt." In: P. Wilkinson and A. M. Stewart, eds. ***Contemporary Research on Terrorism.*** Aberdeen: Aberdeen University Press, 1987. pp. 107-120.
4253. Fritzsche, Peter. "Terrorism in the Federal Republic of Germany and Italy: Legacy of the '68 Movement or 'Burden of Fascism'?." ***Terrorism and Political Violence***, 1:4 (October 1989), 466-481.
4254. George, Bruce. "Working Group on Terrorism: Final Report." In: Y. Alexander and A. H. Foxman, eds. ***The 1987 Annual on Terrorism.*** Dordrecht: Martinus Nijhoff, 1988. pp. 501-524.
4255. Geysels, F. "Europe from the Inside." ***Policing***, 6:1 (Spring 1990), 338-354.
4256. Hoffman, Bruce. "Right-Wing Terrorism in Europe." ***Conflict***, 5:3 (1984), 185-210.
4257. _____. "Right Wing Terrorism in Europe." ***Orbis***, 28 (Spring 1984), 16-27.
4258. Horchem, Hans J. "Terrorism in Western Europe." In: R. Clutterbuck, ed. ***The Future of Political Violence.*** London: Macmillan, 1986. pp. 145-158.
4259. Husbands, Christopher. "Contemporary Right-Wing Extremism in Western European Democracies: A Review Article." ***European Journal of Political Research***, 9 (March 1981), 75-100.
4260. Janke, Peter. "Europe: Regional Assessment." In: R. Clutterbuck, ed. ***The Future of Political Violence.*** London: Macmillan, 1986. pp. 93-101.
4261. Jenkins, Philip. "Under Two Flags: Provocation and Deception in European Terrorism." ***Terrorism***, 11:4 (1988), 275-288.
4262. Kellen, Konrad. "The New Challenge: Euroterrorism Against NATO." ***TVI Journal***, 5:4 (1985), 3-5.
4263. Kriegel, Annie. "Public Opinion, Intellectuals and Terrorism in Western Europe." In: B. Netanyahu, ed. ***International Terrorism: Challenge and Response.*** New Brunswick, NJ.: Transaction Books, 1981. pp. 172-179.
4264. Labich, K. "Coping with the Fear of Terror." ***Fortune***, 113 (May 26, 1986), 57-59.

4339. "Steps Taken to Prevent Terrorist Crimes. (Great Britain)." ***Journal of Criminal Law***, 54:3 (August 1990), 342-244.

4340. Walker, Clive. "The Jellicoe Report on the Prevention of Terrorism (Temporary Provisions) Act 1976." ***Modern Law Review***, 46 (July 1983), 484-492.

4341. _____. "Prevention of Terrorism (Temporary Provisions) Act 1984." ***Modern Law Review***, 47:6 (1984), 704-713.

4342. Warner, Bruce W. "Extradition Law and Practice in the Crucible of Ulster, Ireland and Great Britain: A Metamorphosis?" In: P. Wilkinson and A. M. Stewart, eds. ***Contemporary Research on Terrorism***. Aberdeen: Aberdeen University Press, 1987. pp. 475-509.

4343. _____. "Extradition Law and Practice in the Crucible of Ulster, Ireland and Great Britain: A Metamorphosis?" ***Conflict Quarterly***, 7 (Winter 1987), 57-92.

4344. West, Iain, and Hugh Johnson. "The Iranian Embassy Siege." ***The Medico-Legal Journal***, 51:4 (1983), 202-216.

4345. Wilkinson, Paul. "Introduction." In: P. Wilkinson, ed. ***British Perspectives on Terrorism***. London: Allen & Unwin, 1981. pp. 1-12.

4346. _____. "Introduction." (Issue) ***Terrorism***, 5:1-2 (1981), 1-12.

4347. _____. "British Policy on Terrorism: An Assessment." In: J. Lodge, ed. ***The Threat of Terrorism***. Brighton: Wheatsheaf Books, 1988. pp. 29-56.

4348. Zellick, Graham. "Spies, Subversives, Terrorists and the British Government: Free Speech and Other Casualties." ***William and Mary Law Review***, 31 (Spring 1990), 773-821.

3. Documents and Reports

4349. Colville, J. M. A. ***Review of Operation of the Prevention of Terrorism (Temporary Provisions) Act 1984***. London: H.M.S.O., 1987. 70p.

4350. Dellow, John. "London Perspective on International Terrorism." In: B. G. Curtis, ed. ***Outthinking the Terrorist - An International Challenge, Proceedings***. Rockville, MD.: National Criminal Justice Reference Service, 1985. pp. 39-47.

4351. Great Britain. British Information Services. ***British Policy Towards International Terrorism***. Policy Background, August 8, 1986. New York: British Information Services, 1986. 5p.

4352. Green, P. ***Prevention of Terrorism and Its Legislative Process***. Occasional Paper No. 3. Highfield, Southampton: University of Southampton, 1988. 30p.

4353. Janke, Peter. "Terrorism in the United Kingdom." Paper Presented to the ***European Conference for Human Rights and Self Determination***, held in May 1983, in Bern, Switzerland.

4354. Jellicoe, George P. ***Review of Operation of the Prevention of Terrorism (Temporary Provisions) Act, 1976***. Command Paper, 8803. London: H.M.S.O., 1983. 144p.

4355. McGowan, Robert, et al. ***The Day of the S.A.S.: The Inside Story of How Britain Ended the Siege of Princess Gate***. London: Express Newspapers, 1980. 64p.

b2. IRA

1.Books

4356. Bell, J. Bowyer. ***IRA: Tactics and Targets.*** Dublin: Dufour Poolberg Press, 1990. 117p.

4357. Bishop, Patrick, and Eamonn Mallie. ***The Provisional IRA.*** London: Heineman, 1987. 394p.

4358. Feehan, John M. ***Bobby Sands and the Tragedy of Northern Ireland.*** London: The Permanent Press, 1986. 152p.

4359. Kelley, Kevin. ***The Longest War: Northern Ireland and the IRA.*** Westport, CT.: Lawrence Hill, 1982. 354p.

2. Journal Articles

4360. Bell, J. Bowyer. "Case Study IV: The Irish Republican Army." In: D. Carlton and C. Schaerf, ed. ***Contemporary Terror.*** London: Macmillan, 1981. pp. 215-226.

4361. Browne, Vincent. "The IRA's Twenty Years." ***Magill,*** (August 1982), 8-10.

4362. Crenshaw, Martha. "The Persistence of IRA Terrorism." In: Y. Alexander and A. O'Day, eds. ***Terrorism in Ireland.*** London: Croom Helm, 1983. pp. 246-272.

4363. Feehan, John M. "IRA Terrorism is Justified." In: B. Szumski, ed. ***Terrorism: Opposing Viewpoints.*** St.Paul, MN.: Greenhaven Press, 1986. pp. 96-104.

4364. Forbes, T. E. T. "Provisional IRA - A Study in Contradiction." In: B. G. Curtis, ed. ***Outthinking the Terrorist - An International Challenge, Proceedings.*** Rockville, MD.: National Criminal Justice Reference Service, 1985. pp. 63-71.

4365. "Freedom Struggle by the Provisional IRA." In: W. Laqueur, ed. ***The Terrorism Reader.*** New York: Meridian, 1987. pp. 132-133.

4366. Geldard, Ian, and Keith Craig. ***IRA, INLA: Foreign Support and International Connections.*** London: Institute for the Study of Terrorism, 1988. 97p.

4367. Great Britain. Foreign and Commonwealth Office. "Qadhafi and Irish Terrorism." In: Y. Alexander, ed. ***The 1986 Annual on Terrorism.*** Dordrecht: Martinus Nijhoff, 1987. pp. 247-256.

4368. Guelke, Adrian. "Loyalist and Republican Perceptions of the Northern Ireland Conflict: The UDA and the Provisional IRA." In: P. H. Merkl, ed. ***Political Violence and Terror.*** Berkeley, CA.: University of California Press, 1986. pp. 91-122.

4369. Hachey, Thomas. "A Courtship with Terrorism: The IRA Yesterday, Today and Tomorrow." In: D. Rapoport and Y. Alexander, eds. ***The Rationalization of Terrorism.*** Frederick, MD.: University Publications of America, 1982. pp. 178-187.

4370. Heskin, Ken. "The Terrorists' Terrorist: Vincent Browne's Interview with Dominic McGlinchey." In: Y. Alexander and A. O'Day, eds. ***Ireland's Terrorist Dilemma.*** Dordrecht: Martinus Nijhoff, 1986. pp. 97-108.

4371. "Inside the IRA: How Ireland's Outlaws Fight Their Endless War: Special Report." ***Life,*** 8 (October 1985), 40-46.

4372. Kearney, Robert N. "The IRA's Strategy of Failure." ***The Crane Bag,*** 4:2 (1980), 62-70.

4373. Kelly, Keith J. "The Survival of the IRA." ***America,*** (May 24, 1980), 440-443.
4374. Maloney, Ed. "The IRA." ***Magill,*** (September 1980), 13-28.
4375. Mansfield, Don. "The Irish Republican Army and Northern Ireland." In: B. E. O'Neill, W. R. Heaton and D. J. Alberts, eds. ***Insurgency in the Modern World.*** Boulder, CO.: Westview Press, 1980. pp. 45-86.
4376. McKinley, Michael. "'Irish Mist': Eight Clouded Views of the Provisional Irish Republican Army." ***Australian Quarterly,*** 57:3 (1985), 203-214.
4377. _____. "The Irish Republican Army and Terror International: An Inquiry into the Material Aspects of the First Fifteen Years." In: P. Wilkinson and A. M. Stewart, eds. ***Contemporary Research on Terrorism.*** Aberdeen: Aberdeen University Press, 1987. pp. 186-229.
4378. _____. "Lavish Generosity: The American Dimension of International Support for the Provisional Irish Republican Army, 1968-1983." ***Conflict Quarterly,*** (Spring 1987), 20-42.
4379. Morrison, Danny. "The Provos Will Not Lay Down Their Arms." ***Forthnight,*** 182 (December 1982), 4-5.
4380. Moxon-Browne, Edward. "Terrorism in Northern Ireland: The Case of the Provisional IRA." In: J. Lodge, ed. ***Terrorism: A Challenge to the State.*** New York: St. Martin's, 1981. pp. 146-163.
4381. _____. "The Water and the Fish: Public Opinion and the Provisional IRA in Northern Ireland." In: P. Wilkinson, ed. ***British Perspectives on Terrorism.*** London: Allen & Unwin, 1981. pp. 41-72.
4382. _____. "The Water and the Fish: Public Opinion and the Provisional IRA in Northern Ireland." ***Terrorism,*** 5:1-2 (1981), 41-72.
4383. O'Ballance, Edgar. "IRA Leadership Problems." ***Terrorism,*** 5:1-2 (1981), 73-82.
4384. _____. "IRA Leadership Problems." In: P. Wilkinson, ed. ***British Perspectives on Terrorism.*** London: Allen & Unwin, 1981. pp. 73-82.
4385. O'Brien, Conor Cruise. "Terrorism Under Democratic Conditions: The Case of the IRA." In: M. Crenshaw, ed. ***Terrorism, Legitimacy and Power.*** Middletown, CT.: Wesleyan University Press, 1983. pp. 91-104.
4386. Paisley, Ian, Norah Bradford and John Taylor. "IRA Terrorism is Not Justified." In: B. Szumski, ed. ***Terrorism: Opposing Viewpoints.*** St.Paul, MN.: Greenhaven Press, 1986. pp. 105-112.
4387. Smyth, Jim. "A Discredited Cause? The IRA and Support for Political Violence." In: Y. Alexander and A. O'Day, eds. ***Ireland's Terrorist Trauma.*** New York: Harvester Wheatsheaf, 1989. pp. 101-126.
4388. "TVI Report Profiles: Provisional Irish Republican Army (PIRA)." ***TVI Report,*** 8:2 (1988), 13-16.
4389. Tugwell, Maurice A. "Politics and Propaganda of the Provisional IRA." In: P. Wilkinson, ed. ***British Perspectives on Terrorism.*** London: Allen & Unwin, 1981. pp. 13-40.
4390. _____. "Politics and Propaganda of the Provincial IRA." ***Terrorism,*** 5:1-2 (1981), 13-40.
4391. White, Barry. "From Conflict to Violence: The Re-Emergence of the IRA and the Loyalist Response." In: J. Darby, ed. ***Northern Ireland : The Background to the Conflict.*** Syracuse, NY.: Syracuse University Press, 1983. pp. 181-196.
4392. White, Robert W. "From Peaceful Protest to Guerrilla War: Micromobilization of the Provisional Irish Republican Army." ***American Journal of Sociology,*** 94:6 (1989), 1277-1302.

4393. Wilkinson, Paul. "The Provisional IRA: An Assessment in the Wake of the 1981 Hunger Strike." ***Government and Opposition***, 7:2 (1982), 140-156.

3. Documents and Reports

4394. Collins, Timothy. ***The IRA: An Examination of a Terrorist Organization.*** Washington, D.C.: Defence Intelligence College, 1986. 30p.

4395. Cronin, Sean. ***IRA Ideology and the Roots of Conflict in Northern Ireland, 1956-1962.*** Ph.D. Dissertation. New York: New School for Social Research, [1981].

4396. Schuetz, Laurence N. ***Arms Transfer to the Irish Republican Army.*** Monterey, CA.: U.S. Naval Postgraduate School, 1987. 167p.

4397. White, Robert W. ***From Peaceful Protest to Guerrilla War: Provisional Irish Republicans.*** Ph.D. Dissertation. Bloomington, IN.: Indiana University, 1987.

b3. NORTHERN IRELAND

1. Books

4398. Alexander, Yonah, and Alan O'Day, eds. ***Terrorism in Ireland.*** London: Croom Helm, 1983. 256p.

4399. _____. _____, eds. ***Ireland's Terrorist Dilemma.*** International Studies in Terrorism, 2. Dordrecht: M. Nijhoff, 1986. 286p.

4400. _____. _____, eds. ***Ireland's Terrorist Trauma: Interdisciplinary Perspectives.*** New York: Harvester Wheatsheaf, 1989. 258p.

4401. Bell, J. Bowyer. ***The Gun in Politics: An Analysis of Irish Political Conflict, 1916-1986.*** New Brunswick, NJ.: Transaction Books, 1987. 371p.

4402. Bew, Paul, and H. Patterson. ***The British State and the Ulster Crisis.*** London: Verso, 1985. 151p.

4403. Boal, Frederick, and J. N. H. Douglas. ***Integration and Division: Geographical Perspectives on the Northern Ireland Problem.*** New York: Academic Press, 1982. 368p.

4404. Boyd, Andrew. ***Northern Ireland, Who is to Blame.*** Dublin: Mercier Press, 1984. 132p.

4405. _____. ***The Informers: A Chilling Account of the Supergrasses in Northern Ireland.*** Dublin: Mercier Press, 1984.

4406. Boyle, Kevin, Tom Hadden and H. Paddy. ***Ten Years in Northern Ireland: The Legal Control of Political Violence.*** Nottingham, Eng.: The Cobden Trust, 1980.

4407. Bradford, Norah. ***A Sword Bathed in Heaven: The Life, Faith and Cruel Death of Rev. Robert Bradford B.Th.M.P.*** Hants, Eng.: Pickering and Inglis, 1984. 160p.

4408. Browne, Vincent, ed. ***The Magill Book of Irish Politics.*** Dublin: Magill Publications, 1982.

4409. Cielou, Robert. ***Spare My Tortured People: Ulster and the Green Border.*** Lisnaskea, Ireland: Whitethorn Press, 1983. 286p.

4410. Clarke, Liam. ***Broadening the Battlefield: The H-Blocks and the Rise of Sinn Fein.*** Dublin: Gill and Macmillan, 1987. 270p.

4411. Conroy, John. ***Belfast Diary: War as a Way of Life.*** Boston, MA.: Beacon Press, 1987. 218p.

4412. Coogan, Tim Pat. ***On the Blanket: The H-Block Story.*** Dublin: Ward River Press, 1980.

4413. Darby, John. ***Northern Ireland: The Background to the Conflict.*** Syracuse, NY.: Syracuse University Press, 1983. 272p.

4414. _____. Nicholas Dodge and A.C. Hepburn. ***Political Violence: Ireland in a Comparative Perspective.*** Ottawa: University of Ottawa Press, 1990. 184p.

4415. ***The Divided Province: The Troubles in Northern Ireland, 1969-1985.*** London: Orbis, 1985. 128p.

4416. Doumitt, Donald P. ***Conflict in Northern Ireland: The History, the Problems and the Challenge.*** American University Studies, Series IX; History; Vol. 5. New York: Peter Lang, 1985. 247p.

4417. Downey, James E. ***Us and Them: Britain - Ireland and the Northern Ireland Question, 1969-1982.*** Dublin: Ward River Press, 1983. 246p.

4418. Flackes, W. D., and S. Elliott. ***Northern Ireland: A Political Directory, 1968-88.*** 3rd rev ed. Belfast: Blackstaff Press, 1989. 400p.

4419. Gallagher, Eric, and Stanley Worrall. ***Christians in Ulster, 1969-1980.*** Oxford: Oxford University Press, 1982.

4420. Galliher, John F., and Jerry L. De Gregory. ***Violence in Northern Ireland: Understanding Protestant Perspectives.*** New York: Holmes and Meier, 1985. 208p.

4421. Garvin, Tom. ***The Evolution of Irish Nationalist Politics.*** Dublin: Gill and Macmillan, 1981.

4422. Gifford, Tony. ***Supergrasses: The Use of Accomplice Evidence in Northern Ireland: A Report.*** London: Cobden Trust, 1984.

4423. Guelke, Adrian. ***Northern Ireland: The International Perspective.*** London: Gill and Macmillan, 1989. 236p.

4424. Heskin, Ken. ***Northern Ireland: A Psychological Analysis.*** New York: Columbia University Press, 1980.

4425. Hogan, Gerard, and Clive Walker. ***Political Violence and the Law in Ireland.*** Manchester: Manchester University Press, 1989. 342p.

4426. Holland, Jack. ***Too Long a Sacrifice: Life and Death in Northern Ireland Since 1969.*** New York: Dodd, Mead, 1981.

4427. Hurley, Kark J. ***Blood on the Shamrock: An American Ponders Northern Ireland 1968-1990.*** Frankfurt am Main: Peter Lang, 1990. 384p.

4428. Lee, A. McClung. ***Terrorism in Northern Ireland.*** New York: General Hall, 1983. 253p.

4429. McCafferty, Nell. ***The Armagh Women.*** Dublin: Co-Op Books, 1981.

4430. McCann, Eamonn. ***War and an Irish Town.*** London: Pluto Press, 1980.

4431. McKittrick, David. ***Despatches from Belfast.*** Belfast: The Blackstaff Press, 1989. 219p.

4432. Messenger, Charles. ***Northern Ireland: The Troubles.*** New York: Gallery Books, 1990. 192p.

4433. Moxon-Browne, Edward. ***Nation, Class and Creed in Northern Ireland.*** Aldershot, Eng.: Gower, 1983. 206p.

4434. Nelson, Sarah. ***Ulster's Uncertain Future: Protestant Political, Paramilitary and Community Groups and the Northern Ireland Conflict.*** Belfast: Appletree Press, 1984.

4435. O'Ballance, Edgar. ***Terror in Ireland: The Heritage of Hate.*** Novato, CA.: Presidio Press, 1981. 287p.

4436. O'Dowd, B. R., and Mike Tomlinson. ***Northern Ireland: Between Civil Rights and Civil War.*** London: CSE Books, 1980.

4437. O'Malley, Padraig. ***The Uncivil Wars: Ireland Today.*** Boston: Houghton Mifflin, 1983. 481p.

4438. Shivers, Lynne, and David Bowman. ***More Than the Troubles: A Common Sense View of the Northern Ireland Conflict.*** Philadelphia, PA.: New Society, 1984.

4439. Taylor, Robert W. ***Families at War: Voices from the Troubles.*** London: BBC Books, 1989. 206p.

4440. Wallace, Martin. ***British Government in Northern Ireland: From Devolution to Direct Rule.*** London: David & Charles, 1982. 187p.

2. *Journal Articles*

4441. Alexander, Yonah, and Alan O'Day. "Introduction: The Persistence of Irish Terrorism." In: Y. Alexander and A. O'Day, eds. ***Ireland's Terrorist Trauma.*** New York: Harvester Wheatsheaf, 1989. pp. 1-12.

4442. Arthur, Paul. "Republican Violence in Northern Ireland: The Rationale." In: J. Darby, N. Dodge and A.C. Hepburn, eds. ***Political Violence: Ireland in a Comparative Perspective.*** Ottawa: University of Ottawa Press, 1990. pp. 11-28.

4443. Aughey, Arthur. "Between Exclusion and Recognition: The Politics of the Ulster Defence Association." ***Conflict Quarterly,*** 5:1 (1985), 40-52.

4444. _____, and Colin J. McIlheney. "The Ulster Defence Association: Paramilitaries and Politics." ***Conflict Quarterly,*** 2:2 (1981/82), 32-45.

4445. _____. "Political Violence in Northern Ireland." In: H. H. Tucker, ed. ***Combating the Terrorists.*** New York: Facts on File, 1988. pp. 75-112.

4446. Bew, Paul. "The Problem of Ulster Terrorism: The Historical Roots." In: Y. Alexander and A. O'Day, eds. ***Terrorism in Ireland.*** London: Croom Helm, 1983. pp. 235-245.

4447. Bonner, David. "Combatting Terrorism: Supergrass Trials in Northern Ireland." ***Modern Law Review,*** 61:1 (January 1988), 23-53.

4448. Boyce, D. G. "Water for the Fish: Terrorism and Public Opinion." In: Y. Alexander and A. O'Day, eds. ***Terrorism in Ireland.*** London: Croom Helm, 1983. pp. 149-170.

4449. _____. "'A Gallous Story and A Dirty Deed': Political Martyrdom in Ireland Since 1867." In: Y. Alexander and A. O'Day, eds. ***Ireland's Terrorist Dilemma.*** Dordrecht: Martinus Nijhoff, 1986. pp. 7-28.

4450. Bruce, Steve. "Protestantism and Terrorism in Northern Ireland." In: Y. Alexander and A. O'Day, eds. ***Ireland's Terrorist Trauma.*** New York: Harvester Wheatsheaf, 1989. pp. 13-33.

4451. Buckley, Suzann, and P. Lonergan. "Women and the Troubles, 1969-1980." In: Y. Alexander and A. O'Day, eds. ***Terrorism in Ireland.*** London: Croom Helm, 1983. pp. 75-87.

4452. Cairns, Ed, and Melanie Giles. "Colour Naming of Violence-Related Words in Northern Ireland." ***British Journal of Clinical Psychology***, 28:1 (1989), 87-88.

4453. Carlton, Charles. "Judging Without Consensus: The Diplock Courts in Northern Ireland." ***Law and Policy Quarterly***, 3 (April 1981), 225-242.

4454. Carroll, Terrance G. "Disobedience and Violence in Northern Ireland." ***Comparative Political Studies***, 14 (April 1981), 3-30.

4455. _____. "Regulating Conflicts: The Case of Ulster." ***The Political Quarterly***, 51:4 (1980), 451-463.

4456. Charters, David. "The Changing Forms of Conflict in Northern Ireland." ***Conflict Quarterly***, 1 (Fall 1980), 32-39.

4457. _____. "From Palestine to Northern Ireland: British Adaptation to Low Intensity Operations." In: D. A. Charters and M. Tugwell, eds. ***Armies in Low Intensity Conflict***. London: Brassey's, 1989. pp. 169-250.

4458. Chepesiuk, Ron. "Ulster: Up In Arms." ***Journal of Defense and Diplomacy***, 4:10 (October 1986), 42-47.

4459. Cluskey, Frank. "The Irish Response." In: B. Netanyahu, ed. ***International Terrorism: Challenge and Response***. New Brunswick, NJ.: Transaction Books, 1981. pp. 180-186.

4460. Collum, Danny Duncan. "Growing Terror and Limited Rights in Northern Ireland." ***Sojourners***, 18 (March 1989), 6.

4461. Corfe, Tom. "Political Assassination in the Irish Tradition." In: Y. Alexander and A. O'Day, eds. ***Terrorism in Ireland***. London: Croom Helm, 1983. pp. 106-120.

4462. Darby, John. "Northern Ireland: Internal-Conflict Analyses." In: Y. Alexander and A. O'Day, eds. ***Ireland's Terrorist Trauma***. New York: Harvester Wheatsheaf, 1989. pp. 166-177.

4463. _____. "Intimidation and Interaction in a Small Belfast Community: The Water and the Fish." In: J. Darby, N. Dodge and A. C. Hepburn, eds. ***Political Violence: Ireland in a Comparative Perspective***. Ottawa: Ottawa University Press, 1990. pp. 64-82.

4464. Davis, Richard. "Kilson Versus Marighela: The Debate over Northern Ireland Terrorism." In: Y. Alexander and A. O'Day, eds. ***Ireland's Terrorist Dilemma***. Dordrecht: Martinus Nijhoff, 1986. pp. 179-210.

4465. _____. "Irish Republicanism v. Roman Catholicism: The Perennial Debate in the Ulster Troubles." In: Y. Alexander and A. O'Day, eds. ***Ireland's Terrorist Trauma***. New York: Harvester Wheatsheaf, 1989. pp. 34-74.

4466. De Gregory, Jerry, and John F. Galliher. "Northern Ireland: Corrupt Ideologies and the Failure of Government Cagebuilding." In: Y. Alexander and A. O'Day, eds. ***Ireland's Terrorist Trauma***. New York: Harvester Wheatsheaf, 1989. pp. 159-165.

4467. Diplock Commission Report. "Legal Procedures to Deal with Terrorist Activities." ***International Journal of Politics***, 10:1 (1980), 61-67.

4468. Dodd, Norman L. "The Continuing Problem of Terrorism in Northern Ireland." ***Asian Defence Journal***, 8 (August 1981), 33-38.

4469. Dutter, Lee E. "Northern Ireland and Theories of Ethnic Politics." ***The Journal of Conflict Resolution***, 24:4 (1980), 613-640.

4470. Farrell, M. "A Permanent State of Emergency - The Suppression of the Irish Nationalist Revolt in Northern Ireland." In: H. Kochler, ed. ***Terrorism and National Liberation***. Frankfurt: Verlag Peter Lang, 1988. pp. 171-186.

4471. Fields, Rona M. "Terrorised into Terrorist: 'Pete the Para' Strikes Again." In: Y. Alexander and A. O'Day, eds. ***Ireland's Terrorist Trauma.*** New York: Harvester Wheatsheaf, 1989. pp. 178-212.

4472. Findlay, Mark. "Organized Resistance, Terrorism and Criminality in Ireland: The State's Construction and Control Equation." ***Crime and Social Justice,*** 21 (1984), 95-115.

4473. Finn, John E. "Public Support for Emergency (Anti-Terrorist) Legislation in Northern Ireland: A Preliminary Analysis." ***Terrorism,*** 10:2 (1987), 113-124.

4474. Finnane, Mark. "The Inevitability of Politics: Responses to Terrorism in Northern Ireland." In: Y. Alexander and A. O'Day, eds. ***Ireland's Terrorist Trauma.*** New York: Harvester Wheatsheaf, 1989. pp. 127-148.

4475. Foley, Gerry. "Bernadette and the Politics of H-Block." ***Magill,*** (April 1981), 9-21.

4476. Foley, Thomas P. "Public Security and Individual Freedom: The Dilemma of Northern Ireland." ***Yale Journal of World Public Order,*** 8:2 (1982), 284-324.

4477. Frankel, Norman. "Conversations in Ulster." ***Conflict Quarterly,*** 3:1 (1982), 21-35.

4478. "Green and Unpleasant Land." ***New Republic,*** 198 (April 11, 1988), 7-9.

4479. Greer, D. S. "The Admissibility of Confessions under the Northern Ireland (Emergency Provisions) Act." ***Northern Ireland Legal Quarterly,*** 31 (Autumn 1980), 205-238.

4480. Greer, Steven C. "The Supergrass System in Northern Ireland." In: P. Wilkinson and A. M. Stewart, eds. ***Contemporary Research on Terrorism.*** Aberdeen: Aberdeen University Press, 1987. pp. 510-535.

4481. _____. "Supergrasses and the Legal System in Britain and Northern Ireland." ***Law Quarterly Review,*** 102 (April 1986), 198-249.

4482. _____. "The Rise and Fall of the Northern Ireland Supergrass System." ***Criminal Law Review,*** (October 1987), 663-670.

4483. Hadden, Tom, Paddy Hillyard and Kevin Boyle. "How Fair Are the Ulster Trials?." ***New Society,*** (November 13, 1980), 320-322.

4484. Harbinson, H. J., and H. A. Lyons. "A Comparison of Political and Non-Political Murderers in Northern Ireland, 1974-1984." ***Medicine, Science and the Law,*** 26:3 (1986), 193-198.

4485. Harris, Rosemary. "Anthropological Views on 'Violence' in Northern Ireland." In: Y. Alexander and A. O'Day, eds. ***Ireland's Terrorist Trauma.*** New York: Harvester Wheatsheaf, 1989. pp. 75-100.

4486. Hennen, Christopher. "Terrorism in Northern Ireland." ***Military Intelligence,*** (October-December 1984), 17-22.

4487. Heskin, Ken. "The Psychology of Terrorism in Northern Ireland." In: Y. Alexander and A. O'Day, eds. ***Terrorism in Ireland.*** London: Croom Helm, 1983. pp. 88-105.

4488. Hewitt, Christopher. "Catholic Grievances, Catholic Nationalism and Violence in Northern Ireland During the Civil Rights Period." ***British Journal of Sociology,*** 32 (September 1981), 362-380.

4489. _____, and Kathleen Peroff. "Rioting in Northern Ireland: The Effects of Different Policies." ***Journal of Conflict Resolution,*** 24:4 (1980), 593-611.

4490. Hillyard, Paddy, and Janie Percy-Smith. "Converting Terrorists: The Use of Supergrass in Northern Ireland." ***Journal of Law and Society,*** 11:3 (Winter 1984), 335-355.

4491. Hume, John. "The Irish Question: A British Problem." ***Foreign Affairs,*** (Winter 1979/80), 300-313.

4492. Jennings, Anthony. "Justice Under Fire in Ulster." ***New Law Journal***, 138 (September 9, 1988), 644-645.

4493. Kelley, J., and I. McAllister. "Economic Theories of Political Violence in the Northern Ireland Conflict." In: Y. Alexander and A. O'Day, eds. ***Ireland's Terrorist Dilemma.*** Dordrecht: Martinus Nijhoff, 1986. pp. 75-96.

4494. King, Tom. "Northern Ireland: Security Situation." In: Y. Alexander and A. H. Foxman, eds. ***The 1987 Annual on Terrorism.*** Dordrecht: Martinus Nijhoff, 1988. pp. 377-384.

4495. Lebow, Richard N. "Origins of Sectarian Assassination - The Case of Belfast." In: A. D. Buckley and D. D. Olson, eds. ***International Terrorism: Current Research and Future Directions.*** Wayne, NJ.: Avery, 1980. pp. 41-53.

4496. Lee, A. McClung. "The Dynamics of Terrorism in Northern Ireland, 1968-1980." ***Social Research***, 48 (Spring 1981), 100-134.

4497. _____. "Terrorism's Social-Historical Contexts in Northern Ireland." In: L. Kriesberg, ed. ***Research in Social Change Movements, Conflicts and Change, 1983.*** Greenwich, CT.: JAI Press, 1983. pp. 99-131.

4498. _____. "Human Rights in the Northern Ireland Conflict: 1968-1980." ***International Journal of Politics***, 10:1 (1980), 1-146.

4499. Lippman, Matthew. "The Abrogation of Domestic Human Rights: Northern Ireland and the Rule of British Law." In: Y. Alexander and K. A. Myers, eds. ***Terrorism in Europe.*** London: Croom Helm, 1982. pp. 179-208.

4500. "Living in a Catholic Ghetto." ***TVI Journal***, 1:11 (1980), 7-11.

4501. Maguire, Keith. "The Intelligence War in Northern Ireland." ***International Journal of Intelligence and Counterintelligence***, 4 (Summer 1990), 145-165.

4502. Maloney, Ed. "Paisley." ***The Crane Bag***, 4:2 (1980), 23-27.

4503. Mason, Roy. "The H-Block Protest." ***International Journal of Politics***, 10:1 (1980), 129-131.

4504. McCorry, J., and M. Morrissey. "Community, Crime and Punishment in West Belfast." ***Howard Journal of Criminal Justice***, 28:4 (November 1989), 282-290.

4505. McGarry, John, and Brendan O'Leary. "Northern Ireland's Future: What is to be Done?." ***Conflict Quarterly***, 10:3 (Summer 1990), 42-62.

4506. McIlheney, Colin J. "Arbiters of Ulster's Destiny? The Military Role of the Protestant Paramilitaries in Northern Ireland." ***Conflict Quarterly***, 5:2 (1985), 33-40.

4507. McKeown, Michael. "Chronicles: A Register of Northern Ireland's Casualties, 1969-1980." ***The Crane Bag***, 4:2 (1980), 1-5.

4508. McKinley, Michael. "The International Dimensions of Terrorism in Ireland." In: Y. Alexander and A. O'Day, eds. ***Terrorism in Ireland.*** London: Croom Helm, 1983. pp. 3-31.

4509. Moxon-Browne, Edward. "Alienation: The Case of Catholics in Northern Ireland." In: M. Slann and B. Schechterman, eds. ***Multidimensional Terrorism.*** Boulder, CO.: Lynne Rienner, 1987. pp. 95-110.

4510. _____. "The Case of the Catholics in Northern Ireland." ***Journal of Political Science***, 14:1-2 (1986), 74-88.

4511. Mullan, K. "The Politics of Legitimacy and the Northern Ireland Emergency Provisions Act, 1973." ***Canadian Criminal Forum***, 4 (1982), 133-141.

4512. Munck, Ronnie. "Repression, Insurgency and Popular Justice: The Irish Case." ***Crime and Social Justice***, (1984), 81-94.

4513. Murphy, Simon. "The Northern Ireland Conflict, 1968-1982: British and Irish Perspectives." ***Conflict***, 7:3 (1987), 215-232.

4514. Murray, Russell. "Political Violence in Northern Ireland, 1969-1977." In: F. W. Boal and J. N. H. Douglas, eds. ***Integration and Division: Geographic Perspectives on the Northern Ireland Problem.*** London: Academic Press, 1982. pp. 309-332.

4515. Nelson, William R. "New Developments in Terrorist Trails in Northern Ireland." ***Political Communication and Persuasion***, 7:3 (1990), 167-180.

4516. O'Brien, Conor Cruise. "Bobby Sands: Mutations of Nationalism." In: C. C. O'Brien. ***Passions and Cunning.*** London: Weidenfeld and Nicolson, 1988. pp. 199-212.

4517. _____. "Hands Off." ***Foreign Policy***, 37 (Winter 1979-1980), 101-110.

4518. O'Connor, R. "A Report from the Land of Troubles." ***America***, 158 (May 21, 1988), 527-529+.

4519. O'Donoghue, Joseph, and Marry Ann O'Donoghue. "Toward Understanding Group Conflict in Northern Ireland." ***International Journal of Group Tensions***, 11:1-4 (1981), 117-125.

4520. O'Duffy, Brendan, and Brendan O'Leary. "Violence in Northern Ireland, 1969 - June 1989." In: J. McGarry and B. O'Leary, eds. ***The Future of Northern Ireland.*** Oxford: Clarendon Press, 1990. pp. 318-341.

4521. O'Gara, James. "An Irreligious War." ***Commonweal***, (December 2, 1983), 655-660.

4522. Obradovic, Marija. "Causes of the Conflict in Northern Ireland." ***Review of International Affairs***, 34 (October 5, 1983), 29-31.

4523. Patterson, H. "British Governments and the "Protestant Backlash", 1969-1974." In: Y. Alexander and A. O'Day, eds. ***Ireland's Terrorist Dilemma.*** Dordrecht: Martinus Nijhoff, 1986. pp. 231-248.

4524. Pockrass, Robert M. "Terroristic Murder in Northern Ireland: Who is Killed and Why?." ***Terrorism***, 9:4 (1987), 341-359.

4525. Poole, Michael. "The Geographical Location of Political Violence in Northern Ireland." In: J. Darby, N. Dodge and A. C. Hepburn, eds. ***Political Violence: Ireland in a Comparative Perspective.*** Ottawa: University of Ottawa Press, 1990. pp. 48-63.

4526. Raymond, Raymond J. "The United States and Terrorism in Ireland, 1969-1981." In: Y. Alexander and A. O'Day, eds. ***Terrorism in Ireland.*** London: Croom Helm, 1983. pp. 32-52.

4527. Rees, Merlyn. "Terror in Ireland - and Britains Response." ***Terrorism***, 5:1-2 (1981), 83-88.

4528. _____. "Terror in Ireland - and Britain's Response." In: P. Wilkinson, ed. ***British Perspectives on Terrorism.*** London: Allen & Unwin, 1981. pp. 83-88.

4529. _____. "Terror in Ireland and Britain's Response." In: B. Netanyahu, ed. ***International Terrorism: Challenge and Response.*** New Brunswick, NJ.: Transaction Books, 1981. pp. 276-282.

4530. Rice, Thomas H. "Terrorism in Northern Ireland." ***Humanity and Society***, 8:3 (1984), 366-375.

4531. Robertson, Kenneth. "Northern Ireland: Change, Continuity, and Trends." In: A Kurz, ed. ***Contemporary Trends in World Terrorism.*** New York: Praeger, 1987. pp. 32-42.

4532. Robinson, A. A. "The UDA - Life Through Orange-Colored Glasses." ***TVI Journal***, 1:11 (1980), 2-6.

4533. Schmitt, David E. "Biocommunal Conflict and Accommodation in Northern Ireland." ***Terrorism,*** 9:3 (1987), 263-284.

4534. _____. "Equal Employment Opportunity as a Technique Toward the Control of Political Violence: The Case of Northern Ireland's Fair Employment Agency." ***Current Research on Peace and Violence,*** 3:1 (1980), 33-46.

4535. _____. "Ethnic Minorities and the Potential for Violence and Separatist Activity: The Cases of Northern Ireland and the Southwestern United States." ***Current Research on Peace and Violence,*** 7:23 (1984), 128-148.

4536. Shannon, Catherine. "Catholic Women and the Northern Irish Troubles." In: Y. Alexander and A. O'Day, eds. ***Ireland's Terrorist Trauma.*** New York: Harvester Wheatsheaf, 1989. pp. 234-248.

4537. Shearman, Hugh. "Conflict in Northern Ireland." In: G. W. Keeton and G. Schwarzenberger, eds. ***Year Book of World Affairs, 1982.*** London: Stevens & Sons, 1982. pp. 182-196.

4538. Slack, Kenneth. ""Loyalist" Terrorism in Ireland." ***Christian Century,*** 103:20 (June 18-25, 1986), 573-575.

4539. Smith, William B. "Terrorism: The Lessons of Northern Ireland." ***Journal of Contemporary Studies,*** 5 (Winter 1982), 29-50.

4540. Smyth, Jim. "Stretching the Boundaries: The Control of Dissent in Northern Ireland." ***Terrorism,*** 11:4 (1988), 289-308

4541. _____. "Unintentional Mobilization: The Effect of the 1980-81 Hunger Strikes in Ireland." ***Political Communication and Persuasion,*** 4:3 (1987), 179-189.

4542. Soule, John W. "Problems in Applying Counterterrorism to Prevent Terrorism: Two Decades of Violence in Northern Ireland Reconsidered." ***Terrorism,*** 12:1 (1989), 31-46.

4543. Spillane, Jay M. "Terrorists and Special Status: The British Experience in Northern Ireland." ***Hastings International and Comparative Law Review,*** 9:3 (1986), 481-515.

4544. Spjut, R. J. "Criminal Statistics and Statistics on Security in Northern Ireland." ***British Journal of Criminology,*** 23 (October 1983), 358-380.

4545. Stewart, A. T. Q. "The Mind of Protestant Ulster." In: D. Watt, ed. ***Constitution of Northern Ireland: Problems and Prospects.*** London: Heineman, 1981. pp. 31-45.

4546. Stollard, Paul. "Architecture and Terrorism: A Case Study of the Impact of 'The Troubles' on the Architecture of Northern Ireland." ***International Journal of Comparative and Applied Criminal Justice,*** 13:2 (Fall 1989), 77-85.

4547. Tomkins, Thomas C. "Terrorist Innovation: The Ingenuity of the Irish." ***TVI Journal,*** 5:4 (1985), 52-53.

4548. Townshend, Charles. "Terror in Ireland: Observations on Tynan's 'The Irish Incivilities and Their Times'." In: P. Wilkinson and A. M. Stewart, eds. ***Contemporary Research on Terrorism.*** Aberdeen: Aberdeen University Press, 1987. pp. 179-185.

4549. _____. "The Process of Terror in Irish Politics." In: N. O'Sullivan, ed. ***Terrorism, Ideology, and Revolution.*** Boulder, CO.: Westview Press, 1986. pp. 88-114.

4550. "Ulster: The Counter-Terror." In: W. Laqueur, ed ***The Terrorism Reader.*** New York: Meridian, 1987. pp. 134-136.

4551. Walker, Clive. "Irish Republican Prisoners: Political Detainees, Prisoners of War or Common Criminals." ***The Irish Jurist,*** 19 (Winter 1984), 189-225.

4552. _____. "Political Violence and Democracy in Northern Ireland." ***Modern Law Review***, 51:5 (September 1988), 605-622.

4553. _____. "Arrest and Rearrest." ***Northern Ireland Legal Quarterly***, 35:1 (1984), 1-27.

4554. Wilkinson, Paul. "The Orange and the Green: Extremism in Northern Ireland." In: M. Crenshaw, ed. ***Terrorism, Legitimacy and Power.*** Middletown, CT.: Wesleyan University Press, 1983. pp. 105-123.

4555. Wright, Frank. "Case Study III: The Ulster Spectrum." In: D. Carlton and C. Schaerf, eds. ***Contemporary Terror.*** London: Macmillan, 1981. pp. 153-214.

4556. _____. "Communal Deterrence and the Threat of Violence in the North of Ireland in the Nineteenth Century." In: J. Darby, N. Dodge and A. C. Hepburn, eds. ***Political Violence: Ireland in a Comparative Perspective.*** Ottawa: University of Ottawa Press, 1990. pp. 1-10.

4557. Wright, Steve. "A Multivariate Time Series Analysis of the Northern Irish Conflict, 1969-1976." In: Y. Alexander and J.M. Gleason, eds. ***Behavioral and Quantitative Perspectives on Terrorism.*** New York: Pergamon Press, 1981. pp. 283-321.

3. Documents and Reports

4558. Article 19. ***No Comment: Censorship, Secrecy and the Irish Troubles.*** London: Article 19, The International Centre on Censorship, 1989. 108p.

4559. Bentley-Mussen, Joan A. ***Revolution in Northern Ireland? A Case Study.*** Ph.D. Dissertation. Washington, D.C.: The American University, 1985. 199p.

4560. Fennell, Desmond. ***The Northern Ireland Problem: Basic Data and Terminology.*** Galway: University College, 1981.

4561. Finn, John E. ***Public Support for Emergency (Anti Terrorist) Legislation in Northern Ireland: A Preliminary Analysis.*** Middletown, CT.: Wesleyan University, Department of Government, 1986. 34p.

4562. Furmanski, Louis S. ***The Essence of Conflict: A Theoretical Inquiry into Conflict Analysis: The Case of Northern Ireland.*** Ph.D. Dissertation. West Lafayette, IN.: Purdue University, [1981].

4563. Great Britain. Parliament. House of Commons. ***Northern Ireland (Emergency Provisions) Bill: (As Amended by Standing Committee D).*** London: H.M.S.O., 1987. 20p.

4564. Guelke, Adrian. ""The Ballot Bomb": Terrorism and the Electoral Process in Northern Ireland." Paper Presented at the ***12th World Congress of Sociology***, held on July 3-9, 1990 in Madrid.

4565. Hewitt, Christopher. "Violence in Northern Ireland: Ethnic Conflict and Radicalization in an International Setting." Paper Presented at the ***Spring Conference of the National Capital Area Political Science Association***, held on February 27, 1982 at Mount Vernon College, Washington, D.C.

4566. Hyland, Mary F. ***Terrorism as a Heritage: Northern Ireland.*** Master's Thesis. Long Beach, CA.: California State University at Long Beach, 1986. 65p.

4567. Institute for the Study of Conflict. ***Northern Ireland: Problems and Perspectives.*** Conflict Studies, No. 135. London: Institute for the Study of Conflict, 1982. 48p.

4568. Jackson, Harold, and Anne McHardy. ***The Two Irelands: The Problems of the Double Minority.*** Report No. 2. London: The Minority Rights Group, 1984. 16p.

4569. Lee, A. McClung. "Varieties of Political Terrorism: Northern Ireland Experience." Paper Presented to the ***30th Annual Meeting of the Society for the Study of Social Problems,*** held on August 21-24, 1981, at Toronto.

4570. Macdonald, Michael D. ***Children of Wrath: Political Violence in Northern Ireland.*** Ph.D. Dissertation. Berkeley, CA.: University of California at Berkeley, 1983. 220p.

4571. McKinley, Michael. ***The Ulster Question in International Politics, 1969-1978.*** Ph.D. Dissertation. Australian National University, Canberra, [1980].

4572. Naughton, M. K. ***Government Actions to Control Terrorist Violence: A Case Study on Northern Ireland.*** Master's Thesis. Monterey, CA.: Naval Postgraduate School, 1988. 171p.

4573. New Ulster Political Research Group (NUPRP). ***Supplementary Introduction to Documents for Discussion: Beyond the Political Divide.*** Belfast: NUPRP, 1980.

4574. O'Connell, John. ***Irish Terrorism - A Problem of British Design.*** Carlisle Barracks, PA.: U.S. Army War College, 1986. 28p.

4575. Robinson, Peter, et al. ***Northern Ireland: A War to Be Won.*** Belfast: D.U.P., 1984. 46p.

4576. Workers Research Unit. ***Belfast Bulletin No. II: Supergrasses.*** Belfast: Workers Research Unit, 1984.

4577. Wright, Steve. "The State and Terrorism in Northern Ireland." Paper Presented at the ***24th Annual Convention of the International Studies Association,*** held on April 5-9, 1983 in Mexico City.

4578. _____. ***A Time Series Analysis of the Northern Irish Conflict 1969-1978.*** Ph.D. Dissertation. Lancaster: University of Lancaster, 1980.

b4. SECURITY SERVICES

1. Books

4579. Allen, Charles. ***The Savage Wars of Peace: Soldier's Voices 1945-1989.*** London: Michael Joseph, 1990. Chapter III. pp. 205-281.

4580. Asmal, Kader. ***Shoot to Kill?: International Lawyer's Inquiry into the Lethal Use of Firearms by the Security Forces in Northern Ireland.*** Dublin: Mercier Press, 1985. 173p.

4581. Babington, Anthony. ***Military Intervention in Britain: From the Gordon Riots to the Gibraltar Incident.*** London: Routledge, 1990. 242p.

4582. Barzilay, David. ***The British Army in Ulster. 4 Vols.*** Belfast: Century Services, 1973-1981.

4583. Bonner, David. ***Emergency Powers in Peacetime.*** London: Sweet & Maxwell, 1985,

4584. Geraghty, Tony. ***Who Dares Wins: The Story of the Special Air Services, 1950-1980.*** London: Arms and Armour Press, 1980.

4585. Hamill, Desmonds. ***Pig in the Middle: The Army in Northern Ireland, 1969-1984.*** London: Methuen, 1985. 308p.

4586. Holroyd, Fred, and Nick Burbridge. ***War Without Honor.*** Hull: Medium, 1989. 184p.

4587. Kitchin, Hilary. ***The Gibraltar Report: Inquest into the Deaths of Mairead Farrell, Daniel McCann & Sean Savage.*** London: National Council for Civil Liberties, 1989. 31p.

4588. Ladd, James. ***SAS Operations.*** London: Hale, 1986. 218p.

4589. Lindsay, Kennedy. ***The British Intelligence Services in Action.*** Newtownabbey, County Antrim: Dunrod Press, 1980.

4590. McArdle, Patsy. ***The Secret War: An Account of the Sinister Activities Along the Border Involving Gardai, RUC, British Army and SAS.*** Dublin: Mercier Press, 1984. 104p.

4591. Seymour, William. ***British Special Forces.*** London: Sidgwick and Jackson, 1985. 324p.

4592. Taylor, Peter. ***Beating the Terrorists? Interrogation in Omagh, Gough and Castlereagh.*** Harmondsworth, Eng.: Penguin Books, 1980. 347p.

4593. Walsh, Dermot. ***Arrest, Interrogation and Diplock Courts.*** Belfast: Cobden Trust, 1983.

4594. Williams, Maxine. ***Murder on the Rock: How the British Government Got Away with Murder.*** London: Larkin, 1989. 61p.

2. *Journal Articles*

4595. "Authorized Procedures for the Interrogation of Persons Suspected of Terrorism." ***International Journal of Politics,*** 10:1 (1980), 58-61.

4596. Bonner, David. "Combating Terrorism: The Jellicoe Approach." ***Public Law,*** (Summer 1983), 224-234.

4597. Boyle, Kevin, Tom Hadden and D. Hillyard. "Emergency Powers: Ten Years On." ***Fortnight,*** 179 (December 1979/January 1980), 4-8.

4598. British Information Services. "Security Statistics." ***International Journal of Statistics,*** 10:1 (1980), 42-46.

4599. Findlay, Mark. "Criminalization and the Detention of Political Prisoners: An Irish Perspective." ***Contemporary Crises,*** (:1 (1985), 1-17.

4600. Gardiner Commission. "Measures to Deal with Terrorism." ***International Journal of Politics,*** 10:1 (1980), 98-105.

4601. Garrett, J. Brian. "Ten Years of British Troops in Northern Ireland." ***International Security,*** (Spring 1981), 80-104.

4602. Gregory, F. E. C. "The British Police and Terrorism." ***Terrorism,*** 5:1-2 (1981), 107-124.

4603. _____. "The British Police and Terrorism." In: P. Wilkinson, ed. ***British Perspectives on Terrorism.*** London: Allen & Unwin, 1981. pp. 107-124.

4604. Hart, W. "Ulster's Prison Guards." ***Corrections Magazine,*** 6:3 (1980), 20-27.

4605. _____. "Waging Peace in Northern Ireland." ***Police Magazine,*** 3:3 (1980), 22-32.

4606. Hermon, John. "Policing in a Combative Environment." ***Police Chief,*** (March 1985), 136-138.

4607. Hocking, Jenny. "Counterterrorism as Counterinsurgency: The British Experience." ***Social Justice***, 15 (Spring 1988), 83-97.

4608. Holden Reid, Brian. "The Experience of the British Army in Northern Ireland." In: Y. Alexander and A. O'Day, eds. ***Ireland's Terrorist Dilemma.*** Dordrecht: Martinus Nijhoff, 1986. 249-260.

4609. Mark, Robert. "Policing a Britain Under Threat." In: R. Clutterbuck, ed. ***The Future of Political Violence.*** London: Macmillan, 1986. pp. 159-166.

4610. McCullough, H. M. "Royal Ulster Constabulary." ***Police Studies***, 4:4 (1982), 3-12.

4611. Murray, Russell. "Killing of Local Security Forces in Northern Ireland, 1969-1981." ***Terrorism***, 7:1 (1984), 11-52.

4612. _____. "Police Officer Deaths in Northern Ireland: 1969-1982." ***Police Chief***, 50 (April 1983), 41-47.

4613. O'Halpin, Eunan D. "Anglo-Irish Security Co-Operation: A Dublin Perspective." ***Conflict Quarterly***, 10 (Fall 1990), 5-24.

4614. Pockrass, Robert M. "The Police Response to Terrorism: The Royal Ulster Constabulary." ***Conflict***, 6:4 (1986), 287-306.

4615. Reed, J. "Northern Ireland - Progress in Policing Within a Divided Community." ***Police Journal***, 55:1 (1982), 20-27.

4616. "Security Forces in Northern Ireland." ***Reinsurance***, 17 (June 1985), 51-53.

4617. Spjut, R. J. "The 'Official' Use of Deadly Force by the Security Forces Against Suspected Terrorists: Some Lessons from Northern Ireland." ***Public Law***, (Spring 1986), 38-66.

4618. Stone, J. L. "Irish Terrorism Investigations." ***FBI Law Enforcement Bulletin***, 56 (October 1987), 18-23.

4619. "TVI Interview: British Prison Official Ray Wyre on Terrorists Behind Bars." ***TVI Journal***, 5:3 (1985), 22-25.

4620. "TVI Notebook: Ireland: Keeping the Peace and Keeping Away." ***TVI Journal***, 2:11 (1981), 2-3.

4621. Walsh, Dermot. "Arrest and Interrogation: Northern Ireland 1981." ***Journal of Law and Society***, 9:1 (1982), 37-62.

4622. Weitzer, Ronald. "Policing Northern Ireland Today." ***The Political Quarterly***, 58:1 (1987), 88-95.

4623. Wilson, James. "Pig in the Middle." ***Army Quarterly and Defence Journal***, 115:4 (1985), 429-430.

4624. Wolf, John B. "British Anti-Terrorist Policy in Northern Ireland: Legal Aspects." ***Police Chief***, 50 (April 1983), 36-40.

3. Documents and Reports

4625. Bryett, Keith. ***The Effects of Political Terrorism on the Police of Great Britain and Northern Ireland Since 1969.*** Ph.D. Dissertation. Aberdeen: University of Aberdeen, 1987. 460p.

4626. Hahn, K. S. ***Case Study: The Effects of the British Army Against the Irish Republican Army.*** Master's Thesis. Wright-Patterson AFB, OH.: Air Force Institute of Technology, 1989. 83p.

c. FRANCE

1. Books

4627. Gally, Laurent. ***The Black Agent: Traitor to an Unjust Cause.*** London: Andre Deutsch, 1988. 198p.

4628. Moxon-Browne, Edward. ***Terrorism in France.*** Conflict Studies, No. 144. London: Institute for the Study of Conflict, 1983. 26p.

2. Journal Articles

4629. Cerny, Philip G. "France: Non-Terrorism and the Politics of Repressive Tolerance." In: J. Lodge, ed. ***Terrorism - A Challenge to the State.*** Oxford: Martin Robertson, 1981. pp. 91-118.

4630. Chauvin, Luc. "French Diplomacy and the Hostage Crises." In: B. Rubin, ed. ***The Politics of Counterterrorism.*** Lanham, MD.: University Publications of America, 1990. pp. 91-106.

4631. Cordes, Bonnie J. "Action Directe Comes of Age." ***TVI Journal,*** 5:4 (1985), 6-7.

4632. Francis, Samuel T. "Terrorist Renaissance: France, 1980-1983." ***World Affairs,*** (Summer 1983), 54-58.

4633. "French Terrorism - A Taste of Violence." ***TVI Journal,*** 3:1 (1982), 8+.

4634. Moxon-Browne, Edward. "Terrorism in France." In: J. Lodge, ed. ***The Threat of Terrorism.*** Brighton: Wheatsheaf Books, 1988. pp. 213-228.

4635. _____. "Terrorism in France." In: W. Gutteridge, ed. ***Contemporary Terrorism.*** New York: Facts on File, 1986. pp. 111-134.

4636. Pisano, Vittorfranco S. "Part I: A Case Study in Terrorism of the Left: Action Directe." ***Conflict,*** 9:2 (1989), 155-160.

4637. _____. "Terrorism is as French as Champagne." ***TVI Journal,*** 3:1 (1982), 8-13.

4638. Raufer, Xavier. "Part II: What the Group Olivier Archives Reveal." ***Conflict,*** 9:2 (1989), 161-170.

4639. Savigear, Peter. "Separatism and Centralism in Corsica." ***World Today,*** 36 (September 1980), 351-355.

4640. _____. "Corsica: Regional Autonomy or Violence." ***Conflict Studies,*** 149 (1983), 3-17.

4641. Simpson, Howard R. "Paris: The Terrorist Offensive." ***TVI Report,*** 7:4 (1987), 21-23.

4642. _____. "France 1989: Bad Year for Terrorists?." ***TVI Report,*** 9:1 (1989), 9-11.

4643. "TVI Interview: Massacres Could Bloodstain Europe: A French Terrorist Expert Expresses His Opinion." ***TVI Report,*** 6:3 (Winter 1986), 9-11.

4644. "TVI Report Profiles: Direct Action, Action Direct (AD)." ***TVI Report,*** 8:2 (1988), 1-4.

4645. Wieviorka, Michel. "French Politics and Strategy on Terrorism." In: B. Rubin, ed. ***The Politics of Counterterrorism.*** Lanham, MD.: University Publications of America, 1990. pp. 61-90.

3. Documents and Reports

4646. Savigear, Peter. "Corsican Nationalism and the Uses of Violence." Paper Presented at the ***Panel on the Role of High Risk Violence in Ethnic Nationalism at the Annual Meeting of the International Studies Association,*** held on October 29-31, 1981 at the University of Florida at Gainesville.

d. WEST GERMANY

1. Books

4647. Aust, Stefan. ***The Baader-Meinhof Group: The Inside Story of a Phenomenon.*** London: Bodley Head, 1987. 560p.

4648. Bourgereau, Jean Marcel. ***The German Guerrilla: Terror, Reaction and Resistance.*** Sanday: Cienfuegos Press: Soil of Liberty, 1981. 106p.

2. Journal Articles

4649. "Baader and Meinhof, The Ghosts Still Haunt Germany." ***TVI Journal,*** 2:11 (1981), 9-14.

4650. Becker, Jillian. "Another Final Battle on the Stage of History." ***Terrorism,*** 5:1-2 (1981), 89-106.

4651. _____. "Case Study I: Federal Germany." In: D. Carlton and C. Schaerf, eds. ***Contemporary Terror.*** London: Macmillan, 1981. pp. 122-138.

4652. Billig, Otto. "The Case History of a German Terrorist." ***Terrorism,*** 7:1 (1984), 1-10.

4653. Boehm, T. M., and J. J. James. "The Medical Response to the LaBelle Disco Bombing in Berlin, 1986." ***Military Medicine,*** 153:5 (1988), 235-238.

4654. Bookbinder, Paul. "Economic Inflation and Deflation of Confidence Promoted German Terrorism." ***TVI Journal,*** 1:8 (1980), 4-9.

4655. _____. "Ulrike Meinhof and Andreas Baader: The Idealist and the Adventurer." ***TVI Journal,*** 2:11 (1981), 9-13.

4656. _____. "West German Elections were Key to Future." ***TVI Journal,*** 4:4-6 (1983), 3-5.

4657. Bradshaw, Jon. "The Dream of Terror." ***Esquire,*** 90 (July 18, 1987), 24-45, 47-50.

4658. Cook, Shura. "Germany: From Protest to Terrorism." In: Y. Alexander and K. A. Myers, eds. ***Terrorism in Europe.*** London: Croom Helm, 1982. pp. 154-178.

4659. Falj, Gerhard. "Terror as Politics: The German Case." ***International Review of Politics and Political Science,*** 20:4 (1983), 22-32.

4660. "The Future of Terrorism in West Germany." ***TVI Journal,*** 4:4-6 (1983), 3-6.

4661. Hofmeyer, R. "Terrorism, The West German Experience." In: M. Hough, ed. ***Revolutionary Warfare and Counter Insurgency.*** Pretoria: Institute for Strategic Studies, University of Pretoria, 1984.

4662. Horbatiuk, Kevin G. "Anti-Terrorism: The West German Approach." ***Fordham International Law Journal,*** 3 (Spring 1980), 167-191.

4663. Horchem, Hans J. "The Development of West German Terrorism after 1969: An Overview." ***TVI Journal,*** 5:4 (1985), 10-16.

4664. _____. "European Terrorism: A German Perspective." ***Terrorism,*** 6:1 (1983), 27-52.

4665. _____. "Political Terrorism - The German Perspective." In: A. Merari, ed. ***On Terrorism and Combating Terrorism.*** Frederick, MD.: University Publications of America, 1985. pp. 63-68.

4666. _____. "Terrorism and Government Response: The German Experience." ***Jerusalem Journal of International Relations,*** 4:3 (1980), 43-55.

4667. _____. "Terrorism in Germany: 1985." In: P. Wilkinson and A. M. Stewart, eds. ***Contemporary Research on Terrorism.*** Aberdeen: Aberdeen University Press, 1987. pp. 141-163.

4668. _____. "The Lost Revolution of West Germany's Terrorists." ***Terrorism and Political Violence,*** 1:3 (July 1990), 353-360.

4669. _____. "West Germany's Red Army Anarchists." In: W. Gutteridge, ed. ***The New Terrorism.*** New York: Facts on File, 1986. pp. 199-216.

4670. _____. "European Terrorism: A German Perspective." In: W. Laqueur, ed. ***The Terrorism Reader.*** New York: Meridian, 1987. pp. 289-297.

4671. Kellen, Konrad. "The Road to Terrorism: Confession of a German Terrorist." ***TVI Journal,*** 5:2 (1984), 36-39.

4672. _____. "The RAF in West Germany: Stronger than Ever?." ***TVI Report,*** 7:2 (1987), 24-25.

4673. _____. "Ideology and Rebellion: Terrorism in West Germany." In: W. Reich, ed. ***Origins of Terrorism.*** Cambridge: Cambridge University Press, 1990. pp. 43-58.

4674. _____. "New Revelations About West Germany's Fight Against Terrorists." ***TVI Report,*** 8:1 (1988), 37-38.

4675. Kolinsky, Eva. "Terrorism in West Germany." In: J. Lodge, ed. ***The Threat of Terrorism.*** Brighton: Wheatsheaf Books, 1988. pp. 57-88.

4676. Lochte, Christian. "Fighting Terrorism in the Federal Republic of Germany." In: B. Netanyahu, ed. ***Terrorism: How the West Can Win.*** New York: Farrar, Straus, Giroux, 1983. pp. 171-174.

4677. Merkl, Peter H. "Rollerball or Neo-Nazi Violence?." In: P. H. Merkl, ed. ***Political Violence and Terror.*** Berkeley, CA.: University of California Press, 1986. pp. 229-256.

4678. Miller, Bowman H. "Terrorism and Language: A Text-Based Analysis of the German Case." ***Terrorism,*** 9:4 (1987), 373-407.

4679. Nelson, D. J. "The Problem of Terrorism Against American Forces in Germany." ***Atlantic Community Quarterly,*** (Fall 1985), 275-284.

4680. "A Postscript to "Current Terrorist Activities in Germany"." ***TVI Journal,*** 5:3 (1985), 53+.

4681. Pridham, Geoffrey. "Terrorism and the State in West Germany During the 1970's: A Threat to Stability or Case of Political Over Reaction?" In: J. Lodge, ed. ***Terrorism: A Challenge to the State.*** Oxford: Martin Robertson, 1981. pp. 11-56.

4682. Roberts, Julian. "Terrorism and German Intellectuals." ***Journal of Area Studies,*** 3 (Spring 1981), 21-25.

4683. Scheerer, Sebastian. "The Crime of Claus Croissant." ***Contemporary Crises,*** 4:3 (July 1980), 341-349.

4684. Schiller, David T. "The Current Campaign Against Laboratory Tests in West Germany." ***TVI Journal,*** 5:4 (1985), 36-38.

4685. _____. "Current Terrorist Activities in Germany." ***TVI Journal,*** 5:3 (1985), 14-17.

4686. _____. "The Police Response to Terrorism: A Critical Overview." In: P. Wilkinson and A. M. Stewart, eds. ***Contemporary Research on Terrorism.*** Aberdeen: Aberdeen University Press, 1987. pp. 536-548.

4687. _____. "Germany's Other Terrorists." ***Terrorism,*** 9:1 (1987), 87-99.

4688. _____. "Coping with Terrorism: West Germany in the 1970s and 1980s." In: A. Kurz, ed. ***Contemporary Trends in World Terrorism.*** New York: Praeger, 1987. pp. 132-139.

4689. _____. "West Germany Coping with Terrorism: The Evolution of a Police Organization." ***TVI Report,*** 6:2 (1985), 28-32.

4690. _____. "Hitting the Nerve Center: The Murder of Gerold Von Braunmuehl." ***TVI Report,*** 7:2 (1987), 26-28.

4691. _____. "A Tale of Two Trials." ***TVI Report,*** 9:1 (1989), 19-24.

4692. _____. "Touching a Raw Nerve: An RAF Assassination Attempt in Bonn." ***TVI Report,*** 8:4 (1989), 8-11.

4693. _____. "The Economic Implications of Terrorism: A Case Study of the Federal Republic of Germany." ***TVI Report,*** 7:1 (1987), 37-39.

4694. _____. "Two Bombings in Berlin: More Than Meets the Eye." ***TVI Report,*** 7:1 (1987), 43-44.

4695. _____. "A Tale of Two Trials (Part II)." ***TVI Report,*** 9:3 (1990), 22.

4696. Steinke, W. "The Terrorism of Left-Wingers in the Federal Republic of Germany and the Combat Against the Terrorists." In: ***Anti-Terrorism - IDENTA - 85.*** Boulder, CO.: Westview, 1985. pp. 32-51.

4697. "TVI Report Profiles: Red Army Faction (RAF)." ***TVI Report,*** 8:2 (1988), 17-19.

4698. Wasmund, Klaus. "The Political Socialization of Terrorist Groups in West Germany." ***Journal of Political and Military Sociology,*** 11:2 (Fall 1983), 223-239.

4699. _____. "The Political Socialization of West German Terrorists." In: P. H. Merkl, ed. ***Political Violence and Terror.*** Berkeley, CA.: University of California Press, 1986. pp. 191-228.

4700. Wellmer, Albrecht. "Terrorism and the Critique of Society." In: J. Habermas, ed. ***Observations on The Spiritual Situation of the Age.*** Cambridge, MA.: MIT Press, 1984. pp. 283-307.

4701. Winn, G. F. T. "Terrorism, Alienation and German Society." In: Y. Alexander and J. M. Gleason, eds. ***Behavioral and Quantitative Perspectives on Terrorism.*** New York: Pergamon Press, 1981. pp. 256-282.

4702. Wurth, Don E. "The RAF Strikes Once More: Details of the Braunmuehl Killing." ***TVI Report,*** 7:2 (1987), 28-29.

4703. _____. "The West German RAF Strikes Again." ***TVI Report,*** 7:1 (1987), 40-42.

4704. Zimmermann, Ekkart. "Review Essay: Terrorist Violence in West Germany: Some Reflections on Recent Literature." ***Journal of Political and Military Sociology,*** 14:2 (Fall 1986), 321-332.

3. Documents and Reports

4705. Bay, Charles. ***The Red Army Faction: Four Generations of Terror.*** Washington, D.C.: Defence Intelligence College, 1986. 43p.

4706. Becker, Jillian. ***Terrorism in West Germany: The Struggle for What.*** London: Institute for the Study of Terrorism, 1988. 95p.

4707. Bergenthal, A. ***Is Political Extremism Within the Armed Forces of the Federal Republic of Germany a Threat That Can Be Managed.*** Carlisle Barracks, PA.: Army War College, 1990. 40p.

4708. Defence Systems, Inc. ***Terrorist Innovations and Adaptation: A Case Study of Selected German Red Army Faction Operations: Part II.*** McLean, VA.: Defence Systems, Inc., 1986. 14p.

4709. "A Document Published Recently by the Red Army Faction: West Germany's Leading Terrorist Organization." ***TVI Journal,*** 5:4 (1985), 17.

4710. Elliott, John D. ***Terrorism in West Germany.*** Ph.D. Dissertation. George Washington University, [1981].

4711. Frankel, Norman. "The Terrorist Attack Against Israel at the 1972 Munich Olympics: A Schematic Model." Paper Presented at the ***Annual Meeting of the Midwest Chapter of the International Studies Association,*** held on October 16-18, 1980 at the University of Chicago.

4712. Hoffman, Bruce. ***Right-Wing Terrorism in West Germany.*** RAND P-7270. Santa Monica, CA.: Rand Corporation, 1986. 26p.

4713. Horchem, Hans J. ***Terrorism in West Germany.*** Conflict Studies No. 186. London: Institute for the Study of Conflicts, 1986. 21p.

4714. Kellen, Konrad. ***Ideology and Rebellion: Terrorism in West Germany.*** Washington, D.C.: Woodrow Wilson International Center for Scholars, 1987. 22p.

4715. King, Michael J. ***The Growth of Police Powers in the Federal Republic of Germany: An Analysis of the Relations of the State, Legitimation and Coercion.*** Ph.D. Dissertation. Cardiff: University of Wales, 1987. 367p.

4716. Kraushaar, Dietrich K. ***The Peace Movement and Terrorist Organizations in the Federal Republic of Germany.*** Maxwell Air Force Base, AL.: Air War College, 1986. 32p.

4717. Lewis, Rand C. ***Right-Wing Extremism in West Germany, 1945-1989: A Nazi Legacy.*** Ph.D. Dissertation. Moscow, ID.: University of Idaho, 1990. 329p.

4718. Rupprecht, Reinhard. "Terrorism and Counterterrorism in the Federal Republic of Germany." Paper Presented at the ***10th Annual Symposium on the Role of Behavioral Science in Physical Security,*** held on April 23-24, 1985 in Washington, D.C.. pp.73-75.

4719. "Terrorist Communique: The Red Army Faction Bulletin on the Braunmuehl Assassination in Bonn." ***TVI Report,*** 7:2 (1987), 30-32.

4720. United States. Central Intelligence Agency. ***West Germany's Red Army Faction.*** Washington, D.C.: Federal Aviation Administration, 1987. 19p.

4721. Zimmermann, Ekkart. "Terrorist Violence in West Germany: Some Reflections on Recent Literature." Paper Presented to the, ***13th Annual World Congress of the International Political Science Association,*** held on July 15-20, 1985, in Paris.

e. HOLLAND

1. Books

4722. Barker, R. ***Not Here, But in Another Place.*** New York: St.Martin's Press, 1980. 356p.
4723. Van Kaam, Ben. ***The South Moluccans: Background to the Train Hijacking.*** London: Hurst, 1981.

2. Journal Articles

4724. "Appendix: Summary of a Dutch Case Study." In: A. P. Schmid and J. de Graaf, eds. ***Violence as Communication: Insurgent Terrorism and the Western Media.*** Beverly Hills, CA.: Sage, 1982. pp. 227-234.
4725. Den Uyl, Joop M. P. "The Dutch Response." In: B. Netanyahu, ed. ***International Terrorism: Challenge and Response.*** New Brunswick, NJ.: Transaction Books, 1981. pp. 165-171.
4726. Hauben, Robert. "Hostage Taking: The Dutch Experience." In: L. Z. Freedman and Y. Alexander, eds. ***Perspectives on Terrorism.*** Wilmington, DE.: Scholarly Resources, 1983. pp. 131-142.
4727. Herman, Valentine, and Rob Van der Laan Bouma. "Nationalists Without a Nation: South Moluccan Terrorism in the Netherlands." In: J. Lodge, ed. ***Terrorism: A Challenge to the State.*** Oxford: Martin Robertson, 1981. pp. 119-146.
4728. _____. _____. "Nationalists Without a State: South Moluccan Terrorism in the Netherlands." ***Terrorism,*** 4:1-2 (1980), 223-258.
4729. Rosenthal, Uriel, and P. Hart. "Managing Terrorism: The South Moluccan Hostage Takings." In: U. Rosenthal, M. T. Charles and P. Hart, eds. ***Coping with Crises.*** Springfield, IL.: Charles C. Thomas, 1989. pp. 367-393.
4730. Schmid, Alex P. "Politically-Motivated Violent Activists in the Netherlands in the 1980s." In: J. Lodge, ed. ***The Threat of Terrorism.*** Brighton: Wheatsheaf Books, 1988. pp. 145-178.
4731. Vermaat, J. A. E. "Terrorist Sympathizers in the Netherlands." ***Terrorism,*** 10:4 (1987), 329-336.
4732. Wurth, Don E. "The Heineken Kidnapping: A Case Study." ***TVI Journal,*** 5:1 (1984), 40-42.
4733. Yaeger, Carl H. "Menia Muria: The South Moluccans Fight in Holland." ***Terrorism,*** 13:3 (1990), 215-226.

f. ITALY

1. Books

4734. Collin, Richard O. ***Winter of Fire: The Abduction of General Dozier and the Downfall of the Red Brigades.*** New York: E.P. Dutton, 1990.
4735. Drake, Richard. ***The Revolutionary Mystique and Terrorism in Contemporary Italy.*** Bloomington, IN.: Indiana University Press, 1989. 218p.

4736. Henze, Paul. ***The Plot to Kill the Pope.*** New York: Scribner's, 1984. 224p.

4737. ***Inside a Terrorist Group: The Red Brigades of Italy.*** International Security & Terrorism Series; No. 6. Upland PA.: Diane Publ, 1987. 180p.

4738. Jamieson, Alison. ***The Heart Attacked: Terrorism and Conflict in the Italian State.*** London: Marion Boyars, 1989. 306p.

4739. Katz, Robert. ***Days of Wrath: The Ordeal of Aldo Moro, The Kidnapping, The Execution, The Aftermath.*** Garden City, NY.: Doubleday, 1980. 326.

4740. Meade, Robert C. Jr. ***Red Brigades: The Story of Italian Terrorism.*** London: MacMillan, 1990. 301p.

4741. Moss, David. ***The Politics of Violence in Italy, 1969-1985.*** London: MacMillan, 1989. 317p.

4742. Pisano, Vittorfranco S. ***The Dynamics of Subversion and Violence in Contemporary Italy.*** Stanford, CA.: Hoover Institution Press, 1987. 210p.

4743. Wagner-Pacifici, Robin. ***The Moro Morality Play: Terrorism as a Social Drama.*** Chicago, IL.: University of Chicago Press, 1986. 360p.

4744. Weinberg, Leonard, and William L. Eubank. ***The Rise and Fall of Italian Terrorism.*** Boulder, CO.: Westview Press, 1987. 155p.

2. Journal Articles

4745. Bobbio, Norberto. "Italy's Permanent Crisis.' ***Telos,*** 54 (Winter 1982-83), 123-133.

4746. Boffi, A. "Who Benefits from Terrorism?" ***World Marxist Review,*** 25 (July 1982), 62-66.

4747. Bolton, Catherine. "Italian Terrorism: Dead or Dormant?" ***Journal of Defence and Diplomacy,*** 2:11 (1984), 39-42.

4748. Bookbinder, Paul. "A Red Brigades Mistake." ***TVI Journal,*** 3:5 (1982), 4-5.

4749. Branley, Bill. "Terrorists Mean Business." ***Soldiers,*** (July 1982), 6-10.

4750. Capaccio, Jeffrey M., and William J. Stover. "Terror's Roots are Many, Tangled." ***TVI Journal,*** 3:8 (1982) 8-13.

4751. Cappadocia, E. "Terrorism in Italy: A Commentary." ***Queen's Quarterly,*** (Winter 1982), 770-782.

4752. Codevilla, Angelo. "Italy: Political Violence in the Heart of NATO." ***International Security Review,*** 5 (Spring 1980), 91-110.

4753. Collin, Richard O. "When Reality Came Unglued: Antonio Savasta and the Italian Red Brigades." ***Violence, Aggression and Terrorism,*** 3:4 (1989), 269-294.

4754. _____. "Breaking the Police: Mussolini's Use of Terrorism." ***Violence Aggression and Terrorism,*** 1;1 (1987), 41-60.

4755. Cowan, Suzanne. "Terrorism and the Italian Left." In: C. Boggs and D. Plotke, eds. ***The Politics of Eurocommunism - Socialism in Rransition.*** Boston, MA.: South End Press, 1980. pp. 163-193.

4756. Das, Dilip K. "Impact of Antiterrorist Measures on Democratic Law Enforcement: The Italian Experience." ***Terrorism,*** 13:2 (1990), 89-98.

4757. Della Porta, Donatella, and Sidney Tarrow. "Unwanted Children: Political Violence and the Cycle of Protest in Italy, 1966-1973." ***European Journal of Political Research,*** 14 (1986), 607-632.

4758. _____. "Recruitment Processes in Clandestine political Organizations: Italian Left Wing Terrorism." ***International Social Movement Research,*** 1 (1988), 155-169.

4759. Dozier, J. L. "Opening General Session Address - IACP Conference." ***Police Chief,*** 50 (March 1983), 41-45.

4760. Drake, Richard. "The Red and the Black: Terrorism in Contemporary Italy." ***International Political Science Review,*** 5:3 (1984), 279-298.

4761. _____. "The Red Brigades and the Italian Political Tradition." In: Y. Alexander and K. A. Myers, eds. ***Terrorism in Europe.*** London: Croom Helm, 1982. pp. 102-140.

4762. _____. "Julius Evola and the Ideological Origins of the Radical Right in Contemporary Italy." In: P. H. Merkl, ed. ***Political Violence and Terror.*** Berkeley, CA.: University of California Press, 1986. pp. 61-90.

4763. _____. "Contemporary Terrorism and the Intellectuals: The Case of Italy." In: P. Wilkinson and A. M. Stewart, eds. ***Contemporary Research on Terrorism.*** Aberdeen: Aberdeen University Press, 1987. pp. 130-140.

4764. Eubank, William L., and Leonard Weinberg. "Change and Continuity in the Recruitment of Italian Political Terrorists: 1970-1984." ***Journal of Political Science,*** 14:1-2 (1986), 43-57.

4765. _____. _____. "Italian Women Terrorists." ***Terrorism,*** 9:3 (1987), 241-262.

4766. Evans, Robert E. "Terrorism and Subversion of the State: Italian Legal Responses." ***Terrorism and Political Violence,*** 1:3 (July 1989), 324-352.

4767. Ferracuti, Franco, and Francesco Bruno. "Exit from Terrorism." ***CrimCare Journal,*** 1:1 (1985), 39-48.

4768. _____. "Ideology and Repentance: Terrorism in Italy." In: W. Reich, ed. ***Origins of Terrorism.*** Cambridge: Cambridge University Press, 1990. pp. 59-64.

4769. Ferrarotti, Franco. "Terrorism and the Tradition of Intellectual Elitism in Italy." ***Praxis International,*** 1 (July 1981), 140-159.

4770. Fraser, John. "The Inner Contradictions of Marxism and Political Violence: The Case of the Italian Left." ***Social Research,*** 48:1 (1981), 21-44.

4771. Furlong, Paul. "Political Terrorism in Italy: Responses, Reactions and Immobilism." In: J. Lodge, ed. ***Terrorism: A Challenge to the State.*** Oxford: Martin Robertson, 1981. pp. 57-90.

4772. Gentilone, Filippo, and Jose Ramos Regidor. "The Political Dimension of Reconciliation: A Recent Italian Experience." In: C. Floristan and D. Duquoc, eds. ***Forgiveness.*** McLean, VA.: Books International, 1986. pp. 22-31.

4773. Grassi, Aldo. "Terrorism in Italy and the Government Response." In: R. H. Ward and H. E. Smith, eds. ***International Terrorism: The Domestic Response.*** Chicago, IL.: University of Illinois at Chicago, Office of International Criminal Justice, 1987. pp. 93-98.

4774. Gualdi, C. "Multi-Subject Trials: The Italian Experience." ***Police Chief,*** 55:4 (1988), 13-14.

4775. Harmon, Christopher C. "Left Meets Right in Terrorism: A Focus on Italy." ***Strategic Review,*** (Winter 1985), 40-51.

4776. Henze, Paul. "Origins of the Plot to Kill the Pope." ***Washington Quarterly,*** 6:4 (Autumn 1983), 3-19.

4777. Jamieson, Alison. "The Italian Experience." In: H. H. Tucker, ed. ***Combating the Terrorists.*** New York: Facts on File, 1988. pp. 113-154.

4778. _____. "Political Kidnapping in Italy." ***Conflict,*** 8:1 (1988), 41-48.

4779. Jenkins, Brian M. "Italian Terrorism: Recent Developments." ***TVI Report,*** 7:3 (1987), 12-15.

4780. Jenkins, Philip. "The Assassins Revisited: Claire Sterling and the Politics of Intelligence." ***International and National Security***, 1;3 (1986), 459-471.

4781. La Scala, Frank. "Italy's "Other" Terrorists." ***TVI Journal***, 3:5 (1982), 6-15.

4782. Lovett, Clara M. "Marxism and Culture in Italy." ***Problems of Communism***, 29:6 (November-December 1980), 77-80.

4783. Lumley, B., and Philip Schlesinger. "Press, The State and Its Enemies: The Italian Case." ***Sociological Review***, 30 (November 1982), 603-626.

4784. Melady, Thomas, and John F. Kikoski. "The Attempted Assassination of the Pope?." ***Orbis***, 28:4 (Winter 1985), 775-801.

4785. Melucci, Alberto. "New Movements, Terrorism and the Political System: Reflections on the Italian Case." ***Socialist Review***, 11:2 (1981), 97-136.

4786. Moran, Sue. "Red Brigades Assassination of Economist Ezio Tarantelli." ***TVI Journal***, 5:4 (1985), 8-9.

4787. _____. "The Case of Terrorist Patricio Peci: A Character Sketch." ***TVI Journal***, 5:2 (1984), 34-35.

4788. Moss, David. "The Kidnapping and Murder of Aldo Moro." ***European Journal of Sociology***, 22:2 (1981), 265-295.

4789. Newhouse, John. "The Diplomatic Round - A Freemasonry of Terrorism." ***New Yorker***, (July 8, 1985), 46-49, 51-63.

4790. Noli, Jean. "Imposimato, A Man of Great Courage." ***Reader's Digest (Canada)***, 127 (August 1985), 69-73.

4791. Pasquino, Gianfranco, and Donatella Della Porta. "Interpretations of Italian Left Wing Terrorism." In: H. P. Merkl, ed. ***Political Violence and Terror.*** Berkeley, CA.: University of California Press, 1986. pp. 169-190.

4792. Pisano, Vittorfranco S. "The Italian Experience." In: B. M. Jenkins, ed. ***Terrorism and Personal Protection.*** Stoneham, MA.: Butterworth, 1985. pp. 64-87.

4793. _____. "Libya's Foothold in Italy." ***Washington Quarterly***, 5:2 (1982), 179-182.

4794. _____. "Structure and Dynamics of Italian Terrorism." In: ***Clandestine Tactics and Technology, Vol. 6.*** Gaithersburg, MD.: International Association of Chiefs of Police, 1980. 34p.

4795. _____. "Terrorism in Italy: From Dozier's Rescue to Hunt's Assassination." ***Police Chief***, 51 (June 1984), 35-38.

4796. _____. "Terrorism in Italy: The Dozier Affair." ***Police Chief***, 49 (April 1982), 38-41.

4797. _____. "Terrorism - The Italian Case." ***Police Chief***, (March 1985), 136-138.

4798. _____. "Red Brigades: A Challenge to Italian Democracy." In: W. Gutteridge, ed. ***Contemporary Terrorism.*** New York: Facts on File, 1986. pp. 167-197.

4799. _____. "Clandestine Operations in Italy: The Bulgarian Connection." ***Conflict Quarterly***, 4:1 (1984), 28-38.

4800. _____. "Foreign Links with Italian Terrorists." ***Terrorism Report***, 1:3 (1980), 3-6.

4801. _____. "Interview with Giorgio Almirante, Member of Parliament and Secretary of the Italian Social Movement." ***TVI Journal***, 1:8 (1980), 2-4.

4802. _____. "The Red Brigades: A Challenge to Italian Democracy." ***Conflict Studies***, 120 (July 1980), 1-19.

4803. _____. "Terrorism of the Right in Italy: Facts and Allegations." ***TVI Journal***, 6:1 (1985), 20-23.

4804. _____. "Who's Fighting Italian Terrorism? Are Police and Intelligence Neutralized?" ***TVI Journal***, 1:3 (1980), 18-20.

4805. _____. "Genesis, Rise, and Decline of Italian Terrorism: The Operational Dimension." ***Conflict,*** 10:3 (1990), 227-238.

4806. "Red Brigades are Red Faced." ***TVI Journal,*** 3:5 (1982), 4-6.

4807. Rimanelli, Marco. "Italian Terrorism and Society, 1940s-1980s: Roots, Ideologies, Evolution, and International Connections." ***Terrorism,*** 12:4 (1989), 249-296.

4808. Romano, S. "Roots of Italian Terrorism." ***Policy Review,*** 25 (Summer 1983), 25-27.

4809. Rosen, M. D. "At War With the Red Brigades." ***Police Magazine,*** (March 1982), 42-48.

4810. Salvioni, D., and A. Stephanson. "Reflections on the Red Brigades." ***Orbis,*** 29:3 (1985), 489-506.

4811. Santoro, K., et al. "Italian Attitudes and Responses to Terrorism." ***Terrorism,*** 10:4 (1987), 289-310.

4812. Scherer, John L. "The Plot to Kill the Pope." ***Terrorism,*** 7:4 (1985), 351-366.

4813. Schraub, Kimber M. "The Rise and Fall of the Red Brigades." In: B. Rubin, ed. ***The Politics of Counterterrorism.*** Lanham, MD.: University Publications of America, 1990. pp. 137-162.

4814. Scotti, Tony. "The Aldo Moro Kidnapping." ***TVI Journal,*** 5:3 (1985), 7-8.

4815. Seton-Watson, Christopher. "Terrorism in Italy." In: J. Lodge, ed. ***The Threat of Terrorism.*** Brighton: Wheatsheaf Books, 1988. pp. 89-118.

4816. Sheehan, Thomas. "Italy: Terror on the Right." ***New York Review of Books,*** (January 22, 1981), 23-26.

4817. Silj, Alessandro. "Case Study II: Italy." In: D. Carlton and C. Schaerf, eds. ***Contemporary Terror.*** London: Macmillan, 1981. pp. 139-152.

4818. Sterling, Claire. "Italian Terrorists: Life and Death in a Violent Generation." ***Encounter,*** 57:1 (1981), 18-31.

4819. Stoppa, Paolo. "Revolutionary Culture Italian Style." ***Washington Quarterly,*** 4:2 (Spring 1981), 100-113.

4820. Striker, James R. "Terrorism - An Expression of the Public's Needs." ***TVI Journal,*** 3:9 (1982), 3-10.

4821. "TVI Report Profiles: Red Brigades, Brigate Rosse (BR)." ***TVI Report,*** 8:2 (1988), 5-8.

4822. "Terror on the Italian Right." ***TVI Journal,*** 3:5 (1982), 6+.

4823. Vigna, Piero Luigi. "Italian Responses." In: B. Netanyahu, ed. ***International Terrorism: Challenge and Response.*** New Brunswick, NJ.: Transaction Books, 1981. pp. 196-200.

4824. Villalba, Franco. "The Organizational Structure of the Italian Counter-Terrorist Forces." ***International Defence Review,*** 18:6 (1985), 915-917.

4825. Wagner-Pacifici, Robin. "Negotiation in the Aldo Moro Affair: The Suppressed Alternative in a Case of Symbolic Politics." ***Political Sociology,*** 12:4 (1983), 487-517.

4826. Weinberg, Leonard. "The Violent Life: Left and Right-Wing Terrorism in Italy." In: P. H. Merkl, ed. ***Political Violence and Terror.*** Berkeley, CA.: University of California Press, 1986. pp. 145-168.

4827. _____, and William L. Eubank. "Recruitment of Italian Political Terrorists." In: M. Sloan and B. Schechterman, eds. ***Multidimensional Terrorism.*** Boulder, CO.: Lynne Rienner, 1987. pp. 81-94.

4828. _____. _____. "Neo-Fascist and Far Left Terrorists in Italy." ***The British Journal of Political Science,*** (October 1988)

4829. _____. _____. "Leaders and Followers in Italian Terrorist Groups." ***Terrorism and Political Violence,*** 1:2 (April 1989), 156-176.

4830. "Who's Who in the Agca Affair?" ***Briefing,*** 8 (December 6, 1982), 8-12.

3. Documents and Reports

4831. Buckingham, Larry Allen. ***Red Brigades: A Description of a Terrorist Organization.*** M.A. Thesis. Wright-Patterson AFB, OH.: Air Force Institute of Technology, 1982. 118p.

4832. Della Porta, Donatella. "Left-Wing Political Violence in Italy During the Seventies: The Formation of Terrorist Organizations." Paper Presented at the ***13th World Conference of the International Political Science Association,*** held on July 15-20, 1985, in Paris.

4833. Ferracuti, Franco. "Ideology and Repentance: Terrorism in Italy." Paper Presented at the ***Interdisciplinary Research Conference on the Psychology of Terrorism,*** held on March 16-18, 1987, at the Woodrow Wilson International Center for Scholars, in Washington, D.C., 28p.

4834. _____. "Repentant Terrorist Legislation - A Preliminary Analysis of Problems and Results in Italy." In: B. G. Curtis, ed. ***Outthinking the Terrorist - An International Challenge, Proceedings.*** Rockville, MD.: National Criminal Justice Reference Service, 1985. pp. 57-61.

4835. Friedlander, Robert A. ***An Infinity of Mirrors: Mehmet Ali Agca and the 'Plot to Kill the Pope'.*** Gaithersburg, MD.: International Association of Chiefs of Police, 1983.

4836. Hayes, Richard E., and Thomas S. Schiller. ***The Impact of Government Behavior on the Frequency, Type, and Targets of Terrorist Group Activity: The Italian Experience, 1968-1982.*** McLean, VA.: Defence Systems, 1983. 142p.

4837. Langford, Kenneth R. ***An Analysis of Left and Right Wing Terrorism in Italy.*** Washington, D.C.: Defence Intelligence College, 1985. 94p.

4838. Moran, Sue, ed. ***Court Depositions of Three Red Brigadists.*** RAND N-2391-RC. Santa Monica, CA.: Rand Corporation, 1986. 269p.

4839. Pasquino, Gianfranco. "Italian Terrorism: Competing Explanations." Paper Presented to the ***12th Annual World Congress of the International Political Science Association,*** held in August 1982, in Rio de Janeiro.

4840. Pisano, Vittorfranco S. ***The Red Brigades: A Challenge to Italian Democracy.*** Conflict Studies, No. 120. London: Institute for the Study of Conflict, 1980. 19p.

4841. _____. ***Terrorism and Security: The Italian Experience: Report to the Subcommittee on Security and Terrorism of the Committee on the Judiciary, U.S. Senate.*** Washington, D.C.: U.S. Government Printing Office, 1984.

4842. United States. Congress. Senate. Committee on the Judiciary. Subcommittee on Security and Terrorism. ***Terrorism and Security: The Italian Experience: Report.*** Washington, D.C.: U.S. Government Printing Office, 1984. 20p.

4843. _____._____._____._____._____. ***Terrorism in Italy: An Update Report, 1983-1985.*** Washington, D.C.: U.S. Government Printing Office, 1986. 36p.

4844. Vissicchio, Luigi, et al. ***Italian Attitudes and Responses to Terrorism.*** Philadelphia, PA.: University of Pennsylvania, 1987. 63p.

4845. Wagner-Pacifici, Robin. ***The Moro Morality Play: A Case of Symbolic Politics.*** Ph.D. Dissertation. Philadelphia, PA.: University of Pennsylvania, 1983. 394p.

4846. Weinberg, Leonard. "The Violent Life: An Analysis of Left and Right Wing Terrorism in Italy." Paper Presented to the ***12th Annual World Congress of the International Political Science Association,*** held in August 1982, in Rio de Janeiro.

4847. _____. "An Analysis of Neo-Fascists and Neo-Fascist Violence in Italy." Paper Presented to the ***13th World Congress of the International Political Science Association,*** held on July 15-20, 1985 in Paris.

g. SPAIN

1. Books

4848. Clark, Robert P. ***The Basque Insurgents: ETA, 1952-1980.*** Madison, WI.: University of Wiscounsin Press, 1984.

4849. _____. ***Negotiating with ETA: Obstacles to Peace in the Basque Country, 1975-1988.*** The Basque Series. Reno, NV.: University of Nevada Press, 1990. 278p.

2. Journal Articles

4850. Arango, E. Ramon. "Violence and Terrorism." In: E. R. Arango. ***Spain: From Repression to Renewal.*** Boulder, CO.: Westview Press, 1985. pp. 179-184.

4851. Brunn, Gerhard. "Nationalist Violence and Terror in the Spanish Border Provinces: ETA." In: W. J. Mommsen and G. Hirschfeld, eds. ***Social Protest, Violence and Terror in Nineteenth and Twentieth Century Europe.*** London: Macmillan, 1982. pp. 112-136.

4852. Casas, Tony. "Spain's Prison for Terrorists." ***Corrections Today,*** 51:4 (July 1989), 152-153.

4853. Clark, Robert P. "Patterns in the Lives of ETA Members." ***Terrorism,*** 6:3 (1983), 423-454.

4854. _____. "Patterns of ETA Violence, 1968-1980." In: P. H. Merkl, ed. ***Political Violence and Terror.*** Berkeley, CA.: University of California Press, 1986. pp. 123-142.

4855. _____. "Patterns in the Lives of ETA Members." In: P. H. Merkl, ed. ***Political Violence and Terror.*** Berkeley, CA.: University of California Press, 1986. pp. 283-310.

4856. _____. "Obstacles to Negotiating a Ceasefire with Insurgents: The ETA Case." ***TVI Report,*** 7:1 (1987), 1-11.

4857. Douglass, W. A., and Joseba Zulaika. "On the Interpretation of Terrorist Violence: ETA and the Basque Political Process." ***Comparative Studies in Society and History,*** 32:2 (1990), 238-257.

4858. Fusi, Juan Pablo. "Spain: The Fragile Democracy." ***West European Politics,*** 5:3 (1982), 222-235.

4859. Glos, George E. "Danger Signals for Spain." ***The World Today,*** 38:1 (1982), 26-32.

4860. Heilberg, Marianne. "Saints and Sinners: An Analysis of the Political Violence of ETA." In: E. Ellingsen, ed. ***International Terrorism as a Political Weapon.*** Oslo: The Norwegian Atlantic Committee, 1988. pp. 27-46.

4861. Hollyman, John Llewelyn. "Basque Revolutionary Separatism: ETA." In: P. Preston, ed. ***Spain in Crisis.*** London: Harvester Press, 1976. pp. 212-233.

4862. "Insurgency in Spain." ***TVI Journal,*** 2:6 (1981), 10-17.

4863. Janke, Peter. "Terrorism and the Spanish State: A Plan for Action." In: H. H. Tucker, ed. ***Combating the Terrorists.*** New York: Facts on File, 1988. pp. 173-184.

4864. _____. "Spanish Separatism: ETA's (Euskadi ta Askatasuna) Threat to Basque Democracy." In: W. Gutteridge, ed. ***Contemporary Terrorism.*** New York: Facts on File, 1986. pp. 135-166.

4865. Morn, F., and M. Toro. "From Dictatorship to Democracy: Crime and Policing in Contemporary Spain." ***International Journal of Comparative and Applied Criminal Justice,*** 13:1 (1989), 53-64.

4866. Moxon-Browne, Edward. "Terrorism and the Spanish State: The Violent Bid for Basque Autonomy." In: H. H. Tucker, ed. ***Combating the Terrorists.*** New York: Facts on File, 1988. pp. 155-172

4867. Pisano, Vittorfranco S. "Spain Faces the Extremists: Cannons to the Left and Cannons to the Right." ***TVI Journal,*** 2:6 (1981), 10-16.

4868. Pollack, Benny, and Graham Hunter. "Dictatorship, Democracy and Terrorism in Spain." In: J. Lodge, ed. ***The Threat of Terrorism.*** Brighton: Wheatsheaf books, 1988. pp. 119-144.

4869. Reinares, Fernando. "The Dynamics of Terrorism During the Transition to Democracy in Spain." In: P. Wilkinson and A. M. Stewart, eds. ***Contemporary Research on Terrorism.*** Aberdeen: Aberdeen University Press, 1987. pp. 121-129.

4870. _____. "Nationalism and Violence in Basque Politics." ***Conflict,*** 8:2/3 (1988), 141-156.

4871. "TVI Report Profiles: Basque Homeland and Freedom, Euzkadi Ta Askatasuna (ETA)." ***TVI Report,*** 8:2 (1988), 9-12.

4872. Trevino, Jose A. "Spain's Internal Security: The Basque Autonomous Police Force." In: Y. Alexander and K. A. Myers, eds. ***Terrorism in Europe.*** London: Croom Helm, 1982. pp. 141-153.

3. Documents and Reports

4873. Clark, Robert P. "Patterns of Insurgent Violence in Spain's Basque Provinces." Paper Presented to the ***Annual Meeting of the Southwestern Political Science Association,*** held in March 1981.

4874. _____. "The Roots of Insurgency: The Social Origins of ETA." Paper Presented to the ***Annual Meeting of the International Studies Association,*** held on October 1981.

4875. _____. "Basque Resistance and ETA." Paper Presented at the ***Spring Conference of the National Capital Area Political Science Association,*** held on February 27, 1982 at Mount Vernon College, Washington, D.C.

4876. _____. "The Basque Resistance: Violent and Non-Violent." Paper Presented at the ***Role of Terrorism in Ethnic Nationalism Pannel of the Annual Convention of the International Studies Association, Studies*** A held On October 29-31, 1981 at the University of Florida.

4877. De Ridder, Martine M. "Basque Terrorism: Evaluating Governmental Responses to ETA." Paper Presented at the ***24th Annual Convention of the International Studies Association,*** held on April 5-9, 1983 in Mexico City.

4878. ***Exposing Police Terror in Spain.*** Case # 956.0. Case Program. Cambridge, MA.: Harvard University, Kennedy School of Government, 1990.

4879. Hayes, Richard E., and Melvin Y. Shibuya. ***The Impact of Government Behavior on the Frequency, Type, and Targets of Terrorist Group Activity: The Spanish Experience, 1968-1982.*** McLean, VA.: Defence Systems, 1983. 123p.

4880. Janke, Peter. ***Spanish Separatism: ETA's Threat to Basque Democracy.*** Conflict Studies, No. 123. London: Institute for the Study of Conflict, 1981. 19p.

4881. Jaurequi Bereciartu, Gurutz. "Political Violence in the Basque Country." Paper Presented to the ***13th Annual World Congress of the International Political Science Association,*** held on July 15-20, 1985, in Paris.

4882. Llera Ramo, Francisco J., and Jose M. Mata Lopez. "ETA: From Secret Army to Social Movement or Political Parties." Paper Presented at the ***12th World Congress of Sociology,*** held on July 3-9, 1990 in Madrid.

4883. Moxon-Browne, Edward. ***Spain and the ETA: The Bid for Basque Autonomy.*** Conflict Studies, No. 201. London: Centre for Security and Conflict Studies, 1986. 17p.

4884. Porter, Franz. ***Spain's ETA.*** Washington, D.C,: Defence Intelligence College, 1986. 30p.

4885. Zulaika, Joseba. ***Itziar: The Cultural Context of Basque Political Violence.*** Ph.D. Dissertation. Princeton, NJ.: Princeton University, 1982. 541p.

h. THE REST OF WESTERN EUROPE

1. Journal Articles

4886. Adams, Nathan M. "Greece: Sanctuary of International Terrorism." ***Reader's Digest (Canada),*** 134:806 (June 1989), 62-67.

4887. Cook, Shura. "Interview with Dr. Peter Jankowitsch, Former Minister of Foreign Affairs, Austria." ***TVI Report,*** 7:3 (1987), 19-22.

4888. Dermaut, John. "Terrorism in Belgium: The Communist Combatant Cells." ***TVI Report,*** 6:4 (1986), 27-28.

4889. Dinan, Desmond. "Anti-Terrorist Forces and Operations in the Irish Republic." ***TVI Report,*** 6:4 (1986), 32-35.

4890. Frigaard, Iver. "Terrorism in Nordic Perspective." In: E. Ellingsen, ed. ***International Terrorism as a Political Weapon.*** Oslo: The Norwegian Atlantic Committee, 1988. pp. 47-53.

4891. Jenkins, Philip. "The Assassination of Olof Palme: Evidence and Ideology." ***Contemporary Crises,*** 13:1 (1989), 15-33.

4892. Laufer, David. "The Evolution of Belgian Terrorism." In: J. Lodge, ed. ***The Threat of Terrorism.*** Brighton: Wheatsheaf Books, 1988. pp. 179-212.

4893. Petkovic, Ranko. "Yugoslavia and International Terrorism." ***Review of International Affairs***, 37 (January 30, 1986), 1-3.

4894. Sinclair, Hugh. "False Alarm Keeps Belgians on Edge." ***Terror Update***, 8 (May 1989), 8.

4895. Sundberg, Jacob W. F. "Operation Leo." ***Terrorism***, 5:3 (1981), 197-232.

4896. _____. "Operation Leo: Description and Analysis of a European Terrorist Operation." In: B. M. Jenkins, ed. ***Terrorism and Beyond: An International Conference on Terrorism and Low-Level Conflict.*** Santa Monica, CA.: RAND Corporation, 1980. pp. 174-202.

4897. "Terrorism in Greece." ***Foreign Report***, (March 7, 1985), 1-2.

3. Documents and Reports

4898. United States. Office of Coordinator of Counter-Terrorism. ***Revolutionary Organization 17 November.*** Washington, D.C.: U.S. Government Printing Office, 1989. 9p.

i. SOVIET UNION AND EASTERN EUROPE

1. Books

4899. Adelman, Jonathan. ***Terror and Communist Politics: The Role of the Secret Police in Communist States.*** Boulder, Co.: Westview Press, 1984. 292p.

4900. Francis, Samuel T. ***The Soviet Strategy of Terror.*** Washington, D.C.: The Heritage Foundation, 1981. 78p.

4901. Golan, Galia. ***Gorbachev's "New Thinking" About Terrorism.*** The Washington Papers/141. New York: Praeger, 1990. 117p.

4902. Goren, Roberta. ***The Soviet Union and Terrorism.*** London: Allen & Unwin, 1984. 232p.

2. Journal Articles

4903. Alexander, Yonah. "Some Perspectives on Terrorism and the Soviet Union." In: W. Laqueur, ed. ***The Terrorism Reader.*** New York: Meridian, 1987. pp. 363-368.

4904. Ascher, Abraham. "Lessons of Russian Terrorism." ***Problems of Communism***, 29:6 (1980), 70-75.

4905. Bocharov, Gennady. "Hijacking: Nightmare in the Skies." ***Literary Gazette International***, 1:13 (1990), 10-11.

4906. Ceyba, R. J. "Terrorism - Made in U.S.S.R.." ***Journal of Security Administration***, 5:1 (1982), 75-85.

4907. Filkentscher, Wolfgang. "Terrorism, Marxism, and the Soviet Constitution." In: B. Netanyahu, ed. ***Terrorism: How the West Can Win.*** New York: Farrar, Straus, Giroux, 1986. pp. 52-55.

4908. Golan, Galia. "The Soviet Attitude Toward the Use of Terror." In: A. Kurz, ed. ***Contemporary Trends in World Terrorism.*** New York: Praeger, 1987. pp. 94-102.

4909. Haggman, Bertil. "Soviets Ambivalent About Terrorism: Ivan Wears a Janus Face." ***TVI Journal,*** 1:7 (1980), 2-7.

4910. Henze, Paul. "Bulgaria: An Interlocking Web of Narcotics Trafficking, Terrorism and Subversion." ***Security Systems Digest,*** 15:13 (1984), 4-8.

4911. Holler, Lyman E. "'They Shoot People, Don't They?': A Look at Soviet Terrorist Mentality." ***Air University Review,*** 32:6 (September-October 1981), 83-88.

4912. Holyst, Brunon. "The Abduction of Polish Airlines "LOT" Planes." ***Violence, Aggression and Terrorism,*** 3:1-2 (1989), 119-138.

4913. Ivianski, Zeev. "Fathers and Sons: A Study of Jewish Involvement in the Revolutionary Movement and Terrorism in Tsarist Russia." ***Terrorism and Political Violence,*** 1:2 (April 1989), 137-155.

4914. Kamenetsky, Ihor. "Terrorism as an Instrument of the State in the U.S.S.R." In: H. H. Han, ed. ***Terrorism, Political Violence and World Order.*** Lanham, MD.: University Press of America, 1984. pp. 319-338.

4915. Ludwikowski, Rett R. "State Sponsored Domestic Terrorism: The Case of Poland." ***Terrorism,*** 12:2 (1989), 89-96.

4916. _____. "Glasnost and Terrorism - the Next Phase." ***Terrorism,*** 12:6 (1989), 429-432.

4917. Maley, Robert J. "The Potential for Terrorism Within the Soviet Union in the 21st Century." ***Terrorism,*** 13:1 (1990), 53-64.

4918. Maslic, Andjelko. "Terrorism by Fascist Emigration of Yugoslav Origin." ***Socialist Thought and Practice,*** 3 (1981), 49-64.

4919. Medvedev, Roy. "The Sources of Political Terrorism." ***Dissent,*** 36:3 (Summer 1989), 318-322.

4920. Murphy, John F., and Donald R. Brady. "The Soviet Union and International Terrorism." ***International Lawyer,*** 16 (Winter 1982), 139-148.

4921. Mushkat, M. "Some Aspects of Soviet Views of Guerrilla Warfare and Terrorism." In: R. E. Kanet, ed. ***Soviet Foreign Policy Studies and East - West Relations.*** New York: Pergamon Press, 1982. pp. 166-197.

4922. Pilon, J. G. "The Bulgarian Connection: Drugs, Weapons and Terrorism." ***Terrorism,*** 9:4 (1987), 361-371.

4923. Sadkovic, James J. "Terrorism in Croatia, 1929-1934." ***East European Quarterly,*** 22:1 (1988), 55-79.

4924. Valenta, Jiri. "Terrorism and the U.S.S.R.." ***Terrorism,*** 10:1 (1987), 59-61.

4925. Waller, Kristen L. "Why Austria? An Analysis of Arab Terrorism in a Neutral Country." ***TVI Report,*** 7:3 (1987), 16-19.

3. Documents and Reports

4926. Geifman, Anna. ***Political Parties and Revolutionary Terrorism in Russia, 1900-1917***. Ph.D. Dissertation. Cambridge, MA.: Harvard University, 1990. 413p.

4927. Newell, David A. ***The Russian Marxist Response to Terrorism: 1878-1917***. Ph.D. Dissertation. Palo Alto, CA.: Stanford University, 1981. 514p.

D. LATIN AMERICA

a. GENERAL WORKS

1. Books

4928. Ehrenfeld, Rachel. ***Narco Terrorism.*** New York: Basic Books, 1990. 225p.

4929. Radu, Michael, and Vladimir Tismaneanu. ***Latin American Revolutionaries: Groups, Goals, Methods.*** Washington, D.c.: Pergamon-Brassey's, 1990. 386p.

4930. _____, ed. ***Violence and the Latin American Revolutionaries.*** New Brunswick, NJ.: Transaction Books, 1988. 156p.

4931. Wiarda, Howard J. ***Latin American Politics and Development.*** Boulder, Co.: Westview Press, 1985. 672p.

2. Journal Articles

4932. Anderson, James. "Latin America: Regional Assessment." In: R. Clutterbuck, ed. ***The Future of Political Violence.*** London: Macmillan, 1986. pp. 124-132.

4933. Brock, David. "The World of Narcoterrorism." ***American Spectator,*** 22 (June 1989), 24-28.

4934. Enders, T. "Cuban Support for Terrorism and Insurgency in the Western Hemisphere." ***Department of State Bulletin,*** (August 1982), 73-75.

4935. Finney, Richard A. "Growing Unity Among South American Guerrillas." ***Journal of Defense and Diplomacy,*** 4:7 (July 1986), 21-24.

4936. Ford, John W. "Terrorism in the Western Hemisphere - The Role of the OAS and Its Human Rights Commission." In: H. H. Han, ed. ***Terrorism, Political Violence and World Order.*** Lanham, MD.: University Press of America, 1984. pp. 663-666.

4937. Francis, Samuel T. "Latin American Terrorism: Links with the Terrorists International." ***Terrorism Report,*** 1:1 (1980), 5-6.

4938. Galvin, John R. "Challenge & Response: On the Southern Flank Three Decades Later." ***Military Review,*** 66:8 (1986), 5-15.

4939. Garcia-Passalacqua, Juan M. "Intertwined Futures: Puerto Rico, The United Nations, The Caribbean Basin and Central America." ***Fletcher Forum,*** 9 (Summer 1985), 269-294.

4940. Gillespie, Richard. "A Critique of the Urban Guerrilla: Argentina, Uruguay and Brazil." ***Conflict Quarterly,*** 1:2 (1980), 39-53.

4941. _____. "The Urban Guerrilla in Latin America." In: N. O'Sullivan, ed. ***Terrorism, Ideology, and Revolution.*** Boulder, CO.: Westview Press, 1986. pp. 150-177.

4942. Halperin, Ernst. "Violence in Latin America: Insurgencies." In: T. Adeniran and Y. Alexander, eds. ***International Violence.*** New York: Praeger, 1983. pp. 106-115.

4943. Hudson, Rex A. "Castro's America Department: Systemizing Insurgencies in Latin America." ***Terrorism,*** 9:2 (1987), 125-168.

4944. Huggins, Martha D. "U.S. Supported State Terror: A History of Police Training in Latin America." ***Crime and Social Justice,*** 27 (1987), 149-171.

4945. Levy, Jim, and Peter Ross. "The State of Violence: Terror in Latin America." ***Australian Quarterly,*** 58:3 (Spring 1986), 269-277.

4946. Lopez, George A. "Terrorism in Latin America." In: M. Stohl, ed. ***The Politics of Terrorism.*** New York: Marcel Dekker, 1988. pp. 497-524.

4947. Meyer, Dan C. "Myth of Narcoterrorism in Latin America." ***Military Review,*** 70:3 (March 1990), 64-70.

4948. Morris, D. "Terrorism in Latin America." In: V. S. Pisano, ed. ***Terrorist Dynamics: A Geographical Perspective.*** Arlington VA.: International Association of Chiefs of Police, 1988. pp. 93-125.

4949. O'Keefe, R. B. "Ruben Dario's Dinamita: The Advent of Left-Wing Terrorism in the America's." ***Americas,*** (January 1985), 83-91.

4950. Perez, Jesse M., and Donald B. Vought. "Violence: The Alternate Political Institution." ***Military Review,*** 66:8 (1986), 42-55.

4951. Petras, James. "Political Economy of State Terror - Chile, El-Salvador and Brazil." ***Crime and Social Justice,*** 27-28 (1987), 88-171.

4952. _____. "The Anatomy of State Terror: Chile, El Salvador and Brazil." ***Science and Society,*** 51:3 (1987), 314-338.

4953. Radu, Michael. "Terror, Terrorism and Insurgency in Latin America." ***Orbis,*** 28:1 (1984), 27-40.

4954. _____. "Terror, Terrorism, and Insurgency in Latin America." In: W. Laqueur, ed. ***The Terrorism Reader.*** New York: Meridian, 1987. pp. 298-302.

4955. Reif, Linda L. "Women in Latin American Guerrilla Movements: A Comparative Perspective." ***Comparative Politics,*** 18:2 (1986), 147-170.

4956. Russell, Charles A. "Latin America: Regional Review." ***Terrorism,*** 4 (1980), 277-292.

4957. Sater, William F. "Frente Popular Manuel Rodriguez." ***TVI Report,*** 8:1 (1988), 8-13.

4958. Shackley, Theodore G., Robert L. Oatman and Richard A. Finney. "Narcoterrorism." ***Chief Executive,*** (June 1990), 44-48.

4959. Sloan, John W. "Political Terrorism in Latin America." In: M. Stohl, ed. ***The Politics of Terrorism.*** 2nd ed. New York: Marcel Dekker, 1983. pp. 377-396.

4960. _____. "State Repression and Enforcement Terrorism in Latin America." In: M. Stohl and G. A. Lopez, eds. ***State as Terrorist.*** Westport, CT.: Greenwood Press, 1984. pp. 83-98.

4961. Sutton, James R. "Latin American Insurgencies: A Personal Perspective." ***International Journal of Comparative and Applied Criminal Justice,*** 13:2 (Fall 1989), 87-94.

4962. Taylor, Robert W. "Liberation Theology, Politics and Violence in Latin America." Paper Presented to the ***Terrorism: An International Conference,*** held on April 15-17, 1986 at the University of Aberdeen. pp. 45-54.

4963. Ugalde, Antonio, and Rodolfo R. Vega. "State Terrorism, Torture and Health in the Southern Cone." ***Social Science and Medicine,*** 28:7 (1989), 759-765.

4964. Waghelstein, John D. "Latin American Insurgency - Status Report." ***TVI Report,*** 8:1 (1988), 47-48.

4965. Waldmann, Peter. "Guerrilla Movements in Argentina, Guatemala, Nicaragua, and Uruguay." In: P. H. Merkl, ed. ***Political Violence and Terror.*** Berkeley, CA.: University of California Press, 1986. pp. 257-282.

4966. Weitz, Richard. "Insurgency and Counterinsurgency in Latin America, 1960-1980." ***Political Science Quarterly,*** 101:3 (1986), 397-414.

4967. Wickham-Crowley, Timothy P. "Terror and Guerrilla Warfare in Latin America, 1956-1970." ***Comparative Studies in Society & History***, 32:2 (April 1990), 201-237.

3. Documents and Reports

4968. Fauriol, G. ***Latin American Insurgencies.*** Washington, D.C.: Georgetown University, Center for Strategic and International Studies, 1985. 226p.

4969. ***Latin American Terrorism: A Round-Up.*** Strategic Briefing Paper, No. 132. Cheltenham, Glos.: Intelligence International, 1990. 21p.

4970. ***The Legitimacy of Political Violence?: The Case of Latin America.*** Occasional Paper Series, 22. Amherst, MA.: University of Massachusetts at Amherst, International Area Studies Programs, 1988. 30p.

4971. Radu, Michael. ***Insurgent and Terrorist Groups in Latin America.*** Philadelphia, PA.: Foreign Policy Research Institute, 1984. 355p.

4972. United States. Congress. Senate. Committee on Foreign Relations. ***Administration Proposal for Counterterrorism Assistance for Central America: Hearings.*** 99th Cong., 1st sess. Washington, D.C.: U.S. Government Printing Office, 1986. 262p.

b. ARGENTINA

1. Books

4973. Graham-Yool, Andrew. ***A Matter of Fear: Portrait of an Argentinian Exile.*** Westport, CT.: Lawrence Hill, 1982. 128p.

2. Journal Articles

4974. Abos, A. "Circles of Violence: The Theory and Practice of State Terror in Argentina." ***This Magazine***, (May-June 1981), 10-16.

4975. "The Argentine Military Junta's Final Report on the War Against Subversion and Terrorism, April 1983." ***Terrorism***, 7:3 (1984), 323-340.

4976. Barkey, David W., and D. S. Eitzen. "Toward an Assessment of Multi-National Corporate Social Expenditures in Relation to Political Stability and Terrorist Activity: The Argentine Case." ***Inter American Economic Affairs***, 34:4 (1981), 77-90.

4977. Berman, Maureen R., and R. S. Clark. "State Terrorism: Disappearances." ***Rutgers Law Journal***, 13 (Spring 1982), 531-577.

4978. Buchanan, Paul G. "The Varied Faces of Domination: State Terror, Economic Policy, and Social Rupture during the Argentine "Proceso," 1976-81." ***American Journal of Political Science***, 31:2 (May 1987), 336-382.

4979. Corradi, Juan E. "The Mode of Destruction: Terror in Argentina." ***Telos***, 54 (Winter 1982-83), 61-76.

4980. Cox, Robert. "Total Terror: Argentina, 1969-1979." In: M. Crenshaw, ed. ***Terrorism, Legitimacy and Terror.*** Middletown, CT.: Wesleyan University Press, 1983. pp. 124-142.

4981. Eitzen, D. S., and David W. Barkey. "Terrorist Targeting and Corporate Philanthropy: The Argentine Case." In: B. M. Jenkins, ed. ***Terrorism and Corporate Protection.*** Stoneham, MA.: Butterworth, 1985. pp. 167-175.

4982. Falcoff, Mark. "Between Two Fires: Terrorism and Counter-Terrorism in Argentina, 1970-1983." In: B. Rubin, ed. ***The Politics of Terrorism.*** Lanham, MD.: University Press of America, 1988. pp. 1-26.

4983. Pion-Berlin, David. "The Political - Economy of State Repression in Argentina." In: M. Stohl and G. A. Lopez, eds. ***State as Terrorist.*** Westport, CT.: Greenwood Press, 1984. pp. 99-122.

4984. Purnell, Susanna W. "Business and Terrorism in Argentina, 1969-1978." In: B. M. Jenkins, ed. ***Terrorism and Personal Protection.*** Stoneham, MA.: Butterworth, 1985. pp. 88-98.

4985. Snow, Peter. "Latin American Political Violence: The Case of Argentina." In: H. H. Han, ed. ***Terrorism, Political Violence and World Order.*** Lanham, MD.: University Press of America, 1984. pp. 267-272.

4986. Suarez-Orozco, Marcelo M. "The Treatment of Children in the Dirty War - Ideology, State Terrorism and the Abuse of Children in Argentina." In: N. Scheperhughes, ed. ***Culture, Illness, and Healing: Studies in Comparative Cross-Cultural Research, Vol 11.*** Dordrecht: D. Reidel, 1987. pp. 227-246.

c. CENTRAL AMERICA

1. Books

4987. Black, George. ***Garrison Guatemala.*** New York: Monthly Review Press, 1984. 208p.

4988. Brody, Reed. ***Contra Terror in Nicaragua: Report of a Fact-Finding Mission: September 1984-January 1985.*** Boston, MA.: South End Press, 1985. 204p.

4989. Cabestrero, Teofilo. ***Blood of the Innocent: Victims of the Contras' War in Nicaragua.*** Maryknoll, NY.: Catholic Institute for International Relations, 1985. 104p.

4990. Didion, Joan. ***Salvador.*** New York: Simon & Schuster, 1983. 108p.

4991. Fried, Jonathan L. ***Guatemala in Rebellion: Unfinished History.*** New York: Grove Tree, 1983. 342p.

4992. Jonas, Susanne, Ed McCaughan and Elisabeth Sutherland, eds. ***Guatemala, Tyranny on Trial.*** San Francisco, CA.: Synthesis Publications, 1984. 301p.

4993. McClintock, Michael. ***The American Connection. Vol. 2: State Terror and Popular Resistance in Guatemala.*** Oxford: Zed Press, 1985. 319p.

4994. _____. ***The American Connection. Vol. 1: State Terror and Popular Resistance in El Salvador.*** Oxford: Zed Press, 1985. 388p.

4995. Payeras, Mario. ***Days of the Jungle: The Testimony of a Guatemalan Guerrillero, 1972-1976.*** New York: Monthly Review Press, 1983. 94p.

2. Journal Articles

4996. Aguilera-Peralta, Gabriel. "Terror and Violence as Weapons of Counterinsurgency in Guatemala." ***Latin American Perspective***, 7:2-3 (1980), 91-113.

4997. Anderson, Thomas P. "The Ambiguities of Political Terrorism in Central America." ***Terrorism***, 4 (1980), 267-276.

4998. Benavides, Marta. "The Death of Maria Cristian Gomez." ***Christianity and Crisis***, 49 (July 10, 1989), 210-211.

4999. Black, George. "Guatemala's Silent War." ***Monthly Review***, 35:3 (1983), 3-17.

5000. Booth, J. A. "Guatemalan Nightmare: Levels of Political Violence, 1966-1972." ***Journal of Interamerican Studies***, 22 (May 1980), 195-225.

5001. Bowen, Gordon L. "The Political Economy of State Terrorism: Barriers to Human Rights in Guatemala." In: G. W. Shepherd and V. P. Nanda, eds. ***Human Rights and Third World Development.*** Westport, CT.: Greenwood Press, 1985. pp. 83-124.

5002. _____. "U.S. Approaches to Guatemalan State Terrorism, 1977-1986." In: M. Stohl and G. A. Lopez, eds. ***Terrible Beyond Endurance? The Foreign Policy of State Terrorism.*** Westport, CT.: Greenwood Press, 1988. pp. 119-166.

5003. Brody, Reed. "U.S. Sponsored Terrorism Against Nicaragua." In: Hans Koechler, ed. ***Terrorism and National Liberation.*** Frankfurt: Peter Lang, 1988. pp. 111-125.

5004. Calero, Adolfo, Arturo Jose Cruz and Alfonso Robello Callejas. "U.S.-Sponsored Contras are Freedom Fighters." In: B. Szumski, ed. ***Terrorism: Opposing Viewpoints.*** St Paul, MN.: Greenhaven Press, 1986. pp. 142-144.

5005. Chamoro, Edgar. "U.S.-Sponsored Contras are Terrorists." In: B. Szumski, ed. ***Terrorism: Opposing Viewpoints.*** St.Paul, MN.: Greenhaven Press, 1986. pp. 137-141.

5006. Collazo-Davila, Vincente. "The Guatemalan Insurrection." In: B. E. O'Neill, W. R. Heaton and D. J. Alberts, eds. ***Insurgency in the Modern World.*** Boulder, CO.: Westview Press, 1980. pp. 109-136.

5007. Dew, Edward. "Suriname Tar Baby: The Signature of Terror." ***Caribbean Review***, 12:1 (Winter 1983), 4-7.

5008. Duarte, M. de Jesus. "Terrorism in Central America." ***Terrorism***, 7:1 (1984), 57-62.

5009. Fairbanks, C. H. "Why Is The PLO in Central America." ***Terrorism***, 10:1 (1987), 62-66.

5010. Halperin, Ernst. "Central America: The Role of Cuba and of the Soviet Union." In: U. Ra'anan, et al. ***Hydra of Carnage.*** Lexington, MA.: Lexington Books, 1986. pp. 125-134.

5011. Hoffman, Bruce. "The PLO and Israel in Central America: The Geopolitical Dimension." ***Terrorism and Political Violence***, 1:4 (October 1989), 482-515.

5012. Keller, Frank B. "Terror in Northern Nicaragua." ***Swiss Review of World Affairs***, 25:3 (1985), 11.

5013. Kiracofe, Clifford A. "The Soviet Network in Central America." ***Midstream***, 27 (May 1981), 3-6.

5014. Krane, Dale A., and T. David Mason. "The Political Economy of Death Squads: Toward a Theory of the Impact of State-Sanctioned Terror." ***International Studies Quarterly***, 33:2 (1989), 175-198.

5015. Livingstone, Neil C. "Death Squads." ***World Affairs***, 146:3 (1983-84), 239-248.

5016. McLellan, Andrew C. "Right-Wing Terror Paralyzes Guatemalan Labor." ***AFL-CIO Free Trade Union News***, (September 1980), 8-9+.

5017. Mulgannon, Terry. "Guerrillas in Guatemala." ***TVI Journal***, 5:3 (1985), 39-43.

5018. _____. "Travelling in El Salvador: Personal Glimpses of a Torn Country." ***TVI Journal***, 5:2 (1984), 20-22.

5019. _____. "A Personal Comment on the Contras." ***TVI Report***, 6:4 1986), 36-37.

5020. Palmatier, Malcolm. "El Salvador President Duarte's Account of the Kidnapping of His Daughter." ***TVI Report***, 7:4 (1987), 16-18.

5021. Premo, Daniel L. "Political Assassination in Guatemala: A Case Study of Institutional Terror." ***Journal of Inter-American Studies and World Affairs***, 23:4 (1981), 429-456.

5022. "Revolutionary Aftermath in Nicaragua." ***TVI Journal***, 1:4 (1980), 11-14.

5023. Taylor, Robert W., and H. E. Vanden. "Defining Terrorism in El Salvador - La Matanza." ***Annals of the American Academy of Political and Social Science***, 463 (1982), 106-118.

5024. Torrens, James. "An Education in Terror at El Salvador's Universities." ***America***, 149 (December 24, 1983), 411-413.

5025. Torres-Rivas, Edelberto. "Guatemala: Crisis and Political Violence." ***NACLA Report on the Americas***, 14:1 (1980), 16-27.

5026. Van den Bergh, Harry. "State Policy and the Cult of Terror in Central America." In: P. Wilkinson and A. M. Stewart, eds. ***Contemporary Research on Terrorism***. Aberdeen: Aberdeen University Press, 1987. pp. 256-269.

5027. Villalobos, Joaquin. "The War in Central America and Its Perspectives." ***TVI Report***, 7:3 (1987), 25-30.

5028. Wainstein, Eleanor S. "El Salvador - Attack on the Private Sector." In: B. M. Jenkins, ed. ***Terrorism and Personal Protection***. Stoneham, MA.: Butterworth, 1985. pp. 99-112.

5029. Zelaya-Coronado, Jorge Luis. "Roots of Political Violence: Case of Guatemala." In: H. H. Han, ed. ***Terrorism, Political Violence and World Order***. Lanham, MD.: University Press of America, 1984. pp. 335-338.

3. Documents and Reports

5030. Amnesty International. ***Guatemala: A Government Program of Political Murder***. London: Amnesty International, 1981. 32p.

5031. Ashby, Timothy. ***Nicaragua's Terrorist Connection***. Backgrounder, T-387. Washington, D.C.: The Heritage Foundation, 1986. 9p.

5032. Bouchey, L. Francis. ***Guatemala: A Promise in Peril***. Washington, D.C.: Council for Inter-American Security, 1980. 91p.

5033. Calvert, Peter. ***Guatemalan Insurgency and American Security***. Conflict Studies, No. 167. London: Institute for the Study of Conflict, 1984. 20p.

5034. Davis, Shelton H. ***Witnesses to Political Violence in Guatemala: The Suppression of a Rural Development Movement***. Boston, MA.: Oxfam America, 1983. 68p.

5035. National Lawyers Guild. ***Guatemala: Repression and Resistance***. New York: National Lawyers Guild, 1980.

5036. Raushenbush, Richard. ***The Terrorist War In Guatemala***. Washington, D.C.: Council for Inter-American Security Educational Institute, 1982. 82p.

5037. Salazar, Leonardo A. ***Discourses on Terrorism and Nicaragua: A Case Study of Television News, Ideology, and Cultural Impoverishment.*** Ph.D. Dissertation. East Lansing, MI.: Michigan State University, 1988. 396p.

5038. Tugwell, Maurice A., and David Charters. ***Insurgency and Counter-Insurgency in Central America.*** ORAE Extra-Mural Paper No. 23. Ottawa: Operational Research and Analysis Establishment, Department of National Defence, 1983. 270p.

5039. United States. Congress. House. Committee on Foreign Affairs. ***The Central American Counterterrorism Acts of 1985: Hearings.*** 99th Cong., 1st sess. Washington, D.C.: U.S. Government Printing Office, 1986. 321p.

5040. _____._____._____._____. Subcommittee on Inter-American Affairs. ***Review of the Presidential Certification of Nicaragua's Connection to Terrorism: Hearings.*** 96th Cong., 2nd sess. Washington, D.C.: U.S. Government Printing Office, 1980.

d. COLOMBIA

1. Journal Articles

5041. Danneskiold Lassen, Suzanne Bettina. "Drug Trafficking and Terrorism in Colombia." In: B. Rubin, ed. ***The Politics of Counterterrorism.*** Lanham, MD.: University Publications of America, 1990. pp. 107-136.

5042. Del Olmo, Rosa. "The Attack on the Supreme Court of Colombia: A Case Study of Guerrilla and Government Violence." ***Violence, Aggression and Terrorism,*** 2:1 (1988), 57-84.

5043. Freifeld, S. A. "Diplomatic Hostage Taking: A Retrospective Look at Bogota." ***International Perspective,*** 9 (September-October 1980), 13-18.

5044. Guillermopietro, A. "Letter From Bogota." ***New Yorker,*** 65 (October 16, 1989), 112-120+.

5045. Hoskin, Gary. "Colombia's Political Crisis." ***Current History,*** (January 1988), 9-12, 38-39.

5046. Jenkins, Brian M. "Colombia's Bold Gamble for Peace." ***TVI Journal,*** 5:2 (1984), 10-19.

5047. Lee, R. W. "Narcoterrorism - the Colombian Case." ***Terrorism,*** 12:6 (1989), 435-437.

5048. Lupsha, Peter A. "Towards an Etiology of Drug Trafficking and Insurgent Relations: The Phenomenon of Narco Terrorism." ***International Journal of Comparative and Applied Criminal Justice,*** 13:2 (Winter 1989), 61-75.

5049. Mochary, M. V. "Narcoterrorism - the Next Phase." ***Terrorism,*** 12:6 (1989), 438-440.

5050. Rosenberg, Tina. "A Mess in the Andes." ***New Republic,*** (September 18-25, 1989), 23-26.

5051. Sater, William F. "Terrorist Kidnappings in Colombia." In: B. M. Jenkins, ed. ***Terrorism and Personal Protection.*** Stoneham, MA.: Butterworth, 1985. pp. 113-128.

5052. "TVI Report Profiles: April 19 Movement (M-19)." ***TVI Report,*** 9:1 (1989), 1-4.

5053. "TVI Report Profiles: Revolutionary Armed Forces of Colombia (FARC)." ***TVI Report***, 9:1 (1989), 5-7.

5054. "Terrorism: The New Global War." ***Latin American Times***, 2 (May 1980), 10-15.

5055. Zackrison, James L. "La Violencia in Colombia: An Anomaly in Terrorism." ***Conflict Quarterly***, 9:4 (Fall 1989), 5-18.

2. Documents and Reports

5056. Jenkins, Brian M. ***Colombia's Bold Gamble for Peace***. RAND P-7055. Santa Monica, CA.: RAND Corporation, 1985. 21p.

e. PERU

1. Books

5057. Tarazona-Sevillano, Gabriela. ***Sendero Luminoso and the Threat of Narcoterrorism***. Washington Papers, 144. New York: Praeger, 1990. 168p.

2. Journal Articles

5058. Ash, Robert B. "The Rural Struggle in Latin America: The Case of Peru and Sendero." ***Journal of the Royal United Services Institute for Defence Studies***, 130:2 (1985), 39-45.

5059. Atlin, J., and J. Nef. "Peru's "Shining Path"." ***International Perspectives***, (May - June 1985), 25-28.

5060. Bennett, Philip. "Peru: Corner of the Dead." ***Atlantic***, (May 1984), 28-33.

5061. _____. "Pol Pot in Peru." ***New Republic***, (January 28, 1985), 16-18.

5062. Berg, R. H. "Sendero Luminoso and the Peasantry of Andahnaylas." ***Journal of Interamerican Studies of World Affairs***, 28 (Winter 1986/87), 165-196.

5063. Bourque, Susan C., and Kay B. Warren. "Democracy Without Peace: The Cultural Politics of Terror in Peru." ***Latin American Research Review***, 24:1 (1989), 7-34.

5064. Davis, Robert B. "Sendero Luminoso and Peru's Struggle for Survival." ***Military Review***, 70:1 (January 1990), 79-88.

5065. De Quire, J. "The Challenge of Shining Path." ***Nation***, (December 8, 1984), 610-613.

5066. Gorriti, Gustavo. "The War of the Philosopher-King." ***New Republic***, (June 18, 1990), 15-22.

5067. _____. "Terror in the Andes: The Flight of the Ashaninkas." ***New York Times Magazine***, (December 2, 1990), 40-48, 65-72.

5068. Hazleton, William A., and Sandra Woy-Hazleton. "Terrorism and the Marxist Left: Peru's Struggle Against Sendero Luminoso." ***Terrorism***, 11:6 (1988), 471-490.

5069. Hilton, Isabel. "Shining Path of Insurgency." ***Geographic Magazine***, 61:8 (1989), 22-26.

5070. Mason, T. David, and Janet Swartzfager. "Land Reform and the Rise of Sendero Luminoso in Peru." ***Terrorism and Political Violence***, 1:4 (October 1989), 516-538.

5071. McClintock, Cynthia. "Democracies and Guerrillas: The Peruvian Experience." ***International Policy Report***, September 1983.

5072. _____. "Sendero Luminoso: Peru's Maoist Guerrillas." ***Problems of Communism***, 32 (September/October 1983), 19-34.

5073. _____. "Why Peasants Rebel: The Case of Peru's Sedero Luminoso." ***World Politics***, 37:1 (1984), 48-84.

5074. McCormick, Gordon H. "The Shining Path and Peruvian Terrorism." ***Journal of Strategic Studies***, 10:4 (December 1987), 109-128.

5075. _____. "The Shining Path and Peruvian Terrorism." In: D. C. Rapoport, ed. ***Inside Terrorist Organizations.*** New York: Columbia University Press, 1988. pp. 109-128.

5076. Neier, Aryeh. "Peru's Dirty War." ***Nation***, (February 11, 1984), 148-149.

5077. Palmer, David S. "Rebellion in Rural Peru: The Origins and Evolution of Sedero Luminoso." ***Comparative Politics***, 18:2 (1986), 127-146.

5078. _____. "Terrorism as a Revolutionary Strategy: Peru's Sendero Luminoso." In: B. Rubin, ed. ***The Politics of Terrorism.*** Lanham. MD.: University Press of America, 1988. pp. 129-152.

5079. "Peru's Internal War: A Latin American Democracy's Struggle Against Terrorism." ***World Press Review***, 31 (December 1984), 28-30.

5080. Ranly, Ernest W. "Under the Peruvian Volcano." ***Commonweal***, 113:3 (1986), 78-82.

5081. Rosenberg, Tina. "Guerrilla Tourism." ***New Republic***, (June 18, 1990), 23-25.

5082. Sanders, Thomas G. "Peru Between Democracy and the Sendero Luminoso." ***UFSI Reports***, 21 (December 1984), 1-8.

5083. Szusterman, C. "Soldiers of Peru: Review and Commentary." ***Journal of Latin American Studies***, 16 (May 1984), 157-170.

5084. Werlich, David P. "Peru: The Shadow of the Shining Path." ***Current History***, (February 1984), 78-82, 90.

5085. _____. "Debt, Democracy and Terrorism in Peru." ***Current History***, 86:516 (1987), 29.

5086. Zileri, Enrique. "Peru's Internal War: A Latin American Democracy's Struggle Against Terrorism." ***World Press Review***, (December 1984), 28-30.

3. Documents and Reports

5087. Anderson, James. ***Sendero Luminoso: A New Revolutionary Model.*** London: Institute for the Study of Terrorism, 1987. 87p.

5088. Jones, Frank. ***Sendero Luminoso: Origins, Outlooks, and Implications.*** Monterey, CA.: Naval Postgraduate School, 1986. 147p.

5089. McCormick, Gordon H. ***The Shining Path and Peruvian Terrorism.*** RAND P-7297. Santa Monica, CA.: RAND Corporation, 1987. 21p.

5090. Taylor, Lewis. ***Maoism in the Andes: Sendero Luminoso and the Contemporary Guerrilla Movement in Peru.*** Working Paper, 3. Liverpool: Liverpool University, Center for Latin American Studies, 1983. 40p.

f. URUGUAY

1. Journal Articles

5091. Lopez-Alves, Fernando. "Political Crises, Strategic Choices and Terrorism: The Rise and Fall of the Uruguayan Tupamaros." ***Terrorism and Political Violence,*** 1:2 (April 1989), 202-241.

5092. Miller, James A. "Urban Terrorism in Uruguay: The Tupamaros." In: B. E. O'Neill, W. R. Heaton and D. J. Alberts, eds. ***Insurgency in the Modern World.*** Boulder, CO.: Westview Press, 1980. pp. 137-190.

5093. Ronfeldt, David F. "The Kidnapping of Dan Mitrioni in Uruguay." ***TVI Report,*** 7:4 (1987), 13-16.

2. Documents and Reports

5094. Rizowi, Charles. ***The Effects of Support Withdrawal on Uruguay's Political System: The Tupamaros Urban Guerrilla Warfare, 1960-1973.*** Ph.D. Dissertation. University of Chicago, 1981.

5095. Ronfeldt, David F. ***The Mitrione Kidnapping in Uruguay.*** RAND N-1571-DOS/-DARPA/RC. Santa Monica, CA.: Rand Corporation, 1987. 61p.

g. THE REST OF LATIN AMERICA

1. Books

5096. Asencio, Diego. ***Our Man Is Inside.*** Boston, MA.: Little, Brown, 1983. 244p.

5097. Fontaine, Roger W. ***Terrorism: The Cuban Connection.*** New York: Crane Russak, 1988. 199p.

5098. Prado, Salmon. ***Defeat of Che Guevara: Military Response to Guerrilla Challenge in Bolivia.*** Westport, CT.: Greenwood Press, 1990. 288p.

2. Journal Articles

5099. Askins, William. "Warm Breeze or Hurricane? An Uneasy Wind of Change Stirs Mexico." ***TVI Journal,*** 1:6 (1980), 12-15.

5100. Auguste, Barry D. L. "The Caribbean: A Zone of Peace." In: H. H. Han, ed. ***Terrorism, Political Violence and World Order.*** Lanham, MD.: University Press and World Order, 1984. pp. 633-638.

5101. Baratta, Robert T. "Political Violence in Ecuador and the AVC." ***Terrorism,*** 10:3 (1987), 165-174.

5102. Ehrenfeld, Rachel. "Narco Terrorism and the Cuban Connection." ***Strategic Review,*** 16:3 (1988), 55-63.

5103. Lawton, David. "Political Violence and Revolutionary Activity in the Caribbean: Third World Cauldron." In: H. H. Han, ed. ***Terrorism, Political Violence and World Order.*** Lanham, MD.: University Press of America, 1984. pp. 627-632.

5104. Livingstone, Susan M. "Terrorism: "The Original Cheap Shot": An Interview with Ambassador Diego Assecio." ***World Affairs,*** 146:1 (1983), 42-53.

5105. Monday, Mark. "New Civil War a Possibility." ***TVI Journal,*** 3:8 (1982), 2-4.

5106. Sater, William F. "Terrorism in Chile: The Movement of the Revolutionary Left." ***TVI Journal,*** 5:3 (1985), 18-22.

5107. Wilde, Margaret. "Authority and Excess: Reflections of Paraguay." In: H. H. Han, ed. ***Terrorism, Political Violence and World Order.*** Lanham, MD.: University Press of America, 1984. pp. 273-282.

5108. Williams, Timothy. "The Message of the Bomb." ***Carribean and West Indies Chronicle,*** (April/May 1984), 6-7.

3. Documents and Reports

5109. Evans, Robert D. ***Brazil, The Road Back From Terrorism.*** Conflict Studies, No. 47. London: Institute for the Study of Conflict, 1984. 20p.

5110. Lupsha, Peter A. "Narco-Terrorism? Cuba's Recent Involvement in Drug Trafficking: The Ochoa-La Guardia Cases." Paper Presented at the ***Fourth Annual Symposium on International Terrorism,*** held in 1989 at the University of Chicago, Chicago, IL.

5111. Sater, William F. ***The Revolutionary Left and Terrorist Violence in Chile.*** RAND N-2490-AF. Santa Monica, CA.: Rand Corporation, 1986. 19p.

E. THE MIDDLE EAST

a. GENERAL WORKS

1. Books

5112. Choueiri, Youssef M. ***Islamic Fundamentalism.*** London: Pinter, 1990. 178p.
5113. Dietl, Wilhelm. ***Holy War.*** New York: Macmillan, 1984. 349p.
5114. Hirst, David. ***The Gun and the Olive Branch: The Roots of Violence in the Middle East.*** London: Faber & Faber, 1984. 475p.
5115. Hussain, Asaf. ***Political Terrorism and the State.*** London: Mansell, 11988. 203p.
5116. Kilmarx, Robert A., and Yonah Alexander, eds. ***Business and the Middle East: Threats and Prospects.*** New York: Pergamon Press, 1982. 240p.
5117. Pierce, Joe E. ***Terrorism, the Middle East and You.*** Portland, OR.: Hapi Press, 1986. 132p.
5118. Ruwayha, Walid Amin. ***Terrorism and Hostage Taking in the Middle East.*** Paris: The Author, 1990. 512p.
5119. Wright, Robin. ***Sacred Rage: The Crusade of Modern Islam.*** New York; Simon & Schuster, 1985. 315p.

2. Journal Articles

5120. Abella, Irving. "Terrorism and the West." ***Middle East Focus,*** 9:4 (Spring 1987), 2-3.
5121. Abir, Mordechai. "The Arab World, Oil and Terrorism." In: B. Netanyahu, ed. ***International Terrorism: Challenge and Response.*** New Brunswick, NJ.: Transaction Books, 1981. pp. 135-140.
5122. Ali, Sheikh R., and Jess J. Bowe. "Terrorism in the Middle East." ***International Journal of Comparative and Applied Criminal Justice,*** 12:1-2 (Spring-Winter 1988), 119-129.
5123. Amos, John W. "Terrorism in the Middle East: the Diffusion of Violence." ***Middle East Annual, 1984,*** pp. 149-167.
5124. Ashkenasi, Abraham. "Social - Ethnic Conflict and Paramilitary Organization in the Near East." In: P. H. Merkl, ed. ***Political Violence and Terror.*** Berkeley, CA.: University of California Press, 1986. pp. 311-334.
5125. Askins, William. "Mid-Eastern Muddle: Rebels - With and Without Help - Cloud Area's Future." ***TVI Journal,*** 1:10 (1980), 6-9.
5126. Barakat, Halim I., et al. "Terrorism and the Middle East: Context and Interpretation." ***Arab Studies Quarterly,*** 9 (Spring 1987), 133-187.
5127. _____. "Liberation or Terrorism: Refuting the Language of the Oppressor." ***Arab Studies Quarterly,*** 9:2 (1987), 133-138.
5128. Belfiglio, Valentin J. "Middle East Terrorism." ***International Problems,*** 26 (Summer 1987), 21-28.
5129. Boyle, Francis A. "Upholding International Law in the Middle East." In: H. H. Han, ed. ***Terrorism, Political Violence and World Order.*** Lanham, MD.: University Press of America, 1983. pp. 511-524.

5130. Bremer, L. Paul. "Conference on Middle East Fundamentalism and Terrorism, The Carnegie Endowment for International Peace, April 21, 1988." ***Terrorism,*** 11:5 (1988), 345-347.

5131. Briemberg, Mordecai. "Reshaping the Political Discourse on the Middle East." ***Insurgent Sociologist,*** 14:3 (Fall 1987), 131-137.

5132. Burgin, Maskit. "Shi'ite International Terrorism." In: A. Kurz, et al. ***INTER: International Terrorism in 1989.*** Tel Aviv: Jaffee Center for Strategic Studies, 1990. pp. 36-60.

5133. Burns, Julian H. Jr. "Tripoli to Tehran: Terrorism's Road Well Travelled." ***Joint Perspectives,*** (Fall 1981), 42-53.

5134. Carmichael, D. J. C. "Further Reflections on 'Terrorism and the Defence of Civilized Values': The PLO vs. Israel." In: J. Gross Stein and D. B. Dewitt, eds. ***The Middle East at the Crossroads.*** Oakville, Ontario.: Mosaic Press, 1983. pp. 61-71.

5135. _____. "Terrorism and the Defence of Civilized Values." In: J. Gross Stein and D. B. Dewitt, eds. ***The Middle East at the Crossroads.*** Oakville, Ontario.: Mosaic Press, 1983. pp. 44-51.

5136. Chomsky, Noam. "Middle East Terrorism and the American Ideological System." ***Race and Class,*** 28:1 (1986), 1-28.

5137. Cohn, Haim H. "Holy Terror." ***Violence Aggression and Terrorism,*** 1:2 (1987), 1-12.

5138. Connorton, Alison. "North Africa and the Middle East: Regional Assessment." In: R. Clutterbuck, ed. ***The Future of Political Violence.*** London: Macmillan, 1986. pp. 102-112.

5139. Cooper, Mary H. "Dealing with Terrorism: Opening a New Chapter." ***Editorial Research Reports,*** (May 30, 1986), 391-408.

5140. Delloff, Linda M. "Transplants and Compassion." ***Christian Century,*** 97 (March 5, 1980), 245-246.

5141. Faris, Hani A. "The American and Arab Perspectives on Terrorism." ***Arab Studies Quarterly,*** 9:2 (1987), 149-154.

5142. Gerson, Allan. "Fundamentalism and the Arab-Israeli Conflict." ***Terrorism,*** 11:5 (1988), 355-356.

5143. Gilboa, Eitan. "Terrorism and Trust: How We See the Middle East." ***Public Opinion,*** 9 (November/December 1986), 52-55.

5144. Gilmour, Jan, and Andrew Gilmour. "Terrorism (Book Review)." ***Journal of Palestine Studies,*** 17:2 (Winter 1988), 129-142.

5145. Hamizrachi, Yoram. "Coping with Terror in the Middle East." In: B. Macdonald, ed. ***Terror.*** Toronto: Canadian Institute of International Studies, 1987. pp. 127-136.

5146. Henderson, George. "The Abu Nidal Connection." ***Middle East International,*** 266 (January 10, 1986), 6-7.

5147. Horner, Charles. "The Facts about Terrorism." ***Commentary,*** 69 (June 1980), 40-45.

5148. _____. "Terrorism Analyzed." ***American Zionist,*** 70 (September/October 1980), 16-21.

5149. Hunter, Shireen T. "Terrorism: A Balance Sheet." ***Washington Quarterly,*** 12:3 (Summer 1989), 17-32.

5150. "Islamic Extremists: In the Name of Allah." ***Canada and the World,*** (March 1985), 5-6.

5151. Kechichian, Joseph A. "Terrorism in the Middle East and U.S. Military Responses." ***Journal of South Asian and Middle Eastern Studies***, 10:3 (1987), 38-61.

5152. Kennedy, Moorhead. "Commentary: On Terrorism and Its Causes." ***The Washington Report on Middle East Affairs***, 4:12 (1986), 3-4.

5153. Khadduri, Majid. "Islamic Fundamentalism." ***Terrorism***, 11:5 (1988), 357-358.

5154. Kurz, Anat. "Western Countries' Policies and Middle Eastern Based International Terrorism in 1986." In: A. Kurz, et al. ***INTER 86.*** Tel Aviv: Jaffee Center for Strategic Studies, 1987. pp. 63-78.

5155. Levitt, Geoffrey M. "On Terrorism: Review Article." ***The Middle East Journal***, 42 (Autumn 1988), 677-681.

5156. Lilienthal, Alfred M. "Middle East Terror: The Double Standard." ***Vital Speeches of the Day***, 52:9 (1986), 277-282.

5157. Long, David E. "Middle East Terrorism - The Next Phase." ***Terrorism***, 12:6 (1989), 421-424.

5158. Martin, Richard C. "Religious Violence in Islam: Towards an Understanding of the Discourse on Jihad in Modern Egypt." In: P. Wilkinson and A. M. Stewart, eds. ***Contemporary Research on Terrorism.*** Aberdeen: Aberdeen University Press, 1987. pp. 55-71.

5159. Merari, Ariel. "Political Terrorism and Middle Eastern Instability." In: N. Novick and J. Starr, eds. ***Challenges in the Middle East.*** New York: Praeger, 1981. pp. 101-109.

5160. _____. "Soviet Attitudes Toward Middle Eastern Terrorism." In: S. L. Spiegel, M. A. Heller and J. Goldberg, eds. ***The Soviet-American Competition in the Middle East.*** Lexington, MA.: Lexington Books, 1988. pp. 191-200.

5161. _____, et al. "Perspectives on Terror." ***IDF Journal***, 3:4 (1986), 30-36.

5162. _____. "The Readiness to Kill and Die: Suicidal Terrorism in the Middle East." In: W. Reich, ed. ***Origins of Terrorism.*** Cambridge: Cambridge University Press, 1990. pp. 192-210.

5163. "Mid-Eastern Muddle." ***TVI Journal***, 1:10 (1980), 6-9.

5164. Miller, Judith. "Terrorism Around the Mediterranean." In: R. O'Neill, ed. ***Prospects for Security in the Mediterranean.*** Hamden: Archon Books, 1988. pp. 147-162.

5165. Nelson, Barry. "Kidnapped!." ***Canadian Business***, 56 (June 1983), 31-38.

5166. "The New Terrorists." ***Foreign Report***, (February 14, 1985), 1-3.

5167. Norton, Augustus R., and D. J. Lampros-Norton. "Militant Protest and Political Violence Under the Banner of Islam." ***Armed Forces and Society***, 9 (Fall 1982), 3-19.

5168. _____. "Terrorism in the Middle East." In: V. S. Pisano, ed. ***Terrorist Dynamics: A Geographical Perspective.*** Arlington, VA.: International Association of Chiefs of Police, 1988. pp. 1-44.

5169. Overland, Martha Ann. "New Approach to Mideast Terrorism." ***Editorial Research Reports***, (August 26, 1988), 430-438.

5170. Peck, M. C. "The Middle East and Energy: Sources of Threat." In: Y. Alexander and C. K. Ebinger, eds. ***Political Terrorism and Energy.*** New York: Praeger, 1981. pp. 181-190.

5171. Peleg, Ilan. "Terrorism in the Middle East: The Case of the Arab-Israeli Conflict." In: M. Stohl, ed. ***The Politics of Terrorism.*** New York: Marcel Dekker, 1988. pp. 525-548.

5172. Perry, Victor. "Terrorism Incorporated." ***Midstream: A Monthly Jewish Review***, 28:2 (1982), 7-10.

5173. Pipes, Daniel. "Why Asad's Terror Works and Qadhafi's Does Not." ***Terrorism,*** 11:5 (1988), 364-368.

5174. Post, Jerrold M. "Fundamentalism and the Justification of Terrorist Violence." ***Terrorism,*** 11:5 (1988), 369-370.

5175. Probst, Peter S. "Islamic Extremism and U.S. Security Interests." ***Terrorism,*** 11:5 (1988), 371-373.

5176. Quester, George H. "Some Explanations for State-Supported Terrorism in the Middle East." In: M. Stohl and G. A. Lopez, eds. ***Terrible Beyond Endurance? The Foreign Policy of State Terrorism.*** Westport,CT.: Greenwood Press, 1988. pp. 225-246.

5177. Rabinovich, Itamar. "Syria and Lebanon." ***Current History,*** 86:517 (February 1987), 61-64.

5178. Ramati, Yohanan. "Terror and Peace: The Choice." ***Midstream: A Monthly Jewish Review,*** 28:8 (1982), 3-6.

5179. Reich, Bernard. "Some Observations on Middle East Terrorism." ***Terrorism,*** 12:6 (1989), 425-428.

5180. Rubin, Barry. "The Political Uses of Terrorism in the Middle East." In: B. Rubin, ed. ***The Politics of Terrorism.*** Lanham, MD.: University Press of America, 1988. pp. 27-66.

5181. Rudolph, Ross. "Commentary: Civilization and Defence Against Terrorism." In: J. Gross Stein and D. B. Dewitt, eds. ***The Middle East at the Crossroads.*** Oakville, Ontario: Mosaic Press, 1983. pp. 52-60.

5182. Said, Abdul Aziz. "Western Arrogance, Islamic Fanaticism, and Terrorism." ***Terrorism,*** 11:5 (1988), 378-384.

5183. Sid-Ahmed, M. "The Arab-Israeli Conflict and Terrorism." In: H. Kochler, ed. ***Terrorism and National Liberation.*** Frankfurt: Verlag Peter Lang, 1988. pp. 97-110.

5184. Sinai, Joshua. "The Next Stage in Middle East Terrorism." ***Defense and Foreign Affairs Strategic Policy,*** 18:11 (November 1990), 22-25.

5185. Stohl, Michael. "Terrorism, States, and State Terrorism: The Reagan Administration in the Middle East." ***Arab Studies Quarterly,*** 9:2 (1987), 162-172.

5186. "Through the Barrel of a Gun, Part I." ***Middle East,*** 69 (July 1980), 8-15.

5187. "Through the Barrel of a Gun, Part II." ***Middle East,*** 70 (August 1980), 17-20.

5188. "Through the Barrel of a Gun, Part III." ***Middle East,*** 71 (September 1980), 20-26.

5189. Weinberg, Henry H. "Terrorism and Peace in the Middle East." ***Middle East Focus,*** 6:5 (January 1984), 3, 28.

5190. Windsor, Philip. "The Middle East and Terrorism." In: ***Terrorism and International Order.*** London: Royal Institute of International Affairs, 1986. pp. 26-36.

5191. Yacobovici, Simcha. "The Ideology of Terror." ***Middle East Focus,*** 4:3 (1981), 10-16.

3. Documents and Reports

5192. Dam, Kenneth W. ***Terrorism in the Middle East: October 1, 1984.*** Washington, D.C.: U.S. Department of State, Bureau of Public Affairs, 1984.

5193. Gal-Or, Noemi. ***The Pendulum of Arab International Civil Transportation Terrorism.*** Tel Aviv: International Center for Peace in the Middle East, 1986. 23p.

5194. Hyman, Anthony. ***Muslim Fundamentalism.*** Conflict Studies, No. 174. London: Institute for the Study of Conflict, 1985. 27p.

5195. Jenkins, Brian M. ***Subnational Conflict in the Mediterranean Region.*** RAND P-6858. Santa Monica, CA.: RAND Corporation, 1983. 28p.

5196. McGovern, George. "A Better Answer to Terrorism." Paper Presented at the ***Conference on U.S. - Arab Relations in a Changing World,*** held on October 16-17, 1986 in Houston. Washington, DC.: American - Arab Affairs Council, 1987. pp. 105-109.

5197. Rayfield, Gordon E. ***The Righteous Executioners: A Comparative Analysis of Jewish Terrorists of the 1940's and Palestinian Terrorists of the 1970's.*** Ph.D. Dissertation. New York: City University of New York, 1980. 801p.

5198. Rolef, Susan H. ***Violence as Reality: Assassination and Massacre in the Arab World.*** Jerusalem: Carta, 1983. 35p.

5199. Rosolio, Shaul. "Reflections on International Terrorism as Seen from the Middle East." In: B. G. Curtis, ed. ***Outthinking the Terrorist - An International Challenge, Proceedings.*** Rockville, MD.: National Criminal Justice Reference Service, 1985. pp. 49-55.

5200. Whitehall, Conrad S. ***Terrorism: The Holocaust & the Urgent Need for the Establishment of a Palestinian State.*** Albuquerque, NM.: Institute of Economic & Political World Strategic Studies, 1986. 167p.

b. THE PALESTINIANS AND THE PLO

1. Books

5201. Amos, John W. ***Palestinian Resistance: Organization of a Nationalist Movement.*** New York: Pergamon Press, 1980. 427p.

5202. Bar-Zohar, Michael, and Eitan Haber. ***The Quest for the Red Prince.*** London: Weidenfeld and Nicolson, 1983. 232p.

5203. Becker, Jillian. ***The PLO: The Rise and Fall of the Palestine Liberation Organization.*** London: Weidenfeld and Nicolson, 1984. 303p.

5204. Cobban, Helena. ***The Palestinian Liberation Organization: People, Power and Politics.*** New York: Cambridge University Press, 1984. 305p.

5205. Dhaher, Ahmed. ***The Palestinian Experience.*** Boulder, CO.: Lynne Rienner, 1986. 240p.

5206. Frangi, Abdallah. ***Palestinian Liberation Organization and Palestine.*** London: Zed Press, 1983. 256p.

5207. Golan, Galia. ***The Soviet Union and the Palestine Liberation Organization: An Uneasy Alliance.*** New York: Praeger, 1980. 289p.

5208. Gowers, Andrew, and Tony Walker. ***Behind the Myth: Yasser Arafat and the Palestinian Revolution.*** London: W. H. Allen, 1990. 356p.

5209. Gresh, Alain. ***The PLO: The Struggle Within: Toward an Independent Palestinian State.*** London: Zed Press, 1985. 267p.

5210. Hart, Alan. ***Arafat: Terrorist or Peacemaker.*** London: Sidgwick & Jackson, 1984. 480p.

5211. Kirisci, Kemal. ***The PLO and World Politics: A Study of the Mobilization of Support for the Palestinian Cause.*** London: Frances Pinter, 1986. 198p.

5212. Laffin, John. ***The PLO Connections.*** London: Corgi, 1983. 174p.

5213. Livingstone, Neil C., and David Halevy. ***Inside the PLO: Covert Units, Secret Funds and the War Against Israel and the United States.*** New York: William Morrow, 1990. 336p.

5214. Melman, Yossi. ***The Master Terrorist: The True Story Behind Abu Nidal.*** London: Sidgwick & Jackson, 1987. 232p.

5215. Merari, Ariel, and Shlomi Elad. ***The International Dimension of Palestinian Terrorism.*** JCSS Study; No. 6. Boulder, CO.: Westview Press, 1986. 147p.

5216. Mishal, Shaul. ***The PLO & Arafat: Between Gun and Olive Branch.*** New Haven, CT.: Yale University Press, 1986. 190p.

5217. Sahliyeh, Emil. ***The PLO After the Lebanon War.*** Boulder, CO.: Westview Press, 1985. 268p.

5218. Schoenberg, Harris O. ***A Mandate for Terror: The United Nations and the PLO.*** New York: Shapolsky, 1989. 570p.

5219. Shemesh, Moshe. ***The Palestinian Entity, 1959-1974: Arab Politics and the PLO.*** London: Frank Cass, 1990. 402p.

5220. Wallach, Janet, and John Wallach. ***Arafat: In the Eyes of the Beholder.*** New York: Carol Publishing Group, 1990. 465p.

5221. Yodfat, Aryeh, and Yuval Arnon-Ohana. ***PLO: Strategy and Tactics.*** London: Croom Helm, 1981. 225p.

2. Journal Articles

5222. Abraham, Nabeel. "The Conversion of Chairman Arafat." ***American Arab Affairs,*** 31 (Winter 1989-90), 53-69.

5223. Abu Khalil, As'ad. "Internal Contradictions in the PFLP: Decision Making and Policy Determination." ***The Middle East Journal,*** 41:3 (Summer 1987), 361-378.

5224. Abu, Nidal. "The Palestinian Goal Justifies Terrorism." In: B. Szumski, ed. ***Terrorism: Opposing Viewpoints.*** St.Paul, MN.: Greenhaven Press, 1986. pp. 113-118.

5225. Alexander, Edward. "Professor of Terror." ***Commentary,*** 88 (August 1989), 49-50.

5226. Alexander, Yonah. "The Nature of the PLO: Some International Implications." ***Middle East Review,*** 12:3 (1980), 42-48.

5227. _____. "Some Soviet - PLO Linkages." ***Middle East Review,*** 14:3-4 (1982), 64-69.

5228. Baum, Phil, and Raphael Danziger. "Yasir Arafat and the 'Achile Lauro'." ***American Jewish Monthly,*** (January 1986), 7-8.

5229. _____. _____. "The November 1988 Palestine National Council Resolutions in Algiers and Their Aftermath." ***Terrorism,*** 11:5 (1988), 385-408.

5230. _____. _____. "The Fifth Fath General Congress: Triumph of Moderation or Return to Radicalism?." ***Terrorism,*** 12:2 (1989), 97-106.

5231. Becker, Jillian. "The Centrality of the PLO." In: B. Netanyahu, ed. ***Terrorism: How the West Can Win.*** New York: Farrar, Strauss, Giroux, 1986. pp. 98-102.

5232. Bishop, Vaughn F. "Political Terrorism in the Palestinian Resistance Movement." In: M. Stohl, ed. ***The Politics of Terrorism. 2nd ed.*** New York: Marcel Dekker, 1983. pp. 397-418.

5233. Cobban, Helena. "The PLO in the 1980s: Between the Gun and the Olive Branch." ***International Journal,*** 38:4 (1983), 635-651.

5234. "A Discussion with Yasser Arafat." ***Journal of Palestine Studies,*** 11;2 (1982), 3-15.

5235. Frankel, Norman. "Abu Za'im - Alternative to Yasir Arafat." ***Terrorism,*** 11:2 (1988), 151-164.

5236. _____. "The Reformatory Movement of Fatah: Interviews with Hussein Aweidah." ***Terrorism,*** 11:5 (1988), 409-418.

5237. _____. "An Interview with Nabil Sha'ath." ***TVI Report,*** 9:2 (1989), 22-27.

5238. Gammer, Moshe. "Areas of Armed Conflict: South Lebanon; Palestine Liberation Organization Operations." In: C. Legum, ed. ***Middle East Contemporary Survey, Vol. 4. 1978-80.*** New York: Holmes & Meier, 1981. pp. 233-269.

5239. Gazit, Shlomo. "The Myth and Reality of the PLO." In: B. Netanyahu, ed. ***International Terrorism: Challenge and Response.*** New Brunswick, NJ.: Transaction Books, 1981. pp. 343-349.

5240. Golan, Galia. "The Soviet Union and the PLO Since the War in Lebanon." ***Middle East Journal,*** 40:2 (Spring 1986), 285-306.

5241. _____. "Soviet - PLO Relations." ***Jerusalem Quarterly,*** 16 (1980), 121-136.

5242. Great Britain. Foreign and Commonwealth Office. "Abu Nidal Group and State Terrorism." In: Y. Alexander, ed. ***The 1986 Annual on Terrorism.*** Dordrecht: Martinus Nijhoff, 1987. pp. 283-297.

5243. Habash, George. "The Future of the Palestinian National Movement (Interview)." ***Journal of Palestine Studies,*** 14:4 (1985), 3-10.

5244. Hoffman, Bruce. "The Plight of the Phoenix: The PLO since Lebanon." ***Conflict Quarterly,*** 5:2 (1985), 5-17.

5245. _____. "Recent Trends in Palestinian Terrorism." In: ***International Terrorism and the Drug Connection.*** Ankara: Ankara University Press, 1984. pp. 241-250.

5246. Hussaini, Hatem I. "The Palestine Liberation Organization and the Palestinian Struggle: Present Challenges and Future Outlook." ***The Search: Journal for Arab and Islamic Studies,*** 5:3-4 (1984), 73-82.

5247. Ioannides, Christos P. "The PLO and the Iranian Revolution." ***American Arab Affairs,*** 10 (Fall 1984), 89-105.

5248. Israel. Defence Forces Spokesman. "PLO Terror: Data on the PLO Terrorist Organization." In: Y. Alexander, ed. ***The 1986 Annual on Terrorism.*** Dordrecht: Martinus Nijhoff, 1987. pp. 261-282.

5249. Israeli, Raphael. "The Charter of Allah: The Platform of the Islamic Resistance Movement (Hamas)." In: Y. Alexander and A. H. Foxman, eds. ***The 1988-1989 Annual of Terrorism.*** Dordrecht: Martinus Nijhoff, 1990. pp. 99-134.

5250. Kamin, Jonathon T. "The PLO in the Aftermath of Rebellion." ***SAIS Review,*** 5:1 (1985), 91-105.

5251. Kassim, Anis. "A Response to Professor Robert A. Friedlander; (The PLO and the Rule of Law)." ***Denver Journal of International Law and Policy,*** 10 (Winter 1981), 237-241.

5252. Kelman, Herbert C. "Talking with Arafat." ***Foreign Policy,*** 49 (Winter 1982-83), 119-139.

5253. Kimche, Jon. "The PLO's Second Front." ***Midstream: A Monthly Jewish Review***, 28:2 (1982), 3-6.

5254. _____. "Arafat's Abu Nidal Connection." ***Midstream***, 33:6 (June/July 1987), 3-5.

5255. Kurz, Anat. "Palestinian International Terrorism: Current Trends and Political Implications." In: A. Kurz, et al. ***INTER: International Terrorism in 1988.*** Tel Aviv: Jaffee Center for Strategic Studies, 1989. pp. 17-24.

5256. _____. "Palestinian Terrorism: The Violent Aspects of a Political Struggle." ***TVI Report***, 9:2 (1989), 6-12.

5257. _____. "Palestinian International Terrorism in 1989." In: A. Kurz, et al. ***INTER: International Terrorism in 1989.*** Tel Aviv: Jaffee Center for Strategic Studies, 1990. pp. 78-86.

5258. _____. "The Intifada - Features of the Uprising and Its Implications for the Policy of the Palestine Liberation Organization." ***TVI Report***, 9:2 (1989), 13-21.

5259. Livingstone, Neil C. "The Wolves Among Us: Reflections on the Past Eighteen Months and Thoughts on the Future." ***World Affairs***, 146:1 (1983), 7-23.

5260. Mattar, Philip. "The PLO Since Beirut." In: ***The Middle East Annual, Vol. 3. 1983.*** Boston, MA.: G. K. Hall, 1984. pp. 83-102.

5261. Medoff, Rafael. "Amnesty International's PLO Problem." ***Midstream: A Monthly Jewish Review***, 30:10 (1984), 6-11.

5262. Merari, Ariel. "The Future of Palestinian Terrorism." ***TVI Journal***, 5:3 (1985), 11-13.

5263. _____. Tamar Prat and David Tal. "The Palestinian Intifada: An Analysis of a Popular Uprising After Seven Months." ***Terrorism and Political Violence***, 1:2 (April 1989), 177-201.

5264. _____. "The Future of Palestinian Terrorism." In: W. Laqueur, ed. ***The Terrorism Reader.*** New York: Meridian, 1987. pp. 303-308.

5265. Miller, Aaron D. "Whither the PLO?" ***Middle East Review***, 16:3 (1984), 40-43.

5266. _____. "Portrait of Abu Nidal." In: W. Laqueur, ed. ***The Terrorism Reader.*** New York: Meridian, 1987. pp. 309-314.

5267. Muravchik, J. "Arresting Arafat." ***New Republic***, 193 (December 30, 1985), 12-13.

5268. Nederveen-Pieterse, Jan P. "State Terrorism on a Global Scale: The Role of Israel." ***Crime and Social Justice***, 21-22 (1984), 58-80.

5269. Nisan, Mordechai. "PLO Messianism: Diagnosis of a Modern Gnostic Sect." ***Terrorism***, 7:3 (1984), 299-312.

5270. _____. "The PLO and the Palestinian Issue." ***Middle East Review***, 18:2 (1985), 52-60.

5271. O'Ballance, Edgar. "Arafat and the PLO." ***Journal of the Royal United Services Institute for Defence Studies***, 129:1 (1984), 49-52.

5272. "The PLO after Lebanon: An Interview with Dr. Dan Schueftan." ***The Israeli Economist***, 43 (August 1987), 19-25.

5273. "Palestinian Terrorism in 1985." In: A. Merari, et al. ***INTER 85.*** Boulder, CO.: Westview Press, 1986. pp. 31-54.

5274. Pipes, Daniel. "How Important is the PLO?." ***Commentary***, (May 22, 1983), 17-25.

5275. Prat, Tamar. "Trends in Palestinian Terrorism." In: ***Anti Terrorism - IDENTA - 85.*** Boulder, CO.: Westview Press, 1985. pp. 81-87.

5276. _____. "Palestinian International Terrorism in 1986." In: A. Kurz, et al. ***INTER 86.*** Tel Aviv: Jaffee Center for Strategic Studies, 1987. pp. 36-62.

5277. _____. "Palestinian Armed Struggle: Strategy and Tactics." In: A. Kurz, ed. ***Contemporary Trends in World Terrorism.*** New York: Praeger, 1987. pp. 24-31.

5278. Pryce-Jones, David. "The Gun, Again." ***New Republic,*** (December 14, 1984), 7-9.

5279. Rabinowitz, Dorothy. "The Case of Abu Eain." ***New Republic,*** (December 16, 1981), 12-14.

5280. Rouleau, Eric. "The Future of the PLO." ***Foreign Affairs,*** (Fall 1983), 138-156.

5281. Rubin, Benjamin. "PLO Violence and Legitimate Combatancy: A Response to Professor Green." In: ***Israel Yearbook on Human Rights, Vol. 19. 1989.*** Dordrecht: Martinus Nijhoff, 1989. pp. 167-186.

5282. Said, Edward W. "The Essential Terrorist." In: E. Said and C. Hutchins, eds. ***Blaming the Victims.*** New York: Verso, 1988. pp. 149-158.

5283. Schiller, David T. "Fatah's View of the PLO." ***TVI Journal,*** 5:3 (1985), 36-37.

5284. _____. "A Battlegroup Divided: The Palestinian Fedayeen." ***Journal of Strategic Studies,*** 10:4 (December 1987), 90-108.

5285. _____. "A Battlegroup Divided - The Palestinian Fedayeen." In: D. C. Rapoport, ed. ***Inside Terrorist Organizations.*** New York: Columbia University Press, 1988. pp. 90-108.

5286. Schueftan, Dan. "The PLO After Lebanon." ***Jerusalem Quarterly,*** 28 (Summer 1983), 3-24.

5287. Stein, Kenneth W. "The PLO After Beirut." ***Middle East Review,*** 15:3-4 (1983), 11-17.

5288. Susser, Asher. "The PLO After Lebanon." ***IDF Journal,*** 2:1 (1984), 40-45.

5289. _____. "Palestinian Issues: The Palestine Liberation Organization." In: C. Legum, ed. ***Middle East Contemporary Survey, Vol. 7. 1982-83.*** New York: Holmes & Meier, 1985. pp. 275-330.

5290. _____. "Palestinian Issues: The Palestine Liberation Organization." In: C. Legum, ed. ***Middle East Contemporary Survey, Vol. 6. 1981-82.*** New York: Holmes & Meier, 1983. pp. 317-357.

5291. _____. "Palestinian Issues: The Palestine Liberation Organization." In: C. Legum, ed. ***Middle East Contemporary Survey, Vol. 3. 1980.*** New York: Holmes & Meier, 1980. pp. 283-312.

5292. _____. "The Palestinian Liberation Organization." In: C. Legum, ed. ***Middle East Contemporary Survey, Vol. 4. 1979-80.*** New York: Holmes & Meier, 1981. pp. 233-269.

5293. _____. "Palestinian Issues: The Palestine Liberation Organization." In: I. Rabinovich and H. Shaked, eds. ***Middle East Contemporary Survey, Vol. 9. 1984-85.*** Boulder, CO.: Westview Press, 1986. pp. 181-233.

5294. _____. "Palestinian Issues: The Palestinian Liberation Organization." In: H. Shaked and D. Dishon, eds. ***Middle East Contemporary Survey, Vol. 8. 1983-84.*** Boulder, CO.: Westview Press, 1985. pp. 195-235.

5295. "TVI Report Profiles: Al Fatah." ***TVI Report,*** 8:3 (1989), 1-4.

5296. "TVI Report Profiles: Fatah Revolutionary Council (FRC)." ***TVI Report,*** 8:3 (1989), 5-8.

5297. "TVI Report Profiles: Popular Front for the Liberation of Palestine (PFLP)." ***TVI Report,*** 8:3 (1989), 9-12.

5298. "TVI Report Profiles: Popular Front for the Liberation of Palestine: General Command (PFLP-GC)." ***TVI Report,*** 8:3 (1989), 13-14.

5299. Tal, David. "The International Dimension of PFLP-GC Activity." In: A. Kurz, et al. ***INTER: International Terrorism in 1989.*** Tel Aviv: Jaffee Center for Strategic Studies, 1990. pp. 61-77.

5300. Teitelbaum, Joshua. "Palestinian Issues: The Palestine Liberation Organization." In: A. Ayalon and H. Shaked, eds. ***Middle East Contemporary Survey, Vol. 12. 1988.*** Boulder, CO.: Westview Press, 1988. pp. 229-276.

5301. _____. "Palestinian Issues: The Palestine Liberation Organization." In: I. Rabinovich and H. Shaked, eds. ***Middle East Contemporary Survey, Vol. 11. 1987.*** Boulder, CO.: Westview Press, 1987. pp. 210-249.

5302. _____. "Palestinian Issues: The Palestinian Liberation Organization." In: I. Rabinovich and H. Shaked, eds. ***Middle East Contemporary Survey, Vol. 10. 1986.*** Boulder, CO.: Westview Press, 1986. pp. 165-202.

5303. United States. United States District Court. Eastern District of New York. "In the Matter of the Extradition of Mahmoud Abed Atta, a/k/a "Mahmoud El-Abed Ahmad," Defendant." ***Terrorism,*** 11:5 (1988), 419-440.

5304. Wells, Ronald A. "Terrorism." ***The Reformed Journal,*** 36:9 (September 1986), 6-7.

5305. Yaniv, Avner. "Phoenix or Phantom? The PLO After Beirut." ***Terrorism,*** 7:3 (1984), 313-322.

5306. _____. "The PLO, the Middle East, and the World." ***Middle East Review,*** 18:1 (1985), 51-60.

5307. Yarimi, Offer. "Palestinian Issues: The Palestinian Liberation Organization." In: C. Legum, ed. ***Middle East Contemporary Survey, Vol. 5. 1980-81.*** New York: Holmes & Meyer, 1982. pp. 293-324.

5308. Yerushalmi, Mordechai. "A Statistical Analysis of Palestinian Terrorism and Israeli Counter-Terrorism over Time." ***International Journal of Comparative and Applied Criminal Justice,*** 13:2 (Fall 1989), 95-110.

3. Documents and Reports

5309. American Jewish Congress. Commission on International Affairs. ***The Palestinians: An Essay on the Uses of Propaganda and Terror.*** New York: American Jewish Congress, 1980. 48p.

5310. Downey, Vicki. ***Half Century of Terror.*** Tucson, AZ.: Islamic Association for Palestine, 1986. 8p.

5311. Elomari, Hussein K. ***Terrorism and the Palestinian Experience.*** Ph.D. Dissertation. Cincinnati, OH.: Union for Experimenting Colleges/ Universities Without Walls and Union Graduate Schools, 1989. 153p.

5312. Gruen, George E., ed. ***The Palestinians in Perspective: Implications for Mideast Peace and U.S. Policy.*** New York: Institute of Human Relations Press, American Jewish Committee, 1982. 109p.

5313. Hoffman, Bruce. ***Recent Trends in Palestinian Terrorism.*** RAND P-6981. Santa Monica, Ca.: RAND Corporation, 1984. 17p.

5314. _____. ***Recent Trends in Palestinian Terrorism, II.*** RAND P-7076. Santa Monica, Ca.: RAND Corporation, 1985. 19p.

5315. _____. ***The Other Terrorist War: Palestinian Versus Palestinian.*** RAND P-7175. Santa Monica, CA.: Rand Corporation, 1986. 4p.

5316. Israel. Ministry of Foreign Affairs. Information Division. ***The PLO in Lebanon.*** Jerusalem: Ministry of Foreign Affairs, 1982. 39p.
5317. Kelman, Herbert C. ***Understanding Arafat.*** Tel Aviv: The International Center for Peace in the Middle East, 1983.
5318. Merari, Ariel. ***PLO: Core of World Terror.*** Jerusalem: Carta, 1983. 31p.
5319. Miller, Aaron D. ***The PLO and the Politics of Survival.*** Washington, D.C.: Center for Strategic and International Studies, Georgetown University, 1983. 132p.
5320. Moughrabi, Fouad. "The PLO: A High Risk Insurgency?." Paper Presented at the ***Annual Convention of the International Studies Association***, held on October 29-31, 1981 at the University of Florida.
5321. ***The Palestinians.*** London: Minority Rights Group, 1984. 19p.
5322. Rubenberg, Cheryl. ***The Palestine Liberation Organization: Its Institutional Infrastructure.*** Belmont, MA.: Institute of Arab Studies, 1983. 66p.
5323. United States. Congress. House. Committee on Foreign Affairs. Subcommittee on Europe and the Middle East. ***PLO Commitments and Compliance Report: Hearing.*** 101st Cong., 2nd sess. Washington, D.C.: U.S. Government Printing Office, 1990. 112p.
5324. Wise, Charles D. ***The Impact of Palestinian Terrorism on the Arab/Israeli Conflict.*** Ph.D. Dissertation. Norman, OK.: University of Oklahoma, 1980. 256p.

c. ISRAEL

1. Books

5325. Ben-Rafael, Eliezer. ***Israel - Palestine: A Guerrilla Conflict in International Politics.*** Westport, CT.: Greenwood Press, 1987. 230p.
5326. Eidelberg, Paul. ***The Case of Israel's Jewish Underground.*** Dollard des Ormeaux, Quebec.: Dawn, 1985.
5327. Jonas, George. ***Vengeance: The True Story of an Israeli Counter-Terrorist Team.*** Toronto: Lester & Orpen Dennys, 1984. 376p.
5328. Katz, Samuel M. ***Guards Without Frontiers: Israel's Counter Terrorist Forces.*** London: Arms & Armour Press, 1990. 221p.
5329. Schiff, Zeev. ***A History of the Israeli Army: 1874 to the Present.*** New York: Macmillan, 1986. 274p.

2. Journal Articles

5330. Abraham, Nabeel. "The Bus Hijacking: Disturbing Questions for Israelis and Arabs." ***Middle East International***, (July 13, 1984), 12-14.
5331. Alexander, Edward. "Terror at Home, Letter from Jerusalem." ***Midstream***, 30:7 (1984), 9-11.
5332. Ben-Yehuda, Nachman. "Conflict Resolution in an Underground Group: The Shamir-Giladi Clash." ***Terrorism***, 12:3 (1989), 199-212.

5333. _____. "Violence, Aggression and Conflict Resolution in an Underground Group: The Case of Lehi and Levi." ***Violence, Aggression and Terrorism,*** 3:3 (1989), 173-190.

5334. Bensinger, G. J. "The Israel Police and Terrorism Management." ***Journal of Crime and Justice,*** 6 (1983), 1-15.

5335. Bush, George. "The Challenges of Terrorism and Anti-Semitism." ***American Israel Public Affairs Committee,*** (1987), 49-55.

5336. Cromer, Gerald. "Jewish Underground: At the Center or on the Periphery of Israeli Society." ***Terrorism,*** 11:5 (1988), 350-354.

5337. Cygielman, Victor. "Roots of Jewish Terror." ***New Outlook,*** 27 (June/July 1984), 13-15.

5338. Davidson, Lawrence. "Terrorism in Context: The Case of the West Bank." ***Journal of the Palestine Studies,*** 15:3 (1986), 109-124.

5339. Devries, Bert. "Double-Barreled but Shortsighted." ***The Reformed Journal,*** 35:12 (December 1985), 2-3.

5340. Diskin, A. "Trends in Intensity Variation of Palestinian Military Activity: 1967-1978." ***Canadian Journal of Political Science,*** 16 (June 1983), 335-348.

5341. Don-Yehiya, Eliezer. "Jewish Messianism, Religious Zionism and Israeli Politics: The Impact and Origins of Gush Emunim." ***Middle Eastern Studies,*** 23:2 (1987), 215-234.

5342. Friedland, Nehemia, and Ariel Merari. "The Psychological Impact of Terrorism: The Double-Edged Sword." ***Political Psychology,*** 6:4 (1985), 591-604.

5343. Friedlander, Robert A. "The Armageddon Factor: Terrorism and Israel's Nuclear Option." In: L. R. Beres, ed. ***Security of Armageddon: Israel's Nuclear Strategy.*** Lexington, MA.: Lexington Books, 1986. pp. 151-158.

5344. Gammer, Moshe. "Armed Operations." In: C. Legum, ed. ***Middle East Contemporary Survey, Vol. 3. 1978-79.*** New York: Holmes & Meier, 1980. pp. 184-212.

5345. _____. "Armed Operations." In: C. Legum, ed. ***Middle East Contemporary Survey, Vol. 5. 1980-81.*** New York: Holmes & Meier, 1982. pp. 214-226.

5346. Gershovich, Moshe. "Armed Operations." In: C. Legum, ed. ***Middle East Contemporary Survey, Vol. 7. 1982-83.*** New York: Holmes & Meier, 1985. pp. 176-190.

5347. Glick, Edward B. "Arab Terrorism and Israeli Retaliation: Some Moral, Psychological and Political Reflections." In: D. Rapoport and Y. Alexander, eds. ***The Rationalization of Terrorism.*** Frederick, MD.: University Publications of America, 1982. pp. 154-159.

5348. Greenstein, Edward L. "Jewish Terror: How Did We Get It? An Interview with Uriel Simon." ***Midstream,*** 30:10 (1984), 31-34.

5349. Hazelton, L. "Respectable Terrorism." ***Harpers,*** 261 (October 1980), 28-31.

5350. Inbari, Pinchas. "Underground: Political Background and Psychological Atmosphere." ***New Outlook,*** 27 (June/July 1984), 9-12.

5351. "Israeli Terrorism in the West Bank and Gaza - The Pariah as Poacher." ***Third World Quarterly,*** 8:2 (1986), 9-13.

5352. Karmon, Yigal. "On Problems of Countering Population Support for the Terrorists in Administered Territories." In: A. Merari, ed. ***On Terrorism and Combating Terrorism.*** Frederick, MD.: University Publications of America, 1985. pp. 9-18.

5353. Kidron, Peretz. "Elections and Terrorism." ***Middle East International,*** 225 (May 18, 1984), 5-7.

5354. _____. "The Shin Bet Strikes at Last." ***Middle East International***, (May 4, 1984), 3-4.

5355. Lahav, Pnina. "A Barrel Without Hoops: The Impact Of Counterterrorism on Israel's Legal Culture." ***Cardozo Law Review***, 10:3 (December 1988), 529-560.

5356. Lebowitz, Arieh, and Moshe Kagan. "More Violence on the West Bank." ***Israel Horizons***, 28 (May/June 1980), 3-4.

5357. Ledeen, Michael A. "Europe and Israel: The Effects of Terrorism." ***JINSA Security Affairs***, 4:5 (1986), 1, 5.

5358. Leibel, Aaron, et al. "Terrorism, Settlements and Palestinians." ***Present Tense***, 12:1 (1984), 6-22.

5359. Levenfeld, Barry. "Israel's Counter-Fedayeen Tactics in Lebanon: Self Defence and Reprisal Under Modern International Law." ***Columbia Journal of Transnational Law***, 21 (1982), 1-48.

5360. Linn, Ruth. "Terrorism, Morality, and Soldiers' Motivation to Fight: An Example from the Israeli Experience in Lebanon." ***Terrorism***, 11:2 (1988), 139-150

5361. Lotan, Yael. "Terror in a Small Place." ***New Outlook***, 23 (May 1980), 4-5.

5362. _____. "The Strange Tragedy of Eli the Wolf." ***New Outlook***, 23 (June/July 1980), 17.

5363. Medoff, Rafael. "Gush Emunim and the Question of Jewish Couterterror." ***Middle East Review***, 18:4 (1986), 17-24.

5364. _____. "Negotiating with Terrorism." ***Global Affairs***, 1:2 (1986), 19-26.

5365. Miller, Reuben. "Responding to Terrorism's Challenge: The Case of Israeli Reprisals." ***Virginia Social Science Journal***, 25 (Winter 1990), 109-123.

5366. "The New Terrorism." ***IDF Journal***, 3:1 (Fall 1985), 39-42.

5367. O'Brien, William V. "Israel's Counterterror Strategies, 1967-1987." ***Middle East Review***, 20:1 (Autumn 1987), 23-30.

5368. Occhiogrosso, Paul F. "The Shin Beth Affair: National Security Versus the Rule of Law in the State of Israel." ***Loyola of Los Angeles International and Comparative Law Journal***, 11:1 (Winter 1989), 67-116.

5369. Peres, Shimon. "The Fight Against Terrorism: A Challenge to the Democracies." In: Y. Alexander and A. H. Foxman, eds. ***The 1987 Annual on Terrorism***. Dordrecht: Martinus Nijhoff, 1988. pp. 385-388.

5370. Pieterse, Jan Nederveen. "State Terrorism on a Global Scale: The Role of Israel." ***Crime and Social Justice***, 21 (1984), 58-80.

5371. _____. "The Washington - Tel Aviv Connection - Global Frontier Management." ***Crime and Social Justice***, 27-28 (1987), 201-219.

5372. Rawkins, Phillip. "Terror from the Heart of Zion: The Political Challenge of the Jewish Underground in the West Bank." ***Middle East Focus***, 7:5 (1985), 9-13, 22-23.

5373. Reich, Bernard. "Fundamentalism and the Peace Process: Israel, the West Bank and Gaza." ***Terrorism***, 11:5 (1988), 374-377.

5374. Rosenberg, Robert. "Car Bomb in Jerusalem!." ***Readers Digest***, 130:777 (January 1987), 122-124+.

5375. Sabel, Robbie. "Terrorism and the Law: How Israel Copes with Terrorism." ***International Society of Barristers Quarterly***, 17:2 (1982), 274-282.

5376. Salpeter, Eliahu. "Israel's Unsettling Underground: A Time of Soul Searching." ***New Leader***, 67 (May 28, 1984), 3-4.

5377. Sprinzak, Ehud. "From Messianic Pioneering to Vigilante Terrorism: The Case of the Gush Emunim Underground." ***Journal of Strategic Studies***, 10:4 (December 1987), 194-216.

5378. _____. "The Reemergence of Jewish Terrorism in Israel." In: ***Anti Terrorism - IDENTA - 85***. Boulder, CO.: Westview Press, 1985. pp. 88-114.

5379. _____. "From Messianic Pioneering to Vigilante Terrorism - The Case of the Gush Emunim Underground." In: D. C. Rapoport, ed. ***Inside Terrorist Organizations***. New York: Columbia University Press, 1988. pp. 194-216.

5380. _____. "Fundamentalism, Terrorism, and Democracy: The Case of Gush Emunim." ***New Outlook***, 31:9 (1988), 8-14.

5381. "TVI Interview: Rafi Eitan, March 27, 1985." ***TVI Journal***, 5:4 (1985), 22-25.

5382. Tommer, Yehonathan. "The Underground and Halakha." ***Newsview***, 5:37 (September 18, 1984), 14-15.

5383. "The Treatment of Terrorists in the Israeli Occupied Territories." ***The American University Journal of International Law and Policy***, 3 (Fall 1988), 451-480.

5384. Twersky, David. "Of Tear Gas and the Purity of Arms." ***Jewish Frontier***, 47 (March 1980), 23-27.

5385. "The West Bank Bust." ***New Republic***, (June 25, 1984), 7-8.

5386. "West Bank Terror." ***Impact International***, 10 (June 13, 1980), 7-8.

5387. Yakuel, A. "The Israel National Police Bomb Disposal Unit." In: ***Anti Terrorism - IDENTA - 85***. Boulder, CO.: Westview Press, 1985. pp. 133-137.

5388. Yariv, Aharon. "A Strategy to Counter Palestinian Terrorism." In: A. Merari, ed. ***On Terrorism and Combating Terrorism***. Frederick, MD.: University Publications of America, 1985. pp. 1-8.

5389. Yishai, Yael. "The Jewish Terror Organization: Past or Future Danger?." ***Conflict***, 6:4 (1986), 307-332.

3. Documents and Reports

5390. Alon, Hanan. ***Countering Palestinian Terrorism in Israel: Toward a Policy Analysis of Counter Measures***. RAND N-1567-FF. Santa Monica, CA.: Rand Corporation, 1980. 271p.

5391. _____. ***Countering Palestinian Terrorism in Israel: Toward a Policy Analysis of Countermeasures***. Ph.D. Dissertation. Santa Monica, CA.: Rand Graduate Institute of Policy Studies, 1980. 296p.

5392. Fields, J. L. ***Irgun Zvai Leumi: The Jewish Terrorist Element of Arab Israeli Conflict***. Maxwell AFB, AL.: Air Command and Staff College, 1985. 36p.

5393. Gal-Or, Noemi. ***The Jewish Underground: Innovation or Recurrence***. Tel Aviv: International Center for Peace in the Middle East, 1986. 7p.

5394. Lagerwist, Frank A. ***Israel and the Politics of Terrorism in the Middle East***. Albuquerque, CA.: Institute of Economic & Political World Strategic Studies, 1981. 143p.

5395. Lukacs, Yehuda, ed. ***Documents on the Israeli - Palestinian Conflict, 1967-1983***. Cambridge, MA.: Cambridge University Press, 1984. 247p.

5396. Russ, Shlomo M. ***The 'Zionist Hooligans': The Jewish Defense League***. Ph.D. Dissertation. New York: City University of New York, 1981. 1147p.

5397. Yerushalmi, Mordechai. ***The War Over Israel: Palestinian Terrorism and Israeli Counterterrorism.*** Ph.D. Dissertation. Chicago, IL.: University of Illinois, 1989. 250p.

d. LEBANON

1. Books

5398. Bavly, Dan. ***Fire in Beirut: Israel's War in Lebanon with the PLO.*** New York: Stein and Day, 1984. 261p.

5399. Carlson, Kurt. ***One American Must Die: A Hostage's Personal Account of the Hijacking of Flight 847.*** New York: Congden and Weed, 1986.

5400. Deeb, Marius. ***The Lebanese Civil War.*** New York: Praeger, 1980. 158p.

5401. Fisk, Robert. ***Pity the Nation: Lebanon at War.*** New York: Macmillan, 1990. 662p.

5402. Gilmour, David. ***Lebanon: The Fractured Country.*** Oxford: Martin Robertson, 1983. 209p.

5403. Gordon, David C. ***Lebanon: The Fragmented Nation.*** London: Croom Helm, 1980. 297p.

5404. Hammel, Eric. ***The Root: The Marines in Beirut, August 1982 - February 1984.*** New York: Harcourt, Brace, Jovanovich, 1985. 448p.

5405. Laffin, John. ***The War of Desperation: Lebanon, 1982-85.*** London: Osprey Press, 1985. 213p.

5406. Martin, David C., and John Walcott. ***Best Laid Plans: The Inside Story of America's War Against Terrorism.*** New York: Harper & Row, 1988. 392p.

5407. Pintak, Larry. ***Beirut Outtakes: A TV Correspondent's Portrait of America's Encounter with Terror.*** Lexington, MA.: Lexington Books, 1988. 347p.

5408. Rabinovich, Itamar. ***The War for Lebanon, 1970-1985.*** Ithaca, NY.: Cornell University Press, 1985. 243p.

5409. Thomas, Gordon. ***Journey into Madness: Medical Torture and Mind Controllers.*** London: Bantam Books, 1988. 398p.

2. Journal Articles

5410. "1984 Death Toll: Violence Continues." ***Monday Morning,*** 13:650 (January 7, 1985), 10-12.

5411. Abu Khalil, As'ad. "The Hostage Question in Lebanon." ***TVI Report,*** 7:4 (1987), 11-13.

5412. "Adequacy of U.S. Marine Corps Security in Beirut." ***Terrorism,*** 7:3 (1984), 341-346.

5413. Ajami, Fuad. "The End of the Affair." ***Harpers,*** (June 1984), 53-59+.

5414. Alexander, A. N. "A Personal Account of the Bombing of the American Embassy in Beirut." ***Business America,*** 6 (May 30, 1983), 16-18.

5415. Alexander, Raymond H., Eric R. Frykberg and Joseph J. Tepas. "The 1983 Beirut Airport Terrorist Bombing." ***The American Surgeon,*** 55:3 (1989), 134-141.

5416. Berry, Steve M. "The Release of France's Last Hostages in Lebanon: An Analysis." ***TVI Report,*** 8:3 (1989), 19-22.
5417. Beyaghlou, Kamal A. "Death and Martyrdom in Shi'a Islam." ***Middle East Insight,*** 4:3 (1985), 24-33.
5418. Burgin, Maskit. "Foreign Hostages in Lebanon." In: A. Merari and A. Kurz, et al. ***INTER: International Terrorism in 1987.*** Tel Aviv: Jaffee Center for Strategic Studies, 1988. pp. 33-70.
5419. _____. "Foreign Hostages in Lebanon - An Update." In: A. Kurz, et al. ***INTER: International Terrorism in 1988.*** Tel Aviv: Jaffee Center for Strategic Studies, 1989. pp. 25-30.
5420. Caligaris, Paolo. "Beirut Kidnapping: Rome Cover-Up?" ***Middle East,*** 82 (August 1981), 28-29.
5421. "DOD Commission Reports on Beirut Terrorist Attack." ***Marine Corps Gazette,*** 68 (February 1984), 10-13.
5422. Derickson, Uli, and Jim Gallo. "I'm No Heroine." ***Reader's Digest,*** 127 (November 1985), 131-136.
5423. Dibble, Philo. "Beirut Bombing: Report from Embassy Says 7 Floors 'Collapsed' One After the Other." ***State,*** (June 1983), 2-9.
5424. Elshtain, Jean Bethke. "Reflections on the Stockholm Syndrome." ***Christianity and Crisis,*** 45 (September 16, 1985), 354-356.
5425. Faris, Hani A. "Lebanon and the Palestinians: Brotherhood or Fracticide?" ***Arab Studies Quarterly,*** 3:4 (1981), 352-370.
5426. Farsoun, S. K., and R. B. Wingeter. "The Palestinians in Lebanon." ***SAIS Review,*** 3 (Winter 1981-82), 93-106.
5427. Felton, John. "Hostages Return, But Terrorism Problem Ligers." ***Congressional Quarterly Weekly Report,*** 43 (July 6, 1985), 1327-1329.
5428. Geldard, Ian. "The Fate of Terry Waite." ***Terror Update,*** 8 (May 1989), 1,3.
5429. Gigliotti, Donna. "Victims of Terrorism: American Embassy at Beirut is Bombed." ***State,*** (May 1983), 2-5.
5430. Gruen, George E. "Shi'ite Terrorists Target Lebanese Jews." ***Terrorism,*** 10:3 (1987), 185-188.
5431. Hastedt, Glenn. "Intelligence Failure and Terrorism: The Attack on the Marines in Beirut." ***Conflict Quarterly,*** 8:2 (Spring 1988), 7-22.
5432. Hof, Frederic C. "Beirut Bombing of October 1983: An Act of Terrorism?" ***Parameters,*** 15:2 (Summer 1985), 69-74.
5433. Howell, Leon. "Benjamin Weir and the Message from Lebanon." ***Christianity and Crisis,*** 45 (October 14, 1985), 387-388.
5434. Israel. Defence Forces Spokesman. "Abduction and Hostage-Taking in Beirut." In: Y. Alexander and A. H. Foxman, eds. ***The 1987 Annual on Terrorism.*** Dordrecht: Martinus Nijhoff, 1988. pp. 313-324.
5435. Jacobsen, Eric. "Eric Jacobsen: A Comment." ***Whittier Law Review,*** 8:3 (1986), 763-777.
5436. Jenkins, Brian M., and Robin Wright. "The Kidnappings in Lebanon." ***TVI Report,*** 7:4 (1987), 2-11.
5437. Jureidini, Paul A. "Islamic Fundamentalism and the Lebanese Case." In: A. Kurz, ed. ***Contemporary Trends in World Terrorism.*** New York: Praeger, 1987. pp. 53-65.
5438. Khasan, Hilal. "Do Lebanese Shi'is Hate the West?." ***Orbis,*** 33:4 (Fall 1989), 583-

5439. Kramer, Martin. "The Structure of Shi'ite Terrorism." In: A. Kurz, ed. ***Contemporary Trends in World Terrorism.*** New York: Praeger, 1987. pp. 43-52.

5440. La Monica, Jay. "Life in Limbo: II Lebanon: Betamaxes and Bombs." ***Washington Quarterly,*** 5:1 (1982), 189-191.

5441. McBrien, J. R. "Lebanon, Terrorism, and Future Policy." In: N. C. Livingstone and T. E. Terrell, eds. ***Beyond the Iran-Contra Crisis.*** Lexington, MA.: D.C. Heath & Lexington, 1988. pp. 53-64.

5442. Merari, Ariel, and Josefa Braunstein. "Shi'ite Terrorism: Operational Capabilities and the Suicide Factor." ***TVI Journal,*** 5:2 (1984), 7-9.

5443. Miller, Reuben. "A Tragic Mystery." ***Security Management,*** 34 (March 1989), 58-61.

5444. Norton, Augustus R. "Aspects of Terrorism in Lebanon: The Case of the Shia's." ***New Outlook,*** (January 1984), 19-23.

5445. _____. "Political Violence and Shi'a Factionalism in Lebanon." ***Middle East Insight,*** 3:2 (1983), 9-16.

5446. O'Brian, Lee. "Campaign of Terror: Car Bombings in Lebanon." ***MERIP Reports,*** 13:8 (October 1983), 23-26.

5447. Pipes, Daniel. ""Death to America" in Lebanon." ***Middle East Insight,*** 4:1 (1985), 3-9.

5448. _____. "Iranian Terrorism Hijacks United States Influence - Undeclared War." ***New Republic,*** 192:25 (1985), 12-14.

5449. Schbley, Ayla Hammond. "Resurgent Religious Terrorism: A Study of Some of the Lebanese Shi'a Contemporary Terrorism." ***Terrorism,*** 12:4 (1989), 213-248.

5450. _____. "Religious Terrorists: What They Aren't Going to Tell Us." ***Terrorism,*** 13:3 (1990), 237-242.

5451. "Shi'ite Terrorism in 1985." In: A. Merari, et al. ***INTER 85.*** Boulder, CO.: Westview Press, 1986. pp. 55-70.

5452. "TVI Report Profiles: Hizbollah (Party of God)." ***TVI Report,*** 9:3 (1990), 1-6.

5453. Terrill, W. Andrew. "Low Intensity Conflict in Southern Lebanon: Lessons and Dynamics of the Israeli-Shi'ite War." ***Conflict Quarterly,*** 7:3 (Summer 1987), 22-35.

5454. Wagner, Kathryn. "Beirut in Retrospect." ***Air Force Engineering and Services Quarterly,*** (Winter 1984), 14-15.

5455. Weir, Benjamin M. "Reflections of a Former Hostage on Causes of Terrorism." ***Arab Studies Quarterly,*** 9:2 (1987), 155-161.

5456. Zamir, Meir. "Politics and Violence in Lebanon." ***The Jerusalem Quarterly,*** 25 (Fall 1982), 3-26.

3. Documents and Reports

5457. ***The Beirut Massacre: The Complete Kahn Commission Report.*** Princeton, NJ.: Karz - Cohl, 1983. 136p.

5458. Bloch, Hannah, et al. ***TWA Hijacking: A Chronology of Events.*** Report 85-845F. Washington, D.C.: Library of Congress, Congressional Research Service, 1985. 17p.

5459. Deeb, Marius. ***Militant Islamic Movements in Lebanon: Origins, Social Basis and Ideology.*** Occasional Papers Series. Washington, D.C.: Center for Contemporary Arab Studies, Georgetown University, 1986. 27p.

5460. Gruen, George E. ***The Kidnapping of Lebanese Jewish Leaders.*** New York: The American Jewish Committee, 1985. 3p.

5461. Hoffman, Bruce. ***Shi'a Terrorism, The Conflict in Lebanon and the Hijacking of TWA Flight 847.*** RAND P-7116. Santa Monica, CA.: Rand Corporation, 1985. 3p.

5462. _____. ***The Siege Mentality in Beirut: An Historical Analogy Between the British in Palestine and the Americans in Lebanon.*** RAND P-6953. Santa Monica, CA.: RAND Corporation, 1984. 4p.

5463. _____. ***U.S. Policy Options to the Hostage Crisis in Lebanon.*** RAND P-7585. Santa Monica, CA.: Rand Corporation, 1989. 6p.

5464. Israeli, Raphael, ed. ***PLO in Lebanon: Selected Documents.*** London: Weidenfeld and Nicolson, 1983. 316p.

5465. Mark, Clyde R. ***Marine Security in Beirut: A Comparison of the House Armed Services Committee and the Long Commission Reports.*** Washington, D.C.: Library of Congress, Congressional Research Service, 1984. 14p.

5466. Sayah, Edward N. ***Lebanese Internal Divisions and Palestinian Guerrilla Activity, 1967-1976.*** M.A. Thesis. North Texas State University, 1983. 167p.

5467. Schbley, Ayla Hammond. ***Religious Resurgence and Religious Terrorism: A Study of the Actions of the Shi'a Sectarian Movements in Lebanon.*** Ph.D. Dissertation. Denton, TX.: North Texas State University, 1988. 266p.

5468. Snyder, Robert. ***Negotiating with Terrorists: TWA Flight 847.*** PEW Case No. 333. Pittsburgh, PA.: University of Pittsburgh, 1988.

5469. United States. Congress. House. Committee on Armed Services. ***Beirut Tragedy: "A New Crowd in Town and Beirut Casualties: Care and Identification": Report.*** 98th Cong., 1st sess. Washington, D.C.: U.S. Government Printing Office, 1983.

5470. _____._____._____._____. ***Full Committee Consideration on Report on Terrorist Bombing at Beirut International Airport: Hearing.*** 98th Cong., 2nd sess. Washington, D.C.: U.S. Government Printing Office, 1984.

5471. _____._____._____._____. Investigations Subcommittee. ***Adequacy of U.S. Marine Corps Security in Beirut: Summary of Findings and Conclusions.*** Washington, D.C.: U.S. Government Printing Office, 1983.

5472. _____._____._____. Committee on Foreign Affairs. Subcommittee on International Operations. ***American Hostages in Lebanon: Hearings.*** 101st Cong., 2nd sess. Washington, D.C.: U.S. Government Printing Office, 1990. 22p.

5473. _____._____. Senate. Committee on Armed Services. ***The Situation in Lebanon: Hearings, October 25, 31, 1983.*** 98th Cong., 1st sess. Washington, D.C.: U.S. Government Printing Office, 1984.

5474. _____._____._____. Committee on Foreign Relations. ***The Security of American Personnel in Lebanon: A Staff Report.*** 98th Cong., 2nd sess. Washington, D.C.: U.S. Government Printing Office, 1984.

5475. _____. DOD Commission on Beirut International Airport Terrorist Act. ***Report of the DOD Commission on Beirut International Airport Terrorist Act, October 23, 1983.*** Washington, D.C.: U.S. Government Printing Office, 1984. 141p.

e. SYRIA

1. Journal Articles

5476. Bishop, James, and Karen Harmon. "The Syrian Connection." ***TVI Report***, 7:3 (1987), 23-25.

5477. Bradlee, B., et al. "Terrorism and the Anti-Syria Campaign." ***Journal of Palestine Studies***, 15:4 (1986), 3-16.

5478. Hazo, Robert G. "The Syrian Connection." ***The Washington Report on Meddle East Affairs***, 5:3 (1986), 1, 3-4.

5479. Lay, David. "Syria's Regime Under Pressure." ***Middle East International***, 131 (August 15, 1980), 8-9.

5480. Maoz, Moshe. "State-Run Terrorism in the Middle East - The Case of Syria." ***Middle East Review***, 19:3 (1987), 11-15.

5481. Pipes, Daniel. "Foreign Adventures Shore Up Assad Regime." ***New Republic***, 195: 23 (1986), 13-16.

5482. _____. "Terrorism: The Syrian Connection." ***The National Interest***, 15 (Spring 1989), 15-28.

5483. _____. "Syria: The Cuba of the Middle East?." ***Commentary***, 82:1 (July 1986), 15-22.

5484. Reed, S. F. "Dateline Syria: Fine de Regime?" ***Foreign Policy***, 39 (Summer 1980), 176-190.

5485. Rubin, Barry. "Why Assad Terror Goes Unpunished - The Untouchables." ***New Republic***, 194:22 (November 1986), 16-17.

5486. "Syria and International Terrorism." ***ADL International Report***, (February 1987), 9-13.

5487. Tueller Pritchett, Dianne. "The Syrian Strategy of Terrorism." ***Conflict Quarterly***, 8:3 (Summer 1988), 27-48.

5488. Ya'ari, Ehud. "Behind the Terror." ***Atlantic***, 259 (June 1987), 18-22.

2. Documents and Reports

5489. United States. Department of State. Bureau of Public Affairs. ***Syrian Support for International Terrorism: 1983-1986.*** Special Report, 157. Washington, D.C.: U.S. Government Printing Office, 1986. 4p.

f. TURKEY

1. Books

5490. Chaliand, Gerard, and Yves Ternon. ***The Armenians from Genocide to Resistance.*** London: Zed Press, 1983. 125p.

5491. Derogy, Jacques. ***Resistance and Revenge: The Armenian Assassination of the Turkish Leaders Responsible.*** New Brunswick, NJ.: Transactions Publishers, 1990. 206p.

5492. Feryal, Matbaacilik. ***State of Anarchy and Terror in Turkey.*** Ankara: n.p., 1982. 83p.

5493. Harris, George S. ***Turkey: Coping with Crisis.*** Boulder, CO.: Westview Press, 1985. 240p.

5494. Hyland, Francis P. ***Armenian Terrorism: A Brief History.*** Boulder, CO.: Westview Press. 1990.

5495. ***International Terrorism and the Drug Connection.*** Ankara: Ankara University Press, 1984. 294p.

5496. Kurz, Anat, and Ariel Merari. ***Asala: Irrational Terror or Political Tool.*** Boulder, CO.: Westview Press, 1985. 110p.

5497. Ternon, Yves. ***The Armenian Cause.*** Delmar, NY.: Caravan Books, 1985. 287p.

2. Journal Articles

5498. Alexander, Yonah. "Strategic Responses to Terrorism - The Turkish Experience." In: W. J. Taylor, S. A. Maaranen, G. W. Gong, eds. ***Strategic Responses to Conflict in the 1980s.*** Lexington, MA.: Lexington Books, 1984. pp. 81-92.

5499. "Armenian Terrorism and the International Terrorist Network." ***Turkish Review,*** 4:19 (Spring 1990), 13-50.

5500. Ataov, Turkkaya. "Turkish Perceptions of Terrorism." In: Y. Alexander, ed. ***The 1986 Annual on Terrorism.*** Dordrecht: Martinus Nijhoff, 1987. pp. 101-108.

5501. _____. "Need For a Comprehensive Agreement Against International Terrorism." ***Review of International Affairs,*** 33 (March 5, 1982), 25-26.

5502. _____. "Procurement of Arms for Armenian Terrorism: Realities Based on Ottoman Documents." In: ***International Terrorism and the Drug Connection.*** Ankara: Ankara University, 1984. pp. 169-178.

5503. Breindel, Eric. "Terrorism Does Not Avenge a Tragic Past: Armenians and Turks." ***New Republic,*** 186:22 (1982), 9-10.

5504. Chirac, Jacques. "American Responses are a Little Primitive." ***Middle East Report,*** 17:1 (1987), 39-43.

5505. Corsun, Andrew. "Armenian Terrorism: A Profile." ***Department of State Bulletin,*** (August 1982), 31-35.

5506. Dodd, C. H. "The Containment of Terrorism: Violence in Turkish Politics, 1965-80." In: N. O'Sullivan, ed. ***Terrorism, Ideology, and Revolution.*** Boulder, CO.: Westview Press, 1986. pp. 132-149.

5507. Erdost, Muzaffer. "Eyewitness to Death." ***Index to Censorship,*** 10 (April 1981), 3-6.

5508. Ergil, Dogu. "The Social Profile of Turkish Terrorists." In: Y. Alexander and A. H. Foxman, eds. ***The 1987 Annual on Terrorism.*** Dordrecht: Martinus Nijhoff, 1988. pp. 61-84.

5509. "External Links of Terrorists Documented." ***Outlook,*** (February 1981), 3-6.

5510. Fay, James. "Terrorism in Turkey: Threat to NATO's Troubled Ally." ***Military Review,*** 61 (April 1981), 16-26.

5511. Gunter, Michael M. "Armenian Terrorist Campaign Against Turkey." ***Orbis,*** 27 (Summer 1983), 447-477.

5512. _____. "The Armenian Terrorist Campaign Against Turkey." ***Orient,*** 24:4 (1983), 610-636.

5513. _____. "Contemporary Aspects of Armenian Terrorism." In: ***International Terrorism and the Drug Connection.*** Ankara: Ankara University Press, 1984. pp. 103-144.

5514. _____. "Contemporary Armenian Terrorism." ***Terrorism,*** 8:3 (1986), 213-252.

5515. _____. "Transnational Sources of Support for Armenian Terrorism." ***Conflict Quarterly,*** 5 (Fall 1985), 31-52.

5516. _____. "The Historical Origins of Contemporary Armenian Terrorism." ***Journal of South Asian and Middle Eastern Studies,*** 9:1 (1985), 77-end.

5517. _____. "Turkey and the Armenians." In: M. Slann and B. Schechterman, eds. ***Multidimensional Terrorism.*** Boulder, CO.: Lynne Rienner, 1987. pp. 57-62.

5518. _____. "Cycles of Terrorism: The Question of Conpemporary Turkish Counterterror and Harassment Against the Americans." ***Journal of Political Science,*** 14:1-2 (1986), 58-73.

5519. _____. "Political Instability in Turkey During the 1970s." ***Conflict Quarterly,*** 9:1 (Winter 1989), 63-77.

5520. Gurkan, Ihsan. "Conflict: A Turkish View." In: B. M. Jenkins, ed. ***Terrorism and Beyond: An International Conference on Terrorism and Low-Level Conflict.*** Santa Monica, CA.: RAND Corporation, 1980. pp. 101-114.

5521. Gurun, Kamman. "Causes and Prevention of Armenian Terrorism." In: ***International Terrorism and the Drug Connection.*** Ankara: Ankara University Press, 1984. pp. 251-258.

5522. Harris, George S. "Left in Turkey." ***Problems of Communism,*** 29 (July 1980), 26-41.

5523. Henze, Paul. "The Quest for an Assassin: A Report from Turkey." ***Encounter,*** (May 1983), 9-19.

5524. _____. "Turkey on the Rebound?" ***Wilson Quarterly,*** 6:5 (1982), 109-125.

5525. _____. "The Roots of Armenian Violence." In: ***International Terrorism and the Drug Connection.*** Ankara: Ankara University, 1984. pp. 179-202.

5526. Hoffman, Bruce. "The International Symposium on the Rehabilitation of Terrorists in Turkey." ***TVI Journal,*** 6:1 (1985), 44-50.

5527. "The Internal Threat, 1970-1984: Part 2." ***Briefing,*** 500 (October 1, 1984), 17-18.

5528. Itil, Turan M., et al. "Contemporary Aspects of International Terrorism - Turkish Case - Notes from a Seminar." ***Foreign Policy (Ankara),*** 10:3 (1983), 78-86.

5529. _____. "Terrorism in Turkey with Special Consideration of Armenian Terrorism." In: ***International Terrorism and the Drug Connection.*** Ankara: Ankara University Press, 1984. pp. 29-47.

5530. Johnson, Maxwell D. "The Role of the Military in Turkish Politics." ***Air University Review,*** 33:2 (1982), 49-63.

5531. Kevorkyan, Dikran. "Armenian Terrorism Within the Framework of International Terrorism." In: ***International Terrorism and the Drug Connection.*** Ankara: Ankara University Press, 1984. pp. 95-102.

5532. Kutschera, Chris. "The Price of Security." ***Middle East,*** 83 (September 1981), 32-33.

5533. Landau, Jacob M. "Images of the Turkish Left." ***Problems of Communism,*** 32:5 (1983), 72-74.

5534. Laqueur, Walter Z. "Turkey's Trials." ***New Republic,*** (October 11, 1980), 13-15.

5535. Lowry, Heath W. "Nineteenth and Twentieth Century Armenian Terrorism: 'Threads of Continuity'." In: ***International Terrorism and the Drug Connection.*** Ankara, Turkey: Ankara University Press, 1984. pp. 71-83.

5536. Mackenzie, Kenneth. "Ankara: Hazardous Straits." ***Washington Quarterly,*** 3 (Summer 1980), 192-198.

5537. Mango, Andrew. "Managing the Turkish Crisis." ***World Today,*** 36 (July 1980), 259-265.

5538. McCarthy, Justin. "Armenian Terrorism: History as Poison and Antidote." In: ***International Terrorism and the Drug Connection.*** Ankara: Ankara University Press, 1984. pp. 85-94.

5539. Miller, Judith. "The Istanbul Synagogue Massacre: An Investigation." ***The New York Times Magazine,*** (January 4, 1987), 14-20, 32, 36, 47, 52.

5540. Orlow, Dietrich. "Political Violence in Pre-Coup Turkey." ***Terrorism,*** 6:1 (1982), 53-72.

5541. "PLO Seeks Wider Turkish Support." ***Briefing,*** (January 14, 1985), 15-17.

5542. Papazian, Pierre. "The Armenians and the Ottoman Empire: Roots of Terrorism." ***Midwest Quarterly,*** 27:2 (Winter 1986), 215-229.

5543. Perez, Frank H. "Terrorism: Lingering Threat to Turkey?." ***Terrorism,*** 11:5 (1988), 359-363.

5544. Sayari, Sabri. "The Terrorist Movement in Turkey: Social Composition and Generational Changes." ***Conflict Quarterly,*** 7 (Winter 1987), 21-32.

5545. _____. "Patterns of Political Terrorism in Turkey." ***TVI Journal,*** 6:1 (Summer 1985), 39-43.

5546. Scruton, Roger. "Turkey: Ally Under Siege." ***Policy Review,*** 24 (Spring 1983), 49-55.

5547. Somer, Tarik. "Armenian Terrorism and the Narcotic Traffic." In: ***International Terrorism and the Drug Connection.*** Ankara: Ankara University Press, 1984. pp. 19-27.

5548. Songar, Ayhan. "Terrorism in General and Psychiatric Evaluation of Terroristic Events in Turkey." In: ***International Terrorism and the Drug Connection.*** Ankara: Ankara University Press, 1984. pp. 147-154.

5549. Szaz, Z. Michael. "Armenian Terrorists and the East-West Conflict." ***Journal of Social, Political and Economic Studies,*** 8 (Winter 1983), 387-394.

5550. Taneri, Aydin. "Turks, Byzantines, Armenians." In: ***International Terrorism and the Drug Connection.*** Ankara: Ankara University Press, 1984. pp. 281-288.

5551. Van Bruinessen, Martin. "Between Guerrilla War and Political Murder: The Worker's Party of Kurdistan." ***Middle East Report,*** 18:4 (July-August 1988), 40-46.

5552. Virts, Nancy, and Albert Wohlstetter. "Armenian Terror as a Special Case of International Terror." In: ***International Terrorism and the Drug Connection.*** Ankara: Ankara University, 1984. pp 261-280.

5553. Wilkinson, Paul. "Armenian Terrorism." ***The World Today,*** 39:9 (1983), 344-350.

5554. Wohlstetter, Albert, and Nancy Virts. "Armenian Terror as a Special Case of International Terror." In: ***International Terrorism and the Drug Connection.*** Ankara: Ankara University Press, 1984. pp. 261-280.

3. Documents and Reports

5555. Gruen, George E. ***Combatting Terrorism: Lessons from the Istambul Massacre.*** New York: American Jewish Committee, Institute of Human Relations, 1986. 8p.

5556. Kouyamjian, Dickran. "Armenian Militancy: Present Contexts and Future Conjectures." Paper Presented at the ***17th Annual Meeting of the Middle East Studies Association,*** held on November 4, 1983 in Chicago, IL.

5557. Libaridian, Gerard. "Roots of Political Violence in Recent Armenian History." Paper presented at the ***17th Annual Meeting of the Middle East Studies Association,*** held on November 4, 1983 in Chicago, IL.

5558. Mackenzie, Kenneth. ***Turkey Under the Generals.*** Conflict Studies, No. 126. London: Institute for the Study of Conflict, 1981. 31p.

5559. Sayari, Sabri. ***Generational Change in Terrorist Movements: The Turkish Case.*** RAND P-7124. Santa Monica, CA.: RAND Corporation, 1985. 16p.

5560. United States. Congress. Senate. Committee on the Judiciary. Subcommittee on Security and Terrorism. ***Terrorism, The Turkish Experience: Hearings.*** 97th Cong. 1st sess. Washington, D.C.: U.S. Government Printing Office, 1981.

g. LIBYA

1. Books

5561. Blundy, David, and Andrew Lycett. ***Qaddafi and the Libyan Revolution.*** Boston, MA.: Little, Brown, 1987. 230p.

5562. Cooley, John K. ***Libyan Sandstorm.*** London: Sidgwick & Jackson, 1983. 320p.

5563. Davis, Brian L. ***Qaddafi, Terrorism, and the Origins of the U.S. Attacks on Libya.*** New York: Praeger, 1990. 202p.

5564. Goulden, Joseph C., and A. W. Raffio. ***The Death Merchant: The Rise and Fall of Edwin P. Wilson.*** New York: Simon and Schuster, 1984. 453p.

5565. Haley, Edward P. ***Qaddafi and the United States Since 1969.*** New York: Praeger, 1984. 364p.

5566. Kaldor, Mary, and Paul Anderson. ***Mad Dogs: The U.S. Raids on Libya.*** London: Pluto Press, 1986. 172p.

5567. Lloyd, Richard. ***Beyond the CIA: The Frank Terpil Story.*** New York: Seaver Books, 1983. 256p.

5568. Sicker, Martin. ***The Making of A Pariah State: The Adventurist Politics of Muammar Qaddafi.*** New York: Praeger, 1987. 140p.

2. Journal Articles

5569. Adelman, Kenneth. "Libya: A Source of International Terrorism." ***Department of State Bulletin,*** (January 1983), 60-62.

5570. Alexander, Yonah. "Libyan Terrorism: Some Strategic Considerations." In: Y. Alexander, ed. ***The 1986 Annual on Terrorism.*** Dordrecht: Martinus Nijhoff, 1987. pp. 143-164.

5571. Anderson, Lisa. "Assessing Libya's Qaddafi." ***Current History***, 84:502 (May 1985), 197-200, 226-227.

5572. Aruri, Naseer H., and John J. Carroll. "The Anti Terrorist Crusade." ***Arab Studies Quarterly***, 9:2 (1987), 173-187.

5573. Austin, Granville. "The Libya Raid and the Arab - Israeli Dispute." ***Journal of Palestine Studies***, 15:4 (Summer 1986), 99-111.

5574. Beggs, Sarah J. "On Terrorism and Demons: A Call For Humility." ***Christian Century***, 103:16 (May 7, 1986), 454-455.

5575. Bennett, John C. "On Libya, On Terrorism: Second Thoughts Needed." ***Christianity and Crisis: A Christian Journal of Opinion***, 46:8 (May 19, 1986), 173-174.

5576. Berger, Elena. "Dealing with Libya." ***Editorial Research Reports***, (March 14, 1986), 187-204.

5577. Bishop, Dale L. "Bombing Libya: Wrong Problem, Wrong Solution." ***Christianity and Crisis***, 46:7 (May 5, 1986), 147-148.

5578. Boyle, Francis A. "The Outstanding Crisis Between the United States and Libya over International Terrorism." In: H. Kochler, ed. ***Terrorism and National Liberation***. Frankfurt: Verlag Peter Lang, 1988. pp. 157-170.

5579. Buis, George. "Terrorism and the U.S. Libya Raid." ***Journal of Palestine Studies***, 15:4 (Summer 1986), 112-119.

5580. Cooley, John K. "Qaddafi's Nervous Neighbors." ***Middle East International***, (September 4, 1981), 2-3.

5581. _____. "The Libyan Menace." ***Foreign Policy***, 42 (Spring 1981), 74-93.

5582. Felton, John. "Reagan Tightens Economic Sanctions on Libya." ***Congressional Quarterly Weekly Report***, 44 (January 11, 1986), 59-60.

5583. "Gaddafi and Terrorism: Sampling Global Opinion on the U.S. Raid and the Future." ***World Press Report***, 33 (June 1986), 21-26.

5584. Ghanem, L. "Terrorism and the United States Libya Raid." ***Journal of Palestine Studies***, 15:4 (1986), 112-119.

5585. Henderson, George. "Free to Agree with Colonel Qaddafi." ***Index on Censorship***, (December 1980), 18-24.

5586. Hersh, Seymour. "Target Quaddafi." ***New York Times Magazine***, (February 22, 1987), 16-26.

5587. Jenkins, Brian M. "Libya's Continuing Role in International Terrorism." ***TVI Report***, 7:2 (1987), 1-6.

5588. Jenkins, Philip. "Whose Terrorists? Libya and State Criminality." ***Contemporary Crises***, 12:1 (1988), 5-24.

5589. Juster, Kenneth I., and Jeffrey P. Bialos. "The Libyan Sanctions: A Rational Response to State-Sponsored Terrorism?." ***Virginia Journal of International Law***, 26:4 (1986), 799-855.

5590. Kishtainy, Khalid. "Shi'ism and the Islamic Revolution." ***Contemporary Review***, (1985), 62-66.

5591. Kramer, N. "Shi'ite Terrorism." In: ***Anti Terrorism - IDENTA - 85***. Boulder, CO.: Westview Press, 1985. pp. 127-132.

5592. "Last, Final and Decisive Phase." ***Impact International***, 10 (May 23, 1980), 8-9.

5593. "Libyan Problem." ***Department of State Bulletin***, (October 1983), 71-78.

5594. "Libyan Raid: Americans Sanction More Raids if Libyan Terrorism Continues." ***Gallup Report***, (April 1986), 2-12.

5595. Livingstone, Neil C. "The Raid on Libya and the Use of Force in Combating Terrorism." In: N. C. Livingstone and T. E. Terrell, eds. ***Beyond the Iran-Contra Crisis.*** Lexington, MA.: D.C. Heath & Lexington Books, 1988. pp. 65-84.

5596. Mawyer, Martin. "America Responds to Terrorism." ***Fundamentalist Journal,*** 5:6 (June 1986), 59-60.

5597. Melakopides, Constantine. "Libya Raid and the Western Alliance." ***International Perspectives,*** (July - August 1986), 19-21.

5598. Militaris, Vox. "The U.S. Strike Against Libya: Operation El Dorado Canyon." ***Army Quarterly and Defence Journal,*** 116:2 (1986), 134-148.

5599. Morrison, David. "The 'Shadow War': The Air Attack on Libya Marks a New Phase." ***National Journal,*** 18 (May 10, 1986), 1100-1105.

5600. Perdue, William D. "The Ideology of Terrorism." In: T. Sono, ed. ***Libya: The Vilified Revolution.*** Langley Park, MD.: Progress Press, 1985. pp. 27-55.

5601. Ritchie, David J. "To the Shores of Tripoli; The Second American War in Libya." ***Strategy & Tactics,*** 109 (1986), 14-24.

5602. St. John, Ronald B. "Terrorism and Lybian Foreign Policy, 1981-1986." ***World Today,*** 42:7 (1986), 111-114.

5603. Sterling, Claire. "Qaddafi Spells Chaos." ***New Republic,*** (March 7, 1981), 15-20.

5604. Thatcher, Margaret. "International Terrorism: Britain Supports US Action Against Libya." In: Y. Alexander, ed. ***The 1986 Annual on Terrorism.*** Dordrecht: Martinus Nijhoff, 1987. pp. 303-308.

5605. Ullman, H. K. "Assessing the Raid on Libya." ***Naval Forces,*** 4 (1986), 10-11.

5606. United States. Department of State. "Libya Under Qadhafi: A Pattern of Aggression." In: W. Laqueur, ed. ***The Terrorism Reader.*** New York: Meridian, 1987. pp. 337-344.

5607. Wall, James M. "Libya Raid Undermines Morality and Security." ***Christian Century,*** 103:15 (April 30, 1986), 427-428.

5608. Wapner, Paul. "Problems of U.S. Counter-Terrorism: The Case of Libya." ***Alternatives,*** 13 (April 1988), 271-89.

5609. Zilian, Frederick. "The U.S. Raid on Libya - and NATO." ***Orbis,*** 30 (Fall 1986), 499-524.

3. Documents and Reports

5610. Casford, James. ***America Strikes Back.*** Maxwell Air Force Base, AL.: U.S. Air Command and Staff College, 1987. 35p.

5611. Cordes, Bonnie J. ***Qaddafi: Idealist and Revolutionary Philanthropist.*** RAND--P-7209. Santa Monica, CA.: The Rand Corporation, 1986. 10p.

5612. Grannis, L. A. ***Center of Gravity - Libya 1989.*** Maxwell AFB.: Air War College, 1989. 80p.

5613. Gutteridge, William, ed. ***Libya: Still a Threat to Western Interests.*** Conflict Studies, No. 160. London: Institute for the Study of Conflict, 1984. 25p.

5614. Trebon, G. L. ***Libyan State Sponsored Terrorism - What Did Operation El Dorado Canyon Accomplish.*** Maxwell AFB, AL.: Air Command and Staff College, 1988. 64p.

5615. United States. Congress. Senate. Committee on Foreign Relations. ***Libyan Activities: Libya's Role in Sub-Saharan Africa and the Near East: Hearings.*** 97th Cong., 1st sess. Washington, D.C.: U.S. Government Printing Office, 1981.

5616. _____._____._____. Committee on the Judiciary.Subcommittee on Security and Terrorism. ***Libyan-Sponsored Terrorism: A Dilemma for Policymakers: Hearing.*** 99th Cong., 2nd sess. Washington, D.C.: U.S. Government Printing Office, 1986. 121p.

h. IRAN

1. Books

5617. Koob, Kathryn. ***Guest of the Revolution.*** Nashville, TE.: T. Nelson, 1982. 240p.

5618. Moody, Sid. ***444 Days: The American Hostage Story.*** New York: Routledge Press, 1981.

5619. Sick, Gary. ***All Fell Down: America's Tragic Encounter with Iran.*** New York: Random House, 1985. 366p.

2. Journal Articles

5620. Adams, Nathan M. "Iran Ayatollas of Terror." ***Reader's Digest,*** (January 1985), 36-42.

5621. Bernstein, Alvin H. "Iran's Low-Intensity War Against the United States." ***Orbis,*** 30 (Spring 1986), 149-167.

5622. Bill, James A. "The Politics of Extremism in Iran." ***Current History,*** 81:471 (January 1982), 9-13.

5623. Boyle, Francis A. "The United Nations Charter and the Iranian Hostage Crisis." In: H. H. Han, ed. ***Terrorism, Political Violence and World Order.*** Lanham, MD.: University Press of America, 1983. pp. 537-558.

5624. Christopher, Warren. "Introduction." In: ***American Hostages in Iran.*** New Haven, CT.: Yale University Press, 1985. pp. 1-34.

5625. Cooper, Roger. "Explosive Politics." ***Middle East International,*** 153 (July 3, 1981), 2-3.

5626. Dunn, Michael C. "Until the Imam Comes: Iran Exports Its Revolution." ***Tactics and Technologies,*** (July-August 1987), 43-50.

5627. Elahi, Cyrus. "Political Violence and War: An Overview of the Iranian Revolution." In: H. H. Han, ed. ***Terrorism, Political Violence and World Order.*** Lanham, MD.: University Press of America, 1983. pp. 303-312.

5628. Han, Henry H. "The Shah: A Commentary in Autocratic Abuse of Power." In: H. H. Han, ed. ***Terrorism, Political Violence and World Order.*** Lanham, MD.: University Press of America, 1983. pp. 283-302.

5629. Ioannides, Christos P. "The Hostages of Iran: A Discussion with the Militants." ***Washington Quarterly,*** 3:3 (1980), 12-35.

5630. "Iran's Islamic Fundamentalism and Terrorism." ***Terrorism,*** 12;6 (1989), 401-416.

5631. "Iran's Use of International Terrorism." ***Department of State Bulletin,*** 88 (June 1988), 50-53.

5632. Kazemi, Farhad. "The Fada'iyan-E Islam: Fanaticism, Politics and Terror." In: S. Arjomand, ed. ***From Nationalism to Revolutionary Islam.*** Albany, NY.: University of New York Press, 1984. pp. 158-176.

5633. Kostiner, Joseph. "War, Terror, Revolution: The Iran-Iraq Conflict." In: B. Rubin, ed. ***The Politics of Terrorism.*** Lanham, MD.: University Press of America, 1988. pp. 95-128.

5634. Momayezi, Nasser. "Economic Correlates of Political Violence: The Case of Iran." ***Middle East Journal,*** 40:1 (1986), 68-81.

5635. Rose, Gregory F. "Iran: Revolution, Culture and Collective Action." In: M. Slann and B. Schechterman, eds. ***Multidimensional Terrorism.*** Boulder, CO.: Lynne Rienner, 1987. pp. 73-80.

5636. Rubin, Alfred P. "The Hostage Incident: The United States and Iran." In: G. W. Keeton and G. Schwarzenberger, eds. ***The Year Book of World Affairs, 1982.*** London: Stevens & Sons, 1982. pp. 213-240.

5637. Saunders, Harold H. "The Crisis Begins." In: ***American Hostages in Iran.*** New Haven, CT.: Yale University Press, 1985. pp. 35-71.

5638. _____. "Diplomacy and Pressure, November 1979 - May 1980." In: ***American Hostages in Iran.*** New Haven, CT.: Yale University Press, 1985. pp. 72-143.

5639. Schweitzer, Yoram. "Terrorism: A Weapon in the Shi'ite Arsenal." In: A. Kurz, ed. ***Contemporary Trends in World Terrorism.*** New York: Praeger, 1987. pp. 66-74.

5640. Sick, Gary. "Military Options and Constraints." In: ***American Hostages in Iran.*** New Haven, CT.: Yale University Press, 1985. pp. 144-172.

5641. Timmerman, Kenneth R. "Iran, and International Terror: Trying to Export the Islamic Revolution." ***Journal of Defense & Diplomacy,*** 5:1 (1987), 21-24.

5642. Von Dornoch, A. "Iran's Violent Diplomacy." ***Survival,*** 30:3 91988), 252-266.

5643. Zabih, Seperh. "Aspects of Terrorism in Iran." ***The Annals of the American Academy of Political and Social Science,*** 463 (September 1982), 84-94.

3. Documents and Reports

5644. Bernstein, Alvin H. ***In the U.S. War on Terrorism, Iran is the Enemy.*** Backgrounder No. 452. Washington, DC.: The Heritage Foundation, 1985. 12p.

i. THE REST OF THE MIDDLE EAST

1. Books

5645. Al-Qasimi, Sultan Muhammad. ***The Myth of Arab Piracy in the Gulf.*** London: Croom Helm, 1986. 450p.

5646. Bailey, Clinton. ***Jordan's Palestinian Challenge, 1948-1983: A Political History.*** Boulder, CO.: Westview Press, 1984. 146p.

5647. Ezeldin, Ahmed G. ***Terrorism and Political Violence: An Egyptian Perspective.*** Studies in Terrorism. Chicago, IL.: Office of International Criminal Justice, 1987. 144p.

5648. Heykal, Muhammad H. ***Autumn of Fury: The Assassination of Sadat.*** London: Deutsch, 1983. 290p.

2. Journal Articles

5649. Adams, Nathan M. "Destination Tehran: Anatomy of a (Kuwait Airways) Hijacking." ***Reader's Digest,*** 127 (October 1985), 71-74, 187-188+.

5650. Ayalon, Ami. "Regime Opposition and Terrorism in Egypt." In: B. Rubin, ed. ***The Politics of Terrorism.*** Lanham, MD.: University Press of America, 1988. pp. 67-94.

5651. Cooper, H. H. A. "Whose Hand Behind the Triger Finger?." ***TVI Report,*** 2:9 (1981), 6-8.

5652. Friedlander, Robert A. "A New International Anarchy?." ***TVI Journal,*** 2:10 (1981), 8-10.

5653. Friend, D. "Embassy on the Front Line of Terror: In Kuwait, U.S. Diplomats Take a Crash Course in Self Defence." ***Life,*** 8 (December 1985), 130-134+.

5654. Jansen, Godfrey. "Home to Roost." ***Middle East International,*** 213 (December 23, 1983), 7-8.

5655. Kostiner, Joseph. "The Rise and Fall of Militant Opposition Movements in the Arab Peninsula." In: A. Kurz, ed. ***Contemporary Trends in World Terrorism.*** New York: Praeger, 1987. pp. 75-93.

5656. O'Neill, Bard E. "Revolutionary War in Oman." In: B. E. O'Neill, ed. ***Insurgency in the Modern World.*** Boulder, CO.: Westview Press, 1980. pp. 213-234.

5657. Reid, Donald M. "Political Assassination in Egypt, 1910-1954." ***International Journal of African Historical Studies,*** 15:4 (1982), 625-651.

5658. "Terrorism: 3 National Employees Killed in Kuwait Attack." ***State,*** (January 1984), 8-9.

5659. Viotti, Paul R. "Iraq: The Kurdish Rebellion." In: B. E. O'Neill, W. R. Heaton and D. J. Alberts, eds. ***Insurgency in the Modern World.*** Boulder, CO.: Westview Press, 1980. pp. 191-212.

3. Documents and Reports

5660. Doumergu, Emil. ***Saudia Arabia and the Explosion of Terrorism in the Middle East.*** Great Currents of History Book. Albuquerque, NM.: Institute of Economic & Political World Strategic Studies, 1983. 137p.

j. ENTEBBE RESCUE

1. Journal Articles

5661. Akinsanya, Adeoye A. "The Entebbe Rescue Mission: A Case of Aggression?" ***Journal of African Studies,*** 9 (Summer 1982), 46-57.

5662. Boyle, Francis A. "The Entebbe Hostage Crisis." In: H. H. Han, ed. ***Terrorism, Political Violence and World Order.*** Lanham, MD.: University Press of America, 1983. pp. 559-602.

5663. Maoz, Zeev. "The Decision to Raid Entebbe: Decision Analysis Applied to Crisis Behavior." ***Journal of Conflict Resolution,*** 25:4 (1981), 677-707.

5664. Menarchik, Edward D. "Strike Against Terror! The Entebbe Raid." ***Air University Review,*** 3:1 (1980), 65-76.

5665. "Operation Jonathan: The Rescue at Entebbe." ***Military Review,*** (July 1982), 2-23.

2. Documents and Reports

5666. Menarchik, Edward D. ***The Politics of the Israeli Rescue Operation at Entebbe: Crisis Resolution Between State and Terrorist Organizations.*** Ph.D. Dissertation. Washington, D.C.: The George Washington University, 1983. 423p.

F. AFRICA

a. GENERAL WORKS

1. Books

5667. Davidson, Basil. ***The People's Cause: A History of Guerrillas in Africa.*** Harlow, Eng.: Longman, 1981. 210p.

2. Journal Articles

5668. Alleg, Henri. "Political Violence in Algeria." In: J. Darby, N. Dodge and A. C. Hepburn, eds. ***Political Violence: Ireland in a Comparative Perspective.*** Ottawa: Ottawa University Press, 1990. pp. 103-130.

5669. Denemark, Robert A., and Mary B. Welfling. "Terrorism in Sub-Saharan Africa." In: M. Stohl, ed. ***The Politics of Terrorism.*** New York: Marcel Dekker, 1983. pp. 327-376.

5670. _____. _____. "Terrorism in Sub-Saharan Africa." In: M. Stohl, ed. ***The Politics of Terrorism.*** New York: Marcel Dekker, 1988. pp. 445-496.

5671. Fanthorpe, David. "Africa South of the Sahara: Regional Assessment." In: R. Clutterbuck, ed. ***The Future of Political Violence.*** London: Macmillan, 1986. pp. 113-123.

5672. Igbinovia, Patrick E. "Terrorist Aircraft Hijacking and Sabotage in African States." ***International Journal of Comparative and Applied Criminal Justice***, 10:1-2 (Spring-Winter 1986), 73-93.

5673. Otubanjo, Femi. "African Guerrillas and Indigenous Governments." ***Conflict Quarterly***, 1:4 (1980), 32-41.

5674. Ringquist, Delbert. "A Longitudinal Analysis of the Correlates of Political Violence and Development: The Case of the Former French Colonies." In: H. H. Han, ed. ***Terrorism, Political Violence and World Order.*** Lanham, MD.: University Press of America, 1984. pp. 667-679.

5675. Shaw, Timothy M. "Unconventional Conflict in Africa: Nuclear, Class and Guerrilla Struggles." ***Jerusalem Journal of International Relations***, 7:1-2 (1985), 63-78.

3. Documents and Reports

5676. Wessner, Charles W. ***Bureaucratic Constraints on Police Implementation: The France Response to Urban Terrorism in Algiers 1956-1957.*** Ph.D. Dissertation. Medford, MA.: Fletcher School of Law and Diplomacy, 1981.

b. SOUTHERN AFRICA

1. Books

5677. Cline, Ray, and Darrell Freeman. ***Terrorism: The South African Connection.*** New York: Crane Russak, 1988. 175p.

5678. Henriksen, Thomas H. ***Revolution and Counterrevolution: Mozambique's War of Independence, 1964-1974.*** Westport, CT.: Greenwood Press, 1983. 289p.

5679. Johnson, Phyllis, and David C. Martin. ***Apartheid Terrorism: The Destabilization Report.*** Bloomington, IN.: Indiana University Press, 1990. 164p.

5680. Lan, David. ***Guns and Rain: Guerrillas and Spirit Mediums in Zimbabwe.*** London: James Currey, 1985. 243p.

5681. Munslow, Barry. ***Mozambique, The Revolution and Its Origins.*** London: Longman, 1983.

2. Journal Articles

5682. Alberts, D. J. "Armed Struggle in Angola." In: B. E. O'Neill, W. R. Heaton and D. J. Alberts, eds. ***Insurgency in the Modern World.*** Boulder, CO.: Westview Press, 1980. pp. 235-268.

5683. Arnold, Dave. "Combatting Urban Terrorism in Rhodesia." ***TVI Report,*** 6:3 (Winter 1986), 37-39.

5684. Asmal, Kader. "Apartheid and Terrorism - The Case of Southern Africa." In: H. Kochler, ed. ***Terrorism and National Liberation.*** Frankfurt: Verlag Peter Lang, 1988. pp. 127-156.

5685. Benkes, Herbert. "South Africa's Response." ***Terrorism,*** 10:2 (1987), 125-126.

5686. Campbell, Keith. "Prospects for Terrorism in South Africa." ***South Africa International,*** 14 (October 1983), 397-417.

5687. Clifford Vaughan, Frederick M. "Terrorism and Insurgency in South Africa." In: P. Wilkinson and A. M. Stewart, eds. ***Contemporary Research on Terrorism.*** Aberdeen: Aberdeen University Press, 1987. pp. 270-289.

5688. _____. "Terrorism and Insurgency in South Africa." ***Journal of Social, Political and Economic Studies,*** 12:3 (Autumn 1987), 259-276.

5689. Denemark, Robert A., and H. P. Lehman. "South-African State Terror - The Costs of Continuing Repression." In: M.Stohl and G. A. Lopez. ***State as Terrorist.*** Westport, CT.: Greenwood Press, 1984. pp. 143-166.

5690. Francis, Samuel T. "Communism, Terrorism and the African National Congress." ***Journal of Social Policy and Economic Studies,*** 11 (Spring 1986), 55-71.

5691. Friedland, Elaine A. "South Africa and Instability in Southern Africa." ***Annals of the American Academy of Political and Social Science,*** 463 (1982), 95-105.

5692. Goot, Elisabeth L. "Should South Africa be Named a Terrorist State?." ***Brooklyn Journal of International Law,*** 15:3 (December 1989), 801-841.

5693. Hovey, Gail. "State Terrorism and Its Allies." ***Christianity and Crisis: A Christian Journal of Opinion,*** 48 (May 2, 1988), 147-148.

5694. Howe, Herbert M. "South Africa - Terrorism and State Disintegration." ***Terrorism,*** 12:6 (1989), 419-420.

5695. _____. "Government and Opposition Terrorism in South Africa." In: B. Rubin, ed. ***The Politics of Terrorism.*** Lanham, MD.: University Press of America, 1988. pp. 153-182.

5696. Isaacman, A., and B. Isaacman. "South Africa's Hidden War." ***Africa Report,*** 27 (November/December 1982), 4-8.

5697. Johnstone, Frederick. "State Terror in South Africa." ***Telos,*** 54 (Winter 1982-83), 115-121.

5698. McDougall, Gay, and Carl Soderberg. "South Africa's Death Squads: Special Police and Military Teams are Terrorizing Anti-Apartheid Organizations and Killing Their Leaders." ***Focus,*** 18 (June 1990), 3-4+.

5699. Morris, Michael. "Armed Attacks upon South African Police." ***Terrorism Report,*** 1:1 (1980), 6-8.

5700. Phillips, Jeffrey L. ""Serious Disruptions" in Zimbabwe." ***Christian Century,*** 106:15 (1989), 1038-1039.

5701. Powell, Philip. "People's War in South Africa." ***TVI Report,*** 8:4 (1989), 23-32.

5702. "Renamo-Rural Terrorism at Work - Who is Renamo." ***The Black Scholar,*** 18;6 (November-December 1987), 45-46.

5703. Rich, Paul. "Insurgency, Terrorism and the Apartheid System in South Africa." ***Political Studies,*** 32 (1984), 68-85.

5704. Richardson, Leon D. "The Threat to Peace in South Africa." ***TVI Report,*** 7:4 (1987), 29-36.

5705. Sidler, Peter. "Angola, Namibia and Their Guerrillas." ***Swiss Review of World Affairs,*** 34:10 (1985), 8-11.

5706. Stepherd, George W. "Internal and External Settlements in Southern Africa?" In: H. H. Han, ed. ***Terrorism, Political Violence and World Order.*** Lanham, MD.: University Press of America, 1984. pp. 681-687.

3. Documents and Reports

5707. Cilliers, Jacobus K. ***A Critique on Selected Aspects of the Rhodesian Security Forces' Counter Insurgency Strategy: 1972-1980.*** M.A. Thesis. University of South Africa, 1982.

5708. Friedland, Elaine A. ***A Comparative Study of the Development of Revolutionary Nationalist Movements in Southern Africa - FRELIMO and the National Congress of South Africa.*** Ph.D. Dissertation. City University of New York, 1980.

5709. Hough, M. ***South Africa, Counter-Insurgency, Terrorism, and Publicity: Factual Review.*** Pretoria: Institute for Strategic Studies, University of Pretoria, 1981. 19p.

5710. Minter, William. ***Apartheid's Contras: Rural Terrorism and Mozambique's Struggle for Survival.*** Washington, D.C.: Washington Office on Africa Educational Fund and Mozambique Support Network, 1988. 8p.

5711. Morris, Michael. ***South African Political Violence and Sabotage, 1 July - 31 December, 1982.*** Cape Town: Terrorism Research Centre, 1982. 49p.

5712. Sono, Themba. "State Terrorism and Liberation Movements: The Case of South Africa." Paper Presented to the ***International Progress Organization Conference on the Question of Terrorism,*** held on March 18-20, 1987, at Geneva.

5713. United States. Congress. Senate. Committee on the Judiciary. ***Soviet, East German, and Cuban Involvement in Fomenting Terrorism in Southern Africa: Report.*** 97th Cong., 2nd sess. Washington, D.C.: U.S. Government Printing Office, 1982. 28p.

G. ASIA AND AUSTRALIA

a. INDIA

1. Books

5714. Canandian, Darshan S. ***Terrorism in Punjab: Selected Articles & Speeches.*** Columbia, MO: South Asia Books, 1987.
5715. Dang, Satyapal. ***Genesis of Terrorism: An Analytical Study of Punjab Terrorists.*** New Delhi: Patriot Publishers, 1988. 148p.
5716. Mulgrew, Ian. ***Unholy Terror: The Sikhs and International Terrorism.*** Toronto: Key Porter books, 1988. 250p.
5717. Nath, Shailshwar. ***Terrorism in India.*** New York: Asia Books, 1980. 350p.
5718. Saksena, N. S. ***Terrorism, History and Facets in the World and India.*** Columbia, MO.: South Asia Books, 1986.
5719. Samiuddin, Abida. ***The Punjab Crisis: Challenge and Response.*** Springfield, VA.: Mittal, 11985. 714p.
5720. Tegart, Charles. ***Terrorism in India.*** Calcutta: New Age, 1983. 85p.
5721. Tiwari, S. C., ed. ***Terrorism in India.*** New Delhi: South Asia, 1990. 266p.
5722. Tripathy, Biswakash. ***Terrorism and Insurgency in India: 1900-1986.*** New Delhi: Pacific Press, 1987. 296p.
5723. Vas, E. A. ***Terrorism and Insurgency: The Challenge of Modernization.*** Dehra Dun: Natraj, 1986. 360p.

2. Journal Articles

5724. Bose, N. S. "Morality and the Use of Violence: A Conceptual Dichotomy in the Indian Perspective." In: D. C. Rapoport and Y. Alexander, eds. ***The Rationalization of Terrorism.*** Frederick, MD.: University Publications of America, 1982. pp. 160-177.
5725. Clad, James. "Terrorism's Toll: Continuing Violence Muddies Sikh Activists' Aims." ***Far Eastern Economic Review***, 150 (October 11, 1990), 33-34.
5726. Cloughley, Brian. "The Troubles in Nagaland (India)." ***TVI Journal***, 6:1 (1985), 35-39.
5727. _____. "The Sikh Extremists: Violence at Home and Abroad." ***TVI Report***, 7:2 (1987), 33-39.
5728. Ghosh, Partha S. "Terrorism and Saarc." ***India Quarterly***, 43:2 (April-July, 1987), 121-137.
5729. Hula, Richard C. "Political Violence and Terrorism in Bengal." In: M. Stohl, ed. ***The Politics of Terrorism.*** 2nd ed. New York: Marcel Dekker, 1983. pp. 419-446.
5730. Laushey, David M. "The Terrorist and Marxist Challenges to Gandhian Leadership of the Indian Nationalist Movement in Bengal." ***Journal of Third World Studies***, 3:2 (1986), 32-41.
5731. Leaf, Murray J. "The Punjab Crisis." In: W. Laqueur, ed. ***The Terrorism Reader.*** New York: Meridian, 1987. pp. 318-326.

5732. Mathur, Krishnan. "Law and Order Administration with Special Reference to Terrorism." ***Indian Journal of Public Administration***, 35:2 (April-June, 1989), 233-260.

5733. Mulgannon, Terry. "The Sikhs of Punjab." ***TVI Report***, 6:2 (1985), 14-19.

5734. Nandy, A. "The Discreet Charms of Indian Terrorism." ***Journal of Commonwealth and Comparative Politics***, 28:1 (1990), 25-43.

5735. Noorani, A. G. "Terrorism and Human Rights." ***Economic and Political Weekly***, 25:30 (July 28, 1990), 1621-1622.

5736. Sanyal, S., and V. K. Kathpalia. "Developing a Scale Measuring Attitude Towards Terrorism." ***Indian Journal of Criminology***, 17:2 (July 1989), 118-124.

5737. Subrahmanyam, K. "Hijacking of IC-421." ***Strategic Analysis***, 8:6 (1984), 479-499.

5738. Wheelock, Wade. "The Sikhs: Religious Militancy, Government, Oppression, or Politics as Usual?." ***Conflict***, 8:2/3 (1988), 97-110.

5739. "White Paper on Punjab." In: R. P. Dhokalia and K. N. Rao, eds. ***Terrorism and International Law***. New Delhi: Indian Society of International Law, 1988. pp. 67-79.

3. Documents and Reports

5740. Agarwaal, Ashok, and Ram Narayan Kumar. ***SSP Govind Ram: The Terror in Batala.*** Washington, D.C.: Council of Khalistan, 1989. 12p.

5741. Austin, Dennis, and Anirundha Gupta. ***The Politics of Violence in India and South Asia.*** Conflict Studies 233. London: Research Institute for the Study of Conflict and Terrorism, 1989.

5742. Sharan, Sarojini. "Terrorism as a Political Weapon: India and Sri Lanka." Paper Presented to the ***13th Annual World Congress of the International Political Science Association***, held on July 15-20, 1985, in Paris.

b. JAPAN

1. Books

5743. Farrell, William R. ***Blood and Rage: The Story of the Japanese Red Army.*** Lexington, MA.: Lexington Books, 1990. 265p.

2. Journal Articles

5744. Angel, Robert C. "Japanese Terrorists and Japanese Countermeasures." In: B. Rubin, ed. ***The Politics of Counterterrorism.*** Lanham, MD.: University Publications of America, 1990. pp. 31-60.

5745. Chang, Dae H., and Masami Yajima. "The Japanese Sekigun Terrorists: Red Army Samurai Warriors." ***International Journal of Comparative and Applied Criminal Justice***, 13:1 (Winter 1989), 1-22.

5746. Holloway, Nigel. "The Red Army Returns." ***Far Eastern Economic Review***, 138 (December 17, 1987), 22-24.

5747. Muramatsu, Takeshi. "Japan's Terror Groups." In: B. Netanyahu, ed. ***Terrorism: How the West Can Win.*** New York: Farrar, Strauss, Giroux, 1986. pp. 106-108.

5748. Takagi, Masayuki. "Missiles from the Radical Left." ***Japan Quarterly,*** 33 (October-December 1986), 391-394.

5749. United States. Department of State. "The Japanese Red Army." ***Terrorism,*** 13:1 (1990), 73-78.

3. Documents and Reports

5750. Kincaid, Jo H. ***The Use of Terrorist Tactics as Instruments for Causing Change in Japan: 1920-1936.*** Washington, D.C.: Defence Intelligence College, 1986. 61p.

c. AUSTRALIA AND NEW ZEALAND

1. Books

5751. Crown, James. ***Australia: The Terrorist Connection.*** Melbourne: Sun Books, 1986. 150p.

5752. Dyson, J. ***Sink the Rainbow: An Enquiry into the Greenpeace Affair.*** London: Golancz, 1986. 192p.

5753. Sunday Times Insight Team. ***Rainbow Warrior: The French Attempt to Sink Greenpeace.*** New York: Harcourt, Brace, Jovanovich, 1986. 256p.

2. Journal Articles

5754. Alcalay, Glenn. "Bombs Away." ***Environmental Action,*** 17:3 (1985), 10-11.

5755. Clifford, W. "Terrorism: Australia's Quiet War." ***Reader's Digest,*** (October 1981)

5756. Cloughley, Brian. "The Australian Special Air Service." ***TVI Report,*** 8:2 (1988), 24-26.

5757. Doogan, C. M. "Defence Powers Under the Constitution: Use of Troops in Aid of Police Forces - Suppression of Terrorist Activities." ***Journal of the Royal United Services Institute of Australia,*** 5:2 (October 2, 1982),

5758. Miller, S. (Mick). "Victoria: Terrorism Comes to Melbourne." ***Australian Police Journal,*** 40:2 (1986), 44.

5759. Rowling, W. "New Zealand's Response to Terrorism: A Perspective." ***Terrorism,*** 10:1 (1987), 37-40.

5760. Selth, Andrew. "Australian Diplomats and the Terrorist Threat." ***Pacific Defence Reporter,*** 12 (September 1985), 45-46.

5761. _____. "International Terrorism: A Survey of Foreign Policy Responses." ***Australian Quarterly,*** 58:3 (Spring 1986), 257-268.

5762. _____. "International Terrorism and Australian Foreign Policy: A Survey." In: Y. Alexander, ed. ***The 1986 Annual on Terrorism.*** Dordrecht: Martinus Nijhoff, 1986. pp. 77-100.

5763. _____. "International Terrorism and the Hawke Government: A Survey of Foreign Policy Responses." ***Australian Foreign Affairs Record,*** 57:11 (1986), 1007-1014.

5764. Wardlaw, Grant. "Political Terrorism in the 1980s." ***Reporter,*** 4:3 (1983), 3-6.

5765. _____. "Terrorism and Public Disorder: The Australian Context." In: D. Chappell and P. Wilson, eds. ***The Australian Criminal Justice System: The Mid 1980's.*** Stoneham, MA.: Butterworths, 1986. pp. 150-164.

3. Documents and Reports

5766. Selth, Andrew. ***International Terrorism and Australian Foreign Policy: A Survey.*** Working Paper No. 102. Canberra: Australian National University, Research School of Pacific Studies, 1986. 24p.

d. NORTH AND SOUTH KOREA

1. Books

5767. Bermudez, Joseph S. ***Terrorism: The North Korean Connection.*** New York:Crane, Russak, 1990. 220p.

2. Journal Articles

5768. Hoon, Shin Jae. "After the Massacre." ***Far East Economic Review,*** 122 (October 27, 1983), 14-15.

5769. _____, and John McBeth. "Mausoleum Massacre." ***Far East Economic Review,*** 122 (October 20, 1983), 16-19.

5770. Kim, Jae Taik. "North Korean Terrorism: Trends, Characteristics, and Deterrence." ***Terrorism,*** 11:4 (1988), 309-322.

5771. McBeth, John. "Dress Rehearsal?" ***Far East Economic Review,*** 122 (October 27, 1983), 15-16.

5772. _____. "Anti-terrorism Forces Trained to Olympic Pitch." ***Far Eastern Economic Review,*** 141 (September 8, 1988), 65-66+.

3. Documents and Reports

5773. ***International Renegades: North Korean Diplomacy Through Terror.*** Seoul: Korean Overseas Information Service, 1983.

5774. ***An International Terrorist Clique, North Korea: Attempted Assassination Against a Guest of a State in Rangoon.*** Seoul: Korean Overseas Information Service, 1983.

5775. ***Massacre in Rangoon: North Korean Terrorism.*** Seoul: Korean Overseas Information Service, 1983.

5776. United States. Congress. House. Committee on Foreign Affairs. Subcommittee on Asian and Pacific Affairs. ***The Bombing of Korean Airlines Flight KAL-858.*** Washington, D.C.: U.S. Government Printing Office, 1989. 31p.

e. SRI LANKA

1. Books

5777. Dissanayaka, T. D. S. A. ***The Agony of Sri Lanka: An Inch - Dept Account of the Racial Riots of 1983.*** Colombo: Swastika, 1983. 120p.
5778. Hoole, Rajan, et al. ***The Broken Palmyra: The Tamil Crisis in Sri Lanka: An Inside Account.*** Claremont, CA.: The Sri Lankan Studies Institute, 1990. 481p.
5779. Hyndman, Patricia. ***The Communal Violence in Sri Lanka, July 1983: Report.*** Sydney: Lawaria, 1984. 288p.
5780. O'Ballance, Edgar. ***The Cyanide War: Tamil Insurrection in Sri Lanka, 1973-1988.*** London: Brassey's, 1989. 139p.

2. Journal Articles

5781. Bray, John. "Sri Lanka's Ethnic Conflict: Prospects for a Settlement." ***TVI Report,*** 7:3 (1987), 4-8.
5782. _____. "Sinhalese Terrorism in Sri Lanka." ***TVI Report,*** 8:4 (1989), 19-22.
5783. Bush, Kenneth. "Ethnic Conflict in Sri Lanka." ***Conflict Quarterly,*** 10:2 (Spring 1990), 41-58.
5784. "Ethnic Violence in Sri-Lanka: 1981-1983." ***International Commission of Jurists, IDOC Bulletin,*** 11:12 (1983), 7-13.
5785. Jayasinghe, Nihal. "The Sri Lankan Conflict: Is It Really Ethnic?." ***International Journal of Comparative and Applied Criminal Justice,*** 13:2 (Fall 1989), 27-37.
5786. Jetly, Nancy. "India and the Sri Lankan Ethnic Tangle." ***Conflict,*** 9:1 (1989), 59-76.
5787. Kearney, Robert N. "Tension and Conflict in Sri-Lanka." ***Current History,*** (March 1986), 109-112.
5788. _____. "Sri Lanka in 1984: The Politics of Communal Violence." ***Asian Survey,*** 25:2 (February 1985), 257-263.
5789. _____. "Sri Lanka in 1985: The Persistence of Conflict." ***Asian Survey,*** 26:2 (1986), 219-223.
5790. Kodikara, S. V. "The Separatist Eelam Movement in Sri Lanka: An Overview." ***India Quarterly,*** 37:2 (April-June 1981), 194-212.
5791. Marks, Tom. "Counterinsurgency in Sri-Lanka: Asia's Dirty Little War." ***Soldier of Fortune,*** (February 1987), 38-84.
5792. Nagarajan, K. V. "Troubled Paradise: Ethnic Conflict in Sri Lanka." ***Conflict,*** 6:4 (1986), 333-354.
5793. Oberst, Robert C. "Sri Lanka's Tamil Tigers." ***Conflict,*** 8:2/3 (1988), 185-202.
5794. Otis, Paulette, and Christopher D. Carr. "Sri Lanka and the Ethnic Challenge." ***Conflict,*** 8:2/3 (1988), 203-216.

5795. Richardson, Leon D. "The Tamil Separatist Problem." ***TVI Journal,*** 6:1 (1985), 31-35.

5796. Samarasinghe, S. W. R. "Sri Lanka in 1983: Ethnic Conflict and the Search for Solutions." ***Asian Survey,*** 24:2 (1984), 250-256.

5797. "Sri Lanka: Travails of Peace-Keeping." ***Economic and Political Weekly,*** 22:38 (September 19, 1987), 1571-1576.

3. Documents and Reports

5798. Amnesty International. ***Report of an Amnesty International Mission to Sri Lanka.*** London: Amnesty International, 1983. 72p.

5799. Austin, Dennis. ***Lions and Tigers: The Crisis in Sri Lanka.*** Conflict Studies 211. London: Center for Security and Conflict Studies, 1989. 25p.

5800. Bush, Kenneth. ***Negotiating Ethnic Conflict: The Indo - Sri Lanka Agreement of July 1987.*** Master's Thesis. Ottawa: Carleton University, 1989.

5801. Caspersz, Paul, and Reggie Siviwardena. ***State Terrorism in Jaffna: Report of the MIRJE Mission, 6th - 9th June 1981.*** Colombo: Movement for Interracial Justice and Equality - MIRJE, 1981. 10p.

5802. International Commission of Jurists. ***Ethnic Violence in Sri Lanka, 1981-1983: A Report.*** Geneva: International Commission of Jurists, 1983. 24p.

5803. Jayewardene, C. H. S., and H. Jayewardene. ***Tea for Two: Ethnic Violence in Sri Lanka.*** Ottawa, Ont.: Crimcare, 1984. 157p.

5804. Leary, Virginia A. ***Ethnic Conflict and Violence in Sri Lanka: Report.*** Geneva: International Commission of Jurists, 1981. 87p.

5805. Muttukumaru, Anton. ***Security Considerations in the Context of Ethnic Conflict.*** Colombo: Marga Institute, 1984. 10p.

5806. Rupesinghe, Kumar. ***Notes on "Ethnic" Violence in Sri Lanka.*** PRIO Working Paper no. 7/86. Oslo: International Peace Research Institute (PRIO), 1986. 45p.

5807. Sri Lanka. Ministry of Foreign Affairs. ***Investigations into Acts of Terrorism.*** Colombo: Ministry of Foreign Affairs, 1981. 14p.

5808. _____. Ministry of State. Department of Information. ***Tamil Terrorists: A Record of Murder and Robery.*** Overseas Information Series, No. 6. Colombo: Department of Information, 1983. 10p.

5809. _____._____._____. ***Tamil EElam Terrorists Murder Again: Time Bombs Kill 30 at Madras Airport.*** Overseas Information Series No. 23. Colombo: Department of Information, 1984. 12p.

5810. ***Sri Lanka: Reign of Terror in Jaffna: May - June, 1981.*** Colombo: Colombo Study Circle, 1981. 73p.

5811. Tamil United Liberation Front. ***State Terrorism Against the Tamil Speaking People.*** Jaffna: Tamil United Liberation Front, 1984. 6p.

5812. Tremayne, Penelope, and Ian Geldard. ***Tamil Terrorism: Nationalist or Marxist.*** London: Institute for the Study of Terrorism, 1986. 49p.

5813. World Fellowship of Buddhists - Sri Lanka Regional Centre. ***Terrorism in North Sri Lanka and Racial Riots: An Analysis of Their Causes.*** Colombo: World Fellowship of Buddhists, 1983. 25p.

f. THE REST OF ASIA

1. Books

5814. Psinakis, Steve. ***Two "Terrorists" Meet.*** San Francisco, CA.: Alchemy Books, 1981. 338p.

2. Journal Articles

5815. Abeyratne, R. I. R. "Invasion of the Maldives and International Terrorism." In: Y. Alexander and A. H. Foxman, eds. ***The 1988-1989 Annual of Terrorism.*** Dordrecht: Martinus Nijhoff, 1989. pp. 83-98.

5816. Austin, W. Timothy. "Living on the Edge: The Impact of Terrorism Upon Philippine Villagers." ***International Journal of Offender Therapy and Comparative Criminology,*** 33:2 (1989), 103-119

5817. Bray, John. "Asia: Regional Assessment." In: R. Clutterbuck, ed. ***The Future of Political Violence.*** London: Macmillan, 1986. pp. 133-144.

5818. Dale, Stephen F. "Religious Suicide in Islamic Asia: Anticolonial Terrorism in India, Indonesia and the Philippines." ***Journal of Conflict Resolution,*** 32:1 (1988), 37-59.

5819. De Silva, Manik. "Strike an Counter-Strike." ***Far East Economic Review,*** (December 13, 1984), 14-15.

5820. _____. "Terrorists in the South." ***Far Eastern Economic Review,*** 138 (November 12, 1987), 22-23.

5821. Gregor, A. James. "Terrorism: The View from Taiwan." ***Terrorism,*** 5:3 (1981), 233-265.

5822. Guiart, Jean. "New Caledonia: Behind the Revolt." ***TVI Journal,*** 6:1 (Summer 1985), 23-25.

5823. Haqqani, Husain. "The Hands Behind the Bomb." ***Far Eastern Economic Review,*** 137 (July 30, 1987), 28-29.

5824. Heaton, William R., and Richard Macleod. 'People's War in Thailand." In: B. E. O'Neill, W. R. Heaton and D. J. Alberts, eds. ***Insurgency in the Modern World.*** Boulder, CO.: Westview Press, 1980. pp. 87-108.

5825. Hechanova, Luis G. "Violence in the Philippines: "Kill a Priest, Frighten Thousands"." ***Christianity and Crisis,*** 45 (December 9, 1985), 488-490.

5826. Majul, Cesar Adib. "The Moros of the Philippines." ***Conflict,*** 8:2/3 (1988), 169-184.

5827. Miles, Donna. "Real Hero - Colonel Mike Rowe Assassinated in the Philippines." ***Soldiers,*** 44 (June 1989), 24-25.

5828. Mulgannon, Terry. "Inside the Philippines: A View from the Countryside." ***TVI Report,*** 8:3 (1989), 10-14.

5829. Munro, Ross H. "The New Khmer Rouge." ***Commentary,*** 80 (December 1985), 19-38.

5830. Murphy, Denis. "Violence in the Philippines." ***America,*** 153 (November 2, 1985), 278-281.

5831. Pauker, Guy. "Successes and Failures in the Fight Against Insurgencies: Post-World War II Experiences in Southeast Asia." ***TVI Report,*** 6:2 (Fall 1985), 3-10.

5832. Richardson, Leon D. "Kidnapping in the Colony of Hong Kong." ***TVI Report***, 7:4 (1987), 19-21.

5833. Sadullah, A. M. "Terrorism: A Political Weapon." ***Pakistan Horizon***, 39:4 (1986), 91-97.

5834. Singh, K. R. "International Terrorism and South Asia." ***Strategic Analysis***, 12:10 (June 1989), 1165-1182.

5835. "TVI Report Profiles: The New People's Army (NPA)." ***TVI Report***, 8:4 (1989), 1-3.

5836. "Terrorist Group Profile: The New People's Army." ***Terrorism***, 13:2 (1990), 177-181.

5837. Ustinov, G. "Afghan Rebels are Terrorists." In: B. Szumski, ed. ***Terrorism: Opposing Viewpoints***. St.Paul, MN.: Greenhaven Press, 1986. pp. 167-174.

5838. Vanderkroef, J. M. "Terrorism by Public Authority - The Case of the Death Squads of Indonesia and the Philippines." ***Current Research on Peace and Violence***, 10:4 (1987), 143-158.

5839. "Vietnam's New Guerrillas." ***TVI Journal***, 1:3 (1980), 22+.

5840. Wainstein, Eleanor S. "Muslim Rebels in the Philippines." ***TVI Report***, 6:2 (1985), 11-13.

5841. West, Dalton A. "Terrorism in the Pacific Basin." ***Terrorism***, 12:1 (1989), 66-68.

5842. _____. "Political Violence in the Asia-Pacific: Some Trends, 1988." ***Terrorism***, 12:2 (1989), 134-138.

5843. _____. "Ethnic Strife in Paradise: Fiji 1987." ***Conflict***, 8:2/3 (1988), 217-236.

5844. Wheeler, Jack. "Afghan Rebels are Freedom Fighters." In: B. Szumski, ed. ***Terrorism: Opposing Viewpoints***. St.Paul, MN.: Greenhaven Press, 1986. pp. 159-166.

5845. Whitehall, A. S. "Seduction, Intimidation and Terror in the Philippines." ***Pacific Defence Reporter***, (October 1981), 49-50.

5846. Young, P. Lewis. "New Caledonia: In Conflict." ***TVI Journal***, 6:1 (Summer 1985), 26-30.

5847. Zwick, J. "Militarism and Repression in the Philippines." In: M. Stohl and G. A. Lopez, eds. ***State as Terrorist***. Westport, CT.: Greenwood Press, 1984. pp. 123-142.

3. Documents and Reports

5848. Chan, Henry Y. S. ***Terrorism and Revolution: A Study of Political Assassination in the Late Imperial China, 1900-1911***. Ph.D. Dissertation. Bloomington, IN.: Indiana University, 1987. 236p.

5849. United States. Department of State. Bureau of Public Affairs. ***The New People's Army***. Fact Sheet. Washington, D.C.: U.S. Government Printing Office, 1989. 9p.

5850. Zonozy, Nassrulah Y. ***A Comparative Study of Terrorism in Southwest Asia, 1968-1982***. Ph.D. Dissertation. Denton, TX.: University of North Texas, 1990. 263p.

AUTHOR INDEX

SUBJECT INDEX